VISUAL C++ 6 Programming Blue Book

QA
76.73
.C153
G55
1999

Stephen D. Gilbert
Bill McCarty

CAF7238

Publisher
Keith Weiskamp

Aquisitions Editor
Stephanie Wall

Marketing Specialist
Gary Hull

Project Editor
Michelle Stroup

Technical Reviewer
John Cox

Production Coordinator
Wendy Littley

Cover Design
Anthony Stock

Layout Design
April Nielsen-Hall

CD-ROM Developer
Robert Clarfield

INDIANA-PURDUE LIBRARY
WITHDRAWN
JAN 28 2000
FORT WAYNE

Visual C++ 6 Programming Blue Book

Copyright © The Coriolis Group, 1999

All rights reserved. This book may not be duplicated in any way without the express written consent of the publisher, except in the form of brief excerpts or quotations for the purposes of review. The information contained herein is for the personal use of the reader and may not be incorporated in any commercial programs, other books, databases, or any kind of software without written consent of the publisher. Making copies of this book or any portion for any purpose other than your own is a violation of United States copyright laws.

Limits of Liability and Disclaimer of Warranty

The author and publisher of this book have used their best efforts in preparing the book and the programs contained in it. These efforts include the development, research, and testing of the theories and programs to determine their effectiveness. The author and publisher make no warranty of any kind, expressed or implied, with regard to these programs or the documentation contained in this book.

The author and publisher shall not be liable in the event of incidental or consequential damages in connection with, or arising out of, the furnishing, performance, or use of the programs, associated instructions, and/or claims of productivity gains.

Trademarks

Trademarked names appear throughout this book. Rather than list the names and entities that own the trademarks or insert a trademark symbol with each mention of the trademarked name, the publisher states that it is using the names for editorial purposes only and to the benefit of the trademark owner, with no intention of infringing upon that trademark.

The Coriolis Group, Inc.
14455 North Hayden Road, Suite 220
Scottsdale, Arizona 85260

602/483-0192
FAX 602/483-0193
http://www.coriolis.com

Library of Congress Cataloging-in-Publication Data
McCarty, Bill, 1953 -
Visual C++ 6 blue book / by Bill McCarty and Stephen D. Gilbert.
p. cm.
Includes index.
ISBN 1-57610-324-2
1. Microsoft Visual C++. 2. C++ (Computer program language)
I. Gilbert, Stephen D. II. Title.
QA76.73.C153M329 1998
005.2'768 — dc21 98-29350
CIP

Printed in the United States of America

10 9 8 7 6 5 4 3 2 1

an International Thomson Publishing company

Albany, NY • Belmont, CA • Bonn • Boston • Cincinnati Detroit Johannesburg • London • Madrid
Melbourne • Mexico City • New York • Paris • Singapore • Tokyo • Toronto • Washington

14455 North Hayden, Suite 220 • Scottsdale, Arizona 85260

Dear Reader:

Coriolis Technology Press was founded to create a very elite group of books: The ones you keep closest to your machine. Sure, everyone would like to have the Library of Congress at arm's reach, but in the real world, you have to choose the books you rely on every day *very* carefully.

To win a place for our books on that coveted shelf beside your PC, we guarantee several important qualities in every book we publish. These qualities are:

- *Technical accuracy:* It's no good if it doesn't work. Every Coriolis Technology Press book is reviewed by technical experts in the topic field, and is sent through several editing and proofreading passes in order to create the piece of work you now hold in your hands.
- *Innovative editorial design:* We've put years of research and refinement into the ways we present information in our books. Our books' editorial approach is uniquely designed to reflect the way people learn new technologies and search for solutions to technology problems.
- *Practical focus:* We put only pertinent information into our books and avoid any fluff. Every fact included between these two covers must serve the mission of the book as a whole.
- *Accessibility:* The information in a book is worthless unless you can find it quickly when you need it. We put a lot of effort into our indexes, and heavily cross-reference our chapters, to make it easy for you to move right to the information you need.

Here at The Coriolis Group we have been publishing and packaging books, technical journals, and training materials since 1989. We're programmers and authors ourselves, and we take an ongoing active role in defining what we publish and how we publish it. We hope that you're happy with the book in your hands, and that in the future, when you reach for software development and networking information, you'll turn to one of our books first.

Keith Weiskamp
President and Publisher

Jeff Duntemann
VP and Editorial Director

Look for these books from The Coriolis Group:

Visual C++ 6 Core Language Little Black Book

MFC Black Book

Visual Basic 6 Black Book

Visual Basic 6 Programming Blue Book

Visual Basic 6 Client/Server Gold Book

Visual Basic 6 Object Oriented Programming Gold Book

XML Black Book

Java Studio Blue Book

Several thousand years ago, King Solomon wrote "The end of a matter is better than its beginning, and patience is better than pride." At the end of this matter, I'd like to thank my wife, Kathleen, whose patience is above all, proverbial, along with my co-author, Bill McCarty, without whom the end would still be out of sight. Ultimately, however, all thanks are due to the Beginning and End, the Alpha and Omega, the creator, sustainer, and redeemer of my soul, Jesus Christ.

—Stephen Gilbert

Stephen Gilbert, my co-author, deserves the greatest thanks. All the good parts of the book are his; I did the rest. As always, my family (Jennifer, Patrick, and Sara) has propped me up and kept me going through the rough times. I vow to do the same when each writes his or her first four books; after that, they're on their own. Eternal thanks are due to Jesus Christ, the lover of my soul, who bought me for Himself that I might live with Him forever. My share of the proceeds from this book will be used principally to fund the purchase of a home studio for producing modern (techno/electronica) worship music devoted to His praise.

—Bill McCarty

❧

Acknowledgments

Many have worked with us to bring this book to completion. Coriolis' best Acquistions Editor, Stephanie Wall, gave us this opportunity. Thanks, Stephanie. Our editors were truly world class. We love them, not only for their hard work on this project, but because they're great folks and fun to work with. If we ever write another book, we want them on the team. Thanks to Michelle Stroup (Project Editor), Tiffany Taylor (Copy Editor), and John Cox (Technical Editor). Thanks also to the rest of the production team, namely Wendy Littley (Production Coordinator), and Robert Clarfield (CD-ROM Developer).

Contents At A Glance

Table Of Contents

Introduction

We wrote this book to help you master Microsoft's Visual C++ and its Microsoft Foundation Classes (MFC) application framework. We don't promise that you'll become a Visual C++/MFC Eagle Scout simply by reading this book. But—this book will take you well down the road—and you'll earn at least a couple of merit badges along the way. Truth is, Visual C++ and MFC are too large and complex to be mastered by reading a single book. The trick is to take your time, learning step by step. Begin with the familiar and gradually discover the how-to's and what-for's of MFC.

That's exactly how this book works: It shows you how to use the Visual C++ Interactive Development Environment (IDE) and how to program using MFC, one step at a time. If you've failed to learn MFC programming from another book, don't despair. Instead, work through the first few chapters of this book. Soon, you'll have a working MFC program, NotePod, that you can use to edit text files. Not only that, you'll know how and why the NotePod program works. Subsequent chapters introduce progressively more sophisticated projects, including PaintORama and WordZilla. If you like to learn by doing, this is the book for you.

Despite its simple approach, this is not a beginner's book: We assume that you're familiar with the C++ language and its standard libraries. If you're not, we urge you to grab a copy of Robert Lafore's *Object-Oriented Programming in C++* (Corte Madera, California: The Waite Group Press). If your C++ is simply a little rusty, you'll probably have little trouble understanding the example programs, which are thoroughly explained. But you may find Richard Leinecker's *The Visual C++ 5 Programmer's Reference* (Scottsdale, Arizona: The Coriolis Group) helpful on fine points of C++ syntax or operation.

As you work through this book, you should type in and run each project. Only if you do the steps will you understand and recall them. You'll probably notice that some chapters are mostly project-oriented and some chapters are mostly explanation of the project completed in the previous chapter. If possible, read an explanation chapter soon after completing its associated project chapter. That way, the example projects will be fresh in your mind, helping you understand the explanations more readily.

This book focuses on fundamentals, but MFC fundamentals are far from drab. You'll learn your way around some very exciting technologies, including:

- DocView architecture
- ActiveX controls
- FormView
- ODBC databases
- Networking and the Internet

Be sure to check the CD-ROM, which contains all the source code for the example programs, useful MFC utilities, and last-minute technical information. We hope you enjoy reading this book as much as we enjoyed writing it.

Chapter 1

Building Your First Application: Learning To Use VC++

VC++ enables you to create a clone of the Windows Notepad program without writing a single line of code. See how easy it is to create your own editor.

Does this sound familiar?

It's Christmas day—or, better yet, your birthday. The cake has been eaten, the cards have been read and acknowledged, and your obligations have been forgotten, forgiven, or overlooked. It's time to get down to business. There, on the floor in the center of the room, surrounded by wrapping paper and packing peanuts, sits the object of your desire: the Gizmo-2000. At this point, it doesn't matter exactly what a Gizmo-2000 is—the latest computer, a new ham radio, a riding lawnmower, or an electron microscope. What *does* matter is that it's the biggest, baddest, latest, most awesome Gizmo on the planet, and you can't wait to get started.

Of course, there's one tiny complication. Right next to your shiny new Gizmo-2000 stands the largest pile of books you've ever seen. The top book is titled *The History and Operation of Gizmos: A Depth-First Approach.*

Now, you have a choice. Should you:

a. Neatly pack the Gizmo-2000 back in its carton and start planning a study schedule designed to make you a Gizmo Guru in the most reasonable time?

b. Find an extension cord, plug the Gizmo in, and start pressing a few buttons to see what this baby'll do?

If you answered a, then this book probably isn't right for you. On the other hand, if you answered b without even considering a, then you've come to the right place.

This is a book for explorers—those who want to make the Gizmo work first, and then figure out how or why it works. Of course, exploring can be both time consuming and dangerous. Like those who settled the West in the late 1800s, you need a guide—and that's where we come in. We can help get you to your destination quickly and without getting eaten by bears.

Are you ready? Let's move 'em on out.

Taking VC++ For A Spin

The quickest way to get Visual C++ up and running is to select the shortcut from the Start menu, as you can see in Figure 1.1. Notice that Visual C++ appears inside the Visual Studio 6 folder, which is accessible from the main Programs folder. (You may have purchased your copy of Visual C++ 6 as a standalone product, or you may have acquired it as part of a package that includes C++, Visual Basic, and a host of other development tools.)

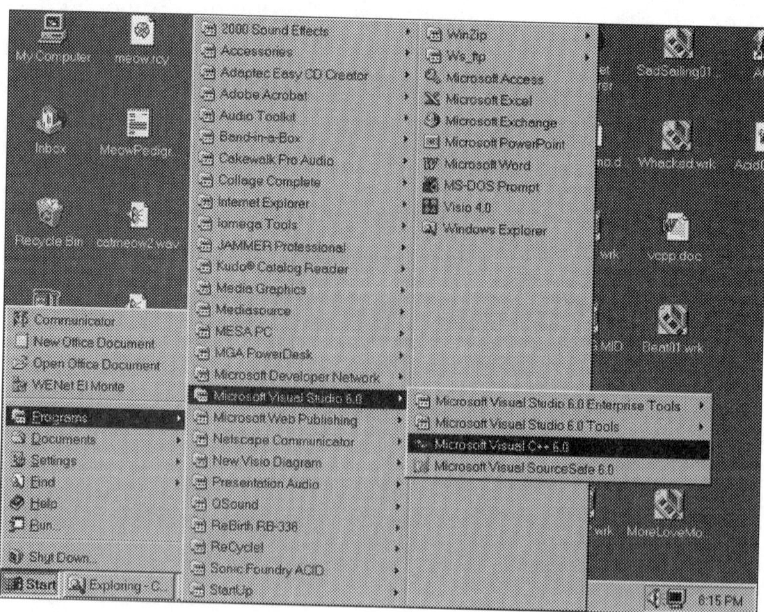

Figure 1.1
Starting Visual C++ 6 from the Start menu.

The Integrated Development Environment (IDE) that you use to create your Visual C++ programs acts a little like an artist's studio: It conveniently puts "under one roof" all the tools you need to write your programs. Let us explain how the various pieces of the Visual C++ IDE work together.

What Is Visual C++?

Visual C++ includes these major components:

- The Editor, which you use to enter, browse, and revise your C++ source code.
- The Compiler, which translates your C++ source code into object code.
- The Linker, which creates executable files by combining object code and library modules.
- The Libraries, which provide prewritten modules that you can incorporate into your programs. One of the most important libraries contains the Microsoft Foundation Classes (MFC), which you use to write programs that run Microsoft Windows. In addition, the standard C++ library supports input/output and other standard features of the C++ language.
- Other tools, including the AppWizard, the ClassWizard, and the Resource Editor. You'll meet the AppWizard in this chapter and additional tools in subsequent chapters.

Using Visual C++

When you start Visual C++, you'll briefly see a colorful splash screen. After the splash screen disappears, Visual C++ looks somewhat austere, as you can see in Figure 1.2. Its only touch of color comes from the ubiquitous Tip Wizard box, which appears each time Visual C++ starts. If you're not into daily self-improvement, you can disable the Tip Wizard by clearing the Show Tips At Startup checkbox.

The Visual C++ screen includes three windows:

- The Project Workspace window appears along the left edge of the screen. It helps you navigate large programs with many source files.

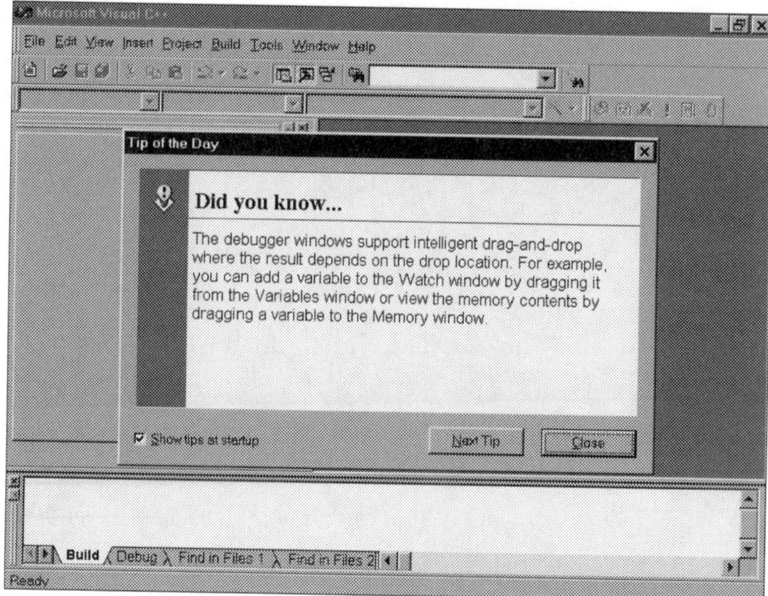

Figure 1.2
The Visual C++ opening screen with Tip Wizard.

- The Editor window appears to the right of the Project Workspace window. You use the Editor window to enter and revise source code.
- The Output window appears along the bottom edge of the screen. It displays progress messages, error messages, and result summaries for commands you issue. For example, compilation errors appear in the Output window if you attempt to compile a program that contains errors.

Project NotePod: Preliminary Briefing

Nothing really happens in Visual C++ until you create a project—so, it's time to do just that. Rather than build a useless example, let's create a real Visual C++ program that does something useful. We're not talking some wimpy "Hello World" program, either. This is an industrial-strength text editor that includes menus and a toolbar—it even sports printing and print-preview. Our project is just like Windows' Notepad program, only better. So, in homage to the classic film *Invasion of the Body Snatchers*, and to be sure no one confuses this example program with Notepad, let's call our program *NotePod*. (After all, from the pod-people's point of view, they were simply improving on the raw material they were given.)

To create a new project in Visual C++, you begin by selecting File|New from the main menu. In the dialog box that subsequently appears, you choose the Projects tab and select a project type from the list that you find there.

Unfortunately, Visual C++ presents a vast number of different project types from which you can choose. Even worse, the offerings are presented in simple alphabetical order, which makes picking the right project type a little like ordering from a large and unfamiliar a la carte menu—unless you're familiar with the restaurant, you have to rely on luck.

Fortunately, you're not in that predicament—you have a guide, remember? Simply search the list until you find the entry "MFC AppWizard (exe)", then select it, as illustrated in Figure 1.3.

In addition to selecting a project type, the New dialog box also asks you to give the project a name and specify its location. Type the name of your project (NotePod) in the Project Name text field. As you type, the name you provide will be added to the end of the Location text field below the Project Name.

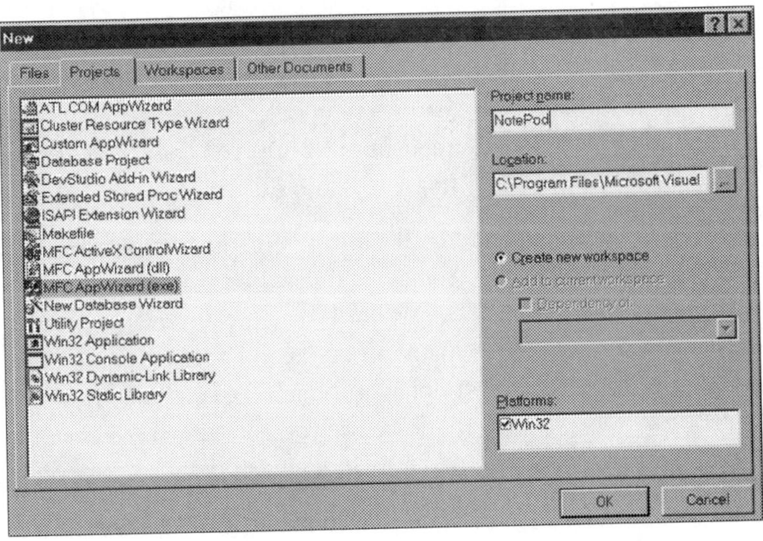

Figure 1.3
Starting an AppWizard project.

The project name you select serves several purposes. First, it serves as the name for your executable program when your project is assembled. Second, it's used as the name of the subdirectory (called a *workspace* in Visual C++ parlance) where your project files will automatically be created. Third, when Visual C++ creates your project, it will use the project name to construct the class names that your application uses.

By default, when you create a new project, Visual C++ creates a new workspace. If you like, you can click on the button at the end of the Location text field to select a different location for your project. For the NotePod project, type "NotePod" in the Project Name text field and use the default values for all the other choices. When you're finished, click on OK and let the Visual C++ AppWizard take over.

Getting Started With AppWizard

The Visual C++ AppWizard is a code generator—you might think of it as your own personal programming assistant. The AppWizard leads you through a series of dialog boxes, asking you what features you want your application to have. Once it has all the information it needs, AppWizard generates a custom skeleton application. This skeleton program includes the features you specify, and you can further customize it to include specific features that set your program apart from every other Windows application. Thus, you can "have it your way" without ever stepping behind the grill.

You'll want to remember an important point about AppWizard: You use it only when you start your project. You can use AppWizard to create a starter application, but you can't use it to maintain or expand your program. Because of this fact, you need to plan ahead and be sure you know what you want your program to do before you get started. You can't rerun the AppWizard to add print-preview or database support after the fact.

With that in mind, let's take a walk with the AppWizard as it constructs the NotePod program.

AppWizard 1: Giving Your Application Some Style

As you can see in Figure 1.4, AppWizard first asks what type of application you want to create. Your choices are as follows:

- *Single Document Interface (SDI)*—This type of application allows you to open only one document at a time. The document automatically fills your application's main window, leaving no room for additional documents. Windows Notepad is an SDI application; when you open a text file from its File menu, the new file replaces the file you were viewing. You'll learn more about SDI applications in Chapter 11.
- *Multiple Document Interface (MDI)*—This type of application can open multiple documents at the same time. All of the familiar Microsoft Office products are MDI applications. In Excel, for instance, you can open several spreadsheets simultaneously—each spreadsheet appears in its own window and each individual document window remains inside the main application window. Our NotePod program is an MDI application.
- *Dialog based*—This type of application uses a dialog box as its main window. Dialog-based applications are frequently used for

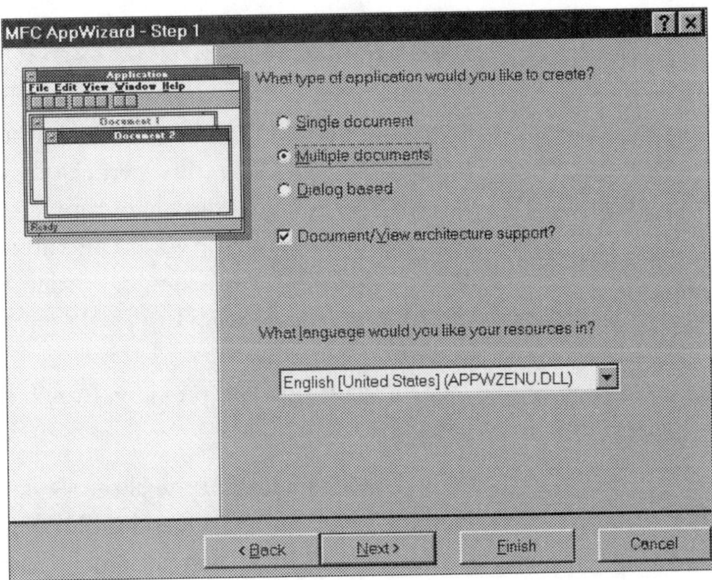

Figure 1.4
AppWizard Step 1: Choosing your application style.

simple utility programs like the Date/Time Properties application that sets the date and time in Windows 95. Visual C++ provides access to its dialog editor to design the look and feel of your dialog-based application. Dialog-based applications contain relatively few classes, so they're easy to understand when you're just starting out. You'll learn how to use dialog-based applications in Chapter 3.

The AppWizard's Step 1 dialog box also allows you to specify two specialized options. First, unchecking the Document/View Architecture Support checkbox—a new option in Visual C++ 6—lets AppWizard generate simpler code for certain kinds of applications. Most of the time, you'll leave this at its default (checked) setting. You'll read more about the Document/View architecture in Chapter 12. Second, you can store your resources, such as menu and system prompts, in a language other than English. You simply select the desired language from the drop-down list box that appears in the dialog box.

For the NotePod program, let's create an MDI application, leave the Document/View checkbox selected, and leave the resource DLL set to English. Once you've made those selections, click on Next and you're ready for Step 2.

AppWizard 2: Data, Data, Everywhere

The next AppWizard screen asks you what kind of database support you'd like. AppWizard will automatically write code to access databases using the Open Database Connectivity (ODBC) standard, which provides almost universal access to hundreds of different databases. AppWizard also allows you to access databases that use Microsoft's Jet Engine, the database engine that's used in Access and Visual Basic. In Visual C++ 6, you can also use ActiveX Data Objects (ADO) to access an Object Linking and Embedding (OLE) DB provider. (You'll learn more about this in Chapters 19 and 20.)

Of course, if you look at the choices offered by AppWizard in Figure 1.5, ODBC, ADO, and OLE DB are nowhere to be found. Instead, you're given a choice among four levels of database support that seem a little vague. After all, how are you supposed

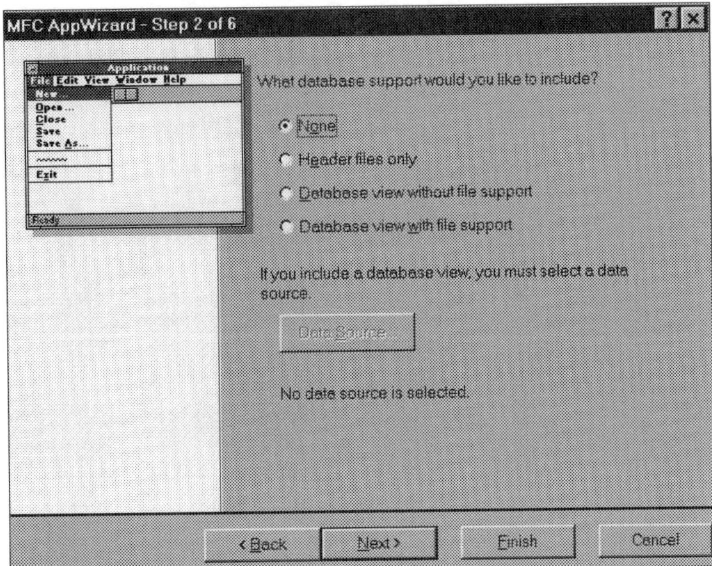

Figure 1.5
AppWizard Step 2: Specifying database support options.

to know whether you need "Header files only" or "Database view with file support"?

Fortunately, for right now, the answer is fairly simple. The NotePod application won't need any database support at all, so we'll defer explanation of these options until Chapter 19. (At that point, you'll use the Visual C++ database support to build a database query-and-update application.) Just select None and click on Next to move along.

AppWizard 3: It's OLE All Over Again

Step 3 in the AppWizard interview allows you to select the level of "Compound document support" that you require. In this screen, you ask AppWizard to add support for Microsoft's Component Object Model (COM).

COM is a huge subject with many different facets, and it more than deserves a book (or perhaps 10 books) of its own. In Chapter 17, you'll see how COM lets your Visual C++ programs use the same kind of ActiveX components used in Visual Basic programs.

COM is more than ActiveX controls, however. Using COM, you can let other programs automatically control your Visual C++

application as if it were a component. Perhaps you've noticed that programs like Microsoft Word allow you to embed in your document a spreadsheet or a drawing from another application: This magic is courtesy of COM. Figure 1.6 shows the COM options available in Visual C++.

We won't use any compound document support in the NotePod program, so uncheck the ActiveX Controls checkbox at the bottom of AppWizard's Step 3 dialog box. Then, click on Next to continue.

AppWizard 4: Bells And Whistles

In Step 4, AppWizard gives you the chance to select from a grab bag of different "gee-whiz" features. Four of these options are selected by default:

- *Docking Toolbar*—Tells AppWizard to create a standard toolbar directly below your application's menu. The toolbar is dockable, meaning that your application's users can detach it, move it, and then reattach it to any edge of the screen. When you ask AppWizard to create a toolbar, it also supplies standard buttons for operations such as clipboard cut, copy, and paste, as well as file open and save.

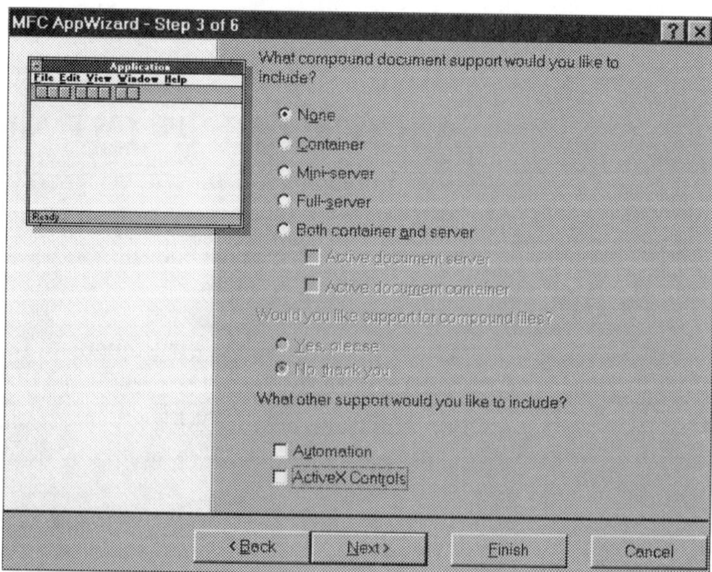

Figure 1.6
AppWizard Step 3: Setting up COM options.

- *Initial Status Bar*—Places a standard Windows status bar at the bottom of your application window. When you enable status-bar support, your application's menu includes an option that allows users to display or hide the status bar.
- *Printing And Print Preview*—Takes care of displaying the standard Windows print-preview window, as well as displaying the Printer dialog box when a user chooses File | Print. In addition, Visual C++ adds routines that make it possible to use the same code for output to either the screen or printer.
- *3D Controls*—Adds code that renders a 3D appearance to Windows controls like checkboxes, text fields, and radio buttons. This option affects only controls used outside of dialog boxes; Windows controls used inside dialog boxes are 3D anyway. By checking this option, you ensure that all of your application's controls have the same look and feel.

In addition to the four selected items, AppWizard also allows you to add context-sensitive help, MAPI support, and Windows sockets support. Because these features are used less often, they aren't selected by default. Unlike the four default items, each of these selections also requires considerable additional work to implement.

A new feature in Visual C++ 6 lets you select Internet Explorer-style ReBar toolbars instead of the traditional Windows toolbars. Finally, at the bottom of the Step 4 screen, you can select how many files you want to appear on the Most Recently Used (MRU) files list. The default (4) is rather puny, so we recommend that you set this option to 16, as you can see in Figure 1.7.

Once you've set the number of files, it's time to move on. However, don't click on Next—instead, click on Advanced and get ready to delve into the world of document templates.

An AppWizard Interlude: Name That Extension

When you click on Advanced in AppWizard's Step 4 screen, the dialog box that appears contains a property sheet with two tabs. One tab—Window Styles—allows you to fine-tune the look of

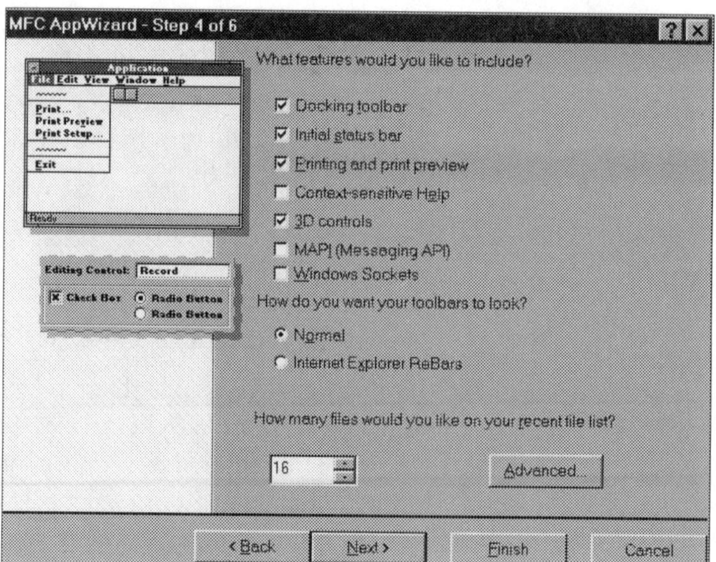

Figure 1.7
AppWizard Step 4: A whole mess of bells and whistles.

your document windows. This option is seldom used, and we won't use it here.

The second option—the Document Template Strings tab—consists of several text fields, and is much more useful. By entering the appropriate value in each field, you can register your custom document type with the Windows shell. As a result, a user can double-click on a file in Windows Explorer to open your application. Let's go ahead and register a document type for the NotePod application. Here are the two steps you'll need to follow:

1. In the File Extension text field, enter "pod". You'll use this file extension for NotePod files. (The files themselves are just plain text).
2. When Windows creates a document type name, it uses a string that's limited to six characters. Thus, the document type is called "NotePo" instead of "NotePod". You can't change that. You can, however, change each of the remaining text fields to display "NotePod" instead of "NotePo". Visual C++ will use these strings when you open a new file and when you look for the POD file type in Windows Explorer.

In Figure 1.8, you can see the completed dialog box as it should appear. Once you've filled in each of the fields, click on Close,

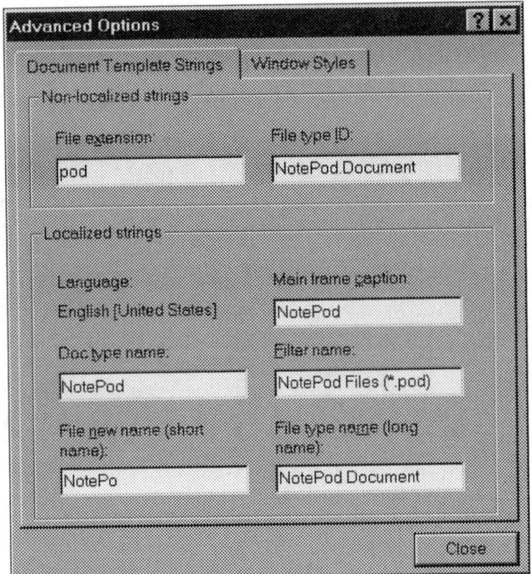

Figure 1.8
An AppWizard interlude: Choosing your advanced document options.

click on Next in Step 4, and get ready for the penultimate AppWizard screen. Don't give up: The completed application is coming soon!

AppWizard 5: Whatever's Left Over

In the previous release of Visual C++, the Step 5 dialog box offered only two options: the ability to automatically generate comments in the source code, and whether to link statically or dynamically to the MFC library. Both of these options have been retained in the current incarnation. And Visual C++ 6 adds another option: the ability to generate either a standard MFC application or a Windows Explorer-style program that features a document window consisting of two panes.

You should generally choose to have AppWizard place comments in your code. When you select this option, AppWizard will insert comments pointing out areas where you need to add code. In addition, it will often give you a hint about the kind of code you need to write.

If you choose to use the MFC library as a shared DLL, your Visual C++ executable programs will be much smaller (because they can share the same copy of the library). However, if you want to distribute an application that you've linked to one or more shared DLLs, you'll need to make provisions to distribute those DLLs as well. In contrast, when you choose to use the statically linked version of MFC, your programs are much larger—but each program is entirely self contained.

For the NotePod project, let's create a standard MFC project, have AppWizard add comments, and use MFC in a shared DLL. Once you've made the selections, which you can see in Figure 1.9, click on Next and get ready for the checkered flag.

AppWizard 6: An App With A View

You thought we were kidding about the checkered flag business, didn't you? As you can see in Figure 1.10, however, you really are at the finish line.

AppWizard's Step 6 dialog box is different in one important way from those before it: This is your last opportunity to back up and change any of the selections you've made on the previous screens. After this, you'll have a chance to bail out, but you won't be able to back up.

The Step 6 dialog box lists each of the C++ classes that AppWizard is about to generate. It also includes several text fields

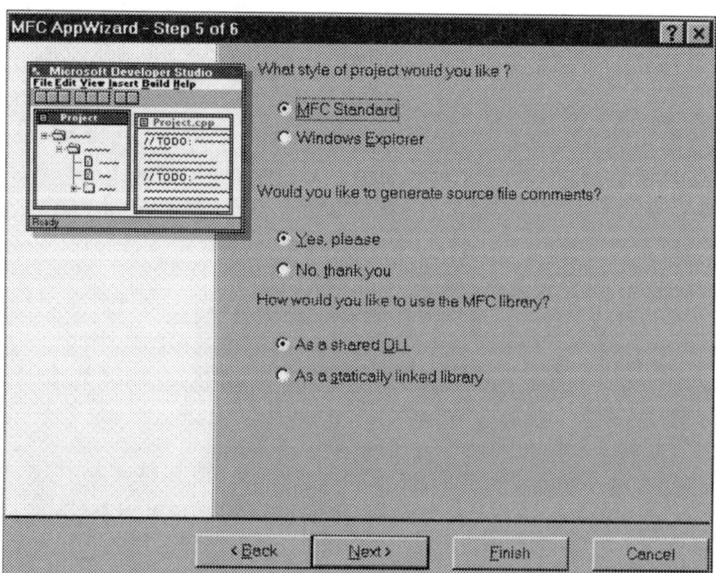

Figure 1.9
AppWizard Step 5: Window styles, comments, and libraries.

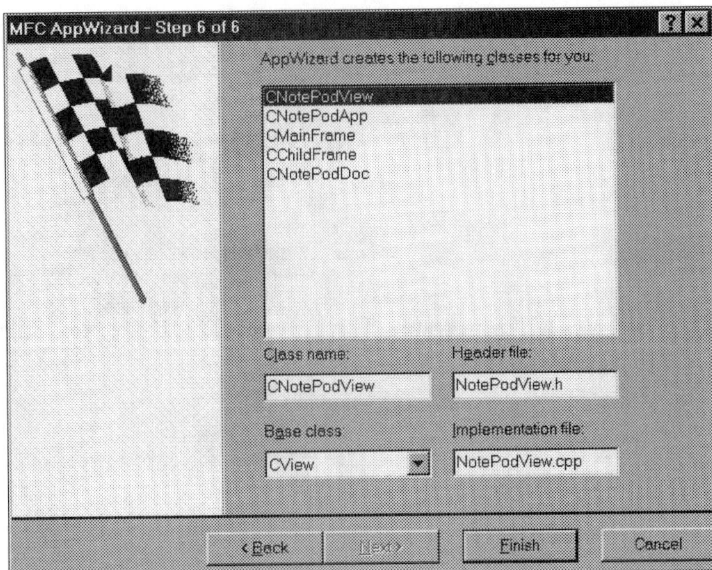

Figure 1.10
AppWizard Step 6: Changing the base view class.

that allow you to change the kind of code that AppWizard generates. As you scroll through the list of class names, each text field displays the name of the class (which you can change if you like), as well as the name of the base class and the files used to store the class header and implementation.

Normally, you'll make only one change on this screen. When you select your application's view class (the class name that ends with "view"), you'll see that a drop-down list box replaces the text field that held the name of the base class. In MFC, the view class represents the way your application interacts with users and the information it presents on screen. By simply selecting a different base class for your application's view, you can easily and dramatically change the way your application works.

Because the NodePod application is a text editor, you'll want to choose a base class that supports that kind of functionality. Fortunately, MFC comes to the rescue with the **CEditView** class. Select **CEditView**, click on Finish, and you're finally done.

Well, almost. As you can see in Figure 1.11, the AppWizard gives you one last chance to bail out. Notice, however, that the New Project Information dialog box has no Back button. If you want to return to Step 6 of the AppWizard, click on Cancel.

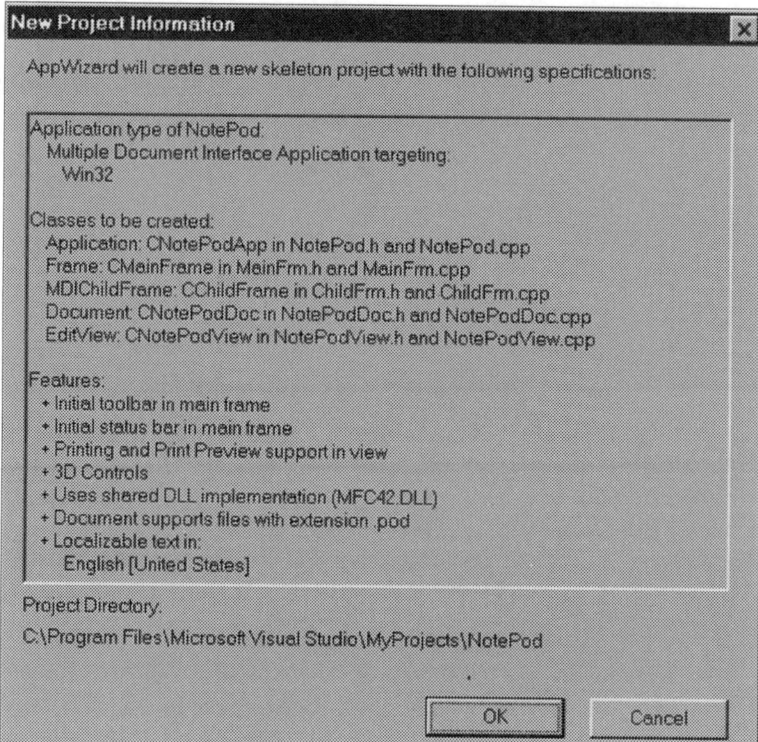
New Project Information

AppWizard will create a new skeleton project with the following specifications:

Application type of NotePod:
Multiple Document Interface Application targeting:
Win32

Classes to be created:
Application: CNotePodApp in NotePod.h and NotePod.cpp
Frame: CMainFrame in MainFrm.h and MainFrm.cpp
MDIChildFrame: CChildFrame in ChildFrm.h and ChildFrm.cpp
Document: CNotePodDoc in NotePodDoc.h and NotePodDoc.cpp
EditView: CNotePodView in NotePodView.h and NotePodView.cpp

Features:
+ Initial toolbar in main frame
+ Initial status bar in main frame
+ Printing and Print Preview support in view
+ 3D Controls
+ Uses shared DLL implementation (MFC42.DLL)
+ Document supports files with extension .pod
+ Localizable text in:
English [United States]

Project Directory:
C:\Program Files\Microsoft Visual Studio\MyProjects\NotePod

OK
Cancel

Figure 1.11
AppWizard: One last chance to change your mind.

The New Project Information dialog box is simply a recapitulation of the selections you've made on all of the previous screens. Read it through, and once you're satisfied, click on OK. AppWizard will create the files that you requested and place them in the directory you specified. Now, you can bid AppWizard a fond farewell—its work on this project is finished.

Exploring Your Project

Although the AppWizard has exited the scene, it left behind more than enough for you to remember it by. As a matter of fact, if you use Windows Explorer to look in the directory you specified when you started the NotePod project, you'll find a whole slew of new files—22 of them—and a couple of new subdirectories as well. How are you supposed to make sense of all these files?

As Nicklaus Wirth, the inventor of Pascal, once wrote, "The details are the jungle where the Devil hides. The only salvation lies in structure." Visual C++ comes to your rescue by providing a structured way to look at your files. The files themselves aren't rearranged—instead, you're given three different "views" on your project structure:

- FileView shows your files arranged in a logical hierarchy of source files, header files, and resource files.
- ClassView presents your project as a logical hierarchy of classes, functions, and data members.
- ResourceView arranges the resources in your program by resource type.

You can access each of these views through the Workspace window that appears by default on the left side of the screen. If you've closed the Workspace window, you can reopen it by choosing the View | Workspace menu item or pressing Ctrl+O. Once the Workspace window is displayed, you switch between the three views of your project by clicking the appropriate tab at the bottom of the window.

Let's briefly take a look at how Visual C++'s Workspace window arranges the files for project NotePod.

Files Galore: The File View

When you select the FileView tab, you'll initially see a single icon with a small + symbol beside it. Click with the mouse to expand each + until there are no more to be found. What you'll see should look like Figure 1.12.

The files for your project are organized in three folders: Source Files, Header Files, and Resource Files. In addition, two files—ReadMe.txt and NotePod.reg—are stored in the "root".

If you took the time to look through your files using Windows Explorer, you might be a little confused at this point. File View doesn't show you the physical organization of your files, as Explorer does—it gives you a logical view, instead.

By clicking on a file icon in the FileView window, you instantly open the file in Developer Studio's main window. Go ahead and

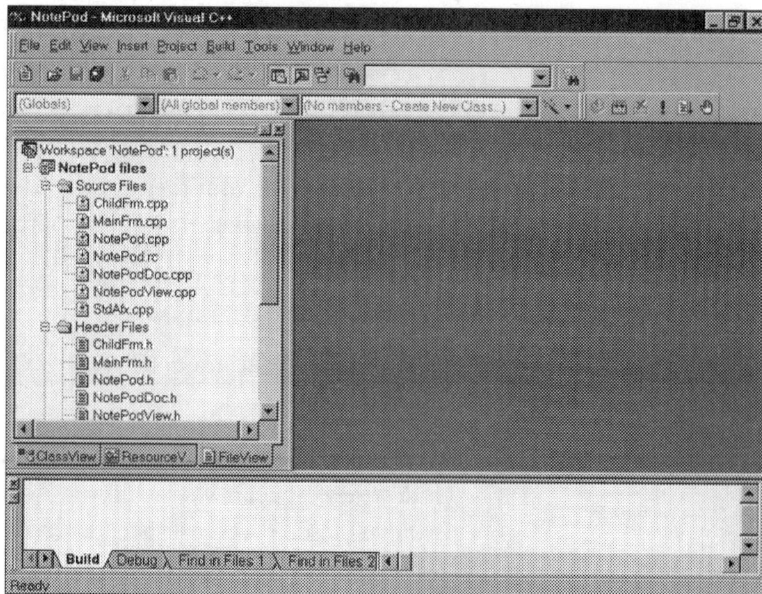

Figure 1.12
Exploring Project NotePod: Looking at the FileView window.

try it yourself: Double-click on the ReadMe.txt file and take a few minutes to browse through it. You'll see that AppWizard has clearly explained the meaning and purpose of each file it generated.

Although FileView, along with AppWizard's ReadMe.txt file, provides a little structure for your application, Visual C++ has a much better treat in store: ClassView. To use File View, you have to know which files contain which class definitions and declarations. On the other hand, the ClassView window lets you view your project as a collection of classes, regardless of the physical files that contain those classes.

Class Consciousness: The ClassView Window

When you click on the ClassView tab in the Workspace window, you'll see a tree that's similar to the FileView window. However, ClassView displays your project as a list of classes, rather than folders. When you expand one of the classes, you'll see a list of methods and data members.

You can see the ClassView window for the NotePod project in Figure 1.13.

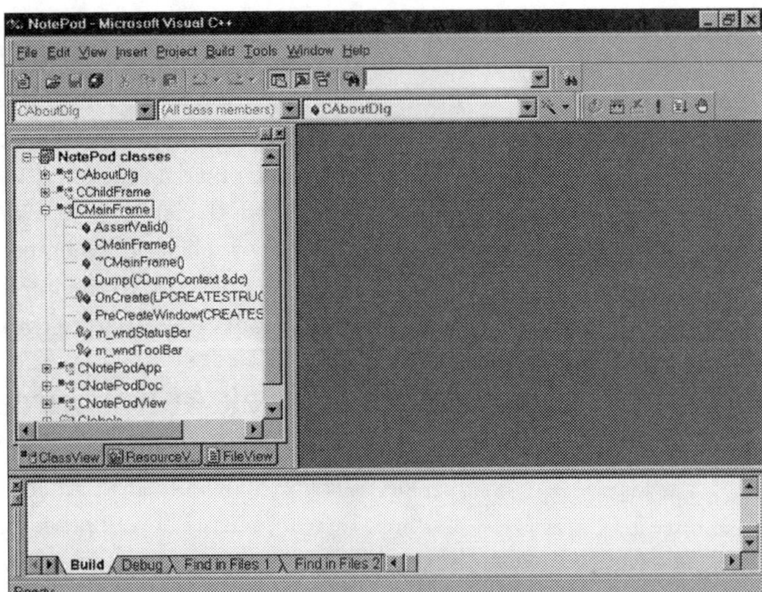

Figure 1.13
Exploring Project NotePod: Looking at the ClassView window.

As you can see from Figure 1.13, the NotePod project contains six classes: **CAboutDlg**, **CChildFrame**, **CMainFrame**, **CNotePodApp**, **CNotePodDoc**, and **CNotePodView**. You'll learn more about these classes and what each of them does in the next chapter. For now, let's just take a quick look around.

If you click on the + that appears next to **CMainFrame**, it will expand into a tree that displays several different icons. Visual C++ uses these icons to help you quickly differentiate among the various parts of your classes. For instance, the small purple block appearing next to the first entry, **AssertValid()**, lets you know that it's a member function. The small cyan (light blue-green) blocks appearing beside **m_wndStatusBar** and **m_wndToolBar** tell you that these are data members of the **CMainFrame** class.

Class View uses two other icons to display the access specifier associated with the data member or function. A small key—such as that appearing beside the **m_wndStatusBar** member—means that the item is protected. If a padlock appears, then the item is private. If neither appears, then the item is public.

As in File View, double-clicking on an item in the ClassView window opens an editing window where you can make changes

There's More To Programs Than Code

If your programming experience has been confined to the command-line DOS or Unix world, you may wonder exactly what constitutes non-code portions of a program—after all, programming is all about code, right? Well, not exactly. In a Windows program, you store the data that defines the "look and feel" or user-interface portions of your application separately from the code that operates on that data. Such data items are called resources and they're automatically bundled into your executable program when you build your application.

to—or simply view—the item's definition. You don't have to be concerned about where the related file is located: Visual C++ tracks that information for you. Exactly which file opens, however, depends on the kind of item you double-click. When you select a class name or a data member, Visual C++ assumes you want to see the class declaration. So, you're taken to the appropriate header file. If you click on a member function, on the other hand, Visual C++ takes you to the implementation file that defines the function, rather than to the class declaration.

A Quick Peek At Resource View

The Workspace window has one remaining view—the ResourceView window. Like the other windows, ResourceView arranges the components of your program in a hierarchical manner. Resource View, however, doesn't work with your project's source code; instead, it organizes the non-code portions of your program.

Rather than talking in generalities, let's look at a few specifics. If you examine Figure 1.14, you'll see the ResourceView window for the NotePod project. Notice that there are seven folders: Accelerator, Dialog, Icon, Menu, String Table, Toolbar, and Version. Like the folders used in the FileView window, these are virtual folders used simply to provide structure for your application—they aren't physical folders that store your files.

If you open one of the folders—Dialog, for instance—you'll see that it contains an item called **IDD_ABOUTBOX**. If you double-click on **IDD_ABOUTBOX**, Visual C++ will open an editing window, just as it did in Class View and File View. The difference is that Resource View sends you to the appropriate kind of editor for the type of resource you double-click. If you open a Dialog resource, Resource View sends you to the dialog editor; if you open the Toolbar resource, you're placed in the toolbar editor. In Figure 1.14, the dialog editor has been activated.

In Chapter 3, you'll walk through each of the resource editors. But for right now, it's time to move on.

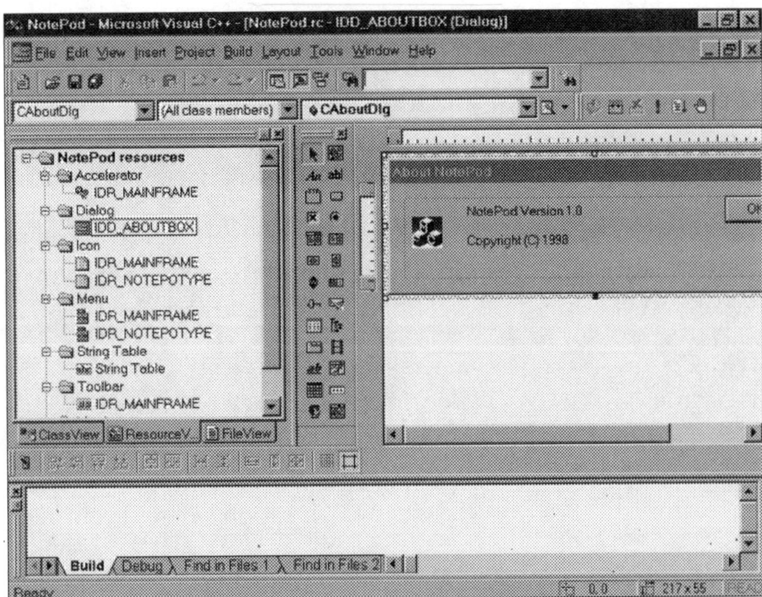

Figure 1.14
Exploring Project NotePod: Looking at the ResourceView window.

Activating Project NotePod

So far, you've looked at the NotePod project from every viewpoint but one: What does NotePod look like when it runs? The time has come to remedy that condition.

To run the NotePod program, you first have to create an executable (you can't run the source code). This process is called *building the application*. (If you come from a Unix background, you'd call it *making the application*.)

Building NotePod

Building the application is easy: Simply choose Build | Build NotePod.exe from the main menu, click on the Build icon on the Build toolbar, or press the F7 accelerator key.

Once you start the build process, Visual C++ keeps you informed by posting messages to the Output window, which normally appears at the bottom of the screen. If you've closed the Output window, you can reopen it by selecting View | Output from the main menu. Once the Output window is displayed, be sure the

Build tab is selected, or you won't be able to watch the progress as Visual C++ compiles your application. You can see the output from building the NotePod project in Figure 1.15. Notice that we've expanded the Output window to show all the messages generated by Visual C++.

The first time you build the NotePod program, you need to be patient—it may take a while, even on a fast machine. On subsequent builds of the same project, Visual C++ is much faster.

If the Visual C++ compiler encounters any errors, it will place the error messages in the Output window. Within Visual C++, however, error messages are special. If you double-click on an error message in the Output window, you'll automatically be taken to the location where the error occurred, so you can fix it.

For now, though, you don't need to worry about errors, because you haven't written any code yet. Instead, let's take NotePod out for a test ride.

A World Of Pods

To run NotePod from within Visual C++, simply select Build|Execute NotePod.exe from the main menu, click on the

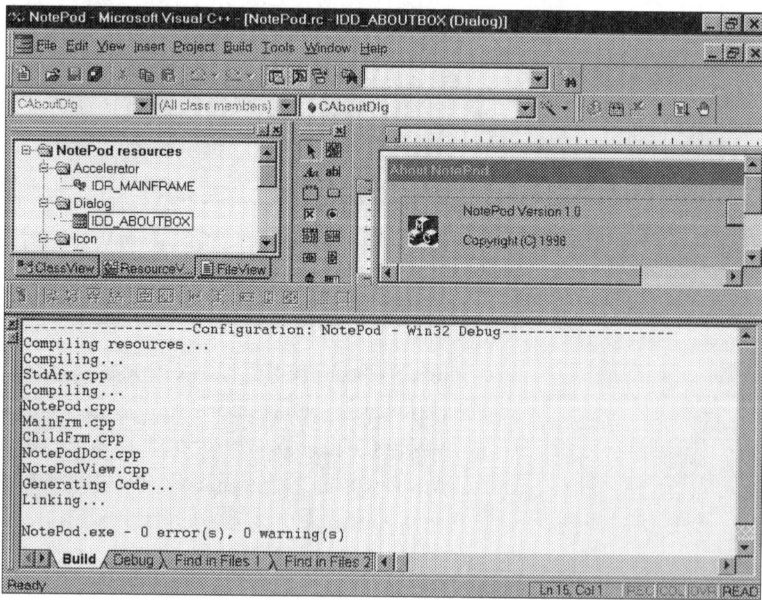

Figure 1.15
Compiler progress in the Output window.

Execute icon (!) on the Build toolbar, or press Ctrl+F5. You'll find that NotePod will start right up. (You don't have to run NotePod from within the IDE, of course. It's a real Windows program, so you can start it by double-clicking its file icon in Windows Explorer or by adding a shortcut to your Start menu.)

The first thing you should notice about NotePod is that you can move it, resize it, minimize it, and maximize it. As we said, it's a regular Windows program—you didn't have to write any code to support these features. You can see the NotePod program at work in Figure 1.16.

Next, write some text in the document window, just as you can with Notepad. Unlike Notepad, though, you can open another document window, then use the Window menu to arrange your documents. You can copy text from one window to another, you can print your documents or use the built in print-preview—you can even fill your entire disk with files, each with the .pod extension.

NotePod does all of this without your writing a single line of code. Of course, there's a price to be paid for this convenience: the price of mindless conformity. While AppWizard gives you a plethora of

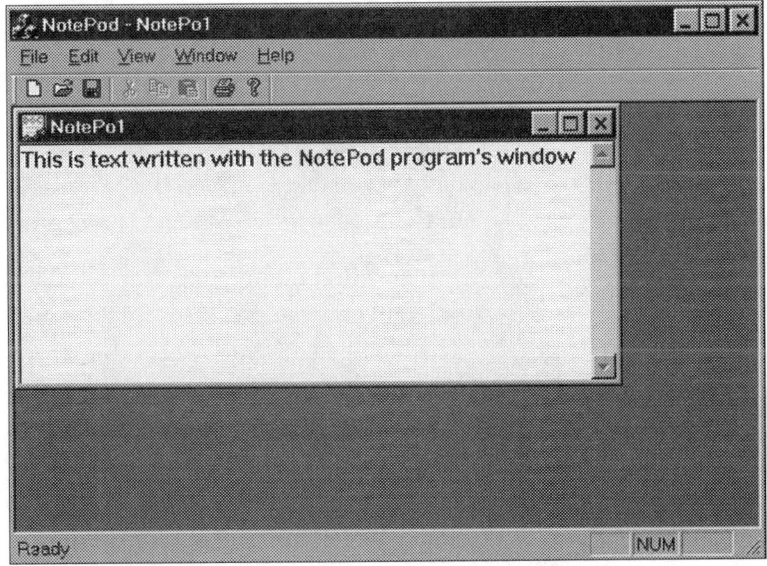

Figure 1.16
The NotePod program: multiple documents with cut and paste already implemented.

options, in the final analysis you have a canned program—NotePod works exactly like every other NotePod pro-gram created by every other "programmer" who clicks on the same AppWizard options. NotePod truly inhabits a world of clones.

The New World Order

Fortunately, that's not the end of the story. (This is, after all, only Chapter 1.) Although AppWizard is a handy, labor-saving device and gets much of the Visual C++ limelight, it's really only a figurehead: The real programming power is wielded behind the scenes, in the never-ending, object-oriented class struggle, by a shadowy figure dubbed the ClassWizard.

All programmers become programmers because, in the final analysis, they want to tell the computer what to do, rather than vice versa. In the pursuit of this goal, the ClassWizard is both your ally and your most powerful weapon. The AppWizard gives you a starting point for your program—but the ClassWizard lets you build your dreams without getting your fingernails dirty.

Meet Me At The WizardBar

Let's see how the ClassWizard can help customize NotePod so that it isn't a mere clone of every other NotePod program produced by AppWizard. Rather than use the full-fledged ClassWizard, which you'll meet in Chapter 3, we'll instead use its more accessible emissary, the WizardBar. The WizardBar appears in the toolbar when Visual C++ is running.

You may find it annoying that when you're using the NotePod program and you press the Tab key, NotePod skips eight spaces. The Notepad program works this way, too. Both programs do this because they are created using the built-in Windows multiline Edit control, and that's the Edit control's default behavior. The Windows Edit control, however, does have the ability to display tabs using a different set of tab stops. You can accomplish this simply by sending it the **SetTabStops()** message.

Here's how you use the WizardBar to modify the NotePod project:

1. Select the ClassView pane in the Workspace window. Double-click on the **CNotePodView** class to open the class definition window in the editor.
2. Click on the down-arrow to activate the drop-down menu at the very right of the WizardBar, as shown in Figure 1.17. From the menu, select the Add Virtual Function option.
3. In the Virtual Functions dialog box that appears, select the **OnInitialUpdate()** function. Then, click on the Add And Edit button, shown in Figure 1.18.
4. Visual C++ adds the new function to your CNotePodView.cpp file, adds a comment, and then places you inside the editor. Add the line

   ```
   SetTabStops(16);
   ```

   inside the function body, as you can see in Figure 1.19. Once you're done, rebuild the project and then try out the new, customized version of NotePod.

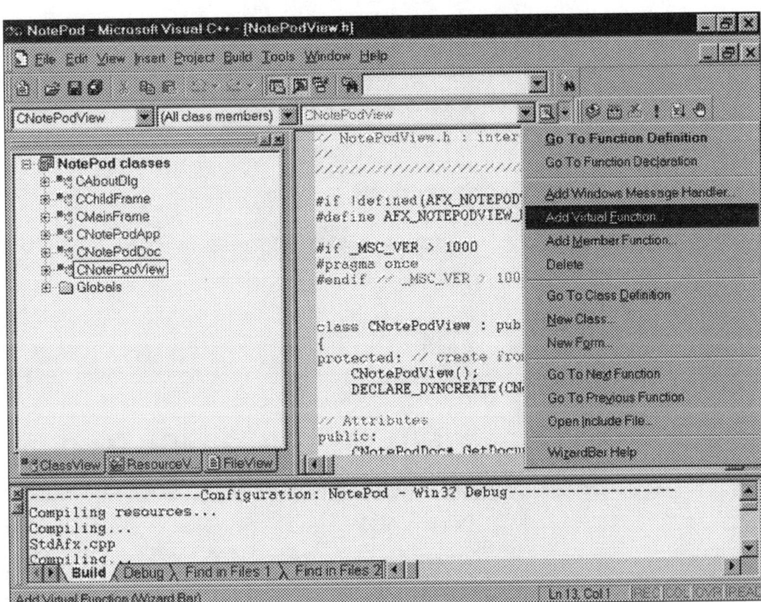

Figure 1.17
Using the WizardBar options menu.

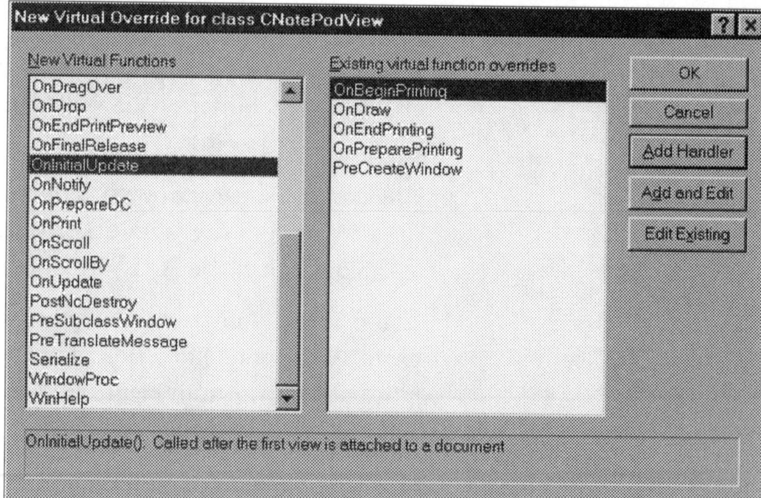

Figure 1.18
Overriding a virtual function using the WizardBar.

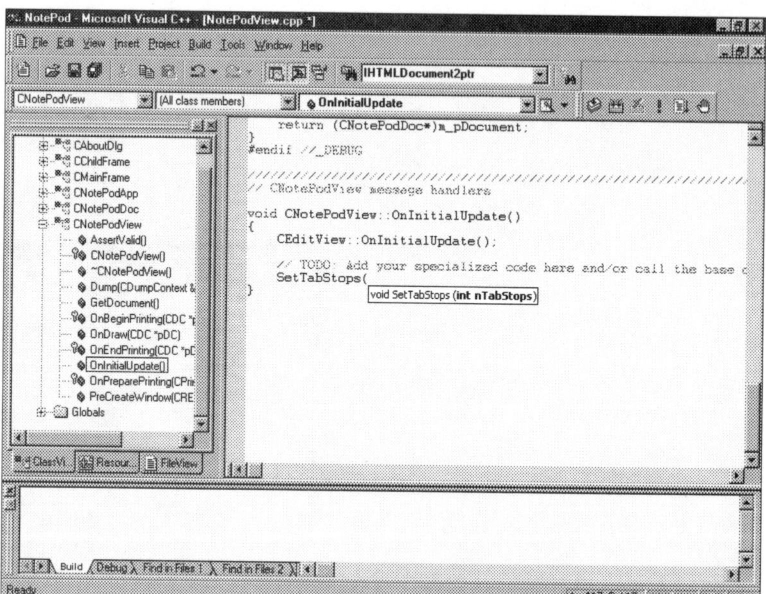

Figure 1.19
Adding code in the Visual C++ editor.

Help From An Unexpected Source

If you've been pointing, clicking, and typing along with the NotePod project, you were probably very surprised when you started typing the **SetTabStops()** function in the last section. As you noticed, once you type a function name, the Visual C++ editor helps you complete the function by displaying the argument types required in a tooltip window, as you can see in Figure 1.19.

Microsoft calls this feature AutoCompletion, and it works like this:

- When you type the name of an object, Visual C++ pops up a list of the member functions applicable to that object type. You can scroll through the list and press the spacebar to have Visual C++ insert the function name for you.
- When you type the name of a function, as you did for **SetTabStops()**, Visual C++ displays the prototype for the function, so you know what kinds of arguments to pass.
- When the function is overloaded, the tooltip box that Visual C++ displays contains a set of arrows. By clicking on the arrows, you can switch between the different argument signatures that this function name accepts.

AutoCompletion is one of those neat ideas that makes your work as a programmer more productive. But, what if you need to know more than just a method name? To help you in that case, Visual C++ comes with a special dedicated version of the Microsoft Developer Network (MSDN) CD, which you can access by pressing the F1 key. Along with the documentation included on the CD, Visual C++ 6 includes a new HTML-based help engine that is a vast improvement over the widely disparaged InfoViewer used in Visual C++ 5.0.

As you can see in Figure 1.20, the new HTML help engine allows you to search the entire CD for a list of topics, and then easily navigate among the resulting documents. Truly, getting help has never been easier.

Card Tricks Or Hat Tricks: What's The Meaning Of This?

If you're new to Windows programming, you may be a little confused—we've covered a lot of ground, with very little explanation. Don't worry, that explanation's coming right up in the next chapter.

On the other hand, if you've had some experience with Windows programming, you may find yourself similarly confused. Perhaps

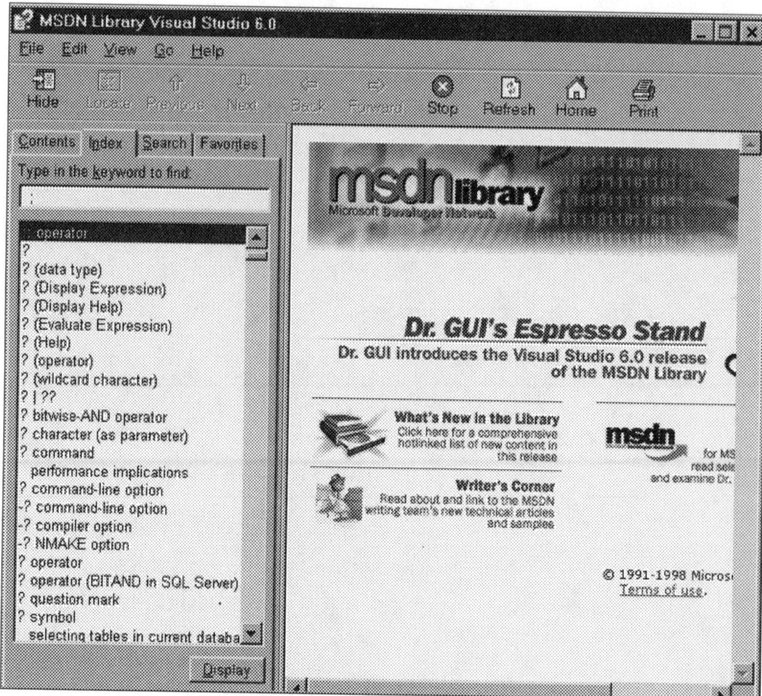

Figure 1.20
Using the online documentation.

all this pointing and clicking seems a little like a card trick. *After all,* you're thinking to yourself, *programming still comes down to writing code.*

You know something? You're absolutely right.

Despite the similar-sounding names, Visual C++ isn't a point-and-click programming environment like Visual Basic. Visual C++ programs usually aren't collections of forms populated by components. Instead, writing Visual C++ programs involves the modification and extension of a common application framework, the MFC. To use the MFC effectively, you must have a thorough understanding of how it works.

That's the subject of the next chapter.

Chapter 2
Windows Programming

Like an old-fashioned wireless operator, Windows programs deal with events by sending messages. In this chapter, you'll begin developing an event vocabulary.

"Window programs are fat and slow!"

If you've been around personal computers for any length of time, you've probably heard this complaint. In fact, you've probably heard it repeatedly. On the face of it, the charge has merit: Your Windows word processor does require more hard disk space and does run less quickly than the DOS version it replaced. But, the operative word here is *replaced*. If your DOS word processor was that great, why did you stop using it?

Therein lies the crux of the matter. All of us would like software that's smaller and faster, but not at the expense of the features Windows provides. Windows wasn't designed to be a smaller and faster version of DOS; rather, it was designed to remedy some of the limitations that DOS imposes on both programmers and users. So, it's only fair to evaluate Windows on those terms. Complaining about Windows' size and speed is a little like criticizing Godzilla for being a clumsy ice skater—it's simply not his calling in life.

In this chapter, we'll start by looking at the problems Windows solves for users and programmers. To follow along, you'll need to understand the basic internal architecture of Windows itself. Then, we'll examine the basic structure of a Windows program—the Windows application architecture. Although the programs we'll write make use of Visual C++ and the MFC libraries, under the skin they'll all share a common ancestry with the very first API-based programs of yesteryear.

Finally, we'll take an in-depth look at MFC itself. Just as all API-based programs share a common internal architecture, so do all MFC programs. We'll first create a very minimal MFC program. Once you've mastered it, we'll move on to consider MFC's document/view architecture and the code generated by AppWizard.

DOS Problems

To fully understand and appreciate Windows, it's necessary to take a time trip back to the 1980s, before Windows became ubiquitous. In those days, both programmers and users worked with DOS and, as a result, both programmers and users had problems.

Users found the command-line programs supported by DOS difficult to use. So, they demanded applications with Graphical User Interfaces (GUIs). DOS programmers found themselves spending more and more of their development time on the GUI "frills" and less on the substance.

Users were understandably upset when their DOS applications failed to support the fancy new monitor or printer they purchased. Meanwhile, the poor DOS programmer spent more and more time writing interface code for new hardware.

Users didn't want to think about their computers; they simply wanted to get their work done. They wanted to run multiple programs simultaneously, and they wanted their programs to be able to share data and work together cooperatively. Faced with ambitious user requirements like these, the exhausted DOS programmer threw up her hands in resignation.

As you can see, the 1980s were far from "the good old days" as far as computing was concerned. In a moment, we'll look at how Windows solves these problems. But first, let's examine each in more detail.

Problems With The User Interface

How do you describe Windows? If you're like most others—users and programmers alike—you describe it, without hesitation, as a graphical user interface in the tradition of the Xerox Star and the Apple Macintosh.

Although the traditional DOS (or Unix) command line is arguably more efficient than the windows, icons, mice, and pointers of GUIs, most users find typing commands at the C:> prompt difficult and intimidating. So, for the majority of users, the Windows GUI makes computers easier to understand and use.

Unfortunately, users' demands for easier-to-use GUI applications posed a problem for programmers: Such applications are difficult to write under DOS. As users asked for a cooler "look and feel," DOS programmers found themselves devoting more of their application development time to writing user-interface code, and less time to the problems that their programs were initially intended to solve.

Problems With Hardware Dependency

Traditional DOS applications also posed a second problem: They were intrinsically tied to the hardware for which they were originally designed. Perhaps you remember when the best-selling word-processing program was the DOS version of WordPerfect. WordPerfect's popularity derived, in part, from the fact that it came with a stack of drivers to support virtually any kind of printer. But, of course, the printer-drivers used for WordPerfect wouldn't work for Lotus 123 or WordStar.

This hardware dependency created a tremendous problem for programmers, as well. If you wanted to develop a DOS application for the PC market, you were faced with three choices. You could:

- Write your application so that it worked at the lowest-common-denominator level. You might support only CGA graphics in your program, for instance. Of course, this meant that users who shelled out cash for a fancy graphics card would likely be disappointed when they discovered your program failed to support its advanced features.

- Support the advanced features of only selected hardware devices, such as Epson printers, for instance. This approach would please those who purchased one of the supported devices, but it would doubly disappoint those who selected some other brand or model.
- Spend an inordinate amount of time and money making sure your application worked as it should on all the new hardware that was released. Doing so would win you customers—but you could find yourself spending much of your profits on software development, as you struggled to keep current with the latest hardware offerings.

As you see, each of these alternatives for dealing with hardware dependency presented difficulties for the user, the programmer, or both.

Problems With Cooperation

DOS is a *single-task operating system*: It runs a single program at a time. Only after one program is finished can you run another. Unfortunately, life isn't single-threaded. Most of us are continually interrupted by telephone calls, email, meetings, and so on. In such an environment, an operating system that requires you to shut one program down before opening another is often a hindrance, not a help.

Not only did DOS refuse to run programs cooperatively, often programs couldn't exchange even the simplest information with one another. Users wanted programs that worked together and seamlessly shared information—but DOS, and DOS programs, were too frequently not up to the task.

Windows was designed to solve these three major problems. Let's take a quick look and see how (and how well) Windows achieved this goal.

Windows Solutions

When Windows was introduced, it implemented features designed to address each failing of DOS. In particular, we'd like to discuss these four features:

- A common user interface.
- A system-wide, queued input and messaging system.
- A device-independent input/output architecture.
- Application multitasking and interprocess communication.

The Common User Interface

The Windows user interface is the part of Windows that gets the most press. That's natural, because it's the only part of Windows that's visible! For users, Windows' common user interface makes their computer easier to understand and work with.

For programmers, though, the effect of Windows is more profound. First, Windows offers an extensive library of common, built-in user-interface routines that are guaranteed to be present on every system that runs Windows. Second, Windows provides you with a built-in windowing/menuing manager. As a consequence, you don't have to worry about user-interface details such as resizing windows or handling menus—you can spend more time concentrating on the functional aspects of your program.

The Windows Messaging Architecture

In addition to supplying you with a built-in window manager, Windows also implements a system of communication known as *queued input*, or Windows messaging. Here's what that means.

If you're writing a traditional DOS program and you want to get input from the mouse or the keyboard, you often must resort to a method known as *polling*. A program that uses polling functions as an endless loop that continually monitors a particular device—in this case, the mouse or the keyboard—and then takes some action when the user moves the mouse or presses a key.

But when you use polling, your computer spends most of its time doing exactly nothing—running in circles, so to speak. Of course, clever DOS programmers know how to eliminate polling loops by directly intercepting or hooking the hardware interrupts generated by devices like the mouse, the keyboard, and the system timer. Unfortunately, such cleverness often leads to its own problems, as programs compete to intercept the same hardware interrupts. Barring incredible luck and superhuman foresight, collisions are inevitable.

Windows does away with such competition by taking exclusive control of all hardware devices. Windows itself receives every system input event—mouse, keyboard, and timer—and constructs event records that are then passed along to applications that need them.

As a consequence of this process, individual programs no longer need to monitor the system input devices—indeed, they can't. Instead, Windows routes timer, keyboard, and mouse messages to the appropriate programs. All your program has to do is to respond appropriately.

Also as a result of this process, Windows eliminates contention for input devices. Under DOS, if several programs installed a mouse handler interrupt-service routine, it was frequently very difficult to determine which program should handle which mouse message. When Windows handles the mouse, however, it's responsible for tracking the location of objects on screen and making sure that mouse events are routed to the correct program. Thus, sharing a hardware device among programs becomes trivial. If your program wants the mouse cursor to turn into a hand, while all other programs want to use an arrow, Windows will ensure that the correct cursor is displayed at the appropriate time.

The Device-Independent Input/Output Architecture

In the old DOS ages, if you bought a fancy 21-inch monitor and wanted to run Lotus or WordPerfect, your monitor vendor would have to supply you with a set of software patches for each application. Otherwise, you were simply out of luck.

If you were on the other side of the fence and were writing the software, the situation was even more difficult. For every application you supported, you had to know the specifics of the hardware attached to the computer, and then write your program to directly access that hardware device.

Of course, this wasn't true for *every* hardware device. For instance, DOS provided very good support for writing to different file systems. You didn't really have to know anything about the number of tracks and cylinders on your hard disk to read and write files. Moreover, you could use exactly the same code to read and write files on a hard disk or a floppy disk (which has a different layout than a hard disk). The operating system (DOS, in this case) provided an abstraction (files and directories) so you didn't have to deal with the hardware at the physical level (tracks and sectors).

So, under DOS, writing to files was device-independent—but writing to the display or to a printer wasn't. Windows set out to fix that shortcoming by introducing the Graphics Device Interface (GDI). When you, as a programmer, want to display output on screen using Windows, you aren't concerned with the physical display device. Instead, you write your code in terms of the GDI; your code should work, unchanged, on every new monitor that's developed.

Interprocess Communication And Cooperation

Finally, Windows tackled DOS's inability to run different programs simultaneously and have those programs cooperate with each other. Earlier versions of Windows supported a weak version of multitasking—a particularly "selfish" application could prevent other programs from getting their fair share of CPU time, for instance. With 32-bit Windows (Windows 95, Windows 98, and Windows NT), Microsoft introduced a stronger form of multitasking.

Under Windows, applications can cooperate in two ways. First, the system Clipboard allows simple data sharing between different applications, even if they were written by different companies. The second way involves the Component Object Model (COM), also known as OLE (for Object Linking and Embedding). COM-enabled programs can act as components of other applications, or as facilitators that help other programs cooperate.

Original Windows Programming: Using The API

Despite what you may have heard, it's possible to use Visual C++ to build Windows applications that are organized in almost exactly the same manner as the DOS applications built in the past. Such programs are called *Win32 console applications*. Unfortunately, console applications don't act like Windows applications: They have none of the user-friendly features that users expect from Windows programs.

Instead, you have to learn to write event-driven applications if you want them to act like other Windows programs. Unfortunately (at least for beginners), the fundamental structure of an event-driven program is very different from the straightforward, hierarchical structure of a traditional procedural application. This structural change is the reason it takes about 80 lines of code to write a simple event-driven "Hello World" program. The program is complex not merely because it operates in graphics mode, but because it's organized in a fundamentally different way.

What *Event-Driven* Means

Traditional programs are organized hierarchically. In C, for instance, a **main()** function sits atop a pyramid of other functions. It acts rather like a general manager, delegating its work to a few top-level routines. Likewise, each of these routines manages other, lower-level routines. Everything is orderly, and it's easy to step through the program—using a debugger, for instance—from start to finish. This is the sort of program most of us learned to write.

A Windows program, however, isn't organized in a (purely) hierarchical manner. It still contains functions, but those functions are designed to respond (somewhat autonomously) to external events. For this reason, we say that Windows programs are *event driven*.

An event can represent any of several occurrences. For example, one sort of event is generated when the user clicks the mouse or presses a key. Another sort of event can be generated by your computer's system clock. Still other events are generated by various modules inside Windows' own system software. Events can even be generated by functions inside your program or other programs.

However, you may find it difficult to get used to the fact that you generally don't call functions in response to these events. Instead, you send messages to Windows objects, asking them to respond to events in a predetermined fashion. And, even more importantly, you leave it up to Windows to deliver those messages.

How Events Are Generated

At the hardware level, each Windows input device is interrupt driven. When you press a key on your keyboard, a hardware interrupt occurs, normal Windows activity is suspended, and control is given to a piece of code called an Interrupt Service Routine (ISR). The ISR acts as device driver for the mouse, keyboard, and timer devices.

When the ISR is given control, it formats specific data and stores it in predefined registers. It then calls a designated routine inside Windows. This routine extracts the data from the registers and places an event record into the Windows hardware queue. Ordinarily, every event generates a new event record, but sometimes, multiple events are compressed into a single record along with a repeat count. Holding down a key until it autorepeats, for instance, causes this reaction.

Hardware events are pulled out of the hardware queue—formatted into normal, serialized Windows messages—and placed on the application input queue by a secondary thread running inside Windows. (Earlier versions of Windows performed this operation only when the application asked for a new message. This allowed an uncooperative Windows application to block other applications from receiving and processing their message events.) Thus, even though the hardware input is interrupt driven, event messages are processed by your application in a first-in, first-out (FIFO) order.

What Are Messages?

Messages are the standard communication mechanism within a Windows program, just as function calls are the standard communication mechanism in a traditionally organized DOS program. Messages are usually generated by one of three different sources:

- Hardware input events are generated by the keyboard, mouse, or timer. These events are sometimes called *enqueued events*, because they pass through the hardware input queue.
- Window manager events are generated by Windows itself in response to a user performing an operation such as moving or resizing a window, or selecting a menu item. Perhaps the most common of these messages—**WM_PAINT**—is sent to update your window area.
- Individual windows can send messages to other windows. For example, to tell a text field to erase its text, you send it the **WM_SETTEXT** message. The text field would also use this mechanism to tell you when its text has changed—it notifies you by sending an **EN_CHANGE** message.

As you can see, Windows messages are identified by a set of mnemonic identifiers. As you might guess from the capitalization, each name stands for an integer constant used to identify the particular message. Messages generated by Windows itself usually start with "WM_", which stands for *Windows Message*. Messages generated by specific kinds of Windows controls use different prefixes. For instance, messages generated by an edit control carry the prefix "EN_", which stands for *Edit Notification*.

Originally, all of these constants were defined in the master Windows header file, windows.h. As Windows grew, however, this header file became too large and was broken into pieces. Currently, you can find the message definitions in the header file winuser.h. Here are the first several entries in that file:

```
#define WM_NULL                          0x0000
#define WM_CREATE                        0x0001
#define WM_DESTROY                       0x0002
#define WM_MOVE                          0x0003
#define WM_SIZE                          0x0005
```

Although Windows messages are identified by a single integer, the actual message used for communication is a C structure named **MSG** that contains six different fields. These fields are as follows:

```
typedef struct tagMSG {
    HWND        hwnd;
    UINT        message;
    WPARAM      wParam;
    LPARAM      lParam;
    DWORD       time;
    POINT       pt;
} MSG;
```

Each of the fields inside a **MSG** structure is, in turn, defined in terms of other data types also defined by Windows. Using these data types facilitates porting Windows programs to processors where the fundamental data sizes might differ. Here's what each of these six fields does:

- ***HWND hwnd***—In Windows, every window has a unique identifier called its *window handle*. The value stored in this field is the handle of the window that the message should go to.
- ***UINT message***—An unsigned integer that stores the message identifier (for example, **WM_PAINT**) that designates the type of message.
- ***WPARAM wParam***—Additional information that may be needed to process the message. For instance, this field may contain the identifier of a selected menu item. Each message type uses this field for its own particular purpose. The **WPARAM** type is a 32-bit number.
- ***LPARAM lParam***—Used like the **wParam** field, to hold auxiliary information that varies with the message type. The **LPARAM** type is a 64-bit number. A given message type will use either or both of **WPARAM** and **LPARAM** according to types of its parameters.
- ***DWORD time***—The system time when the message was generated. This value is used to organize messages in the message queue.
- ***POINT pt***—The location of the mouse cursor at the time the message was generated.

Now that you know what events and messages are, let's take a look at how Windows programs are organized using the Software Developer's Kit approach, which involves directly using the Windows API.

The Windows Application Architecture

Not surprisingly, a Windows program is mainly a collection of windows. What, exactly, is a window? Glad you asked. A *window* is a rectangular area of the screen that contains different features and regions. Here are some window-related terms you'll need to know:

- *Client and non-client areas*—Every window has parts that Windows takes care of and parts for which your program is responsible. The part your program is responsible for is called the *client area*—you'll do input and output there. The rest of the window is the *non-client area*, which Windows maintains without help from you.
- *Window style*—A window's style is assigned when the window is created. There are three main window styles:
  - ***WS_OVERLAPPEDWINDOW***—used for a "main" window, the top-level window of your application. Such windows are movable and resizable, and can appear anywhere on screen. The WS_OVERLAPPEDWINDOW style denotes a top-level window; such windows don't have *parent windows* that contain them and may restrict their movement.
  - ***WS_POPUPWINDOW***—used for dialog boxes. A pop-up window has a parent, but it "floats" in front of its parent and can be moved outside of its parent's screen area.
  - ***WS_CHILDWINDOW***—used for window controls. A command button (such as the OK button in a typical dialog box) is a child window, as is a text field or a scrollbar. A child window gets its screen space from its parent—you can't move it outside of its parent's space.

Figure 2.1 shows each of the main window styles.

As you might expect, windows are central to Windows programs. In a Windows program, all keystrokes, mouse movements, and

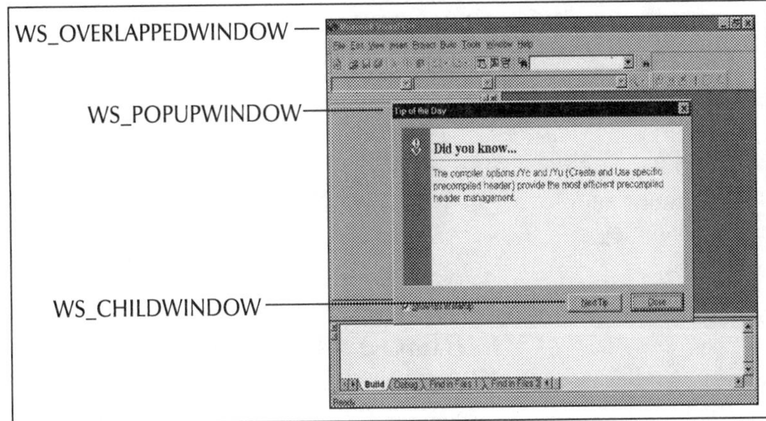

Figure 2.1
The main window styles.

timer activities are sent as messages to some designated window that's responsible for handling that particular activity. Even the user-interface elements, such as buttons and text fields, are just specialized kinds of child windows.

How It's Done

As we mentioned, Windows programs are organized differently than DOS programs. Writing an API-based Windows application essentially boils down to writing code to handle these four tasks:

- Initialization
- Instantiation
- Invoking the message loop
- Responding to messages

The first three tasks always take place in a function named **WinMain()**. **WinMain()** is the entry point to every Windows program, just as **main()** is the entry point to every traditional C program. The fourth task is carried out in a function that's traditionally named **WndProc()** (but you're free to name it as you'd like). Figure 2.2 shows the organization of a typical Windows program.

Your program may have additional functions if you like, but every Windows program must have at least these two. Let's take a look at a minimal API-based Windows program, and see how these two functions work.

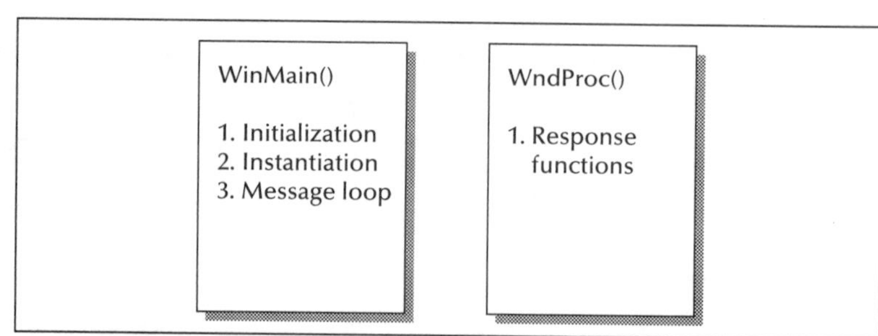

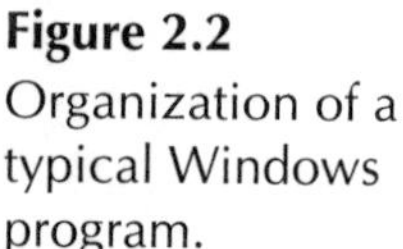

Figure 2.2
Organization of a typical Windows program.

Inside The WinMain() Function

After Windows loads your program into memory, it calls the **WinMain()**function. **WinMain()**'s first job is to define an application-specific window class for your program's main window. Let's see how that works.

Initialization

To define a window class, you first choose a name—say, "MyWindowClass". Then, you associate that name with a window style (**WS_OVERLAPPEDWINDOW**, for instance) and the procedure that will handle all of the messages for the window class. After you've done this, Windows uses your class definition as a template when you ask it to create an instance of your class.

In some ways, window classes are similar to C++ classes—at least in theory—because they act like templates for creating objects (windows), and because you have to define both the attributes and behaviors of your new class. But in another way, they're completely unlike C++ classes, because the attributes you must define are pre-declared—you're just filling in the values. In the final analysis, window classes and C++ classes are quite different animals indeed.

To define a class, you first create an instance of Windows' **WNDCLASS** type. The **WNDCLASS** type is a structure that contains various fields you need to fill in. The most important fields are the name of the class and the address of the function (which you'll write) that will respond to messages. Here's an abbreviated version:

```
static char MyClassName[] = "MyWindowClass";
WNDCLASS wc;
```

```
wc.lpfnWndProc = WndProc;
wc.lpszClassName = MyClassName;
// Additional fields omitted
```

In this case, **WndProc** is the address of the procedure to which you want Windows to send messages. You also need to complete eight other fields, specifying such items as the application's icon, the brush used to paint the background, and the mouse cursor to be used when the mouse is moved over the window.

Once you've defined all the attributes of your Window class, you then pass the structure on to Windows, which retrieves and records the information. You initiate this process, called *class registration*, by using the Windows API function **RegisterClass()** like this:

```
RegisterClass(&wc);
```

Instantiation

Once you've defined and registered your application's main window class, the next step is to create and display an instance of your application's main window.

To create a window instance, you use the API function **CreateWindow()**, which requires 11 arguments. If **CreateWindow()** succeeds, it returns a handle to the newly created window—you can use this handle to perform operations on the window. Here's the code to create an instance of the window class **MyWindowClass**:

Hungarian Notation

As you work with Windows, you'll often notice strange names like **lpfnWndProc** and **lpszClassNam**e. These are instances of *Hungarian Notation*—named in honor of legendary Microsoft programmer Charles Simonyi, who invented the system. In Hungarian Notation, variable names are prefixed with type and scope information. In this case, **lpfnWndProc** means that **WndProc** is a long pointer to a function, and **lpszClassName** means that **ClassName** is a long pointer to a zero-terminated character string. In a way, Hungarian Notation is a relic of ages past, when compilers were unable to perform the strict type checking that modern C++ compilers accomplish. Nevertheless, the idea lives on—even in MFC, where all class names start with "C" and all data members are prefixed with "m_".

```
HWND hwnd = CreateWindow( MyClassName,          // Name
                          "Hi Mom",             // Title
                          WS_OVERLAPPEDWINDOW,  // Style
                          CW_USEDEFAULT,        // Left
                          CW_USEDEFAULT,        // Top
                          CW_USEDEFAULT,        // Width
                          CW_USEDEFAULT,        // Height
                          NULL,                 // Parent
                          NULL,                 // Menu
                          hInstance,  // App Handle
                          NULL);      // Addl. data
```

Once your main window is created, you need to accomplish a couple more steps before your program will run. First, when a window is created, it's usually invisible. You can easily make your window visible by calling the method **ShowWindow()** like this:

```
ShowWindow(hwnd, nCmdShow);
```

The first argument is simply the handle that was returned by **CreateWindow()**. The second argument, **nCmdShow**, is one of the arguments received by the **WinMain()** function itself. Its value determines whether the window is displayed normally, minimized, or maximized.

Now, you might think that after politely asking Windows to display your new window, things would be fine. That's not entirely the case, however. The **WM_PAINT** message, which causes the window to repaint itself, is one of the lowest-priority messages—so it may be a while before your window gets around to displaying itself. You can speed the process up considerably by following your **ShowWindow()** call with a call to

```
UpdateWindow(hwnd);
```

which tells Windows, in essence, "Do it *now!*"

At this point, you've defined a new window class and created and displayed an actual window, but **WinMain()** still lacks one important feature: a message loop.

The Message Pump

As you recall, whenever an event occurs—whenever the user moves the mouse or presses a key—Windows creates a message and places it in the input queue of the proper application. Your program is responsible for fetching the message from the input queue and then processing it.

A Windows API procedure called **GetMessage()** handles these tasks. When you call **GetMessage()**, you pass it the address of a **MSG** structure. If there's a message waiting in the input queue for your program, Windows fills in all the fields of the **MSG** structure and returns **TRUE** to **WinMain()**. If, however, there's a **WM_QUIT** message waiting in the message queue, the **GetMessage()** function returns **FALSE**, and your program ends. At its most basic, your loop looks like this:

```
MSG msg;
while(GetMesssage(&msg, NULL, 0,0,))
{
    // process messages here
}
// end up here when GetMessage() receives WM_QUIT
```

So far, as you can see, this code doesn't look too strange. You may be curious about the additional arguments to **GetMessage()**(you'll usually use the ones we've shown), or you may wonder how a **WM_QUIT** message is generated (when the main window of an application is closed). But, all in all, the loop isn't much different than you'd expect—because you haven't seen the really weird stuff yet.

The "weird stuff" goes where the comment says *process messages here*. Here's what you probably expect to find at that point:

```
while(GetMesssage(&msg, NULL, 0,0,))
{
    switch(msg.message)
    {
        case WM_PAINT:
           // handle WM_PAINT messages
        case WM_SIZE:
```

```
            // handle WM_SIZE messages
            // and so forth
    }
}
```

Instead of this rather pedestrian but understandable code, however, you find these two inscrutable lines inside the message loop:

```
TranslateMessage(&msg);
DispatchMessage(&msg);
```

If your first reaction is "Huh?" then rest assured that you're not alone—it's not at all obvious what's going on. Well, be confused no longer; here's what happens.

Suppose that the user of your program presses capital B on the keyboard. As you saw previously, Windows leaps into action and intercepts that event, turns it into a message, and places the message in the queue. In this case, Windows will generate a **WM_KEYDOWN** message. (When the user releases the key, Windows will generate another message: **WM_KEYUP**.) Now, Windows doesn't have the faintest idea what your program wants to do when the user presses the B key. However, most of the time you use the keyboard for typing, so it's likely that the program will retrieve the ASCII value of the character B. So far, so good. Unfortunately, this is where things get sticky.

The **WM_KEYDOWN** message tells you only that the user pressed the key. However, the character B and the character b share the same physical key. Thus, if you want to find out the ASCII value of the key entered, you must also determine the state of the Shift key. Worse yet, the problem doesn't stop there—what if the Caps-Lock key is on? In that case, holding down the Shift key should produce the ASCII value for the lowercase b. So, you need to know the state of the Shift key *and* the state of the Caps-Lock key.

As you can see, just reading the ASCII value of a keystroke can become relatively complex. Because this is such a common task, Windows provides the **TranslateMessage()** function. When you pass the address of your message to **TranslateMessage()**, the function checks whether the message is about a keypress. If so, it calculates the proper ASCII value for the keystroke (taking into account the Shift key, the Caps-Lock, and even non-English keyboard layouts). Once it has calculated the proper ASCII value, **TranslateMessage()** generates another message—called **WM_CHAR**—that contains the proper ASCII value. It then sends the new message to your program. Figure 2.3 summarizes this process.

These steps make some sense. Unless you call **TranslateMessage()**, you don't incur the overhead of translating between keystrokes and their ASCII representations. So, you can call the function or not call it, according to your preference. Of course, translating the message on your own may turn out to be more than you bargained for.

But, what's that second line in the message loop, **DispatchMessage()**? And where do you actually process your messages?

DispatchMessage() works like this. Do you remember when you filled in the **WNDCLASS** structure and registered the main window for your application? You filled in a field with the address of a **WNDPROC**, or *window procedure*. But, oddly, you don't call a window procedure directly—instead, you ask Windows to call it for you. Functions of this kind are called *callback procedures*. The window procedure is a callback procedure that handles messages sent to it by Windows.

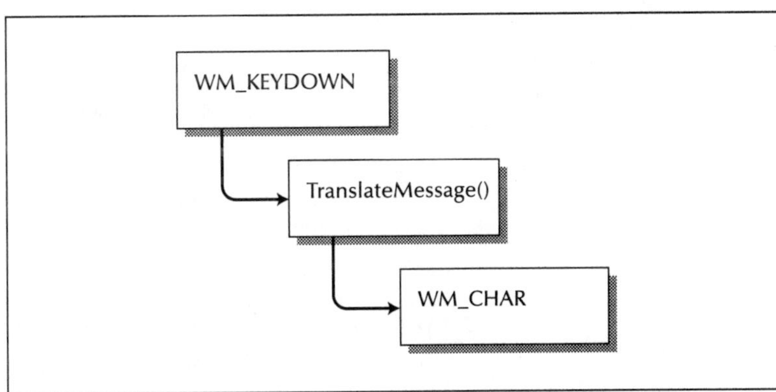

Figure 2.3
Operation of **TranslateMessage()**.

As you may have guessed by now, calling **DispatchMessage()** simply hands the message you retrieved from Windows' message queue back to Windows with instructions to deliver it to your window procedure. The window procedure actually processes each such message. Let's take a look at that procedure now.

Inside The WndProc() Function

Now that you've seen how the **WinMain()** function works, it's time to examine the second function that's part of every Windows program: the **WndProc()** procedure. In the **WndProc()** procedure, you'll process each of the messages that Windows sends your way. Again, you can't call **WndProc()** directly: Only Windows can call the **WndProc()** procedure.

Structurally, **WndProc()** is simpler than **WinMain()**. When Windows calls **WndProc()**, it first unpacks and passes four fields of the **MSG** structure you passed to **DispatchMessage()**. These four fields are:

- ***hwnd***—the handle to the window instance that's dispatching the message.
- ***wParam** and **lParam***—parameter information for the particular message.
- ***message***—the actual message identifier.

Inside **WndProc()** the code is set up as a simple switch on the message parameter, like this:

```
switch (message)
{
    case WM_PAINT:
        // handle WM_PAINT message
        return 0;
    case WM_DESTROY:
        PostQuitMessage(0);
        return 0;
}
```

As you can see, the code looks (at least, conceptually) very similar to the code we proposed to insert in the **WinMain()** message loop.

If you're paying close attention, there may be one detail bothering you: What happens to messages for which there's no **case**? Do you have to write a **case** for every message? No, you don't—and, that's a good thing, because there are more than 200 messages. Instead, Windows defines default actions for all the messages that can be generated. But these actions don't occur automatically: If you don't write code to respond to an event, you're responsible for invoking the default code for that event. You do that by calling the function **DefWindowProc()**, passing it the same arguments that Windows passed to your **WndProc()** function. This is usually coded as the last line of **WndProc()**, so that any messages you don't explicitly handle are passed on back to Windows for default handling.

A Windows API Programming Recap

Let's recap the main points about Windows API programming before we turn our attention to Visual C++ and the Microsoft Foundation Classes:

- Windows programs are organized in a fundamentally different way than hierarchical, straightforward, procedural programs.
- A Windows program is a collection of windows, each of which is attached to a window procedure that responds to events generated by Windows.
- Every Windows program starts at the mandatory **WinMain()** function, which is responsible for defining the characteristics of the application's main window. **WinMain()** initially displays the main window, then runs a loop to retrieve messages from Windows and hand them back for subsequent processing.
- Every window in a Windows program is associated with a procedure designed to respond to Windows messages. This procedure, by tradition called **WndProc()**, is always called by Windows itself, never by your program.

Windows Programming: MFC

Although you can use Visual C++ to write traditional API programs like the ones you saw in the previous section, its real forte is writing programs based on the Microsoft Foundation Classes (MFC). In fact, when most people talk about Visual C++ programming, they really mean programming using MFC.

In this section, we'll first take an overall look at MFC—what it is, what it does, and why you'll want to use it. After that, we'll examine a minimal MFC program. Just as plain API programs have an overall architecture, so, do MFC programs; understanding the MFC way of doing things is one of the keys to making effective use of Visual C++. Finally, we'll discuss MFC's document-view architecture—why it's important and why you'll use it.

What Is MFC?

At its heart, the Windows API is a C API. Windows was developed long before C++ came into widespread use. However, as more developers began using C++ and discovering the benefits and power of encapsulation, inheritance, and polymorphism, demand grew for an object-oriented approach to developing Windows applications.

One of the first companies to respond was the Whitewater Group, with its object-oriented programming language known as Actor. While Actor never achieved great success, the set of class libraries it used was adapted by Borland for use in Pascal and C++—the libraries became the basis for their Object-Windows class libraries.

Microsoft weighed in with Version 1.0 of MFC, released concurrently with its C/C++ compilers. This first version of MFC was simply a thin wrapper around the Windows API. For instance, instead of using an **HWND**, programmers could create **CFrameWnd** objects. Instead of calling API functions and passing an **HWND**, they could call the member functions of the **CFrameWnd** class. MFC 1.0 wasn't a resounding success, mainly because the tools it used to build applications were relatively primitive and Spartan.

All of that changed with the release of Visual C++ 1.0. For Microsoft, Visual C++ broke new ground in ease of use. More importantly, however, the Visual C++ tools were designed to work together to create and maintain applications based upon

MFC. And, MFC itself was extended to include an application framework or architecture.

Class Library Vs. Application Framework

Application frameworks have been around for a long time. An application framework is a little like an upside-down library, as you can see in Figure 2.4. A class library contains classes that can create objects for use inside your application—for example, **Button** objects, **Time** objects, or **Socket** objects. But a class library doesn't dictate the overall shape and organization of your program.

An application framework, on the other hand, is a complete application that you can customize to meet your needs. The framework itself controls the programming flow—you customize it by changing (or, in an object-oriented world, overriding) the way that those functions work.

The big difference between an application framework and a traditional class library lies in the amount of code you write and the amount of code you can reuse. Generally, if the application framework does what you want it to, you'll write much less code than if you provide the framework and use the class library's relatively independent objects.

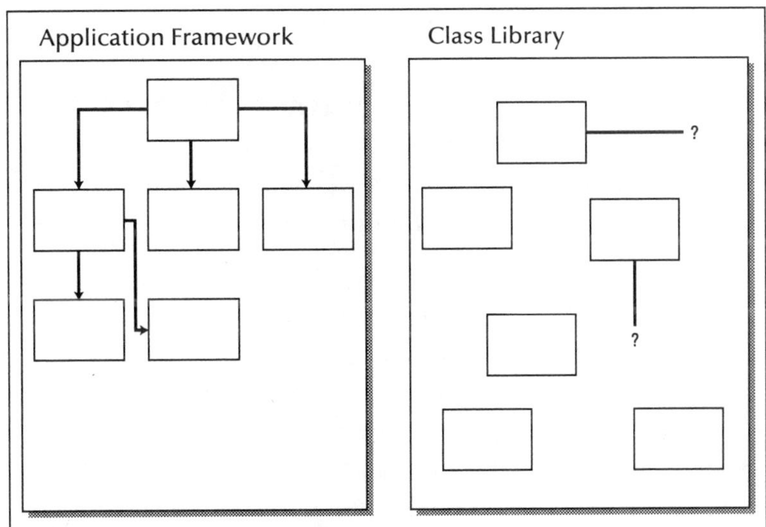

Figure 2.4
A class library versus an application framework.

Why Use MFC?

Throughout the rest of this book, you'll be learning about the classes and features provided by MFC. So, we'll just touch on them here.

In Chapter 1, you saw the primary advantage gained by using the MFC application framework. How much code did you have to write to add a toolbar to your NotePod application? None. The code for handling the toolbar was inherited from the application framework.

How much code did you write to support displaying the File Open and File Save dialog boxes? To support reading and writing your files to disk? To add tiling or cascading to the document windows in NotePod?

Again and again and again, none. And that's not only true for the NotePod program—in general, it's true for all MFC programs built using the MFC class libraries and application frameworks.

Writing programs using MFC isn't no-code programming, and it isn't primarily visual point-and-click programming. Instead, programming in MFC involves understanding the MFC programming model and using the Visual C++ tools to modify the application framework to do what you want. You might call this *programming by exception.*

A Minimal MFC Program

Before we move on to the next chapter, let's take a few moments to look at the minimal structure of an MFC program, much as we did for the API-based program earlier.

First, remember that an MFC program is a Windows program just like the API-based version you saw earlier. This means that every MFC program also has a **WinMain()** function and a **WndProc()** function that handles messages. In an MFC program, though, you never see either of these functions (unless you go rooting through the MFC source code, searching for them). Instead, they're buried inside the application framework.

If you don't see **WinMain()** and **WndProc()**,what *do* you find when you look at an MFC program? Well, basically there will always be two objects: a main Window object and an application object. (Technically, the main Window object isn't absolutely essential, though in practice it's almost always present. However, every MFC program must have an application object.)

To create a minimal MFC program (without using the AppWizard), you select Win32 Application from the New|Projects list box. Name your new project BDSimpleMFC and click on OK. See Figure 2.5.

As shown in Figure 2.6, Visual C++ asks what kind of Windows application you'd like to create. Choose the An Empty Project radio button and click on Finish.

Visual C++ presents the New Project Information dialog box, as shown in Figure 2.7. Click on OK to proceed.

Your workspace will be empty, as shown in Figure 2.8. To add your C++ source, choose File|New and select the C++ Source option. Fill in the file name BDSimpleMFC as shown in Figure 2.9, then click on OK.

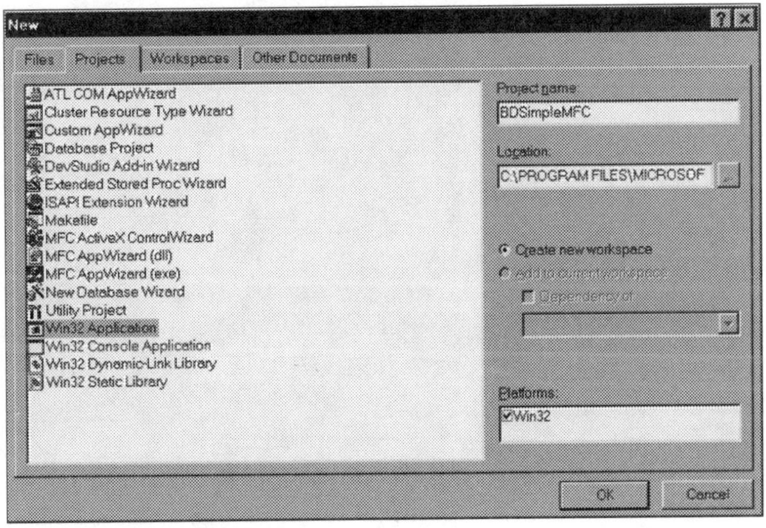

Figure 2.5
Creating a minimal MFC program.

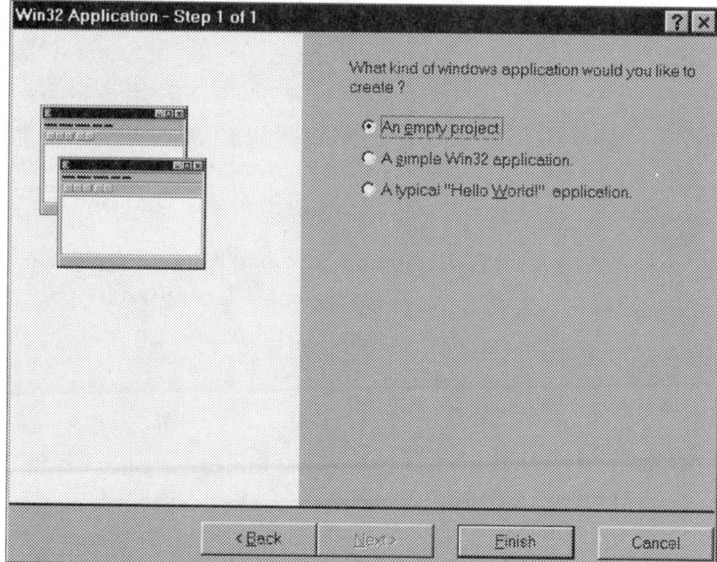

Figure 2.6
Choosing the application type.

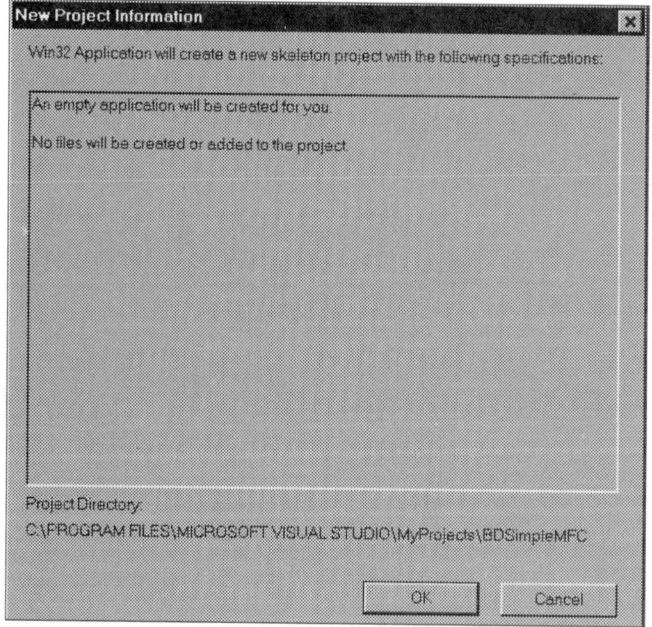

Figure 2.7
The New Project Information dialog box.

Now, add the code shown in Listing 2.1 to the editor window. It's best if you type the code, because that way you'll pay attention to every jot and tittle. However, you can access the CD-ROM to obtain the file, if you prefer.

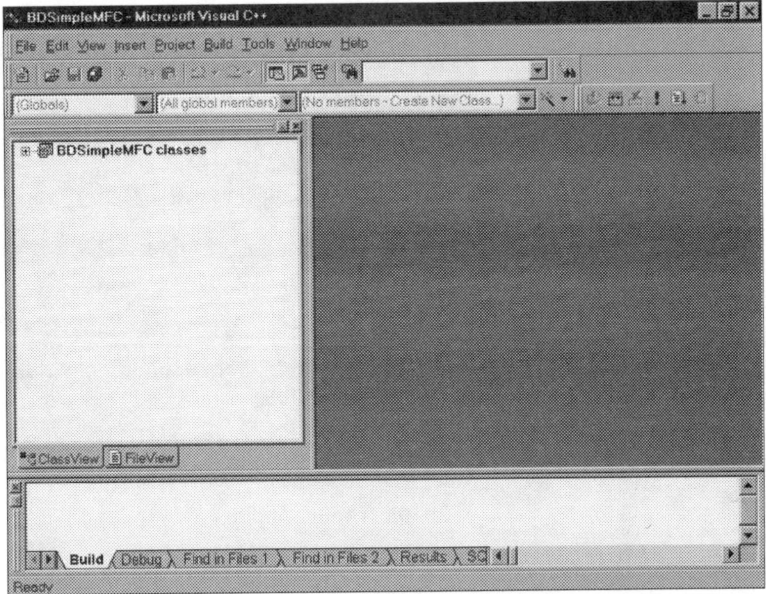

Figure 2.8
An empty workspace.

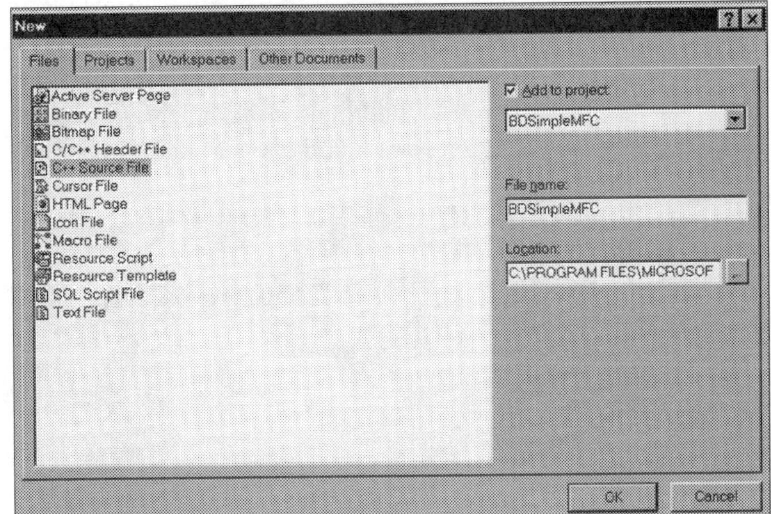

Figure 2.9
Adding a C++ source file.

Listing 2.1 The Brain-Dead MFC App.

```
#include <afxwin.h>

// Our Main Window Class
class CBDWindow:public CFrameWnd
{
public:
  CBDWindow()
```

```
    {
      Create(0, "A Brain-Dead MFC Window");
    }
};

// Our Application Class
class CBDApp:public CWinApp
{
public:
  virtual BOOL InitInstance()
  {
    m_pMainWnd = new CBDWindow();
    m_pMainWnd->ShowWindow(SW_SHOWMAXIMIZED );
    return TRUE;
  }
};

CBDApp TheOneAndOnlyBrainDeadMFCApp;
```

Next, use the Project|Settings menu item to access the Project Settings dialog box. Select the Use MFC In A Shared DLL option from the list box, as shown in Figure 2.10. Click on OK.

Now, you can compile and run your program. As in Chapter 1, use Build|Build BDSimpleMFC to compile the source code. Check for and correct any compilation errors, and recompile as

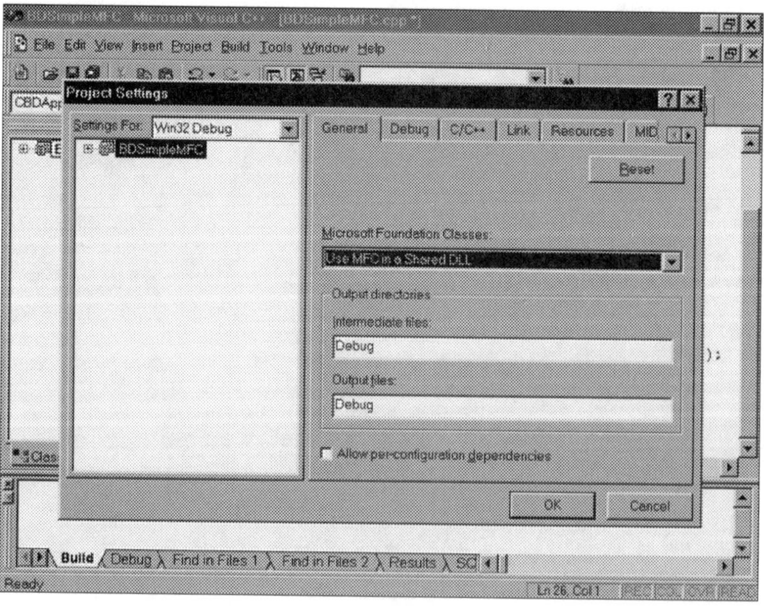

Figure 2.10
Revising the project settings.

needed. Once you have a successful compile, use Build | Execute to run the program. You'll see your own Brain-Dead MFC Window, as shown in Figure 2.11. (Initially, the window is maximized—we've resized the window in the figure.)

Now that you've got a functioning MFC program, let's spend a few moments examining how it works. First, notice that the source code defines two classes: **CBDWindow**, which represents the application's top-level window, and **CBDApp**, which represents the application itself. Each of these classes is derived from a base class, from which it inherits considerable functionality. The **CBDWindow** class is derived from the MFC class **CFrameWnd**, and the **CBDApp** class is derived from the MFC class **CWinApp**. (The declarations for the base classes **CFrameWnd** and **CWinApp** are included in the application framework's header file, afxwin.h.)

Because each class inherits so much functionality, each is quite small and simple. The **CBDWindow** class just defines a public constructor that calls the **Create()** member function, which it inherits from an ancestor class. The **Create()** function specifies a name for the window, which appears in the window title bar (see Figure 2.11).

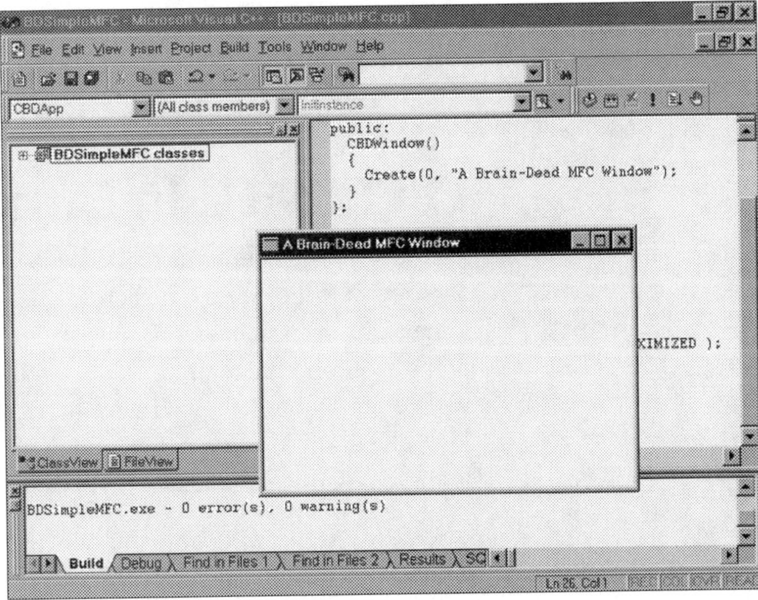

Figure 2.11
A brain-dead MFC window.

The **CBDApp** class simply overrides the virtual method **InitInstance()**. In the body of the method, it constructs an instance of the **CBDWindow** class and assigns the returned pointer to the inherited data member **m_pMainWnd**. It then uses this pointer to invoke the **ShowWindow()** function, passing an argument that causes the window to display itself at maximum size. Finally, the method returns the value **TRUE**, which signals successful completion.

One detail remains, which is often forgotten by beginning MFC programmers. Notice that the program creates an instance of the application (a **CBDApp** object) with *global scope*. The creation of this global instance makes the program run.

If you find this confusing, consider the following object-oriented Hello World program:

```
class HelloWorld
{  public:
   HelloWorld() { cout << "Hello World"; )
};
int void main() { }
HelloWorld h;
```

Notice how the construction of the global **HelloWorld** object entails printing *Hello World* even though the body of the **main()** method is empty. MFC works the same way. If you fail to create the global instance of your application object, your program won't run.

On To MFC In Earnest

We hope that this brief introduction to MFC has whetted your appetite. If things seem a little fuzzy, that's okay. You'll see these same techniques many more times before the book is done. The purpose of this chapter, rather like a tour of the homes of Hollywood stars, was to let you know where things are and what they look like from a distance. If you don't yet feel yourself entirely at home, that's understandable.

The next chapter will show you how to build FourUp, a simple Windows program using MFC, which lets you play video poker. Are you up for FourUp? Let's go!

Chapter 3

Building A Simple Dialog-Based Application

The FourUp application resembles a video-poker machine except in one important detail: It won't siphon away your savings.

An old adage suggests that there are two things you never want to see being made: laws and sausages. But, when you think about it, this saying applies to many areas. To bring a feature film to your local cinema, for instance, requires months (or years) of drudging, painstaking effort, none of which is especially glamorous or romantic, even if the finished result appears so. Laws, sausages, films, books, software—in every venue, much goes on behind the scenes before the curtain rises.

Windows programs are no different—it's not all code and glory. As a matter of fact, a significant portion of every Windows program consists of items that aren't code: bitmaps, cursors, icons, dialog boxes, and strings. These Windows elements are known as *resources*.

You can think of Windows resources as a very special kind of initialized data. Suppose you have this line of code in your C++ program:

```
static int nCards[] = { 1, 2, 3, 4, 5 };
```

When you compile your program, the data that makes up the values stored in the array **nCards** will be stored along with the program code in the executable program on your disk. When the program loads into memory, the values will be read from the EXE file into memory, so you can read them.

Windows resource data works somewhat differently. It *is* stored on your hard disk in the EXE file, just like initialized data. However, when your program loads, the resource data is *not* loaded into memory along with the rest of the program. Instead, the resource data remains on disk until it's needed. For instance, when your program displays a dialog box, the dialog box template data is dynamically retrieved from disk and used to build the dialog box you see on screen.

This scheme offers two advantages. First, because resource data is read-only, it can be discarded from memory when it isn't in use—if the data is needed again, it's automatically reloaded from disk. That means your program requires less memory. Second, you don't need a lot of little files hanging around. Can you imagine the difficulty of trying to distribute a Windows program if you had to include each image file used for every toolbar, button, and icon? The job would be a mess. Instead, resource data lets you deliver a single package to your users. They don't have to know all the messy details—indeed, it's probably better if they don't.

Resources And Dialog Boxes

In Chapter 1, you saw how easy it is to use the AppWizard to create a fairly sophisticated text editor. However, although the program was easy to create, if you looked through the code, you discovered it wasn't that easy to understand.

This difficulty isn't really the fault of MFC. As you saw at the end of Chapter 2, a minimal MFC program is simpler and easier to understand than an equivalent API-based Windows program. So, who is the culprit? It's tempting to lay the blame for the complexity of the NotePod code at the foot of the AppWizard. But in fact, the code is complex simply because NotePod supports many sophisticated functions—certainly it's more involved than the minimal MFC program.

No one working to understand MFC should have to struggle with that kind of complexity. So, in this chapter we'll continue to use the AppWizard, but we're going to ask the AppWizard to generate a dialog-based program. A dialog-based program is simpler than

NotePod because it has only two main classes: the main application class (derived from **CWndApp**) and the main window class (in the case of a dialog-based application, derived from **CDialog**). Dialog-based applications don't need the extra document and view classes that the NotePod project required. Because they're simpler, dialog-based applications are also easier to understand.

Dialog-based applications have one other advantage over most MFC programs: You can design the entire user interface using the Visual C++ resource editors rather than writing code. In creating a dialog-based application, you visually place bitmaps, buttons, text fields, and other Windows controls, and then you visually size and position them.

Sound fun? One last thing before we get started. Don't get the idea that just because a dialog-based application has a simpler structure than an application based on the document/view architecture, the dialog-based program must be less sophisticated. Dialog-based programs are every bit as capable as their more complex brethren—you can bet on it.

Starting The FourUp Project

Now, speaking of betting, let's introduce this chapter's project: FourUp. The FourUp program is similar to the video-poker games so beloved of casino operators in Las Vegas and Atlantic City. FourUp is slightly simpler, though, so you can concentrate on programming and learning to use Developer Studio's resource editors.

FourUp isn't really a game of skill. When the game begins, the player is given $100. At each deal (which costs $2), the player receives four cards. The values of the cards are irrelevant—only the suits matter. If the player gets two pair (two Hearts and two Clubs, for instance), the payout is $3. If the player gets three of a single suit, the payout is $6. If the dealer lays out four cards of the same suit, the payout is $9.

Of course, the game doesn't use real money. If you want to write the program so it dials into the player's bank to deposit winnings (or cover losses), then you're on your own.

In this chapter, you'll begin creating the FourUp program; you'll complete it in Chapter 5. You'll start by using Visual C++'s Dialog Editor and Bitmap Editor to build a professional-looking About dialog box. If you're impatient to see the finished program, you can turn to Chapter 5. Or, even better, you can run FourUp off the CD-ROM and try it out for yourself.

Creating A Dialog-Based Application In AppWizard

Start Visual C++ and use AppWizard to create the initial files for the FourUp application. You begin a dialog-based application just the way you started the NotePod project in Chapter 1:

- Choose File|New from the main menu.
- Select MFC AppWizard (Exe) from the list of projects available on the Project property sheet.
- Name your project FourUp.

In the first AppWizard window, click on the bottom radio button when you're asked what kind of application to create. Notice that when you select the Dialog Based radio button, the Document/View checkbox turns gray. This happens because the document/view architecture and the dialog-based application architecture aren't compatible. In a document/view application, you can always use dialog box resources. But in a dialog-based application, there's no document or view—there's only the dialog box. Figure 3.1 shows the first AppWizard window that appears when you create a dialog-based application.

Dialog-Based Options

When it creates a dialog-based application, AppWizard doesn't need to write as much code—so it asks you fewer questions. Rather than six windows, dialog-based applications require only four.

In the second window, you choose whether to add several different features. Here's a list of features, and the choices you should make for the FourUp program:

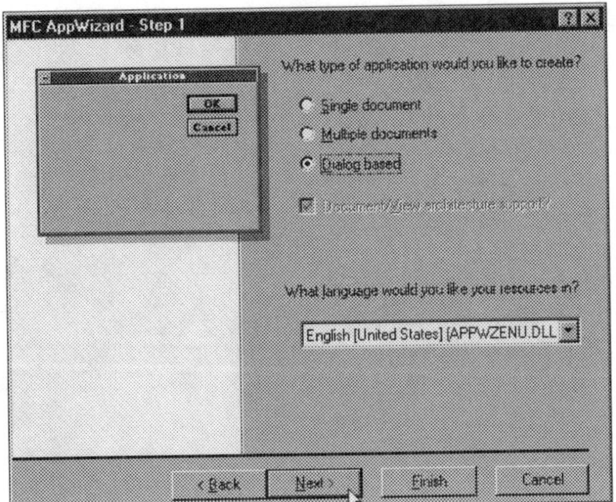

Figure 3.1
Starting a dialog-based project.

- Select the About Box checkbox to add an identifying screen. You'll get started using Visual C++ resource editors by giving FourUp's About dialog box a professional look.
- You won't use context-sensitive help. It's not selected by default, so you can leave the checkbox as it is.
- You do want to use the 3D controls, so leave the corresponding checkbox selected.
- You aren't going to use OLE Automation, ActiveX, or Windows sockets, so you can uncheck each of those boxes.
- At the bottom of the dialog box, you can enter the title for your dialog window. You want to attract players to your game, so enter "FourUp - Get Rich Now!!!!". Be sure you include the exclamation points—research has shown them to be an effective marketing tool.

You can see the completed AppWizard dialog in Figure 3.2.

Step 3 is the same as Step 5 was when you created the NotePod AppWizard program, except you're not given an opportunity to create a Windows Explorer-style project. The Explorer style is incompatible with a dialog-based application, as is the document/view architecture. Select Yes for source code comments and specify that you want to use the MFC library as a shared DLL. Then, click on Next.

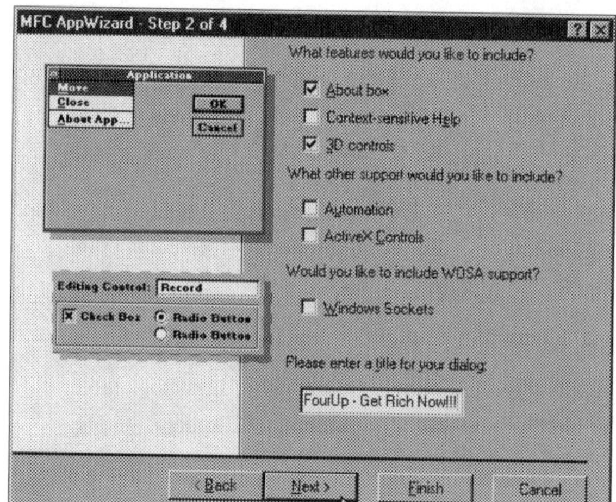

Figure 3.2
AppWizard dialog box options.

Class Review

Figure 3.3 shows AppWizard's class-review window for the FourUp application. As with the NotePod project, this checkered-flag window gives you a chance to review the classes your application uses and to change your mind about options you chose in previous steps. You might want to compare this window to the similar one generated for NotePod. AppWizard listed five classes for the NotePod project—but it lists only two for the FourUp application. Simpler indeed.

The class-review window has one other difference. In the NotePod project, you were able to change the base class used to

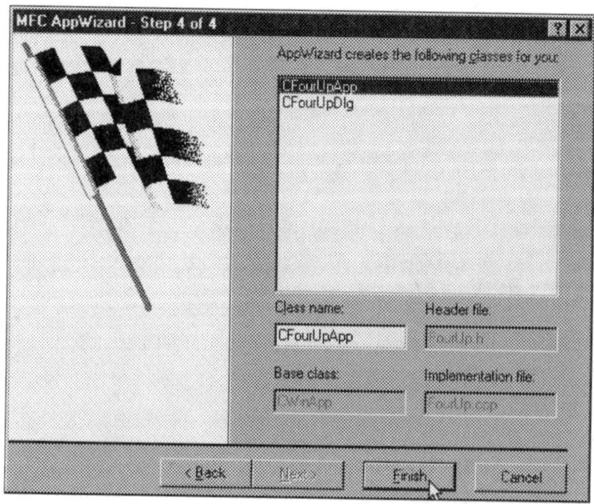

Figure 3.3
The MFC dialog-based project files.

derive your application's view class. As we mentioned previously, a dialog-based application has no view class—so, the only customization option available lets you change the name of the class that AppWizard generates. (For the **CFourUpDlg** class, you can also change the names of the files used to store the header and implementation files. You can change only the name of the **CFourUpApp** class.)

Click on Finish in the class-review window and click on OK in the New Project Information dialog box. AppWizard will generate the files needed for your program and activate the project workspace, just as it did previously. In the workspace, you find the ClassView, ResourceView, and FileView panes, as you saw in NotePod. If you click on the ClassView pane and expand all the classes, you'll see that FourUp truly is simpler than NotePod—there are only three classes, compared to NotePod's six. (Neither NotePod nor FourUp listed the class used to create the application's About dialog box in class-review window.) You can see Visual C++'s initial configuration of the FourUp project in Figure 3.4.

When you look at Figure 3.4, one thing is immediately obvious: Instead of a blank work area to the right of the project workspace

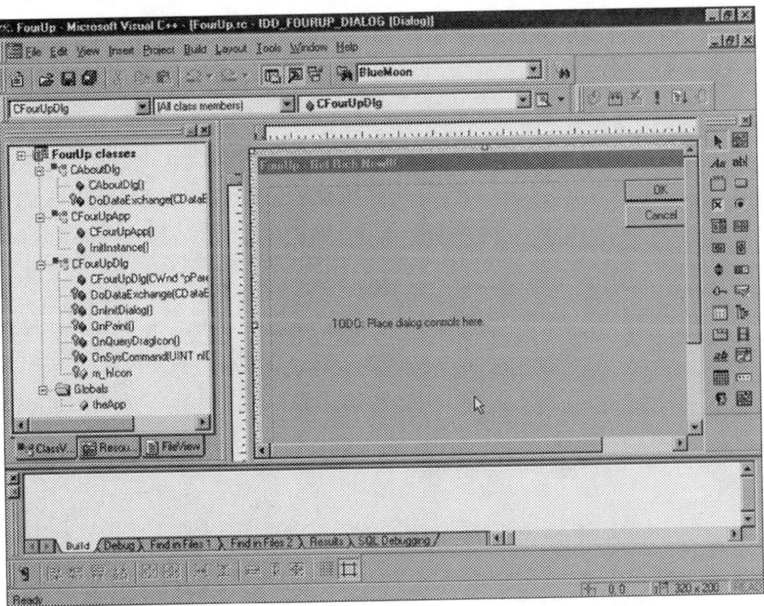

Figure 3.4
Visual C++'s opening dialog-based configuration.

window, you see a form with OK and Cancel buttons. A label on the form says:

TODO: Place dialog controls here

Next to the form you'll find a toolbar of buttons that resemble the controls in Visual Basic or Delphi.

Because FourUp is a dialog-based application, Visual C++ knows to start you out in the Dialog Editor. The Dialog Editor is one of several specialized editors you can use to create and maintain the resources inside your Windows programs. Let's take a closer look.

Starting The Dialog Editor

Before we start working on the FourUp slot, er..., video game, let's take a quick look at the Dialog Editor. Then, we'll use its tools to modify the application's About dialog box before we tackle the more difficult main screen in Chapter 5.

Meet The Control Toolbar

The toolbar full of buttons in the Dialog Editor is called the *Control Toolbar*. Like most of the toolbars in Visual C++, it's dockable—when you place it against the side of the screen, it appears as part of the border.

But look closely at the top of the toolbar. Do you see the small Close button and the set of raised ridges? Take your mouse and "grab" the toolbar by the raised ridges—you can tear it away from its docking position and use it as a floating toolbox. If you move it back against one of the sides, it will dock itself again, melding into the border.

Each button on the Control Toolbar is a component (or *control*, as they're generally called in Visual C++) that you can place on your dialog box. You can use two techniques to place a component—such as a command button or a text label—on the surface of your dialog box:

- Click on the control you want. The control button will remain depressed, and the mouse cursor will become a cross-hair when you move it over your dialog box. Position the mouse pointer over your dialog box and click to "drop" the control at that location.

- Drag a control from the Control Toolbar. When you drag a control and move the mouse cursor over the dialog window, you'll see an outline of the control. Releasing the mouse button places the control at that location.

The Control Toolbar contains 25 controls. In this chapter, we'll look at only 4 of these 25 controls—we'll cover the others throughout the remainder of the book. Figure 3.5 shows the Control Toolbar and identifies each of its controls.

> **▶Tip**
>
> ***Finding Your Tool***
>
> *The Control Toolbar has so many controls that you may find it hard to find the control you need, especially if you're unfamiliar with the icon used to designate the control. However, Visual C++ can rescue you. As you move your mouse cursor over the Control Toolbar, allow the cursor to hover over a button you're interested in: Visual C++ will pop up a tooltip window giving you the name of the control.*

Starting The About Box

Okay, enough looking around. Let's get started on that About dialog box. If you haven't already done so, be sure that the ResourceView tab is selected in the project workspace. Expand the folders so that you can see what they contain. Inside the Dialog folder you'll find two small icons that resemble screen forms. Each is identified by two unusual names: **IDD_ABOUTBOX** and **IDD_FOURUP_DIALOG**.

Resource Identifiers

These strange names are *resource identifiers*. As their style suggests (all caps, connected by underscores), these aren't variable names, but preprocessor manifest constants: constants created using the C++ preprocessor directive **#define**. Almost all resources are named using such identifiers.

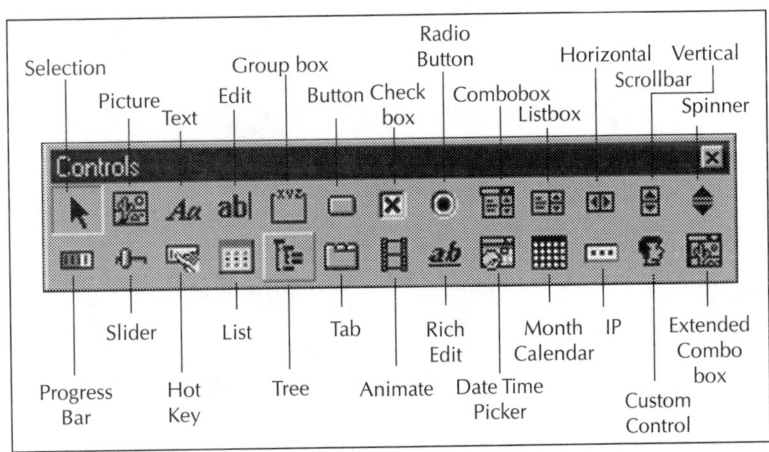

Figure 3.5
The Developer Studio Control Toolbar.

The first part of a resource identifier, in this case "**IDD_**", stands for a *ID*entifier for a *D*ialog. If the resource were an icon, the name would (usually) start with "**IDI_**", and so forth. As with most **#defined** constants, the actual value of **IDD_ABOUTBOX** is an integer constant stored in a header file—in this case, the header file resource.h. From your point of view, however, that makes no difference—Visual C++ maintains the definition of the constant and the contents of the file resource.h, so you don't have to think about them.

Double-click on **IDD_ABOUTBOX**, and we'll start editing the About dialog box designed by AppWizard. Your window should look like that pictured in Figure 3.6.

The IDR_MAINFRAME Identifier

You probably first notice the MFC icon in the About dialog box. All MFC projects use this standard icon as both the application icon and the icon appearing in the default About dialog box, but you'll almost always choose to replace it with one of your own.

If you look back at the ProjectView window, you'll see that the icon is named using the identifier **IDR_MAINFRAME**. Given the previous discussion of identifiers, you'd probably expect the

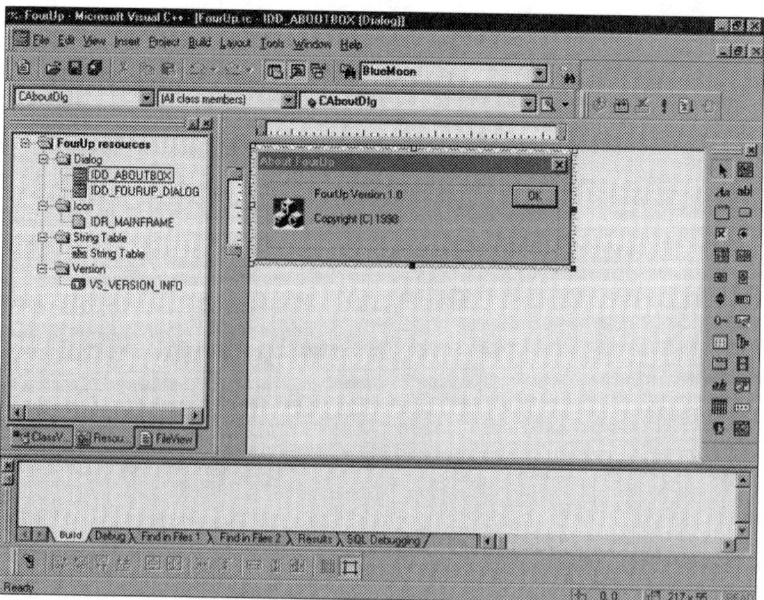

Figure 3.6
Opening the Dialog Editor with **IDD_ABOUTBOX**.

icon to be named **IDI_MAINFRAME**. However, this is an exception to the standard naming conventions: **IDR** stands for *ID*entifier for a *R*esource, because the same identifier is used for icons, cursors, accelerator tables, and several other resources. Can you guess why MFC would have several resources with the same name? If you look at the rest of the name, it might make sense. Any resource that uses the identifier **IDR_MAINFRAME** is the default resource for your application's main window. Icons, cursors, and other resources can share this name.

Adding New Resources

To replace the built-in MFC icon, you need to create one of your own. When you installed Visual C++, you had the option of installing a set of resources for use in your programs. These are installed in your Visual Studio directory, in the subdirectory Common\Graphics. (If you didn't install the resources, you can find this directory on your CD-ROM and simply copy the necessary files to your hard drive.) Underneath that directory are other subdirectories for icons, bitmaps, and other graphic resources. To create a new icon (and to create the images you'll use for our card display), you'll use four images found in the Icon\Misc subdirectory: Misc34.ico, Misc35.ico, Misc36.ico, and Misc37.ico. They represent the Heart, Club, Diamond, and Spade images, respectively. You can, of course, use any images you like, provided they are stored as ICO files.

To add these icons to your project, select the Insert | Resource menu item, and then select Icon from the list of resources displayed in the Insert Resource dialog box. Next, click on Import and use the standard file dialog box to locate the icons to load. You can select multiple files by holding down the Ctrl key as you click. The Insert Resource dialog box is shown in Figure 3.7.

Meet The Bitmap Editor

As soon as you load an icon, you'll notice another change in the appearance of Visual C++. The Dialog Editor and the Control Toolbar unceremoniously disappear, only to be replaced by a palette of painting colors and a toolbox containing drawing implements.

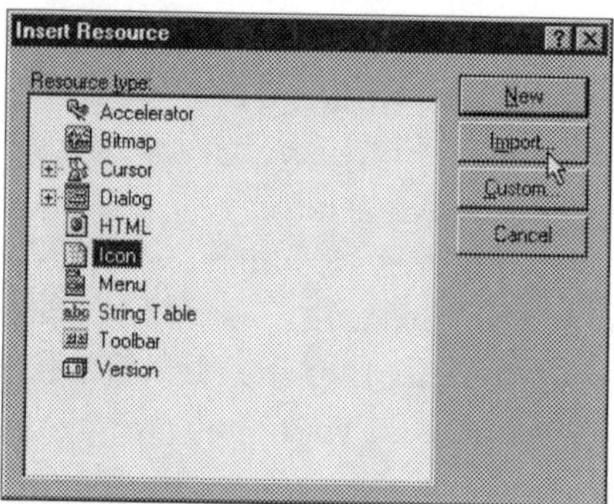

Figure 3.7
The Insert Resource dialog box.

This is the Visual C++ Bitmap Editor. You'll use the Bitmap Editor to create or manipulate cursors, icons, and (as you might expect) bitmaps. Rather than provide separate tools for each type of resource, the behavior of the Bitmap Editor changes subtly as you switch from resource type to resource type.

In addition to the Drawing and Color palettes, you'll also notice that the drawing area—the place where you'll paint—is split into two panes. One pane shows the icon enlarged about six times normal size, whereas the other pane shows the resource at actual size. You can paint in either pane, but most of the time you'll draw in the larger pane and watch the smaller pane to see the effects of your work.

You can get to the Bitmap Editor by double-clicking on any bitmap-type resource (icon, cursor, and so on) in the ResourceView window. Select the ResourceView window, if necessary, and double-click on the icon named **IDR_MAINFRAME**. You'll see a screen like that shown in Figure 3.8.

Adding New Icons

As Figure 3.8 shows, you can also insert a new resource into your project by right-clicking on the Icon folder in the ResourceView window. You can then choose Import from the context menu that appears, and save yourself the work of choosing a resource type from the Insert Resource menu.

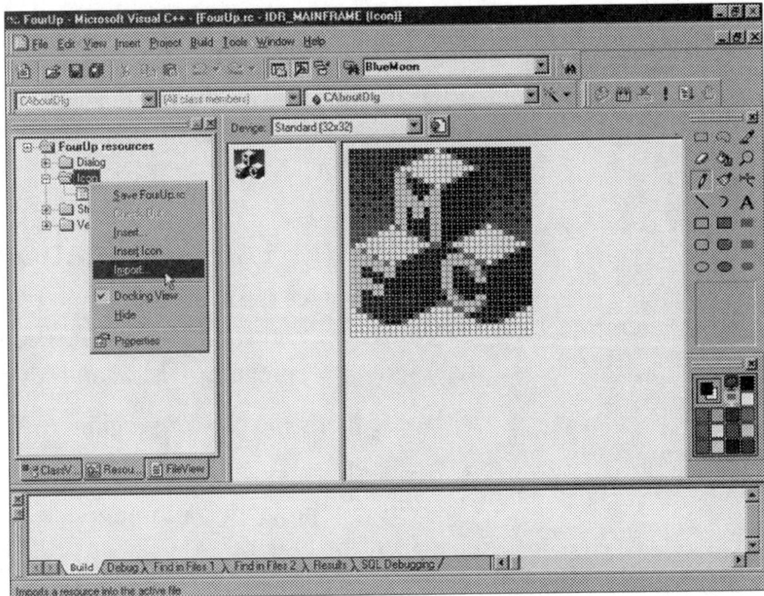

Figure 3.8
The Visual C++ Bitmap Editor.

When you add resources to your project, each is given a default name. The first icon you add to your project receives the identifier **IDI_ICON1**. Admittedly, that's not a very meaningful name. For some resources, the name doesn't matter—you'll never use it. However, sometimes you'll need to work with your resources and manipulate them as your program runs. That's the case for each of the four new icons that the FourUp project needs—a meaningful name makes such resources easier to work with.

Changing Resource IDs

At first, it may not be obvious how you change the name of an icon. If you double-click on its name in the ResourceView window, you just start up the Bitmap Editor. The simplest method, as with much of Windows, is to employ a right-click:

- In the ResourceView window, select the name of the icon you wish to rename.
- Right-click to open the context menu for the icon.
- Select Properties from the list.
- In the Properties dialog box that appears, type your new name in the ID drop-down list box.

In Figure 3.9, you can see the first of the icons—**IDI_ICON1**—being renamed **IDI_HEART**. After you've done this, load the other three icons (unless you loaded them earlier by using multiple selection) and rename them **IDI_CLUB**, **IDI_DIAMOND**, and **IDI_SPADE**.

Modifying The Application Icon

Now that you've retrieved and named the four icons you'll need, let's turn our attention to modifying the application icon that represents your program. This icon is displayed in several places:

- Beside the name of your program in Windows Explorer.
- Beside the name of your program in the Windows 95 Taskbar, when your program is running.
- In the title bar of your application's window.
- On the desktop if you create a shortcut to your application.
- In the About dialog box.

Icons come in several sizes. The normal size is 32 pixels wide by 32 pixels high—such an icon appears on the desktop, or when the user selects Large Icons from Windows Explorer's View menu.

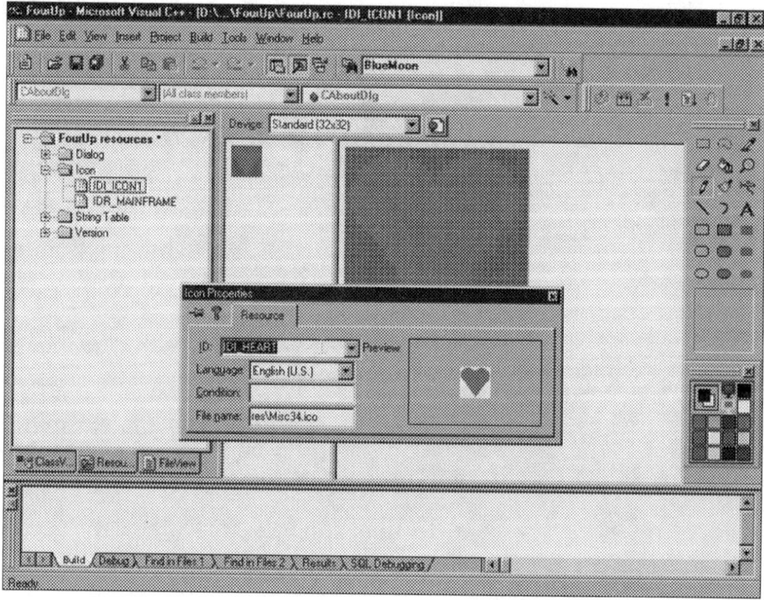

Figure 3.9
Changing a resource ID.

Each side of the smaller icon is half that size, 16 pixels—it appears when the user selects Windows Explorer's Small Icons or List view, as well as in the application's title bar and the Windows 95 Taskbar.

An icon image file can contain both types of images, though you'll see only one identifier in the ResourceView window. To switch between icon image sizes, you select an item from the drop-down list box that appears above the image when you're editing an icon. As you'll see if you try this yourself, AppWizard generates both a 16×16 and a 32×32 icon.

Because you don't want to create a custom icon for both sizes, let's just delete the small icon from the file. That way, when Windows runs FourUp and doesn't find a small icon, it will simply scale your larger one appropriately. First, make certain that the **IDR_MAINFRAME** icon is loaded. Then, you can delete the small icon by choosing the 16×16 icon from the drop-down list box, and then selecting Delete Device Image from the Image menu. (Be sure you don't select the 32×32 icon when you do this—otherwise, you'll have to redraw it from scratch.)

You're going to create your custom FourUp icon in three steps:

1. Take the existing MFC icon and use some Bitmap Editor tools to create a custom background.
2. Combine the background with the heart icon you imported earlier to create a new composite icon.
3. Add some special effects to make the FourUp icon instantly recognizable.

Ready? Let's go.

Step 1: Creating A Custom Background

Follow these steps to modify the MFC icon so it acts as a custom background for the FourUp icon:

1. Double-click on **IDR_MAINFRAME** in the Icons folder in the ProjectView window. This will open the Visual C++ Bitmap Editor, as you saw in Figure 3.8.

2. Choose the Rectangle Selection tool from the Drawing palette. This tool looks like a rectangle drawn with a dashed line, and it appears by default in the upper-left corner of the palette. (If necessary, use the tooltip to identify it.)
3. Move your mouse cursor over the icon image—it will change to a large cross-hair. Place your cursor in the upper-left corner of the default **IDR_MAINFRAME** icon and click the left mouse button. Holding down the left button, drag down and to the right until you've selected as much of the dark blue background as possible, without selecting any of the MFC blocks. Your selection should extend about one quarter of the way from the left and almost half-way down the icon. Release the mouse button.
4. Copy the selected block to the clipboard, using either Edit|Copy or Ctrl+C.
5. Paste the block back into your image using either Edit|Paste or Ctrl+V. When you do, the image will return to the position it came from. Notice the selection rectangle surrounding the block—move your cursor inside the block, and it will become a compass. Move the pasted block to the right, covering as much of the M block as possible, but keeping the selection at the top of the icon.
6. Continue to paste and move the same selection until you've covered the top half of the icon. At this point, repeat the same process on the bottom half of the icon. Don't worry about filling the center part—you'll take care of that in a minute. Be sure to fill the blue area to the bottom edge of the icon.
7. Using the selection tool, select the bottom half of the icon, being careful to select only the blue and black pixels you've pasted—don't select any of the white pixels remaining in the middle of the icon. Your selection should extend across the width of the icon.
8. Select Image|Flip Vertical from the main menu. Now you have two mirror image backgrounds, fading from black on the top and bottom to blue in the middle. To cover the left-over "garbage" in the middle of your icon, select a few blue pixels,

then copy and paste them over the middle until your image looks like the one in Figure 3.10. This would be a good time to save your project workspace, so that an unexpected system crash will be less painful.

Step 2: Combining Two Icon Images

Now, you'd like to take the **IDI_HEART** icon, which you added to your project earlier, and combine it with the new background you just created. To do that, just follow these steps:

1. Double-click on the icon name **IDI_HEART** in the ResourceView window. (If you've been following along, that's the icon originally named **IDI_ICON1**.)
2. Be sure the image is selected in the Bitmap Editor. (Either the large or small image can be selected—it doesn't make any difference.)
3. Copy the image to the clipboard using Edit|Paste or Ctrl+C.
4. Select the **IDR_MAINFRAME** icon by double-clicking on its name in the ResourceView window.
5. Select the modified image (again, it doesn't matter whether you select the large or small image) and paste the **IDI_HEART** image from the clipboard.

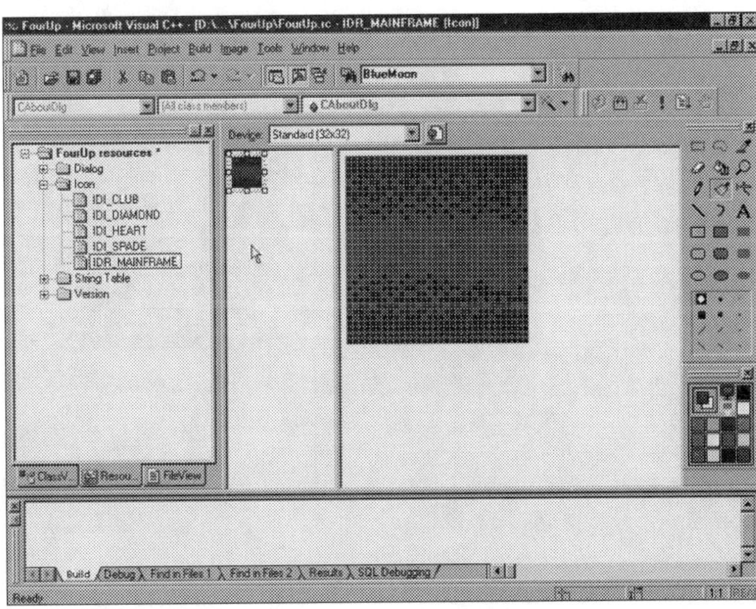

Figure 3.10
Modifying the **IDR_MAINFRAME** icon in the Bitmap Editor.

Opaque And Transparent Backgrounds

That's almost all there is to it, but there's one potential complication. For icons and cursors (but not for regular bitmaps, as you'll see shortly), the Bitmap Editor can treat the background as an opaque area or as a transparent area. You want the gradient blue background of your new, custom icon to show up behind the heart image, so you need to make sure the background of the overlaid image is transparent.

When you select an image using the Rectangle Selection tool, the Drawing palette changes a little from the way it appears when you're using one of the line-drawing or freehand-drawing tools. If you select the Pencil tool or the Brush tool, the region separating the Drawing palette and the Color palette changes to let you select the pencil or brush width you want to paint with. But when you use the Rectangle Selection tool, a *transparency selection indicator* appears in this region. If the top image displayed in this area is highlighted, the image you paste will use an opaque background. If the bottom image in the indicator area is highlighted, the pasted image will use a transparent background. You can see the result of dropping the **IDI_HEART** icon over the gradient blue icon using a transparent background in Figure 3.11.

The rest of the tools in the Drawing palette work as you'd expect in a drawing program such as Windows' Paint. You may have

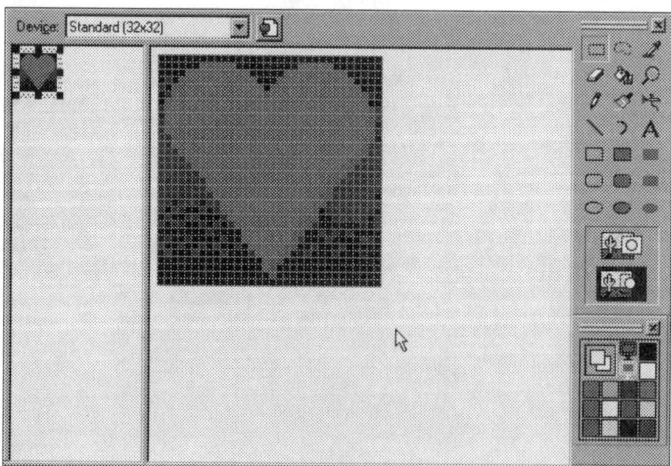

Figure 3.11
Combining two icons.

difficulty with the tiny icons—it takes a special talent to make such a small image look good. Take a little time to experiment with each of the tools, and see if you have that talent.

Step 3: Using The Type Tool

If you find your drawing skills lacking, you can make a good-looking icon with the Type tool. To use the Type tool, you type in a small floating dialog box that overlays the main Bitmap Editor window. The dialog box has a Font button that lets you select any of the type fonts installed on your system. After you select a font, you can enter any characters you wish. As you type, the characters appear on your icon, surrounded by a selection rectangle. You can position the text anywhere you want—its position isn't fixed until you close the Text tool's dialog box.

Let's add a little text to the icon before we move on. Just follow these instructions:

1. Select the Text tool from the Drawing palette.
2. Using the Color palette, set the foreground color to black by clicking on the black color swatch with the left mouse button. (If you click with the right mouse button, you'll change the background color.)
3. Using the Font button in the Text tool dialog box, choose any 20-point font that appeals to you. Then, type and position the character "4" in the center of the heart image.
4. When you've positioned the black 4 to your satisfaction, click on the Text tool button again to fix the letter.
5. Now, change the foreground color on the Color palette to yellow.
6. Using the same font, type the character "4" again, and this time position it a little to the left and up from the black 4. The first image will act as a drop-shadow, peeking out behind the yellow 4. When you've positioned the letter to your satisfaction, close the Type tool dialog box by selecting a different control (any one will do), and you're finished. Figure 3.12 shows the repositioned yellow 4.

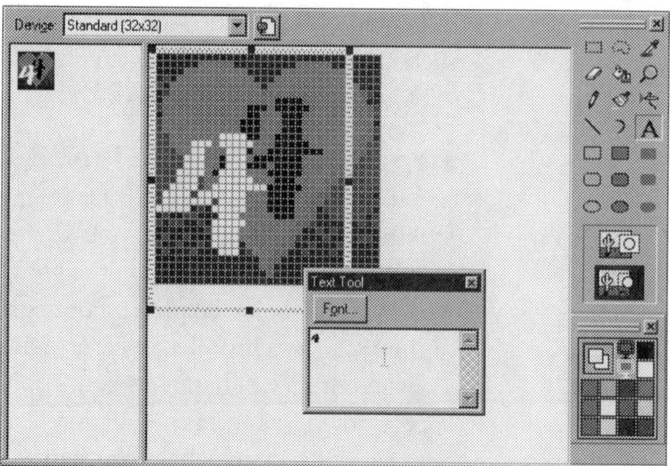

Figure 3.12
Adding text to an icon.

Dialog Editor Déjà Vu

Congratulations! Your application has a new icon. Now, let's finish up the About dialog box, so we can get on with the rest of the application. Let's start by adding the new icon to the About dialog box. Here's how to do that:

1. In the ResourceView window, double-click on **IDD_ABOUTBOX** to open the Dialog Editor.
2. Select the icon displayed in the About dialog box. Then, right-click to open the context menu. Select Properties to open the Picture Properties dialog box. See Figure 3.13.
3. In the Picture Properties dialog box, be sure that the Type drop-down list displays the value Icon, then select any value *except* **IDR_MAINFRAME** from the Image drop-down list. You'll notice that the icon displayed in your About dialog box changes. (You may have to tab out of the field before the change takes effect.) Now, reselect **IDR_MAINFRAME** from the Image drop-down list. Close the dialog box, and you should see your new icon displayed in the About dialog box.

Selecting, Sizing, And Moving Components

Now that you're a bitmap image master, it's time to learn how to work with controls. Throughout this chapter, we've been telling

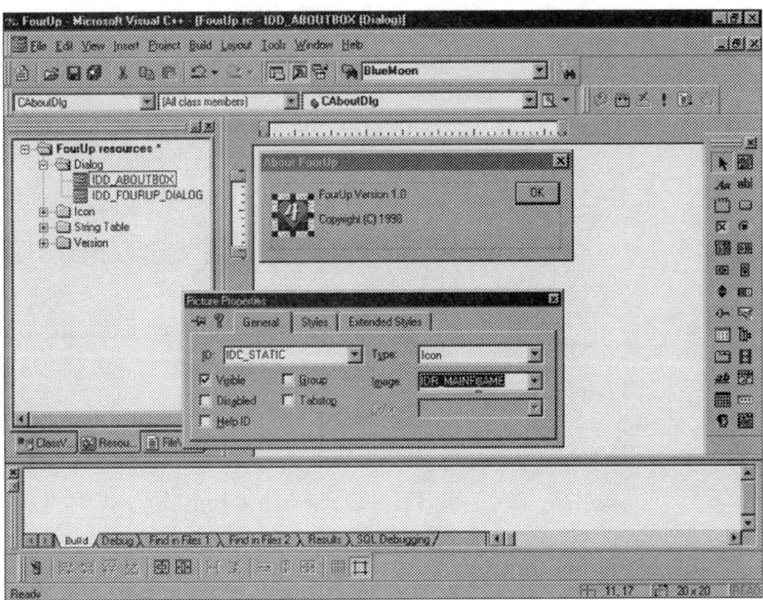

Figure 3.13
Changing the icon in the About dialog box.

you to select items—but haven't talked much about what you should see when you've selected a particular item.

When you select a control, a bitmap, or a dialog box in any of the resource editors, you'll notice two things. First, the selected item has a fairly thick, "fuzzy" white line surrounding it—this is the *selection rectangle*. Second, a small rectangle appears at each corner of the selection rectangle, as well as at the mid-points of the top and sides—these rectangles are *sizing handles*.

The sizing handles at the midpoints of the lines let you resize the selection rectangle in a particular direction—horizontal or vertical. The sizing handles at the corners reshape the control diagonally so that it becomes larger (or smaller) in both the horizontal and vertical dimensions.

When you place your cursor over one of the sizing handles, the cursor will change to tell you the direction in which you can move the given line. If you move the cursor over a vertical sizing handle, you'll see a north-south arrow. (That is, the cursor will change to a double-headed arrow, pointing both up and down.) If you move the cursor over one of the horizontal sizing handles, it changes to an east-west arrow; and, depending on the corner you pick, the cursor can also change to a northwest-southeast or a northeast-southwest arrow.

Besides having a direction, the sizing handles also have an *activation status*. An active sizing handle appears as a filled rectangle, and an inactive one appears as a hollow rectangle. An inactive sizing rectangle doesn't really do anything except let you know it's there.

Let's see how these handles work in your About dialog box. Look at Figure 3.14, and notice:

- The selection rectangle around the outside of the About dialog box.
- The active sizing handles on the bottom and right side, as well as the lower-right corner.
- The five inactive sizing handles on all the other sides and corners.
- The north-south arrow cursor being used to enlarge the dialog box.

Resize the About dialog box so that it's a little taller, to provide room for new controls. Don't fret about the exact size: You can easily resize it again.

To move a control without resizing it, you first need to make sure it's selected. Then, move your cursor so that it rests on the

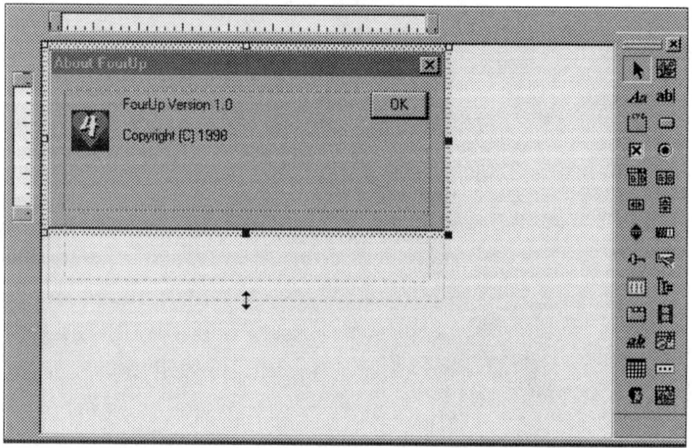

Figure 3.14
Resizing the About dialog box in the Dialog Editor.

The Secret Of Correct Cursor Placement

How, you may wonder, can you tell where to place the cursor? It's easy. You just look at the mouse cursor. When a control is prepared to move, the cursor changes to a compass cursor (four arrows pointing north-east-west-south). When you see the compass, you can drag the control wherever you like.

selection rectangle, but not on one of the sizing handles. You may also be able to move some controls by placing your cursor *inside* the selection rectangle—that is, on the control itself.

Introducing The Dialog Toolbar

It's hard to reposition and resize controls accurately. As you might expect, though, Visual C++ provides several tools that make up for your inaccuracy. Perhaps the handiest is the Dialog Toolbar.

The Dialog Toolbar is usually docked at the bottom of the screen. Most of its controls serve to help you align controls individually and with each other. You'll use the Dialog Toolbar throughout the rest of this chapter to make your dialog boxes look neat and professional.

Let's start by moving the OK button from its position in the upper-left corner to the bottom of your dialog box. Moving it to the bottom is easy, because the dialog box's border keeps you inside the lines. The problem comes when you want to center the button—if you're off even a single pixel in one direction or the other, your screens will look sloppy. Fortunately, by using the Dialog Toolbar's Center Horizontal tool, which you can see in Figure 3.15, you can avoid the tedium of manually counting pixels.

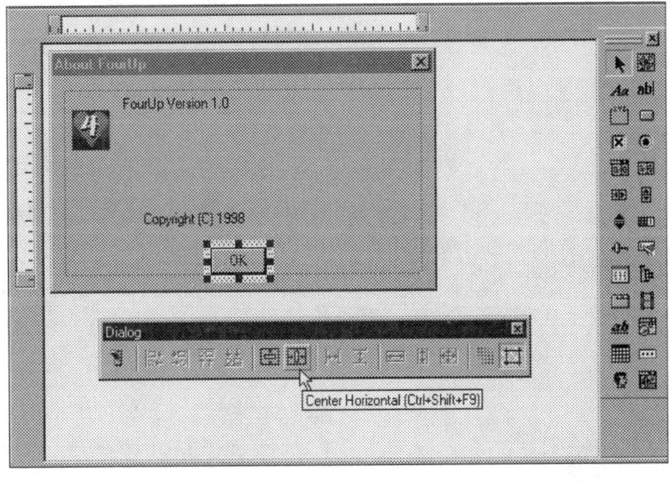

Figure 3.15
Dragging and aligning controls in the Dialog Editor.

Working With Static Text

You'll often use the *static text* component in your dialog boxes. Static text, as its name suggests, is simply a label that holds an unchanging text value. In the About dialog box, the lines that hold the version number of FourUp and the copyright information are both static text.

On the Control Toolbar, the static text icon consists of the letters *Aa* in italic text. (Two other icons appear similar: the text box control, also known as the edit control, consists of the letters *ab* followed by a vertical line, and the rich-text edit control consists of the letters *ab* in underlined italic text.) To add a new static text control, simply select the static text icon on the Control Toolbar and then drag and drop it onto your dialog box.

Like most other controls you use in the Dialog Editor, you can change the properties of static text by first selecting the control, then right-clicking and choosing Properties from the context menu. The Text Properties dialog box has three pages. The first page—General—allows you to change the ID and the caption displayed on screen. Let's try it and see how it works.

1. Select the text containing the copyright information and drag it to the bottom of the screen. Place it above the OK button. (Don't worry about exact alignment at this point.)
2. Open the Text Properties dialog box by choosing Properties from the context menu or by choosing the View | Properties menu item.
3. Notice that the control's ID **IDC_STATIC**. **IDC_STATIC** is defined as -1, which is a shorthand way of saying, "I want this control to sit here and look good. I'm never going to communicate with it again." Because you have no intention of modifying the copyright information at runtime, you'll leave this value alone.
4. When you change the caption, you can put in any characters you want. To create multiple lines of text, you can insert the C++ escape sequence **\n** into your text. You can also insert special ANSI characters if you like, by using the proper octal escape sequence—you enter the escape character followed by

the three-digit octal value of the character you wish to display. You can find a list of useful escape sequences in the Visual C++ online help.

Figure 3.16 shows these modifications to the copyright line. Notice that as you type in the Text Properties dialog box, your changes are reflected in the actual text displayed on your dialog. The figure uses the octal escape sequence **\251** to start the line with a copyright symbol.

Static Text Styles

In the Text Properties dialog box, the Styles property page lets you choose alignment options. Most frequently, you'll choose to change the alignment of the text by using the Align Text drop-down combo box, especially if you need to center your text.

As you can see in Figure 3.17, this page also lets you choose a number of other options. Here's what those options mean:

- *Center Vertically* tells Windows to automatically center your text within the area defined by the selection rectangle.
- *No Prefix* allows you to enter text that contains ampersands (&). Normally, if you put an ampersand in text, Windows

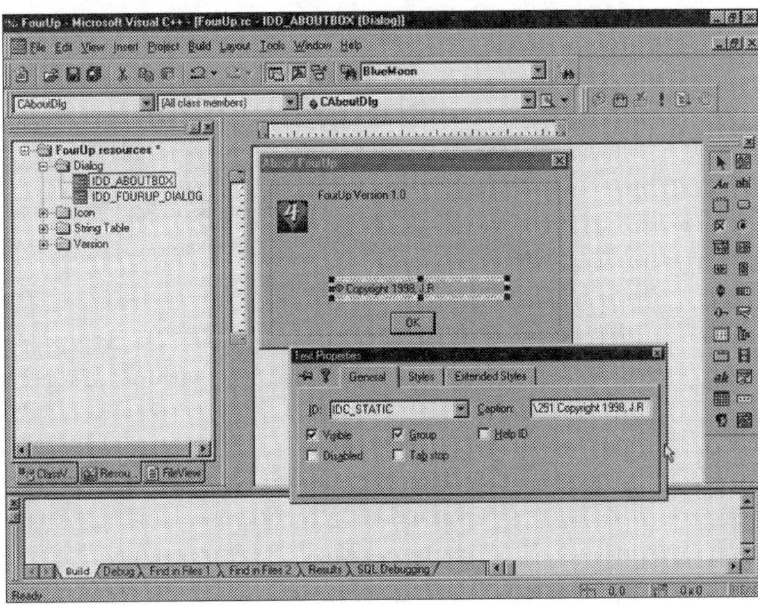

Figure 3.16
Static text. Changing a caption.

interprets it as a sign that you want to underline the next character and make that character a shortcut key. This option is sometimes useful for static text, as you'll see later in the book, but it's more often used with buttons and other controls that can take some action.

- *No Wrap* prevents automatic word wrapping. Normally, if the text in the caption area is too large to appear on one line, Windows will break the text between lines. Notice, however, that Windows doesn't resize the selection rectangle to accommodate those extra lines—you have to do that yourself. You can see how this works by taking any piece of static text and resizing the selection rectangle to make Windows wrap the lines. If you check the No Wrap option, this behavior is eliminated.
- *Simple* creates a text control that Windows can display more quickly than other types of text controls. However, a simple text control can't do some of the fancier tricks its not-so-simple brethren can perform.
- *Notify* creates a text control that can send a message to its parent when it's been clicked or double-clicked. Normally, static text controls don't generate any messages.
- *Sunken* adds a 3D depressed border that follows the static text selection rectangle.
- *Border* works like Sunken, but it inserts a thin single-line border that outlines the selection area.

For the FourUp copyright line, let's set the alignment to center and leave all the other selections at their default values. You can see the result in Figure 3.17.

Now, similarly use the Align Text property to center the phrase "FourUp Version 1.0" within the static text control that contains it.

Alignment And Multiple Selection

So far, you've worked only with individual controls. Frequently, however, you'll need to work with multiple controls as a group. Fortunately, the Dialog Toolbar has a bevy of tools that let you easily align and work with multiple components.

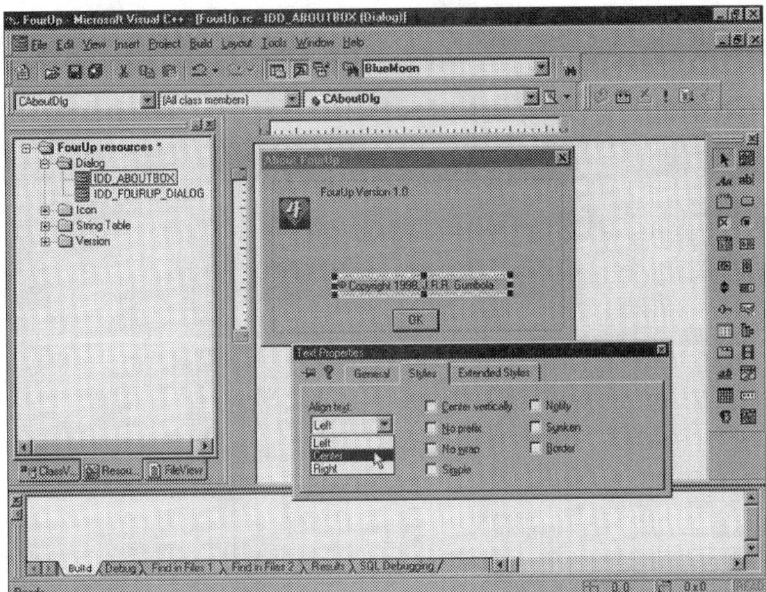

Figure 3.17
Changing the alignment of static text.

Normally, when you select a component like a static text control, any controls that were previously selected are released. To work with multiple controls, you need some way of selecting multiple controls. You can use either of these two techniques:

- Hold down the Shift key or the Ctrl key as you select the second and subsequent controls. Notice that when you select multiple controls, the sizing handles of the last-selected control are active, whereas the sizing handles of all the other controls become inactive. The control with active sizing handles is called the *dominant control*.
- Drag the mouse cursor so that it draws a selection rectangle around any controls you wish to select. (If the selection rectangle only partially surrounds a control, that control won't be selected). When you release the mouse button, the control closest to the starting point of the selection rectangle becomes the dominant control.

Once you've selected multiple items, you can move them around your dialog box as a group by using either the mouse or the cursor keys. You can also copy, cut, and paste the group using the clipboard. Even more interesting, you can use the Dialog Toolbar to align and space controls relative to one another. Let's see how

Avoiding Alignment Woes

Watch out for one potential pitfall as you use the alignment controls—you must be sure that the button you click on is appropriate to the situation. For instance, if you click on the Align Top button using the selected label in Figure 3.18, you'll be unhappily surprised when the title text label covers the copyright label. Of course, you can use Edit|Undo to escape the consequences of your misdeed. In general, avoid using the Align Top or Align Bottom commands with controls that are stacked vertically, and avoid using the Align Left or Align Right commands with controls that are stacked horizontally.

that works with our About dialog box. You can follow along by looking at Figure 3.18.

1. Select the text containing the application title: FourUp Version 1.0.
2. Drag the control so it appears in roughly the same position shown in Figure 3.18.
3. Holding down the Shift or Ctrl key, select the copyright static text control so that it becomes the dominant control. Be sure that the title text control is still selected.
4. On the Dialog Toolbar, click on the Align Left button. You can get the same result by choosing Layout|Align|Left from the main menu, or by using the Ctrl+Left Arrow shortcut key.

When you do this, the title text arranges itself so its left edge is in line with the left edge of the copyright text. The title text moves, rather than the copyright text, because the copyright text is the dominant control.

As you can see, other Dialog Toolbar controls work in a similar way: Align Right, Align Top, and Align Bottom. (In Chapter 5, you'll see a set of related buttons that evenly space a group of selected controls.)

The Dialog Toolbar does offer one last alignment option you may find handy: The Grid button (perhaps you noticed it in Figure 3.18). The Grid button allows you to create a form grid. When you move and place controls with the grid active, the controls must line up on the grid lines. Furthermore, you can change the spacing of the grid lines by using the Guide Settings dialog box, which you reach from the Layout menu.

But, What About A Font Property?

As you can see from Figure 3.18, your About dialog box is starting to look really nice. All that's left is to center the FourUp icon above the application name, then set the title in a nice, big, flashy font. Select the title text and open the Text Properties dialog box. Now, simply choose the new font and size you want to use from the font list.

Oh.

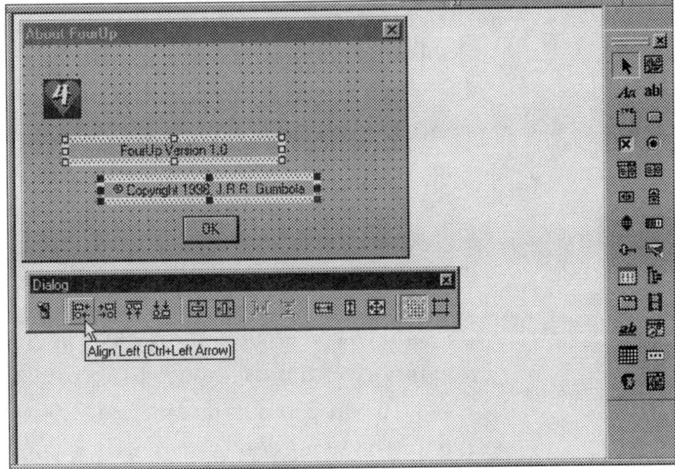

Figure 3.18
Aligning controls with the Dialog Toolbar.

There isn't any font list. As a matter of fact, there's no easy way to select a font for individual components in a dialog box. If you select the About dialog box and open its properties, you'll see that you can set the font properties for the dialog box as a whole. However, you'll seldom do this because it has two unpleasant side effects:

- It makes all of the text in your dialog box appear in the new font you've selected. Choosing the DinoBots font for your title might look cool, but it probably doesn't look so hot on the face of all your buttons and text fields.
- The size of the dialog box is calculated in units based on the font. If you change the font from 8-point MS Sans Serif to 12-point, for instance, your dialog box will swell to accommodate the new units of measure. This is probably not what you had in mind.

So, how can you add a nice flashy font for your About dialog box title? The answer is staring you in the face, exalted bitmap master: Use the Visual C++ Bitmap Editor.

Creating Bitmap Resources

Because you're already familiar with the basic operation of the Bitmap Editor, we don't have to rehash those details. Instead, we'll point out places where the Bitmap Editor works differently with bitmap resources than it does with icons.

To start things off, drag a new picture control from the Control Toolbar. The Picture control is the control that looks like a still life with the sun and a cactus in the foreground. The picture control serves several purposes. When you originally drop it on your dialog box, you'll see that it's just a hollow black frame. When you open the Properties dialog box, however, you'll see that you can choose to display various kinds of pictures. Choose Bitmap, as shown in Figure 3.19.

As soon as you change the Type property from Frame to Bitmap, you'll notice that the Image list box becomes active. Unfortunately, when you pull down the list, you'll find it empty. As you did for the icons you loaded earlier, you'll have to create a bitmap resource before you can use it as part of a control.

To add a new bitmap, choose Insert|Resource from the main menu, and then select Bitmap in the Insert Resource dialog box. Because you're going to construct the bitmap from scratch, rather than modify an existing bitmap, click on New instead of Import. You can see this in Figure 3.20.

Because the FourUp project had no previous bitmap resources, you'll see a new Bitmap folder in the ResourceView window. Open it, and you'll find your new bitmap with the identifier

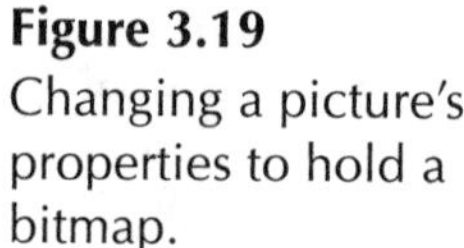

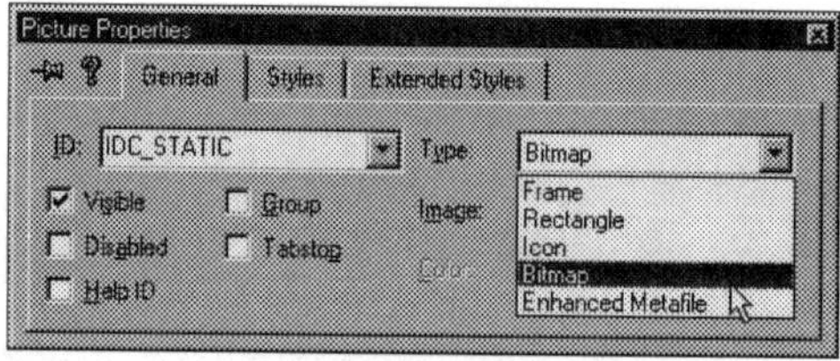

Figure 3.19
Changing a picture's properties to hold a bitmap.

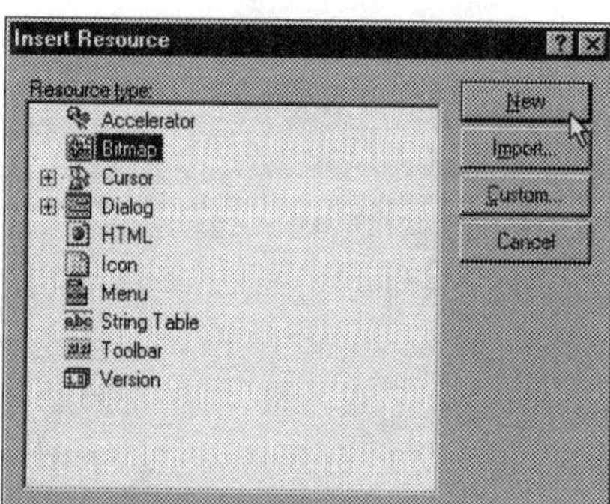

Figure 3.20
Inserting a Bitmap with the Insert Resource dialog box.

IDB_BITMAP1. (By now, you can guess what the **IDB** stands for.) You really don't care about the name, because you won't be using it in your program—simply double-click on it to open the Bitmap Editor, unless the Bitmap Editor is already open.

When you first open a bitmap resource—as opposed to an icon resource—you'll notice two changes in the way the Bitmap behaves:

- The drawing area (or *canvas*) is resizable. That wasn't true with icons, which have a fixed and determined size.
- The drawing area has a background color. Icons use the default transparent background color, but bitmaps have an opaque background.

Follow these steps to create your new logo for the FourUp application:

1. Stretch the drawing area to about 100 units wide and 35 units high, as indicated by the dimensions shown in the lower-right corner of the window. You can make it bigger if you like, then cut it down to size later. If you can't see the entire text area in the larger drawing pane, select the Magnify icon (it looks like a magnifying glass) from the Drawing palette and choose a lower resolution from the list that appears.
2. Select a background color by right-clicking on the light gray color swatch. The same color appears as the background of your dialog box, so the edges of your bitmap won't show.
3. Use the Fill tool (it looks like a spilled paint bucket) to color the background. To do this, click on the tool in the Drawing palette, and then right-click anywhere on your drawing surface. (If you left-click, you'll paint using the foreground color.)
4. Change the foreground color to black by left-clicking on the black color swatch.
5. Choose the Text tool, then select an appropriate font style and size (about 14 points). Type the word "FourUp" in the Text tool dialog box. Then, click on the Text tool to set the new contents.

6. Position the text close to the lower-right margin of your drawing area. If the text is too big, choose a smaller font size. If it doesn't nearly fill the drawing area, choose a larger one.
7. Change the foreground color again, this time to red.
8. Select the Text tool and retype "FourUp" using the same font and size. Now, position the red text over the black text, so the black text peeks out like a shadow. You can see how it looks in Figure 3.21.
9. After you finish your bitmap (and after you've saved it using File|Save, just to be safe), go back to the Dialog Editor and reselect the Picture control you dropped onto your form. In the Picture Properties dialog box, you'll now find **IDB_BITMAP1** in the drop-down list of images. Select it, and your new snazzy title will appear in your dialog box.

One Last Control: The Groupbox

By now, your About dialog box looks pretty good. You've got your icon, you've got your custom bitmap title, you've got your static text, and you've even got a button. What more could you need?

Well, before we take leave of the About dialog box, let's look at one more control on the Control Toolbar: the groupbox control.

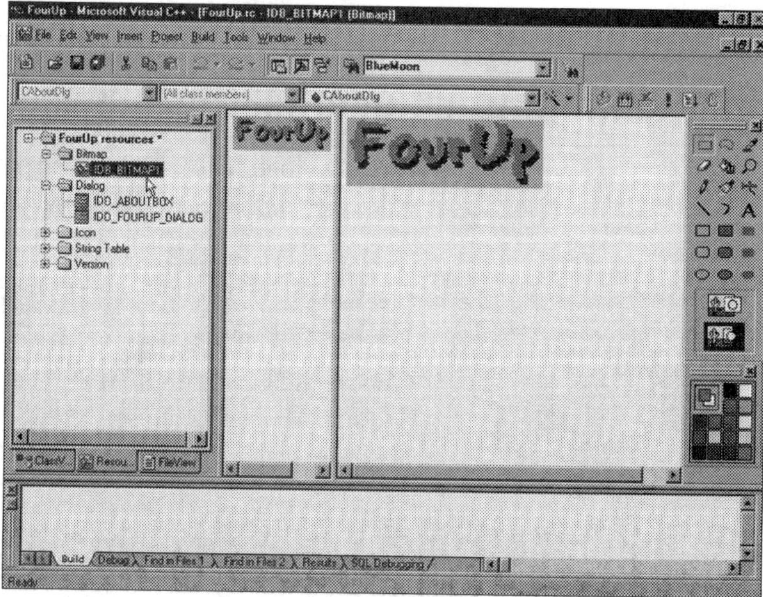

Figure 3.21
Using the Bitmap Editor to create a title for the main dialog box.

Its toolbar icon looks like a rectangle with the letters xyz centered in the top, as we showed you in Figure 3.5.

Groupbox controls are like static text controls and icons and bitmaps, in that they really don't *do* anything—they exist merely to look good. Let's put a groupbox around the controls in FourUp's About dialog box. Just follow these steps:

1. Drag a groupbox control from the Control Toolbar and drop it on your About dialog box.
2. Use the Dialog Toolbar to turn on the alignment grid. This will help you place the groupbox control evenly.
3. Select and expand the control so that it appears equidistant from all four sides (about two units from each edge, where each grid dot represents a single unit). You should note two things. First, the line goes right through the OK button—don't worry, we'll fix it in a moment. Second, you'll have to place your selection rectangle closer to the top than to the other three sides, because the drawn rectangle is inset to make up for the text that appears in its title bar.
4. Open the groupbox's property sheet and erase the caption. By default, each groupbox has the word *Static* as its caption, as you can see in Figure 3.22.
5. Expand the dialog box vertically, so as much space appears between the top of the OK button and the bottom of the groupbox outline as between the bottom of the OK button and the bottom of the dialog box.

Final Checkout

Well, you've finished your About dialog box and explored a lot of new tools on the way. In the next chapter, you'll take some time dissecting the code produced by AppWizard, to give you a better idea of what the MFC classes **CWinApp**, **CWnd**, and **CDialog** actually do.

Before we leave, though, let's take one last look at FourUp and its About dialog box. If you compile and run FourUp, you'll see that it uses your new icon—but it doesn't have a menu. How are you supposed to see the About dialog box?

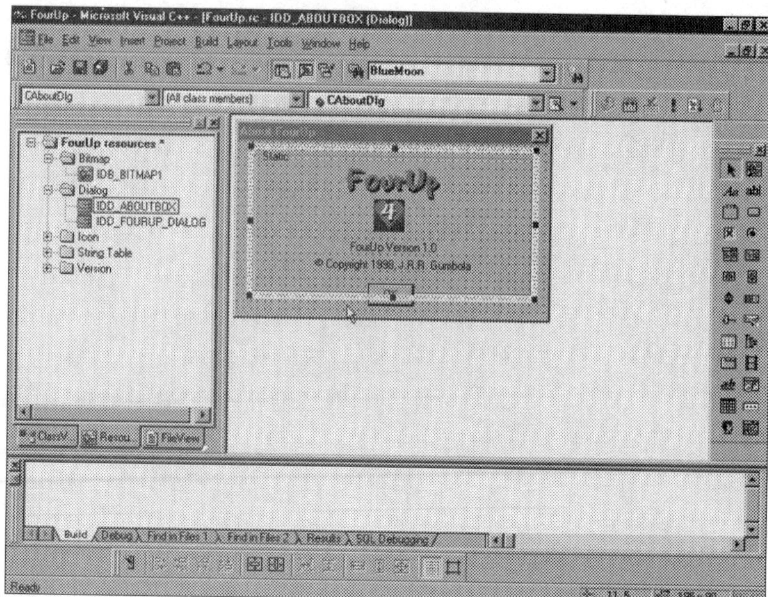

Figure 3.22
Adding a groupbox control.

That's easy. When AppWizard creates a dialog-based application, it adds your About dialog box to the application's *system* menu. Just click on the icon that appears in the title bar, then choose About FourUp from the menu that appears.

There's your finished dialog box, which you can see in Figure 3.23. All that remains is to give the rest of the application some life. But that will have to wait for the next project chapter.

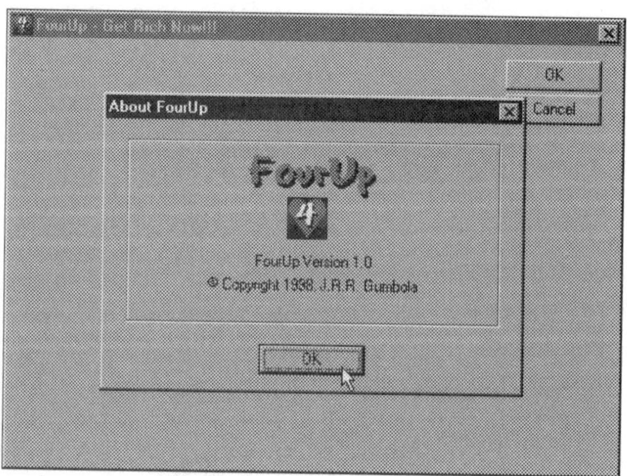

Figure 3.23
Displaying the finished About dialog box.

Chapter 4

Dialog Boxes

Dialog boxes enable users to converse with an application program. In this chapter, you'll learn how to make interesting conversation.

Perhaps—and we do mean perhaps—the greatest movie of all time is Louis Malle's *My Dinner with Andre*, starring Wallace Shawn and Andre Gregory. Shawn plays a struggling playwright/actor who accepts a dinner invitation from Gregory, an old friend who has just returned from years overseas. Gregory recounts to Shawn the circumstances of his sudden departure and the many odd things that transpired thereafter—essentially, the film consists of this rambling dialogue, as Gregory recalls his extravagantly fantastic experiences and Shawn strives to make sense of his friend's motivations and behavior. The audience, right up to the film's last few minutes, expects action—but there is only dialogue. The joke, it seems, is on them. Except, that is, for those few who enjoy a superlatively dry style of humor, who declare the film a veritable monument to creative genius at its apex.

The FourUp application, which you began in the previous chapter, is a little like that. It, too, is all dialog. But don't be misled, like Malle's; all-dialogue film, an all-dialog application can be plenty interesting, even if your tastes run to the normal.

The Structure Of The FourUp Application

There's no doubt about it: MFC is huge, containing well over 200 classes, some of which have hundreds of data members and functions. On the face of it, MFC does little to reduce the complexity of the raw Windows API. But, in fact, MFC significantly reduces the complexity of Windows programs because it provides an *application architecture*. There may be many pieces, but all of the pieces fit together in a similar way. Almost every MFC program you build—from the simplest to the most complex—can be reduced to the basic structure shown in Figure 4.1.

The Required Pieces

On the left side of the illustration you can see the two required pieces: the application object and the window object. Every MFC program *must* have an application object, which is responsible for starting and stopping the application.

The application usually creates the other required object, the program's main window. (Technically, the application object is the only required part of an MFC application—but you'll probably never encounter such a solitary application object. If a graphical user-interface program has no window, it would probably be better implemented using a non-graphical user interface.)

Once the application has created and displayed the main window, both objects continue to work together. The application object

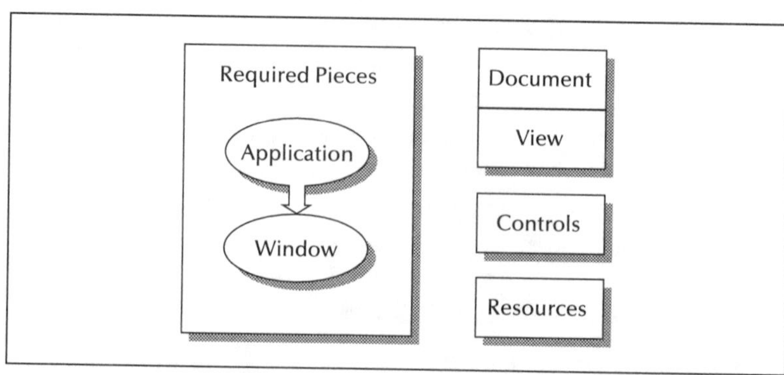

Figure 4.1
The basic MFC application architecture.

runs the message pump, retrieving messages from Windows. The window object responds to messages, or passes them on to other portions of the application.

In MFC programs, you'll usually implement these two required pieces as subclasses of the **CWinApp** and **CWnd** classes, as you can see (somewhat abbreviated) in Figure 4.2. We'll look at these classes as well as their ancestors, **CCmdTarget** and **CObject**, later in this chapter.

The Usual Suspects

Most programs contain additional pieces beyond those required by a minimal application. The NotePod project from Chapter 1, for instance, also included a document class and a view class, which were responsible for managing and displaying the application's data. The document-view classes are usually inseparable—if you use one of them, you almost always use both.

The document-view architecture is ideally suited for complex applications, because it lets you divide the work your program has to accomplish into smaller, self-contained pieces. Nevertheless, the architecture does add some complexity of its own, which can get in the way of understanding MFC basics. Because of that, we won't return to the document-view architecture until Chapter 11.

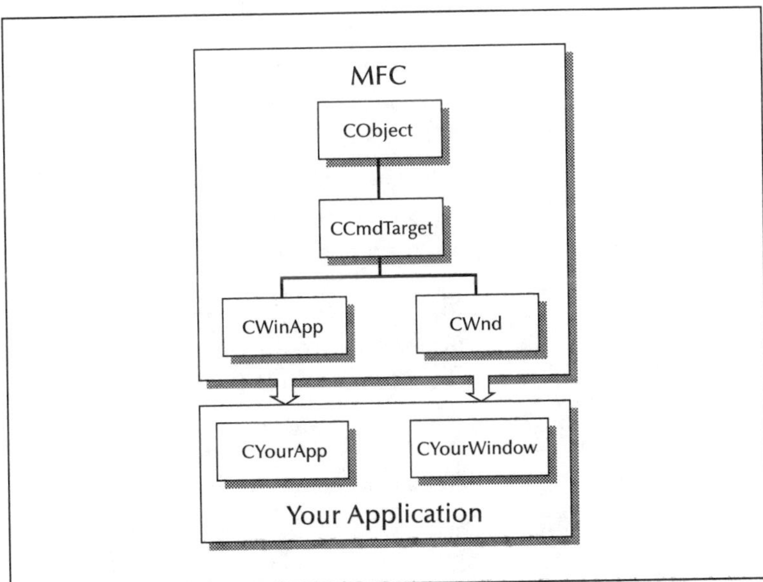

Figure 4.2
The MFC application class hierarchy.

But don't prematurely suffer separation anxiety. As it turns out, two other pieces—components and resources—are even more common in MFC applications than the document and view classes. For now, we'll focus the investigation on them.

Components Or Controls?

Components are specialized, self-contained window objects, which most often form part of the user interface. In other words, components typically provide interaction with the user, who uses the components to control the program. Therefore, components are normally known as *controls*. Even though controls are self-contained, they can't exist on their own—they must be contained inside another window, which takes on the role of *parent window*. For that reason, controls are sometimes called *child-window controls*. MFC supports six built-in families of child-window controls:

- **CStatic**—controls that display text or icons, such as the picture control on the Control Toolbar.
- **CButton**—push buttons, checkboxes, radio buttons, and groupboxes.
- **CListbox**—controls that display a scrolling list of items.
- **CComboBox**—controls that display a retractable list of items.
- **CScrollBar**—horizontal and vertical scroll bars.
- **CEdit**—single-line and multiline text-editing controls.

All versions of Windows support these basic controls. With the introduction of Windows 95, and continuing through Windows NT 4.0 and Windows 98, the list of available controls continues to expand. Indeed, by using ActiveX controls (available from a wide variety of sources), you can find the right component for almost any eventuality.

Figure 4.3 shows the six common child-window control classes. It also shows two other commonly used classes derived from **CWnd**: the **CFrameWnd** class and the **CDialog** class.

Resources

In addition to controls, most applications make use of *resources*. In a Windows program, resources are a special form of read-only

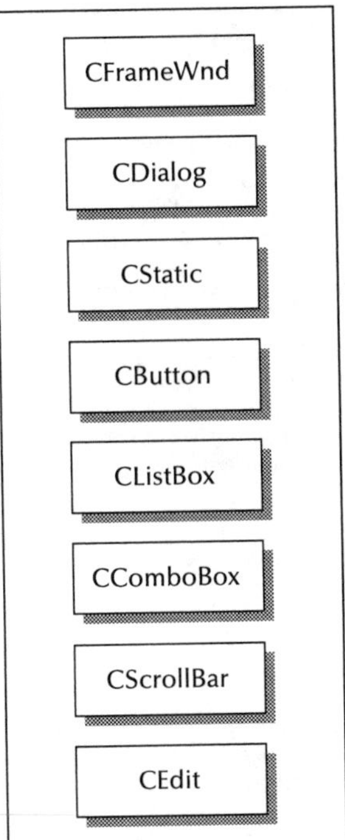

Figure 4.3
Window classes derived from **CWnd**.

data, bound into the executable file by a program called the *resource compiler*. Resources come in two basic varieties:

- *Binary*—graphics resources, including icons, cursors, and bitmaps.
- *Text*—structured resources, including dialog boxes, menus, string tables, and accelerator tables.

Binary resources are stored in separate files, whereas text resources are stored in a plain ASCII text file that describes the structure of each element. This ASCII file is called the *resource script*—it normally has the same name as your project, with the extension .rc.

Every program that uses resources has a resource script. Text resources are fully contained within the resource script; binary resources are simply referenced by their file names. When you compile your program, the resource compiler combines your text resources and binary resources into a single binary image (stored in an res file), which it attaches to your executable during the linking step. Figure 4.4 illustrates this process.

The FourUp Family

Before we buckle down and start examining these application pieces in detail, let's take a quick look at the classes of the FourUp program, and identify which part of the puzzle each fits into.

Here's a short outline:

- *Application object*—Like almost every application, the FourUp application uses a class derived from **CWinApp** as its application object. The class is named **CFourUpApp**, and its definition and implementation are contained in the files FourUp.h and FourUp.cpp.
- *Window object*—FourUp uses a **CDialog**-derived class as its main window. **CDialog** is a subclass of the **CWnd** class. FourUp's main window class is named **CFourUpDlg**; the class's definition and implementation are contained in the files FourUpDlg.cpp and FourUpDlg.h.
- *Components*—FourUp uses several child-window controls, in addition to a second **CDialog**-derived class (**CAboutDlg**) that implements the program's About box. The classes include

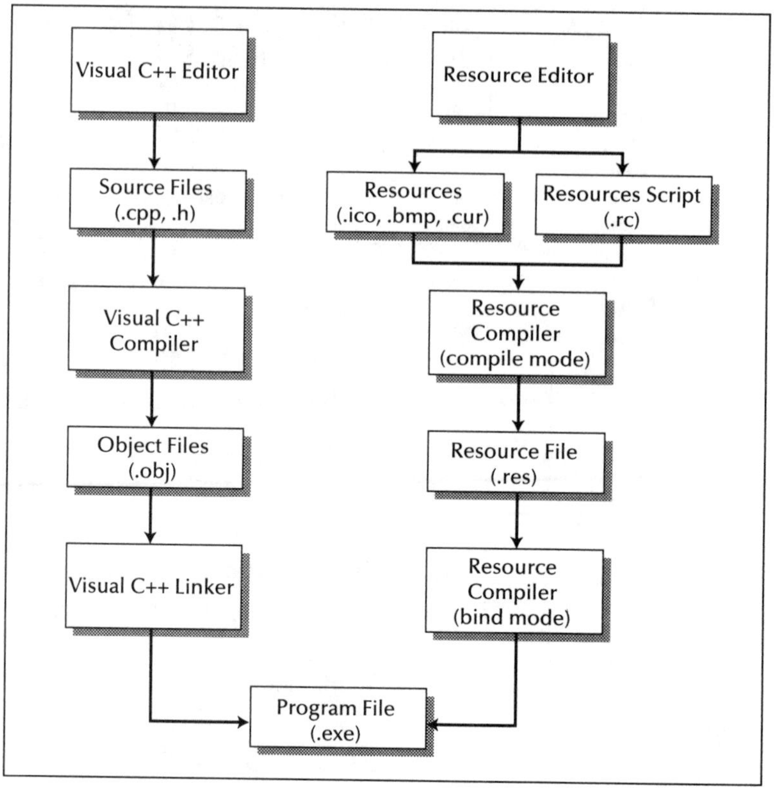

Figure 4.4
Source code, resources, and programs.

CStatic (bitmap, icon, and plain-text varieties) and **CButton** (groupbox and push-button varieties). These components are distributed between two files: layouts for **CAboutDlg** and **CFourUpDlg** in the resource script, and class definitions and implementation in FourUpDlg.cpp.

- *Resources*—FourUp uses both binary and text resources. Its binary resources include the bitmap used for the custom title and the icons representing each playing-card suit, as well as the application icon. Text resources include the layout for the main screen and the About dialog box, as well as some resources generated by Visual C++ (such as version information). The text resources are stored in the file named FourUp.rc, and the binary resources are stored in the project's res subdirectory.

Now that you've seen the FourUp program from a height (so to speak), let's drill in on the details. We'll start with the project's application class, **CFourUp**.

Meet The Application Object

Even if you're an experienced C/C++ programmer, you're likely to be surprised the first time you open an AppWizard-generated file. You might say that the code is very weird—what *are* those extremely strange comments, like this one?

```
//{{AFX_MSG(CAboutDlg)
//}}AFX_MSG
```

And what are you supposed to do with a line like this?

```
#define
AFX_FOURUP_H__2965C9C5_FBA4_11D1_837C_8CAD2F77F2B1
  __INCLUDED_
```

When you think about it, though, the code AppWizard generates is logical. It was written to help automated tools like ClassWizard work better—it wasn't written for humans to decipher.

Because the code intended for ClassWizard is so odd, you're unlikely either to confuse it with code you've written or to be tempted to change it. It's also unlikely that one of your identifiers will accidentally clash with an identifier chosen by AppWizard (unless your taste in identifier names is strange beyond description). Reading a program written by AppWizard is like reading a letter written in two different languages: If you don't understand one of the languages, you just skip through looking for the pieces that make sense.

We're going to start our look at FourUp's application object by examining the source code for the **CFourUpApp** class.

Looking At CFourUp.h

The FourUp project uses **CFourUpApp** as its application class. AppWizard projects follow the generally accepted C++ practice of storing a class definition in a header file that uses the .h extension, and storing the implementation (or actual function definitions) for the class in a separate .cpp file. Header files may contain inline functions, but they don't create variables or allocate memory.

The FourUp application follows this convention by storing the header file for the **CFourUpApp** class in the file FourUp.h. The header file appears in Listing 4.1—let's walk through it line by line.

Listing 4.1 FourUp.h: the main header file for the FourUp application.

```
// FourUp.h : main header file for the FOURUP application
//

#if \
!defined(AFX_FOURUP_H__2965C9C5_FBA4_11D1_837C_8CAD2F77F2B1__INCLUDED_)
#define \
AFX_FOURUP_H__2965C9C5_FBA4_11D1_837C_8CAD2F77F2B1__INCLUDED_

#if _MSC_VER > 1000
#pragma once
#endif // _MSC_VER > 1000

#ifndef __AFXWIN_H__
    #error include 'stdafx.h' before this file for PCH
#endif

#include "resource.h"       // main symbols

/////////////////////////////////////////////////////////
// CFourUpApp:
// See FourUp.cpp for the implementation of this class
//

class CFourUpApp : public CWinApp
{
public:
    CFourUpApp();

// Overrides
    // ClassWizard generated virtual function override
    //{{AFX_VIRTUAL(CFourUpApp)
    public:
    virtual BOOL InitInstance();
    //}}AFX_VIRTUAL

// Implementation

    //{{AFX_MSG(CFourUpApp)
        // NOTE - the ClassWizard will add and remove
        //        member functions here.
```

```
        // DO NOT EDIT what you see in these blocks of
        //       generated code !
        //}}AFX_MSG
    DECLARE_MESSAGE_MAP()
};

/////////////////////////////////////////////////////////////////////////////
//{{AFX_INSERT_LOCATION}}
// Microsoft Visual C++ will insert additional
// declarations immediately before the previous line.

#endif //
!defined(AFX_FOURUP_H__2965C9C5_FBA4_11D1_837C_8CAD2F77F2B1__INCLUDED_)
```

The Header Guards

Let's start with the preliminaries: that strange stuff at the beginning and end of the file. In C++, it's not uncommon for a header file to be included more than once during a single compile. Usually this is done indirectly, by including two header files that each require a common header.

To avoid processing a header file a second time—which can result in compilation errors—you can *guard* your C++ headers by using conditional compilation. Here's how the technique works. Suppose you have a header file named junk.h containing these lines:

```
#if !defined(JUNK)
// conditional header lines here
#endif
```

If you include the header file from another file like this

```
#include "junk.h"
#define JUNK
#include "junk.h"
```

then the compiler will process the lines between the first **#if** and the ending **#endif** during the first include, but it won't process them during the second include. The preprocessor will "eat" them. So far, so good.

Of course, this scheme relies on *you* to know when a file is being included a second time. After all, in the case you just saw, you can fix the code far more easily by not including junk.h a second time.

You really want the header file to automatically keep track of whether it has already been included. And, as it turns out, that's really very simple. Just change the original lines like this:

```
#if !defined(JUNK)
#define JUNK
// conditional header lines here
#endif
```

Now, the first time the header is included (during a single compilation), the identifier **JUNK** won't be defined, so the code between the **#if-#endif** will be executed. That code immediately **#defines JUNK**. So, the next time the file is read, its contents will be skipped.

However, this technique raises the possibility of name clashing. Suppose that the identifier **JUNK** was already defined in some other header file you hadn't seen for years, and that header file was included before junk.h. Suddenly, the compiler no longer reads your header file. There are several ways to avoid this problem. AppWizard generates a long, incomprehensible string and uses it as the guardian identifier. Here are the (slightly modified) header guards for FourUp.h:

```
#if\
!defined(AFX_FOURUP_H_2965C9C5_FBA4_11D1_837C_8CAD2F77F2B1_INCLUDED_)
#define\
AFX_FOURUP_H_2965C9C5_FBA4_11D1_837C_8CAD2F77F2B1_INCLUDED_
// ....
// Header body here
// ....
#endif //\
!defined(AFX_FOURUP_H_2965C9C5_FBA4_11D1_837C_8CAD2F77F2B1_INCLUDED_)
```

We think that it's unlikely you've **#defined** the identical identifier elsewhere in your program.

Resource.h

Next, we're interested in the inclusion of the resource.h header file, with the line:

```
#include "resource.h"
```

Hands Off The Resource.h Header File

Resource.h is a machine-maintained header file. It contains all the identifiers for the resources you work with in the resource editors. You shouldn't edit this file yourself.

Listing 4.2 shows FourUp's resource.h file, as it existed at the end of Chapter 3. (It will grow as we add more controls in Chapter 5.)

Listing 4.2 The FourUp application resource.h file.

```
// Microsoft Developer Studio generated include file.
// Used by FourUp.rc
//
#define IDM_ABOUTBOX                    0x0010
#define IDD_ABOUTBOX                    100
#define IDS_ABOUTBOX                    101
#define IDD_FOURUP_DIALOG               102
#define IDR_MAINFRAME                   128
#define IDI_HEART                       129
#define IDI_CLUB                        130
#define IDI_DIAMOND                     131
#define IDI_SPADE                       132
#define IDB_BITMAP1                     133

// Next default values for new objects
//
#ifdef APSTUDIO_INVOKED
#ifndef APSTUDIO_READONLY_SYMBOLS
#define _APS_NEXT_RESOURCE_VALUE        134
#define _APS_NEXT_COMMAND_VALUE         32771
#define _APS_NEXT_CONTROL_VALUE         1006
#define _APS_NEXT_SYMED_VALUE           101
#endif
#endif
```

The Class Definition

The definition for the **CFourUpApp** class takes up the major part of CFourUp.h. Rather than repeat each piece of code, let's look at the high points:

- Note from the header that the class is publicly derived from **CWinApp**. That means you can call any of the methods inherited from **CWinApp** or **CWinApp**'s superclasses.
- The header files that AppWizard writes are divided into sections to help you find what you're looking for. The header begins with the constructor section. Next comes a section marked with the comment.

```
// Overrides
```

which contains virtual functions designed for you to extend. The section marked with the comment

```
// Implementation
```

holds AppWizard code that may change from release to release. You shouldn't rely on code in the implementation section—and you generally won't modify code found here.

- Finally, you'll notice the *AFX* comments. Here, the ClassWizard will add or remove functions, and so on. As one of the comments points out, you shouldn't edit anything appearing between comment markers that look like this:

```
//{{
//}}
```

- The last line of the header file contains the cryptic line

```
DECLARE_MESSAGE_MAP()
```

This macro tells Visual C++ that the class will respond to Windows messages. This entry, and the corresponding message-map entries in the implementation file, are part of a sophisticated macro system for building *message response tables*. A message response table ensures that Windows messages are routed to the appropriate member function. You don't need to know any more than that to effectively use the message-mapping system (although we'll cover the subject in more depth when we discuss keyboard and mouse messages). Instead, you'll normally use the ClassWizard to connect your functions with the appropriate messages—ClassWizard will maintain the message response tables for you.

Looking At FourUp.cpp

The implementation of the **CFourUpApp** class appears in the file FourUp.cpp. Rather than show you the whole listing at once, we'll go through each section, explaining what each piece does. We'll start with the preliminaries.

Includes And Defines

The first section of FourUp.cpp includes files and defines special constants. Let's look at the three **#include** lines. The first line

```
#include "stdafx.h"
```

is the standard application framework header file used for all MFC programs. It brings in the definitions for the standard MFC components, the most commonly used extensions, and the Internet Explorer 4 common controls.

The next two lines bring in the header files for the two files that make up our project:

```
#include "FourUp.h"
#include "FourUpDlg.h"
```

You may wonder why you have to include FourUpDlg.h, when this is the implementation file for the application class, not the window class. The reason will be apparent shortly—suffice to say that we'll need the definitions stored in FourUpDlg.h before we're finished with this file.

When you build a C/C++ project, you have the option of defining a *release build* or a *debug build*. By default, the initial build is a debug build. During a debug build, MFC generates extra code to check common programming errors. When you switch to creating a release build, that code is removed. (You can switch between build types by using the Build|Set Active Configuration dialog box.)

You can track memory allocations and deletions only during debug builds. If you dynamically allocate an object using the **new** operator, and then forget to delete that object, MFC's debug version of **new** will tell you where and when the error occurred. These features are activated for the **CFourUpApp** class by the following lines of code:

```
#ifdef _DEBUG
#define new DEBUG_NEW
#undef THIS_FILE
static char THIS_FILE[] = __FILE__;
#endif
```

The Class Message Map

Following the header files and the debug **#defines** comes the class message map, which you can see in Listing 4.3.

Listing 4.3 The CFourUpApp message response table.

```
/////////////////////////////////////////////////////////////
// CFourUpApp

BEGIN_MESSAGE_MAP(CFourUpApp, CWinApp)
    //{{AFX_MSG_MAP(CFourUpApp)
        // NOTE - the ClassWizard will add and remove
        //mapping macros here.
        //    DO NOT EDIT what you see in these blocks of
        generated code!
    //}}AFX_MSG
    ON_COMMAND(ID_HELP, CWinApp::OnHelp)
END_MESSAGE_MAP()
```

The message response table starts with the **BEGIN_MESSAGE_MAP** macro and finishes with the **END_MESSAGE_MAP** macro. On the lines in between appear macros that *map* individual messages to particular functions.

For instance, in the **CFourUpApp** message map, the **ON_COMMAND** macro (highlighted in the listing) connects the **ID_HELP** message to the function **CWinApp::OnHelp()**. When the program runs, if the **CFourUpApp** object receives an **ID_HELP** message from Windows—generated by pressing the F1 key—then the inherited **CWinApp::OnHelp()** member function is called.

Although you can add your own message-map entries by hand—as long as you don't enter them in ClassWizard's "hands off" area—you'll rarely need to. ClassWizard can do a much better job than you of setting everything just right.

The CFourUpApp Constructor And Application Object

The next section of CFourUp.cpp includes the class constructor and a single, global instance of **CFourUpApp**, named **theApp**. The code is shown in Listing 4.4.

Listing 4.4 The CFourUpApp Constructor and application object.

```
/////////////////////////////////////////////////////////////
// CFourUpApp construction

CFourUpApp::CFourUpApp()
{
    // TODO: add construction code here,
    // Place all significant initialization in
    // the Init Instance function
}

/////////////////////////////////////////////////////////////
////////////////////
// The one and only CFourUpApp object
CFourUpApp theApp;
```

Because the **CFourUpApp** class represents your application, you might be surprised to find so little code in the class constructor. Actually, *little* is an understatement—there's *none*. If you're trying to make the mental jump from the API's **WinMain()** function to the **CFourUpApp** constructor, then you're probably even more confused.

The confusion arises from not understanding exactly when the **CFourUpApp** constructor is called. If you think back to your C++ class, you know the answer: The constructor is called when a **CFourUpApp** object is created. But exactly *when* is a **CFourUpApp** object created? The answer lies in the last line of Listing 4.4, which we'll see soon.

First, remember that every program can have only one application object. After all, the application object really *is* the program. Second, note that the **CFourUpApp** object **theApp** is created as a global object. As a result, its constructor is called when the program loads—before **WinMain()** is called, and before many of the MFC subsystems have had a chance to finish initializing themselves. It's only *after* the main application object is constructed that **WinMain()** is called at all. Thus, if you need to do some initialization inside your application class, the constructor isn't the place to do it. Instead, the **CFourUpApp** class overrides the virtual function **InitInstance()**. In **InitInstance()**, you'll do the kind of application initialization that an API program performs in **WinMain()**.

As luck would have it, **InitInstance()** is the only function we have left to explore in the **CFourUpApp** class. Let's look at it now.

The CFourUpApp::InitInstance() Function

Every Windows program starts, you'll recall, with a **WinMain()** function. MFC programs are no different—they also have a **WinMain()** function. But unlike an API-based Windows program, an MFC program's **WinMain()** function is buried deep inside the MFC library itself.

If you're concerned that MFC programs are somehow less powerful or less flexible than API programs, you can put your fears to rest. In almost every API program, the **WinMain()** function is, essentially, identical. MFC hides the boilerplate code, then gives you "hooks" to the parts of **WinMain()** you're likely to want to change. These hooks take the form of virtual functions, called from MFC's own **WinMain()** function. When we look at the **CWinApp** class in a bit, you'll see a few more of these virtual functions. The most important, however, is the **InitInstance()** function.

When MFC's version of **WinMain()** begins, it first obtains a pointer to the application object. Because the application object is a global variable, it already exists by the time **WinMain()** starts up. **WinMain()** then uses this pointer to call the application object's **InitInstance()** method. Because **InitInstance()** is a virtual function, **WinMain()** actually calls the version you create in your overridden application.

Listing 4.5 shows the **CFourUpApp** version of **InitInstance()**. Read through it, and then we'll point out some of the highlights.

Listing 4.5 The CFourUpApp::InitInstance() function.

```
/////////////////////////////////////////////////////////////////
// CFourUpApp initialization

BOOL CFourUpApp::InitInstance()
{
```

```
    // Standard initialization
    // If you are not using these features and wish to
    // reduce the size of your final executable, you
    // should remove from the following the specific
    // initialization routines you do not need.

#ifdef _AFXDLL
    Enable3dControls();      // Call when using MFC shared
#else
    Enable3dControlsStatic();    // When static linking
#endif

    CFourUpDlg dlg;
    m_pMainWnd = &dlg;
    int nResponse = dlg.DoModal();
    if (nResponse == IDOK)
    {
        // TODO: Place code here to handle when the
        // dialog is dismissed with OK
    }
    else if (nResponse == IDCANCEL)
    {
        // TODO: Place code here to handle when the
        // dialog is dismissed with Cancel
    }

    // Since the dialog has been closed, return FALSE
    // so that we exit the application, rather than
    // start the application's message pump.
    return FALSE;
}
```

How InitInstance Works

In an API application, the **WinMain()** function has three tasks. It has to:

1. Register a new main window class.
2. Create an instance of the main window and display it.
3. Run the message pump.

The **InitInstance()** function carries out the second of these requirements for MFC's **WinMain()** function. Here's how the **CFourUpApp::InitInstance()** function carries out that task.

First, it creates a new main window with the line

```
CFourUpDlg dlg;
```

Second, it initializes its **m_pMainWnd** data member so that it points to the new window, like this:

```
m_pMainWnd = &dlg;
```

Third, it displays the main window by using the main window's **DoModal()** member function:

```
int response = dlg.DoModal();
```

Because the FourUp application's main window is based on the **CDialog** class, that's all the code required. The **DoModal()** function displays the main window, then handles all of the message routing until the user clicks on OK or Cancel in the main window. When that occurs, the main window closes and **DoModal()** returns the identifier of the button the user clicked on to close the dialog box. The **InitInstance()** method stores that value in a local variable named **response**, and AppWizard writes a skeleton handler for both the OK and Cancel buttons, based on the value returned. If you don't want to do anything, of course, you don't have to—or you can do something entirely different, if you prefer. All you need do is change the code provided by AppWizard.

The last line in **InitInstance()** returns **FALSE**. This is appropriate only for dialog-based applications. Non-dialog-based applications return **TRUE** to start the **WinMain()** message pump.

All About CWinApp

As you saw in Figure 4.1 at the beginning of this chapter, **CFourUpApp** is derived from **CWinApp**. If you look at the MFC documentation, you'll see several virtual functions or "overridables" defined in the **CWinApp** class. Here are the four most interesting ones:

- ***InitInstance()***—will always be overridden.

- ***Run()***—scans the message loop and processes messages.
- ***OnIdle()***—called by **Run()** when no messages are found. **OnIdle()** can seize the opportunity to perform background tasks that might otherwise slow system response.
- ***ExitInstance()***—called by **Run()** when an application terminates.

CFourUpApp overrides only the **InitInstance()** function. Most programs don't need to override any of the remaining functions—they're provided so that MFC can respond to even the unusual situations.

What's A CCmdTarget?

If you look back at Figure 4.2, you can see that the **WinApp** class is derived from a class named **CCmdTarget**. **CCmdTarget** is a base class for objects that receive and respond to messages. It provides member data and functions that all such objects must possess. It's a prolific parent class—its subclasses include **CWinApp**, **CWnd**, **CFrameWnd**, **CView**, and **CDocumen**t. And, **CCmdTarget** has a great many grandchild classes: Because controls are generally derived from the **CWnd** class, they too are descendants of **CCmdTarget**.

Where Does CObject Fit In?

Again, looking at Figure 4.2, you can see that **CCmdTarget** is derived from **CObject**. The **CObject** class is the root class of MFC objects—every MFC object is a descendant of **CObject**, and **CObject** has no parent class. If you need to create a new kind of MFC object and none of the existing MFC objects seem like a good starting place, you can derive your new class from **CObject**. That way, it will peacefully coexist with other MFC classes.

Looking At Windows

The FourUp application uses two types of windows: a main window and a dialog box. Main windows trace their lineage from the prolific **CWnd** class, whereas dialog boxes descend from the

CDialog class. Let's learn a bit more about these two important and common classes.

All About CWnd

CCmdTarget's most noteworthy child class is **CWnd**, the base class for main windows. **CWnd**, as we mentioned, is also the parent class of many other important MFC classes, including **CFrameWnd**, **CMDIFrameWnd**, **CView**, **CDialog**, **CButton**, **CContolBar**, **CToolbar**, and so on. Look back to Figure 4.3 to refresh your memory.

The FourUp application uses a dialog box as its main window, so its window object is an instance of the **CWnd** subclass **CDialog**. Let's meet this versatile class.

Meet The CDialog Class

Dialog boxes have two associated program entities: a resource and an object, which is an instance of a class derived from **CDialog**. The resource records the properties of the dialog box, such as the controls that it holds and their screen positions. The object inherits data and function members from **CDialog** and its ancestors: **CWnd**, **CCmdTarget**, and **CObject**.

The FourUp application contains two dialog boxes: one that serves as the application's main window, **CFourUpDlg**, and the application's About box, **CAboutDlg**. Let's look first at **CAboutDlg**, then come back to **CFourUpDlg**.

A Quick Look At CAboutDlg

The source code for the **CAboutDlg** class is shown in Listing 4.6. Spend a few moments studying it, and then we'll give you the cook's tour.

Listing 4.6 The CAboutDlg class.

```
/////////////////////////////////////////////////////////////////////////////
// CAboutDlg dialog used for App About

class CAboutDlg : public CDialog
{
```

```
public:
    CAboutDlg();

// Dialog Data
    //{{AFX_DATA(CAboutDlg)
    enum { IDD = IDD_ABOUTBOX };
    //}}AFX_DATA

    // ClassWizard generated virtual function overrides
    //{{AFX_VIRTUAL(CAboutDlg)
    protected:
    virtual void DoDataExchange(CDataExchange* pDX);
    //}}AFX_VIRTUAL

// Implementation
protected:
    //{{AFX_MSG(CAboutDlg)
    //}}AFX_MSG
    DECLARE_MESSAGE_MAP()
};

CAboutDlg::CAboutDlg() : CDialog(CAboutDlg::IDD)
{
    //{{AFX_DATA_INIT(CAboutDlg)
    //}}AFX_DATA_INIT
}

void CAboutDlg::DoDataExchange(CDataExchange* pDX)
{
    CDialog::DoDataExchange(pDX);
    //{{AFX_DATA_MAP(CAboutDlg)
    //}}AFX_DATA_MAP
}

BEGIN_MESSAGE_MAP(CAboutDlg, CDialog)
    //{{AFX_MSG_MAP(CAboutDlg)
        // No message handlers
    //}}AFX_MSG_MAP
END_MESSAGE_MAP()
```

First, you probably noticed that **CAboutDlg** contains no message maps:

```
BEGIN_MESSAGE_MAP(CAboutDlg, CDialog)
    //{{AFX_MSG_MAP(CAboutDlg)
        // No message handlers
    //}}AFX_MSG_MAP
END_MESSAGE_MAP()
```

The **BEGIN_MESSAGE_MAP** and **END_MESSAGE_MAP** lines are there, just as in **CFourApp**. But **CAboutDlg** doesn't need to handle any Windows messages, so it has no message handlers, just as the comment states.

Another novelty comes in the lines

```
protected:
    virtual void DoDataExchange(CDataExchange* pDX);
```

which provide a function override for the inherited **DoDataExchange()** function. This function supports dialog data exchange (DDX) and dialog data verification (DDV), which you'll learn about in Chapter 18. DDX and DDV facilitate working with dialog boxes containing controls that provide input data or display output data. DDX lets you bind a member variable to a control, such as a text field, so that the value of the member variable always reflects the contents of the control. DDV lets you check user-supplied data against a set of validation rules, helping ensure that only valid data is processed. Because the About dialog box has no dynamic controls, it doesn't require DDX or DDV support—nevertheless, the hooks are there so that you can add support if needed.

Walking Through CFourUpDlg

Listing 4.7 shows the header file FourUpDlg.h. More accurately, it shows an abridged version of the file, which contains quite a few lines that aren't relevant here. Study the listing for a bit. If your curiosity is whetted, you can use the Visual C++ editor to open the file from the CD-ROM and see the lines we've omitted.

Listing 4.7 The header file FourUpDlg.h (abridged).

```
/////////////////////////////////////////////////////////////
// CFourUpDlg dialog

class CFourUpDlg : public CDialog
{
// Construction
public:
    CFourUpDlg(CWnd* pParent = NULL);    // standard
```

```
    // Dialog Data
    //{{AFX_DATA(CFourUpDlg)
    enum { IDD = IDD_FOURUP_DIALOG };
    //}}AFX_DATA

    // ClassWizard generated virtual function overrides
    //{{AFX_VIRTUAL(CFourUpDlg)
    protected:
    virtual void DoDataExchange(CDataExchange* pDX);
    //}}AFX_VIRTUAL

// Implementation
protected:
    HICON m_hIcon;

// Generated message map functions
    //{{AFX_MSG(CFourUpDlg)
    virtual BOOL OnInitDialog();
    afx_msg void OnSysCommand(UINT nID, LPARAM lParam);
    afx_msg void OnPaint();
    afx_msg HCURSOR OnQueryDragIcon();
    //}}AFX_MSG
    DECLARE_MESSAGE_MAP()
};
```

The file contains five major sections of interest:

- *Construction*— contains the **CFourUpDlg** constructor.
- *Dialog Data*— defines a C++ enumeration that refers to the dialog box.
- *Virtual function overrides generated by ClassWizard*— contains the only overridden function, **DoDataExchange()**, which you don't really need because DDX/DDV support isn't required.
- *Implementation*— defines a data member that refers to the dialog box's icon.
- *Message map functions*— associate messages and handlers.

Because CFourUpDlg.h is a header file, it includes only the prototypes for its functions. The implementation file CFourUpDlg.cpp provides bodies for the functions that appear in the header file. Let's look at the implementation file piece by piece, starting with Listing 4.8, which shows the class constructor.

Listing 4.8 The CFourUpDlg class constructor.

```
CFourUpDlg::CFourUpDlg(CWnd* pParent /*=NULL*/)
    : CDialog(CFourUpDlg::IDD, pParent)
{
    //{{AFX_DATA_INIT(CFourUpDlg)
    //}}AFX_DATA_INIT
    m_hIcon = AfxGetApp()->LoadIcon(IDR_MAINFRAME);
}
```

Whereas **CFourUpApp**'s constructor was empty, **CFourUpDlg**'s constructor contains a line that loads a value into the data member **m_hIcon**. This data member holds the icon used to represent the dialog box when it's minimized. You obtain the value using the MFC application framework function **AfxGetApp()**, which returns a pointer to the application object. You then use the pointer to access the **LoadIcon()** member function, which returns the appropriate icon as defined in the application's resource data.

Consistent with **CFourUpApp**, the bulk of **CFourDlg**'s initialization happens within its **OnInitDialog()** function, shown in Listing 4.9. Recall that the application framework automatically invokes this function after the application is loaded.

Listing 4.9 The CFourUpDlg::OnInitDialog() function.

```
BOOL CFourUpDlg::OnInitDialog()
{
    CDialog::OnInitDialog();

    // "Add About..." menu item to system menu.

    // IDM_ABOUTBOX must be in the system command range.
    ASSERT((IDM_ABOUTBOX & 0xFFF0) == IDM_ABOUTBOX);
    ASSERT(IDM_ABOUTBOX < 0xF000);

    CMenu* pSysMenu = GetSystemMenu(FALSE);
    if (pSysMenu != NULL)
    {
        CString strAboutMenu;
        strAboutMenu.LoadString(IDS_ABOUTBOX);
        if (!strAboutMenu.IsEmpty())
        {
            pSysMenu->AppendMenu(MF_SEPARATOR);
            pSysMenu->AppendMenu(MF_STRING, IDM_ABOUTBOX,
                                 strAboutMenu);
```

```
        }
    }

    // Set the icon for this dialog.  The framework does
    // this automatically the application's main window
    // is not a dialog
    SetIcon(m_hIcon, TRUE);         // Set big icon
    SetIcon(m_hIcon, FALSE);        // Set small icon

    // TODO: Add extra initialization here

    return TRUE;  // return TRUE  unless you set the
                  // focus to a control
}
```

OnInitDialog() first adds an About menu item to the application's system menu. However, before jumping into this task, **OnInitDialog()** executes a pair of **ASSERT** macros that check whether the message code assigned to the About menu item (the value of **IDM_ABOUTBOX**) is appropriate. Unless you've mischievously fiddled with the resource properties, this shouldn't be an issue—but MFC is careful here, looking before it leaps. (It's not always so obligingly cautious.)

To add the menu item, the **OnInitDialog()** function gets a pointer to the application's system menu. If this is null, it avoids a doomed attempt to add the menu item. Otherwise, it uses the **LoadString()** function to load a text resource—identified by the value of **IDS_ABOUTBOX**—that contains an appropriate description of the menu item. Recall that you requested the AppWizard to generate code for an About box when you created the FourUp application. AppWizard automatically created the text resource in response to your request, along with the very code you're studying.

Now, the **OnInitDialog()** function calls the **AppendMenu()** function once to add a menu separator (a horizontal rule) and again to add the menu item. (Recall that this is simply a tour, not a complete explanation of all that's happening—you'll learn about menus later.) Finally, the function sets the dialog box's icon, using the previously loaded value of **m_hIcon**, and returns **TRUE**.

All that remains of the **CFourUpDlg** class are its message map and message handler functions. The message map is shown in Listing 4.10. Notice that it provides linkage for three messages:

- **WM_SYSCOMMAND**
- **WM_PAINT**
- **WM_QUERYDRAGICON**

You can simply drop the prefix **ON_** to discover the name of a message from the information in the message map. Let's look at each handler for these messages in turn.

Listing 4.10 The CFourUpDlg message map.

```
BEGIN_MESSAGE_MAP(CFourUpDlg, CDialog)
    //{{AFX_MSG_MAP(CFourUpDlg)
    ON_WM_SYSCOMMAND()
    ON_WM_PAINT()
    ON_WM_QUERYDRAGICON()
    //}}AFX_MSG_MAP
END_MESSAGE_MAP()
```

Listing 4.11 shows the **OnSysCommand()** function, which handles the **WM_SYSCOMMAND** message. It's called whenever the user selects a menu item from the system menu. The function checks whether the user selected the About menu item. If so, it creates an instance of **CAboutDlg** and invokes its **DoModal()** function, which opens the dialog box; if not, it passes the message parameters to the message handler implemented in its superclass (**CDialog**) for default processing.

Listing 4.11 The CFourUpDlg::OnSysCommand() function.

```
void CFourUpDlg::OnSysCommand(UINT nID, LPARAM lParam)
{
    if ((nID & 0xFFF0) == IDM_ABOUTBOX)
    {
        CAboutDlg dlgAbout;
        dlgAbout.DoModal();
    }
    else
    {
        CDialog::OnSysCommand(nID, lParam);
    }
}
```

Listing 4.12 shows the **OnPaint()** function, which handles the **WM_PAINT** message. The application framework automatically handles this message when sent to a document-view application's main window. However, FourUp isn't a document-view application, so AppWizard generated code to handle the message. The **WM_PAINT** message indicates that a window needs to be repainted. In **CFourUpDlg**, this arises only when the application has been minimized, in which case the application's icon needs to be drawn. The painting code is somewhat complex, so we'll pass it by for the moment—you'll learn about painting in Chapter 7.

For now, notice that the painting is performed only if the function **IsIconic()** returns true, indicating that the application has been minimized. Otherwise, the **WM_PAINT** message is handed off to the parent class.

Listing 4.12 The CFourUpDlg::OnPaint() function.

```
// If you add a minimize button to your dialog, you will
// need the code below to draw the icon.  For MFC
// applications using the document/view model, this is
// automatically done for you by the framework.

void CFourUpDlg::OnPaint()
{
    if (IsIconic())
    {
        CPaintDC dc(this); // device context for painting

        SendMessage(WM_ICONERASEBKGND,
                    (WPARAM) dc.GetSafeHdc(), 0);

        // Center icon in client rectangle
        int cxIcon = GetSystemMetrics(SM_CXICON);
        int cyIcon = GetSystemMetrics(SM_CYICON);
        CRect rect;
        GetClientRect(&rect);
        int x = (rect.Width() - cxIcon + 1) / 2;
        int y = (rect.Height() - cyIcon + 1) / 2;

        // Draw the icon
        dc.DrawIcon(x, y, m_hIcon);
    }
    else
    {
```

```
        CDialog::OnPaint();
    }
}
```

The last message handler of the **CFourUpDlg** class is **OnQueryDragIcon()** (see Listing 4.13), which handles the **WM_QUERYDRAGICON** message. The application framework sends this message to discover the icon that should be displayed when the user drags the application's minimized window. Because the application's icon is usually an appropriate choice, AppWizard has obligingly included code that returns a pointer to the icon (obtained from the data member **m_hIcon** that the class constructor initialized), cast to an appropriate type (**HCURSOR**, which represents a handle to a cursor).

Listing 4.13 The CFourUpDlg:: OnQueryDragIcon() function.

```
// The system calls this to obtain the cursor to display
// while the user drags the minimized window.
HCURSOR CFourUpDlg::OnQueryDragIcon()
{
    return (HCURSOR) m_hIcon;
}
```

Introducing Resources

The FourUp application uses three principal kinds of resources: icons, bitmaps, and dialog boxes. You'll learn about several other types of resources in subsequent chapters, including cursors, menus, and strings. In this section, we'll discuss resource scripts and the resource compiler. You'll also get a first-hand look at the resource data managed by Visual C++ for each type of resource used in the FourUp application.

The Resource Script And The Resource Compiler

If you look back at Figure 4.4, you'll see that the CPP files and OBJ files that make up the C++ part of an MFC program are only half the story. A second compilation process runs in parallel with the process that handles your source code. This second compilation process concerns the resources used by your application.

You've already used the Resource Editor to create an icon, a bitmap, and a dialog box. But you didn't see that behind the scenes, Visual C++ created a resource script file that recorded your work. Your icon and bitmap were stored in an ICO and BMP file, respectively. But, in addition, Visual C++ created an RC file that identifies the resources used in your program, specifies their properties, and tells what file contains each icon and bitmap.

When you compile your program, this RC file is compiled—by a program appropriately known as the resource compiler—into a binary RES file. Later, the linker merges this file into your application's EXE file, so that all the resource data is available at runtime.

To give you some insight into how Visual C++ manages resources, let's look at the resource file entries for each resource type used by the FourUp application.

Icon Resources

Listing 4.14 shows the portion of FourUp's resource file that pertains to icons. Notice that the application defines four icons—precisely those you created earlier. The file describes the icons using a four-column layout that includes, from left to right:

- The name of the icon, given by its manifest constant.
- The type of resource (ICON).
- Properties of the resource (for example, **DISCARDABLE**, which indicates a read-only resource that can be discarded from memory without first saving a copy).
- The file containing the icon, expressed as a relative path starting from the project directory.

Because a resource file is a text file, you can edit it using an ordinary text editor. In fact, early Windows programmers had to do just that. However, Visual C++'s Resource Editor makes it much easier to create and update resource files—for one thing, you're spared the possibility of a typographical error that causes a resource compilation error.

Listing 4.14 The FourUp.rc ICON script entries.

```
/////////////////////////////////////////////////////////////
//
// Icon
//

// Icon with lowest ID value placed first to ensure
// application icon remains consistent on all systems.
IDR_MAINFRAME    ICON    DISCARDABLE    "res\\FourUp.ico"
IDI_HEART        ICON    DISCARDABLE    "res\\Misc34.ico"
IDI_CLUB         ICON    DISCARDABLE    "res\\Misc35.ico"
IDI_DIAMOND      ICON    DISCARDABLE    "res\\Misc36.ico"
IDI_SPADE        ICON    DISCARDABLE    "res\\Misc37.ico"
```

All About Bitmap Resources

Listing 4.15 shows the portion of FourUp's resource file that pertains to its solitary bitmap resource. Notice that the format of the bitmap entry is essentially the same as that of the icon entry we described previously.

Listing 4.15 The FourUp.rc BITMAP script entries.

```
/////////////////////////////////////////////////////////////
//
// Bitmap
//

IDB_BITMAP1    BITMAP  DISCARDABLE    "res\\bitmap1.bmp"
```

Dialog Resources

Listing 4.16 shows the portion of FourUp's resource file that pertains to the About dialog box. Notice that the file records a greater volume and variety of information for dialog boxes than for icons or bitmaps. In particular, the resource file records the type, position, and size of every control appearing on the dialog box.

Listing 4.16 The FourUp.rc DIALOG script entries.

```
/////////////////////////////////////////////////////////////
//
// Dialog
//

IDD_ABOUTBOX DIALOG DISCARDABLE  0, 0, 217, 125
STYLE DS_MODALFRAME | WS_POPUP | WS_CAPTION | WS_SYSMENU
```

```
CAPTION "About FourUp"
FONT 8, "MS Sans Serif"
BEGIN
  CTEXT   "FourUp 1.0",IDC_STATIC,49,61,119,8,SS_NOPREFIX
  CTEXT    "© 1998, Bill and Steve",IDC_STATIC,49,72,119,8
  CONTROL  133,IDC_STATIC,"Static",SS_BITMAP,74,15,69,22
  ICON     IDR_MAINFRAME,IDC_STATIC,95,35,21,20
  GROUPBOX "",IDC_STATIC,11,5,195,90
END
```

If the simplicity of the resource records for icons and bitmaps had you seriously considering using a text editor rather than the Resource Editor, we hope this listing has dissuaded you. The Resource Editor is truly powerful, yet easy to use.

The End Of Resources: Reprise

This chapter has covered a lot of ground—ground we'll continue tilling throughout the remainder of the book. You've learned about the structure of a simple, dialog-based application. And, you've learned about the key objects that comprise any MFC application: the application object (an instance of a subclass of **CWinApp**) and the main window object (an instance of a subclass of **CWnd**). You've also gotten an up-close look at sample subclasses of **CWinApp** and **CWnd**. Finally, you've looked behind the scenes at how Visual C++ manages resource data.

In the next chapter, you'll complete the FourUp application. The remaining work focuses on controls: the buttons, labels, and other elements that distinguish graphical user-interface applications. So hang in there—before you know it, you'll have a complete, working MFC application.

Chapter 5

Controls And ClassWizard: Bringing Your Dialog Boxes To Life

Just as your English vocabulary determines your ability to communicate, your MFC control vocabulary determines your ability to write powerful yet easy-to-use Windows programs. In this chapter, you'll develop a working knowledge of the most common MFC controls.

Perhaps you've seen the movie cliché in which the lonely guy or girl comes home every night to an empty apartment and hopefully presses the replay button on the answering machine, only to hear the mechanical voice say again and again, "You have no messages. To play your messages, press 1. To record a new greeting...."

At this point, our FourUp application is a lot like that cinematic answering machine. It has an application object—it has a main window object—it even has some controls. It just doesn't do anything. To put FourUp to work, it needs some messages.

In this chapter, you'll learn about another of Visual C++'s tools for simplifying Windows application development: ClassWizard. ClassWizard helps you create and manage classes in your applications. But, that's not ClassWizard's most important role in an MFC application. ClassWizard acts as a kind of universal "event matchmaker," hooking up Windows controls and events with the code that handles them.

To finish FourUp, here's where we'll be going in this chapter:

- We'll start by revisiting the Dialog Editor from Chapter 3. You'll get a quick refresher as we design FourUp's main dialog box.
- Next, you'll learn how to use MFC's **CButton** class. You've already seen how to add push buttons to your application.

Now, by adding a member function to your dialog class, you'll make your push buttons perform actions.

- We'll explain how you use ClassWizard to create *control variables*: C++ data members that act as proxies for user-interface objects such as **CButton**s and **CEdit** controls.
- Then, you'll learn how to use one of Windows' most useful general-purpose methods—the **MessageBox()** function—in all its varieties.

Planning The Effort

Before we rush headlong to the Dialog Editor, let's take a few moments to plan both how we want our application to look and how we want it to act. Although visual user-interface development certainly beats the alternative, it's no substitute for careful planning. And, planning is best carried out with paper and pencil—even if the paper is simply the back of an old envelope, or a paper napkin from a fast-food emporium. After all, it's easier to revise a plan than to change a finished program.

So, let's first decide how we want FourUp's main dialog box to look. We've already decided how the game will be played:

- When the game starts, the player will receive a fixed amount of money. As the game progresses, the program should tally the player's winnings and/or losses. That means FourUp needs an area to display the amount of money the player has left.
- Each player will be dealt four cards, so the program should have a playing area to display the cards and a button the player can click on to get a new deal. You'll also provide a button that lets the player quit the game.
- Each combination of cards has a different payout ratio. To let the player know what those payouts are, you'll include a payout display area.
- Finally, you want to attract players to the game. You'll do this by incorporating all those flashy graphics you created in

Chapter 3. (You didn't think we were just going to leave them in the About dialog box, did you?)

That does it for the user-interface plan. We'll plan the functions and data members we need when we get around to writing code. For right now, however, we can work from the rough sketch shown in Figure 5.1.

As you can see by looking at the figure, FourUp's main dialog box is divided into four areas. You'll put the graphics at the top, in the title area. Below the title is the playing area, where FourUp will deal the four cards. As play progresses, you'll also display the player's winnings and losses in the playing area. Below the playing area is the payout table, which is simply a table of static text listing the payout for each possible combination of cards. Finally, at the bottom of the window are the buttons the player will use to operate the game. The text on the Deal button will let players know how much they're risking.

By now, you should be fairly comfortable working with the Dialog Editor, so we'll go quickly through the dialog-box layout steps. Ready? Let's get started.

The Dialog Editor Revisited

If you don't have the FourUp workspace open, open it now by using the File|OpenWorkspace menu choice. (Okay: There's

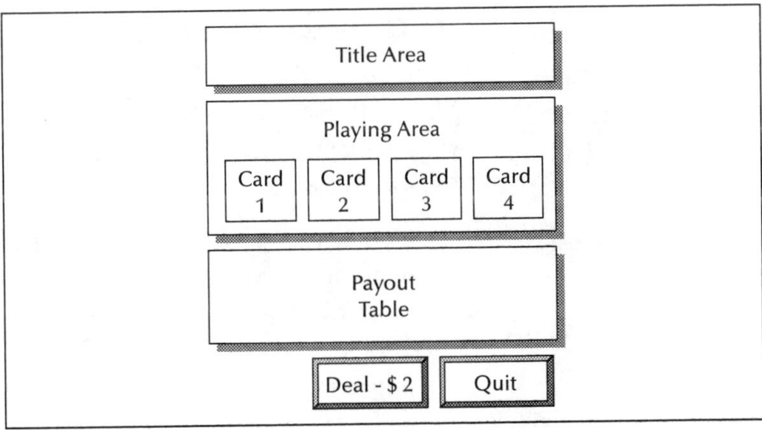

Figure 5.1
FourUp's main dialog box.

nothing we can do to stop you if you merely want to read along. But you'll be sorry later—working with tools like the Dialog Editor is a skill, learned only through hands-on experience. So, boot that computer and get going.) Once you've opened the FourUp project, select the ResourceView window and double-click on **IDD_FOURUP_DIALOG** to open the Dialog Editor. Then, follow these steps:

1. Delete the static text control that says TODO: Place Controls Here. To do that, simply select it and then press Delete or Ctrl+X.
2. Resize the main dialog window so that it's 200 units wide and 175 units high. You can read the units in the lower-right corner as you resize the dialog box. Remember that these units aren't pixels—they're called *Dialog Units*. Every Dialog Unit is roughly twice as high as it is wide, and the actual size is based on the font used in the dialog box. To see this effect illustrated, remember that FourUp's main dialog box is only 175 units high, but 200 units wide—yet the dialog box appears slightly taller than it is wide.
3. Turn on the Grid by clicking on Toggle Grid on the Dialog Toolbar.
4. Next, drag the OK and Cancel buttons to the lower-right corner and arrange them a little more attractively. You can see the results in Figure 5.2.

Adding The Cards

To represent the playing cards, you'll use **CStatic** controls (as MFC calls picture controls). You initially fill each **CStatic** control with one of the playing suit icons you loaded earlier. Here are the steps to follow:

1. Drag four picture controls from the Control Toolbar to the main dialog box. Place them in a horizontal row near the top. (Don't worry about spacing or alignment—in fact, the more disorganized the better. That way, you'll see how the Dialog Editor's alignment tools can space and arrange the components.) Notice that when you drop each control, it appears as a small black frame.

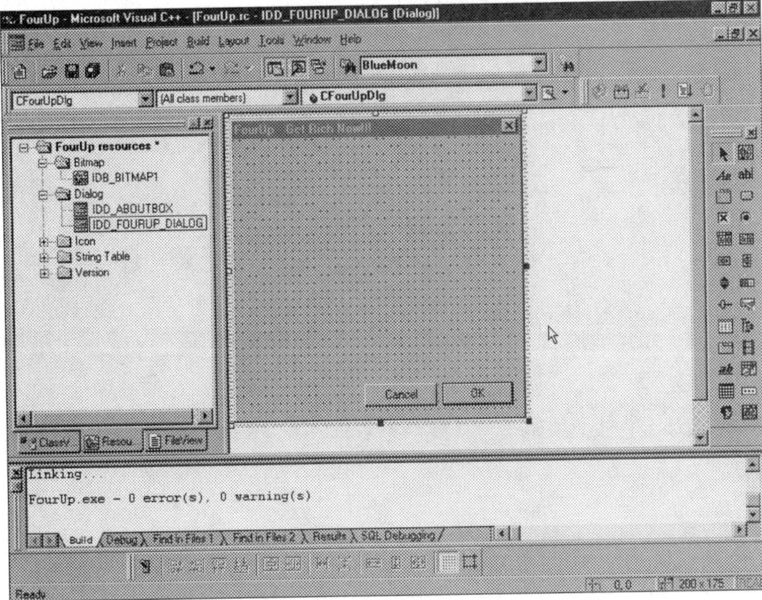

Figure 5.2
The main dialog box after resizing and repositioning the controls.

2. Select the first picture box. (You'll have to click along the edge—if you click in the middle, you'll select the dialog box.) Right-click to open the context menu for the first picture box, and select Properties from the menu.
3. In the Picture Properties dialog box, pull down the Type combo box and change the selection from Frame to Icon. When you do this, note that the picture box control's appearance changes.
4. The Image list box is now active—use it to select **IDI_HEART** from the list of available icons. When you close the Properties dialog box, note that the heart icon replaces the frame in the FourUp window.
5. Change the ID field from **IDC_STATIC** to **IDC_CARD1**. Within your program, you'll use this identifier to refer to the **CStatic** control.

Once you've completed the work for **IDC_CARD1**, go through the same routine for each of the remaining icons: **IDI_CLUB**, **IDI_DIAMOND**, and **IDI_SPADE**. Your dialog box should look like Figure 5.3 when you're finished.

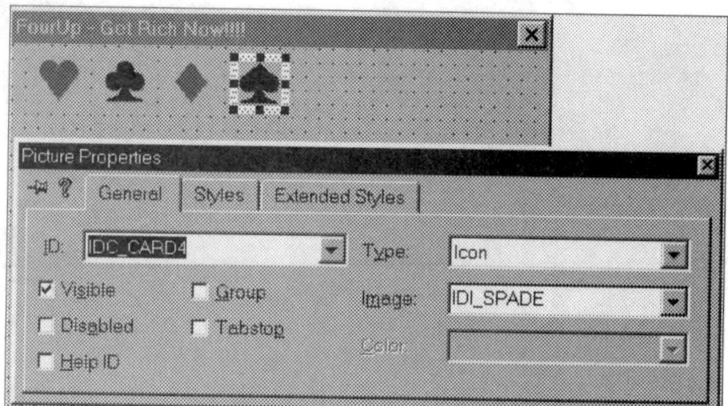

Figure 5.3
Adding icons to the picture controls.

NOTE

*Be sure you assign each control the proper unique ID. Give the control holding **IDI_CLUB** the identifier **IDC_CARD2**, the control holding **IDI_DIAMOND** the identifier **IDC_CARD3**, and the control holding **IDI_SPADE** the identifier **IDC_CARD4**.*

Arranging The Cards

Now, you need to arrange your cards. You'll call upon the good graces and talents of the Dialog Toolbar to accomplish this. Here's how:

1. Place the "end" cards first. Select and move **IDC_CARD1** (the Heart) and **IDC_CARD4** (the Spade), into position at the left and right of the dialog box, respectively. Don't worry about the spacing between the cards, or their alignment—just be sure there's sufficient room between **IDC_CARD1** and **IDC_CARD4** to fit the other two cards.
2. Next, select all four cards. Do you remember how? Click on the first card, and then hold down the Control (or Shift) key as you click on the other three controls. The last card selected becomes the dominant card—remember that you can recognize it by its active sizing handles.
3. Now, turn off the grid so that the controls can be moved to any location within the dialog box, not merely to grid points. To arrange the cards, start by using the Space Across button on the Dialog toolbar, as shown in Figure 5.4. (You can also press Alt+Right Arrow or choose Layout|Space Evenly|Across from the main menu.) Look ahead to Figure 5.5, and notice how the controls are evenly spaced between **IDC_CARD1** and **IDC_CARD4**.
4. Now that the cards are evenly spaced, you can align their tops and bottoms. Because the controls are the same size, it doesn't matter if you use the Align With Bottom or Align With Top

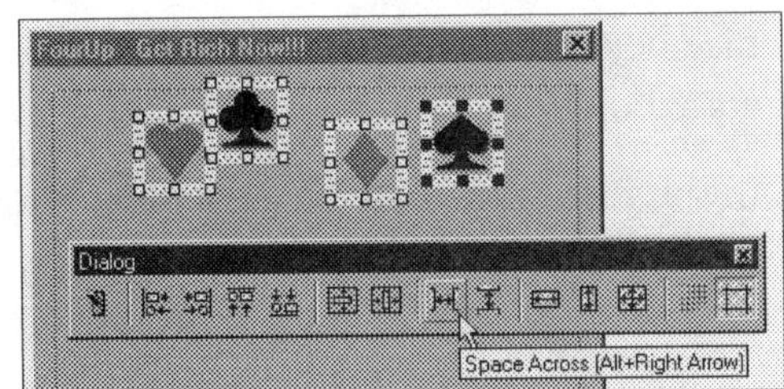

Figure 5.4
Evenly spacing controls using the Dialog toolbar.

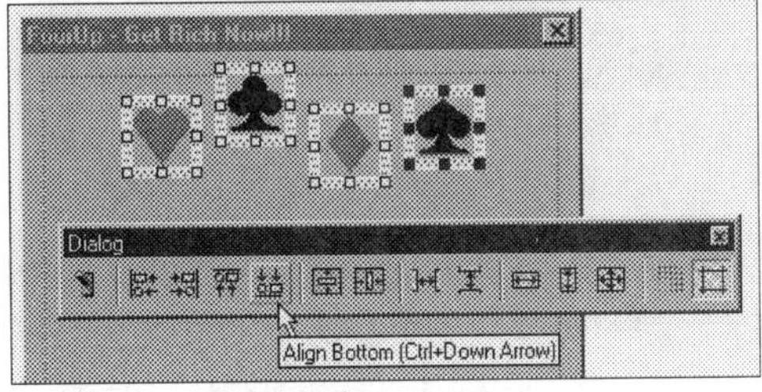

Figure 5.5
Aligning a group of controls using the Dialog toolbar.

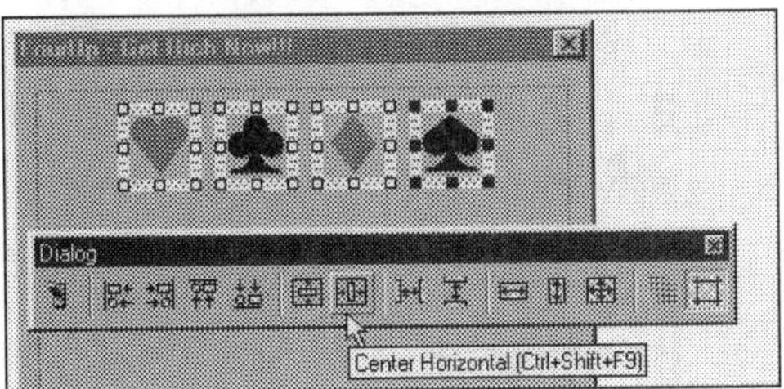

Figure 5.6
Centering a group of controls inside the main window by using the Dialog toolbar.

command. In Figure 5.5, you can see the Align With Bottom button being selected. (You can get the same effect by pressing Ctrl+Down Arrow or by selecting Layout|Align|Bottom from the main menu.) You can see the effect of lining up the card bottoms in Figure 5.6.

5. Center the group of controls horizontally on the playing surface. That's not hard, either—simply use the Center Horizontal button that you used to center an individual button in Chapter 3, as shown in Figure 5.6.

Adding The Playing Area

As you saw in our sketch, you're going to arrange the cards on a playing area, represented by a groupbox control. Recall that when you worked with the groupbox control in Chapter 3, you wanted a nice beveled line around the About box. To get that look, you erased the text that appears by default at the top of the groupbox.

In the case of the playing area, however, you can put that text to good use: It can act as the display area to let players know how much money they've los..., er, won. Here are the steps to follow:

1. Drag a groupbox control from the Control Toolbar and size it to evenly surround your set of cards.
2. Open the Properties dialog box for the groupbox. Change the control's ID to **IDC_AMT_LEFT** and its caption to "Amount Remaining $ 100.00".
3. Now, let's move the playing area down to roughly the same position shown in Figure 5.1. That will leave room to add the title and icon across the top of the dialog box. To move the cards as a group, first select them by drawing a selection rectangle (with the mouse) that completely encloses the **IDC_AMT_LEFT** groupbox. (That will select all the cards and the groupbox at the same time.) Once you've selected the controls, shift-click on the groupbox to make it the dominant control. Then, move the controls down until the position indicator reads about 10, 50. Rather than using the mouse, you'll probably find it easier to use the arrow keys.

Adding The Title Area

Now that the playing area is out of the way, you can add the title. You'll simply make a copy of the icon and the FourUp logo from the About dialog box, and arrange them across the top. Here are the steps to accomplish that:

1. Access the About dialog box by double-clicking on **IDD_ABOUTBOX** in the ResourceView window.
2. Select the FourUp logo and the FourUp icon by clicking on one and shift-clicking on the other. Both should be selected before you go to the next step.
3. Copy both items to the Windows clipboard by using Ctrl+C or Edit|Copy from the main menu.
4. Switch back to the main dialog window by double-clicking on **IDD_FOURUP** in the ResourceView window.

5. Press Ctrl+V or select Edit|Paste from the main menu to place the logo and icon into the **IDD_FOURUP** dialog box. Position each as you like.

Creating The Payout Table

Under the playing area, you'll place another groupbox to show the amount that the players can expect to win when they receive two pair, three of a kind, or four of a kind. (We won't pay anything if the player gets only one pair.) Here are the steps:

1. Drag another groupbox control from the Control Toolbar and place it under the playing area. Title the groupbox "Payouts".
2. Drag three static text labels from the Control Toolbar and place them in the Payouts group box. Inside the three labels, add text as follows:
   - "2 pair 3.00"
   - "3 of a kind 6.00"
   - "4 of a kind 9.00"
3. Use several Tab character escape sequences (`\t`) to position the payout amount to the right of the descriptive text. This will allow you to line up the amounts without messing around with spaces—a task doomed to failure because of the vagaries of variable-pitch type. Move the Properties dialog box to the side so you can see the FourUp dialog box as you enter the escape sequences—that way, you'll know how many to enter. You can see the results in Figure 5.7.

Labeling The Buttons

At this point, our interface is pretty much done. The only thing left is to change the text on the two buttons. Here's what to do:

1. Change the caption on the OK button to "Deal - $ 2.00". (Select Properties from the right-click context menu, just as you do for other controls.)
2. Before you close the OK button's Properties dialog box, change the button's identifier from **IDOK** to **IDC_DEALCARDS**.

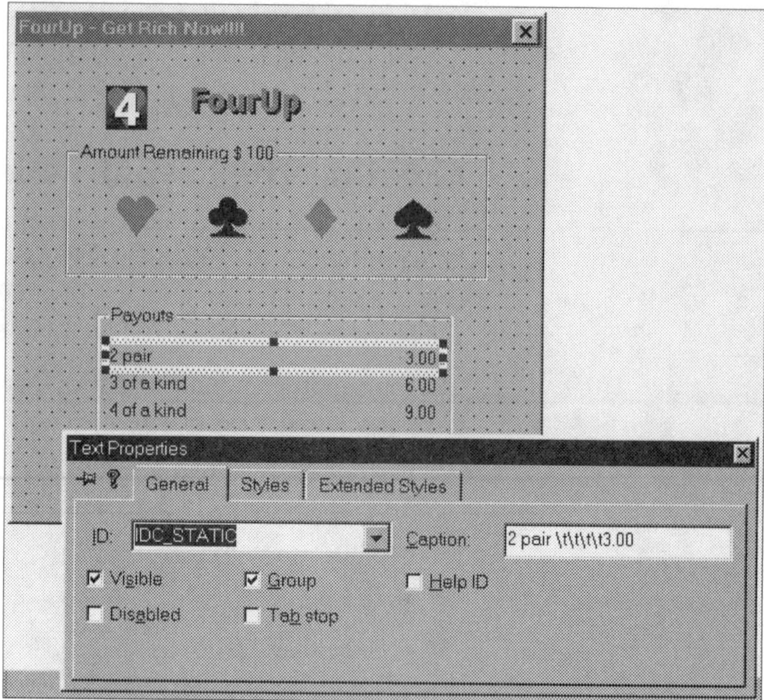

Figure 5.7
Adding text to the Payouts group box.

3. Open the Properties dialog box for the Cancel button, as well. Change its caption to "Cash Out", but leave its identifier as **IDCANCEL**.
4. Finally, swap the position of the two buttons, so that the Deal button is in the center and the Cash Out button is on the right.
5. Center the buttons by using the Center Horizontal tool.

Well, that's it. You're done with the user interface, and it went a lot more quickly than building the About dialog box. You must be getting good at this! Compile the program and try it out. As you can see, the program runs, and you can open the About dialog box as before, but nothing much happens otherwise. You can see the finished results in Figure 5.8.

Writing Code

The user interface for FourUp is finished. Now, your assignment is to write the code that implements the logic of the game as

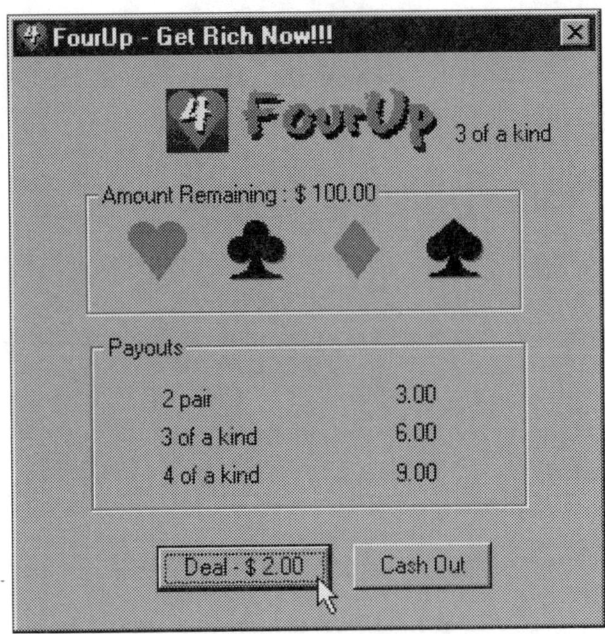

Figure 5.8
Running the FourUp application.

previously described. You'll be graded on how short your code is and how well it meets the specifications.

Actually, we're just kidding—we wouldn't leave you stranded here after coming so far. As it turns out, writing the code for the application is probably the easiest part of the whole thing, thanks to the ClassWizard, which you'll meet shortly.

But first, as we did with the user interface, we need to take a few minutes to plan our strategy. When you're designing a user interface, a few crude drawings can be a world of help. However, when you're planning what a program should do, nothing beats a simple outline, just as your English 101 teacher claimed. Only this time, instead of the acts of the play *Julius Caesar*, the headings are *events* and the subpoints are *responses*.

Planning For Events

Let's start by asking, "What do we want to happen when the player does X?". Because X in this case can be only one of two possible events, our list is short:

- What do we want to happen when the player *clicks on Cash Out*?
    1. Thank the player and indicate how much money remains.
- What do we want to happen when the player *clicks on Deal*?
    1. Check to be sure the player can afford to play. If not, tell the player to raise more money somewhere. (We'll leave it as an exercise for the reader to add money back into the player's account.)
    2. If the player has at least $2 remaining, charge the player for the deal.
    3. Randomly choose a suit for each of the 4 cards.
    4. Update the image of each card to indicate its suit.
    5. Calculate whether the player has won, and if so, add the winnings to the player's account.

Now, take a few moments and ask yourself:

- What data members will I need?
- What member functions will I need?

Writing Code By Hand: Adding A Data Member

Even brief consideration should convince you that, if nothing else, you'll need to keep track of how much money the player has left. To do that, you create a plain old data member—there's nothing special about it, except that you have to decide the class in which you want it to be located.

From studying the structure of the FourUp application in Chapter 4, you know you have two choices: the application class (**CFourUp**) or the dialog class (**CFourUpDlg**). Because you'll mostly interact with components that are (or will be) part of the dialog box itself (and thus, the **CFourUpDlg** class), let's put the new data member there.

Here are the steps to follow. You'll start by defining the variable inside the header for **CFourUpDlg**:

1. Select the ClassView pane in the Project Workspace window.
2. Find the **CFourUpDlg** class and double-click on the class name. (Be sure you double-click on the class name and not the constructor name or one of the other member functions. Double-clicking on a function name takes you to the CPP implementation file. Double-clicking on either the class name or a data member name takes you to the class declaration in the header file.)
3. Now, add a **private** section to the class definition. Define a data member named **m_Amt_Remaining**, of type **double**. You can see the field being added to the class definition in Figure 5.9. Notice that the data member appears in the ClassView pane as you type it.

Next, you need to initialize the **m_Amt_Remaining** field. You can do that in the class constructor. Simply double-click on the constructor name in the ClassView pane to go to the CPP file where the constructor is defined. Initialize the **m_Amt_Remaining** data member by adding the highlighted code shown in Listing 5.1.

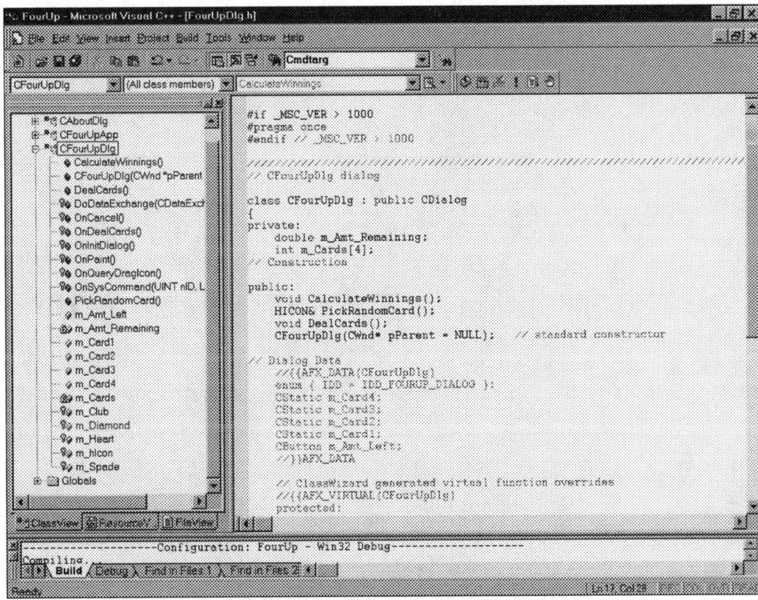

Figure 5.9
Adding a private data member to the **CFourUpDlg** class.

Listing 5.1 Initializing the m_Amt_Remaining data member in the CFourUpDlg constructor.

```
/////////////////////////////////////////////////////////////
// CFourUpDlg dialog

CFourUpDlg::CFourUpDlg(CWnd* pParent /*=NULL*/)
    : CDialog(CFourUpDlg::IDD, pParent)
{
    //{{AFX_DATA_INIT(CFourUpDlg)
    //}}AFX_DATA_INIT
    m_hIcon = AfxGetApp()->LoadIcon(IDR_MAINFRAME);

    // Initialize m_Amt_Remaining field
    m_Amt_Remaining = 100.0;
}
```

Responding To BN_CLICKED Events

Sometimes, Windows programming is confusing: You wonder why something happens the way it does. Handling button events is one of the pleasant exceptions: It's obvious to almost everyone that when the user clicks on a push button, that interaction should generate an event. In Windows, it's called a **BN_CLICKED** event. Fortunately, working with buttons is so easy, you don't even have to know *that*. ClassWizard knows that you normally want an event-handler function for button clicks. To see how it responds, let's return to the Dialog Editor where you'll get a lesson in mind-reading.

Generating The OnCancel() Method

We've already decided what should happen when the player clicks on Cash Out—that's simple. However, it looks like there's a lot to be done when the player clicks on Deal. So, let's handle the Cash Out button first.

To do so, you're going to use the ClassWizard to generate a method that's called whenever the player clicks on Cash Out. Here's how you do it:

1. Return to the Resource View.

2. Double-click on **IDD_FOURUP_DIALOG** to open the Dialog Editor.
3. Double-click on the button labeled Cash Out.

As soon as you do this, the Add Member Function dialog box will open (as you can see in Figure 5.10), with a suggestion that you add a function called **OnCancel**.

If you closely examine the dialog box, you'll see that Windows generated a message called **BN_CLICKED**; this stands for *button clicked*. You should also notice that the button's ID is still **IDCANCEL**, because you didn't change the Cancel button's *name*—you changed only the caption that appears on the button.

You might wonder why you changed the name of the OK button from **IDOK** to **IDC_DEALCARDS**, but you didn't make a similar change to the Cancel button. The reason lies with the special way that Visual C++ handles the OK and Cancel buttons. Most of the time, when VC++ suggests a name, you can change it with impunity. If you change ***OnCancel*** to ***OnCashOut***, however, clicking on Cash Out will no longer quit the application. Leave the name at **OnCancel** so that the default quit processing is available.

As soon as you click on OK in the Add Member Function dialog box, Visual C++ writes a new empty function with the proper prototype in the class header. Then, it opens the code editor, where you can write the code necessary to handle the event. Listing 5.2 shows the code written by the ClassWizard.

Listing 5.2 The ClassWizard-generated OnCancel() function.

```
void CFourUpDlg::OnCancel()
{
    // TODO: Add extra cleanup here

    CDialog::OnCancel();
}
```

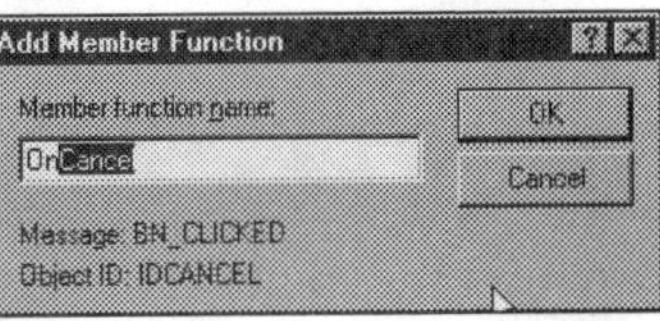

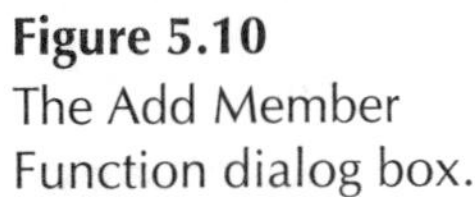
Figure 5.10
The Add Member Function dialog box.

Writing Code: Completing The OnCancel() Function

When the player clicks on the Cash Out button, our plan is to thank them for playing and tell them how much money they have left. So, how do you thank the player for using your program?

Fortunately, Windows comes with a complete set of functions—the **MessageBox()** functions—designed to facilitate operations such as this. **MessageBox()** comes in several versions, one of which is a member function of the **CWnd** class. Luckily, the class you're using—**CFourUpDlg**—is a direct descendent of **CWnd**, so it can invoke **MessageBox()** with no problems. If you were in another class that wasn't descended from **CWnd()**, you'd have to invoke the universal version of **MessageBox()**, called **AfxMessageBox()**.

The **MessageBox()** function takes three arguments:

- The message to display
- The title for the message box pop-up window
- An integer specifying what kind of buttons you want displayed in the message box

You have to pass only the first argument, because the other two are given default values. For the **OnCancel()** method, you'll pass the first two arguments.

Converting The m_Amt_Remaining Data

The **OnCancel()** function has one complication: You want to display the player's remaining nest-egg as well as the friendly parting message. If you're an experienced C programmer, you'd probably use the C standard library function **sprintf()** to accomplish that:

```
char buffer[80];
sprintf(buffer, "Good game. You have $ %.2 left",
m_Amt_Remaining);
```

This code will work fine, but it requires you to link with the **sprintf()** code from the standard C library—which isn't automatically available to MFC programs. If you've previously done any Windows API programming, you know that Windows already contains a similar function, **wsprintf()**. Unfortunately, **wsprintf()** is inadequate for this particular task, because it doesn't handle floating-point formatting.

Fortunately, MFC provides a better way to handle this problem: the **CString** class. **CStrings** are dynamic, variable-length strings that you can use throughout MFC wherever previous versions of Windows would have required a C-style null-terminated string. With the **CString** class, you don't have to worry about how long to make your buffer—you simply create a **CString** object and use its **Format** method. The **CString** will size itself appropriately, handling all memory allocation and deallocation behind the scenes.

Using the **CString** class and the **MessageBox()** member function, you can finish the **OnCancel()** member function by adding the highlighted lines shown in Listing 5.3. You can see the **OnCancel()** method at work in Figure 5.11.

Listing 5.3 The completed OnCancel() function.

```
void CFourUpDlg::OnCancel()
{
    // TODO: Add extra cleanup here
    CString s;
    s.Format("Great game! You have $ %.2f left.",
            m_Amt_Remaining);
    MessageBox(s, "Thanks for playing FourUp!");

    CDialog::OnCancel();
}
```

Writing The OnDealCards() Function

Well, handling the Cash Out button wasn't too bad, was it? Let's see if the code to handle the Deal button is just as easy. Start by returning to the Dialog Editor and double-clicking on the Deal button.

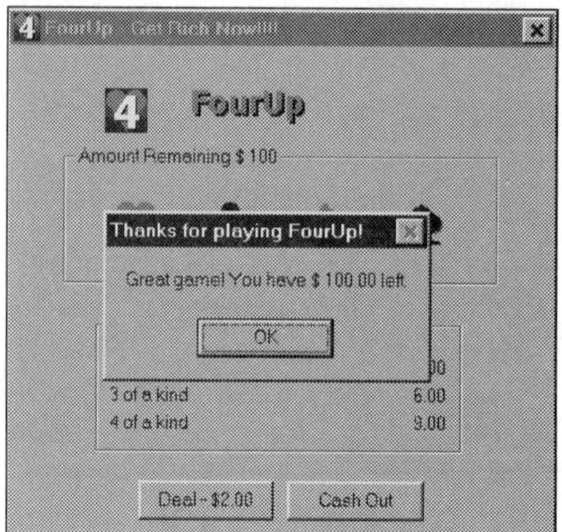

Figure 5.11
Testing the **OnCancel()** method.

Just as before, the Add Member Function dialog box will appear. The Windows message displayed is still **BN_CLICKED**, but this time the name of the function is **OnDealcards()**, because you changed the button's name from **IDOK** to **IDC_DEALCARDS**. If you'd left the name as **IDOK**, ClassWizard would have written the standard dialog-closing code normally used for dialog boxes—every time the player requested a new deal, the game would shut down! Definitely not what you want if you're going to get all of your player's mon... if you're going to give players a quality gaming experience.

Just to be consistent with your naming conventions, change the function's name to **OnDealCards()** (notice the capital C), and then click on OK. Now you're ready to deal!

OnDealCards(): A First Draft

One of the first rules of programming is, "Do the easy stuff first!" If you flout this rule, you risk getting stuck on a point that you could have solved easily after you'd worked on the obvious stuff for a while.

So, in this case, what's the obvious stuff? That's easy—you need to

- Subtract $2 each time the player clicks on Deal.
- Redisplay the player's total amount after dealing the cards and calculating any winnings.

Listing 5.4 shows all you know how to do so far.

Listing 5.4 The first draft of the OnDealCards() function.

```
void CFourUpDlg::OnDealCards()
{
    // 1. Subtract our 2.00, whatever else happens
    m_Amt_Remaining -= 2.00;

    // 2. Deal the cards. Don't know how, just yet

    // 3. Calculate winnings, add to m_Amt_Remaining

    // 4. Display total m_Amt_Remaining
    CString s;
    s.Format("Amount Remaining $ %.2f", m_Amt_Remaining);
}
```

As you can see, you've already made sure you got your money, so Step 1 is finished. Steps 2 and 3 seem a little difficult, so let's simplify matters for the time being and assume the players always lose. That means you simply have to display the total amount remaining. As you can see, the message is already formatted—the only question remaining is how to get it on screen.

Rather than using **MessageBox()** as you did when the player cashed out, this time you'll display the total amount remaining in the caption at the top of the group box (named **IDC_AMT_LEFT**) that surrounds the playing area where the cards are dealt. To do that, you're going to need to learn about *control variables*.

Introducing ClassWizard And Control Variables

Although you don't know it yet, groupbox objects are windows (derived from **CWnd**), just like almost everything else in Windows. As is true for other windows, you can change the text the groupbox uses for its caption by calling its **SetWindowText()** member function.

That sounds simple, right? In the **OnDealCards()** function, you'll just call **SetWindowText()**, passing the formatted **CString**, s. (Look just after Step 4 in Listing 5.4.)

Unfortunately, as you probably guessed, things aren't that simple. **SetWindowText()** is a *member function*—you have to call it by using a **CWnd**-derived object. The problem is, **IDC_AMT_LEFT** isn't really a groupbox object. Instead, as is true of all the identifiers assigned by the Dialog Editor, **IDC_AMT_LEFT** refers to the data used by Windows to construct the groupbox object at runtime.

Before you can send the **SetWindowText()** message to the groupbox represented by **IDC_AMT_LEFT**, you must obtain a reference to the actual groupbox object created by Windows, and then send the message to that object. To do that, you'll use ClassWizard to create a *control variable*, which provides you with a reference to the control constructed at runtime. Here's how you do it:

1. Open the main dialog box in the Dialog Editor. Highlight the **IDC_AMT_LEFT** groupbox and right-click on it to display its context menu. Select ClassWizard from the context menu, as you can see in Figure 5.12.
2. The ClassWizard is a tabbed dialog box. Select the Member Variables tab. Your window should look like Figure 5.13.

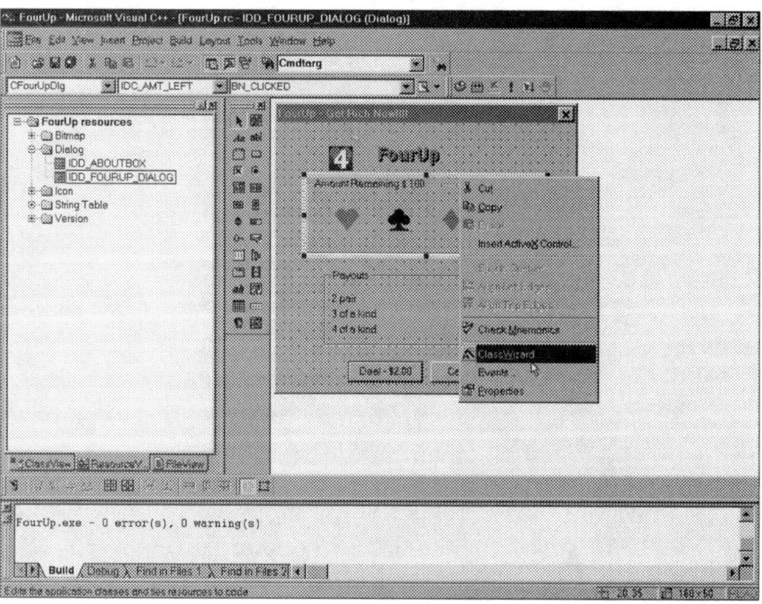

Figure 5.12
Starting ClassWizard with the **IDC_AMT_LEFT** groupbox.

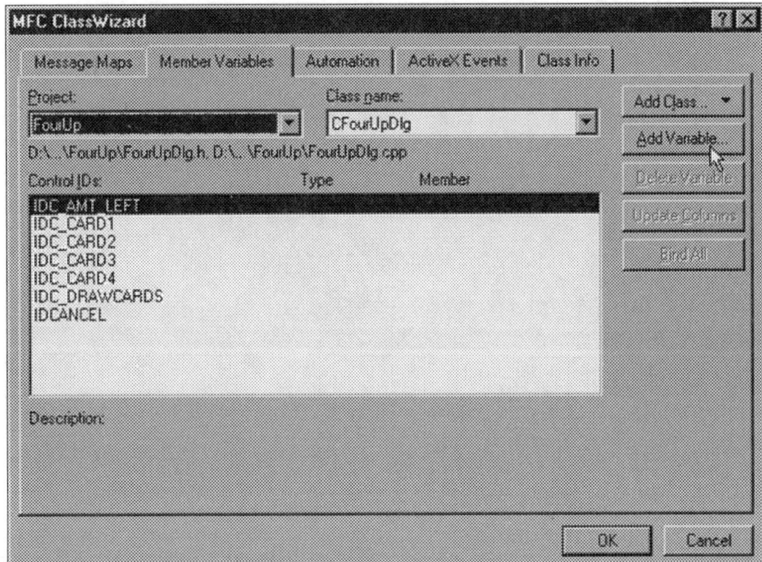

Figure 5.13
Adding a new data member to access **IDC_AMT_LEFT**.

3. Locate and select **IDC_AMT_LEFT** in the list of control ID. Then, click on Add Variable, as you can see in Figure 5.13.
4. When the Add Member Variable dialog box opens, enter "m_Amt_Left" in the Member Variable Name field, choose Control from the Category drop-down list, and choose **CButton** from the Variable Type dropdown list, as shown in Figure 5.14.
5. Add the following line at the end of the **OnDealCards()** function:

```
m_Amt_Left.SetWindowText(s);
```

6. Recompile and run the program. As you can see, each time the player clicks on Deal, FourUp reduces the variable **m_Amt_Remaining** by $2 and displays the new result in the groupbox surrounding the playing area.

Writing Code: Dealing Cards, Totaling Winnings

Well, you're getting near the goal—all you need to do is complete Steps 3 and 4 in the **OnDealCards()** function. Now that you

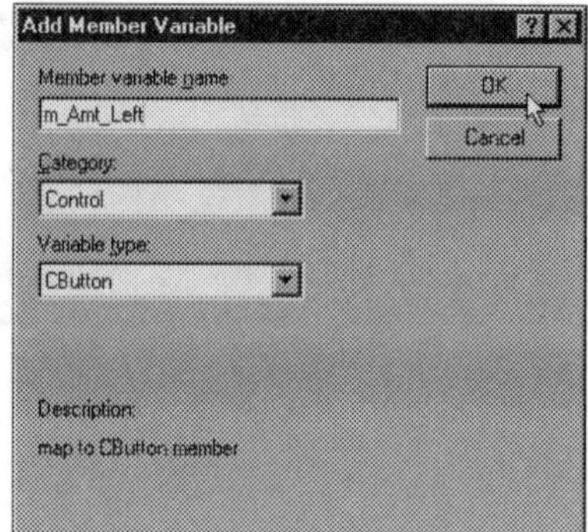

Figure 5.14
Using the Add Member Variable dialog box.

know how to use ClassWizard to construct control variables, writing the rest of the code should be easy (even though there's more of it).

Creating The Card Variables

You'll begin by creating control variables for each of the cards, **IDC_CARD1** through **IDC_CARD4**. You could select each control in turn and then open ClassWizard using the context menu as you did previously. You can also open ClassWizard by pressing Ctrl+W or choosing ClassWizard from the View menu. Let's do that now:

1. Open ClassWizard from the View menu.
2. Add variables for **IDC_CARD1** through **IDC_CARD4**, naming them **m_Card1** through **m_Card4**. Be sure that the Category field always says Control, and the Variable Type field always says **CStatic**—ClassWizard unhelpfully resets the defaults to Value and **CString**, which won't work for this application.

Examine Figure 5.15 to double-check your variable definitions.

Creating The Icon Variables

In addition to the control variables for each card, you'll also need a variable for each card image. Because you already added the four icons (**IDI_HEART** to **IDI_SPADE**), you'd expect to find them in ClassWizard's Member Variables page.

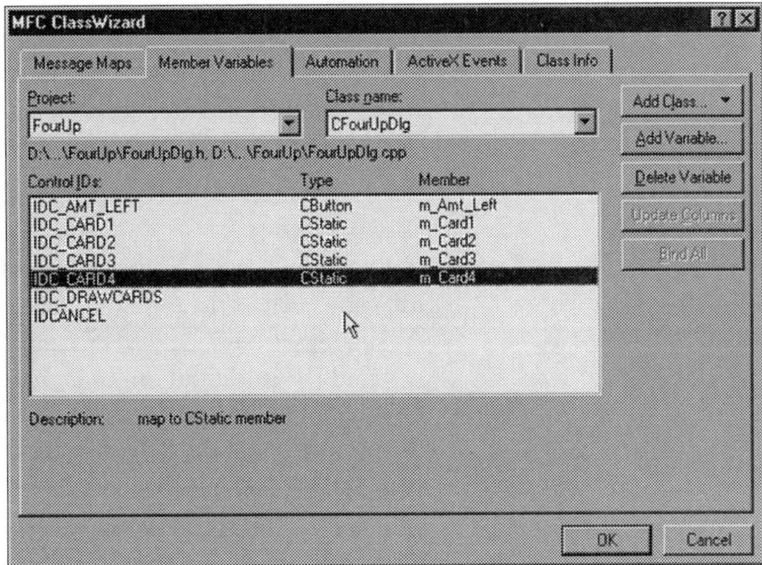

Figure 5.15
Adding a control variable for each playing card image.

No such luck. ClassWizard handles only controls—it doesn't handle the more prosaic resources, such as icons and bitmaps. You'll have to do that by hand. Fortunately, you're not entirely on your own. AppWizard wrote code to handle the original icon; all you have to do is find it, and emulate whatever AppWizard did.

Here are the steps to follow:

1. Find the **m_hIcon** variable in the ClassView window. This variable stores the original icon.
2. Double-click on **m_hIcon**. You'll go to the definition file for the **CFourUpDlg** class, where you'll see these lines of code:

```
// Implementation
protected:
    HICON m_hIcon;
```

3. The **HICON** type stands for a **H**andle to an **ICON**. You'll need one variable for each of your own icons, so add four more **HICON** variables. Name them **m_Heart**, **m_Club**, **m_Diamond**, and **m_Spade**. Your code should now look like this:

```
// Implementation
protected:
    HICON m_hIcon;
    HICON m_Club;
    HICON m_Diamond;
    HICON m_Heart;
    HICON m_Spade;
```

4. Data members must be initialized before use, so you'll have to initialize each of these new variables before you can use it. Again, let's follow the lead of AppWizard, and find out how it handled the initialization for **m_hIcon**. Double-click on the **CFourUpDlg()** class constructor in Class View and find the line that initializes **m_hIcon**. Create similar lines to load **IDI_HEART** and the other icons. You can see the required changes to **CFourUpDlg()** in Listing 5.5.

Listing 5.5 Initializing additional icons in CFourUpDlg().

```
CFourUpDlg::CFourUpDlg(CWnd* pParent /*=NULL*/)
    : CDialog(CFourUpDlg::IDD, pParent)
{
    //{{AFX_DATA_INIT(CFourUpDlg)
    //}}AFX_DATA_INIT
    // Note that LoadIcon does not require a subsequent
    //DestroyIcon in Win32
    m_hIcon      = AfxGetApp()->LoadIcon(IDR_MAINFRAME);
    m_Club       = AfxGetApp()->LoadIcon(IDI_CLUB);
    m_Diamond    = AfxGetApp()->LoadIcon(IDI_DIAMOND);
    m_Heart      = AfxGetApp()->LoadIcon(IDI_HEART);
    m_Spade      = AfxGetApp()->LoadIcon(IDI_SPADE);

    // Initialize m_Amt_Remaining field
    m_Amt_Remaining = 100.0;
}
```

Writing The DealCards() Member Function

If you look back at the **OnDealCards()** button event-handler function, you'll see that you still haven't done anything for the intermediate Steps 2 and 3. Let's remedy that now by adding a **DealCards()** function to handle Step 2 and a **CalculateWinnings()** function to handle Step 3.

You'll write **DealCards()** first. Here are the steps:

1. Choose Add Member Function from the WizardBar menu. (Remember that the WizardBar appears on the toolbar—you can access its menu by clicking on the down-arrow located to its right.)
2. When the Add Member Function dialog box opens (as you can see in Figure 5.16), make the return type of the function **void**, and name the function **DealCards**.
3. Click on OK. At this point, Visual C++ will take you into the code editor, where it has written a skeleton function. Add the code in Listing 5.6 to complete the **DealCards()** function.

Listing 5.6 The DealCards() member function.

```
void CFourUpDlg::DealCards()
{
    // Initialize the m_Cards array
    for(int i = 0; i < 4; i++)
        m_Cards[i] = 0;

    m_Card1.SetIcon(PickRandomCard());
    m_Card2.SetIcon(PickRandomCard());
    m_Card3.SetIcon(PickRandomCard());
    m_Card4.SetIcon(PickRandomCard());
}
```

A Brief Explanation Of The DealCards() Member Function

The **DealCards()** member function performs two tasks. First, for scoring purposes, you need a way to keep track of which cards have been dealt. Because there are four suits, an array of four integers serves nicely. The first integer in the array represents the number of Clubs dealt, the second the number of Diamonds, and so forth. Every time FourUp deals the cards, however, you need to

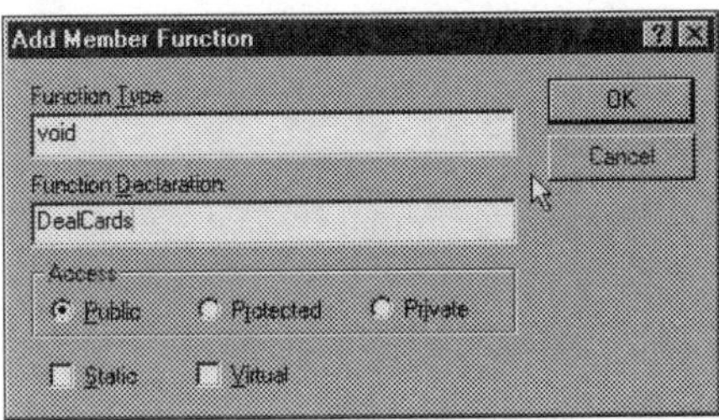

Figure 5.16
The Add Member Function dialog box.

reset the array values to 0. The first loop in **DealCards()** performs this task.

After that, you'll display a random card in each of the card-control variables, **m_Card1** through **m_Card4**. Each control variable is a member of the **CStatic** class, which has a member function called **SetIcon()**. The **SetIcon()** function takes an **HICON** as its argument. Fortunately, you already have four **HICON**s as the member variables **m_Club**, **m_Diamond**, and so forth. You'll simply create a helper function that chooses one of these at random and returns a reference to it.

Completing The DealCards() Member Function

As we explained, to complete the **DealCards()** function, you'll create the array used for scoring and write the helper function, **PickRandomCard()**, to do the actual selection. Here are the steps to follow:

1. Add an **int** array called **m_Cards[4]** to the **CFourUpDlg** class definition next to where you defined the data member **m_Amt_Remaining**.
2. Add the code shown in Listing 5.7 to create the **PickRandomCard()** helper function, which picks a random card. (Remember to add the function by using the WizardBar menu's Add Member Function selection. If you add the code manually, you'll also need to modify the class header file. When you use the WizardBar, it completes that task for you.) Notice that the function returns a reference to an **HICON**, a handle for an icon.

Listing 5.7 The PickRandomCard() member function.

```
HICON& CFourUpDlg::PickRandomCard()
{
    int num = (rand() % 4);
    m_Cards[num] ++;    // Update scoring array

    switch(num)
    {
        case 0: return m_Club;
        case 1: return m_Diamond;
        case 2: return m_Heart;
```

```
    }
    return m_Spade;
}
```

A Random Diversion

Because the **PickRandomCard()** function uses the C library **rand()** function to generate pseudorandom numbers, be sure to "seed" the function so it produces a different sequence of numbers each time the application runs. You can do that by adding the following lines of code to the **CFourUpDlg** class constructor:

```
// seed the random number generator
srand( (unsigned) time(NULL));
```

Writing The CalculateWinnings() Member Function

The last step in your program calculates the player's winnings. Let's see how to do that.

Whenever **DealCards()** is called, it clears the **m_Cards** array by setting the four values to 0. Then, it calls the **PickRandomCard()** function four times. Each time, **PickRandomCard()** generates a random number from 0 to 3 by using the modulus operator (%). This random number decides which card to display, using a **switch** statement. However, before FourUp displays the card, the random number is used to update the "score" for that particular suit by using the lines

```
int num = (rand() % 4);
m_Cards[num] ++;     // Update scoring array
```

Thus, after all four calls to **PickRandomCard()** are complete, each of the four elements in **m_Cards** will have a value between 0 and 4. All you have to do is step through the elements using a loop, and then calculate the correct winnings based on the values you find.

So, how do you calculate the winnings? Here's the logic:

- If you encounter the value 4 in any element, then FourUp dealt four of a kind—you can immediately calculate the payout.

- Likewise, if you encounter the value 3 in any element, FourUp dealt three of a kind, and you can immediately calculate the payout.
- If you encounter the value 0 or 1, it doesn't affect the score (you can ignore the value).
- If you encounter the value 2, you need to know if this is the first pair or the second pair. If it's the second pair, you can calculate the winnings. If it's the first pair, you'll make note of it, but keep checking to see if there's another pair. You can do this by using a local counter variable called **pairs**.

You can see the code for **CalculateWinnings()** in Listing 5.8. When you enter it, remember to let the WizardBar get you started.

Listing 5.8 The CalculateWinnings() member function.

```
void CFourUpDlg::CalculateWinnings()
{
    int pairs = 0;
    for (int i = 0; i < 4; i++)
    {
        if (m_Cards[i] == 2)
        {
            if (pairs > 0)
            {
                m_Amt_Remaining += 3.00;
                break;
            }
            else
            {
                pairs++;
            }
        }
        else if (m_Cards[i] == 3)
        {
            m_Amt_Remaining += 6.00;
            break;
        }
        else if (m_Cards[i] == 4)
        {
            m_Amt_Remaining += 9.00;
            break;
        }
    }
}
```

The Last Things

After you've entered all of these pieces, you still need to "hook them up" by changing the **OnDealCards()** function so that it calls your new member functions. Listing 5.9 shows the changes you need to make.

Listing 5.9 The final OnDealCards() member function.

```
void CFourUpDlg::OnDealCards()
{
    // 1. Subtract our 2.00, whatever else happens
    m_Amt_Remaining -= 2.00;

    // 2. Deal the cards
    DealCards();

    // 3. Calculate winnings, add to m_Amt_Remaining
    CalculateWinnings();

    // 4. Display total m_Amt_Remaining
    CString s;
    s.Format("Amount Remaining $ %.2f", m_Amt_Remaining);
    m_Amt_Left.SetWindowText(s);
}
```

Take A Chance

That's all there is to it. Save your workspace, build the application, and take it out for a spin. Fortunately, FourUp never tries to collect on your losses—so, if things get too grim, just cash out and start over.

You've now seen how to create a complete MFC application. Congratulations: You're ready to create MFC programs of your own. Of course, you'll want to learn more about the MFC classes and facilities.

In the next chapter, we'll explore creating and manipulating windows. You'll also get further acquainted with two of MFC's most popular controls: **CStatic** and **CButton**. As you'll see, **CButton** is actually an entire family of controls that includes push buttons, check boxes, radio buttons, and groupboxes.

Chapter 6
Understanding Controls

In the previous chapter, you met several members of the Windows control menagerie. In this chapter, you'll learn more about their habits and haunts.

Spying has been a tactic of governments since Moses sent two spies into the promised land. Yet spying has rarely been a daytime activity conducted in view of the world—instead, most governments conceal their cloak-and-dagger activities behind a veil of secrecy.

However, during the cold war of the 1950s and 1960s, Americans became fascinated with the world of espionage, as numerous real (and supposed) cases of Communist espionage surfaced. Dramatic accusations and trials—like those of Julius and Ethel Rosenberg and Alger Hiss—dominated the evening news.

Public interest in espionage usually focuses on the spy, or agent; but the role of spy is arguably not the most important one in the espionage play. Every spy has a *control*—a second agent who acts as a contact point with the sponsoring government. The control passes instructions from the government to the spy, and information from the spy to the government.

The controls in a Windows program are a little like those in the world of espionage. They may appear to be rather mundane objects, yet they form the vital information conduit between the application program and the user: Nothing gets to or from the user except by means of controls.

In this chapter, you'll begin building a detailed knowledge of Windows controls. Specifically, you'll learn more about the important **CStatic** and **CButton** controls. So, grab your Walther PPK, leap into your Astin Martin DB5, and we're off. Oh, and watch out for the ejection seeeaaaat!

A Short CWnd Interlude

In Chapter 4, you looked at the basic structure of a dialog-based application, which uses a **CDialog**-derived class as its main window. As you recall, the **CDialog** class is derived from **CWnd**, so an instance of **CDialog** inherits all the attributes and behaviors of a **CWnd**. However, the **CDialog** class also differs from **CWnd**. For example, Visual C++ creates **CDialog** windows differently than **CWnd** windows. Let's take a look, using our FourUp application as an example.

When the **CFourUpApp** class starts running, it calls the virtual **InitInstance()** method, which creates the main window for the application. The code to accomplish that looks something like this:

```
CFourUpDlg dlg;      // Create the window
m_pMainWnd = &dlg;   // Store a pointer to our main window
```

If FourUp's main window were directly derived from **CWnd**, rather than being derived from the **CDialog** subclass, the **InitInstance()** method would look very similar:

```
m_pMainWnd = new CMainWindow;
```

The **CDialog**-based window is created as a local variable on the stack, whereas the **CWnd**-based window is created as a dynamic variable in the freestore—otherwise, the two pieces of code aren't *that* different. Each calls the default constructor of its main window class, then stores the address of the main window object in the **m_pMainWnd** data member of the **CWinApp** class. Only when we look inside the two constructors do we see the real difference between the two.

Window Construction

Let's start by examining how the **CFourUpDlg** class constructor really works. The parts we're interested in are as follows:

```
CFourUpDlg::CFourUpDlg(CWnd* pParent /*=NULL*/)
    : CDialog(CFourUpDlg::IDD, pParent)
{
    // Details omitted
}
```

Notice that the **CFourUpDlg** class doesn't really perform any construction tasks. Instead, it uses its initialization list to call the **CDialog** constructor, passing two pieces of information. The piece of interest to us is the first argument, **CFourUpDlg::IDD**.

The value **CFourUpDlg::IDD** is an enumeration (defined in the header file for **CFourUpDlg**) that contains the resource ID for the dialog template (contained in the resource script, CFourUp.rc). The **CDialog** constructor reads information from the dialog template, and then constructs a window, using the specifications given by the template. To create the main dialog window (and all of the controls contained in the dialog template), the **CDialog** constructor uses the **CWnd::Create()** or the **CWnd::CreateEx()** function, calling the function once for the main dialog window and again for each control it encounters.

The CWnd::Create() Function

Even though you don't need to explicitly use the **CWnd::Create()** function to create controls that you place in a dialog box, you need to understand how the function works, simply because Windows and MFC use it so frequently.

Here's the prototype for **CWnd::Create()**:

```
virtual BOOL Create( LPCTSTR lpszClassName,
                     LPCTSTR lpszWindowName,
                     DWORD dwStyle,
                     const RECT& rect,
                     CWnd* pParentWnd,
                     UINT nID,
                     CCreateContext* pContext = NULL);
```

As you can see, the **Create()** function takes seven arguments, the last of which defaults to **NULL**. Briefly, here's what each argument does:

- *lpszClassName*—A string that names the window "class," a data structure that Windows dynamically creates to simplify building multiple windows that share the same properties. Because this isn't a true C++ class, you should probably think of it as a data structure—but the Windows documentation consistently uses the term *class*.

  Normally, in MFC, you'll pass **NULL**, which directs **Create()** to use the default **CWnd** window class. If you've registered a custom class, you can pass its name here. If you're creating an instance of a built-in control, such as a Windows edit control, you pass the **WNDCLASS** name **"EDIT"** here.
- *lpszWindowName*—The "text" attribute associated with the window. If the window is a main window, this string appears in the title bar. If the window is a push button, on the other hand, this string appears on the face of the button. Some windows—a rectangle static control, for instance—have no text property. In such cases, just pass the empty string, "".
- *dwStyle*—The most important characteristic to understand (we'll further discuss it in a moment). The **dwStyle** argument enables you to specify options for a particular window object upon its creation. You may, for instance, specify that a particular window has a close button or is resizable. Such attributes aren't characteristics of the window's class, but are defined when each window is created.
- *rect*—Defines the coordinates of the window. A **RECT** is a C **struct** that contains four public members: **left**, **top**, **bottom**, and **right**. If you're creating a top-level or main window, these coordinates are measured from the upper-left corner of your screen. If you're creating a child window or control, the coordinates are relative to the parent window.
- *pParentWnd*—A pointer to the window's parent. For child windows, you'll always need to provide the proper value; for top-level windows, you can pass **NULL**.
- *nID*—An integer identifier that identifies the window to its parent and allows the parent to send messages to its child. This argument isn't used for top-level windows—you can pass **NULL** if the window has no parent.

- *pContext*—Used only when you need to override the normal process of connecting a document and its views. You'll rarely use this argument, and never outside the document-view architecture.

Looking At Window Styles

Window styles—the **dwStyle** argument passed to the **CWnd::Create()** method—let you customize various attributes of a window. The general window styles (those applicable to a wide variety of window classes) consist of a set of identifiers that begin with **WS_**. Each identifier refers to a specific attribute; Table 6.1 shows some of the more common styles.

Three window styles specify a window's relationship to other windows. If you apply the **WS_OVERLAPPED** style, then the window doesn't have a parent: It's a top-level window. If you assign the **WS_POPUP** style, you normally give the window a parent, but the window isn't restricted to the parent's space—instead, it floats above the parent. If a window has the **WS_CHILD** style, it must have a parent, and it's "clipped" to the parent's screen space. If you move such a window outside the

Table 6.1 Commonly used window styles.

Window Style	Description
WS_BORDER	Adds a border to the window.
WS_CAPTION	Adds a title bar to the window.
WS_CHILD	Creates a child window.
WS_HSCROLL	Adds a horizontal scroll bar to the window.
WS_MAXIMIZEBOX	Adds a Maximize button to the window.
WS_MINIMIZEBOX	Adds a Minimize button to the window.
WS_OVERLAPPED	Creates an overlapped window.
WS_POPUP	Creates a pop-up window.
WS_SYSMENU	Adds a system menu to the window title bar.
WS_THICKFRAME	Creates a resizable window.
WS_VISIBLE	Makes the window visible when it's created.
WS_VSCROLL	Adds a vertical scroll bar to the window.

parent's area, it isn't displayed. These three styles are mutually exclusive.

Other styles specify various characteristics of the windows they describe. For instance, assigning the **WS_CAPTION** style adds a title bar, and also makes the window movable. The user can move a window with the keyboard or mouse only if it has the **WS_CAPTION** style. In a similar way, if you assign a window the **WS_THICKFRAME** style, the user can resize it. Windows with the **WS_BORDER** style aren't resizable.

Normally, you'll create windows that have more than one style. To do that, you combine different styles using the bitwise **OR** operator, |. Here's an example. Suppose you want a top-level window that has a title bar and a Maximize box, that has no Minimize box or system menu, and that isn't resizable. You'll pass the following window style to **CWnd::Create()**:

```
WS_OVERLAPPED | WS_CAPTION | WS_MAXIMIZEBOX | WS_BORDER
```

To make typing a little less work, several styles combine the most used options. **WS_OVERLAPPEDWINDOW** creates a movable, resizable, top-level window with all the trimmings, whereas **WS_POPUPWINDOW** creates your standard dialog-box style window.

Creating Child Windows

As you saw in Chapter 4, Windows includes six universal child-window control classes. In MFC, those classes are represented by the C++ classes **CStatic**, **CButton**, **CEdit**, **CListBox**, **CComboBox**, and **CScrollBar**. Each of these classes is derived from **CWnd**, and therefore inherits all of **CWnd**'s non-private functions.

However, every control overrides the **CWnd::Create()** function and provides its own distinctive window styles. You use these class-specific window styles, along with the general window styles, to create the specific attributes you want your child-window controls to have.

Here's an example. Suppose you want to create an OK push-button, similar to the one used in the **CAboutDlg** class. Using the **CButton** class, you'll write this code:

```
CButton okBtn;
// Set size: x,y = 100,100, x1,y1 = 200, 150
CRect rect(100, 100, 200, 150);
okBtn.Create( "OK",
          WS_CHILD | WS_VISIBLE | BS_DEFPUSHBUTTON,
          rect, this, IDOK);
```

These lines create a default push button (an OK button) that contains the text "OK", is 100 units wide (x1 - x = 100) and 50 units high (y1 - y = 50), with its upper-left corner at position 100, 100. The window has a runtime identifier given by the value **IDOK**.

You may be saying to yourself, "This is a lot of work!" You're right—it is. It's also very difficult to write such code with any accuracy, because you have to position each control "sight unseen" using x-y coordinates. Working with the Dialog Editor is quite a bit easier.

You'll want to learn about the **Create()** function, even if you don't use it, to become familiar with the control-specific window styles. Did you see the style **BS_DEFPUSHBUTTON** used in the second argument of **Create()**? It specifies that you want to create a default push button. The **BS_** prefix identifies this as a Button Style identifier. Like all child-window controls, this control-specific window identifier is combined with the general **WS_VISIBLE** and **WS_CHILD** styles.

When you use the Dialog Editor to create your controls, you don't have to use the button-style identifiers. Instead, you check a particular box in the control's Properties dialog box. You still need to know about the various styles, however, because the Windows documentation refers to them—it won't ask you what option you selected in the Dialog Editor.

Useful CWnd Functions

Controls derived from **CWnd** inherit the **CWnd** member functions. However, such inheritance often makes it difficult for you to find a particular function. If you want to change the font of a **CStatic** control, for instance, you won't find the **SetFont()** method implemented in the **CStatic** class.That doesn't mean you can't change the font—you'll simply have to look a little further up the inheritance hierarchy.

Sure enough, in the **CWnd** class, you'll find **SetFont()**, along with a host of other useful methods. Table 6.2 presents the methods you'll use to work with child-window controls. **CWnd** is one of the largest classes in the MFC hierarchy, however, so finding things can be difficult. If you don't see what you want in Table 6.2, look through the online-documentation—the method you seek may be there, somewhere!

Now, let's get started looking at the universal Windows control classes. We'll start with the **CStatic** class.

A CStatic Refresher

You've already had a lot of experience using **CStatic** class objects. In the FourUp application, you used **CStatic** controls to display

Table 6.2 Useful CWnd member functions.

Function Name	Description
CenterWindow	Centers a window relative to its parent.
EnableWindow	Enables or disables a window or control.
GetClientRect	Retrieves the dimensions of a control.
GetDlgCtrlID	Retrieves the ID associated with a control.
GetDlgItem	Retrieves the control associated with an ID.
GetFont	Retrieves the font used by a window.
GetParent	Retrieves a control's parent.
GetWindowText	Retrieves the caption associated with a window.
MoveWindow	Changes both the position and size of a window or control.
SetFont	Changes the font used by a window.
SetWindowText	Changes the caption associated with a window.
ShowWindow	Shows or hides a window or control.

text information, bitmaps, and icons—quite a variety of functions. And, **CStatic** objects can do even more.

CStatic controls come in three distinct types: those that display text, those that display rectangles, and those that display images. As you might expect, you differentiate between the types by using window styles. Let's start by looking at how you create **CStatic** controls programmatically. Then, we'll examine the three types.

Creating CStatic Controls

To construct a **CStatic** control programmatically, you use its overridden **Create()** function. The **CStatic::Create()** function only takes five arguments (down from **CWnd**'s seven). Here's an example:

```
m_Mom.Create("Hi Mom",                          // Text
   WS_CHILD | WS_VISIBLE | SS_CENTER,           // Styles
   rect,                                        // Position
   this,                                        // Parent
   IDC_MOM);                                    // Control ID
```

As with all controls, you specify the **WS_CHILD** and **WS_VISIBLE** window styles. You can also specify window-style attributes particular to the **CStatic** class—their names start with the prefix ***SS_***.

Let's see this creation process at work in a mini-application. We won't walk you through an entire project, but if you want to follow along, you can easily do so. (The other examples in this chapter will modify this one.) Here are the steps you'll follow to make the mini-app:

1. Use AppWizard to create a new dialog-based application. Name it TestBedOne.
2. Delete the TODO:... label on the main dialog window.
3. Manually add a **CStatic** data member named **m_Mom** to the **CTestBedOneDlg** class header, using this line of code:

   ```
   CStatic m_Mom;
   ```

4. In the **TestBedOneDlg::OnInitDialog()** function, look for the comment that says: *// TODO: Add extra initialization here.*

Below the comment, add the following lines of code to create the static label:

```
CRect rect;
GetClientRect(&rect);
rect.bottom = 25;
rect.right -= 100;
rect.left += 100;
m_Mom.Create("Hi Mom", WS_CHILD | WS_VISIBLE |
                    SS_CENTER,
           rect, this, IDC_MOM);
```

5. When you're finished, choose View|Resource Symbols from the main menu and add a new **IDC_MOM** symbol with the value 2000.

Now, you should be able to compile and run your application. The result is shown in Figure 6.1.

Most of the time, of course, you won't do all this work. You'll just drag a text control from the Control Toolbar, drop it on the form, size it, and let the Visual C++ Dialog Editor worry about the details.

Now, let's look at the **CStatic** styles you have to choose from.

CStatic Text Styles

You can specify a **CStatic** *text style* control using five styles: **SS_CENTER**, **SS_LEFT**, **SS_RIGHT**, **SS_LEFTNOWORDWRAP**, and **SS_SIMPLE**. Most of these

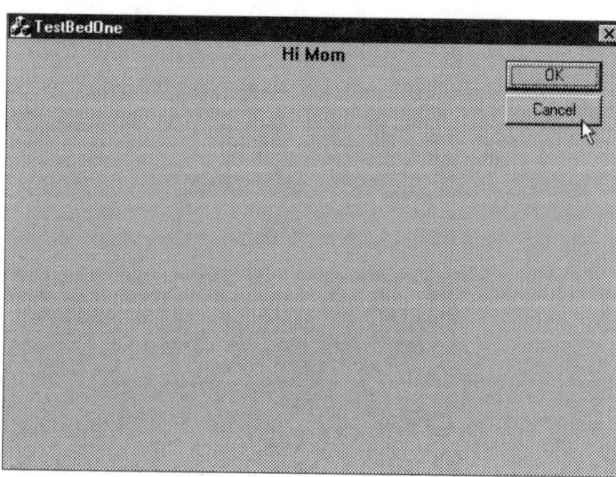

Figure 6.1
The TestBedOne application.

styles have self-explanatory names; we covered the corresponding Dialog Editor choices in Chapter 2. The **SS_SIMPLE** style is useful because it displays a little more quickly and uses fewer resources.

The **SS_LEFT**, **SS_CENTER**, and **SS_RIGHT** styles perform word-wrapping if the specified text doesn't fit on one line; the other two styles don't wrap. If the text doesn't fit inside the rectangle specified when you create the **CStatic** object, the remaining text is *not* displayed.

You can combine these text styles with **SS_NOPREFIX** to prevent automatic translation of the ampersand character to an underline, with **SS_CENTERIMAGE** to center text vertically inside the control, or with **SS_SUNKEN** to display a recessed box around the control.

When you're working with the Dialog Editor, you use the Text Properties dialog box to manage **CStatic** controls belonging to the text family. Take a look at Figure 6.2 to see the Text Properties dialog box.

CStatic Frame Styles

The **CStatic** frame styles use the same **Create()** function as the text styles, but they ignore the first (text) argument. The frame family consists of three frame varieties: filled, hollow, and etched.

Filled frames simply draw a solid rectangle on screen. There are three options: **SS_BLACKRECT**, **SS_GRAYRECT**, and **SS_WHITERECT**. Despite the names, these frames don't always draw in black, gray, and white (although they may). Instead, they use the system colors (defined by the user through the Control Panel) identified as **COLOR_WINDOWFRAME**, **COLOR_BACKGROUND**, and **COLOR_WINDOW**.

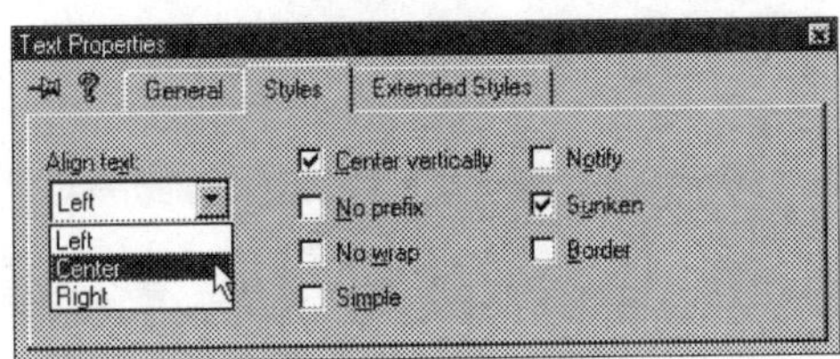

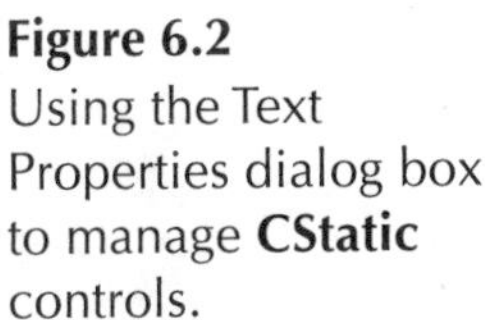
Figure 6.2
Using the Text Properties dialog box to manage **CStatic** controls.

NOTE

Don't confuse the ***CStatic::SetCursor()*** *method with the* ***CWnd::OnSetCursor()*** *function that allows you to associate a Windows cursor with a control.* ***CStatic::SetCursor()*** *simply displays the cursor image, as it would any other bitmap resource.*

Hollow frames come in the same three colors, and draw a one-pixel-wide frame in the given dimensions. The hollow styles are **SS_BLACKFRAME**, **SS_GRAYFRAME**, and **SS_WHITEFRAME**.

The three etched styles—**SS_ETCHEDFRAME**, **SS_ETCHEDHORZ**, and **SS_ETCHEDVERT**— display 3D hollow frames that look best displayed on the standard gray dialog box. The **SS_ETCHEDHORZ** and **SS_ETCHEDVERT** styles display the etched 3D effect only at the top and bottom or the left and right borders.

The CStatic Image Styles

In addition to text and frames, you can use the **CStatic** class to easily and quickly display images, as you discovered in Chapter 3. The three image styles are: **SS_BITMAP**, **SS_ENHMETAFILE**, and **SS_ICON**.

Creating a **CStatic** object that displays an image requires multiple steps. You must load the image resources (bitmaps, metafiles, or icons) separately. Then, you use the **CStatic** functions **SetIcon()**, **SetBitmap()**, **SetCursor()**, and **SetEnhMetaFile()** to display the image.

In the Dialog Editor, both the **CStatic** frame styles and the **CStatic** image styles display the Picture Properties dialog box to let you select the proper style. Rather than using check boxes, as the Text Properties dialog box did, the Picture Properties dialog box offers a pair of interacting combo boxes. First, you select the type of image you want to display: a frame, an icon, and so on. Then, depending on your Type selection, either the Image or the Color combo box will become active. The Picture Properties dialog box is shown in Figure 6.3.

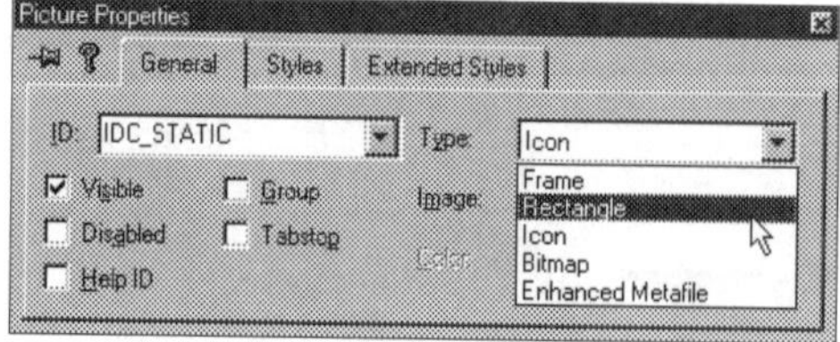

Figure 6.3
Using the Picture Properties dialog box to manage a **CStatic** control.

Working With CStatic Controls

CStatic controls don't really do much—mostly, they sit there and look nice. Often, that's enough. Sometimes, however, you'd like a label or a picture to tell you if it was clicked. To do that, you have to add one more style when you create your **CStatic** control: the **SS_NOTIFY** style.

However, even when you specify the **SS_NOTIFY** style, **CStatic** controls are close-mouthed. They'll respond only to the events **STN_CLICKED**, **STN_DBLCLK**, **STN_DISABLE** and **STN_ENABLE**—and to get those to work, you must add the message response tables by hand.

Most of us would rather avoid such hard work. Fortunately, ClassWizard will help you detect single clicks (as if the control were a button). Here's an example that modifies the TestBedOne program we built earlier:

1. Add a text label to the center of the TestBedOne main dialog box. Change the name of your control to **IDC_CLICKME**, and have it say *Click me, if you dare!!!*. Also check Notify in the Text Properties dialog box.
2. Double-click on your control to make ClassWizard open the Add Member Function dialog box. Accept the name it offers (**OnClickMe**), and then add the following highlighted line to complete the method it writes:

```
void CTestBedOneDlg::OnClickme()
{
    // TODO: Add your control notification handler
    // code
    m_Mom.SetWindowText(
"What? Do I look like a button?");
}
```

3. Compile and run the application. When you click on the label in the center of the screen, you'll see that the dynamic label at the top of the screen changes. Figure 6.4 shows how this looks.

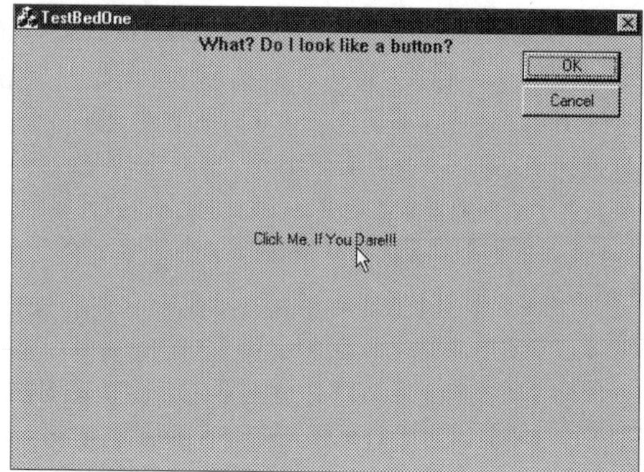

Figure 6.4
Detecting mouse clicks using a **CStatic** label.

CStatic Member Functions

Not only are **CStatic** objects relatively quiet, they also don't have a lot of talents. If you look up **CStatic** in the online help, you'll see that only eight member functions are defined. Of course, as we mentioned, every **CStatic** object is also a **CWnd**, so you have all of the **CWnd** functions at your disposal.

Each **CStatic** member function either displays or retrieves one of the four image-types that the **CStatic** class can handle. The methods to display an image in a **CStatic** control are **SetBitmap()**, **SetCursor()**, **SetEnhMetaFile()**, and **SetIcon()**. The complementary retrieval methods are **GetBitmap()**, **GetCursor()**, **GetEnhMetaFile()**, and **GetIcon()**.

In the FourUp application, you used these methods with the playing cards, which you needed to change each time the player clicked on Deal. From walking through that example, you know that the process of displaying an icon is a little more complex than simply passing the name of the image file. (Just so you know, the process of obtaining an enhanced metafile is even worse.)

Just to refresh what you learned in the last chapter, to display an image programmatically you must follow these steps:

1. Add the image file to your project as a resource, using the Insert|Resource menu item.

2. Obtain a handle to the resource at runtime. For icons, you can do this using **CWinApp::LoadIcon()**. For a bitmap, you can attach the bitmap to a **CStatic** control using the Dialog Editor (as you did for the custom FourUp text logo), then call the member function **GetBitmap()** to get the required **HBITMAP**.
3. Call the **CStatic** member function **SetIcon()** or **SetBitmap()**, passing the **HICON** or the **HBITMAP** obtained in Step 2 as an argument.

That pretty much exhausts the capabilities of the **CStatic** class. Let's go on to another class that's a bit more active, but which—like the **CStatic** class—tries to fit several very different personalities into one package.

The CButton Family

The **CButton** class is composed primarily of various members that do things when you click on them. The glaring exception to this generality is the groupbox side of the family, which seems to belong in the **CStatic** class, but ended up with the buttons by historical accident.

The **CButton** class has four members: push (or command) buttons, checkboxes, radio buttons, and groupboxes.

- Push buttons trigger an action when you click on them. Since Windows 3.0, push buttons have had a 3D appearance. When you click on a push button, it seems to sink into the screen surface; when you release it, it springs back.
- Checkboxes retrieve non-exclusive true-false input from the user of your application. A checkbox has both a caption and an *action area*. The action area is a small box that fills with a graphic check-mark when selected and clears when deselected. A checkbox acts like a toggle, and retains state information—it's either checked or unchecked. When placed in a dialog box, checkboxes have a 3D appearance; when placed in a normal window, they don't.

- Radio buttons are another form of checkbox, used to make an exclusive choice among several alternatives. When several radio buttons belong to the same group, you can select only one of them at a time. Windows will deselect the other members of a group when a member is selected. Like checkboxes, radio buttons individually retain their state information. Also like checkboxes, radio buttons appear with a 3D effect in a dialog box (their preferred and persistent haunt), but not naturally otherwise.
- Groupboxes, the last member of the **CButton** family, are very similar to the **SS_ETCHEDFRAME** style **CStatic**. The only difference is that **CButtons** have a caption property that works. **CButtons** have no state and send no messages, but you can (as you saw in **CFourUp**) send them messages.

Creating CButton Controls

To create a **CButton** object programmatically, you use the default constructor, then call **Create()** as you did for the **CStatic** class. The differences, of course, are in the details—but those differences are slight. Most of them, as you might expect, are concerned with the styles use to create the different varieties of **CButtons**.

Here, for instance, is code you can add to the TestBedOne application to create a push-button style **CButton** object called **m_Dad**:

```
GetClientRect(&rect);
rect.top = rect.bottom - 55;
rect.bottom -= 25;
rect.left = (rect.right - 175);
rect.right -= 25;
m_Dad.Create("Daddy Dearest",                   // Text
    WS_CHILD | WS_VISIBLE | BS_PUSHBUTTON,  // Style
    rect,                                   // Position
    this,                                   // Parent
    IDC_DAD);                               // Control ID
```

As before, follow these steps to try this code in TestBedOne:

1. Add a **CButton** data member named **m_Dad** to the **CTestBedOneDlg** class definition:

```
CButton m_Dad;
```

2. Add a new **IDC_DAD** resource ID, using the View|Resource Symbols menu item. Give it the value 2001.
3. Add the code listed previously to **CTestBedOneDlg::OnInitDialog()**, just after the code that set up dear old **m_Mom**.

You can see the result in Figure 6.5.

The CButton Push-Button Styles

There are two push-button styles: **BS_PUSHBUTTON**, and **BS_DEFPUSHBUTTON**. You can use either when you create a **CButton** control. These two styles have only one real difference: In a dialog box template, like that created by the Dialog Editor, the **BS_DEFPUSHBUTTON** style indicates that the **CButton** should become the *default button*.

The default button will be notified if the user presses the Enter key without first selecting another push button. However, if the user does select another push button (by navigating with the Tab key), then pressing Enter has the effect of clicking on the selected button, rather than the default button.

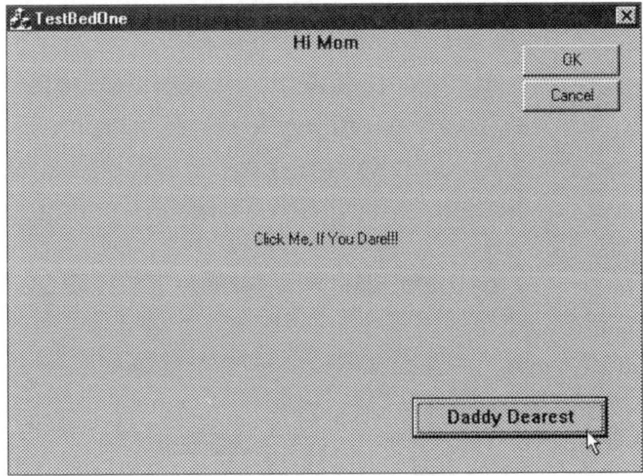

Figure 6.5
Adding a push-button style **CButton** to TestBedOne.

Windows allows only one default push button in a dialog box. If you define more than one, then the last one created becomes the default. When the default push button is displayed, it's drawn with a bold border.

When you're working with the Dialog Editor, you specify the attributes of **CButton** push-button controls by using the Push Button Properties dialog box, shown in Figure 6.6. We'll discuss the appearance styles in the next section.

The Appearance Of Style

Like most other controls, **CButton** controls have several styles that determine the appearance of a button, rather than its type or behavior. Most of these "appearance" styles first made their appearance with the advent of Windows 95.

The first group of appearance styles affects the alignment of text or images within the **CButton** object. The styles **BS_LEFT**, **BS_RIGHT**, and **BS_CENTER** control horizontal alignment, whereas **BS_TOP**, **BS_BOTTOM**, and **BS_VCENTER** control vertical alignment. Two additional alignment styles work only with checkboxes and radio buttons: The **BS_LEFTTEXT** and **BS_RIGHTBUTTON** styles place the caption of such a control on the left, rather than at its default position on the right.

Two styles allow you to use a bitmap or icon instead of the text that normally appears on the face of the button. You can use the **BS_BITMAP** or **BS_ICON** styles with push buttons, check boxes, and radio buttons. Using a bitmap or icon with a button isn't as convenient as using **CStatic** controls in the Dialog Editor. With **CStatic** controls you can pick your images from a drop-down list—but with **CButtons**, you must use the member

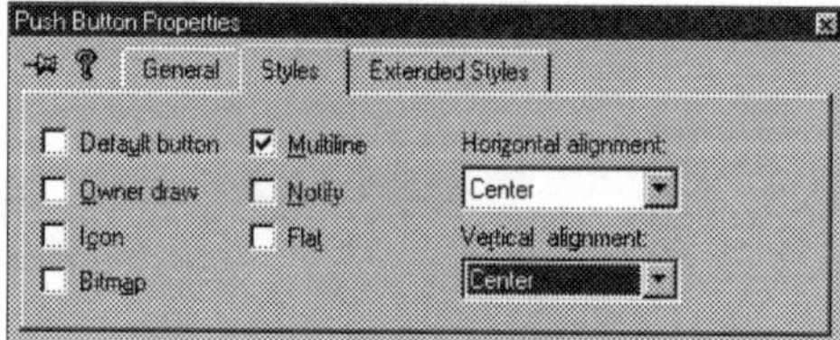

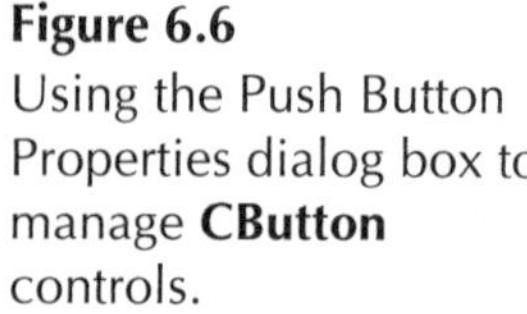

Figure 6.6
Using the Push Button Properties dialog box to manage **CButton** controls.

functions **CButton::SetIcon()** and **CButton::SetBitmap()** to display the images.

Three additional new button styles deserve mention:

- The **BS_MULTILINE** style allows you to create buttons with text that spans multiple lines. You can manually create a line break by inserting the new-line escape sequence (\n), or you can simply allow the automatic line-wrapping to take effect. The **BS_MULTILINE** style has one rather disconcerting effect, however: Multiple lines aren't individually centered when the **BS_CENTER** style is used as well (although the overall text block is centered).
- The **BS_FLAT** style lets you use the new-style checkboxes and radio buttons featured on the Internet Explorer options page. You can use this style with push buttons, as well.

Fast And Easy BS_ICON And BS_BITMAP Buttons

Despite the new Developer Studio ease-of-use features, creating buttons that use the **BS_ICON** or **BS_BITMAP** style is still a bit of a chore. There are just too many pieces floating around. Here's a tip that may help you keep track of all the pieces.

Suppose you want to create a new **BS_BITMAP**-style button to invoke a spelling checker. You name the button **IDC_SPELL_BTN**. To display the bitmap, you'll need four additional pieces of information:

1. The bitmap resource.
2. A static control to hold the bitmap.
3. A control variable that allows you to retrieve the bitmap from the static control.
4. A control variable for the **IDC_SPELL_BTN** button, so that you can set its bitmap.

By using a consistent naming convention, you can easily tell at a glance which "part" of the puzzle you're looking at. When you add the bitmap resource, name it **IDB_SPELL_BM**, and name the static control that contains it **IDC_SPELL_BM**. When you create the control variables, name the static control **m_SpellBM** and the button **m_SpellBtn**.

When you have to set the bitmap on the button in your **InitDialog()** function, it's then a simple matter of writing

```
m_SpellBtn.SetIcon(m_SpellBM.GetBitmap());
```

- The **BS_PUSHLIKE** style has no effect on push buttons. However, it causes radio buttons and checkboxes to behave normally—but look like push buttons. When you click on a check box with the **BS_PUSHLIKE** style, the button depresses, just like a regular push button. Instead of springing back, however, the button stays depressed until you click on it again. When used with radio buttons, the style works similarly, but clicking on one button in a group causes all the others to spring out.

Most of us have learned that just because we have 200 fonts on our system, we don't have to use every one of them when we write a letter. In a similar way, all of these formatting options give you a great deal of control over your finished interface—but it's up to you to exercise restraint. You can see several of the different button styles applied to push buttons in Figure 6.7, but in real life we advise you to select a single button style and stick to it throughout your application.

The CButton Checkbox Button Styles

When you're creating a checkbox **CButton**, you can choose from four different styles: **BS_CHECKBOX**, **BS_AUTOCHECKBOX**, **BS_3STATE**, or **BS_AUTO3STATE**. Ninety-nine and nine-tenths of the time, you'll simply use the **BS_AUTOCHECKBOX** style. You'll use the two **3STATE** styles when a checkbox can have an intermediate state: yes, no, or maybe. You won't use them

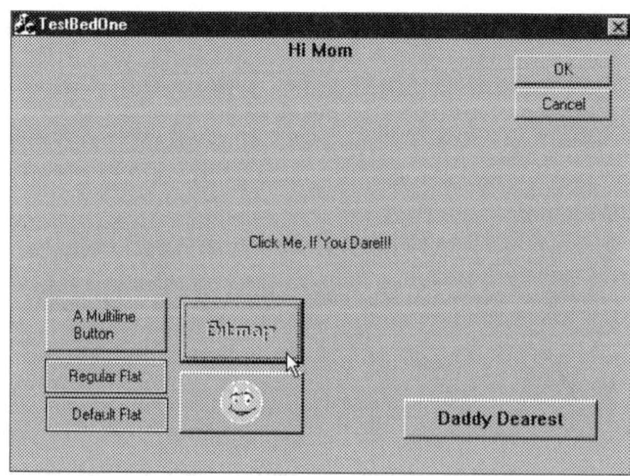

Figure 6.7
Displaying different **CButton** appearance styles.

often, because handling the "maybe" case complicates the rest of the logic in your program. For those times when the intermediate choice is "not applicable," disabling the control is a better option than applying a **3STATE** style.

When you use the **BS_AUTOCHECKBOX** style, Windows takes care of checking and unchecking your checkbox. With the **BS_CHECKBOX** style, you have to do it yourself. In both cases, you can choose to be notified when the state of the checkbox changes—so there's usually no good reason to use the **BS_CHECKBOX** style.

In Visual C++, of course, you don't worry about all of these different styles. Instead, you use the Check Box Properties dialog box, which you can see in Figure 6.8. Note that you can use the same appearance items with checkboxes as with push buttons. Figure 6.9 shows several of the checkbox styles.

The CButton Radio Button Styles

When you create a radio button **CButton**, you have only half as many choices as you enjoyed with the checkbox styles: the two styles **BS_RADIOBUTTON** and **BS_AUTORADIOBUTTON**. If you have fewer styles available, however, you also have twice the reason to use **BS_AUTORADIOBUTTON** and eschew **BS_RADIOBUTTON**. As with checkboxes, the **AUTO** style leaves all the checking and unchecking to Windows. With the **BS_RADIOBUTTON** style, you have to perform these tasks yourself. But, doing it yourself means more than monitoring a single radio button and clearing it or setting it as necessary—instead, you must monitor a whole set of radio buttons. If the user clicks on one of them, you have to cycle through all the others to deselect each of them, in addition to selecting the fortunate one. That's a lot of unnecessary work.

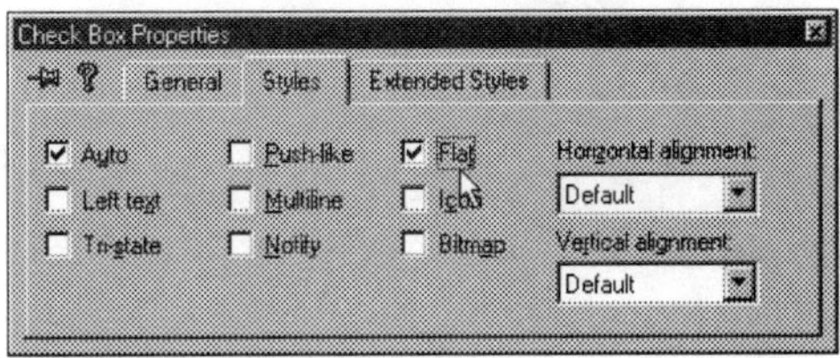

Figure 6.8
Using the Check Box Properties dialog box.

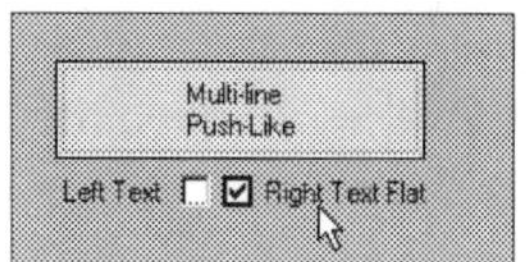

Figure 6.9
Different checkbox styles at work.

To make Windows magically check and clear the **BS_AUTORADIO** buttons you create, you need to be aware of one other style: **WS_GROUP**. Windows uses this style to determine which radio buttons belong to a particular group. After all, you don't want Windows clearing every other radio button in your dialog box when you select one—you want it to clear only the other buttons related to that particular group.

If you're creating your **CButtons** programmatically, apply the **WS_GROUP** style to the first radio button in your radio button group and to the first control after the end of your radio button group. Be sure that no other radio button in that group has the **WS_GROUP** style.

As usual, in Visual C++, you use a dialog box to set the properties of your radio buttons. You can select the styles, as well as adjust the **WS_GROUP** style, using the Radio Button Properties dialog box, which you can see in Figure 6.10.

You can see several of the radio button styles available for the **CButton** class in Figure 6.11.

The CButton Groupbox Styles

We need to talk about one more style: **BS_GROUPBOX**. As we mentioned earlier, a button control that has the **BS_GROUPBOX** style doesn't do much of anything. A groupbox appears as a hollow box with a caption in the upper-left corner.

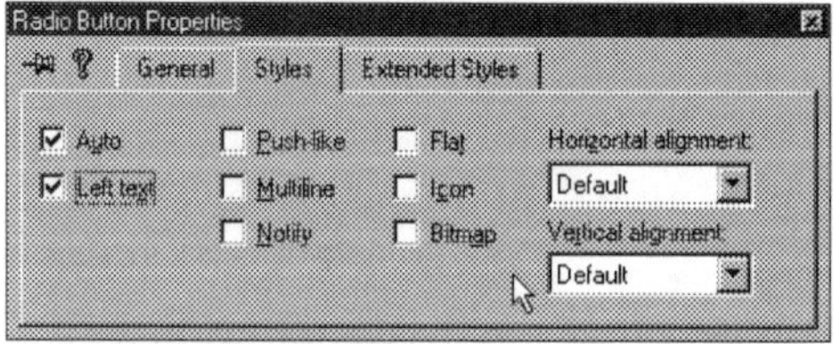

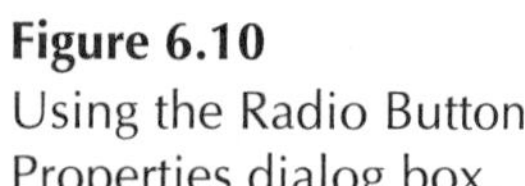

Figure 6.10
Using the Radio Button Properties dialog box.

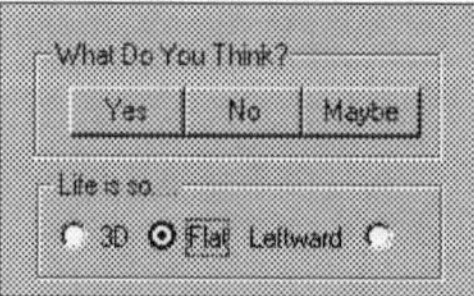

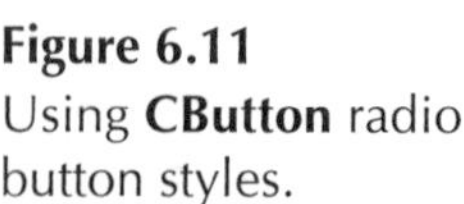

Figure 6.11
Using **CButton** radio button styles.

As their name suggests, groupboxes usually group radio buttons and checkboxes together to form a visual whole. It's important to remember, however, that just because you put your radio buttons in a group box, they don't automatically become part of a group. Groupbox buttons let you visually group controls—but you must use the **WS_GROUP** style to logically group your radio buttons and checkboxes.

> **▶Tip**
>
> ***WS_GROUP And Tab Stops***
>
> *Just because two radio buttons are next to each other doesn't necessarily mean they're in the same group. Grouping doesn't depend upon screen position, but upon the order in which you add components to your dialog box. When creating your dialog boxes, you can reset the tab order (the order in which controls are traversed, using the Tab key) by choosing Layout|Tab Order from the main menu. You should always reset the tab order before setting and clearing **WS_GROUP** settings, unless you've added your controls in a strictly sequential order.*

Like everything else in Visual C++, even the lowly groupbox has its own dialog box. You can see the Group Box Properties dialog box in Figure 6.12.

Working With CButton Controls

As you saw in the FourUp application, working with push buttons is easy—especially when you have ClassWizard to help out. When the user clicks on a button (other than a groupbox button), it generates a **BN_CLICKED** event. (More precisely, it's not an event, but a *notification*—a kind of event generated by a control. For our current purposes, the distinction is unimportant.)

In Visual C++, you can write a method to handle the **BN_CLICKED** event by simply double-clicking on the button in the Dialog Editor. ClassWizard will open its Add Member Function dialog box and offer to create a new member function for you. It will even supply a default name. (As you saw, the name takes the form **On*CtrlName*()**). All you have to add is code.

If you apply the **BS_NOTIFY** style when you create your button (or click on the Notify checkbox in Developer Studio), your button will generate three additional events:

- **BN_DOUBLECLICKED** when the button is double-clicked.

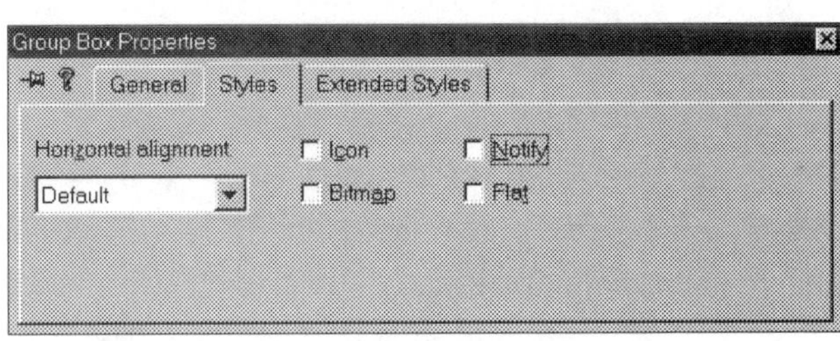

Figure 6.12
The Group Box Properties dialog box.

- **BN_SETFOCUS** when the user tabs to your button or selects it with the mouse.
- **BN_KILLFOCUS** when the keyboard focus leaves your control because the user has selected another control with the keyboard or mouse.

CButton Member Functions

CButtons not only notify you when something happens, they also have a few member functions you may find helpful. The most commonly used are the **GetCheck()** and **SetCheck()** member functions. You'll use these primarily for checkboxes and radio button groups.

The **SetCheck()** member function takes a single argument, which can be either **BST_CHECKED** or **BST_UNCHECKED**. (The **3STATE** checkboxes can also take the **BST_INDETERMINATE** argument value.) To find out whether a checkbox is checked, you can use the **GetCheck()** function, which returns the same values. For example, to take an action if the user checks the **m_check** checkbox control, you'd write:

```
if (m_check.GetCheck() == BST_CHECKED) { ... }
```

Unless you want to take a particular action when a checkbox is selected or deselected, you normally won't respond to notifications from checkboxes. Radio buttons, however, are a different matter. To find out which radio button is selected, you'll use the **GetCheck()** method on each individual button. You can't directly discover which radio button is selected out of all the radio buttons in a group. Because of this fact, you'll often intercept the **BN_CLICKED** message for radio buttons.

Wrap Up

In this chapter, you've been jostled by a plethora of information on windows, **CStatic** controls, and **CButton** controls. Remember that you're not expected to memorize such information—merely understand it. It's the task of the Visual C++ on-line documentation to refresh your memory concerning constructors and methods and their arguments. So, continue to focus on the "big picture," and you'll do well.

The next chapter begins a new project—a draw-by-numbers program—that will take several chapters to complete. However, you'll develop a limited-function version of the program right away. Working with the project, you'll learn about the Windows Graphical Device Interface (GDI) and how to use it to draw lines, shapes, and text.

Chapter 7

Draw By Numbers: Building An Application That Paints

Graffiti artists draw on walls. MFC programmers draw on windows.

A popular bumper sticker during the 1960s read, "Human Being: Do Not Fold, Spindle, Or Mutilate." The words were a play on those printed on the face of the ubiquitous IBM punch card, which was familiar to almost every American at the time. Government checks, utility bills, and even overdue library book notices were delivered via drab, identical cards.

More than anything else, the punch card came to represent the impersonal face of the computer and its insistence that human beings order their lives to suit its demands, and not vice versa. And, people, being people, quite naturally rebelled. The personal computer revolution drove out the forces of tyranny and darkness, and colorful, friendly software reigned supreme throughout the land.

More or less.

As George Orwell pointed out in his novel *Animal Farm*, the more things change, the more they stay the same. The punch card has gone the way of history, but its spiritual descendent, the computerized form, lives on. Thanks to products like Visual Basic, creating form-based computer applications is less work than ever before—and as a result (to the probable delight of the unimaginative bureaucrats who littered punch cards across the world), nearly identical forms are *everywhere*. But, although we may have to accept these form-based applications as the bread-and-butter of Windows software development, we can find a creative outlet through the soul of programming: *graphical applications*.

What is a graphical application? Glad you asked. The popular PC game "Myst" is a graphical application—as are most games developed since the demise of text-based adventure games. Adobe's PhotoShop and Windows' Paint are both obviously graphical applications. So are Lotus Freelance and Microsoft PowerPoint. Screen savers, page-layout programs, even WYSIWYG word-processors and spreadsheets—all of these are graphical applications. Graphical applications depend on the skills of a programmer who writes code that draws the output, whether it's the exciting 3D labyrinths of Doom or the more mundane bar-charts of 1-2-3.

In this chapter, you'll learn to paint on your computer screen, a task that's a little more difficult than placing a label or a button. To make the process as painless as possible, we're going to start slowly, drawing some simple lines and shapes.

So, grab your beret, your smock, and your easel, and prepare to have some fun.

Graphics On LineOne

By tradition, the first text-based program written by programmers learning any language is the "Hello World" application that simply prints the aforementioned words on the computer display. When programmers made the transition from text-based to graphic-based programs, the "Hello World" tradition came along. The only problem with this particular tradition is that it's *booorrrring*. Merely drawing a bunch of random lines would be more interesting. So, with the intent of being *marginally* more interesting, we'll do that!

The LineOne Project

The LineOne program is a dialog-based application that draws 50 randomly sized lines on screen. Despite its simplicity, the LineOne program introduces a host of fundamental concepts that you'll have to master before going on to more complex graphical applications. If it helps, just think of LineOne as "Computer

Painting 100." To pass the class, you'll have to correctly answer these questions:

- What is a *device context*, and what is it used for?
- What is the **WM_PAINT** message, and how do you handle it?
- What functions do you use to draw simple lines on your display?

Building The Project Skeleton

To start the LineOne project, use the AppWizard to create your program skeleton. Follow these steps:

1. Use File|Close Workspace to close any projects that are open. Click on Yes when asked if you want to close all document windows.
2. Select File|New to open the New dialog box. Select the Projects tab from the available pages, then choose MFC AppWizard (exe) from the list of project types. Name your project LineOne. Your screen should look like that shown in Figure 7.1.
3. Click on OK to start AppWizard. In the MFC AppWizard - Step 1 dialog box, choose Dialog-based Application and click on Next.

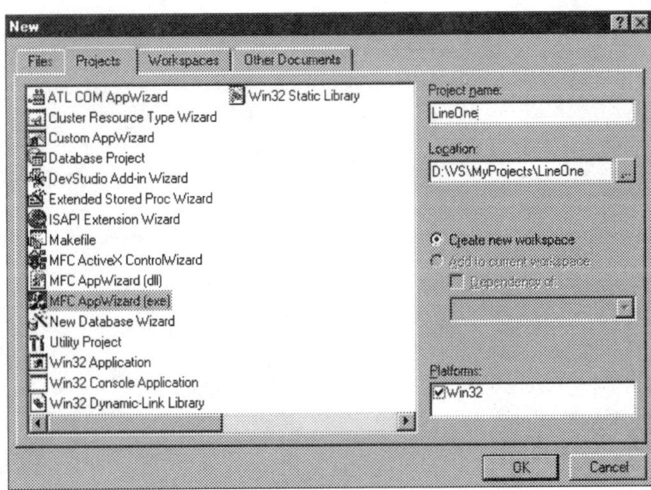

Figure 7.1
Starting the new LineOne application.

4. In the MFC AppWizard - Step 2 dialog box, clear all the checkboxes. Leave LineOne as the title. Your dialog box should look like that shown in Figure 7.2. Now, click on Finish. When the New Project Information dialog opens, click on OK.
5. In the Dialog Editor, which launches automatically, select and delete the TODO: label, as well as the OK and Cancel buttons. Your dialog box should contain no controls, and your screen should look like the one shown in Figure 7.3.
6. Compile and run your application to ensure that this "skeleton" works. When you've explored its presently very limited capabilities, close it by clicking on the Close box in the title bar.

Adding Some Lines

Because you've seen the operation of the basic LineOne application, you might find it hard to believe that it already contains some painting code. After all, it looks—and behaves—like a plain, gray canvas. But that plain, gray, canvas is where you're going to draw your lines.

To add your own drawings to LineOne, follow these steps:

1. Select the ClassView pane in the Project Workspace window. Expand the **CLineOneDlg** class and double-click on the

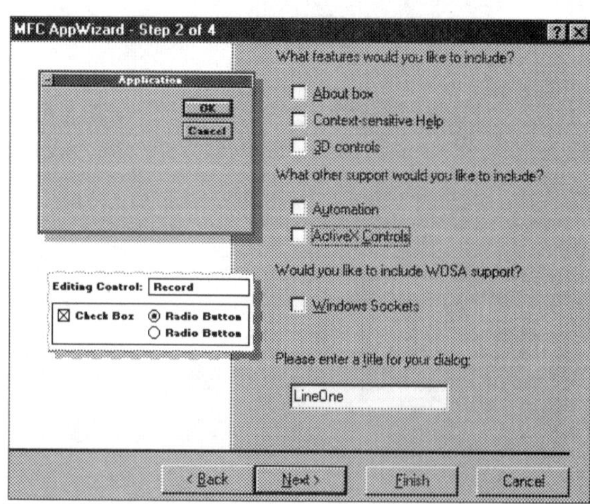

Figure 7.2
MFC AppWizard Step 2 options.

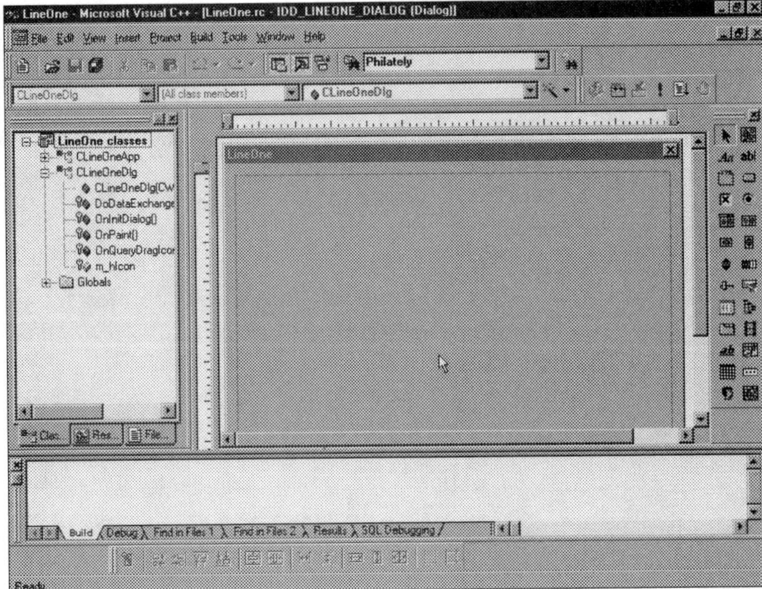

Figure 7.3
Deleting unnecessary dialog box controls.

OnPaint() method you find there. This is where you'll put your line-drawing code.

2. Notice that the **OnPaint()** method already contains quite a bit of code. If you read the comments inserted by AppWizard, you'll see that this code merely draws the application icon when you minimize the application. Because your application has no Minimize button, the code it contains is superfluous. Delete the **OnPaint()** code and replace it with the code shown in Listing 7.1.

Listing 7.1 The CLineOneDlg::OnPaint() member function.

```
void CLineOneDlg::OnPaint()
{
    // 1. Create a device context for the screen
    CPaintDC dc(this);

    // 2. Measure the client area
    CRect rect;
    GetClientRect(&rect);

    // 3. Draw 50 lines
    for (int line = 0; line < 50; line++)
    {
        // 4. Position the start of the line
```

```
        dc.MoveTo(rand() % rect.right, rand() %
            rect.bottom);

        // 5. Draw to the endpoint
        dc.LineTo(rand() % rect.right, rand() %
        rect.bottom);
    }
}
```

3. Compile and run your application. Voilà! You have art! Your results should appear something like those shown in Figure 7.4.

A Quick Peek Inside LineOne

There's not much code in the LineOne program. Of course, if you don't know what the code means, or why it's there, the fact that it consists of only five or six lines is cold comfort indeed—the most intractable riddles are often the shortest.

Fortunately, in this case, things aren't so bleak. Just as the discovery of the Rosetta Stone unlocked the meaning of the ancient Egyptian hieroglyphics, the LineOne **OnPaint()** function unlocks the secrets of Windows Graphical Device Interface, or GDI. Once you understand how the GDI works, the rest is just simple "translation."

To help you get started, we'll divide the explanation into two parts. First, we'll go through each line in the **OnPaint()** function,

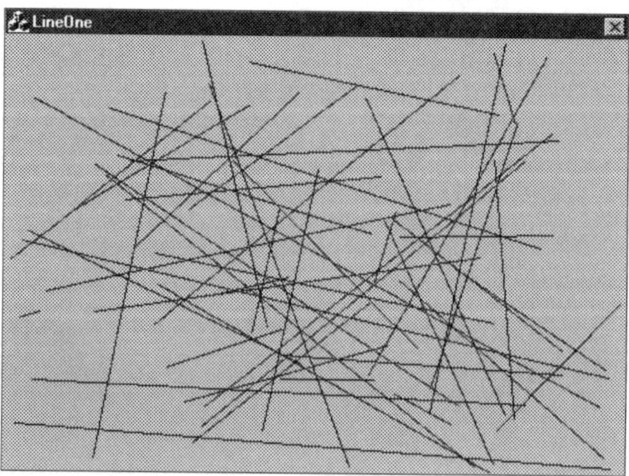

Figure 7.4
Running the LineOne application.

giving a sentence or two of explanation. Then, in the next chapter, you'll embark on a more in-depth exploration of the GDI.

What Is OnPaint()?

In Windows, every window is divided into two parts: the non-client area (which includes the title bar and window border) and the client area (the area "inside the lines," so to speak). You can see this illustrated in Figure 7.5.

Windows draws the non-client area—you don't have to do anything special. On the other hand, *you* are responsible for painting the client area. Whenever Windows wants to paint a window's client area, Windows sends the window a **WM_PAINT** message. To handle that message, you'll normally write an **OnPaint()** member function.

Windows sends a **WM_PAINT** message when a window is first displayed; it also sends a **WM_PAINT** message when a portion of a window's client area is uncovered after having been obscured by another window. In either case, when a window receives a **WM_PAINT** message, it should be prepared to repaint its client area.

As you can imagine, the code you write to display a GIF file is quite a bit different than the code you write to display a bar chart. Despite those differences, most of the code in **OnPaint()** breaks down into these three tasks:

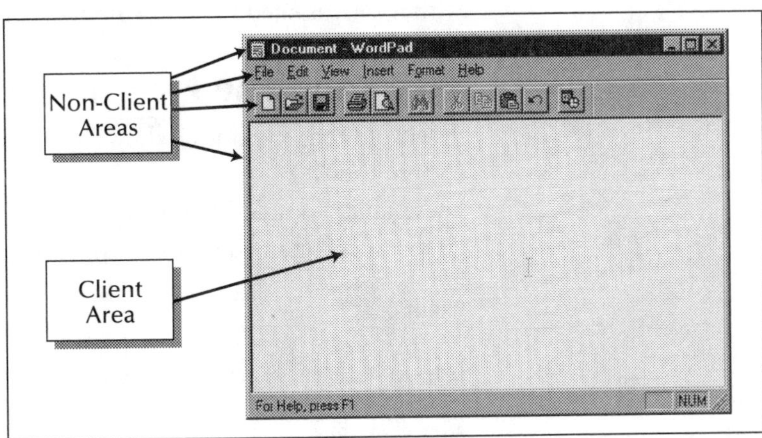

Figure 7.5
The client and non-client areas of a window.

1. Obtain a canvas or painting surface. In Windows, the painting surface you'll use is called a *device context*.
2. Set up your environment. This includes gathering all the pens and brushes you'll need, as well as measuring your work surface so you can properly align the painting on the surface.
3. Paint the window by using the functions available in the Windows graphics library, GDI.

Let's look at LineOne and see if you can identify each of these steps.

Obtaining A Canvas

Just as in real life, if you're going to paint, you need something to paint on. The Windows equivalent of the real-life painter's canvas is the *device context*. You must obtain a device context before producing *any* output in Windows.

The LineOne **OnPaint()** function uses the **CPaintDC** class to construct a device context object named **dc**. The argument passed to the **CPaintDC** constructor is a pointer to the window you want to paint. Because LineOne paints its main window, it passes **this**.

```
// Create a device context for the screen
CPaintDC dc(this);
```

As you'll see later, the **CPaintDC** class is just one of several classes you can use to create a device context. The **CPaintDC** class is used *only* in the **OnPaint()** method, and it provides you with a canvas sized to your window's client area.

Preparing The Environment

To ensure that the lines it draws appear inside the client area (where they'll be visible), the LineOne program must measure its client area. To hold the dimensions of the client area, it creates an instance—named **rect**—of the **CRect** class:

```
CRect rect;
```

It then calls the function **GetClientRect()**:

```
GetClientRect(&rect);
```

The **GetClientRect()** function fills **rect** with the dimensions of the client area, storing them in the public data members **top**, **left**, **bottom**, and **right**.

Painting The Lines

Because the LineOne program draws 50 lines, it requires a loop in its **OnPaint()** function. Each iteration of the loop draws a new line.

The Windows line-drawing functions draw from the current position of the GDI "pen" to a specified position. Therefore, drawing a line in Windows is a two-step process. First, you call the **MoveTo()** function to move the pen to the place where you want to start drawing. The LineOne program uses **MoveTo()** like this:

```
// Start the line at a random location
dc.MoveTo(rand() % rect.right, rand() % rect.bottom);
```

LineOne uses the **rand()** function and the values of the fields **rect.right** and **rect.bottom** to ensure that each line starts somewhere in the window's client area.

In the second step of the two-step process of drawing a line, you call the device context member function **LineTo()**. When you call **LineTo()**, you pass the ending position of the line. **LineTo()** draws a line between the current pen position and the new ending position you specify. As a side effect, this ending position becomes the new current pen position.

Like **MoveTo()**, the **LineTo()** function uses **rand()** to generate a random ending point that falls within the client area. Here's the line-drawing step:

```
// Draw to a second random location
dc.LineTo(rand() % rect.right, rand() % rect.bottom);
```

Because the **LineTo()** function updates the current pen position, you don't really need to call **MoveTo()** before calling **LineTo()**. Each time you create a new device context, the default current pen position is set to 0,0—located in the upper-left corner of the client area. If you comment out the **MoveTo()** line in the

LineOne application, each new line will begin where the previous line left off, as you can see in Figure 7.6.

Inclusive/Exclusive, Or, What Happened To The Last Pixel?

*Beginning Windows programmers are often surprised and frustrated to find that a line drawn from 0,0 to 100,100, doesn't paint the pixel located at 100,100. When drawing lines, Windows uses a method called inclusive/exclusive—it includes the starting position in the area to be painted, but excludes the ending position. Because the **LineTo()** function resets the device context's current pen position, excluding the ending position ensures that a series of **LineTo()** calls paints each pixel only once.*

The Paradox On LineTwo

Before we leave line drawing, let's take a look at another short example program that uses repeated **LineTo()** calls without any intervening **MoveTo()** calls. The LineTwo application works much like LineOne—but rather than draw 50 random lines, it draws a series of diamonds, each one slightly offset and twisted from the one before. The result is definitely "Escher-esq."

Building LineTwo

The instructions for building LineTwo are very similar to those you followed to build LineOne:

1. Use the MFC AppWizard to create a new application named LineTwo.
2. Select Dialog Based Application from the MFC AppWizard Step 1 dialog box and click on Next.
3. Clear all the checkboxes in the MFC AppWizard Step 2 dialog box, then click on Finish. Click on OK when the New Project Information window appears.
4. Remove all the controls from the main dialog window.
5. Open the Dialog Properties dialog box by right-clicking on the main dialog box in the Dialog Editor. Select the Styles

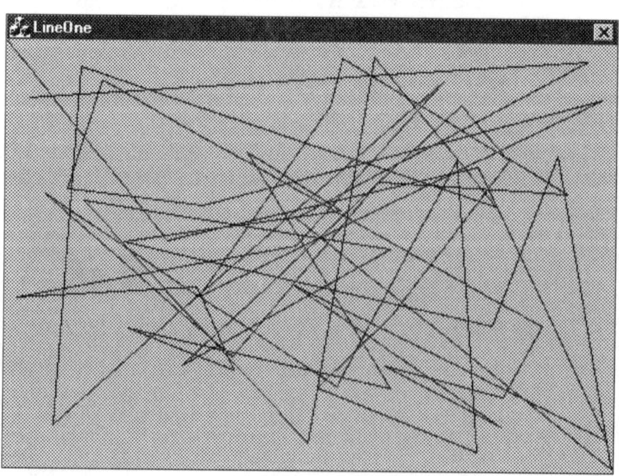

Figure 7.6
Running LineOne without **MoveTo()**.

tab, then select Resizing from the Border drop-down list. You can see this step illustrated in Figure 7.7.

6. Select the ClassView pane in the Project Workspace window. Expand the **CLineTwoDlg** class and double-click on the **OnPaint()** function. Replace the code you find there with the highlighted code shown in Listing 7.2.

Listing 7.2 The CLineTwoDlg::OnPaint() member function.

```
void CLineTwoDlg::OnPaint()
{
    // Drawing lines using LineTo
    // 1. Get client area device context
    CPaintDC dc(this);

    // 2. Measure the client area
    CRect rect;
    GetClientRect(&rect);

    // 3. Start drawing at the top-center
    dc.MoveTo(rect.right / 2, 0);

    // 4. Draw 50 diamonds, offsetting each one
    for(int lines = 0; lines < 50; lines++)
    {
        dc.LineTo(rect.right - lines,     rect.bottom / 2
           + lines);
        dc.LineTo(rect.right / 2 - lines, rect.bottom -
           lines);
        dc.LineTo(lines,                  rect.bottom / 2
           - lines);
        dc.LineTo(rect.right / 2 + lines, lines);
    }
}
```

7. Compile and run your application. You can see the results in Figure 7.8.

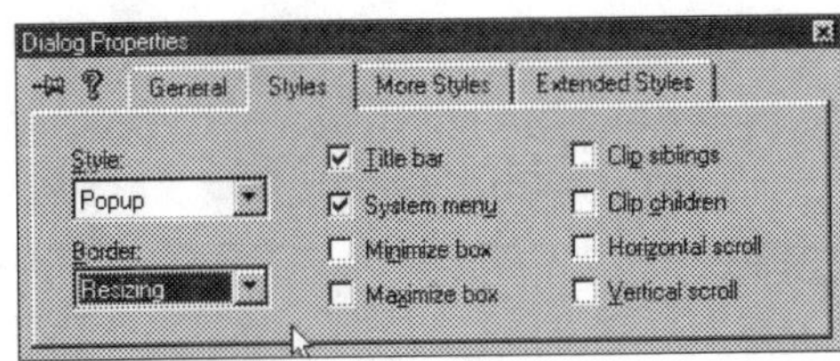

Figure 7.7
Setting the LineTwo dialog box properties.

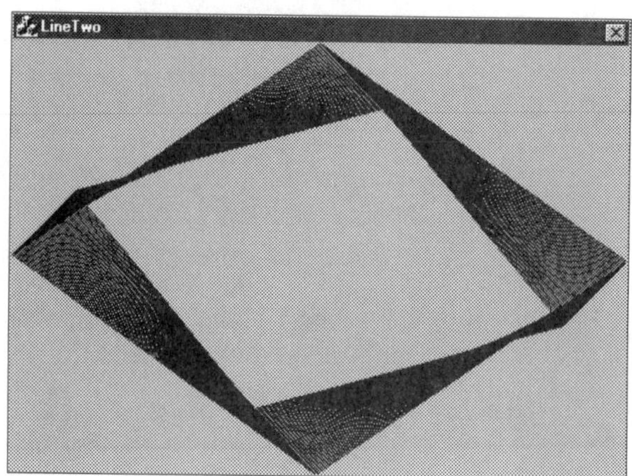

Figure 7.8
Running the LineTwo application.

How LineTwo Works

As in LineOne, all the action in LineTwo occurs in its **OnPaint()** method. LineOne used the client area window dimensions (stored in the **CRect** object **rect**) to ensure that every line fell inside the client area. LineTwo uses the same dimensions to calculate the new ending position for each set of four lines making up one diamond.

Here's how it works:

- First (in Step 3 of Listing 7.2), LineTwo moves the current pen position to the center of the top row. The center is calculated as **rect.right / 2**, and the top row is 0. These values are passed to the **MoveTo()** function.
- Next, LineTwo employs the same loop used in LineOne. The loop executes 50 times, with the local variable **lines** taking on the values from 0 to 49.
- The loop contains four **LineTo()** calls. The first draws from top-center to right-center, the second draws from right-center to bottom-center, the third goes from bottom-center to left-center, and the last returns to top-center.
- Each time through the loop, the ending point of each line shifts clockwise by the amount stored in the variable **lines**. The first time through the loop, **lines** contains 0, so each line ends in the middle—there's no offset. The second time through (and each subsequent time), each end-point shifts. For instance, the

diamond's right endpoint moves left one pixel and down one pixel, by the time LineTwo reaches the line of code that reads

```
dc.LineTo(rect.right - lines, rect.bottom / 2 +
  lines);
```

The same kind of transformation occurs on each of the remaining endpoints.

How LineTwo Doesn't Work

Now, it's time to try a little experiment. When you built LineTwo, you changed the dialog border style to Resizing—so, let's see what happens when you actually resize the program window. To find out, move the dialog box to the screen's upper-left corner, and then pull down the right corner of the dialog box until it almost fills the screen. When you let go of the border, the LineTwo **OnPaint()** function is called, and it handily repaints the dialog box, as you can see in Figure 7.9.

Hmmm. That doesn't look too good does it? Instead of drawing the entire window, your **OnPaint()** method repainted only the *new* areas—even though **OnPaint()** repainted every line. In

Figure 7.9
Resizing the LineTwo application.

Chapter 8, we'll explain in a little more depth exactly how and why this occurs. Here, we'll give you the short and sweet version.

Your **OnPaint()** method is called *only* by Windows, and only when Windows thinks that part of your window needs to be repainted. When you create a **CPaintDC** object in your **OnPaint()** handler—the only place you can use a **CPaintDC** object, remember—Windows obligingly gives you a *clipped* device context.

The clipped device context allows you to paint only the portion of your window that Windows feels needs to be updated. It's as if Windows hands you a canvas, but first places a stencil over it. No matter where you apply paint, it will reach the canvas only in the regions with holes.

Obviously, Windows' behavior isn't appropriate for this application. Is there a way to tell Windows you want to repaint the *whole* window? Yes there is—simply call the **CWnd::Invalidate()** function. It tells Windows that the whole window needs to be repainted, not simply the newly exposed portion.

Because the LineTwo **OnPaint()** function calculates its lines based on the size of its window, it needs to completely redraw the screen whenever the window size changes. Let's make the necessary changes to LineTwo now.

Adding A Windows Message Handler With ClassWizard

Adding the painting code to LineOne and LineTwo was easy, because the **OnPaint()** method already existed—all you did was add new code. However, if you open the LineTwo project and browse through the ClassView pane in the Project Workspace window, you won't find any methods that handle resizing. You'll have to add your own.

When you resize a window, Windows sends a **WM_SIZE** message to notify the window of its new size. (This happens after you're finished resizing, not continuously.) To handle the **WM_SIZE** message, you'll add a Windows message handler, using ClassWizard. Here's how you do it:

1. Open the LineTwo project and select the ClassView pane in the Project Workspace window. Locate the **CLineTwoDlg** class and right-click on the class name.
2. From the context menu that appears, select Add Windows Message Handler.
3. A dialog box with the ponderous title New Windows Message And Event Handlers For Class CLineTwoDlg" will open. From the New Windows Messages/Events list box, select **WM_SIZE,** then click on Add And Edit. (You can see this dialog box in Figure 7.10.)
4. Add the highlighted code to the new **OnSize()** member function shown in Listing 7.3, then recompile. When you run your program, you'll see that it now correctly repaints each time you resize the main window.

Listing 7.3 The CLineTwoDlg::OnSize() member function.

```
void CLineTwoDlg::OnSize(UINT nType, int cx, int cy)
{
    CDialog::OnSize(nType, cx, cy);

    // TODO: Add your message handler code here
    Invalidate();
}
```

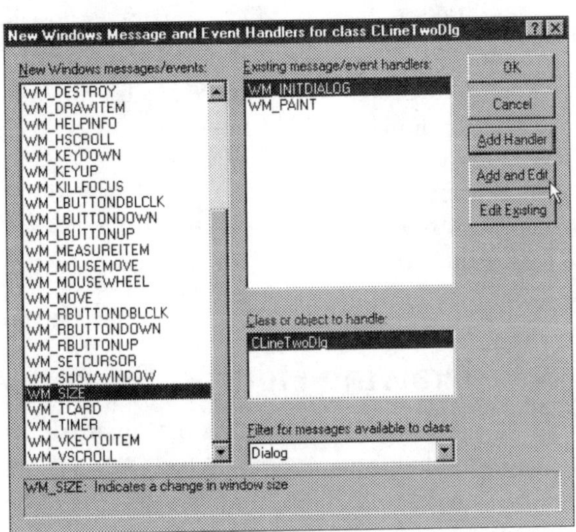

Figure 7.10
The New Windows Message And Event Handlers dialog box.

Windows Figure Drawing

Now that you know how to draw basic lines, let's expand your repertoire by learning how to draw closed figures—simple shapes like rectangles, circles, ellipses, and polygons.

Closed figures differ from lines in two ways:

- Closed figures use a drawing pen, just as lines do, but they also use a "brush" to fill the interior of the shape with color. Later in this chapter, you'll see how to change the built-in pen and brush used to draw lines and shapes.
- Most closed figures are drawn using an imaginary rectangle called a *bounding box*.

Let's start by looking at how a bounding box works. To draw a rectangle, for instance, you use the device context **Rectangle()** function like this:

```
CPaintDC dc(this); // Get a device context
dc.Rectangle(0, 0, 50, 50);
```

The four arguments passed to the **Rectangle()** function represent the coordinates of the upper-left and lower-right corners of the bounding box. When the rectangle is drawn, the current pen is used to draw four lines starting at position 0,0 and going up to—but not including—row 50 and column 50. (Windows uses the same inclusive/exclusive philosophy for drawing closed figures as for drawing simple lines.)

The area enclosed by these lines is filled with the device context's current brush. By default, Windows uses a 1-pixel-wide pen to draw the figure outline and a solid white brush to fill the interior of your shapes.

Drawing Figures: SquaresAndCircles

Let's start our exploration of figure drawing by drawing some random squares and circles. (Actually, you'll be drawing rectangles and ellipses, but SquaresAndCircles sounds better as a program name.) You'll follow the same basic pattern used in LineOne, which should be familiar by now:

- Get a device context using the **CPaintDC** class.
- Measure the client area.
- Use a loop to draw 50 randomly sized rectangles and ellipses. SquaresAndCircles will use the same logic employed by LineOne to ensure that each figure falls completely inside the window's client area.

Here are the step-by-step instructions:

1. Create a dialog-based application named SquaresAndCircles using the AppWizard, just as you did for LineOne. Don't forget to uncheck all the options in the MFC AppWizard Step 2 dialog box.
2. Remove all the controls from the main dialog box in the Dialog Editor. Don't bother changing the style of the dialog border to Resizing.
3. Locate the **CSquaresAndCirclesDlg::OnPaint()** member function in the Project Workspace ClassView window.

Read The Documentation, But Keep Your Powder Dry

Despite the massive amount of documentation available on the Windows API and MFC, you can't always rely on accurate or complete information. **The CDC::Rectangle()** function—along with all the other graphics functions that use a bounding box—is a case in point.

The documentation that comes with Visual C++ contains the following prototype for the **Rectangle()** function:

```
BOOL Rectangle( int x1, int y1, int x2, int y2 );
```

The documentation identifies x1, y1 as the location of the upper-left corner, and x2, y2 as the location of the lower-right corner. In fact, however, the x1,y1 coordinates don't have to represent the upper-left corner of your rectangle—the point can just as easily be the lower-right, lower-left, or upper-right corner. You simply pass two sets of x,y coordinates, and MFC draws a rectangle connecting them. You don't have to spend time making sure that the x1,y1 point is to the left and above x2,y2, as you would if x1,y1 was *really* the upper-left corner.

The moral of this is that you should read the documentation, but shouldn't rely on it. Write a program and see what MFC actually does.

Double-click to open the function, then replace the existing code with that shown in Listing 7.4.

Listing 7.4 The CSquaresAndCirclesDlg::OnPaint() member function.

```
void CSquaresAndCirclesDlg::OnPaint()
{
    // Drawing figures using Rectangle() and Ellipse()
    // 1. Get client area device context
    CPaintDC dc(this);

    // 2. Measure the client area
    CRect rect;
    GetClientRect(&rect);

    // 3. Draw 50 rectangles and 50 ellipses
    int middle = rect.right / 2;
    for(int shapes = 0; shapes < 50; shapes++)
    {
        dc.Rectangle(rand() % middle, rand() %
                     rect.bottom,
                     rand() % middle, rand() %
                     rect.bottom);

        dc.Ellipse(middle + rand() % middle, rand() %
                     rect.bottom,
                   middle + rand() % middle, rand() %
                     rect.bottom);
    }
}
```

4. Compile and run your program. Figure 7.11 shows the SquaresAndCircles program running.

Inside SquaresAndCircles

The SquaresAndCircles program isn't much different from LineOne. The main differences (highlighted in Listing 7.4) are these:

- Rather than mingle the rectangles and ellipses, the program draws the rectangles on the left and the ellipses on the right. To aid in this calculation, you create a local variable called **middle** and initialize it with the value **rect.right / 2**.
- On each iteration, the loop draws one rectangle and one ellipse. Like LineOne, SquaresAndCircles uses random numbers to

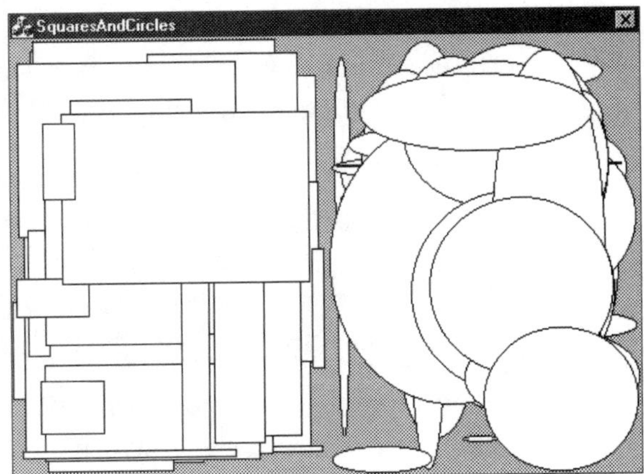

Figure 7.11
Running the SquaresAndCircles program.

calculate the bounds of the closed figure. When the program calls **Rectangle()**, both horizontal arguments (**x1** and **x2**) are calculated modulus **middle**, to ensure that they fit in the left half of the dialog box. When the program calls **Ellipse()**, the horizontal arguments are also calculated modulus **middle**, but the resulting value is added to **middle** to ensure that each ellipse is drawn in the right half of the dialog box.

Drawing Tools

You'll notice that all the lines are visible in LineOne (Figure 7.4), but many of the figures aren't visible in SquaresAndCircles (Figure 7.11). Instead, the figures on top obscure those beneath them, because of the opaque white color that fills each figure. Windows calls the color used to draw a line or outline a figure a *pen*. The color used to fill a figure or paint the background of a window is called a *brush*. Windows provides several built-in pens and brushes called *stock objects*; let's look at how to use them. (Windows also allows you to define custom brushes and pens—we'll look at those in Chapter 8.)

Stock Pens And Brushes

Windows supplies three built-in pens that you can use to draw lines or outline figures. Each of the stock pens is 1 pixel wide.

The default pen—which you've been using so far—is called **BLACK_PEN**. If you'd rather draw white lines, you can use

WHITE_PEN. The third pen, **NULL_PEN** (which draws nothing), might seem puzzling at first—after all, why would you go to all the trouble of drawing invisible lines?

NULL_PEN may not be much good for drawing lines, but its real utility comes into play when you want to draw solid, filled figures. Every time you use the **Rectangle()** or **Ellipse()** function, it draws a filled figure with an outline. If you want the figure without the outline surrounding it, you use the built-in **NULL_PEN**.

In addition to the three stock pens, Windows provides seven stock brushes. Their names—which are pretty self explanatory—are **BLACK_BRUSH, DKGRAY_BRUSH, GRAY_BRUSH, HOLLOW_BRUSH, LTGRAY_BRUSH, NULL_BRUSH,** and **WHITE_BRUSH**.

Both **NULL_BRUSH** and **HOLLOW_BRUSH** do essentially the same thing: They create a brush that does nothing. You use these brushes when you want to draw *unfilled* figures.

Using Stock Pens And Brushes

Using a stock pen or brush is simple. When you draw a line or shape, you use a member function of the device context class, such as **LineTo()** or **Rectangle()**. You can't draw a line or rectangle without first obtaining a device context object.

Your device context object then uses its current pen and brush to draw your line or shape. To draw with a different pen or brush, you simply tell the device context which pen or brush you desire, by calling the device context's **SelectStockObject()** function.

For instance, here's how you instruct a device context to paint black rectangles outlined in white:

```
CPaintDC dc(this);
dc.SelectStockObject(WHITE_PEN);
dc.SelectStockObject(BLACK_BRUSH);
// Draw white-rimmed, black-filled shapes here
```

To see how this works, open the SquaresAndCircles program and make the changes highlighted in Listing 7.5. Before drawing each rectangle, the code sets the device context brush to **HOLLOW_BRUSH**; before drawing each ellipse, the code sets the brush to **DKGRAY_BRUSH**. All shapes are drawn using the stock pen, **WHITE_PEN**. You can see the result in Figure 7.12.

Listing 7.5 Adding stock pens and brushes to the CSquaresAndCirclesDlg::OnPaint() member function.

```
void CSquaresAndCirclesDlg::OnPaint()
{
    // Drawing figures using Rectangle() and Ellipse()
    // 1. Get client area device context
    CPaintDC dc(this);

    // 2. Measure the client area
    CRect rect;
    GetClientRect(&rect);

    // 3. Draw 50 rectangles and 50 ellipses
    int middle = rect.right / 2;
    dc.SelectStockObject(WHITE_PEN);
    for(int shapes = 0; shapes < 50; shapes++)
    {
        dc.SelectStockObject(HOLLOW_BRUSH);
        dc.Rectangle(rand() % middle, rand() %
                      rect.bottom,
                     rand() % middle, rand() %
                      rect.bottom);

        dc.SelectStockObject(DKGRAY_BRUSH);
        dc.Ellipse(middle + rand() % middle, rand() %
                     rect.bottom,
                   middle + rand() % middle, rand() %
                     rect.bottom);
    }
}
```

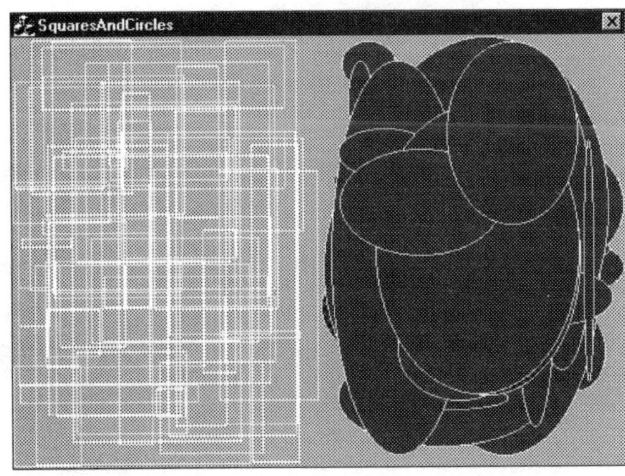

Figure 7.12 Running the SquaresAndCircles program using stock pens and brushes.

Continuous Drawing

All of the programs we've looked at in this chapter do their painting in the **OnPaint()** method. Each program also draws a fixed number of lines or figures. For most programs, that's perfectly okay. However, in screen savers and other programs that include animation, you want to draw continuously.

There are several ways to implement continuous drawing. One of the easiest is to simply write the statement

```
Invalidate(FALSE);
```

as the last line in your **OnPaint()** method. Add this statement to the end of SquaresAndCircles, for instance, to see how it works.

You used the **CWnd::Invalidate()** method when you added resizing to the LineTwo application. If you look up the documentation for **Invalidate()**, you'll see that it takes a single **BOOL** argument called **bErase**. (In the Windows API, **BOOL** is a **typedef** for **int**, used because Windows predates the C++ built-in **bool** data type.) The argument **bErase** specifies whether the background should be automatically erased before drawing the new image. MFC gives the argument the default value **TRUE**, which is why you can call it without providing an argument. When you're doing continuous drawing, however, you don't want the background erased each time, so you call **Invalidate()** with **FALSE**.

If you're an experienced C or C++ programmer, sticking an **Invalidate()** at the end of your **OnPaint()** method probably makes you a little nervous. After all, it does seem perilously close to recursively calling the **OnPaint()** method. Perhaps, you think, it would be better to use an endless loop. If you harbor such thoughts, congratulations! You've just pinpointed the difference between a traditional, function-call-based application and an event-driven, message-passing system.

When you call the **Invalidate()** function, you don't (even indirectly) call the **OnPaint()** method. Instead, you tell Windows that you want a window repainted. It's up to Windows, not you, to decide when the repainting occurs.

If you try to subvert the way that Windows works by adding your own endless loop inside the paint method, you'll find yourself with a locked-up computer, because Windows won't ever get a chance to handle other messages. Windows gives a very low processing priority to the **WM_PAINT** messages produced by a call to **Invalidate()**, meaning that Windows will process any other pending messages before returning to repaint your window.

Meet Windows Timers

You'll usually draw continuously by using a Windows timer. If you use the **Invalidate()** method, you have no way to control how often Windows repaints your display. However, if you use a timer, you can repaint your display every second or every minute, if you choose. With a timer, you can even paint outside of the **OnPaint()** method, leaving it free for other uses.

To use a timer in Windows, you have to know how to:

- Create a timer.
- Destroy a timer.
- Respond to a timer message.

Creating A Timer

To create a timer, you use the **CWnd** member function **SetTimer()**, which has three arguments:

- *The timer ID*—An integer argument that differentiates one timer instance from another when responding to their messages. You can use any positive number you want.
- *The timer interval*—The amount of time you want to wait between timer messages, expressed in milliseconds. If you use 1000 for the second argument, your timer will "go off" roughly every second. Windows timers have a maximum resolution (that is, a minimum interval) of 55 milliseconds, which means you can, at best, get about 18 hits per second.
- *The timer callback function*—The address of a special *callback function* to which you want timer messages sent. If you pass **NULL**, as you'll do here, Windows will notify you with a **WM_TIMER** message, instead. This is the easy way out,

because you can send the **WM_TIMER** message to a regular Windows message-handling function.

Because **SetTimer()** begins sending messages immediately, you should use **SetTimer()** only after your main window has been created. In dialog-based applications, the **OnInitDialog()** function is the perfect place to create a timer. If it's successful, the **SetTimer()** method returns the same timer ID you passed as an argument. Timers are a limited resource, and so it is possible—but unlikely—for there to be no more timers available. If **SetTimer()** is unable to create a timer, it returns 0.

Destroying A Timer

When you're finished with a timer, you should call the **CWnd** member function **KillTimer()**, passing the timer ID you used when you constructed the timer. Timers are a limited global resource, and calling **KillTimer()** when you're finished using a timer is simply common courtesy.

You should call **KillTimer()** before your window is destroyed. For dialog-based applications, AppWizard doesn't generate a suitable function in which to place your **KillTimer()** call. This oversight is easily remedied, however, by using ClassWizard to add a Windows message-handler function for the **WM_DESTROY** message and putting your call to **KillTimer()** there.

Responding To Timer Messages

Windows uses its system clock to "count down" the timer interval value you pass to the **SetTimer()** function. When the interval expires, Windows places a **WM_TIMER** message in the program's event queue and resets the timer value. If the timer interval expires again before the program handles the last message, Windows doesn't generate another **WM_TIMER** message. (What actually happens is a little more complex, but the final result is the same.)

To process a timer message, you simply use ClassWizard to write a Windows message-handler function—normally named **OnTimer()**—for the **WM_TIMER** message. If you plan to paint on the display in your **OnTimer()** function, you can use almost the same code you wrote for **OnPaint()**. Because you're painting outside the **OnPaint()** method, you'll need to use a **CClientDC** object as your device context instead of a **CPaintDC**.

PaintItGray

Before we go on to the next chapter, let's write an application that uses a timer to continuously update the screen with an interesting pattern. The algorithm used is based loosely on Doug Cooper's Pascal TVCure program. It uses timers, a new form of device context, and even a new painting mode. In homage to the old Rolling Stones song, we'll call the program PaintItGray. (The authors of this book are both middle-aged.)

To start the PaintItGray application, create a dialog-based application using the same options you used for the previous programs in this chapter. Once you've removed the unneeded controls from the main window, follow these instructions to finish the application:

1. Use ClassWizard to add to the **CPaintItGrayDlg** class a new Windows message-handler function to handle **WM_TIMER** messages. Add the code highlighted in Listing 7.6 to the **OnTimer()** function produced by ClassWizard.

Listing 7.6 The CPaintItGrayDlg::OnTimer() member function.

```
void CPaintItGrayDlg::OnTimer(UINT nIDEvent)
{
    // TODO: Add your message handler code here and/or
    // call default
    CClientDC dc(this);

    CRect rect;
    GetClientRect(&rect);

    dc.SetROP2(R2_XORPEN);
    dc.SelectStockObject(WHITE_PEN);

    for(int row = rect.bottom - m_boxes; row > m_boxes;
        row--)
    {
        dc.MoveTo(m_boxes, row);
```

```
        dc.LineTo(rect.right - m_boxes, rect.bottom -
          row);
    }
    for(int col = m_boxes; col < rect.right - m_boxes;
          col++)
    {
        dc.MoveTo(col, m_boxes);
        dc.LineTo(rect.right - col, rect.bottom -
          m_boxes);
    }

    m_boxes++;
    m_boxes %= 5;
}
```

2. Open the **OnInitDialog()** method and create a new timer. Assign your timer the ID 1 and an interval of 120. Pass **NULL** for the timer callback procedure. Listing 7.7 shows the modified **OnInitDialog()** method with the new line highlighted.

Listing 7.7 The CPaintItGrayDlg::OnInitDialog() member function.

```
BOOL CPaintItGrayDlg::OnInitDialog()
{
    CDialog::OnInitDialog();

    // Set the icon for this dialog.  The framework does
    // this automatically
    // when the application's main window is not a
    // dialog
    SetIcon(m_hIcon, TRUE);         // Set big icon
    SetIcon(m_hIcon, FALSE);        // Set small icon

    // TODO: Add extra initialization here
    SetTimer(1, 120, NULL);
    return TRUE;  // return TRUE  unless you set the
                  // focus to a control
}
```

3. Using ClassWizard again, add another Windows message-handler function, this time for the **WM_DESTROY** message. In your **OnDestroy()** method, add the line necessary to kill your timer, as shown in Listing 7.8.

Listing 7.8 The CPaintItGrayDlg::OnDestroy() member function.

```
void CPaintItGrayDlg::OnDestroy()
{
    CDialog::OnDestroy();

    // TODO: Add your message handler code here
    KillTimer(1);
}
```

4. In the ClassView window, right-click on **CPaintItGrayDlg** and select Add Member Variable. In the dialog box that opens, create a variable named **m_boxes**. Make the variable type **int** and give it Private access.
5. In the ClassView window, double-click on the **CPaintItGrayDlg** constructor. Add a line initializing the new member variable, as shown by the highlighted line in Listing 7.9.

Listing 7.9 The CPaintItGrayDlg constructor.

```
CPaintItGrayDlg::CPaintItGrayDlg(CWnd* pParent /*=NULL*/)
    : CDialog(CPaintItGrayDlg::IDD, pParent)
{
    //{{AFX_DATA_INIT(CPaintItGrayDlg)
        // NOTE: the ClassWizard will add member
        // initialization here
    //}}AFX_DATA_INIT
    // Note that LoadIcon does not require a subsequent
    // DestroyIcon in Win32
    m_hIcon = AfxGetApp()->LoadIcon(IDR_MAINFRAME);
    m_boxes = 0;
}
```

6. Compile and run your application—try not to become too mesmerized. You can see the program running in Figure 7.13.

Onward And Upward

You've come a long way in this chapter—but, let's face it, there's still a long way to go. After all, the world isn't all shades of gray.

In Chapter 8, we'll take a little time to explore Windows' painting mechanism, the GDI, and the CDC device context classes in

Figure 7.13
Running the PaintItGray application.

more depth. Then, you'll learn how to create custom brushes and pens, and even paint in color. As promised, Chapter 8 will put the painting skills you've learned here to work creating some screen savers you can run from the Windows Control Panel.

Far out!

Chapter 8

Graphics And Text

Computer programs usually require both input and output. Input lets your users "talk" to your program; output lets your program talk back.

Back in the DOS age, your programs had to ask for input. For instance, you called a function like **getch()** to get input via the keyboard. In the Windows world, the situation is quite different. Your program no longer has to *ask* for input—instead, user input is *delivered* to your program, tied to specific events. Your users click on a button, press a key, or move the mouse. Each action generates an event, which Windows automatically sends to your program.

As you might expect, in the Windows world, output is also handled differently. In the DOS age, output came in two varieties: text and graphics. In text mode, you could use functions like **printf()** or **putch()** to place characters on screen. Your computer hardware was responsible for creating and displaying the actual letters on the screen or printer. In graphics mode, you could draw lines and shapes, as well as display text using different fonts. To use graphics mode under DOS, you'd use a graphics library containing functions like **putpixel()** and **drawline()**. However, DOS programmers would often bypass their general-purpose graphics library for performance reasons, writing code to directly manipulate the video adapter and monitor.

Under Windows, you no longer have to deal with text mode—all output is graphical. But, to produce graphical output, your application must use Windows' Graphical Device Interface (GDI) library; there's simply no other way to access the screen or printer.

Windows And GDI: Behind The Scenes

GDI is a *device-independent* graphics library. Under Windows, all output is graphical—you use the same library (GDI) whether you're directing output to the screen, a printer, a plotter, or some more exotic device. Every letter, every line, and every mark displayed by your program is funneled through the routines of the GDI library, which is responsible for ensuring that the output displays correctly. It doesn't matter whether you're using a 640×480 pixel VGA display or the latest high-resolution photo typesetter.

To make this flexibility possible, GDI uses three mechanisms:

- *Device context*—The device context (DC) is the *logical canvas* you'll use for Windows output. Rather than write directly to the screen or printer, you'll always use a device context. You'll learn more about DCs in the next section.
- *Device driver*—The DC (the logical output device) is connected to the physical output device via a Windows device driver. The device driver translates GDI commands into the physical instructions that the device executes to display your output. As this process implies, when you write your program, you don't need to know the ultimate output device. On the other hand, you may sometimes ask an output device to do something that it's not capable of—although your monitor can easily display a yellow circle, your black-and-white laser printer can't. The Windows device driver gracefully handles such requests by doing the best it can. For instance, if you ask your black-and-white laser printer to print color output, its device driver may print shades of gray or use some other pattern.
- *Mapping mode*—Physical output devices come in a variety of resolutions, from the 72 dpi (dots per inch) resolution of a standard CRT to the 4000 dpi resolution of a photo typesetter. Consequently, a device-independent graphics library must perform coordinate transformation. A 100-pixel square displayed on screen is slightly larger than an inch, but the same

square displayed on a photo typesetter appears infinitesimally small. GDI handles this problem by providing a variety of *logical mapping modes*. When producing graphical output, the programmer may specify the scale (pixels/inches/millimeters), as well as the coordinate origin and scaling direction. You'll learn to use mapping modes in Chapters 9 and 10.

In addition to these three features, GDI incorporates all the bells and whistles you'd expect from a full-featured graphics library—everything from primitive graphics functions like **SetPixel()** to complex bitmap- and color-management functions.

What Is A Device Context, And Why Do You Need One?

If you look back at the **OnPaint()** function in any of the programs you wrote in Chapter 7, you'll see that its first order of business is obtaining a device context. At its simplest, a DC is the "canvas" you use for output. However, the DC isn't simply a passive recipient of your artistic endeavors, but an active participant—a sort of co-artist.

When it comes to painting, the DC plays three distinct roles:

- It provides a logical connection to a physical device (via the device driver).
- It provides a collection of drawing tools and attributes.
- It acts as a "traffic cop" to ensure that your painting efforts stay "inside the lines."

Before we examine the DC classes themselves, let's take a quick look at each of these roles.

The Logical Connection

If you've programmed in C or C++ for any length of time, you've had to read and write disk files. In C, to open a file, you first create a file pointer:

```
FILE* fp;
```

Then, you connect that pointer to a specific file or device by using the **fopen()** function, like this:

```
fp = fopen("myfile.txt", "w");
```

To write a character—stored in the variable **ch**—to the file, you use the **fputc()** function:

```
fputc(ch, fp);
```

This code is fairly elementary and seems unremarkable simply because it's so familiar. However, in reality, it is *quite* remarkable. Think about these points—you can use a FILE * without knowing too many points:

- The different fields it points to. Instead, you simply use it as a *handle* to give you access to a particular output device.
- Anything about tracks and sectors, the physical arrangement your disk uses to store information.
- What kind of device is at the other end. For instance, output to a printer doesn't involve tracks and sectors at all. Instead, your character is simply printed.

In Windows, the role of the DC is similar to that of the **FILE ***. However, rather than provide you with a handle to a storage medium, the DC provides you with a handle to a particular output display device.

The Artistic Collection

When you use **fopen()** to connect a **FILE *** to a particular physical file, the fields of the **FILE** structure are initialized with information about the file. To access that information, you use functions from the standard I/O library—such as **ftell()**—that return the position of the current file pointer.

In a similar way, a DC specifies a collection of drawing tools, including a current pen to draw lines, a current brush to fill areas of the display, and a current font to display text. You can use any number of different pens, brushes, and fonts, but a DC can specify only one pen, brush, or font at a time.

In addition to these three drawing tools, every DC contains a collection of more than 20 attributes that affect the operation of the tools. These attributes include such features as the drawing background color, the background mode (opaque or transparent), the text alignment, the color used for text output, and the current mapping mode.

By making these attributes part of the DC, GDI makes the tools simpler to use. For instance, the GDI function **TextOut()**, which draws text, takes only three arguments: the text to display and the x, y coordinates where the text should appear. All the other attributes needed—the color of the text, the color of the background, the mapping of the x, y coordinates, and the font—are part of the DC. Without the GDI attributes, a simple function like **TextOut()** would require a much larger parameter list.

The Clipping Connection

The device context's last important role is that of traffic cop, mediating disputes among programs vying to use the same piece of screen real estate. Because Windows allows multiple programs to run at the same time, no program can be permitted unrestricted access to the entire display. You can imagine the mess that would ensue if you decided to draw an image at the same location where another application was producing its output.

To mediate among programs, GDI uses a strategy called *clipping*. When you obtain a DC, it contains a *clipping region*—a rectangle in which you're allowed free rein to draw and paint as you like. If your window is the active window, then the clipping region is usually the area inside your window's borders: the so-called *client area*. However, part of a window's client area may be obscured by another window that partially overlaps it. When this occurs, the clipping region and the client area aren't identical. In this case, the clipping region includes only the visible portion of the client area.

So, what happens if you paint outside the lines? Well, that's the really neat thing about clipping—nothing happens! Instead of giving you a slap on the wrist, Windows simply ignores your request. This occurs behind the scenes, so you don't have to worry about it. You simply draw as if the entire window were visible, and let Windows handle the rest.

Introducing The CDC Family

Now that you know what a device context is, how do you get one? In MFC, a DC is an instance of one of four children of the **CDC** class: **CPaintDC**, **CClientDC**, **CWindowDC**, and **CMetaFileDC** (see Figure 8.1). Although exceptions exist, most of your painting will involve the **CPaintDC** class or the **CClientDC** class. Either will let you paint anywhere inside the borders of a window.

To construct a **CPaintDC** object or **CClientDC** object, you call the class constructor, passing as an argument a pointer to the window on which you want to draw. The code is just like that you wrote throughout Chapter 7:

```
CPaintDC dc(this);
```

You can use the **CPaintDC** object (**dc**) to paint anywhere within the client area of the main window. However, you can't use it to paint locations outside the client area, such as the title bar or the window borders. When you use a **CPaintDC** or **CClientDC** object, the position 0,0 represents the upper-left corner of the client area, not the actual location on screen. If you want to paint the entire window, including the title bar and borders, you must create a **CWindowDC** rather than a **CPaintDC**. For a **CWindowDC**, the position 0,0 refers to the upper-left corner of the window, not the upper-left corner of the client area.

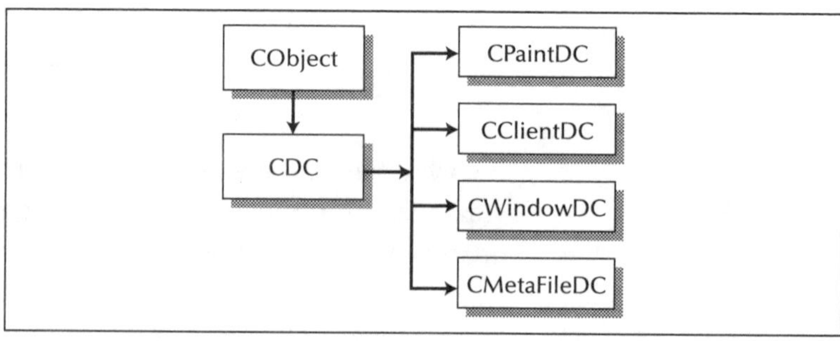

Figure 8.1
The Windows device context classes.

The WM_PAINT Message And The CPaintDC Class

Both **CPaintDC** and **CClientDC** construct a DC whose clipping region includes your window's client area. Although it may seem strange, be assured that there really is a purpose behind having two classes: You use **CPaintDC** only when responding to a **WM_PAINT** message. Typically, you'll do that in a method called **OnPaint()**.

Windows generates a **WM_PAINT** message whenever part of a window's client area needs to be redisplayed. This can occur when the window is restored after being minimized, or when another window that obscured part (or all) of the window's client area is closed or moved.

Rather than make you paint the entire client area, Windows keeps track of the portion that needs to be repainted, called the *invalid region*. To let Windows know that you've received the **WM_PAINT** message and responded appropriately, you must call the **CWnd** member functions **BeginPaint()** and **EndPaint()** within your painting function. If you don't do this, Windows believes that your window still has an invalid region and sends you **WM_PAINT** messages indefinitely.

Nevertheless, if you look closely at the **OnPaint()** functions in Chapter 7, you won't find calls to **BeginPaint()** or **EndPaint()**. The constructor for the **CPaintDC** class automatically calls **BeginPaint()**, and its destructor automatically calls **EndPaint()**. However, the **CClientDC** doesn't make these automatic calls, so you should never use a **CClientDC** object in a function designed to handle **WM_PAINT** messages. Conversely, you should use the **CPaintDC** class only in an **OnPaint()** function.

The GDI Drawing Toolbox

As you saw in Chapter 7, you don't have to use the default black pen or white brush every time you create a DC. Instead, you can use **GetStockObject()** to change, for example, to a **WHITE_PEN** or a **BLACK_BRUSH**. These are both built-in or default graphical drawing objects, meaning that Windows has already created them for your use. Unfortunately, the palette of built-in tools is rather sparse. For almost any serious work, you'll need to create your own brushes, pens, fonts, and other tools.

In MFC, the tools used for drawing on a DC are members of the **CGdiObject** class. As with the **CDC** class, you won't normally create **CGdiObject**s directly. Instead, you'll use one of the six subclasses of **CGdiObject** provided by MFC: **CBitmap**, **CBrush**, **CFont**, **CPalette**, **CPen**, or **CRgn** (see Figure 8.2). In this chapter, we'll take a closer look at **CBrush**, **CFont**, and **CPen**.

Let's start by looking at pens and colors.

CPen, Color And Other CDC Attributes

In Windows, the object responsible for drawing lines and curves is the GDI pen, represented in the Win32 API by the **HPEN** (*H*andle to a *PEN*) data type. In MFC, you don't have to work with pen handles (although you can if you like)—instead, you use the **CPen** class.

A GDI pen has three characteristics:

- *Style*—The kind of line that the pen will draw: solid, dashed, dotted, and so forth.
- *Width*—How wide the pen stroke will be. When you create a pen, you specify its width in logical units. Right now we're

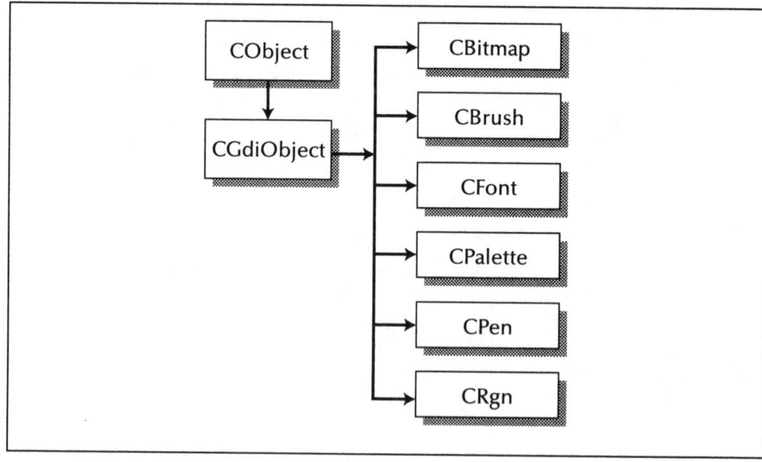

Figure 8.2
MFC's graphics drawing classes.

using pixels as our logical unit, but you'll soon learn how to work with other, more convenient, logical units.

- *Color*—The color of the line you draw.

Not all of these attributes are available in every context. For instance, *styled lines* (lines drawn using dashes, dots, and so on) work only when the line is one pixel wide. A second type of pen, called a *geometric pen*, allows finer control, but is more complex to create and use.

Creating Custom Pens

You can use three techniques to create a non-geometric custom pen using the **CPen** class.

First, you can use the three-argument constructor that allows you to pass arguments giving the pen style, width, and color. Here's an example that constructs a 10-unit-wide green pen (in a moment, you'll learn how to specify a pen's style and color):

```
CPen greenPen(PS_SOLID, 10, RGB(0, 255, 0));
```

This is the simplest method, but it suffers from a serious weakness: If the function fails—because Windows has run out of resources, for instance—the **CPen** constructor will throw an exception, causing your program to end (unless you use **try-catch** to handle the exception). To avoid this potential exception, Microsoft recommends that you use *two-step construction*.

Two-step construction—commonly used for all GDI drawing objects, not just pens—breaks construction into an object creation step and an object initialization step. To use two-step construction with the **CPen** class, first create a **CPen** object using the default constructor:

```
CPen greenPen;
```

Then, use the **CPen::CreatePen()** member function to initialize the attributes of the pen, like this:

```
greenPen.CreatePen(PS_SOLID, 10, RGB(0, 255, 0));
```

The default constructor is guaranteed to succeed, so you don't have to deal with a possible exception. The **CreatePen()** function simply returns **FALSE (0)** if it fails.

You can also construct a **CPen** by creating an instance of the **LOGPEN** structure, supplying values for each of the three relevant fields, and then using **CreatePenIndirect()** as follows:

```
LOGPEN lp;
lp.lopnStyle = PS_SOLID;
lp.lopnWidth = 10;
lp.lopnColor = RGB(0, 255, 0);
CPen greenPen;
greenPen.CreatePenIndirect(&lp);
```

This code is obviously a lot more work than simply using **CreatePen()**, but it makes sense if you need to create several pens with the same style and color but different widths. You have to call **CreatePenIndirect()** for each **CPen** object, but you can reuse the same **LOGPEN** structure repeatedly:

```
CPen pens[10];
lp.opnWidth = 1;
for (int i = 0; i < 10; i++)
{
    pens[i].CreatePenIndirect(&lp);
    lp.opnWidth++;
}
```

Recreational Use Of CPens Is Hazardous To Your Health

As a C++ programmer, you know that when an object is created, its constructor is called. Once an object is created, you can't *re*-create it. Construction usually involves two tasks: allocation and initialization. Allocation sets aside memory for an object, and initialization sets the starting (initial) value for each of the object's fields. Each of these tasks can be performed *only once*.

When performing allocation and initialization in two distinct steps, as in the GDI two-step construction technique, programmers often confuse initialization with assignment. Assignment puts new values into existing fields, whereas initialization sets the starting values. The **CPen::CreatePen()** function performs initialization, not assignment—so, you can call **CreatePen()** only once for each **CPen** object you create.

Pen Styles

The first argument to the **CreatePen()** function is the pen style. You have your choice of seven styles: **PS_SOLID**, **PS_DASH**, **PS_DOT**, **PS_DASHDOT**, **PS_DASHDOTDOT**, **PS_NULL**, and **PS_INSIDEFRAME**.

The **PS_NULL** style creates a pen just like the stock **NULL_PEN**, except that you can create a **PS_NULL** pen wider than one pixel.

The **PS_DASH**, **PS_DOT**, **PS_DASHDOT**, and **PS_DASHDOTDOT** styles create pens that are one pixel wide and composed of combinations of dashes and dots. You can't create wider styled pens. When you draw with a styled pen, the space between each dash or dot is painted with the default background color of the device context. This may or may not be the same color as the brush used to paint the background of the window. If you want the window background color to show between line segments, you can set the DC background mode to transparent, like this:

```
dc.SetBkMode(TRANSPARENT);
```

To set the background color to a specific color, you can use the DC function **SetBkColor()**.

The final two pen styles, **PS_SOLID** and **PS_INSIDEFRAME**, each create a solid pen. **PS_SOLID** and **PS_INSIDEFRAME** differ in two ways. First, **PS_INSIDEFRAME** is the only style that can use *dithered colors* for wide pens. A dithered color results when your graphics hardware can't exactly reproduce the color you specify, so Windows generates a pattern to match your color as closely as possible.You don't have to worry about dithering if your video card supports 24-bit color, but for lower resolution video modes, dithering can be an issue.

The other difference between these two pen styles manifests itself only when you're drawing a figure that uses a bounding rectangle. In such cases, a **PS_SOLID** pen wider than one pixel will attempt to straddle the bounding rectangle—half the line thickness will be drawn outside, and the other half will be drawn inside. When you use the **PS_INSIDEFRAME** style, however, the entire thickness of the line appears inside the rectangle.

You can see this difference illustrated in Figure 8.3. We drew the two rectangles on the left using the same coordinates. However, we drew the black rectangle with a 1-pixel black pen and the white rectangle with a 10-pixel **PS_INSIDEFRAME** white pen. (We used the black pen on top of the white pen so it would be visible.) Note that the entire thickness of the white rectangle appears inside the frame delineated by the black pen.

The two rectangles on the right side of Figure 8.3 differ from those on the left in only one respect: We assigned the **PS_SOLID** style to the white pen used to draw the 10-pixel line. Note how the white rectangle straddles the black line.

Pen Widths And Colors

The second argument to the **CPen()::CreatePen()** member function is the thickness of the pen. You specify the thickness in logical units, the meaning of which changes depending on the mapping mode. For instance, if you set the mapping mode to **MM_LOENGLISH**, a thickness of 10 logical units is roughly 1/10 of an inch, regardless of the display resolution. If you use the default mapping mode (called **MM_TEXT**), the thickness represents 10 pixels. You'll learn more about mapping modes throughout the next several chapters.

Sometimes, you may want to create a pen that's exactly one pixel wide, even though you're using a mapping mode other than

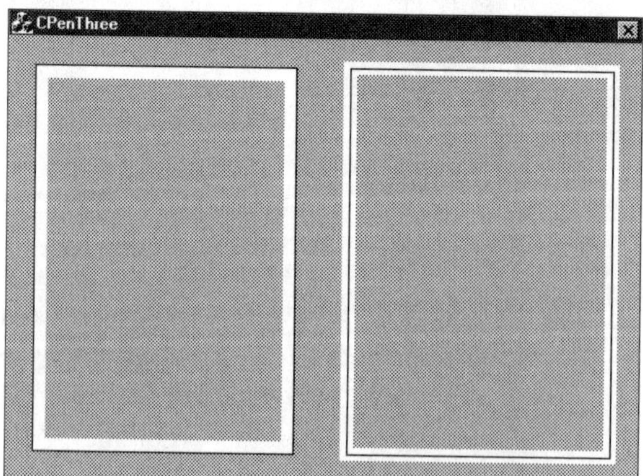

Figure 8.3
PS_INSIDEFRAME and **PS_SOLID** pen styles.

MM_TEXT. In such a case, you can pass 0 for the width; Windows will then create a 1-pixel pen regardless of the current mapping mode.

The third argument passed to **CreatePen()** (or to the **CPen** three-argument constructor) is the pen color. Windows represents a color as a 32-bit unsigned number called a **COLORREF**, of which only 24 bits are actually used. To construct a color, you use the **RGB()** macro, which takes three arguments: the amount of red, the amount of green, and the amount of blue you want the color to contain. You pass any number from 0 to 255 for each of the three colors; to turn a color off, set its value to 0. The **COLORREF**

```
RGB(255, 0, 0);
```

produces a fully saturated red color, because the first argument (*R*ed) is at its maximum value, and the other two arguments (Green and *B*lue) are turned off.

By specifying equal amounts of each color, you can create a set of gray tones ranging from black (**RGB(0, 0, 0)**) to white (**RGB(255, 255, 255)**).

Using CPens

Once you've created a **CPen** object—or any other **CGdiObject**, for that matter)—you activate it by using the **CDC** member function **SelectObject()**. **SelectObject()** works much like **SelectStockObject()**, which you used in Chapter 7. However, instead of passing one of the predefined identifiers, you pass the address of your newly constructed **CPen** object, like this:

```
SelectObject(&greenPen);
```

Because the DC can hold only one pen at a time, **SelectObject()** returns a pointer to the previously selected pen. A custom pen's destructor will automatically return the pen's resources to the operating system when the pen goes out of scope. When this occurs, be sure the DC contains either its original pen, or one of the stock pens. You can select the original pen as follows:

```
CPen * oldPen, bluePen(PS_SOLID, 5, RGB(0, 0, 255));
oldPen = dc.SelectObject(&bluePen);
// Paint here
dc.SelectObject(oldPen);
```

Or, you can select a stock pen:

```
CPen bluePen(PS_SOLID, 5, RGB(0, 0, 255));
dc.SelectObject(&bluePen);
// Painting with blue pen
dc.SelectStockObject(BLACK_PEN);
```

CPenOne: Different Pen Styles

Sometimes, you can most easily understand how an object works by writing a simple example program that exercises its capabilities. Take a look at the **OnPaint()** function for CPenOne, an application you can find on this book's CD-ROM, and notice the following points:

- The function creates six one-pixel black pens, one for each style (except **PS_NULLPEN**):

  ```
  // Create each of the six CPens
  CPen p1, p2, p3, p4, p5, p6;
  p1.CreatePen(PS_SOLID,       1, RGB(0, 0, 0));
  p2.CreatePen(PS_DASH,        1, RGB(0, 0, 0));
  p3.CreatePen(PS_DOT,         1, RGB(0, 0, 0));
  p4.CreatePen(PS_DASHDOT,     1, RGB(0, 0, 0));
  p5.CreatePen(PS_DASHDOTDOT, 1, RGB(0, 0, 0));
  p6.CreatePen(PS_INSIDEFRAME,1, RGB(0, 0, 0));
  ```

- One by one, each pen is selected into the DC. CPenOne then draws a horizontal line using the previously computed values **x**, **y**, **width**, and **height**. After each line is drawn, the program increments the vertical position in anticipation of the next line. Here's how the first pen is used:

  ```
  dc.SelectObject(&p1);
  dc.MoveTo(x, y);
  dc.LineTo(x + width, y);
  y += height;
  ```

- After all six lines have been drawn, CPenOne selects the stock **BLACK_PEN** into the DC in anticipation of the end of the age (or, at least, the end of the **OnPaint()** function):

```
dc.SelectStockObject(BLACK_PEN);
```

You can see the program running in Figure 8.4. Notice how the styled pens—**PS_DOT**, **PS_DASH**, **PS_DASHDOT**, and **PS_DASHDOTDOT**—use a white brush to fill the spaces between their line segments, even though the background color of the dialog box is gray. If you find this objectionable, you can remedy it by using the **CDC** function **SetBkMode()** or **SetBkColor()** as previously described. If, instead, you'd rather paint the dialog box with a white background, you can add the following line to your application's **InitInstance()** method:

```
SetDialogBkColor(RGB(255,255,255));
```

CPenTwo: Different Pen Widths

Like CPenOne, CPenTwo is a simple program that demonstrates the use of various **CPens**. CPenTwo creates five **PS_SOLID** pens, with sizes ranging from 1 to 32 units:

```
// 4. Create each of the five CPens
CPen p1, p2, p3, p4, p5;
p1.CreatePen(PS_SOLID,   1, RGB(0, 0, 0));
p2.CreatePen(PS_SOLID,   4, RGB(0, 0, 0));
p3.CreatePen(PS_SOLID,   8, RGB(0, 0, 0));
p4.CreatePen(PS_SOLID,  16, RGB(0, 0, 0));
p5.CreatePen(PS_SOLID,  32, RGB(0, 0, 0));
```

Remember that these are logical units, which (because we haven't changed the mapping mode) correspond to pixels.

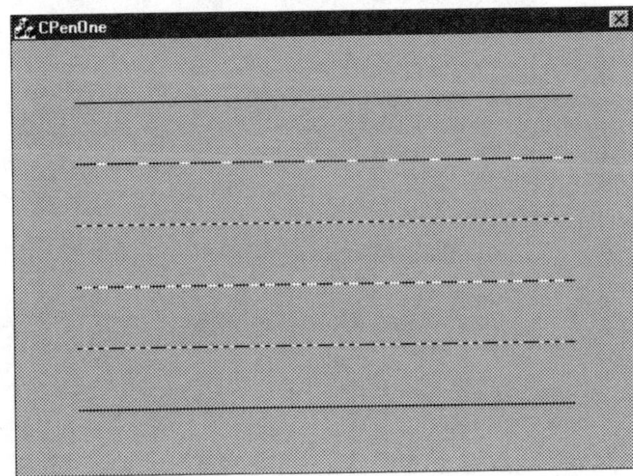

Figure 8.4
Different **CPen** styles.

The rest of the code in CPenTwo is the same as that in CPenOne. You can see each of the five pens in Figure 8.5.

The GDI CBrush Class

You use brushes to fill solid areas. Working with brushes is very similar to working with pens—as with the **CPen** class, you may pass arguments to the **CBrush** constructor or use the default **CBrush** constructor and then call one of the **CBrush** initialization functions.

CBrushes come in three varieties: solid, hatch, and pattern brushes. Solid brushes display either a solid color or a dithered color, depending on your hardware. Hatched brushes use one of six different fill styles, similar to the hatching in architectural drawings. Pattern brushes fill their area with a repeated eight-pixel-square bitmap. We'll cover pattern brushes in a later chapter; right now, let's look at solid brushes and hatch brushes.

Creating Solid Brushes

Using the **CBrush** initialization functions, you can create two kinds of solid brushes: those whose color is specified using a **COLORREF**, and those specified as one of the Windows system colors.

Creating a standard solid brush is very similar to the process you followed to create a **PS_SOLID**-style pen: Create a **CBrush** object using the default constructor, then call the

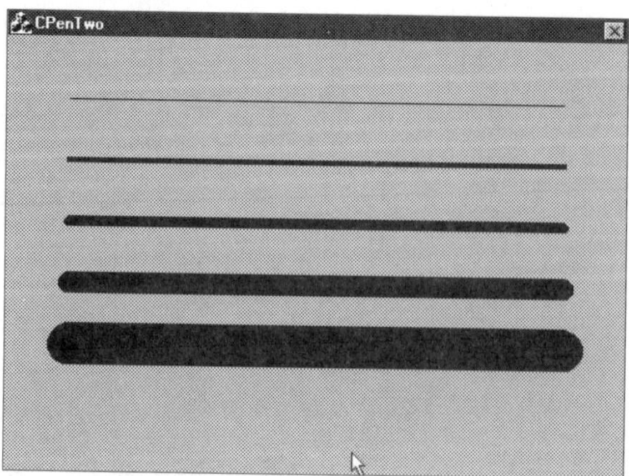

Figure 8.5
Different pen sizes in the CPenTwo application.

CreateSolidBrush() function, which takes a single argument specifying the desired color. Here's an example that creates a nice pink brush:

```
CBrush pinkBrush;
pinkBrush.CreateSolidBrush(RGB(255, 192, 192));
```

In addition to supplying your own **COLORREF** values, you can use one of the 31 built-in Windows system colors, listed in Table 8.1. The Windows Control Panel allows users to choose preferred colors for the graphical elements used throughout Windows. By using system color brushes in your application (rather than hard-coded solid brushes), you make your application much more responsive to users.

To use a system color, call the **CreateSysColorBrush()** function, like this:

```
CBrush bkgrndBrush;
bkgrndBrush.CreateSysColorBrush(COLOR_WINDOW);
```

Creating Hatch Brushes

To create a hatch-style brush, you use the **CreateHatchBrush()** function, which takes two arguments: the hatch style, chosen from the values given in Table 8.2; and the color of the hatch lines (expressed as an **RGB COLORREF**). The current background color will appear between the hatches. If you want to change it, use the **CDC::SetBkColor()** method.

Here's an example that creates a light-blue grid as a background brush:

```
CBrush blueGrid;
blueGrid.CreateHatchBrush(HS_CROSS, RGB(192, 192, 255));
```

The CBrushOne Example: Using Hatch Brushes

Before we leave brushes and pens, let's look at a short example that uses hatch brushes. As with the pen examples, you can find the complete code for CBrushOne on this book's CD-ROM. CBrushOne creates six hatch-style brushes, each using a different color, as follows:

Table 8.1 Windows system colors.

Color ID	Description
COLOR_3DDKSHADOW	Dark shadow for 3D items
COLOR_3DFACE, COLOR_BTNFACE	Surface of 3D items
COLOR_3DHILIGHT COLOR_3DHIGHLIGHT COLOR_BTNHILIGHT COLOR_BTNHIGHLIGHT	Highlight for 3D items
COLOR_3DLIGHT	Light for 3D items
COLOR_3DSHADOW COLOR_BTNSHADOW	Shadow for 3D items
COLOR_ACTIVEBORDER	Border of active window
COLOR_ACTIVECAPTION	Title bar of active window
COLOR_APPWORKSPACE	Background of MDI main window
COLOR_BACKGROUND COLOR_DESKTOP	Desktop
COLOR_BTNTEXT	Text on buttons
COLOR_CAPTIONTEXT	Text in window caption
COLOR_GRAYTEXT	Disabled (grayed out) text
COLOR_HIGHLIGHT	Background of selected items in a control such as a list box
COLOR_HIGHLIGHTTEXT	Text of selected items in a control such as a list box
COLOR_INACTIVEBORDER	Border of inactive window
COLOR_INACTIVECAPTION	Caption of inactive window
COLOR_INACTIVECAPTIONTEXT	Text in an inactive caption
COLOR_INFOBK	Background of tooltip controls
COLOR_INFOTEXT	Text on tooltip controls
COLOR_MENU	Background of menus
COLOR_MENUTEXT	Text in menus
COLOR_SCROLLBAR	Scroll bar gray area
COLOR_WINDOW	Window background
COLOR_WINDOWFRAME	Window frame
COLOR_WINDOWTEXT	Text in windows

Table 8.2 Hatch brush style constants.

Hatch Style ID	Description
HS_BDIAGONAL	45-degree lines from lower-left to upper-right
HS_CROSS	Perpendicular horizontal and vertical lines
HS_DIAGCROSS	Perpendicular 45-degree lines
HS_FDIAGONAL	45-degree lines from upper-left to lower-right
HS_HORIZONTAL	Horizontal lines
HS_VERTICAL	Vertical lines

```
CBrush b1, b2, b3, b4, b5, b6;
b1.CreateHatchBrush(HS_BDIAGONAL,   RGB(255,   0,   0));
b2.CreateHatchBrush(HS_FDIAGONAL,   RGB(  0, 255,   0));
b3.CreateHatchBrush(HS_CROSS,       RGB(  0,   0, 255));
b4.CreateHatchBrush(HS_DIAGCROSS,   RGB(255, 255,   0));
b5.CreateHatchBrush(HS_HORIZONTAL,  RGB(255,   0, 255));
b6.CreateHatchBrush(HS_VERTICAL,    RGB(  0, 255, 255));
```

Once the program has created the six brushes, it divides the main window into two rows and paints three rectangles on each row, using a different brush for each rectangle. The code to paint the first rectangle looks like this:

```
// 4. Paint with all six brushes
dc.SelectObject(&b1);
dc.Rectangle(0, 0, rect.right / 3, rect.bottom / 2);
```

The code for the remaining rectangles is similar—only the brush and the coordinates change. You can see the finished application running in Figure 8.6.

CDC Painting Modes

What color do you expect to see on your display if you create a red pen and then draw a line? If you're like most people, you'll readily answer, "red." But the answer isn't necessarily that easy.

Painting in Windows has a lot in common with painting using water colors. When you paint with water colors, the color on your brush is only one of the factors that determine the final color that appears on your masterpiece—the wetness of the paper, the

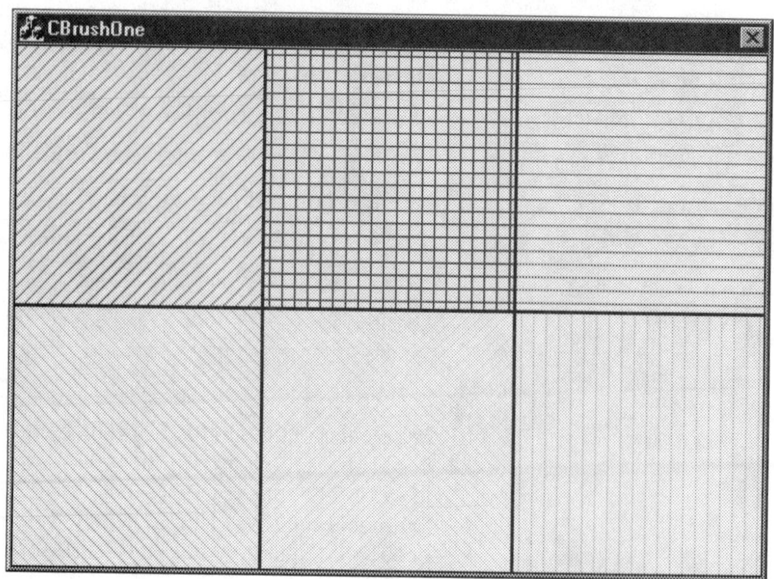

Figure 8.6
Running the CBrushOne application.

previous colors you've laid down, and the relative wetness of your brush all combine to produce the final effect.

When you paint in Windows, the *drawing mode* determines how the color in your pen (and brush) combine with the colors already on screen to produce the finished result. You set the drawing mode by using the **CDC::SetROP2()** function. (**ROP** stands for *R*aster *Op*eration, and refers to the method that displays colors on a CRT device.) You can choose from 256 raster operations, but only 16 of them are used often enough to have names (which start with **R2_**). The most common raster operations are:

- ***R2_COPYPEN***—Paints the pen color directly on the surface. If you choose a red pen, you get red pixels. This mode is like painting on dry paper with a dry brush.
- ***R2_BLACK***, ***R2_WHITE***, *and* ***R2_NOP***—Ignore the pen selected in the device context and always paint with black, white, or nothing.
- ***R2_NOT*** *and* ***R2_NOTCOPYPEN***—Paint using the "inverse" of the screen color and the pen color, respectively. These modes are useful when you want to ensure that a line is visible, regardless of the color of lines and figures behind it.

- **R2_XORPEN**—Performs an exclusive or operation (**XOR**) with the pen color and the screen pixel color. When you use **R2_XORPEN**, drawing the same line twice erases it.

Creating Your Own Screen Saver

In the next chapter, you'll learn how to respond to mouse and keyboard messages, using them to create an interactive painting program. Let's get a head start now by using what you've learned about colors, pens, and brushes in this chapter to write a screen saver program.

If you look in the online Visual C++ documentation under "screen savers," you'll see that several articles walk you through the complications. Our screen saver will be a little simpler—you'll have to press a key or click with the mouse to deactivate it, for instance—but otherwise it will act just like the store-bought variety.

The SuperSaver Skeleton

Let's call our application SuperSaver. Here are the steps you need to follow to create it:

1. Use AppWizard to create a dialog-based application called SuperSaver.
2. Remove all the controls from your dialog window. Open the Dialog Properties dialog box and set the Border to None, as you can see in Figure 8.7.

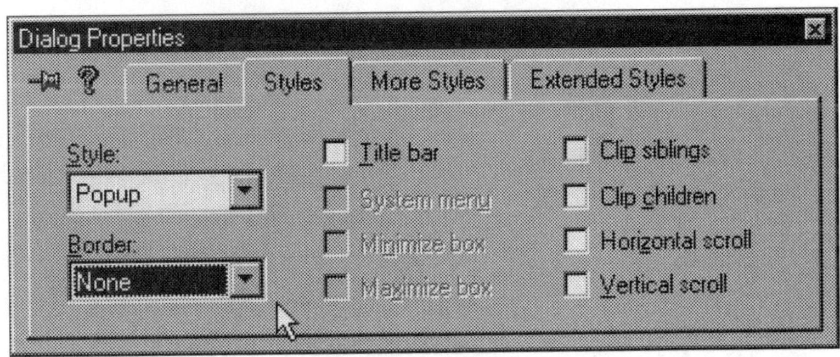

Figure 8.7
Setting the SuperSaver Border property to None.

3. Change the **CSuperSaverApp::InitInstance()** function so it looks like Listing 8.1. Here's how the code works. When you run your screen saver via the Control Panel, the Control Panel will start your program by passing it a command-line argument: "c" to configure your screen saver or "s" to run your code in screen-saver mode. Because you aren't going to do any configuration, you just need to test for the "s" switch and run your program only when it's present. To test for the existence of the switch, use the standard C function **strcmpi()** to check the value of the command line, which the MFC framework automatically captures as **m_lpCmdLine**. (You may want to comment out the conditional code until you're sure the program works as you'd like.) The call to **SetDialogBkColor()** makes the background black. Because you aren't using the return value from **DoModal()**, you don't need to save it.

Listing 8.1 The CSuperSaverApp::InitInstance() function.

```
BOOL CSuperSaverApp::InitInstance()
{
    if (!strcmpi(m_lpCmdLine, "/s") ||
        !strcmpi(m_lpCmdLine, "-s") ||
        !strcmpi(m_lpCmdLine, "s" ))
    {
        SetDialogBkColor(RGB(0,0,0));

        CSuperSaverDlg dlg;
        m_pMainWnd = &dlg;
        dlg.DoModal();
    }
    return FALSE;
}
```

4. In your dialog box's **OnInitDialog()** method, you maximize the main dialog window to fill the screen, and put it on top of all other windows. Listing 8.2 shows how to do this. To put your dialog box on top, use the **SetWindowPos()** function, passing **&wndTopMost** as the first argument. You can call the **GetSystemMetrics()** API function to get the proper size for the window. Use the **SWP_SHOWWINDOW** flag to cause the window to be immediately displayed. In addition to sizing

your window, you should initialize a timer that will paint the display, and initialize the field **m_boxes** to 0.

Listing 8.2 The CSuperSaverDlg::OnInitDialog() member function.

```
BOOL CSuperSaverDlg::OnInitDialog()
{
    CDialog::OnInitDialog();

    // Set the icon for this dialog.  The framework does
    // this automatically
    // when the application's main window is not a
    // dialog
    SetIcon(m_hIcon, TRUE);  // Set big icon
    SetIcon(m_hIcon, FALSE);     // Set small icon

    // TODO: Add extra initialization here
    SetWindowPos(&wndTopMost, 0, 0,
                 ::GetSystemMetrics(SM_CXSCREEN),
                 ::GetSystemMetrics(SM_CYSCREEN),
                 SWP_SHOWWINDOW);

    SetTimer(1, 250, NULL);
    m_boxes = 0;
    return TRUE;  // return TRUE  unless you set the
                  // focus to a control
}
```

5. Add **m_boxes** to the **CSuperSaverDlg** class as a **private, int** data member.
6. Right-click on the **CSuperSaverDlg** class in the ClassView window and select Add Windows Message Handler from the context menu. Add the code that closes the screen saver when you click a mouse button or press a key. Let's start with the key press first. In the dialog box, select the **WM_KEYDOWN** message, then click on Add and Edit. In the body of the method, replace the code with the single statement

   ```
   CDialog::EndDialog(IDOK);
   ```

   Repeat this process for the **WM_LBUTTONDOWN** and **WM_RBUTTONDOWN** messages. Your code should look like Listing 8.3.

Listing 8.3 Member functions to close the screen saver window.

```
void CSuperSaverDlg::OnKeyDown(UINT nChar, UINT nRepCnt,
UINT nFlags)
{
    CDialog::EndDialog(IDOK);
}

void CSuperSaverDlg::OnLButtonDown(UINT nFlags, CPoint
point)
{
    CDialog::EndDialog(IDOK);
}

void CSuperSaverDlg::OnRButtonDown(UINT nFlags, CPoint
point)
{
    CDialog::EndDialog(IDOK);
}
```

7. Add a Windows message handler for the **WM_TIMER** message. The code is similar to that from the PaintItGray application you wrote in the last chapter. Because you want to use color rather than plain gray, make the changes shown in Listing 8.4.

Listing 8.4 The OnTimer() function for the SuperSaver screen saver.

```
void CSuperSaverDlg::OnTimer(UINT nIDEvent)
{
    CClientDC dc(this);

    CRect rect;
    GetClientRect(&rect);

    dc.SetROP2(R2_XORPEN);

    CPen randomPen;
    randomPen.CreatePen(PS_SOLID, 1, RGB(rand() % 255,
                                         rand() % 255,
                                         rand() % 255));
    dc.SelectObject(&randomPen);

    for(int row = rect.bottom - m_boxes; row > m_boxes;
        row—)
    {
        dc.MoveTo(m_boxes, row);
```

```
        dc.LineTo(rect.right - m_boxes, rect.bottom -
           row);
    }
    for(int col = m_boxes; col < rect.right - m_boxes;
           col++)
    {
        dc.MoveTo(col, m_boxes);
        dc.LineTo(rect.right - col, rect.bottom -
           m_boxes);
    }
    m_boxes++;
    m_boxes %= 5;
    dc.SelectStockObject(BLACK_PEN);
}
```

8. Add a final Windows message handler to handle the **WM_DESTROY** message. In the **OnDestroy()** method, kill your timer by adding the line

   ```
   KillTimer(1);
   ```

9. Be sure the Control Panel recognizes your program as a screen saver. Select Insert | Resource from the menu, then choose String Table from the Insert Resources dialog box. Open the String Properties dialog box by double-clicking on the first entry in the string table. Change the ID of the string to **IDS_DESCRIPTON** and check that **IDS_DESCRIPTION** has the value 1, as you can see in Figure 8.8.

10. Comment out the conditional statements at the beginning of the **CSuperSaverApp::InitInstance()** method, build the program, and be sure it runs correctly. When you're satisfied, copy the executable file to the Windows\System directory

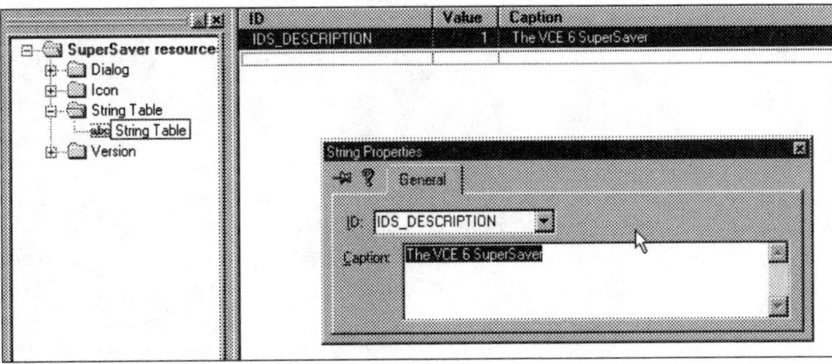

Figure 8.8
Adding a string-table resource entry.

and rename the program using the extension .scr. Now, right-click on your system's desktop to open the Display Properties dialog box. Select the Screen Saver page and add your new screen saver. You can see the SuperSaver program running in Figure 8.9.

What's Next?

As you can see, the Windows GDI library gives you the power you need to generate impressive graphical effects. MFC and Visual C++ make it easy to harness the power of the API, by taking care of many of the details that distracted an earlier generation of programmers from their tasks. However, as with any labor-saving device, a potential danger lurks, as well. Unless you make the effort to understand what your tool is doing and why it's doing it, you'll never completely master the craft of Windows programming. Exploring is good, but you also need to take time for reflection.

As you saw in the SuperSaver project, adding code to recognize keystrokes and mouse clicks takes just a few short steps in Visual C++. In the next chapter, you'll tap into that power and make your drawings interactive, putting your users in charge for a change.

Figure 8.9
Running the SuperSaver screen saver.

Chapter 9

Picasso's Nightmare: Building An Interactive Paint Program

Still-life graphics are fine, but moving graphics are even better—and interactive graphics are best of all. The computer is magical because, unlike the VCR, the user can control what happens. It's not just playback, it's real play.

Do you remember the first time you saw a computer game? I do. In the summer of 1960, when I was 10, my parents—who were school teachers—saved their money and took me and my 7-year-old brother on a driving tour of Europe. We bought a new VW Beetle, and my brother and I spent the next six weeks together in the back seat. (I'm sure the trip seemed like a good idea to my parents when they first conceived it, but it turned out to be the last one we took for a very long time.)

Because the car was so small, we stopped frequently and visited museums and other attractions. One of our stops was the Museum of Science and Industry in Geneva, Switzerland, and there I saw my first computer—a machine that could play tic-tac-toe.

I'm sure that it was a very primitive machine, but to my 10-year-old mind, a number-crunching Cray couldn't have been better. Here was something I could *play* with. And, because it was interactive, it was more than simply a toy. I was captivated. Unfortunately, it was rather large, and I'm sure quite expensive. I pointed out that it wouldn't take up any more room in the car than my brother did, but my quite reasonable arguments fell on deaf ears. It would be almost 20 years before I got my own tic-tac-toe machine.

In Chapter 8, you learned how to draw lines, shapes, and colors—all necessary elements of a good interactive program. But those elements handle only the output side of your program. What about input?

In Windows, your users can generate input two ways: by using the mouse or the keyboard. Most of the time, you don't deal with the "raw" input messages sent by the mouse or keyboard—instead, you use a button, a text control, or a menu to capture the user's mouse clicks and keyboard presses. The controls notify your program when something interesting happens.

However, in this chapter, you'll build an interactive drawing program that handles raw user input. You'll learn how to respond to mouse clicks and mouse movement. You'll also discover how to coordinate the output skills you learned in the last several chapters with your new skill in acquiring user input, creating an experience your users will long remember.

The PaintORama Version 1

Before we dive in, let's take a few moments to outline where we're going. In this chapter, we'll begin work on five versions of the PaintORama program. Each version adds new features to the one before it. On this book's CD-ROM, you'll find each version in its own directory, so you can take it out and play with it if you're so inclined.

Here's what each version does:

- Version 1 creates the main screen, then adds a canvas to hold your drawings and a Clear button to erase them. It allows you to do basic freehand drawing using the default one-pixel black pen. When you finish this section, you'll know how to handle Windows *mouse messages*.
- Version 2 adds variable-width pens to the PaintORama. Along the way, you'll learn about the new Windows *spin control*.
- Version 3 begins by adding color to your pens, introducing you to the Windows *common dialog boxes*. It then moves beyond freehand drawing to incorporate lines and shapes. You'll learn how to use the **CComboBox** class to add drop-down lists to

your programs. We'll also show you how to add visual feedback to your graphics programs by using *rubber-banding*.

- Because you've already learned how to use pens, Version 4 adds support for brushes. In addition, we'll explain how to use Windows' **CListBox** control.
- Version 5 takes you back to your roots—handling the PaintORama's **WM_PAINT** message—by recording and replaying all of your graphics operations. To do this, you'll use the **CMetaFileDC** classes (such as **CPaintDC** and **CClientDC**), each of which is a subclass of the all-seeing **CDC** itself.

To avoid reader stress, we've spread this ambitious project over two chapters. You'll build the first two versions of the PaintORama in this chapter. As in a good TV series, you'll have to wait 'til the next chapter to see how it all comes out.

All the versions of PaintORama in this chapter and the next are dialog-based applications. In Chapter 11, we'll further improve the PaintORama by making the jump to document-view programs.

Building PaintORama

Let's get started by building the basic PaintORama skeleton. Here are the steps:

1. Use the AppWizard to start a new, dialog-based project. In AppWizard's Step 2 window, be sure that the 3D Controls checkbox is checked and unselect everything else, as you can see in Figure 9.1. Name the project PaintORama and click on Finish. When the New Project Information dialog box appears, click on OK.
2. Use the ResourceView window to select the Dialog Editor and the **IDD_PAINTORAMA_DIALOG** template. When the Dialog Editor appears, delete the "TODO:" label as well as the OK and Cancel buttons. Leave the dialog box's caption set to PaintORama.
3. Drag the lower-right corner of the dialog box until the box measures 460 wide by 275 high, using the coordinates in the lower-right status-bar window to check the size. If you have

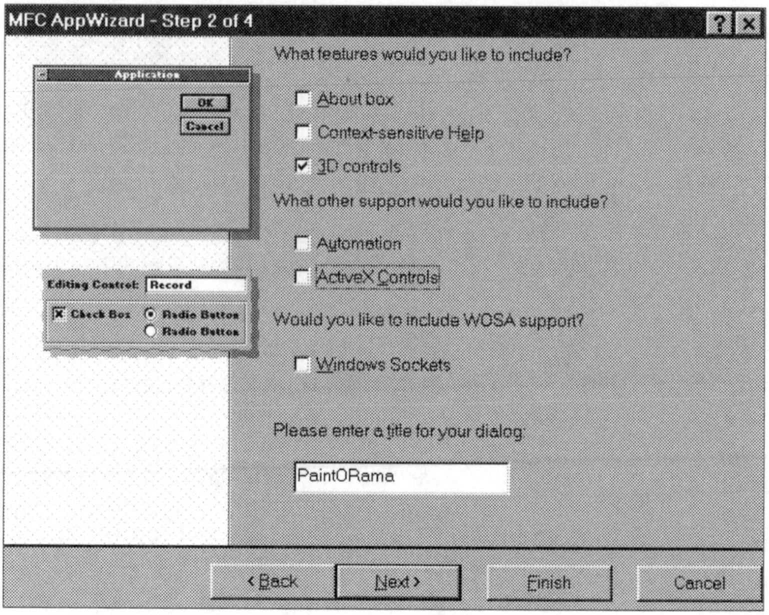

Figure 9.1
AppWizard Step 2. The PaintORama application.

difficulty sizing your dialog box because the Dialog Editor window is so small, select View|Full Screen from the menu and then maximize the Dialog Editor. To get back to the IDE, press Esc or click on the small icon that appears in the upper-left corner. Full Screen mode has only one real drawback: The status bar no longer shows the size of your dialog box, as you can see in Figure 9.2.

4. Drag a picture control from the Control toolbar onto your dialog box. Change its ID to **IDC_CANVAS**, its type to Frame, and its color to Gray, as you can see in Figure 9.3. On the Extended Styles page of the Picture Properties dialog box, check Client Edge and deselect all the other checkboxes. On the Styles page, select only Sunken.
5. Position and size the **IDC_CANVAS** frame control so that it occupies the right side of the dialog box. The control should be about 295 units wide and 253 units high, with the upper-left corner at 150, 7. You don't have to match these dimensions exactly, of course—just be sure to leave about 150 units on the left side of your dialog box free for the PaintORama controls. If you look back at Figure 9.2, you'll see the basic dimensions.

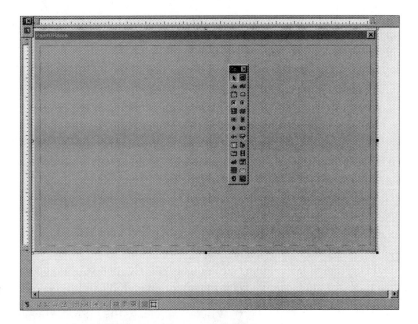

Figure 9.2
Using the Dialog Editor in Full Screen mode.

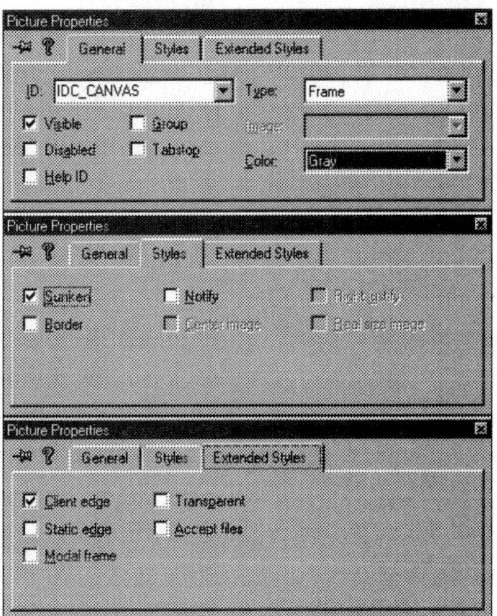

Figure 9.3
Properties for the **IDC_CANVAS** static control.

6. Add a push-button control in the upper-left corner. Assign the button the ID **IDC_CLEARBTN** and add the caption "Clear". You'll use this button to erase your drawings when you want a clean canvas.

That's all there is to this part of the interface. You can compile your program, if you like, just to be sure you didn't make any mistakes. Once you're finished, we'll turn our attention to making the PaintORama do some painting—and that means working with the mouse.

Adding Member Variables

In PaintORama Version 1, we'll do only freehand drawing, using the mouse. Here's how the freehand drawing will act:

- When you click the left mouse button in the canvas area—the area bounded by **IDC_CANVAS**—the program will act as if you've dropped your pen on the canvas.
- You draw with the pen by *dragging*—holding down the left button while you move the mouse.
- When you release the button, the mouse stops drawing.

To accomplish this, you'll need the assistance of three member variables: one to keep track of the canvas boundaries, one to determine where the last line portion was drawn, and one to be sure that the user really wants to initiate line drawing. After a quick refresher on adding new member variables, we'll look at each of these in turn.

You'll start coding by adding three member variables to the **CPaintORamaDlg** class, like this:

1. Right-click on the class name **CPaintORamaDlg** in the ClassView window and choose Add Member Variable from the context menu, as shown in Figure 9.4.
2. When the Add Member Variable dialog box opens, enter "**CRect**" for the type and "**m_Canvas**" for the variable name. Also specify **private** access, using the radio buttons. Figure 9.5 shows the completed Add Member Variable dialog box. The **m_Canvas** variable holds the dimensions of the paintable portion of your canvas. You'll check its value to ensure that the mouse is "inside the lines."

Many programmers like to include comments describing program variables, but you can't do this using the Add Member Variable

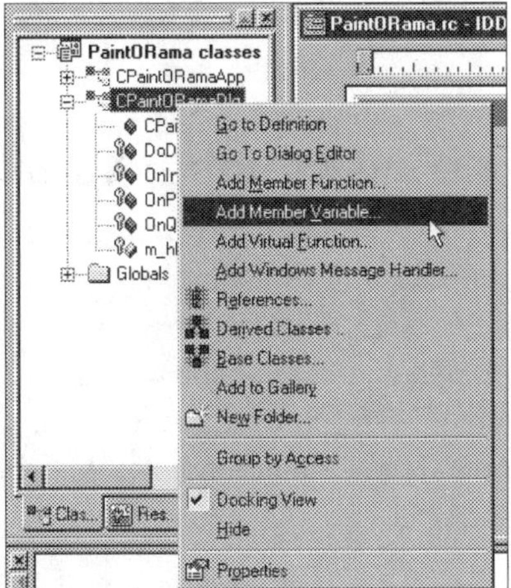

Figure 9.4
Adding a member variable to the **CPaintORamaDlg** class.

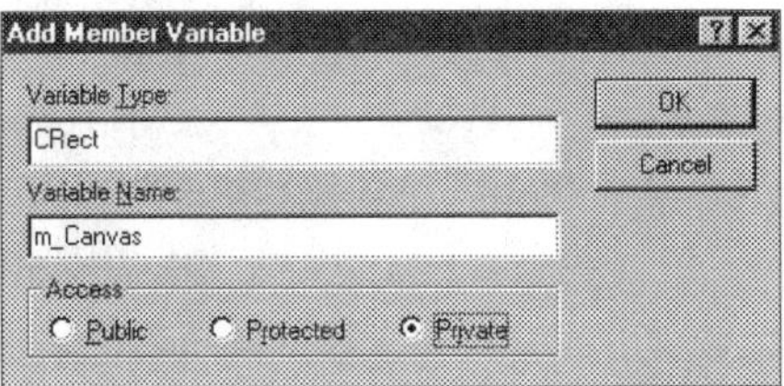

Figure 9.5
Using the Add Member Variable dialog box.

dialog box. For that reason, many programmers prefer to add member variables to the class definition by hand, so they can format and comment each data member to their liking. Whether you use the dialog box or enter the variables by hand, Visual C++ will notice the change and display your variable in the ClassView pane as soon as you finish typing it. If you remove a variable (which you must do manually), it disappears from the ClassView window once its declaration is gone.

Use whichever method you choose to add the two remaining variables to the **CPaintORamaDlg** class:

- ***m_LineStart***—A **private CPoint** that holds the position of the starting position of the line segment you're currently drawing.
- ***m_IsDrawing***—A **private bool** that lets you differentiate between valid and invalid mouse movements. When the user clicks the left mouse button in the canvas area, you'll set **m_IsDrawing** to **true** and store the location of the mouse in **m_LineStart**. Then, when you see a mouse-drag event, you'll

be able to tell whether you should be drawing or not and, if so, where the line should start.

Initializing Member Variables

If you've been programming for any length of time, you've learned that failure to initialize variables is one of the chief causes of software anomalies (*bugs*, for the scrupulously truthful). As a C++ programmer, you've probably had drilled into your head that a constructor's purpose is to make sure objects are "well formed." You know that a constructor should, whenever possible, give every member variable a meaningful value.

The key phrase here, however, is "whenever possible." In Windows and MFC programming, it often *isn't* possible. In the case of a dialog-based application, the main window controls haven't yet been created when the constructor runs. Therefore, most MFC classes include an auxiliary function that gives you a chance to ensure all your data members are initialized. For dialog-based

BOOL, bool, int: Telling The Truth

As every C programmer knows, "Everything is true, nothing is false." Well, in the brave new world of Standard C++, even that is false.

C++ and C have long used integer types to represent Boolean (true/false) values. When you're making a decision or evaluating a loop condition, the integer value 0 is considered false, and every other value is true. The Windows API uses the **typedef BOOL**, along with the manifest constants **TRUE** and **FALSE**, to represent Boolean quantities.

ANSI Standard C++ (which is still being finalized as of this writing) adds a new intrinsic Boolean type called **bool**, which has been present in Visual C++ since Version 5. Variables of type **bool** can have the value **true** or **false**. You can increment a **bool** variable—which sets its value to **true**—but you cannot decrement it.

Most programmers won't be affected by the change from **BOOL** to **bool**. However, if you're upgrading from Visual C++ 4.2, you need to be aware of one pitfall. In version 4.2, the Standard C++ header files used a **typedef** for type **bool**, equating it to an **int**. In Visual C++ 4.2, therefore, the **sizeof(bool)** was four bytes. In Visual C++ 5.0 and following, the **sizeof(bool)** is one byte. This change should affect you only if you have structures that contain **bool** data members. In such cases, data files from earlier versions of Visual C++ can become corrupt.

applications, that function is the **OnInitDialog()** virtual function. The MFC application framework calls the **OnInitDialog()** function after all your application's child controls have been created. **OnInitDialog()** is just what we need in the PaintORama.

You needn't initialize the **m_LineStart** field—it will be initialized when you click the mouse button to begin drawing. But you do have to initialize the **m_IsDrawing** variable, or the first time you drag your mouse pointer over your canvas, you may find yourself drawing lines, even if you don't mean to. To initialize **m_IsDrawing**, add the lines

```
// 1. Assume we aren't drawing
m_IsDrawing = false;
```

to the **CPaintORama::OnInitDialog()** function, where you see the comment

```
// TODO: Add extra initialization here.
```

Calculating A Value For m_Canvas

The **m_Canvas** member variable is a **CRect** that stores the position of the canvas. Your canvas will be the interior of the static frame control **IDC_CANVAS**. Because static frame controls are regular **CWnd** windows under the skin, you can get the location and size of the client area by using the **GetClientRect()** method, just as you've done previously. The only difference is that you want to get the client area for the **IDC_CANVAS** control, not the client area for the **CPaintORama** dialog box. To do that, you must get hold of the **IDC_CANVAS CWnd** object itself.

Because Windows programmers often need to get the **CWnd** object, it's quite easy to do. The function **GetDlgItem()**, when sent to a dialog-based window and passed the ID of a control, returns a **CWnd** pointer to the control. **GetDlgItem()** works only on windows that are derived from **CDialog**, as **CPaintORamaDlg** is. Thus, to get the **IDC_CANVAS** window, you write

```
CWnd* pCanvas =  GetDlgItem(IDC_CANVAS);
```

Now, using the pointer **pCanvas**, you can easily find the screen location of the control. Instead of using **GetClientRect()**, you call the **GetWindowRect()** function, which returns the location of the control in screen coordinates:

```
pCanvas->GetWindowRect(&m_Canvas);
```

After this, **m_Canvas** contains the location of **IDC_CANVAS** on screen. Because you need coordinates relative to the **CPaintORamaDlg** client area, you must translate the returned value. The **ScreenToClient()** function takes the address of a **CRect** object—in this case, **m_Canvas**—and replaces every screen coordinate with its equivalent client-area coordinate. Here's how that looks:

```
ScreenToClient(&m_Canvas);  // Store client coordinates
```

Finally, you have the coordinates of your canvas—almost. Even though Windows controls are really **CWnd** objects, they lack the borders that top-level and pop-up windows have. Instead, the entire window is the client area. You'll leave the two-pixel border drawn by the sunken static frame control in place. Thus, you need to move the **CRect** field named **left** two spaces to the right, and move the field named **right**, two spaces to the left, and so on. The **CRect** class provides the member function **DeflateRect()** for exactly this purpose. Because the inclusive-exclusive drawing functions you'll use to clear the canvas don't actually draw the right or bottom row of pixels, you'll deflate the right and bottom sides by only one pixel, using **DeflateRect()** like this:

```
m_Canvas.DeflateRect(2, 2, 1, 1);
```

You can see the finished **OnInitDialog()** function in Listing 9.1. We've highlighted the added lines.

Listing 9.1 The CPaintORamaDlg::OnInitDialog() function.

```
BOOL CPaintORamaDlg::OnInitDialog()
{
    CDialog::OnInitDialog();

    // Set the icon for this dialog.  The framework does
    // this automatically when the application's main
```

```
    // window is not a dialog
    SetIcon(m_hIcon, TRUE);      // Set big icon
    SetIcon(m_hIcon, FALSE);     // Set small icon

    // TODO: Add extra initialization here
    // 1. Assume we aren't drawing
    m_IsDrawing = false;

    // 2. Calculate the true location of the Canvas
    // Get a pointer to IDC_CANVAS
    CWnd* pCanvas =  GetDlgItem(IDC_CANVAS);
    // Find its location on screen
    pCanvas->GetWindowRect(&m_Canvas);
    // Store client coordinates
    ScreenToClient(&m_Canvas);
    m_Canvas.DeflateRect(2, 2, 1, 1);

    return TRUE;  // return TRUE  unless you set the
                  // focus to a control
}
```

Adding A Clear Button

Let's activate the Clear button to be sure you got the **m_Canvas** calculation right. When you click on Clear, the PaintORama should paint white the entire area bounded by **m_Canvas**. To activate the button, follow these steps:

1. Open the main **CPaintORamaDlg** dialog box in the Dialog Editor.
2. Double-click on the **IDC_CLEARBTN** button. When the Add Member Function dialog opens, accept its suggestion of **OnClearbtn()** and click on OK.
3. Add the code shown in Listing 9.2 to the **OnClearbtn()** function.

Listing 9.2 The CPaintORamaDlg::OnClearbtn() function.

```
void CPaintORamaDlg::OnClearbtn()
{
    // TODO: Add your control notification handler code
    // Clear the canvas when we start
    CClientDC dc(this);
    dc.SelectStockObject(NULL_PEN);
    dc.Rectangle(m_Canvas);
}
```

The **OnClearbtn()** function gets a device context bound to the dialog window. It then selects a **NULL_PEN** into the device context so only the strokes of the default white fill brush will appear. Finally, it uses the **Rectangle()** function you met in the last few chapters to clear the canvas area. Notice that the **Rectangle()** function is overloaded—you can pass it either the alternate corners of a bounding box or a **CRect** object containing those coordinates. Here you pass **m_Canvas**.

Compile the program and click on Clear a few times, to convince yourself that it really does work Now, get ready to do some drawing.

How Mouse Messages Work

Whenever you move the mouse or click a mouse button, Windows generates one or more messages and sends them to the window under the mouse cursor. There are more than 20 types of mouse messages, which seems an intimidating number. But, mouse messages aren't as complicated as they seem. Windows makes a distinction between mouse activities that occur in the client area and activities that occur in the non-client area of windows, such as title bars and borders. Half of the mouse message types correspond to events occurring in the non-client area—except in a few special situations, you can ignore them.

The 10 remaining client-area mouse messages include **WM_MOUSEMOVE**, which is sent to a window whenever you move the mouse pointer over the window's client area. You'll soon use this message to determine where to draw lines. When you move the mouse pointer over a Windows control such as a push button, Windows generates **WM_MOUSEMOVE** messages—but rather than going to the application window, those messages are sent to the push button, which handles them internally.

Each of the remaining nine client-area mouse messages is generated by clicking a mouse button. Clicking the button, releasing the button, and double-clicking the button generate distinct messages. The three mouse buttons have associated mouse messages for each of these three actions, for a total of nine messages.

When you click a mouse button, it generates a **WM_LBUTTONDOWN**, **WM_RBUTTONDOWN**, or **WM_MBUTTONDOWN** message, depending upon which button you clicked—**L**eft, **R**ight, or **M**iddle. (If your mouse has no middle button, you'll never get the set of button messages that begin with "**WM_M**".)

When you release a mouse button, it generates a **WM_LBUTTONUP**, **WM_RBUTTONUP**, or **WM_MBUTTONUP** message. If you quickly click and release a mouse button twice, you won't get the expected pair of **DOWN/UP** messages. For example, suppose you perform this experiment with the left mouse button. Windows will replace the second **WM_LBUTTONDOWN** message with a **WM_LBUTTONDBLCLK** message. The sequence of messages your program receives is as follows:

- **WM_LBUTTONDOWN**
- **WM_LBUTTONUP**
- **WM_LBUTTONDBLCLK**
- **WM_LBUTTONUP**

WM_LBUTTONDOWN: Starting To Draw

When the user of the PaintORama program clicks the mouse within the canvas, you want to start drawing a line. You'll have to intercept the **WM_LBUTTONDOWN** message to do that. Here are the steps to follow:

1. Select the **CPaintORamaDlg** class in the ClassView pane. Right-click to open the context menu, then choose Add Windows Message Handler. This opens the New Windows Message And Event Handlers dialog box, which you can see in Figure 9.6. (You can get the same result several ways: You can use the Wizard Bar pull-down menu you met in Chapter 1 or the main ClassWizard window. It's valuable to learn about all these methods—eventually, you'll probably come to prefer one over the others.)
2. Scroll down the list of available messages until you locate **WM_LBUTTONDOWN**. Select it and click on Add and Edit.

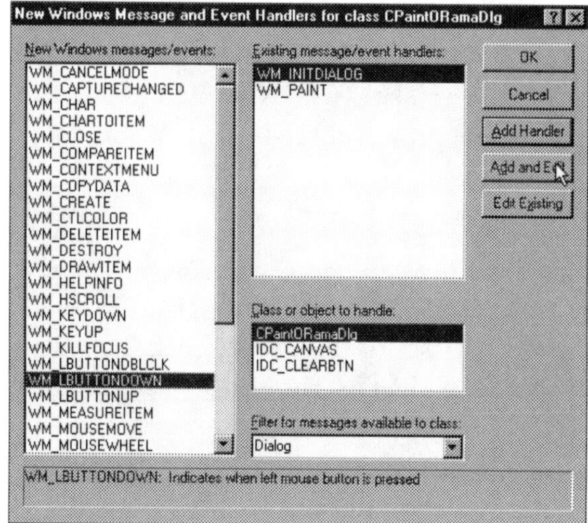

Figure 9.6
Adding a Windows message handler.

3. Replace the code in the Visual C++-generated **OnLButtonDown()** function with the highlighted code shown in Listing 9.3.

Listing 9.3 The CPaintORamaDlg::OnLButtonDown() function.

```
void CPaintORamaDlg::OnLButtonDown(UINT nFlags, CPoint
point)
{
    if (m_Canvas.PtInRect(point))   // If the point is on
                                    // the canvas
    {
        m_IsDrawing = true;         // Then we're drawing
        m_LineStart = point;        // And this is the
                                    // new starting point
        SetCapture();               // Make sure we get a
                                    // WM_LBUTTONUP
    }
    // Otherwise, do nothing
}
```

When Windows calls the **OnLButtonDown()** function, it passes two arguments. The first, **nFlags**, determines whether the Shift or Ctrl key was pressed at the same time the button was clicked. For instance, if you want to take some action on a Ctrl+Click, you can write this code:

```
if ( nFlags & MK_CONTROL ) { /* Ctrl+Click processing */
}
```

The other test constants are **MK_SHIFT**, **MK_LBUTTON**, **MK_RBUTTON**, and **MK_MBUTTON**. For instance, use **MK_RBUTTON** if you want to take an action when both the left and right buttons are clicked.

The second argument, **point**, is a **CPoint** object containing the location of the mouse cursor at the time the button was clicked.

The **CPaintORama::OnLButtonDown()** function does four things:

1. It checks to see if the button was clicked within the **m_Canvas** rectangle. The **CRect** function **PtInRect()** returns **true** if the specified point is in the rectangle and **false** otherwise.
2. If the click occurs within **m_Canvas**, then the user wants to start drawing a line. So, you set **m_IsDrawing** to **true**.
3. Because **OnLButtonDown()** marks the start of the line, you initialize the member variable **m_LineStart** using the **point** argument.
4. Mouse messages are sent to the window under the mouse. Thus, if you click the mouse while you're on the canvas, but then release it after moving off the PaintORama window, the program's start/stop logic will become confused. The **SetCapture()** function ensures that your program will get the final **WM_LBUTTONUP** message, no matter where the button is released.

WM_LBUTTONUP: When Your Line Is Over

In a moment, we'll come back to the code that actually does the drawing. For now, let's look at the **WM_LBUTTONUP** message—the message that stops what **WM_LBUTTONDOWN** began.

Add an **OnLButtonUp()** message handler, using the same procedures you followed to create **OnLButtonDown()**. The **OnLButtonUp()** function contains only two lines: one to set the **m_IsDrawing** field to **false** (because you've stopped drawing) and one to release the mouse from the capture you imposed in **OnLButtonDown()**. You can see the entire method in Listing 9.4.

Listing 9.4 The CPaintORamaDlg::OnLButtonUp() function.

```
void CPaintORamaDlg::OnLButtonUp(UINT nFlags, CPoint
point)
{
    m_IsDrawing = false; // Set the drawing mode to false
    ReleaseCapture();    // Free the mouse
}
```

If you forget to release the mouse capture, you'll discover that you can't close the application after you start drawing. Don't panic—simply switch to any other application, and Windows will release the mouse capture.

WM_MOUSEMOVE: Pixels All In A Row

To draw the pixels on screen, add an **OnMouseMove()** function to intercept the **WM_MOUSEMOVE** method. Replace the code supplied by ClassWizard with the highlighted code in Listing 9.5.

Listing 9.5 The CPaintORamaDlg::OnMouseMove() function.

```
void CPaintORamaDlg::OnMouseMove(UINT nFlags, CPoint
point)
{
    // Draw if m_IsDrawing and on the canvas and
    // the left-mouse button is pressed
    if (m_IsDrawing && (nFlags & MK_LBUTTON) &&
        m_Canvas.PtInRect(point))
    {
        CClientDC dc(this);       // Get a DC
        dc.MoveTo(m_LineStart); // Move to the start of
                                  // the line
        dc.LineTo(point);         // Draw to current
                                  // position
        m_LineStart = point;      // Update current mouse
                                  // position
    }
}
```

How It Works

Three preconditions must be met before you can draw a line:

- The mouse must be in the canvas area. You check that using the **PtInRect()** function.

- The variable **m_IsDrawing** must be **true**. If it is, you know that the user clicked in the **m_Canvas** rectangle and that the initial drawing position is valid.
- The user is *dragging* instead—not just *moving*—the mouse. Windows doesn't provide a separate **WM_MOUSEDRAG** message, so you must distinguish moving from dragging. That's easy to do, though: Just use the **nFlags** argument (which can contain the same possible values as with the **WM_LBUTTONDOWN** message), along with the **MK_LBUTTON** constant. This combination tests whether the left button was down when the mouse moved—exactly the criteria that define a mouse drag. Combining **nFlags** and **MK_LBUTTON** using the bitwise **AND** operator (&) yields an expression that returns 0 if the left mouse button is up and a non-0 value if it's down.

Once you've met all three conditions, drawing the line segment is easy. Simply follow these steps:

1. Get a device context using **GetClientDC()**.
2. Move to the point saved in **m_LineStart**, using the **MoveTo()** function. Notice that **MoveTo()** is overloaded so it can take a **CPoint** (as you've done here) or a pair of integer coordinates (as you did in the last chapter).
3. Pass the current mouse position—passed as the function argument named **point**—to the **LineTo()** function, another overloaded device context method.
4. Update the **m_LineStart** member variable with the mouse's new position, so the next time the mouse moves it will start from the new position. (If you want to have some fun, comment out this line and try the program. You'll end up with some really nifty fan-shaped patterns.)

You might wonder why we use the **LineTo()** function instead of, say, **SetPixel()**. If you use **SetPixel()** in place of **LineTo()**, you'll find that rather than drawing freehand lines, you scatter pixel-dust all over your display. This occurs because the **WM_MOUSEMOVE** message isn't sent every time your mouse moves a single pixel—that many **WM_MOUSEMOVE** messages would overwhelm the system. Exactly how many messages are actually sent depends on your hardware, and how far and quickly you move the mouse. Using **LineTo()** avoids this problem.

Once you're done, compile and run the application. You can see the PaintORama application running in Figure 9.7—we used it to create a charming seascape. (If you think PaintORama is no match for Photoshop, rest assured that the image produced by PaintORama is in no way inferior to that produced by Photoshop. The fault lies not with the tool, but with the wielder.)

The PaintORama Version 2: Pens On Demand

The PaintORama has one noticeable failing: It uses the same black pen for everything. You already know how to make solid-colored pens and hatch-brush pens, as well as how to create pens that use special styles. To apply your expertise to the PaintORama, you merely need to add an interface so your users can select the pen *they* want to use.

Remember that a pen has three characteristics: style, width, and color. You'll use a different Windows control to let the user

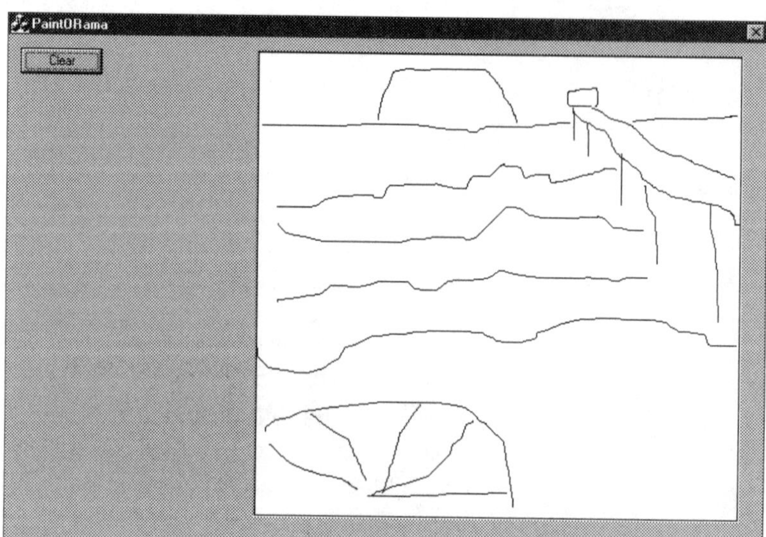

Figure 9.7
Running the PaintORama Version 1.

change each characteristic. Let's start in this chapter by using a spin control and its buddy to change pen thickness.

Spin Doctors: Just What Your Buddy Ordered

The spin control is one of 15 new Windows controls introduced in Windows 95. These new controls are called the *Win32 common controls*, to differentiate them from the older Windows common controls implemented as part of the core Windows libraries. The new controls are implemented in the file Comctl32.dll, and in MFC you generally use them like the older controls.

A spin control is similar to a very small scroll bar with the center portion removed. You use it in combination with a second control—called the *spin buddy*—to accept and display integer values. A spin control can be either vertical—with its arrows pointing up and down—or horizontal—with its arrows pointing right and left. When you click on one of the arrows, the spin control increments or decrements the integer number displayed in its buddy. Usually, you'll use an edit control or a static text control as a spin buddy.

Pens In A Group

Before you add any new controls to the PaintORama, let's add a groupbox to keep everything organized. Here's how:

1. Open the Dialog Editor window, and be sure that the main PaintORama dialog box is displayed.
2. Drag a groupbox from the Control toolbar. The groupbox is pictured in Figure 9.8.
3. Place the groupbox under the Clear button and expand it, using Figure 9.9 as a placement guide. (The status-bar position

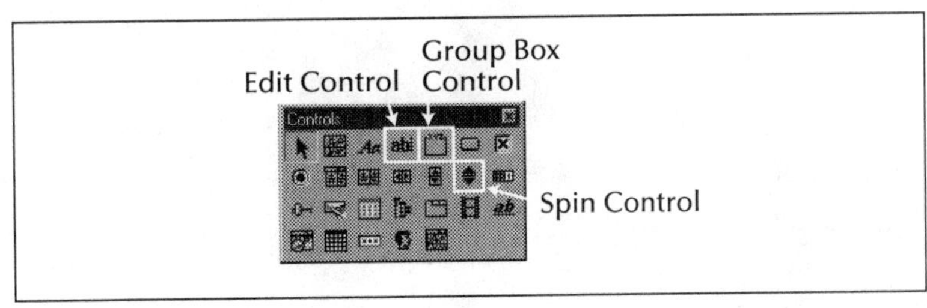

Figure 9.8
The groupbox, edit, and spin controls.

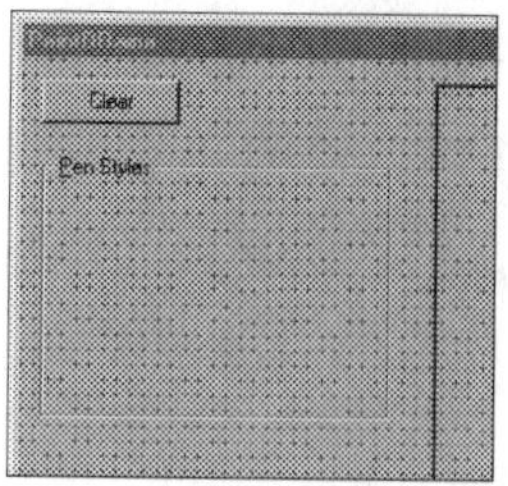

Figure 9.9
Placing the Pen Styles groupbox.

indicator should read about 7, 31—7 units from the left and 31 down from the top—and the size indicator should read about 128, 87.) Give the groupbox the title "Pen Styles". (If you precede the "P" with an ampersand, Windows will underscore the character and let you easily switch to the controls in the groupbox by using the keyboard.)

Adding Spin And His Buddy

Once you've situated the groupbox, drag an edit control and a spin control onto the dialog box and place them as shown in Figure 9.10. (It will probably help you to turn on the layout grid, as shown in the figure.) It's important that you add the edit control first, followed by the spin control—the spin control will look for the control added immediately before it and adopt that control as its buddy. If you add the spin control first, it will adopt the Pen Styles groupbox rather than the edit control—not a happy result.

Lay out the edit control as you want it to appear—then, at runtime, the spin control will jump inside the edit control and display itself there. If you make the edit control too small, you run the risk of filling it with your spinner.

Setting The Spin Properties

Use the Spin Properties dialog box to set the values for the spin control. You can leave the default name, **IDC_SPIN1**, but you should assign these properties:

- Check the Auto Buddy box. If you don't, you'll have to explicitly assign a buddy to your spin control in code.

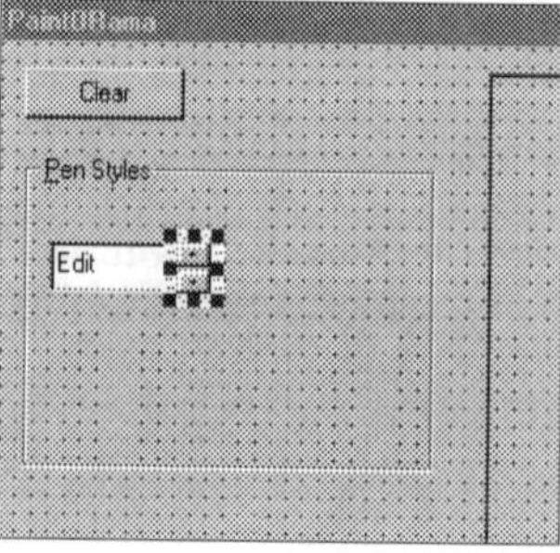

Figure 9.10
Arranging the pen-width controls.

- Check the Set Buddy Integer option. Normally, you'll use spin controls with integers. Checking this box makes the process automatic. If you want to manage another kind of value, such as floating-point numbers, don't check this box—in such a case, you'll have to manually write the code to set and retrieve the buddy values.
- Check the Arrow Keys box. Doing so allows you to operate the spin control from the keyboard as well as with the mouse. All of the other checkboxes should be unchecked.
- Set the Orientation drop-down list to Vertical, so that the little spin arrows point up and down.
- Set the Alignment drop-down list to Right. This option causes the spin control to hop inside its buddy when the screen is painted. If you choose Left, the control will hop inside its buddy and align itself along the buddy's left side when the screen is painted.

You can see the Spin Properties options in Figure 9.11.

Setting The Edit Properties

Once the spinner is happy, it's time to take care of its buddy. Visual C++ IDE makes this easy. Here are the steps to follow:

1. Set the name of the edit control to **IDC_PENWIDTH**.
2. Open ClassWizard and select the Member Variables page. Find and select **IDC_PENWIDTH** and click on Add Variable. In the Add Member Variable dialog box, set the name to **m_PenWidth**, the category to Value, and the variable type to **int**. Figure 9.12 shows the screen as it should appear. Click on OK when you're done.

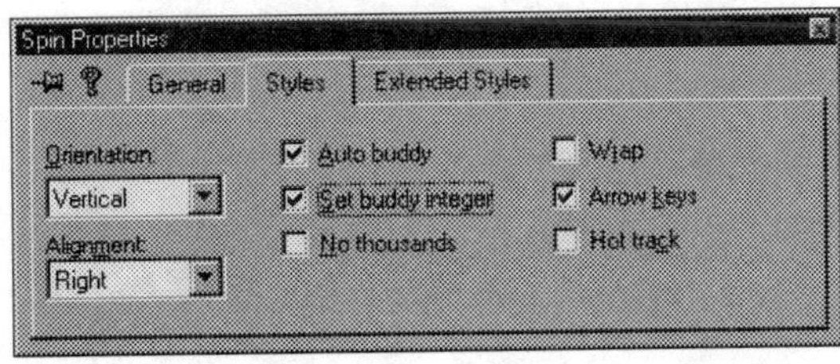

Figure 9.11
The Spin Properties dialog box.

3. When ClassWizard reappears, the dialog box will contain a pair of edit controls in which you can enter the minimum and maximum values for your variable, which MFC will validate. Set the minimum value to 1 (the thinnest pen you'll use) and the maximum value to 32 (the thickest pen you'll use)—Windows can display wider pens, so feel free to experiment with different values. If the user tries to enter a value outside this range or a non-integer value, Windows will display an error message. The dialog box should look like Figure 9.13. Click on OK when you're done.

Hooking Up The Code

Once your spin control is hooked to its buddy, you have to do only three things to generate different pen widths:

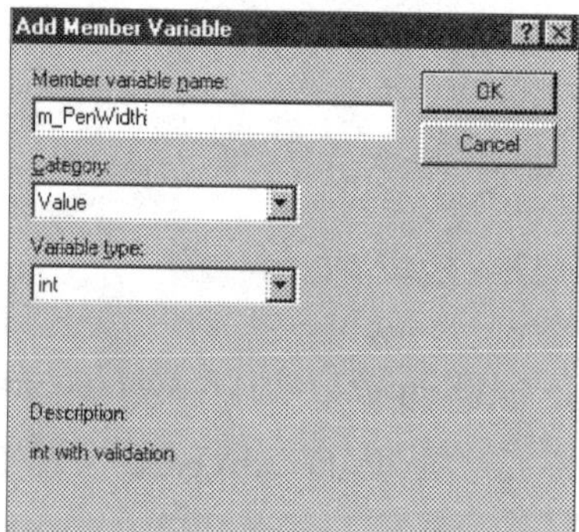

Figure 9.12
Adding the **m_PenWidth** member variable.

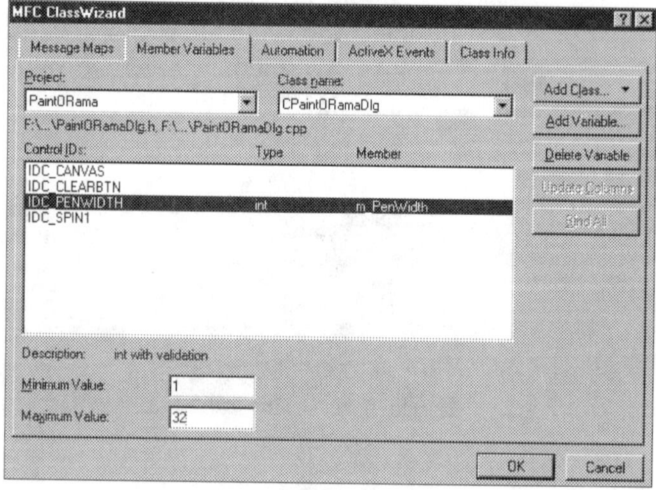

Figure 9.13
Adding validation to an integer text box.

- Initialize both the spin control and the buddy control with acceptable values at startup. Otherwise, your program will greet users with a range-check error each time it starts, which won't inspire confidence in your abilities.
- Set the spin control range so that it agrees with the range used by the buddy control. (Setting the minimum and maximum values in ClassWizard affects only the edit control, not the spin control.)
- Whenever you draw, be sure you're using a pen that matches the width the user specified. You can easily do this by retrieving the width from the buddy control, then creating a new pen in the **OnMouseDown()** function each time you draw a line.

Let's handle these issues one at a time.

Initializing The m_PenWidth Variable

You might think that because ClassWizard creates and validates the **m_PenWidth** variable, it should initialize it as well. Unfortunately, the initialization performed by ClassWizard is less than wizardly.

When ClassWizard creates a variable associated with a control such as **m_PenWidth**, the MFC framework takes care of transferring the value from the variable to the control and from the control back to the variable. This happens automatically at specific times during the life of a dialog box. Or, you can make it happen manually by calling the **UpdateData()** function and passing either **TRUE** (to move information from a control to a variable) or **FALSE** (to move the information from the variable to the control).

When your dialog box is first created, the framework calls **UpdateData(FALSE)** to move the value from **m_PenWidth** to the control **IDC_PENWIDTH**. That means that the **int** variable **m_PenWidth** must exist prior to window creation and must have a valid value. That can occur only in the **CPaintORamaDlg** class constructor.

When you look at the constructor for the dialog class, shown in Listing 9.6, you'll see a section in the middle bracketed by a pair

> **Tip**
>
> ***Don't Tamper With The Sacred Code***
>
> *Although the editor won't prohibit you from manually changing the "sacred" code within the special ClassWizard-maintained blocks, neither will it guarantee that your changes will be there next time you look for them. As a rule, if the code appears "grayed-out" in the editor, you shouldn't change it.*

of comments containing the word **AFX_DATA_INIT**. Between these comments, you'll see that **m_PenWidth** is initialized to **0**. Here ClassWizard automatically initializes all the control member variables it creates. Unfortunately, it ignores the fact that the valid values for **m_PenWidth** are between 1 and 16.

Listing 9.6 The CPaintORamaDlg class constructor.

```
CPaintORamaDlg::CPaintORamaDlg(CWnd* pParent /*=NULL*/)
    : CDialog(CPaintORamaDlg::IDD, pParent)
{
    //{{AFX_DATA_INIT(CPaintORamaDlg)
    m_PenWidth = 0;
    //}}AFX_DATA_INIT
    // Note that LoadIcon does not require a subsequent
    // DestroyIcon in Win32
    m_hIcon = AfxGetApp()->LoadIcon(IDR_MAINFRAME);
    m_PenWidth = 1;
}
```

You may be tempted to simply "fix" ClassWizard's oversight by editing the code contained in the **AFX_DATA_INIT** section. Resist that temptation. Instead, simply give **m_PenWidth** the value you prefer, after the automatic initialization block, as you can see highlighted in Listing 9.6.

Initializing The Spin Control

You can't initialize the spin control in the constructor, as you did the member variable **m_PenWidth**, because the spin control doesn't exist yet. Instead, you have to initialize it in the **OnInitDialog()** method, after the initialization for **m_Canvas** and **m_IsDrawing**.

As you saw with the **m_Canvas** variable, you can get a pointer to your spin control by calling the function **GetDlgItem (IDC_SPIN1)**. Recall that **GetDlgItem()** returns a **CWnd** pointer. Because the **CSpinButtonCtrl** spin control class is derived from **CWnd**, that works fine. However, if you want to call any spin-control-specific functions, you must cast the returned pointer to a **CSpinButtonCtrl *** like this:

```
CSpinButtonCtrl* pSpin =
  (CSpinButtonCtrl*)GetDlgItem(IDC_SPIN1);
```

Once you've retrieved a pointer to your spin control, you can use it to call the functions **SetRange()** and **SetPos()**. **SetRange()** takes two arguments: the lower and upper values for the spin control. If you fail to call **SetRange()**, the spin control default range of 100 to 0 is used. Needless to say, it's disconcerting for your users to find the up-arrow sending their numbers on a downward spiral, so you'll generally call **SetRange()**. The **SetPos()** function simply assigns an initial starting value to the spin control. Just add these two lines following the **GetDlgItem()** call:

```
pSpin->SetRange(1, 32);
pSpin->SetPos(1);
```

Initializing The Drawing Pen

Whenever the user begins drawing a new line, you'll create a new drawing pen in **OnMouseDown()**. So, you need some way to ensure that the pen still exists when it's time to draw. You'll do this by adding a new **CPen** field to the **CPaintORamaDlg** class.

Because you're already an old hand at adding member variables to the class, we won't go over the steps again. Name your member variable **m_Pen**. You don't have to initialize it.

Do you remember how two-step initialization works? You first create a **CPen** object using the default constructor, and then use the **CreatePen()** method to complete the initialization. You can't call **CreatePen()** a second time on an existing **CPen**. But, that's exactly what you'd like to do here—every time **OnMouseDown()** is called, you want to call **m_Pen.CreatePen()** and pass in the new (possibly changed) pen characteristics. To do this, you can simply "unhook" the previous pen attached to **m_Pen**, by calling the member function **DeleteObject()**. Then, you call **CreatePen()** again.

As TV detective Colombo would say, "There's just one more thing." Because you want to use the **m_PenWidth** variable to construct the new pen, you need to be sure you have the latest information from spin and his buddy. To do that, you must call **UpdateData(TRUE)** before constructing the new pen.

You can see the revised code for the **OnLButtonDown()** function in Listing 9.7.

Listing 9.7 Constructing a new pen in OnLButtonDown().

```
void CPaintORamaDlg::OnLButtonDown(UINT nFlags, CPoint
point)
{
    if (m_Canvas.PtInRect(point))   // If the point is on
                                    // the canvas
    {
        m_IsDrawing = true;         // Then we're drawing
        m_LineStart = point;        // And this is the
                                    // new starting point
        SetCapture();               // Make sure we get a
                                    // WM_LBUTTONUP

        // Construct m_Pen
        UpdateData(TRUE);           // Get values from
                                    // controls
        m_Pen.DeleteObject();
        m_Pen.CreatePen(PS_SOLID, m_PenWidth, RGB(0, 0,
          0));
    }
    // Otherwise, do nothing
}
```

Activating Your Pen

It's been a long road, but the end is in sight. There's only one more coding task to master before you have those thick lines in hand: You must activate your new pen. Fortunately, that's easy to do.

All the drawing code for the PaintORama currently resides in the **OnMouseMove()** method. To activate your new pen, simply add the following lines after you create the new device context:

```
// Prepare the DC here
dc.SelectObject(&m_Pen);
```

Now, whenever you draw, you'll use your new pen instead of the default pen. There's one itty-bitty little problem though. To see it, compile and run PaintORama (after adding the line that selects the new pen, of course). Then, select a very thick pen—say, 16 or 32 pixels wide—and draw a line close to the edge of the drawing area. You can see the resulting effect in Figure 9.14, where the point of our arrow spills out of the canvas area.

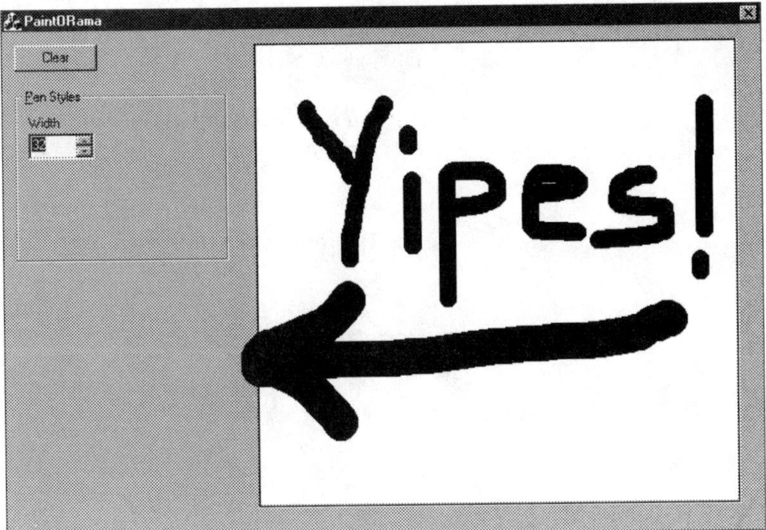

Figure 9.14
Line drawing spill-over.

Obviously, checking to see whether the pen is in the canvas area isn't sufficient when the pen is wider than a single pixel. Even though the line origin is within the canvas area, the width of the pen causes it to spill out onto the wall (so to speak).

Fortunately, the solution is simple: You can ask Windows to employ its clipping mechanism to ensure your output doesn't spill where it's not wanted. To do so, add the line

```
dc.IntersectClipRect(m_Canvas);
```

to the **OnMouseMove()** method, after the line that creates the device context. Now, Windows will clip its output to the rectangle specified by the **m_Canvas** variable.

Tune In Next Week When...

Like any good cliff-hanging sequel, the PaintORama Version 2 leaves you wanting more. You've got variable-width pens, but what about colors? What about styled pens? What about brushes? What about...?

Sorry, you'll have to wait. But, not for long—tune in to the first exciting episode of Chapter 10 to discover everything you always wanted to know about pens (and to get a look at some shapely lines).

Chapter 10

PaintORama: The Next Generation

Some people believe that a sequel is never as good as the original. Often, they're right. But, sometimes, a sequel isn't merely as good as the original—it's better.

When Gene Roddenberry created the first *Star Trek* television show, he couldn't foresee the deep vein of material he'd uncovered—a vein still being mined 30 years later. That doesn't happen with most TV shows or movies. Few people think that the beach movies of the 1960s were as good as the original *Gidget* or that the biker-movie knock-offs of the 1970s were in the same league as *The Wild Bunch*.

However, "Star Trek" has proven to be a different sort of progenitor. Although its premise and characters have been worked and reworked, it has grown and expanded, rather than collapsing into a hollow shell.

Software, too, must evolve and change, if it is to survive. In this chapter, the PaintORama application takes a quantum leap forward, adding color, styled lines, brushes, and shapes. Along the way, you'll meet some new MFC characters:

- *The* **CColorDialog** *class*—An emissary of a whole race of complex, yet subservient, creatures known as the Windows common dialog boxes.
- *The* **CComboBox** *and* **CListBox** *classes*—Close cousins on the evolutionary tree of Windows controls.

The PaintORama Version 3: Colors And Styles

When we last left the humble but honest PaintORama program, it had just hooked up with the venerable Spin Control and its loyal buddy, Edit. However, despite the presence of these new friends, things looked bleak for Paint—almost monochromatic, you might say. "What I need is some color in my life," said Paint to himself, and he set out that very day to find some, with Spin and Edit tagging along behind.

A Colorful Addition

For the PaintORama color control, let's implement a *clickable color swatch*. This isn't a built-in Windows control—it's simply a little square that displays the color of the current pen, mimicking a hardware-store paint swatch. But when you click on the digital swatch, it changes the color of the drawing pen.

You'll see how that works in a few moments. For now, let's built the infrastructure you'll need, by adding variables and laying out the interface.

Building The Foundation

To start with, you need at least one new variable to hold the current pen color, because you build a new pen every time you draw a line. The new variable—**m_PenColor**—should be a private **COLORREF**. You can use the Add Member Variable dialog box to add the variable, or simply insert this line at the bottom of the **CPaintORamaDlg** class definition:

```
COLORREF m_PenColor;
```

You'll need to initialize **m_PenColor**, as well. The best place to do so is in the class constructor, where you should add the following line to ensure that the initial pen color is black:

```
m_PenColor = RGB(0, 0, 0);
```

Now, let's begin the interface. Open the Dialog Editor and drag a static text control and a picture control from the Control toolbar, then drop them to the right of your spin control. (Don't be concerned about their exact positions.) Change the caption of the static text control to "Color"; you can leave its ID set to **IDC_STATIC**. Change the ID of the picture control to **IDC_PENCOLOR**, its Type to Rectangle, and its Color to Black, as shown in Figure 10.1.

Also, check the boxes for Sunken and Notify on the Styles page of the Picture Properties dialog box, as you can see in Figure 10.2.

Finally, before you write any code, arrange your new controls so they look like those pictured in Figure 10.3.

Color On Demand: The CColorDialog

Now, you're finally ready to write the code that lets users pick their own colors. You can offer users this feature several ways—by adding some radio buttons corresponding to the color options, or

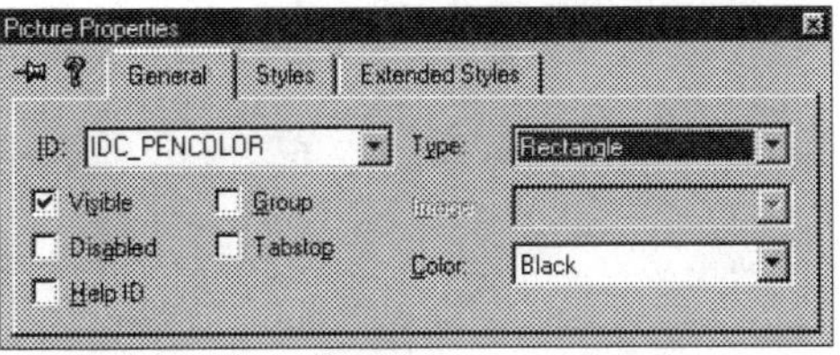

Figure 10.1
Picture Properties dialog box settings for the **IDC_PENCOLOR** control.

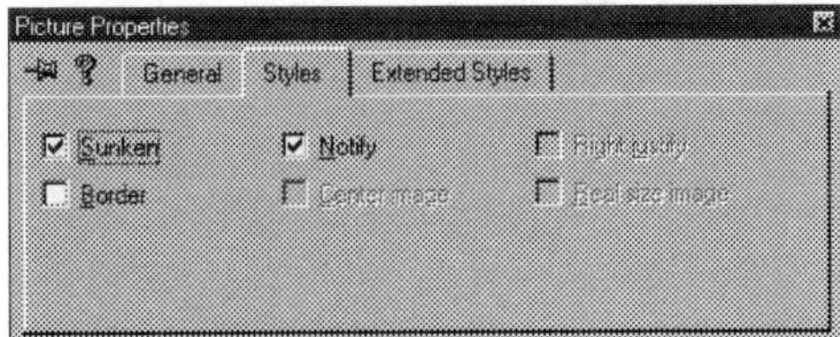

Figure 10.2
Additional Picture Properties dialog box settings for the **IDC_PENCOLOR** control.

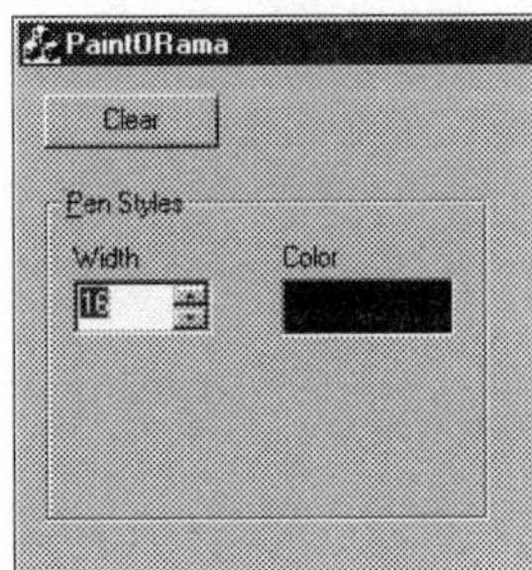

Figure 10.3
Positioning the PaintORama pen-color controls.

maybe providing a combo box or a list box. All of those are feasible choices, and we'll use each of them before the PaintORama is finished. But, there's a better way to display color selections: an instance of the built-in **CColorDialog** class, one of Windows' *common dialog boxes*.

What Are The Common Dialog Boxes?

One of the original goals of Windows (and graphical user interfaces in general) was to standardize the way applications work. For example, when different applications use the same menu structure, users can more easily learn the programs and switch between them.

However, early Windows programs fell short of this goal when it came to dialog box design. Every Windows program used a different design for the dialog boxes that opened files or printed documents, even though those operations were basically the same on every machine. So, beginning in Windows 3.0, Microsoft added six built-in dialog boxes to Windows, each designed to perform a particular common operation. Table 10.1 shows the six dialog boxes and their MFC class names.

As you can see, each dialog box allows you to select a particular resource, such as a font, a color, or a printer.

Using CColorDialog

In the PaintORama, you'll use an instance of the **CColorDialog** class to let the user pick a color, opening the dialog box when the user clicks on the **IDC_PENCOLOR** rectangle. (For this

Table 10.1 The Windows common dialog boxes.

Dialog Box Class	Description
CColorDialog	Interactive color selection
CFileDialog	Interactive file selection for opening or saving a file
CFindReplaceDialog	Interactive string searching and replacing
CFontDialog	Interactive font selection
CPageSetupDialog	Interactive page dimension selection
CPrintDialog	Interactive printer selection

technique to work, the **IDC_PENCOLOR** control must have the **SS_NOTIFY** style, which you can assign by clicking on the Notify checkbox in the Picture Properties dialog box, as shown in Figure 10.2. If you fail to do this, you won't get an error message—the Color dialog box simply won't appear.)

Open the Dialog Editor with the PaintORama main dialog box displayed, and then follow these steps:

1. Double-click on the **IDC_PENCOLOR** control in the Dialog Editor. Because no function is associated with this control, the Add Member Function dialog box appears, as shown in Figure 10.4, offering to add an **OnPencolor** function. Accept the default, and click on OK.
2. Add the highlighted code shown in Listing 10.1 to that produced by ClassWizard.

Listing 10.1 The CPaintORamaDlg::OnPencolor() function.

```
void CPaintORamaDlg::OnPencolor()
{
    CColorDialog dlg(m_PenColor);
    if (dlg.DoModal() == IDOK)
    {
        m_PenColor = dlg.GetColor();
    }
}
```

3. Locate the line that calls the **CreatePen()** function, near the end of the **OnLButtonDown()** function. Change the hard-coded color argument from **RGB(0, 0, 0)** to **m_PenColor**. The completed line should look like this:

```
m_Pen.CreatePen(PS_SOLID, m_PenWidth, m_PenColor);
```

4. Compile and run the PaintORama application. Click on the color swatch, and the Windows common Color dialog box

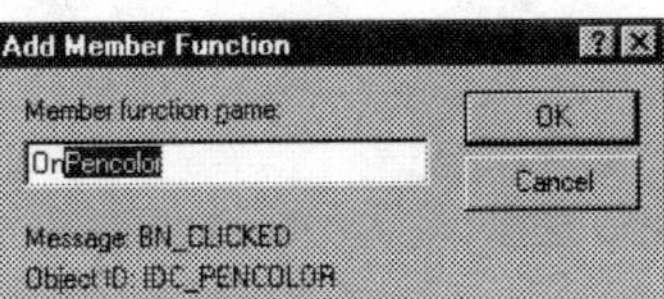

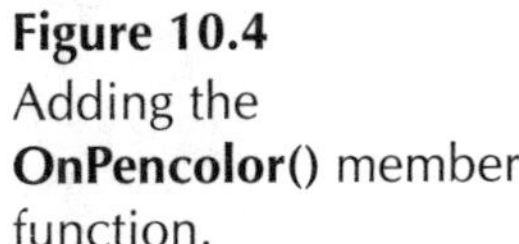
Figure 10.4
Adding the **OnPencolor()** member function.

will open, as shown in Figure 10.5. (The figure shows the dialog box fully expanded, after clicking on Define Custom Colors.)

5. Select a color in the Color dialog box, then click on OK. Change the pen width, using your spin control, and try drawing a few lines. You should be able to create a pen of any thickness and color, as you can see in Figure 10.6. Once you've scribbled for a few moments, let's take a look at how the **CColorDialog** class works. Then, we'll tackle painting the color swatch, which remains a dreary black, no matter how brilliant your pen.

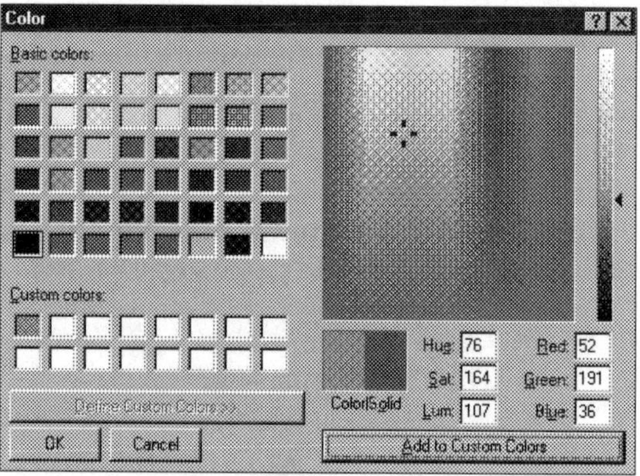

Figure 10.5
The Windows Color dialog box.

Figure 10.6
Drawing with colored pens.

How CColorDialog Works

The **CColorDialog** class is one of the easiest classes to use. You create a **CColorDialog** object like this:

```
CColorDialog dlg(RGB(255, 0, 0));
```

The constructor actually takes three arguments, but all three are given default values—so, you don't have to pass any of them. However, it's common to pass the first argument, which sets the initial selection used by the **CColorDialog**. The second argument specifies a set of flags that let you customize the way the **CColorDialog** works; it's used less often. You'll seldom need the third argument, a pointer to the parent window.

Once you've constructed a **CColorDialog** object, it exists in the computer's memory, but doesn't appear on screen. When you call **DoModal()**, the dialog box opens and allows the user to select a color. If the user closes the dialog box by clicking on OK, **DoModal()** returns the value **IDOK**—in this case, you update the color variable with the value selected by the user. If the user closes the dialog box by pressing Esc, clicking on Cancel, or using the Close box, then the **DoModal()** function returns the value **IDCANCEL**.

By using the **GetColor()** function, you can retrieve the color the user chose. It's common practice to do this only if the value returned by **DoModal()** is **IDOK**. But, because canceling the dialog box doesn't change the chosen color, you could replace the code you used in **OnPenColor()** with this:

```
CColorDialog dlg(m_PenColor);
dlg.DoModal();
m_PenColor = dlg.GetColor();
```

Even though the dialog box is no longer on screen after **DoModal()** returns, the dialog object itself—**dlg**, in this case—remains in memory. As long as the **dlg** variable remains in scope, you can retrieve its color with **GetColor()**.

Swatch Painting

Before leaving colored pens and turning to styles, let's look at what's needed to paint the **IDC_PENCOLOR** swatch with the current color. You'll need to perform three tasks:

- Create and initialize a **CRect** member variable to hold the dimensions of the swatch, as you did earlier for the canvas structure.
- Create a temporary brush, using the same color as the pen you're drawing with.
- Use the temporary brush to fill the **CRect** whenever the pen color changes.

Revise the PaintORama like this:

1. Create a new **CRect** member variable named **m_PenColorSwatch**.
2. Initialize the variable by adding the code shown in Listing 10.2 to the end of the **OnInitDialog()** function. Alert readers will notice that the code is obviously stolen from the code used to initialize the **m_Canvas** variable—only the names have been changed.

Listing 10.2 Initializing the m_PenColorSwatch variable (code added to the end of OnInitDialog()).

```
// 4. Calculate the true location of the color swatch
// Get a pointer to CWnd
CWnd* pPenColor =  GetDlgItem(IDC_PENCOLOR);
// Find its location on screen
pPenColor->GetWindowRect(&m_PenColorSwatch);
// Store client coordinates
ScreenToClient(&m_PenColorSwatch);
m_PenColorSwatch.DeflateRect(2, 2, 1, 1);
```

3. Make the highlighted additions to the **OnPencolor()** function, as shown in Listing 10.3. The **FillRect()** function takes a pointer to a **CRect** object and a pointer to a **CBrush** object, and then fills the rectangle using the brush.

Listing 10.3 Painting the pen-color swatch in OnPencolor().

```
void CPaintORamaDlg::OnPencolor()
{
    CColorDialog dlg(m_PenColor);
    if (dlg.DoModal() == IDOK)
    {
        m_PenColor = dlg.GetColor();
```

```
        CBrush swatch;
        swatch.CreateSolidBrush(m_PenColor);
        CClientDC dc(this);
        dc.FillRect(&m_PenColorSwatch, &swatch);
    }
}
```

That's all there is to it. Now, when you select a color for your pen, the color swatch visually represents your selection. Compile the program and try it.

Radio Buttons And Styled Pens

All right—you've got thick pens and colored pens. Now, all you need is some stylish pens. Because MFC provides only seven pen styles, you can easily represent them using radio buttons. (This won't work with colors—a dialog box with 256 radio buttons looks crowded. And, if your user has a 24-bit color card, you don't want to even think about using one radio button for each color.)

Adding The Interface

Here are the steps to add the color-style radio buttons to the PaintORama:

1. Drag seven radio buttons from the Control toolbar and drop them in the bottom of the Pen Styles groupbox. Arrange them in two columns, with the first four buttons in the first column and the others in the next column.
2. Name your buttons as follows, working down the first column and then returning to the second: Solid Pen, Dash Pen, Dot Pen, Dash-Dot, Dash-Dot-Dot, Null Pen, Inside Frame. Your dialog box should look like Figure 10.7.

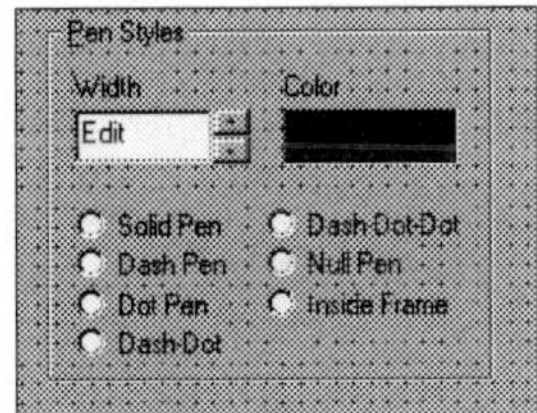

Figure 10.7
The Pen Styles radio buttons.

3. Change the ID of the *first* radio button to **IDC_SOLID_PEN**. While you're changing the name, click on the Group checkbox, as well—if you don't, the automatic radio-button transfer won't take place. Your Radio Button Properties dialog box should look like that shown in Figure 10.8.
4. With the **IDC_SOLID_PEN** radio button selected, open ClassWizard and go to the Member Variables page. Locate **IDC_SOLID_PEN**, then click on Add Variable. In the Add

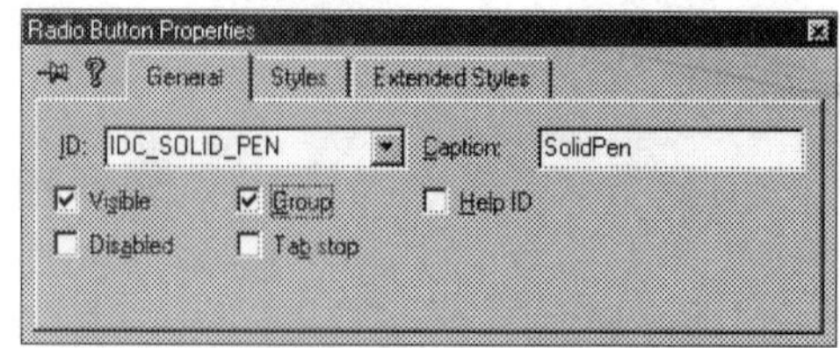

Figure 10.8
The **IDC_SOLID_PEN** Radio Button Properties dialog box options.

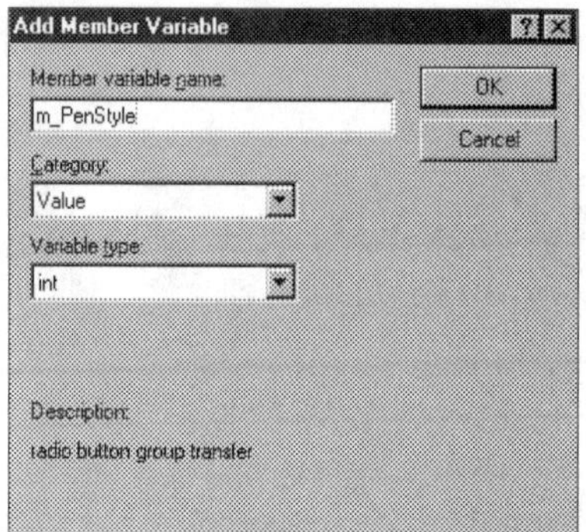

Figure 10.9
Adding the **m_PenStyle** member variable to the PaintORama application.

Member Variable dialog box, enter "**m_PenStyle**" for the dialog box name, "Value" for the Category, and "int" for the Type. At the bottom of the dialog box, you should see the message "radio button group transfer" displayed, as shown in Figure 10.9. Click on OK. Click on OK to exit ClassWizard.

5. For the radio-button transfer to work correctly, it's very important that the control *tab order* be correct. Windows and MFC use this information internally to determine which controls belong together. To set the control tab order, be sure the PaintORama dialog box is selected and then choose Layout | Tab Order from the menu (or press Ctrl+D). A set of small, blue, numbered labels will appear, as you can see in Figure 10.10. Click on each of the controls in the order shown in Figure 10.10 to set the tab order. Your screen should look like the figure when you're done.

Writing The Code

In Chapter 6, you met the radio button, but perhaps you didn't appreciate how easy radio buttons are to work with in Visual C++. When you click on any of the seven radio buttons in the PaintORama, MFC takes it upon itself to store the button's index in the variable **m_PenStyle**. This number will be 0 for the first

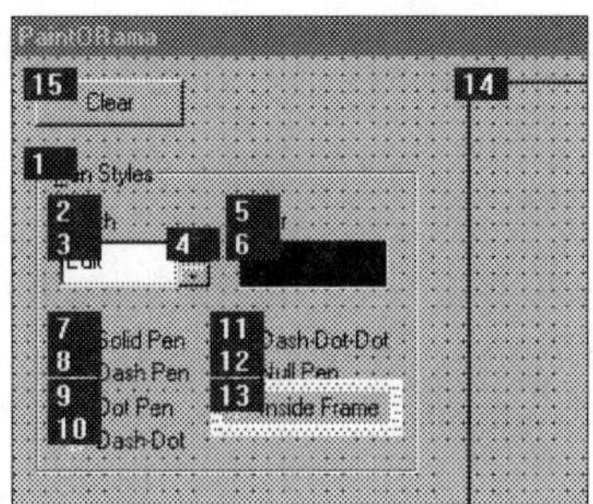

Figure 10.10
Changing the dialog box tab order.

button, 1 for the second, and so forth. Because the pen-style constants are also integers, starting with 0 for **PS_SOLID**, you don't have to do any translation—you can use the index number as is to represent the pen style.

As with the spin control, this transfer of data from the radio button controls to the **m_PenStyle** variable is accomplished automatically when the dialog box is first created, and can be performed programmatically by calling **UpdateData(TRUE)**. Because you're already doing that for the **m_PenWidth** variable, you get the **m_PenStyle** variable updated for free.

Well, not exactly for free—you do have to change two lines of code. To the dialog box constructor, add the line

```
m_PenStyle = PS_INSIDEFRAME;
```

In addition, change the line in **OnLButtonDown()** that constructs the pen to read

```
m_Pen.CreatePen(m_PenStyle, m_PenWidth, m_PenColor);
```

When you're finished, compile and run your new pen-complete version of the PaintORama. Notice that you can create styled pens in any color, but the width must be set to 1. If you try to create styled pens with a width other than 1, you get the plain old solid pen.

At this point, you won't notice any difference between the solid pen style and the inside frame pen style—this difference will become apparent only when you draw shapes and figures. Which, coincidentally, is the subject for the next section. How fortuitous!

PaintORama: Lines and Shapes

As you've seen in the last few chapters, drawing lines and figures isn't really difficult—you can do it with just a few functions. Because the PaintORama can already do freehand drawing, all you need is a control to let the user switch between freehand and lines or rectangles.

You could use radio buttons, but let's try something new: a combo box. As before, you'll build the interface first, then come back and add the necessary code to make it work.

A Nice Little Combo

Be sure the PaintORama project's main dialog form is open in the Dialog Editor. When you're all set, follow these steps to build the lines-and-shapes interface:

1. Drag and drop a groupbox from the Control toolbar to your form. Place it below the Pen Styles groupbox, and make it 40 units high and 128 units wide to match the width of the Pen Styles groupbox (you may have to turn off the grid).
2. Change the caption to "&Lines and Shapes". (As with the Pen Styles groupbox, the ampersand causes Windows to underline the "L" in the caption. You can use the keyboard to switch to the control contained in the groupbox by typing Alt+L.) You can leave the groupbox ID set to **IDC_STATIC**, but be sure to click the Group checkbox in the Group Box Properties dialog box. This makes the groupbox act as a terminator, or bookend, for the group of radio buttons at the bottom of the Pen Styles groupbox.
3. Select a combo box control and drag it from the Control toolbar, dropping it in your groupbox. You can see the combo box control highlighted in Figure 10.11.
4. Size and position the combo box within your groupbox. For a combo box, this is a two-step process: Stretch the control so that it fills the width of the groupbox (leaving a suitable border), then position your mouse over the combo-box button and click. Another rectangle will appear. Use this rectangle to specify the size of the open combo box's list. If

Figure 10.11
Selecting the combo box control in the Control toolbar.

you fail to do this, the combo box won't open when you click on it. Figure 10.12 shows the combo box activation area being resized.

5. When you've adjusted the size of the combo box to your satisfaction, open the Combo Box Properties dialog box by right-clicking on the control and selecting Properties from the context menu. On the General tab, change the name to **IDC_SHAPES** and be sure the Tab Stop and Visible boxes are checked. All the others should be unchecked.

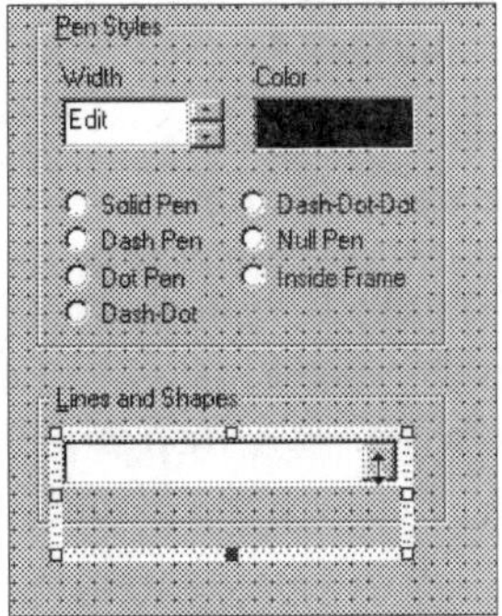

Figure 10.12
Sizing the combo-box activation rectangle.

6. On the Data tab, enter the following strings, each on a separate line: "Freehand", "Lines", "Ovals", and "Rectangles". Use Ctrl+Enter to end each line. (If you use Enter alone, you simply close the dialog box.) Your dialog box should look like Figure 10.13.
7. On the Styles tab, change the combo box's Type to Drop List. (Other combo-box styles let the user enter a new value as well as pick from a list, but in this case you don't want to allow new values.) Set the Owner Draw combo box to No. The Vertical Scroll checkbox should be checked, but all the other boxes should be unchecked.
8. Use ClassWizard to add a new member variable for the combo box. Name the variable **m_ShapesCombo**, set its Category to Control, and set its Type to **CComboBox**.
9. Add the following lines of initialization code to the **OnInitDialog()** method:

```
// 5. Initialize the m_ShapesCombo
m_ShapesCombo.SetCurSel(0);
```

Because **m_ShapesCombo** is a control variable, you can't initialize it in the constructor—it doesn't exist yet. You must

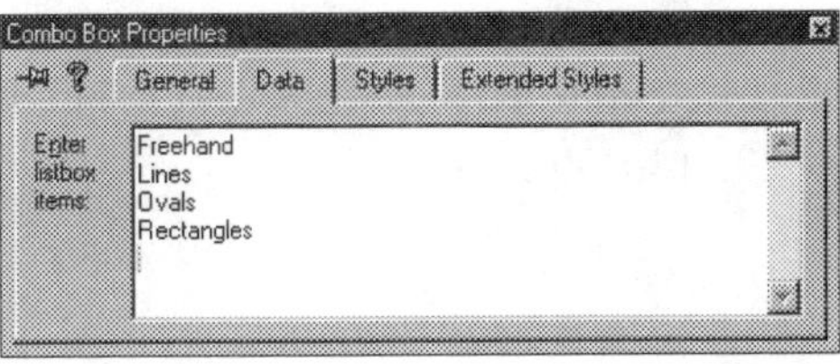

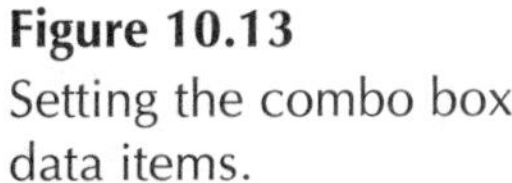

Figure 10.13
Setting the combo box data items.

initialize it in the **OnInitDialog()** method. The **CComboBox SetCurSel()** method sets the current selection of the combo box, with the first item being 0, the second 1, and so on. If you don't do this, the combo box will be empty until the user clicks on it.

Lines And Shapes

Drawing lines and shapes is a little different from freehand drawing. When you're drawing freehand, each time the mouse moves, the PaintORama draws a small line segment connecting the current mouse position with the position recorded in the variable **m_LineStart**. Then, the program updates **m_LineStart** so that it "follows" the mouse around the screen as you draw.

With lines and shapes, however, you want to draw the finished shape only when the mouse button is released. So, you won't update the value of **m_LineStart** as the mouse moves—instead, you'll add another variable, **m_LineEnd**, and then write a general function **DrawShapes()** that draws a shape between any two lines.

Here are the steps to follow:

1. Add a new private **CPoint** variable named **m_LineEnd** to the **CPaintORamaDlg** class definition. You can use the Add Member Variable dialog box or simply enter the variable by hand.
2. In the **OnLButtonDown()** function, locate the line that initializes the **m_LineStart** variable. Below it, add the following line to initialize **m_LineEnd**:

   ```
   m_LineEnd   = point;   // This is the new ending point
   ```

3. Delete the call to **SetCapture()**.
4. Modify the **OnLButtonUp()** function to set the **m_LineEnd** variable and then call the new **DrawShape()** function. Delete the call to **ReleaseCapture()**. The revised function is shown in Listing 10.4.

Listing 10.4 The revised OnLButtonUp() function.

```
void CPaintORamaDlg::OnLButtonUp(UINT nFlags, CPoint
point)
{
    // Set the drawing mode to false
    m_IsDrawing = false;

    // Update the line end
    m_LineEnd = point;

    // Draw the appropriate line or shape
    DrawShape();
}
```

5. Add the **DrawShape()** member function to the **CPaintORamaDlg** class by right-clicking on the class name in the ClassView window, then choosing Add Member Function from the context menu. In the Add Member Function dialog box, the return type should be **void**, and the function declaration should read

   ```
   DrawShape(bool stretch = false);
   ```

6. Add the code shown in Listing 10.5 to that produced by the ClassWizard. We'll discuss how the code works in the next section.

Listing 10.5 The DrawShape() member function.

```
void CPaintORamaDlg::DrawShape(bool stretch)
{
    CClientDC dc(this);
    dc.IntersectClipRect(m_Canvas);

    // Find out what the drawing mode is
    int drawMode = m_ShapesCombo.GetCurSel();

    // Prepare the DC here
    dc.SelectObject(&m_Pen);
    if (stretch && drawMode != 0)
    {
        dc.SetROP2(R2_NOT);
    }

    // Draw the appropriate shape
    switch(drawMode)
    {
```

```
        case 0: // Freehand
            // Move to the start of the line
            dc.MoveTo(m_LineStart);
            // Draw to current position
            dc.LineTo(m_LineEnd);
            // Update current mouse position
            m_LineStart = m_LineEnd;
            break;
        case 1: // Lines
            dc.MoveTo(m_LineStart);
            dc.LineTo(m_LineEnd);
            break;
        case 2: // Ovals
            dc.Ellipse(CRect(m_LineStart, m_LineEnd));
            break;
        case 3: // Rectangles
            dc.Rectangle(CRect(m_LineStart, m_LineEnd));
            break;
        }
}
```

7. Make the changes to the **OnMouseMove()** function shown in Listing 10.6.

Listing 10.6 The Revised OnMouseMove() function.

```
void CPaintORamaDlg::OnMouseMove(UINT nFlags, CPoint
point)
{
    // Draw if m_IsDrawing and on the canvas and
    // the left-mouse button is pressed
    if (m_IsDrawing && (nFlags & MK_LBUTTON) &&
        m_Canvas.PtInRect(point))
    {
        DrawShape(true); // Erase first line
        m_LineEnd = point;
        DrawShape(true); // Stretch it
    }
}
```

8. Compile and run your program. As you'll see when you switch from freehand drawing to rectangles or ellipses, the PaintORama gives you visual feedback with a "stretchy" shape that doesn't settle down until you release the mouse button. In the next section, you'll see how this *rubber-banding* works. In the meantime, try out the new features, which you can see in Figure 10.14.

Figure 10.14
Using rubber-banding to draw ellipses in the PaintORama program.

Rubber-Banding Secrets

The **DrawShape()** function is a little longer than functions we've shown you previously, but once you grasp the general structure, it's easy to understand. The **DrawShape()** function works in concert with the **OnMouseMove()** and **OnLButtonUp()** functions to produce the rubber-banding effect.

Let's go through **DrawShape()** one step at a time:

- The first two lines simply set up the device context. These are the same lines you used previously in **OnMouseMove()**.
- The second step (the third line of code) retrieves the current state of the combo box by using the **GetCurSel()** function. **GetCurSel()** returns the number of the item selected in the combo box, starting with 0. You need that value to decide what kind of shape to draw, so you save it in the **drawMode** local variable.
- The third step sets up the device context. Here, you select the current pen, just as you did before. Then, if you're *not* drawing freehand, and if you *are* in "stretch" mode, you use the **SetROP2()** function to set the drawing mode to **R2_NOT**, which reverses every pixel on the screen. (You'll see why this is important in a moment.) Notice that the code skips **SetROP2()** if you're drawing freehand.

- The fourth, and final, step is a **switch** statement built around the value of **drawMode** (the value retrieved from the combo box). In each case, you draw a particular figure. In the first case (0), you use the code for freehand drawing, which comes from the original **OnMouseMove()** function. The second case (1) draws a line by using **MoveTo()** and **LineTo()**. The third and fourth cases are even simpler, drawing ovals and rectangles with the **Ellipse()** and **Rectangle()** functions.

In order to understand rubber-banding, keep the **DrawShape()** function in mind while looking at the **OnMouseMove()** function. In **OnMouseMove()**, the first statement (provided the mouse is moved into the canvas area) calls **DrawShape(true)**. When the combo box is set to draw a line or shape, passing **true** means to turn on the **R2_NOT** (reverse) drawing mode. In reverse mode, drawing a line or figure twice erases the line or figure—this trick makes rubber-banding possible.

Notice that the first time you call **OnMouseMove()**, both **m_LineStart** and **m_LineEnd** contain the same value, so nothing is drawn. However, after calling **DrawShape(true)**, **OnMouseMove()** updates **m_LineEnd** with the new pen position, and calls **DrawShape(true)** again. This time, **m_LineEnd** and **m_LineStart** *don't* have identical values, so the line or shape is drawn "reversed" on screen.

The next time you call **OnMouseMove()**, it calls **DrawShape (true)** again. Because **m_LineEnd** hasn't been updated since the last call to **DrawShape()**, the current call draws the new rectangle or oval directly on top of the previous one. The drawing mode is **R2_NOT**, so the drawing operation restores each pixel to the color it had before the first rectangle was drawn, thereby erasing the figure. Then, the **m_LineEnd** variable is updated again, and the whole process starts over.

When the mouse is finally released in the **OnLButtonUp()** method, **DrawShape()** is called one last time, with no argument. Because the default argument is **false**, the regular pen and drawing mode are used. The final shape or line is drawn with the correct color and thickness, and won't be erased again.

PaintORama: The Final Brush-Off

Having added the pen-style controls, you should find it easy to add the brush style. You'll pick the brush style from a list box and then use a color swatch to choose the color, just as you did for the pens.

Because you're an old hand at this by now, our instructions will be brief. As Sgt. Friday used to say, "Just the facts."

Making A List

Grab the following controls from the Control toolbar and drop then below the Lines And Shapes groupbox:

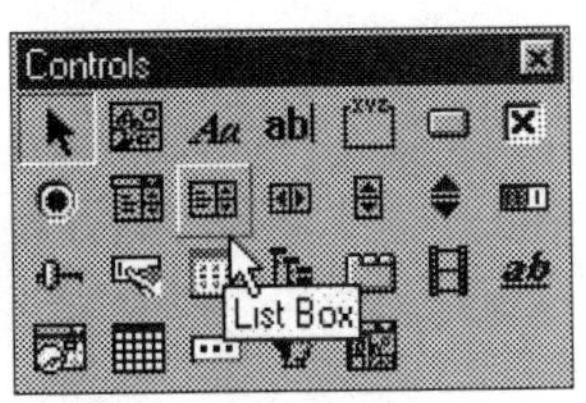

Figure 10.15
The list box control on the Control toolbar.

- A *groupbox*—Give it the caption "&Brush Styles". Leave the ID set to the default, **IDC_STATIC**.
- A *list box*—You can see the list box selected in Figure 10.15. You'll set its properties later.
- *Two pictures*—Change their Type to Rectangle and their Color to Black. Give one the ID **IDC_BRUSHCOLOR** and the other the ID **IDC_BRUSHPREVIEW**. Assign **IDC_BRUSHCOLOR** the Notify Style.
- *Three static text*—Leave their names set to the default value, **IDC_STATIC**. Change their captions to "Styles", "Color", and "Preview". Size and arrange the controls as shown in Figure 10.16. The picture control at the upper right is **IDC_BRUSHCOLOR**, and the picture at the lower right is **IDC_BRUSHPREVIEW**.

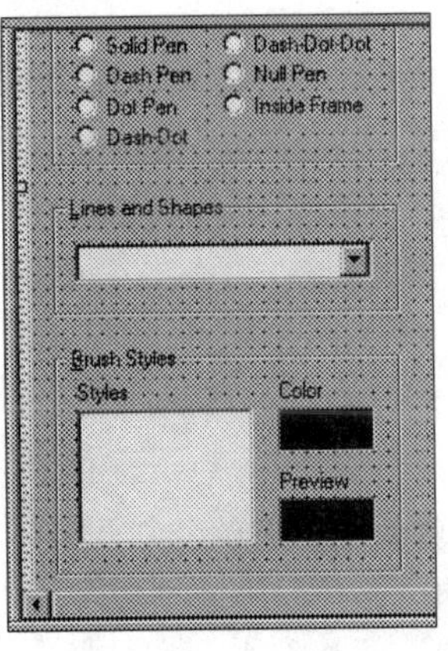

Figure 10.16
Arranging the Brush Styles controls.

Setting The List-Box Properties

Now, set the properties for the list box control. On the General tab, change the list box's ID to **IDC_BRUSHSTYLE**. Be sure the Tab Stop and Visible checkboxes are selected and all the rest are clear.

On the Styles tab, choose Single from the Selection drop-down list and No from the Owner Draw drop-down list. Check the

Border, Notify, Vertical Scroll, and No Integral Height checkboxes and clear all the others. You can see this in Figure 10.17.

Initializing The List Box Control

Although Visual C++ can automatically populate a combo box, it can't populate a list box—you have to do it in code by using the **CListBox::AddString()** function. Here are the two steps to follow to initialize your list box control:

1. Using ClassWizard, add a new member variable for the **IDC_BRUSHSTYLE** list box. Name your variable **m_BrushStyleList** and set its Category to Control and its Type to **CListBox**.
2. Add the code in Listing 10.7 to the **OnInitDialog()** function. This code adds to the list box a description of each possible brush style. The last line makes the ninth item (the stock White brush at index position 8, starting from 0) the default selection.

Listing 10.7 Initializing the IDC_BRUSHSTYLE list box control.

```
// 6. Initialize the m_BrushStyleList Listbox
m_BrushStyleList.AddString("(none)");
m_BrushStyleList.AddString("Solid");
m_BrushStyleList.AddString("LL-UR Diagonal");
m_BrushStyleList.AddString("UL-LR Diagonal");
m_BrushStyleList.AddString("Grid");
m_BrushStyleList.AddString("Grid Diagonal");
m_BrushStyleList.AddString("Horizontal");
m_BrushStyleList.AddString("Vertical");
m_BrushStyleList.AddString("White");
m_BrushStyleList.AddString("Light Gray");
m_BrushStyleList.AddString("Medium Gray");
m_BrushStyleList.AddString("Dark Gray");
m_BrushStyleList.AddString("Black");
m_BrushStyleList.SetCurSel(8);
```

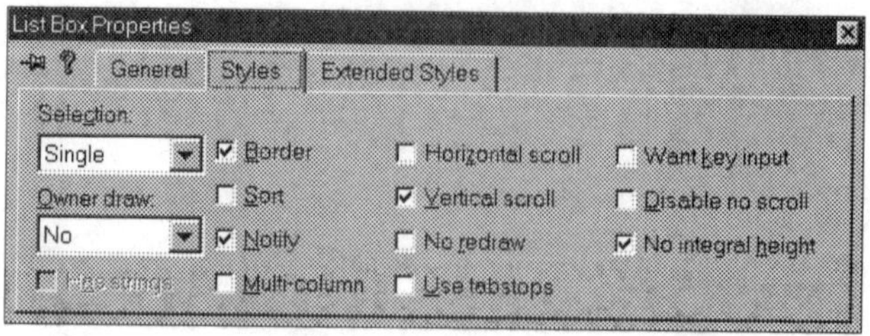

Figure 10.17
The **IDC_BRUSHSTYLE** list-box properties.

Adding Brush Variables

You'll need much the same set of variables for your brushes as you needed for the pens you created earlier. Table 10.2 shows the variables you need to add, along with their types and descriptions. You can either add these by hand or use the Add Member Variable dialog box.

Initializing The Brush Variables

You can initialize four of the brush variables—**m_BrushColorSwatch**, **m_BrushPreviewSwatch**, **m_BrushColor**, and **m_Brush**—in the **OnInitDialog()** function. Listing 10.8 shows the code you need to add. The remaining variable, **m_BrushStyle**, will be initialized when you make changes to the list box.

Listing 10.8 Initializing the brush member variables.

```
// 7. Calculate the true location of the brush color
// swatch
CWnd* pBrushColor = GetDlgItem(IDC_BRUSHCOLOR);
pBrushColor->GetWindowRect(&m_BrushColorSwatch);
ScreenToClient(&m_BrushColorSwatch);
m_BrushColorSwatch.DeflateRect(2, 2, 1, 1);

// 8. Calculate the true location of the brush preview
// color swatch
CWnd* pPreviewColor =  GetDlgItem(IDC_BRUSHPREVIEW);
pPreviewColor->GetWindowRect(&m_BrushPreviewSwatch);
ScreenToClient(&m_BrushPreviewSwatch);
m_BrushPreviewSwatch.DeflateRect(2, 2, 1, 1);

// 9. Initialize the m_BrushColor variable
```

Table 10.2 Brush-related member variables.

Variable Name	Type	Description
m_Brush	**CBrush**	Fills all filled figures.
m_BrushColor	**COLORREF**	Constructs the **m_Brush**.
m_BrushStyle	**int**	Differentiates among the hatch-style brushes.
m_BrushColorSwatch	**CRect**	Stores the coordinates of the brush color swatch.
m_BrushPreviewSwatch	**CRect**	Stores the coordinates of the brush preview swatch.

```
m_BrushColor = RGB(255, 255, 255);

// 10. Use the stock white brush as the default.
m_Brush.CreateStockObject(WHITE_BRUSH);
```

The code in Listing 10.8 calculates the dimensions for the two brush-color swatches. This is the same code you used for the pen-color swatch—with the names changed appropriately, of course. The **m_BrushColor** variable is set to white (**RGB(255, 255, 255)**), but **m_Brush** is initialized by using the stock white brush, rather than constructing a solid brush using **m_BrushColor**.

Brushing Up Your Code

The code to use brushes is simpler than that required for pens. All you have to do is add the single line

```
dc.SelectObject(&m_Brush);
```

to the **DrawShape()** function, right after the line that selects **m_Pen** into the device context.

Although painting with a brush is simpler than using a pen, creating a brush involves more work. However, the code isn't complex—it's just long. Here, in a nutshell, is the basic idea:

1. Delete the old brush. You do this using the line

   ```
   m_Brush.DeleteObject();
   ```

2. Find out which brush style is currently selected in the **m_BrushStyleList** list box, using the **GetCurSel()** function. Store the variable in a local **int** called **style**.
3. Write a big **switch** that creates a different brush for each possible value of **style**.
4. Call the function **PaintBrushPreview()** to display the new brush style in the **m_BrushPreviewSwatch**.

Handling The LBN_SELCHANGE Message

That process looks pretty straightforward, and it is. The question is, where are you going to *put* the code? Well, it turns out that when you change selections in a list box, the list box fires a

LBN_SELCHANGE message. If you double-click on your list box in the Dialog Editor, ClassWizard will offer to add a new member function called **OnSelchangeBrushstyle()** to handle that message for you. Take the Wizard up on the offer and put your code there.

You can see the finished function in Listing 10.9.

Listing 10.9 The OnSelchangeBrushstyle() member function.

```
void CPaintORamaDlg::OnSelchangeBrushstyle()
{
    m_Brush.DeleteObject();

    int style = m_BrushStyleList.GetCurSel();

    switch(style)
    {
    case 0:
        m_Brush.CreateStockObject(NULL_BRUSH);
        break;
    case 1:
        m_Brush.CreateSolidBrush(m_BrushColor);
        break;
    case 2:
        m_Brush.CreateHatchBrush(HS_BDIAGONAL,
          m_BrushColor);
        break;
    case 3:
        m_Brush.CreateHatchBrush(HS_FDIAGONAL,
          m_BrushColor);
        break;
    case 4:
        m_Brush.CreateHatchBrush(HS_CROSS, m_BrushColor);
        break;
    case 5:
        m_Brush.CreateHatchBrush(HS_DIAGCROSS,
          m_BrushColor);
        break;
    case 6:
        m_Brush.CreateHatchBrush(HS_HORIZONTAL,
          m_BrushColor);
        break;
    case 7:
        m_Brush.CreateHatchBrush(HS_VERTICAL,
          m_BrushColor);
        break;
```

```
    case 9:
        m_Brush.CreateStockObject(LTGRAY_BRUSH);
        break;
    case 10:
        m_Brush.CreateStockObject(GRAY_BRUSH);
        break;
    case 11:
        m_Brush.CreateStockObject(DKGRAY_BRUSH);
        break;
    case 12:
        m_Brush.CreateStockObject(BLACK_BRUSH);
        break;
    default:
        m_Brush.CreateStockObject(WHITE_BRUSH);
        break;
    }
    PaintBrushPreview();
}
```

Adding Brush Preview And Color Support

To change the brush color, do exactly the same thing you did with the pens. Double-click on the **IDC_BRUSHCOLOR** control (after making sure its Notify check box is selected), and accept ClassWizard's default function name, **OnBrushcolor()**. Add to the function the code from Listing 10.10.

Listing 10.10 Changing the brush color with OnBrushcolor().

```
void CPaintORamaDlg::OnBrushcolor()
{
    CColorDialog dlg(m_BrushColor);
    if (dlg.DoModal() == IDOK)
    {
        m_BrushColor = dlg.GetColor();
        CClientDC dc(this);
        CBrush b(m_BrushColor);
        dc.FillRect(&m_BrushColorSwatch, &b);
    }
    OnSelchangeBrushstyle();
}
```

Notice that this code is almost identical to that used in the **OnPencolor()** method at the beginning of the chapter. The only significant difference is that every time the brush color changes, you want to make a new brush—so, the function ends with a call to **OnSelchangeBrushstyle()**. When you worked with pens, you created a new pen every time a line was drawn, so you didn't worry about creating a new pen when the pen color changed.

The last function needed before you can try out the PaintORama is **PaintBrushPreview()**. This function isn't a Windows message handler, like most of the other functions you've written in this chapter. To add it, you'll need to use the class context menu's Add Member Function command, or add the function manually. (If you add the function manually, remember to declare it in the class definition [the header file] as well as add the code to the implementation [CPP] file.)

The **PaintBrushPreview()** function is all of five lines, including the braces:

```
void CPaintORamaDlg::PaintBrushPreview()
{
    CClientDC dc(this);
    dc.FillRect(&m_BrushPreviewSwatch, &m_Brush);
}
```

Once you've finished, compile and run your program, and fix any errors. Figure 10.18 shows the PaintORama program at pla..., er..., work.

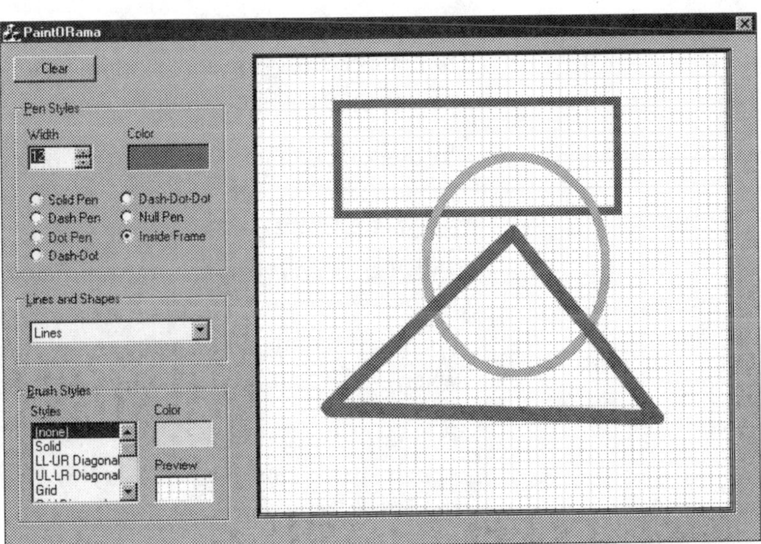

Figure 10.18
Running the PaintORama program.

Coming Soon: Only In Theaters

Let's face it, this has been a looong chapter, with a whole bunch of details. And, unfortunately, the PaintORama still has a few limitations whose solutions will have to wait for future episodes. But, because you've hung in there this long, we'll give you a preview of the next chapter. We can't promise you the secrets of the universe, but you'll learn a neat solution to an annoying problem that even experienced Windows programmers wrestle with.

Here's the problem: When you paint outside the **OnPaint()** function, how do you repaint the screen when a stray window inadvertently messes up your masterpiece? With an interactive painting program like the PaintORama, moving the painting code to **OnPaint()** seems fraught with problems.

In the long term, there's an easy answer to the dilemma: the document-view architecture. With document-view, which you'll begin studying in the next chapter, every program separates data handling from data presentation.

For instance, consider the PaintORama. Each line and shape, along with its characteristics, could be a piece of data—that's how vector graphics programs like Adobe Illustrator and CorelDRAW! work. On the other hand, the PaintORama document could simply be a data structure that allows you to reconstruct the bitmapped image on screen at any time—that's a little like how paint programs like Windows Paint or Adobe Photoshop work.

In the next chapter, we'll again improve the PaintORama, by showing you a quick and efficient solution to the repainting problem: the **CMetaFileDC** class. But, introducing **CMetaFileDC** will also mean the swan-song for dialog box-based applications in these pages—one last cameo appearance, and it's time to move on. You'll see the **CDialog** class and the Dialog Editor once more when we look at ActiveX controls and the **FormView** class.

But, until then, it's time to bid the Dialog Editor goodbye. Tomorrow's a new day, and you'll want to be fresh when you take the PaintORama to meet the document-view.

Chapter 11

Building Documents And Views

The very first computers—not so many years ago—had no software programs as we know them. Instead, programmers rewired the hardware each time they wanted to teach the behemoth a new trick.

The invention of the stored software program, which led to the general-purpose programmable computer, was the first step on the road to the software nirvana we enjoy today. Okay, so perhaps *nirvana* is a tad hyperbolic. But, programming has greatly improved since those early days.

For example, most modern programs are more *structured*. Early programs were monsters of monolithic, straight-line code, with no procedures or local variables. Programmers found this kind of code very hard to maintain. For example, changing a variable at line 25,435 required the programmer to laboriously trace through the rest of the program, looking for subtle side-effects that might arise from a remote jump instruction targeting the modified region of code.

As programmers learned more about the kinds of problems associated with unrestrained jumps (**gotos**) and global variables, they developed informal rules for writing maintainable code. Some of these rules were enshrined in new programming languages—such as the scoping rules associated with Pascal—but others were merely rules of thumb based on previously successful programs. The most interesting rules concerned program structure, and helped programmers decide how many procedures to include in their programs, how big those procedures should be, and how those procedures should communicate with one another.

Modern object-oriented programming has its own set of rules. When programmers began creating classes and objects, the old rules—developed in an age of procedural code—didn't seem to apply. So, programmers sought new ways to arrange the pieces that made up their programs. Programmers working with Smalltalk (one of the original object-oriented languages) developed the widely used *Model-View-Controller* (MVC) architecture.

Just as an earlier generation of programmers learned to separate their programs into self-contained procedures, the developers of MVC proclaimed that modern programmers should separate their programs into three specific kinds of objects:

- *Model objects*—To store a computerized representation of an account, a customer, or whatever real-world entities the program deals with.
- *View objects*—To display information.
- *Controller objects*—To respond to user input.

MFC supports the MVC architecture by means of the *Document-View architecture* (usually known simply as *DocView*). The DocView architecture handles documents: Its model part stores documents and its view part displays them. If you wonder what happened to the controller part of MVC, never fear—Windows components and Windows itself comprise the controller. You don't need to write a controller class to gather input and queue messages for delivery to the document or view, because Windows performs those functions automatically.

Rather than begin work on a DocView application, we're going to revisit the PaintORama program and take a look at how you can use a Windows precursor to DocView—the **CMetaFileDC** class—to record the state of each PaintORama masterpiece you create.

PaintORama: WM_PAINT All Over Again

The document part of a DocView program stores the user's data. For example, in a word-processing program, the document part stores the characters and any formatting they contain. In a spreadsheet program, the document stores the formulas and data the user entered. In the PaintORama program, the document stores the color, shape, pen style and thickness, and the brush used for each line, rectangle, and ellipse.

The PaintORama program has no document part. Thus, when it becomes necessary to repaint the canvas after switching to another application, all the user's work is lost. Try it for yourself. Draw a few lines using the current version of the PaintORama. Drag the window down so that only the title bar is visible, then drag it back to its original position. Surprise—your drawing has vanished. To ameliorate this problem, let's give the user the ability to save the painting.

You could start by creating a set of classes to model each drawing shape, and then create a collection that stores each class. But, Windows offers a much quicker and easier approach: using the **CMetaFileDC** class to create and store a metafile. A *metafile* is simply a data structure that holds GDI commands like **LineTo()** or **Rectangle()**. Using the **CMetaFileDC** class, you can automatically record lines and shapes as the user draws them. When the image needs to be redrawn, the program can play back the metafile in its **OnPaint()** method. Let's take the PaintORama and add this feature, giving the world the new version of PaintORama.

A PaintORama Overview

Adding metafile support to your application requires only three steps. (Of course, actually implementing the code will involve many details, as always.) Here's an overview of those steps:

- You'll add a new **CMetaFileDC** pointer as a class member variable. This variable points to a **CMetaFileDC** object created in the freestore (heap). You'll also write the code that allocates and destroys the **CMetaFileDC** object.
- You'll record every GDI operation in the metafile.
- In the **OnPaint()** function, you'll use the metafile to redisplay the lines and shapes that make up the painting. After the

painting is redisplayed, you'll reinitialize the metafile, so it can continue to record each painting stroke.

Let's walk through each step. You can make the changes directly to the PaintORama application. Or, better yet, you can copy the whole project directory to a new folder so you don't inadvertently mess up the earlier version. On the CD, you'll find the new PaintORama version in a separate directory.

Creating The CMetaFileDC

Begin by opening the PaintORama application and selecting the ClassView pane. Expand the **CPaintORamaDlg** class and then follow these instructions:

1. Open the Add Member Variables dialog box by right-clicking on the **CPaintORamaDlg** class and choosing Add Member Variable from the context menu. In the dialog box, add a **private** pointer to a **CMetaFileDC** (data type **CMetaFileDC ***). Name your pointer **m_pMF**, as you can see in Figure 11.1.
2. Use the ClassView window to locate and open the **OnInitDialog()** function. At the end of the function (before you return **TRUE**), add the initialization for the **m_pMF** variable, which creates a new **CMetaFileDC** object on the heap:

```
// 11. Add the MetaFile
m_pMF = new CMetaFileDC;
m_pMF->Create();
```

3. Right-click on the **CPaintORamaDlg** class in the ClassView window once more, and choose Add Windows Message Handler from the context menu. In the dialog box that appears, select the **WM_DESTROY** message, as shown in

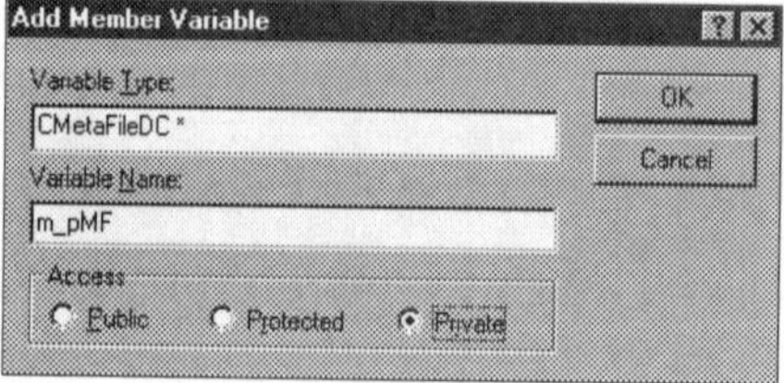

Figure 11.1
Adding the **m_pMF** member variable.

Figure 11.2. Click on Add And Edit and use the Editor window to insert the highlighted code from Listing 11.1.

Listing 11.1 The CPaintORamaDlg::OnDestroy() member function.

```
void CPaintORamaDlg::OnDestroy()
{
    CDialog::OnDestroy();

    // TODO: Add your message handler code here
    m_pMF->Close();
    delete m_pMF;
}
```

As you see, the infrastructure code needed for a **CMetaFileDC** object is pretty straightforward. You use **new** and **Create()** to initialize the metafile and **Close()** and **delete** to free it before your program exits. That's Step 1; in the next step, you record the GDI operations.

Recording With A CMetaFileDC

The base device context class, **CDC**, associates two device contexts with each **CDC**-derived object (for example, instances of **CPaintDC** or **CClientDC**). One device context (DC), whose handle is stored in the member variable **m_hDC**, is known as the *output device context*. DC methods that produce output—such as

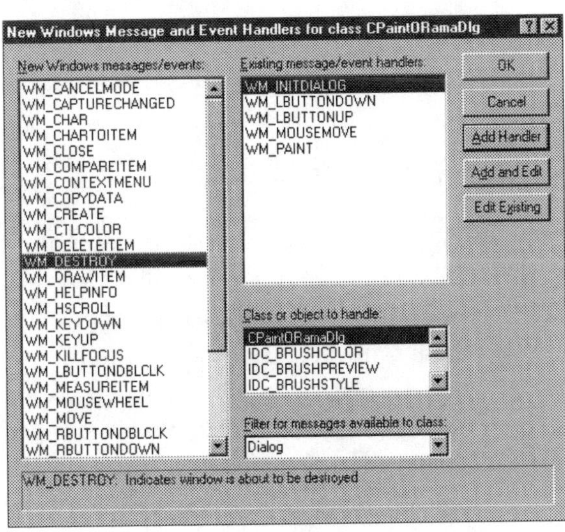

Figure 11.2 Creating the **WM_DESTROY** Windows message handler.

LineTo() or **Rectangle()**—use this output DC. A second DC, whose handle is stored in **m_hAttribDC**, is known as the *attribute device context*. As its name suggests, you use it to change the attributes of the output DC. For instance, to change the thickness of a pen, you use the attribute DC.

When using a standard DC, you don't have to be aware of the output DC and the attribute DC, because both of them refer to the same device. However, the **CMetaFileDC** class normally has no attribute DC (its value is **NULL**). When you use a function that changes a DC attribute—such as **SetBkMode()** or **SelectObject()**—a **CMetaFileDC** ignores the call.

This built-in behavior obviously won't work for the PaintORama application. For example, you want the thick red lines you originally drew to appear as thick red lines when you play back your drawings. Fortunately, even though the **CMetaFileDC** class doesn't record attribute settings automatically, it makes them easy to record. Let's see how to record output operations and attribute changes.

Recording Device Context Output

The PaintORama program produces all GDI output in a single function: **DrawShape()**. At first glance, hooking up metafile recording would seem to be a simple matter of echoing each call to the screen DC with an equivalent call to the metafile DC, like this:

```
dc.MoveTo(m_LineStart);
dc.LineTo(m_LineEnd);
m_pMF->MoveTo(m_LineStart);
m_pMF->LineTo(m_LineEnd);
```

This code is fine, as far as it goes. But it doesn't take into account the rubber-banding code you added to provide visual feedback. You want the metafile to record only the final line or figure, not the intermediate steps. Fortunately, you can easily tell whether a shape is permanent or merely a rubber band. If the function argument **stretch** is **true**, then the shape is a rubber band and shouldn't be recorded in the metafile. So, if **stretch** is **false** or the drawing mode is set to freehand (which provides no rubber-banding), you'll echo each output call to the metafile DC.

The necessary code, which goes in the **DrawShape() switch** statement, is shown in Listing 11.2. We've highlighted the added lines.

Listing 11.2 The DrawShape() switch statement using a CMetaFileDC.

```
// Draw the appropriate shape
switch(drawMode)
{
case 0: // Freehand
    dc.MoveTo(m_LineStart); // Move to the start of the
                            // line
    dc.LineTo(m_LineEnd);   // Draw to current position
    m_pMF->MoveTo(m_LineStart);
    m_pMF->LineTo(m_LineEnd);
    m_LineStart = m_LineEnd;// Update current mouse
                            // position
    break;
case 1: // Lines
    dc.MoveTo(m_LineStart);
    dc.LineTo(m_LineEnd);
    if (! stretch)
    {
        m_pMF->MoveTo(m_LineStart);
        m_pMF->LineTo(m_LineEnd);
    }
    break;
case 2: // Ovals
    dc.Ellipse(CRect(m_LineStart, m_LineEnd));
    if (! stretch)
    {
        m_pMF->Ellipse(CRect(m_LineStart, m_LineEnd));
    }
    break;
case 3: // Rectangles
    dc.Rectangle(CRect(m_LineStart, m_LineEnd));
    if (! stretch)
    {
        m_pMF->Rectangle(CRect(m_LineStart, m_LineEnd));
    }
    break;
}
```

Painting to a DC occurs in several other places. For instance, to paint the pen color swatch or the brush preview swatch, the program issues GDI output commands. However, you don't want to record those in the metafile, because they don't affect the document you're trying to record (the painting on the canvas). But, in one case, this other painting *does* affect the canvas: The **OnClearbtn()** function clears the canvas to white. You'll handle the Clear button after you deal with the DC attribute commands.

Device Context Attribute Commands

Just as you duplicated the GDI output commands, reflecting them to the **CMetaFileDC** as well as to the screen DC, you need to duplicate the commands that change GDI attributes. However, you can't simply issue the GDI attribute calls to the **CMetaFileDC** object, because the default **CMetaFileDC m_hAttribDC** field is set to **NULL**. Instead, you must first create an appropriate DC.

To create an attribute DC for a **CMetaFile**, follow these steps:

1. Create a non-metafile DC. This DC will be associated with the **CMetaFileDC** object, which will look to this proxy DC for its environmental attributes.
2. Associate the non-metafile DC with the metafile by calling the **CMetaFile::SetAttribDC()** function, passing the non-metafile DC as an argument.
3. As with the GDI output commands, echo to the metafile each command that changes the DC environment. (If you want to see why this is necessary, comment out the lines that reflect the GDI attribute commands to the metafile. You'll discover that your image can be saved, but all your lines will be redrawn as one-pixel black lines.)

To record the DC attribute commands, make the changes highlighted in Listing 11.3 to the **DrawShape()** function. Notice that this is a partial listing—don't delete the remainder of the **DrawShape()** function.

Listing 11.3 Changing the CMetaFileDC attribute DC in DrawShape().

```
void CPaintORamaDlg::DrawShape(bool stretch)
{
    CClientDC dc(this);
    m_pMF->SetAttribDC(dc);
    dc.IntersectClipRect(m_Canvas);
    m_pMF->IntersectClipRect(m_Canvas);
```

```
    // Find out what the drawing mode is
    int drawMode = m_ShapesCombo.GetCurSel();

    // Prepare the DC here
    dc.SelectObject(&m_Pen);
    dc.SelectObject(&m_Brush);
    m_pMF->SelectObject(&m_Pen);
    m_pMF->SelectObject(&m_Brush);

    // Rest of function omitted
}
```

Playing Back The Metafile

Now that you've added code to record the GDI commands, you can write code to play them back. The new code belongs in the **OnPaint()** method. In the screen saver program you created in Chapter 8, you deleted the code that AppWizard placed in **OnPaint()**—you can do the same here. In its place, you'll add code that plays back the metafile and prepares it to accept more input.

Here are the steps to follow:

1. Locate the **OnPaint()** method and remove all the code it contains. Create a DC for the canvas; the DC will play back the metafile. Because the code is in an **OnPaint()** function, it uses a **CPaintDC** rather than a **CClientDC**. Here's the code to add:

   ```
   void CPaintORamaDlg::OnPaint()
   {
       CPaintDC dc(this);
       // Remaining lines go here
   }
   ```

2. The **PlayMetaFile()** function, which displays the GDI commands accumulated in a metafile, takes a **HMETAFILE** (handle to a metafile) as its argument, rather than a **CMetaFileDC**. Create an **HMETAFILE** named **hmf** by using the **CMetaFileDC**'s **Close()** function, as follows:

   ```
   HMETAFILE hmf = m_pMF->Close();
   ```

3. Once you call **Close()**, the original metafile stops recording. Call the DC function **PlayMetaFile()** to re-execute the GDI commands that were previously recorded. When you call **PlayMetaFile()**, pass it the new variable like this:

```
dc.PlayMetaFile(hmf);
```

At this point, the recorded GDI commands have been displayed on screen, the user is ready to resume drawing, and the program should once again echo the user's drawing operations to the metafile. Unfortunately, there's no way to reopen a metafile once it's been closed. So, you'll create a new **CMetaFileDC** object (on the heap), copy the contents of the old metafile to the new, and then delete the old **HMETAFILE** *and* the old **CMetaFileDC** that produced it. Finally, you'll make the new **CMetaFileDC** object active.

To accomplish these tasks, make these further additions to the **OnPaint()** method:

4. Create a new **CMetaFileDC** object to record additional commands. Use **new** and **Create()**, just as you did with the original **CMetaFileDC**. Here's the code to add to **OnPaint()**:

```
CMetaFileDC* temp = new CMetaFileDC;
temp->Create();
```

5. To update the new **CMetaFileDC**, use **PlayMetaFile()**, specifying the **CMetaFileDC** as the receiver, like this:

```
temp->PlayMetaFile(hmf);
```

   When **PlayMetaFile()** is done, the new **CMetaFileDC** will contain all the drawing operations contained in the metafile.

6. Delete **HMETAFILE** by using the API function **DeleteMetaFile()**, free the old **CMetaFileDC** that's located on the heap, and then assign the new **CMetaFileDC** to the **m_pMF** pointer. Here are the three necessary lines of code:

```
DeleteMetaFile(hmf);
delete m_pMF;
m_pMF = temp;
```

When you're finished, compile and run the application. As you can see in Figure 11.3, each time you minimize the application or drag the Color dialog box across the canvas, the PaintORama redisplays the image when the canvas is uncovered.

Odds And Ends

You've greatly improved the PaintORama. However, the program doesn't yet paint the background correctly when the user clicks on Clear. The pen and brush preview swatches also don't work properly. Let's handle the problem of the Clear button first.

Handling The Clear Button

When the user clears the canvas, the PaintORama should start a new document. This new document shouldn't carry around the old GDI commands—it should start fresh, with a new DC.

This task is almost as easily done as said. Simply add the new (highlighted) code shown in Listing 11.4 to the **OnClearbtn()** function.

Listing 11.4 The revised OnClearbtn() function.

```
void CPaintORamaDlg::OnClearbtn()
{
    CClientDC dc(this);
    HMETAFILE hmf = m_pMF->Close(); // Close the old
                                    // metafile
    ::DeleteMetaFile(hmf);          // Free the GDI
                                    // resource
    delete m_pMF;                   // Free the C++
                                    // resource
    m_pMF = new CMetaFileDC;        // Allocate a new
                                    // object
```

Figure 11.3
The PaintORama application with repainting active.

NOTE

*The **Rectangle()** function call is slightly different than that we presented previously. Remember that in the **DrawShape()** function, the clipping region is set to the coordinates stored in the member variable **m_Canvas**. The clipping region lets you draw anywhere within those coordinates. When you clear the canvas, however, you use the **Rectangle()** function. Like other GDI output functions that use a bounding box, **Rectangle()** is inclusive-exclusive: It doesn't paint the last column of pixels on the right or the last row of pixels on the bottom. The code presented here compensates for that "off-by-one" error.*

```
    m_pMF->Create();                    // Create the GDI
                                        // resources
    m_pMF->SetAttribDC(dc);             // Hook up with
                                        // current dc

    // Draw to the screen
    dc.SelectStockObject(NULL_PEN);
    dc.Rectangle(m_Canvas.left, m_Canvas.top,
                 m_Canvas.right+1, m_Canvas.bottom+1);

    // Draw to the metafile
    m_pMF->SelectStockObject(NULL_PEN);
    m_pMF->Rectangle(m_Canvas.left, m_Canvas.top,
                     m_Canvas.right+1,
                     m_Canvas.bottom+1);
}
```

Notice that the code to clear the canvas looks almost exactly like the code that creates the new **CMetaFileDC** object in the **OnPaint()** function. However, here you associate the **CMetaFileDC** with the current canvas DC and then clear the canvas.

Starting Out Fresh

The new code in **OnClearbtn()** works just fine when you click on Clear. Now, is it possible to use this code to clear the canvas when the program starts? After all, you really don't want the gray background—you're using it only because that's the **CDialog** class's default behavior.

Using **OnClearbtn()** this way poses a problem: You must determine where to call it. You can't call it in the constructor, because **m_Canvas** and **m_pMF** don't yet exist. You might try to call it at the end of **OnInitDialog()**, but unfortunately, that doesn't work, either.

You might try to call **OnClearbtn()** at the beginning of **OnPaint()**, so that the window starts fresh the first time it's painted. That technique works, but it also erases your previous painting any time a **WM_PAINT** message is received.

MFC provides a DocView function—**OnNewDocument()**—to handle exactly this problem. Unfortunately, you aren't yet writing a DocView application, so you'll have to be a little more creative.

You can implement a straightforward solution by calling **OnClearbtn()** within the **OnPaint()** method, but executing the call only once. A strategically placed **static** local variable makes it simple to do so:

```
static bool firstTime = true;
if (firstTime)
{
    OnClearbtn();
    firstTime = false;
}
```

Because **firstTime** is static, it's initialized only once: when the program is loaded. Place this code in **OnPaint()**, before the code that replays the metafile, and you'll provide a white background for all your paintings.

That solves the problem of gray backgrounds. We could also demonstrate a fix for the problem of wrong-colored paint swatches, but you'd learn little from that side trip. Instead, let's move on to the DocView architecture, which will help you write much more sophisticated programs.

SDIOne: Moving To DocView

The time has come to bid adieu to the PaintORama. You'll be able to bring many of its basic ideas and skills with you, but we need to strike out in a new direction. So, let's pull out the map and see what lies ahead.

In the remainder of this chapter, you're going to build the first in a series of DocView applications. Like the very first version of the PaintORama, your first DocView application will be a simple, monochromatic drawing program.This time, however, you'll include a document class and a view class along with the main window and application classes of previous projects. These new classes will greatly increase the program's power.

In the next chapter, you'll take an in-depth look at the document and view classes. And, in the chapters that follow that, you'll learn to use the Visual C++ Menu Editor to restore PaintORama features you've left behind and add new ones.

Building Your First SDI Application

Now that you know where we're heading, let's not waste any time. Close your current project, choose File | New from the main menu, and create a new MFC AppWizard (exe) project named SDIOne.

Here are the rest of the steps you need to follow:

1. In the AppWizard Step 1 dialog box, select the Single Document radio button and be sure the Document/View Architecture Support check box is selected. Check your screen against Figure 11.4.
2. Accept the default values in the AppWizard Step 2 dialog box—you won't use database support just yet.
3. Select None from the compound document support options in the AppWizard Step 3 dialog box. Also, clear the ActiveX Controls checkbox, as you can see in Figure 11.5.
4. In the AppWizard Step 4 dialog box, accept the default values. The Docking Toolbar, Initial Status Bar, Printing And Print Preview, and 3D Controls options should all be checked, whereas the other checkboxes should be cleared. Choose Normal toolbars instead of ReBar style. Before you leave this screen, click on Advanced.
5. In the Advanced Options dialog box, choose the Document Template Strings tab. All of the existing values are

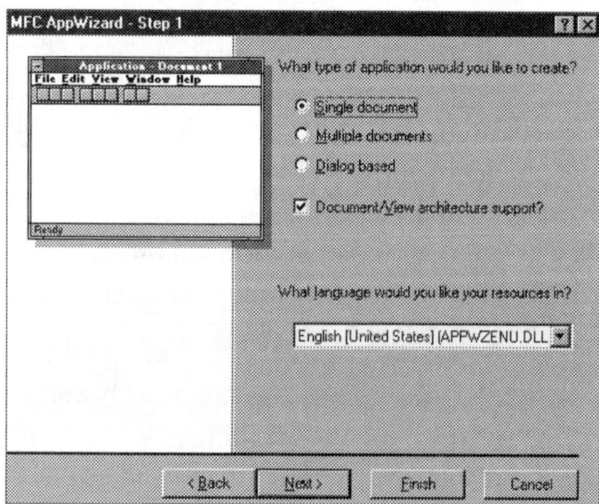

Figure 11.4
The SDIOne application, MFC AppWizard Step 1.

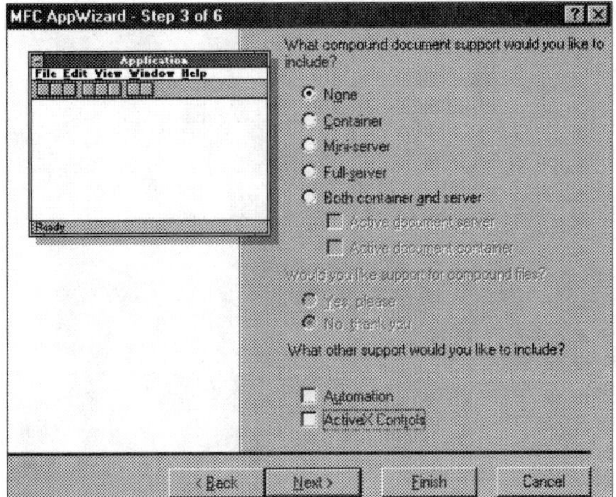

Figure 11.5
The SDIOne application, MFC AppWizard Step 3.

acceptable, but you must provide a file extension. Enter "sdi1", as you can see in Figure 11.6. Click on Close when you're ready to go on. Back in the AppWizard Step 4 dialog box, click on Next.

6. Accept the default values in the AppWizard Step 5 dialog box. Click on Next to advance to the Step 6 dialog box, which lets you review the class. Accept the default values here, as well. Click on Finish to display the New Project Information dialog box shown in Figure 11.7. Except for the project directory, which will be tailored to your system, you should see the same information displayed on your screen.

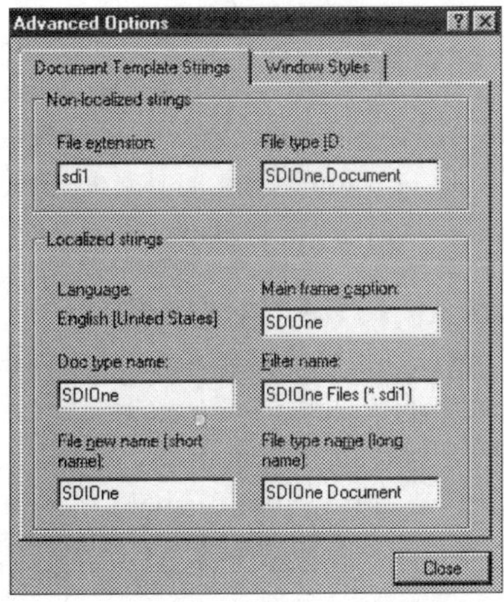

Figure 11.6
The SDIOne application, MFC AppWizard Step 4.

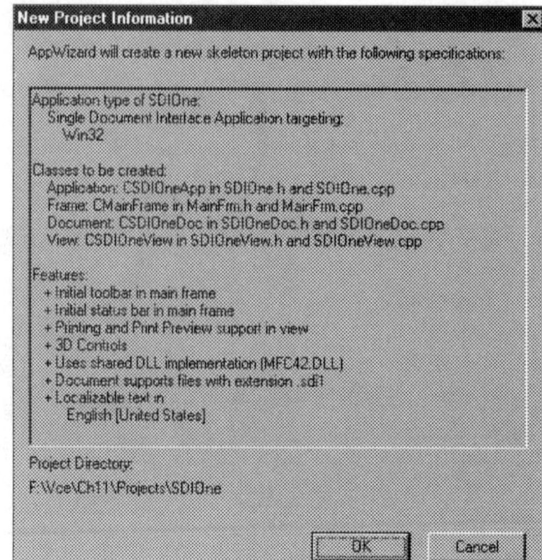

Figure 11.7
The SDIOne application, New Project Information.

Handling The Document In SDIOne

The dialog-based applications you've built so far had only two main classes—the application and the application window. On the other hand, the SDIOne application has five classes: an application class, a main window class, a view class, a document class, and an About dialog box class.

You'll learn more about the responsibilities of each class in the next chapter. For right now, let's simply say that you'll use the view class— **CSDIOneView**—to paint, and the document class— **CSDIOneDoc**—to store the data about your painting.

Because the view class requires the cooperation of the document class, but not vice-versa, you'll start with the document class. SDIOne will implement only the freehand drawing portion of the PaintORama program. So, in the document, you'll store only line segments—you can store them as pairs of **CPoint** objects.

CPoints And The CArray Class

MFC comes equipped with several collection classes, arranged in two broad categories. Early versions of MFC included collection classes based on storing pointers to objects or simple types. In MFC Version 3, however, Visual C++ introduced a new set of collection classes based on C++ templates.

Template-based collection classes have several advantages over the earlier, non-template-based classes. For example, template-based classes enable you to create type-safe collections. The earlier collection classes stored only generic pointers, requiring you to perform potentially hazardous type casts. For instance, when you retrieved an object from a collection, you had to cast that object to the correct type, or write a helper function to do so. When you use template-based classes, C++ performs type checking and conversion for you, ensuring that your collection holds only the correct kind of object.

For the SDIOne application, you'll use a template-based collection class called **CArray**. A **CArray** object works like a regular C-style array, with one exception: **CArray** objects automatically resize themselves, whereas the built-in C++ arrays don't.

Writing The Document Methods

To store the data so the view class can work with it, the document class needs functions to:

- *Store a* ***CPoint***. The view class doesn't know or care that the document class stores the **CPoint** in a **CArray**. The view class simply passes a **CPoint** to the document, and the document stores it for later recall and use. You'll call this function **AddPoint()**.
- *Find out how many* ***CPoint*** *objects the document contains*. When called to repaint itself, the view class must repaint each line individually. But, the view shouldn't root around the document to find these lines. Instead, you'll apply the design principle of encapsulation, making the array stored in the document class a private member variable. Because the view can't access this private member variable, it requires a public accessor function that provides a count of the number of **CPoint** objects. You'll call this function **NumPoints()**.
- *Retrieve a particular* ***CPoint****, given its index value*. After finding out how many points there are, the view will retrieve each one. You'll call this function **GetPoint()**.

In addition, you'll need to add code to create and initialize the **CArray** collection variable. Here are the steps to follow:

1. Open and expand the **CSDIOneDoc** class in the ClassView window, as you can see in Figure 11.8.
2. Manually add a new private member variable to the **CSDIOneDoc** class (you must add the variable manually because the Add Member Variable wizard doesn't support templates). Name the variable **m_data**, and make it a **CArray** type. Because **CArray** is a template class, you must supply the arguments (within angle brackets) to instantiate the template. The **CArray** class requires two arguments: the type of value you intend to store in the array and the type of argument used to access objects stored in the array. Typically, the second argument is a reference to the type of value stored in the array. In this case, both arguments will be **CPoint** objects. Here's what the declaration looks like when you add it to CSDIOneDoc.h:

```
private:
    CArray<CPoint, CPoint> m_data;    // Document
                                      // stored here
```

3. Add the following **#include** statement to the top of CSDIOneDoc.h. It's required whenever you include a template class:

```
#include <afxtempl.h>
```

4. In principle, you don't have to initialize a **CArray** like the **m_data** array. By default, when you add an item to a full **CArray**, the size of the array grows by a single element.

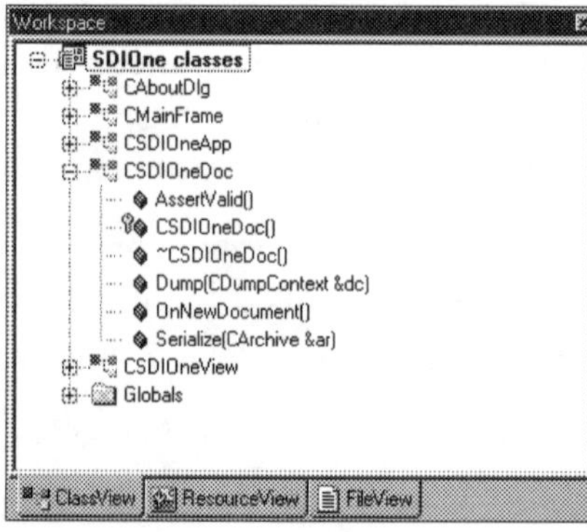

Figure 11.8
Looking at **CSDIOneDoc** in the ClassView window.

Because the elements are kept in contiguous memory, the whole array must be reallocated. To avoid this, you can use the **SetSize()** method to specify an initial size as well as a *growth factor* that determines how many elements are added when the array expands. Using the ClassView window, locate the **OnNewDocument()** function, which is called every time you create a new document. Add this line just before the return statement:

```
m_data.SetSize(0, 128);
```

This statement initializes **m_data** as an empty array that grows by 128 elements each time it expands.

5. Use the Add Member Function dialog box to create the declaration and skeleton for the **AddPoint()**, **GetPoint()**, and **NumPoints()** functions. The return types for the functions are void, **CPoint**, and **int**, respectively. **AddPoint()** takes a single **CPoint** as an argument, whereas **GetPoint()** takes an **int** index. **NumPoints()** takes no arguments. When you've added the function skeletons, complete each function using the lines highlighted in Listing 11.5.

Listing 11.5 The AddPoint(), GetPoint(), and NumPoints() member functions.

```
void CSDIOneDoc::AddPoint(CPoint point)
{
    m_data.Add(point);
}

CPoint CSDIOneDoc::GetPoint(int item)
{
    return m_data[item];
}

int CSDIOneDoc::NumPoints()
{
    return m_data.GetSize();
}
```

6. If you looked through the **CSDIOneDoc** functions, you may have noticed **Serialize()**. The **Serialize()** function is called when the DocView application framework thinks you should

save your document. To enable a document to be saved or retrieved, you must write code that interacts with the **CArchive** class to read/write your data. Fortunately, the **CArray** class already knows how to do that. You can take all the code in the **CSDIOneDoc::Serialze()** function and replace it with the single line highlighted in Listing 11.6.

Listing 11.6 The CSDIOneDoc Serialize() member function.

```
void CSDIOneDoc::Serialize(CArchive& ar)
{
    m_data.Serialize(ar);
}
```

Handling The View In SDIOne

Good news: The code to paint using a view class is much easier than the code in the PaintORama program. For instance, you don't have to worry about whether you're inside the drawing area, as you did in the PaintORama—the entire view-class window is the painting area, so there's no concern about clipping or testing for the mouse position.

You must write four functions for the **CSDIOneView** class. Three of them—**OnLButtonDown()**, **OnMouseMove()**, and **OnLButtonUp()**—work like those in the PaintORama. The other—**OnDraw()**—is very similar to the **OnPaint()** function you worked with in the last few chapters.

Working With Button Handlers

Here are the steps to follow to get your view class up and running:

1. Select the **CSDIOneView** class from the ClassView window, as you can see in Figure 11.9. Expand the class so you can see all the functions.
2. Add a private **CPoint** data member named **m_LineStart** to the class. (Either use the Add Member Variable dialog box or simply add the data member to the CSDIOneView.h file by hand.) This variable serves the same purpose as the similar variable in the PaintORama.
3. Using the context menu, add a Windows message handler for **WM_LBUTTONDOWN**, as shown in Figure 11.10. The

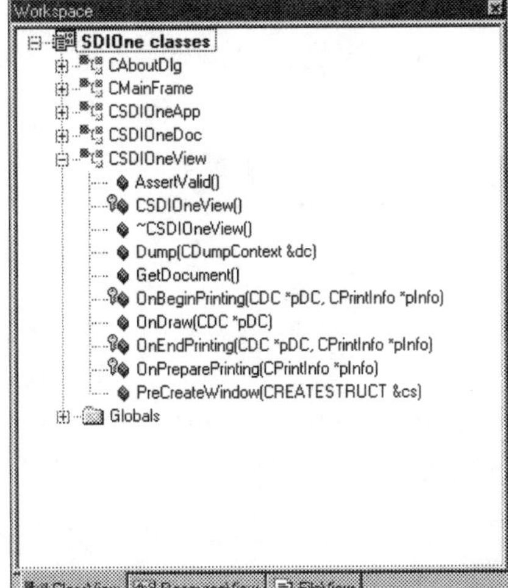

Figure 11.9
Looking at **CSDIOneView** in the ClassView window.

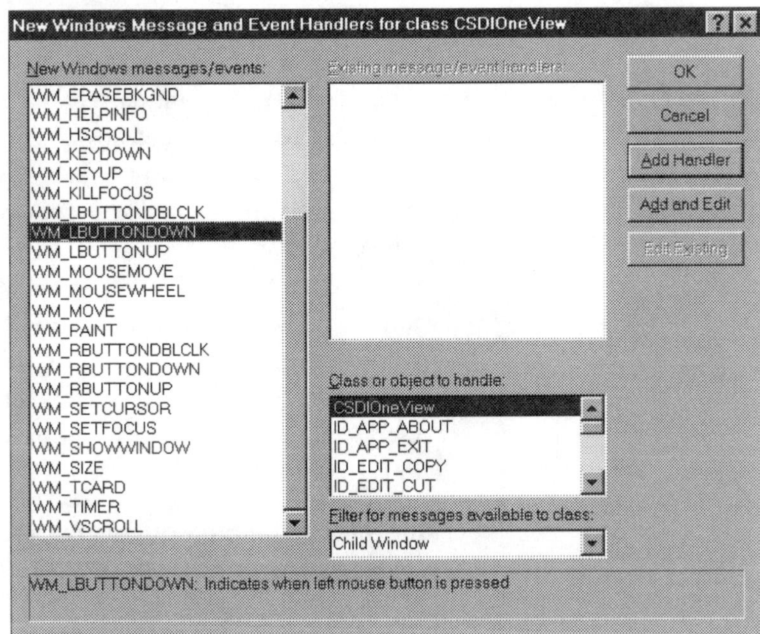

Figure 11.10
Adding a Windows message handler for **WM_LBUTTONDOWN**.

OnLButtonDown() function performs two tasks: It sets the starting position for a line segment and captures the mouse so that you can be sure of getting a **WM_LBUTTONUP** message. Replace the code in the **OnLButtonDown()** function with the lines highlighted in Listing 11.7.

Listing 11.7 The OnLButtonDown() function.

```
void CSDIOneView::OnLButtonDown(UINT nFlags, CPoint
point)
{
    m_LineStart = point;
    SetCapture();
}
```

4. Add a similar method for the **WM_LBUTTONUP** message. The replacement code is shown in Listing 11.8, and it's even simpler than **OnLButtonDown()**—it just releases the mouse capture.

Listing 11.8 The OnLButtonUp() function.

```
void CSDIOneView::OnLButtonUp(UINT nFlags, CPoint point)
{
    ReleaseCapture();
}
```

5. The third Windows message handler does the actual drawing, as before. You don't need any code to ensure you're within the canvas area, but you must check whether the left button is down—that's how you'll know you're dragging the mouse. The code that displays the line segment (by first getting a device context and then using the **MoveTo()** and **LineTo()** functions) is unchanged from the PaintORama. However, before the line segment is drawn, the two end-points are sent to the document object, which is retrieved by calling the **GetDocument()** method. You can see the completed function in Listing 11.9.

Listing 11.9 The OnMouseMove() function.

```
void CSDIOneView::OnMouseMove(UINT nFlags, CPoint point)
{
    if (nFlags & MK_LBUTTON)
    {
        // Save to the document class
        CSDIOneDoc* pDoc = GetDocument();
        ASSERT_VALID(pDoc);
        pDoc->AddPoint(m_LineStart);
        pDoc->AddPoint(point);

        CClientDC dc(this);
        dc.MoveTo(m_LineStart);
```

```
        dc.LineTo(point);
        m_LineStart = point;
    }
}
```

Working With OnDraw()

In DocView applications, the view class doesn't handle **WM_PAINT** messages as your previous applications have. Instead, the DocView framework handles those messages itself. Of course, you still need to write painting code. In a DocView application, you include that code in the virtual function **OnDraw()** rather than in **OnPaint()**.

You'll notice an oddity about **OnDraw()**: You don't have to retrieve your own device context. That's because the DocView framework uses the code you put in **OnDraw()** in several different DCs. The actual context used is passed as a pointer to the base DC class, **CDC**. The same code is used for drawing on screen, drawing on the printer, and in print-preview mode. It's almost like getting two extra contexts for free!

As a result, the code for **OnPaint()** is simpler than the analogous code you wrote for the PaintORama. The framework passes you a pointer to your DC, and it retrieves a pointer to your document class for you, using the lines

```
CSDIOneDoc* pDoc = GetDocument();
ASSERT_VALID(pDoc);
```

To complete **OnDraw()**, you simply ask your document how many points it has, then retrieve and plot each of them using the DC functions you're already familiar with. Add the necessary lines of code to the **OnDraw()** function, as highlighted in Listing 11.10.

Listing 11.10 The CSDIOneView class OnDraw() function.

```
void CSDIOneView::OnDraw(CDC* pDC)
{
    CSDIOneDoc* pDoc = GetDocument();
    ASSERT_VALID(pDoc);

    // TODO: add draw code for native data here
    int nPoints = pDoc->NumPoints();
    CPoint start, stop;
    for (int item = 0; item < nPoints; item += 2)
```

```
    {
        start = pDoc->GetPoint(item);
        stop  = pDoc->GetPoint(item + 1);
        pDC->MoveTo(start);
        pDC->LineTo(stop);
    }
}
```

Coming Soon

Compile and run the SDIOne application. Although it may have fewer features than the PaintORama, it's built on a firmer foundation. The PaintORama program became more fragile and complicated as we added features, yet it couldn't perform all the tasks SDIOne can. Here are some of the tests you should try:

- Create a new painting using either File | New or the New File toolbar icon. In the PaintORama, you had to add additional code—in the **OnClearbtn()** function—to handle new documents.
- Draw a few squiggles and then resize your window. Notice that the **OnDraw()** code keeps everything in sync, even when you minimize or maximize, as you can see in Figure 11.11.
- Print your document or use print-preview. Again, these functions work without any programming on your part (although you may be unhappy with the way your image is scaled). You can see print-preview mode in Figure 11.12.

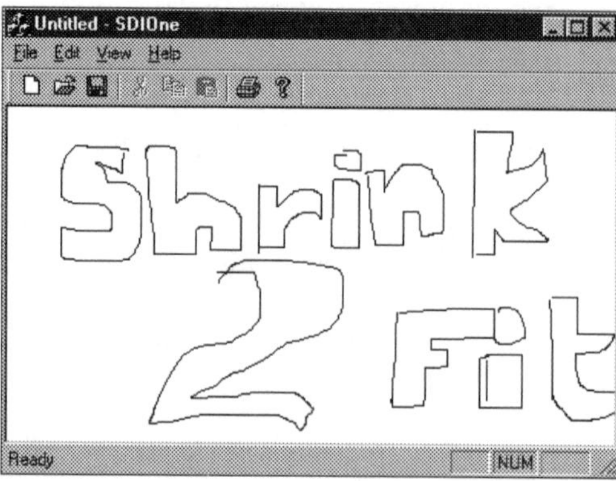

Figure 11.11
Resizing a window using the SDIOne application.

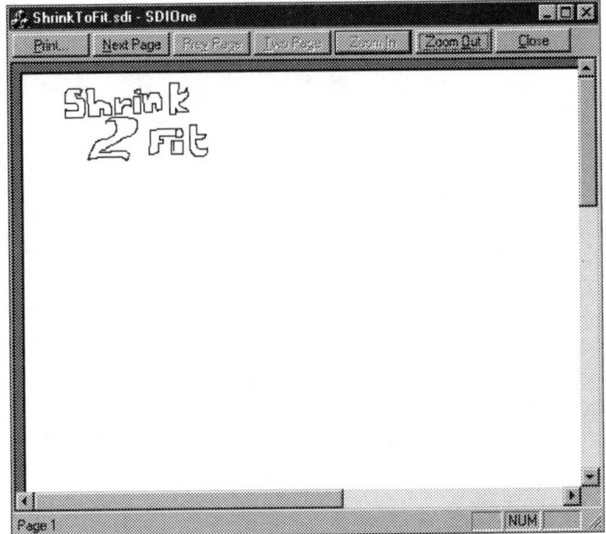

Figure 11.12
Using print-preview with the SDIOne application.

- Use File|Save or File|Save As, and you'll see that the code you added to your document's **Serialize()** method can both read and write the files you create. Because you specified a custom extension (.sdi1) when you set up your project, you can also double-click on your files in Windows explorer to launch the SDIOne application.

As you can see, there's more to DocView than meets the eye. In the next chapter, we'll peel away some of the mystery, and take a closer look inside SDIOne and the classes that it uses.

Chapter 12

The DocView Milieu

Think of a very small company—the proverbial Mom-and-Pop business. At first, Mom and Pop have their hands in every job, from washing the windows to cooking the books. But, as the business grows, they hire specialists—lawyers, accountants, and janitors—to be more efficient. DocView is like that.

Non-DocView programs feature two general-purpose "Mom" and "Pop" classes derived directly from **CWnd** and **CWinApp**. In the more sophisticated DocView world, programs have at least four specialized classes. Each class cooperates closely with the others, but each has clear and distinct responsibilities.

In this chapter, you'll learn about the four major DocView players: the application class, the frame window class, the document class, and the view class. We'll emphasize the big picture for most of the chapter. Then, near the end of the chapter, we'll take a close-up look at the application class, using the previous chapter's SDIOne program as an example. Studying the **CSDIOneApp** class and its **InitInstance()** function will give you a good introduction to the new features added by DocView.

However, before we start, let's get one question out of the way: What is this DocView thing, anyway? So far, it seems more complex than the dialog-based applications you've been building. What's the payoff?

Who, What, Why?

Non-DocView programs lack the document class and view class typical of DocView programs. What do these new classes contribute to your programs?

In the DocView universe, every application works with some kind of data: Your word processor works with character data, your spreadsheet works with numeric data, and your graphics program works with graphics data. In a DocView application, the *document class* manages one kind of data, manipulating it and saving it to—or retrieving it from—external files, such as disk files.

You can write programs that have no user interface—programs that retrieve data, process it, and then send it off to its destination. However, the DocView architecture wasn't designed for that kind of application. Rather, it was designed for interactive programs that let users view and manipulate documents. In a DocView program, the *view class* displays the document to the user.

Types Of DocView Programs

Using the DocView classes, you can write several kinds of programs:

- *Programs that work with a single document type or several different document types*—Microsoft Works is a good example of a multiple-type program. Single-type programs are more common by far.
- *Single Document Interface (SDI) programs*—Such programs (Windows Notepad, for example) can open only one document at a time, even if they're capable of working with several document types.
- *Multiple Document Interface (MDI) programs*—Such programs can open multiple documents at the same time. Such a program has one main window and several subsidiary child windows in which documents appear. Microsoft Word, Microsoft Excel, and even our own NotePod program are MDI applications. Note carefully the distinction between simultaneously opening multiple *types* of documents and simply opening multiple documents.
- *Programs with a single view or multiple views*—In an MDI application, each document automatically has at least one view. In an SDI application, you can use *splitter windows* to provide multiple views of the same document.

- *Programs with different types of views*—Such programs may use only one view at a time. A program that supports multiple view types lets the user view a document in several ways—as a table or a chart, for instance. Users who've worked with a modern spreadsheet package are familiar with this type of program.

Advantages Of DocView

Now that you understand the *who* and *what*, let's take a crack at the *why*. Here are two reasons you should invest the time it takes to become proficient using DocView.

First, "It's good for you." DocView applications help you to apply the program design principle of *modularity*. Programs divided into modules with clearly defined boundaries, responsibilities, and paths of communication are easier to understand, more reliable, and easier to fix than non-modular programs. The dialog-based architecture works okay for small programs—but, for larger programs, you need the assistance of DocView to keep all the elements organized.

Advertisers long ago discovered that the slogan "It's good for you" seldom boosts product sales. Fortunately, there's a more compelling reason to use DocView: You'll become irresistible to the opposite sex, acquire a fancy new convertible sports car, and spend the rest of your life frolicking on the Maui beach.

Oops..., wait. That's not DocView; that's Doc White's Anti-Plaque Tooth Grit. If you use DocView, you'll simply find it easier to develop applications. Of course, simpler application development means more free time. If you want to spend that time on the Maui beach, that's up to you.

Seriously, only by using DocView can you take full advantage of MFC, which builds many framework enhancements on the DocView foundation. Do you want to use toolbars and status bars in your program? You can spend an inordinate amount of time brewing up your own concoction—or you can use the straightforward framework supplied by MFC. Guess what? The MFC version assumes you're working with DocView. Do you want simplified printing? Again, MFC bases its printing framework upon

NOTE

*Figure 12.1 doesn't show all the classes that participate in creating a DocView application. We don't discuss some intermediate classes—such as **CWinThread**, which sits between **CCmdTarget** and **CWndApp**—in this chapter, and we've omitted them to avoid cluttering the figure. We discuss other classes—such as **CSingleDocTemplate**—in the text where they're used.*

DocView. By adopting the MFC DocView framework, you gain access to thousands of lines of pre-written code, covering the most commonly needed application features. And, you don't have to do any extra work to use them.

There you have it: "DocView—tastes great, and it's good for you, too!" Who says advertising is a dying art?

DocView: Who Talks To Whom?

Let's begin our excursion into DocView-land by looking at the four major players. When you asked AppWizard to create the SDIOne application in Chapter 11, it created four classes: an application class, a frame or main window class, a document class, and a view class. You can see these four classes in the bottom panel of Figure 12.1. The top panel contains the MFC framework classes from which your application classes are derived.

Let's briefly look at the four classes created by AppWizard.

The Application Class

Every DocView program has an application class derived from **CWinApp**. Like the application classes you've seen in non-DocView programs, it handles the program start-up and creation

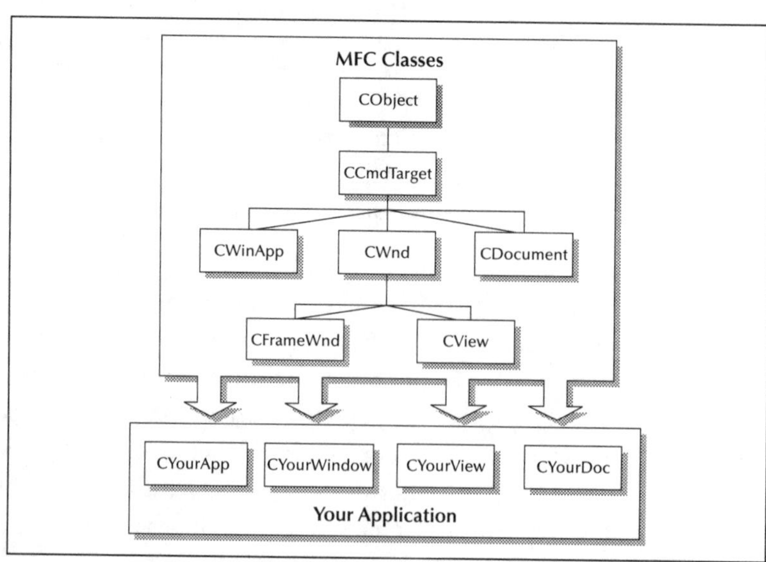

Figure 12.1
The SDI application architecture.

tasks, retrieves messages from Windows, and dispatches messages to the appropriate destination.

In Figure 12.1, this class is called **CYourApp**, but this name is merely an example. Each application names its class differently. For instance, in the SDIOne application, the application class is named **CSDIOneApp** and its files are SDIOne.h and SDIOne.cpp. We discuss the application class and its **InitInstance()** function in detail later in this chapter.

The Main Window Class

Until now, you've been using **CDialog**—a **CWnd** subclass—as your program's main window class. DocView programs derive their main window (frame) class from **CFrameWnd**, also a subclass of

---

What's In A Name?

When AppWizard creates a new project, it uses some simple rules for naming the classes it creates and the files that contain those classes. In most cases, you can override AppWizard's choices. For instance, you might want to do this to comply with company-wide naming conventions.

When AppWizard creates an instance of one of the four DocView classes, it writes a header (.h) file and an implementation (.cpp) file. The class declaration appears in the header file and each function definition appears in the implementation file. (Some programmers call the header file the *interface* file, because it provides all the information a programmer needs to use the class.)

AppWizard names your main window class **CMainFrame** no matter what the name of your project. The window class's header file is named MainFrm.h and its implementation file is named MainFrm.cpp. To name the remaining classes, AppWizard uses several simple rules. It uses the name of your project—SDIOne, for example—as the *base name* for naming classes and files. It then prefixes each class name with a capital "C", which stands for class. The class is then given a suffix describing its type: Doc, View, or App. The files containing the document and view classes are named by removing the "C" from the front of the class name, and the application class is stored in a file that uses the base name of the project.

For the most part, you aren't required to use AppWizard's naming conventions. You can change the name of any class or file, except those belonging to the application class. The main application class must be stored in header and implementation files that have the same base name as your project.

CWnd. Just as the **CDialog** class supports visual interface design via the Dialog Editor, the **CFrameWnd** class has its own special talents.

By default, each DocView program derives **CMainFrame**, which is a subclass of **CFrameWnd**. The **CMainFrame**—a top-level, overlapped, resizable window—holds one or more instances of the application's view class. The **CMainFrame** may also hold controls such as menus, toolbars, and status bars. In addition, it acts as a dispatcher for the messages generated by menus and toolbars, automatically routing them to the appropriate recipient.

You'll take a closer look at the **CFrameWnd** class in Chapters 13 and 14, when you learn to work with menus. For now, let's take an abbreviated look at SDIOne's **CMainFrame** class.

Because the **CMainFrame** class inherits much useful functionality from **CFrameWnd**, it's relatively simple. **CMainFrame** defines a default constructor, a virtual destructor, a virtual **PreCreateWindow()** function, and a Windows message handler for the **WM_CREATE** function **OnCreate()**. In addition, the class has two protected member variables—**m_wndStatusBar** and **m_wndToolBar**—that refer to the main window's status bar and toolbar.

The CMainFrame Constructor

Surprisingly, the constructor for the **CMainFrame** class is **protected**. Therefore, you can't create **CMainFrame** objects using **new** or as local variables on the stack. This certainly seems peculiar. It seems even more peculiar when you realize that the constructors for the document and view classes are also **protected**. What's the purpose of having these classes, if you can't make objects from them?

As with much of MFC, the answer lies out of sight. If you closely examine the header file that defines **CMainFrame**, you'll discover this cryptic line immediately following the constructor declaration:

```
DECLARE_DYNCREATE(CMainFrame)
```

A similar line appears in the MainFrm.cpp implementation file:

```
IMPLEMENT_DYNCREATE(CMainFrame, CFrameWnd)
```

As their all-uppercase names suggest, these are MFC macros. These particular macros add a set of hidden functions to class definitions, enabling dynamic ("on-the-fly") object creation. We'll discuss this in greater depth when we examine the application's **InitInstance()** function and the operation of the document template class.

In the final analysis, the constructors for the document, view, and frame window classes are protected simply because you'll never need to create document, view, or frame objects—that's the application framework's job. Hiding object creation behind the **DYNCREATE** macros leaves you one less thing to worry about.

CMainFrame Member Functions

The **CMainFrame** class is unusual in the MFC world, because you can write a full-featured MFC application that doesn't modify **CMainFrame**. The same is certainly not true for the document and view classes—those classes don't do anything interesting until you add special behavior.

Programmers sometimes modify the **CMainFrame** class, often to add a member function that responds to a menu or toolbar selection. Similarly, if your command-handler functions require member variables (which they usually do), you'll use the **CMainFrame** constructor to initialize them. And, if you allocate memory for a member variable, you can use the **CMainFrame** destructor to safely return the allocated memory via **delete**.

Programmers seldom modify the two member functions written by AppWizard, **PreCreateWindow()** and **OnCreate()**. MFC calls **PreCreateWindow()** before creating the frame window, giving you an opportunity to change its window style by modifying the **CREATESTRUCT** MFC passes as an argument.

The **OnCreate()** method calls the base class creation method—**CFrameWnd::OnCreate()**—and then installs the toolbar and status bar. You can modify **OnCreate()** to change the characteristics of the toolbar or status bar windows. For instance, you might change the number of panes displayed in the status bar. The last three lines in **OnCreate()**

```
m_wndToolBar.EnableDocking(CBRS_ALIGN_ANY);
EnableDocking(CBRS_ALIGN_ANY);
DockControlBar(&m_wndToolBar);
```

make the window toolbar *dockable*. The user can grab a dockable toolbar and attach it to a side of the frame window or make it into a free-floating window, as you can see in Figure 12.2. If you want a non-dockable toolbar, simply delete the three lines shown previously.

The Document Class

As you saw earlier, your program can support a single type of document, or it may support many different document types. However, AppWizard creates a single document class for each application you write—whether you create an SDI application or an MDI application. It's up to you to add any additional document types your program requires.

In Figure 12.1, the document class **CYourDoc** is derived from MFC's **CDocument** class. In the SDIOne application, MFC named the analogous class **CSDIOneDoc** and stored it in the files CSDIOneDoc.h and CSDIOneDoc.cpp.

When you receive your document class, straight from the MFC factory, it doesn't know how to do much. After all, AppWizard

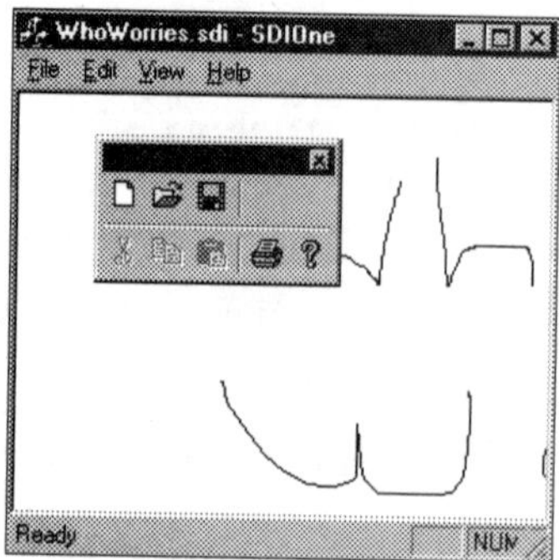

Figure 12.2
Using a docking toolbar with the SDIOne application.

has no idea whether you're writing a word processor, a spreadsheet application, or a painting program. Obviously, the documents for such applications would vary immensely. You must modify the document class by adding member variables that store your application's data and member functions that modify and manipulate the data.

Even though AppWizard can't generate application-specific code for you, the document class it provides contains a framework that makes it easy to add the necessary code. The **CSDIOneDoc** class written by AppWizard includes the following member functions:

- A *protected constructor*—As a member of the DocView trio, the **CSDIOneDoc** class permits object creation only via the dynamic **CreateObject()** method, which is enabled by the **DYNACREATE()** macro pair. In almost all cases, the application framework will create the objects you need.
- A *virtual destructor*—Despite having an empty body, the virtual destructor is important because it ensures that the base-class **CFrameWnd** destructor is called whenever a pointer to a **CSDIOneDoc** object is deleted. Without the virtual destructor, your program would have a memory leak.
- *Two virtual functions,* ***OnNewDocument()*** *and* ***Serialize()***—You'll almost always override these functions. MFC calls the **OnNewDocument()** function each time a new document is loaded. You can use **OnNewDocument()** to initialize the data members of your document class, placing them in a proper pristine state. The **Serialize()** member function performs the messy details required for transferring your documents to and from permanent files. You simply ensure that your document member variables are *serializable* and then send them off to the provided **CArchive** object—the framework takes care of the rest. You'll learn more about what *serialization* means, as well as how to handle files, in Chapters 15 and 16, when we further expand the **CSDIOneDoc** class.
- *Two virtual debugging functions,* ***AssertValid()*** *and* ***Dump()***—You can use these functions for diagnostic output. They're present only when you create a debug release of your program.

The framework will call them if a problem arises. You can override the **AssertValid()** function to check the state of a variable inside your document object. Use the **Dump()** method to print to a debugger window the value of a document field.

CDocument Inherited Methods

In addition to these locally defined functions, which you can override, your **CSDIOneDoc** class inherits several important methods from the **CDocument** class. You'll use these inherited methods as you work with documents and views in subsequent chapters. This section serves as an introduction, so you'll know what to expect.

You'll frequently work with seven important **CDocument** methods. These methods fall into three categories: access to views, document information, and modification status:

- *Access to views*—The **CDocument** class provides three methods that make it easy to work with the view (or views) attached to the document. Recall that a document can be associated with several views, but each view can be attached to only a single document. You can obtain the view attached to a document by calling the **GetFirstView()** function. If there are multiple views, call **GetNextView()** until the return value is **NULL**. Frequently, the document has changed some data and is interested in telling its views to update themselves. The aptly named **UpdateAllViews()** method serves this purpose.
- *Document information*—Two methods allow a document to find out about the file to which it's attached: **GetPathName()** and **GetTitle()**. **GetPathName()** returns the document's fully qualified path, and **GetTitle()** returns the document's title, which is usually based on its file name. If a new document has never been saved, then these functions return **NULL**.
- *Modification status*—The **CDocument** class contains two functions that allow you to monitor whether a document has been changed since the last time it was saved. If the data has changed, then the **IsModified()** function returns a non-zero value. For this to work, however, each function that changes a document's data must cooperate by calling the **SetModifiedFlag()** function when the function changes the data.

The CSDIOneDoc Class

The **CSDIOneDoc** class is a rather minimal implementation of a document class. It would be difficult to make it smaller, and still have it work. Like every document class, **CSDIOne** contains two parts: member variables that store the document information, and member functions that manipulate and provide access to the member variables.

The important object-oriented design principle of encapsulation states that member variables should be **private** or **protected**, never **public**. Unfortunately, this principle is routinely ignored by MFC; for instance, it makes all ClassWizard dialog data members **public**. Even the MFC tutorial program, Scribble, makes its data members **public**. However, you don't have to follow MFC's bad example—in the CSDIOneDoc class, you'll make the single data member, **m_data, private**.

The **m_data** member variable is a **CArray** object. The **CArray** class is a template class, so its class definition is written at compile time—invisibly and behind the scenes—based upon arguments you provide when you instantiate the template. The declaration for the **m_data** member variable

```
private:
    CArray<CPoint,CPoint> m_data;
```

creates a **private**, automatically resized array of **CPoint** objects.

Because the **m_data** member variable is **private** and, therefore, can't be accessed by other classes, the **CSDIOneDoc** class provides three operations that other classes can use to change the document. You can add a new **CPoint** to the document by calling its **AddPoint()** function. You can find out how many points the document contains by calling its **NumPoints()** function. And, you can retrieve a particular **CPoint** object by calling the **GetPoint()** function and providing an index. It might not seem that making **m_data private** and using *accessor* and *mutator* functions yields much improvement over simply making the variable **public**. But, doing so does help you in two ways:

- You're able to change the internal representation of **m_data** simply by changing the implementation of the **AddPoint()** and

GetPoint() functions. Because the **CSDIOne** interface doesn't change, you won't have to revise other classes that depend on it.

- You avoid the headaches that accompany unrestricted **public** access. Because you supply the only functions that operate on **m_data**, you know where to look when something goes wrong. If you allowed **public** access, you'd have to search through the entire application looking for references (direct and indirect) to **m_data**.

The View Class

The final member of the DocView quartet is the view class. As you can see in Figure 12.1, the default view class is a subclass of **CView**—which, in turn, is a subclass of **CWnd**. In Figure 12.1, the view class is called **CYourView**. In the SDIOne program, MFC named the analogous class **CSDIOneView** and stored it in the files SDIOneView.h and SDIOneView.cpp.

When you create an SDI application, you may choose to base your view class on a class other than **CView**. For instance, in the NotePod program you created in Chapter 1, you used the **CEditView** class as the base view class. As you recall, you chose the view class from within AppWizard before the program was generated. In an SDI application, the AppWizard Step 6 dialog box lets you highlight each individual class. When you highlight the application's view class, a combo box opens, replacing the base-class edit box—you can then select a different kind of view. You can see this illustrated in Figure 12.3.

The CView Class

Like the document class, the view class AppWizard writes for your application needs to be customized. The **CView** class is a simple window class with no border. When you start an SDI application, your application's view window sizes itself so that it fits inside and covers the client area of the main window.

Because the view class window has no borders, it's not readily apparent that your frame-window's client area has been covered in this manner. However, it becomes obvious when you interact with the window. Mouse messages are sent to the view class, not

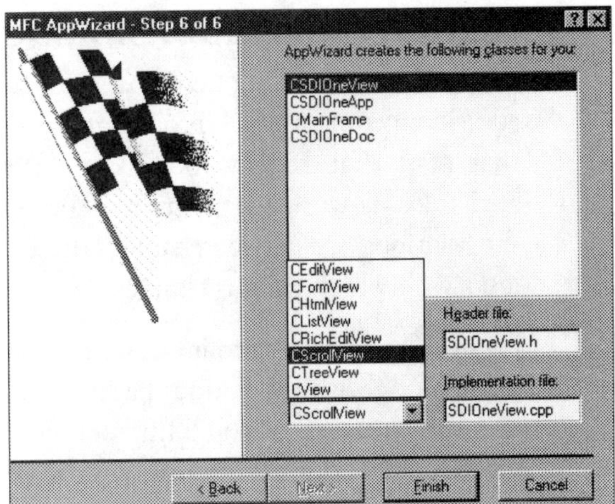

Figure 12.3
Selecting a different base class for your view class in AppWizard.

the frame window, so if you paint on the surface of your frame window's client area, you'll never see the output—it's entirely obscured by the view window.

Like the **CDocument** class, the **CView** class includes a protected constructor, virtual destructor, and diagnostic methods. In addition, it includes the **OnDraw()** method, which fills the place occupied by the **OnPaint()** function in a plain, non-DocView application. **OnDraw()** provides a place for you to render your document. In Chapter 11, the **CSDIOneView** class overrode this method, as do the view classes of most DocView programs.

In addition to the **OnDraw()** method, the **CSDIOneView** class contains three methods devoted to printing. The **OnDraw()** function renders the print image in the same way it renders the screen image. The three printing functions—**OnPreparePrinting()**, **OnBeginPrinting()**, and **OnEndPrinting()**—let you make the adjustments that accompany the move from the big screen to the printed page, such as scaling and pagination.

Finally, the **CSDIOneView** class includes a **GetDocument()** method that returns a pointer to the **CDocument** object, properly cast to a **CSDIOneDoc** pointer. When you build a release version of your program, MFC inlines this function, improving efficiency but reducing runtime error checking.

Rights And Responsibilities

As you can see, adding new classes to the mix does involve some additional complexity. Unfortunately, it's not uncommon to find that a task that *should* work—like painting your window's client area—*doesn't* work. To program accurately, you must keep in mind the relationships between each of the DocView classes and the tasks with which each is charged.

Figure 12.4 shows the four classes involved in a DocView program, along with the various paths of communication. (This isn't the whole picture, as you'll find out when we talk about menus, toolbars, and command routing in the next two chapters. But, it's a good beginning approximation.)

As with non-DocView applications, the DocView application class retrieves messages from the Windows message queue and routes them to window objects. This occurs in the **Run()** method of the application framework, which encapsulates the standard Windows message loop. When the application dispatches messages, most of the messages go to the main window, which forwards them to other objects for processing. However, mouse and keyboard messages are dispatched to the view window.

Besides the standard route through the message loop—a route that any two objects can use to communicate with each other—the document and view classes set up a direct, back-channel hot-line. When a document and view are linked, each contains a pointer to the other. Thus, a document can tell its view to repaint itself by calling the view's **OnUpdate()** function. In a similar way,

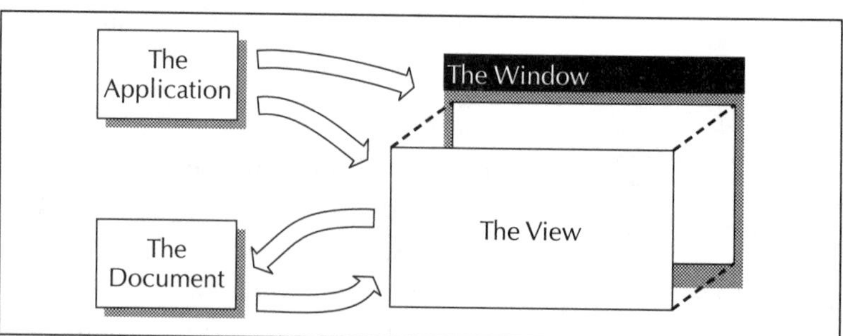

Figure 12.4
The DocView SDI architecture.

the view class communicates directly with the document object to obtain the data it needs to render itself.

Now that you have an overall idea of what a DocView application looks like, let's take a closer look at one of the classes contained in the SDIOne application. Because the classes are relatively large, even for such a simple application as SDIOne, we won't reprint the listings for every class. When we do reprint a listing, we'll show only the code that's pertinent to the point at hand.

As we did with the simplest MFC application from Chapter 2, let's start with the application class: **CSDIOneApp**.

CSDIOneApp: You Call *That* InitInstance()?

MFC named the SDIOne application class **CSDIOneApp**, placing its declaration in the file SDIOne.h and its implementation in the file SDIOne.cpp. The **CSDIOneApp** class contains three overridden methods: the constructor **CSDIOneApp()**, the virtual **InitInstance()** function, and the function **OnAppAbout()**, which displays the application's About dialog box.

The SDIOne.cpp implementation file also defines a global **CSDIOneApp** object. When the application object is created at global scope, its constructor is called before your application's **WinMain()** function. Because of this early construction, SDIOne can't initialize its application class in the **CSDIOneApp** constructor. Instead, it initializes it in the **InitInstance()** function, which is shown in Listing 12.1.

Listing 12.1 The CSDIOneApp::InitInstance() member function.

```
/////////////////////////////////////////////////////////////
// CSDIOneApp initialization

BOOL CSDIOneApp::InitInstance()
{
    // 1. The setup section
    Enable3dControls();            // Call this when using
                                   // MFC in a shared DLL
```

```
    SetRegistryKey(_T(
      "Local AppWizard-Generated Applications"));
    LoadStdProfileSettings();  // Load standard INI file
                               // options

    // 2. Connect the pieces together
    CSingleDocTemplate* pDocTemplate;
    pDocTemplate = new CSingleDocTemplate(
        IDR_MAINFRAME,
        RUNTIME_CLASS(CSDIOneDoc),
        RUNTIME_CLASS(CMainFrame),       // main SDI frame
                                         // framewindow
        RUNTIME_CLASS(CSDIOneView));
    AddDocTemplate(pDocTemplate);

    // 3. Connect to Windows Explorer
    EnableShellOpen();
    RegisterShellFileTypes(TRUE);

    // 4. Retrieve and process command line arguments
    CCommandLineInfo cmdInfo;
    ParseCommandLine(cmdInfo);

    if (!ProcessShellCommand(cmdInfo))
        return FALSE;

    // 5. Work with the window
    m_pMainWnd->ShowWindow(SW_SHOW);
    m_pMainWnd->UpdateWindow();
    m_pMainWnd->DragAcceptFiles();

    return TRUE;
}
```

If you recall the **InitInstance()** method of the minimal MFC program shown in Chapter 1, you might be shocked by what you see here—only a few things look similar. But, the difference is only on the surface. The minimal MFC **InitInstance()** method took three lines to create and display a new window. The **CSDIOneApp::InitInstance()** method performs several additional operations.

In Listing 12.1, we've divided **InitInstance()** into five sections, each devoted to a particular task. Let's look at them in turn.

Application Setup

The set-up section of **InitInstance()** contains three lines:

```
Enable3dControls();          // Call this when using MFC
                             // in a shared DLL
SetRegistryKey(_T(
"Local AppWizard-Generated Applications"));
LoadStdProfileSettings();  // Load standard INI file
                           // options
```

AppWizard added these lines to your program in response to a selection made when you generated your initial program. The **Enable3dControls()** line is created when you select the 3D Controls checkbox in the MFC AppWizard Step 4 dialog box, as shown in Figure 12.5.

AppWizard actually wrote two lines of code, based on your selection. If you dynamically link your program, then the function shown previously is called; if you statically link your program, the function **Enable3dControlsStatic()** is called.

The **Enable3dControls()** function creates the gray, chiseled 3D effect for controls used in dialog boxes and toolbars, as first popularized by Microsoft Excel. Calling **Enable3dControls()** loads the dynamic-link library Ctrl3D32.dll, which automatically subclasses the dialog class (and others). Surprisingly, if you fail to

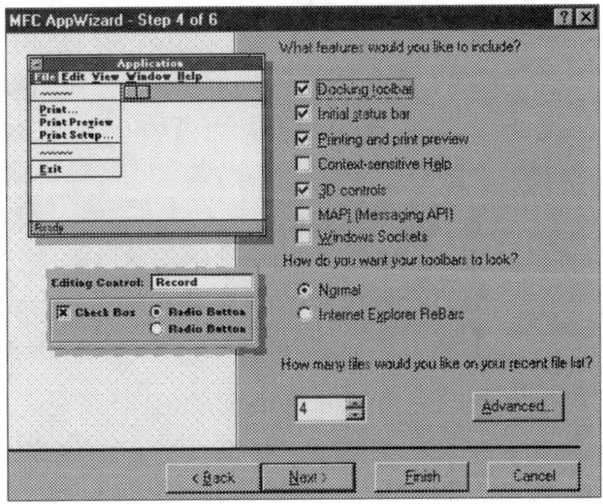

Figure 12.5
The MFC AppWizard Step 4 dialog box.

call **Enable3dControls()**, your dialog boxes will *still* have the 3D effect when run under Windows 95, Windows 98, or NT 4.0; they will have the flat 2D style only when run under Windows NT 3.5.

Enable3dControls() has no effect on controls that are created programmatically and displayed outside a dialog box. Such controls default to the original 2D appearance unless you use the **CreateEx()** function and add the **WS_EX_CLIENTEDGE** attribute when creating the control.

Registration With Mr. _T()

The next two lines in the setup section enable the *MRU list.* MRU stands for Most Recently Used, and refers to the names of the last several files opened by your application. By default, the MRU list contains four files. If you don't want an MRU list, set the number at the bottom of the AppWizard Step 4 dialog box to 0 (you can set the value to any number from 0 to 16). MFC uses this number when calling the **LoadStdProfileSettings()** function. If you set the number to 16, AppWizard will add the line

```
LoadStdProfileSettings(16);
```

to your program. You can easily change the line by hand if you decide you aren't happy with the selection you made in AppWizard. If you default the argument, **LoadStdProfileSetting()** assumes a value of 4.

Once you've called **LoadStdProfileSettings()**, Windows saves the name of the last several files you've opened, along with their paths. This information appears on the File menu, as you can see in Figure 12.6.

Because Windows remembers which files you opened last, even after you've closed and reopened your application, it's obvious that Windows is saving the information somewhere. That somewhere turns out to be the Windows Registry.

The Registry is a single binary file that stores an enormous variety of configuration information in Windows NT, Windows 95, and Windows 98. Information stored in the Registry is organized as a hierarchical database, much like the file system you're used to.

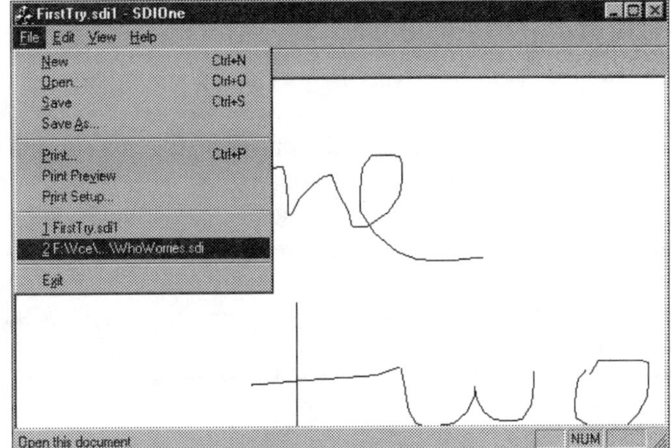

Figure 12.6
Displaying the MRU file list for the SDIOne application.

Instead of folders, however, there are *keys*, and, instead of files, there are *values*. The function call

```
SetRegistryKey(_T(
  "Local AppWizard-Generated Applications"));
```

instructs Windows to create a key (think *folder*, if you like) with the enormous name HKEY_CURRENT_USER1 \Software\ Local AppWizard-Generated Applications\SDIOne. That's certainly a mouthful, isn't it? The key will contain two subkeys: Recent File List and Settings.

When you call **SetRegistryKey()**, you pass it a string defining the *family* key, not the key for the particular application. Several applications may comprise a family, each having its own application key and subkeys. If you change the current argument from **_T("Local AppWizard-Generated Applications")** to **_T("Steve 'n' Bill's Scintillating Software")** the MRU list will be saved under the key shown in Figure 12.7.

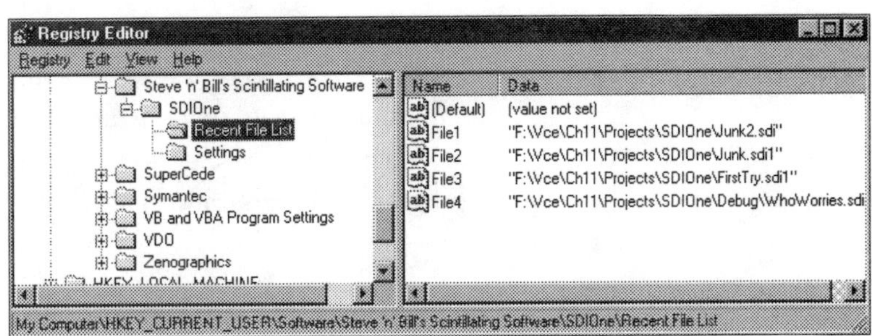

Figure 12.7
Locating the SDIOne Registry key using the Regedit program.

How About Those Extensions?

If you look closely at Figure 12.7 you'll notice that some of the files have the extension .sdi1 and others have the extension .sdi. Because you specified the extension .sdi1 as the application file extension on AppWizard's Advanced Options dialog box—only files with the extension .sdi1 show up by default in the File Open dialog box. However, when you create a new drawing and save it without specifying an extension, Windows will provide one for you. Unfortunately, the default extension Windows provides is only three characters long, apparently for compatibility with previous operating-system releases. Surely you wondered why three-letter extensions are still so prevalent, several years after Windows 95 introduced long file names—now you know at least one reason.

If you don't call **SetRegistryKey()**, the call to **LoadStdProfileSettings()** will cause Windows to create an INI file named SDIOne.ini, place it in the Windows subdirectory, and write the MRU file list to the INI file, instead. If you detest the Windows Registry, your program doesn't have to use it. Just skip the call to **SetRegistryKey()**.

Finally, you may be wondering about the **_T()** stuff. Programs written for the international market no longer use the single-byte ASCII character set for strings and characters, because the 256 characters it provides are insufficient for many world languages. Windows supports two international character sets: MBCS (the Multi-Byte Character Set), and Unicode, a 16-bit universal character encoding. Unfortunately, Unicode is available only in Windows NT, not in Windows 95 or Windows 98.

MFC comes with a special header file—TCHAR.h—that defines a set of macros to transparently convert embedded strings and characters between Windows' character sets. To use these macros, you place all character constants in the **_TCHAR()** macro, like this:

```
_TCHAR('A')
```

Place all embedded string constants in the **_TEXT()** or **_T()** macros. Then, when you define the constant **_UNICODE** in your program, your characters and constants will be correctly represented as Unicode characters. Without it, they remain regular single-byte characters.

Unfortunately, writing software for the international market is considerably more difficult and complex than adding a few macros to your code. On the other hand, they don't hurt anything, and, if you use them, that's one less thing you have to worry about down the road when your application becomes a world-wide success.

Connecting The Pieces

Now that all the preliminaries are out of the way, it's time to create the pieces of your application: the frame, the view, and the document. Remember that a DocView application tightly couples each piece to the others. For the view class and the document class to carry on their bi-directional conversation, each must point correctly to the other. Rather than require you to perform this delicate, precise, and tedious initialization, MFC employs a helper class called a *document template*.

MFC provides two document template classes: the **CSingleDocTemplate** class, designed to hook a view, frame window, and document together in an SDI arrangement; and the **CMultiDocTemplate**, which does the same thing for MDI applications.

Using a document template is a three-step process:

- Create a pointer to a document template.
- Create a new document template by using the **new** operator and references to the instances of your document, view, and frame window classes.
- Add the document template to your application object, so it can manage your object menagerie.

Let's see how this works in practice.

Creating the document template pointer isn't difficult. For the SDIOne application, the line looks like this:

```
CSingleDocTemplate* pDocTemplate;
```

The last step—adding the document template to the application—is also straightforward, merely requiring a call to the application's **AddDocTemplate()** function, as follows:

```
AddDocTemplate(pDocTemplate);
```

It's the step that lies between these that looks confusing. Here's the statement that creates the new document template for the SDIOne application (AppWizard formatted the code over several lines, so it's easier to read):

```
pDocTemplate = new CSingleDocTemplate(
    IDR_MAINFRAME,
    RUNTIME_CLASS(CSDIOneDoc),
    RUNTIME_CLASS(CMainFrame),    // main SDI frame window
    RUNTIME_CLASS(CSDIOneView));
```

The constructor for the **CSingleDocTemplate** class takes four arguments: an integer representing a resource ID, and three **CRuntimeClass** pointers.

The resource ID is a multi-purpose ID used by the framework to identify the application icon, main menu, accelerator table, and document string created using your input from the AppWizard Advanced Options dialog box. At runtime, this ID is used to locate and install each of these items. Okay, so this part is fairly straightforward, after all. However, the use of **CRuntimeClass** pointers and the **RUNTIME_CLASS()** macro is a bit different.

When you pass the **RUNTIME_CLASS()** macro the name of a class, such as **CSDIOneDoc**, it returns a pointer that you can use to create an instance of that class, using a process called *dynamic object creation*. Classes intended for dynamic object creation contain a static pointer to a **CRuntimeClass** structure describing the class, and two functions: **GetRuntimeClass()** and **CreateObject()**. MFC adds this structure to your classes when the **DECLARE_DYNAMIC()** and **IMPLEMENT_DYNAMIC()** macros appear in the header and implementation files. Provided the class complies, you can create an instance by calling the **CreateObject()** function instead of **new**.

By now, you may be wondering, "What does this have to do with me?" Fortunately, the answer is, "Almost nothing." You'll rarely—if ever—use dynamic object creation in your own programs. Most of the time, you won't even have to modify the code that AppWizard writes to set up the document, view, and frame window for your program. But, it's useful to know what MFC is up to behind the scenes, particularly when a program misbehaves or crashes.

Shell Games

The third section of **CSDIOneApp**'s **InitInstance()** method connects your program to the Windows shell. (The Windows Explorer program is called the *shell*, because it provides your primary interface to the operating system.) You've probably noticed that when you double-click on a DOC file in Windows Explorer, Microsoft Word opens and automatically loads the document you double-clicked. Adding the lines

```
EnableShellOpen();
RegisterShellFileTypes(TRUE);
```

to your program make this possible. Because of these lines, you can double-click on a file with the extension .sdi1 to open the SDIOne program. Moreover, if you drag a file with the .sdi1 extension and drop it on a printer icon, the file will be printed, just as if you'd chosen Print from the File menu.

Command Lines

The fourth section in **InitInstance()** processes the program command line—the arguments passed to your program when it starts. You might wonder what this piece of code is doing here. After all, in this age of drag and drop, few of us pass command-line arguments to our programs.

That's certainly true, as far as it goes. But, even though you pass no command-line arguments to your programs, Windows may do so behind your back. For instance, the Windows screen-saver control panel passes a switch to your application, letting it know whether to run as a screen saver (**s**, **/s**, or **-s**) or in configuration mode (**c**, **/c**, or **-c**). DocView programs do something similar.

In a DocView program, MFC breaks the command line into pieces by creating a **CCommandLineInfo** object and passing it to the **ParseCommandLine()** function. MFC passes the fully parsed command line to the **ProcessShellCommand()** function.

The **ProcessShellCommand()** function examines the **CCommandLineInfo** object to determine whether one of the arguments is a file name. If so, **ProcessShellCommand()** attempts to load the document. If no file names are specified, **ProcessShellCommand()** tries to start the application with a blank document. If **ProcessShellCommand()** is unable to accomplish either of these tasks, it returns **FALSE**, and your program terminates.

Working With Windows

The last section in **InitInstance()** should look familiar. The two lines

```
m_pMainWnd->ShowWindow(SW_SHOW);
m_pMainWnd->UpdateWindow();
```

are the same as those used to display your application's main window in Chapter 2's minimal MFC application. The last line

```
m_pMainWnd->DragAcceptFiles();
```

activates drag-and-drop support for your program. Of course, that's not really all there is to drag and drop, but it's all you have to know—the framework calls the correct methods to open dragged files without you doing any more work.

Postscript And Preview: The CSDIOneApp Message Map

In Chapter 4, you saw the message response table, or *message map* for the FourUp application. Recall that a message map is a sophisticated set of macros designed to route Windows messages to the appropriate member function.

One of the most common message map macros is **ON_COMMAND()**, which responds to menu and toolbar selections that generate **WM_COMMAND()** messages. Because each menu command generates the same message, MFC needs a way to associate a particular menu command with the function that handles that command.

Normally, you inform MFC what function handles a menu command by using the **ON_COMMAND()** macro, which takes arguments specifying a menu resource ID—which you'll meet in the next chapter—and the name of the handler function. As you can see in Listing 12.2, the DocView framework has already anticipated you by hooking up **ON_COMMAND()** handlers for the File|New, File|Open, and File|Print Setup menu commands.

Listing 12.2 The CSDIOneApp message map.

```
/////////////////////////////////////////////////////////////
/////////////////////
// CSDIOneApp

BEGIN_MESSAGE_MAP(CSDIOneApp, CWinApp)
    //{{AFX_MSG_MAP(CSDIOneApp)
    ON_COMMAND(ID_APP_ABOUT, OnAppAbout)
    //}}AFX_MSG_MAP
    // Standard file based document commands
    ON_COMMAND(ID_FILE_NEW, CWinApp::OnFileNew)
    ON_COMMAND(ID_FILE_OPEN, CWinApp::OnFileOpen)
    // Standard print setup command
    ON_COMMAND(ID_FILE_PRINT_SETUP,
CWinApp::OnFilePrintSetup)
END_MESSAGE_MAP()
```

In addition to the menu commands automatically hooked up by AppWizard, the framework itself contains several "magic" IDs that you can use to initiate an action. For instance, if you assign the **ID_APP_EXIT ID** to a menu item, selecting the item will cause MFC to call the **CWinApp OnAppExit()** function. Similar automatic IDs include **ID_FILE_SAVE** and **ID_FILE_SAVE_AS**.

What's Next On The Menu?

If you read through the message map for the **CSDIOneApp** class, you'll notice that it handles the printer-setup command, but not the printing or print-preview commands. Why?

The reason lies in MFC's command-routing mechanism. With command routing, you don't have to handle menu commands in the application class, the frame window class, or the view class—you're free to handle them wherever it's easiest or makes the most sense. Because all the painting code is in the **CSDIOneView** class, it's simple to handle printing there. Sure enough, if you look at the message map for the view class, you'll see the command handlers for print-preview and printing.

If all this talk about menus has stimulated your appetite to learn more, you're in luck. The next thing on the menu is...well..., menus!

Chapter 13

Picasso's Dream: The MiniSketch Program

Menu-driven programs are the software incarnation of Joseph Heller's famous novel Catch-22*—the visual equivalent of voice-mail hell.*

If you worked on an early computerized bookkeeping system or airline reservation system, you understand that in a *menu-driven* system, the program does the driving—not you. And, all too often, the program isn't going where you want to go.

Windows programs aren't menu-driven. Sure, menus are a big part of the Windows graphical user interface (GUI). In the early days, when computers were iron and programmers were "real men," the GUI was sometimes called the WIMP interface, because of its reliance on Windows, Icons, Mice, and Pull-down menus. Of course, these days, even the most diehard detractor is more likely to have a mouse than a manual of op-codes.

Rather than menu driven, Windows programs are *user driven.* In a user-driven program, the user controls the order in which actions are performed. Menu-driven programs were popular for so long because—compared to event-driven programs—they were easy to write.

Fortunately, once you've made the jump from hierarchical, procedurally organized programs to event-driven, object-oriented programs, creating menus that put the user in control turns out to be a piece of cake. And, with the tools provided by Visual C++, doing so is even easier.

In this chapter, you'll learn how to create several kinds of menus and how to handle the messages they produce. In the next chapter, we'll carry on and expand your menu expertise, learning about Windows toolbars. But first, we have some old business to take care of.

What's In A Name?

Now that the SDIOne program has served its purpose, let's move on to SDITwo, where you'll add menus and toolbars. Here's what you'll need to do—*read through the entire procedure before you begin.*

Create a new directory named SDITwo and copy into it the files from the SDIOne directory. Now, change the names of the files from SDIOne to SDITwo, leaving each file-name extension intact. Gee..., there are a lot of file names to change, aren't there? Now, open each file using a program editor and change each occurrence of "SDIOne" to "SDITwo". Open the resource file in text mode and change all its references. Wow.., there are an *awful* lot of changes.... And, some of those files are binary, aren't they? Well, if you have a hex editor, you could probably use it, but if not, there's a program called debug....

You get the picture. It's not that there's no way to change the name of a project once AppWizard has finished its work. There's just no *practical* way.

So, here are your choices:

- Each time you add a new feature, start a new project under a different name and redo all the steps from the previous project. If you like, you can think of it as practice.
- Keep the name SDIOne as the program grows and expands, so you're constantly reminded of the necessity to plan ahead—kind of like 6-character date fields and the 640K memory limit.
- Bite the bullet now and come up with a name that will suffice—if not through the next millenium, at least through the next several chapters. You'll have to reenter the code from SDIOne, but only this once.

As you may have guessed, we're going to choose door number three and reenter the code from SDIOne. Of course, *you* can follow a much easier route: Simply copy the starter files from the

CD. But, in case you want to do it all yourself, we'll present the steps to build the MegaloMatic. No...wait, that sounds a little off, somehow. How about StupendousPainter? No, too pretentious. ScintillatingSketcher? Too hard to say—too hard to type, as well.

We need a name that's simple and descriptive: Let's go with MiniSketch.

Here are the instructions for creating the MiniSketch program. For a longer explanation, simply turn back to Chapter 11—except for some of the set-up options, only the names have changed since SDIOne.

1. Create a new MFC AppWizard (exe) project and name it MiniSketch.
2. In the Step 1 dialog box, choose Single Document With Document/View support. In the Step 2 dialog box, choose None and click on Next. In the Step 3 dialog box, deselect the ActiveX Controls checkbox and click on Next. In the Step 4 dialog box, accept the defaults, but click on Advanced to open the Advanced Options dialog box.
3. You can see the Advanced Options dialog box for the MiniSketch program in Figure 13.1. You'll use a three-character file extension, .msk. Change each field so that it matches the figure. Click on Close when you finish, then click on Next.

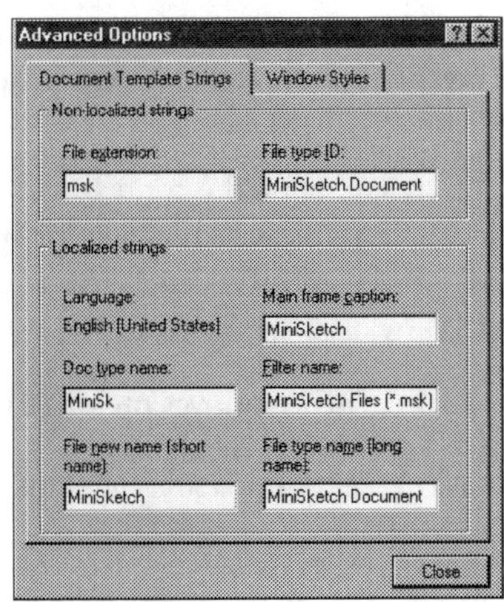

Figure 13.1
The MiniSketch Advanced Options dialog box.

4. Accept the defaults in the Step 5 dialog box. In the Step 6 dialog box, you'll change the class names to shorten them. Instead of **CMiniSketchView**, let's use the initials "MS" for MiniSketch. Thus, your view class will be named **CMSView**. One by one, select each class from the list box and change its name in the Class Name edit box. In Figure 13.2, you can see that we've changed the view class's name. Leave the frame window class's name set to **CMainFrame**. Don't change the names of any of the files—change *only* the three class names, which become **CMSView**, **CMSApp**, and **CMSDoc**. When you've changed all the names, close the App Wizard.
5. Add a private **CPoint** member variable named **m_LineStart** to the **CMSView** class. Add the **m_data CPoint** array to the **CMSDoc** class definition by manually typing in the following two lines (you can't use the Add Member Variable dialog box to create this template-based variable):

   ```
   private:
       CArray<CPoint, CPoint> m_data;
   ```

6. Select the FileView tab in the Workspace window and find the file StdAfx.h in the Header Files folder. Open the file, then add the following line after the other includes:

   ```
   #include <afxtempl.h>
   ```

   This line ensures that the template collection classes you'll use in the next several chapters are available to every class, not just the **CMSDoc** class.
7. Right-click to open the context menu for the **CMSView** class. Add Windows message handlers for **WM_LBUTTONDOWN**, **WM_LBUTTONUP**, and **WM_MOUSEMOVE** to the **CMSView** class, as shown in Listing 13.1.

Listing 13.1 The Windows message handlers for the CMSView class.

```
void CMSView::OnLButtonDown(UINT nFlags, CPoint point)
{
    m_LineStart = point;
```

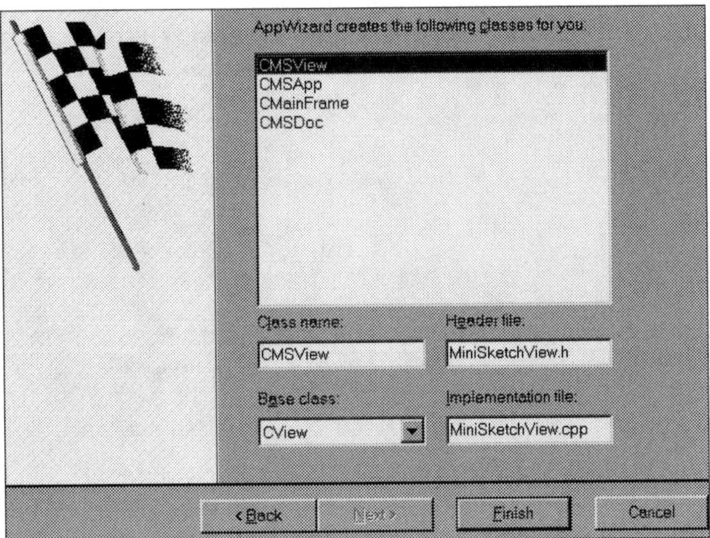

Figure 13.2
Changing the MiniSketch class names.

```
    SetCapture();
}

void CMSView::OnLButtonUp(UINT nFlags, CPoint point)
{
    ReleaseCapture();
}

void CMSView::OnMouseMove(UINT nFlags, CPoint point)
{
    if (nFlags & MK_LBUTTON)
    {
        CMSDoc* pDoc = GetDocument();
        ASSERT_VALID(pDoc);
        pDoc->AddPoint(m_LineStart);
        pDoc->AddPoint(point);

        CClientDC dc(this);
        dc.MoveTo(m_LineStart);
        dc.LineTo(point);
        m_LineStart = point;
    }
}
```

8. Override the virtual **OnDraw()** function in the **CMSView** class by inserting the highlighted code shown in Listing 13.2 into the **OnDraw()** function.

Listing 13.2 The CMSView OnDraw() virtual member function.

```
void CMSView::OnDraw(CDC* pDC)
{
    CMSDoc* pDoc = GetDocument();
    ASSERT_VALID(pDoc);

    int nPoints = pDoc->NumPoints();
    for (int index = 0; index < nPoints; index += 2)
    {
        pDC->MoveTo(pDoc->GetPoint(index));
        pDC->LineTo(pDoc->GetPoint(index+1));
    }
}
```

9. Add the member functions shown in Listing 13.3 to the **CMSDoc** class. You can do so by inserting the code at the end of the file MiniSketchDoc.cpp or by using the Add Member Function dialog box. If you insert the code manually, remember to add a declaration for each function to the **CMSDoc** class definition in the file MiniSketchDoc.h.

Listing 13.3 Member functions for the CMSDoc class.

```
int CMSDoc::NumPoints()
{
    return m_data.GetSize();
}

CPoint CMSDoc::GetPoint(int index)
{
    return m_data[index];
}

void CMSDoc::AddPoint(CPoint point)
{
    m_data.Add(point);
    SetModifiedFlag();
}
```

10. Override the definition of the **CMSDoc::Serialize()** function by replacing the body of the function with the line

```
m_data.Serialize(ar);
```

Also add the following line to the **CMSDoc:: OnNew Document()** function, just before the return statement:

```
m_data.SetSize(0, 128);
```

Compile and run the finished program: It should work just like SDIOne. If you have trouble, recall that you can obtain a starter file from the CD-ROM. *Now* you're ready to make some changes.

MiniSketch Gets Menus

In the transition from the PaintORama program to SDIOne and MiniSketch, we left behind improvements such as colored pens and brushes, along with the ability to draw shapes and figures. Part of the reason lies with the user interface. Because PaintORama was a dialog-based application, it used dialog-box controls such as radio buttons, combo boxes, and list boxes. An SDI application has no *room* for such features, because the "canvas" takes up most of the screen.

Rather than shoehorn the PaintORama interface into MiniSketch, let's go with the flow (so to speak) and learn to do things the SDI way—by using menus and toolbars. Although you'll generally follow the same process you used while developing the PaintORama, you'll see that the scenery looks much different on the SDI trail.

Adding A Menu Item: Clear Drawing

When you developed the PaintORama program, the first thing you added was a button to clear the drawing and start over. Let's do something similar to MiniSketch: You'll add a Clear Drawing menu item that works like the PaintORama's Clear button.

"Wait a minute," you say. "Doesn't the application already have a Clear button? When you select File|New, or click on the New File icon, the program clears the drawing."

Well, that's mostly correct—but not entirely. Choosing File | New creates a new document, which isn't the same as erasing the contents of an existing document. For instance, if you attempt to save a new document, the Save As dialog box opens, because a new file has no name. If you erase the contents of a document and then select File|Save, MiniSketch saves the document under its existing name.

You can see another difference when you click on MiniSketch's File | New menu item: A file confirmation dialog box appears, as shown in Figure 13.3, and prompts you to save your changes. Unlike SDIOne, MiniSketch knows that you've changed your painting (this fact is recorded by the **SetModifiedFlags()** method, which the **CMSDoc** class calls whenever you change the document) and won't let you abandon the changes without confirmation.

Using The Menu Editor

Windows stores menus as resources in your RC file, just like dialog-box templates. A menu template describes the structure of the entire menu system and the characteristics of each menu item. You can edit the menu template in the resource script, if you like—some programmers prefer this—but for MiniSketch, you'll use the specialized Menu Editor.

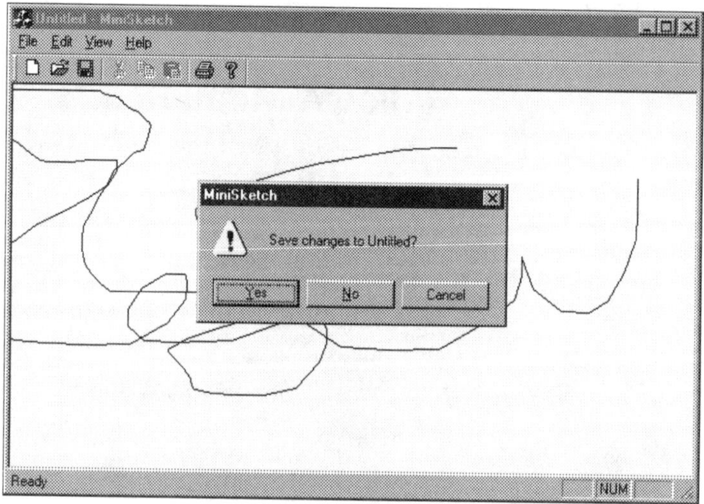

Figure 13.3
The MiniSketch abandon-file confirmation dialog box.

NOTE

*MFC uses the resource ID **IDR_MAINFRAME** for the main application icon, the toolbar, and the accelerator key table. You can use the same ID for several resources, provided they're different resource types. When the document-template class hooks up the frame window, the document, and the document's views, it uses this trick to locate all the required resources.*

To start the Menu Editor, open the MiniSketch project and select the ResourceView tab in the Workspace window. Find the Menu folder and expand it. You'll see a single menu resource named **IDR_MAINFRAME**. Double-click on **IDR_MAINFRAME** in the Menu folder to open the Menu Editor in the Editor window, as you can see in Figure 13.4.

The Menu Editor visually represents the structure of your main menu. Along the top are the pull-down menu captions that will appear in the menu bar when your program runs. To the right of the top-level menu captions you'll see an outlined rectangle, indicating where you can add a new pull-down menu. You'll do that shortly, but now, let's add the Clear Drawing command to the Edit menu.

Here are the steps to follow:

1. Click on the Edit caption in the Menu Editor. When you do, the Edit menu appears. At the bottom of the Edit menu is another outlined rectangle: Click on it, and its outline will change from a black dotted outline to a white outline containing a double row of embedded black dots. Select the menu item, right-click to open the context menu, and choose

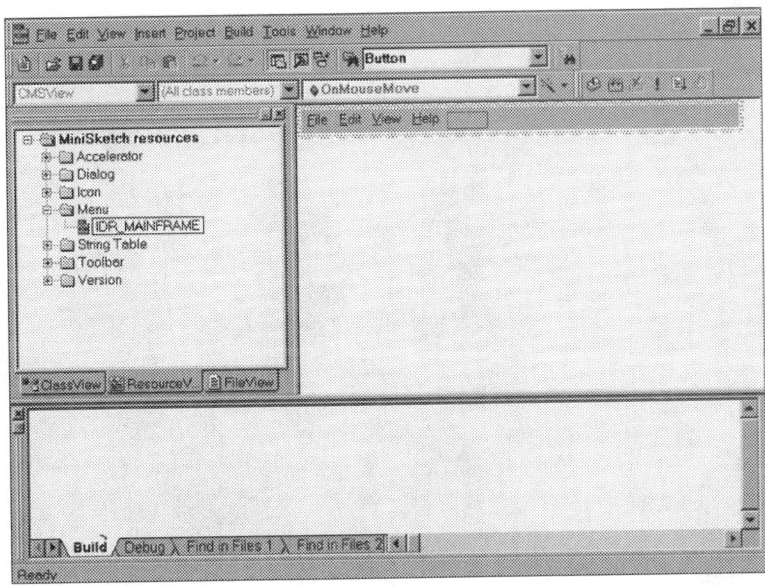

Figure 13.4
Starting the Menu Editor.

Properties. The Menu Item Properties dialog box will open, as shown in Figure 13.5. (You can also simply begin typing the menu-item caption as soon as the new menu item is selected. When you do this, the Menu Item Properties dialog box automatically opens.)

2. In the Caption field, enter "Clear &Drawing". (The ampersand adds an underline below the "D" when it's displayed, so users can choose the menu command by pressing Alt+E and then pressing D.)
3. In the Prompt field, enter the string "Erase the current drawing\nErase Drawing". The first half of this string will appear in the status bar when the user navigates over this menu item using the mouse or keyboard, giving the user information that clarifies the purpose of the menu selection. The second part of the string contains the tooltip text. (Tooltip text appears over a toolbar button if the button has the same resource ID as the menu selection. You should always add tooltip help, even if you don't plan to include a toolbar button for a particular command. That way, you don't have to remember to add it if you *do* insert the toolbar button.) You separate the menu prompt from the tooltip with the newline escape sequence (\n).
4. Drop down the ID combo box. You'll see that the Menu Editor has anticipated you by creating an ID called **ID_EDIT_CLEARDRAWING**, combining the name of the

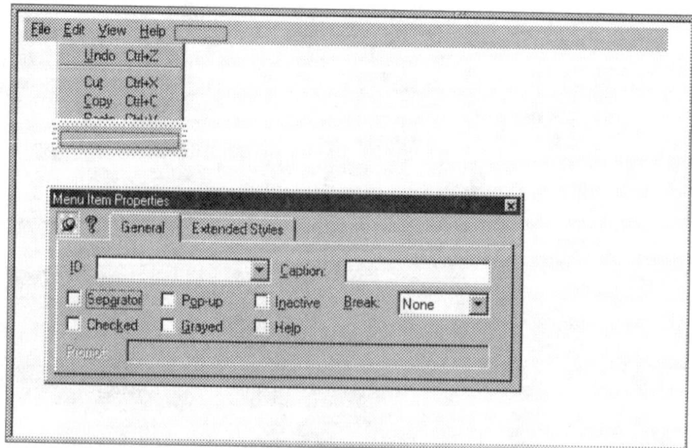

Figure 13.5
The Menu Editor and Menu Item Properties dialog box.

menu (Edit) with the prompt you've used. If you don't like the suggested resource ID, you can simply type in one of your own. In this case, Visual C++'s suggestion is just right. Look at Figure 13.6 to see the completed Menu Item Properties dialog box—be sure your example looks like the figure before going on.

Adding A Menu-Item Handler

When you add a menu item to the menu template by supplying a caption and a resource ID, you don't have to do any additional work. At runtime, Windows will display the menu and handle user interaction. You don't even need to monitor the keyboard or the mouse—only when the user actually selects a menu item do you need to wake up and take notice.

When the user selects a menu item—whether by mouse-click or keyboard shortcut—Windows sends your program a **WM_COMMAND** message. With the message, Windows passes the resource ID of the menu item that triggered the message.

Command Routing

In a traditional C-style Windows program, Windows sends the **WM_COMMAND** message to the window that contains the menu. Under DocView, this would create a problem. The frame window class—which contains the menu—wouldn't be able to handle the message (because it's not a document class) and would have to pass it to a class that could. In effect, the message would

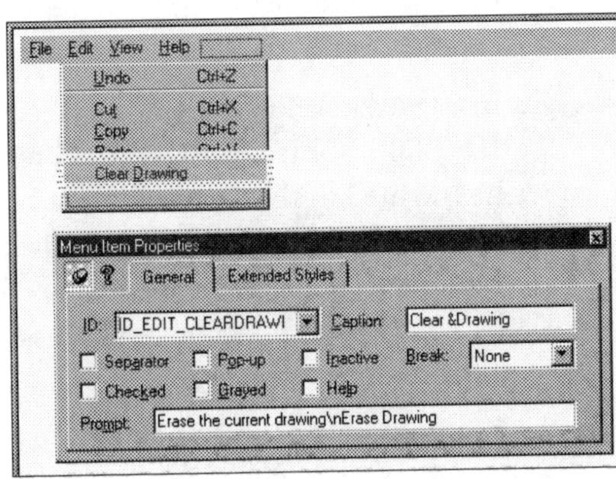

Figure 13.6
The completed Menu Item Properties dialog box for the Clear Drawing menu selection.

be handled twice. For example, to handle the Clear Drawing command in MiniSketch, you'd need to write a handler function inside the **CMainFrame** class to receive the message from Windows, and then write another handler function inside the **CMSView** class, where the work could actually be carried out.

MFC works around this limitation in an elegant way, by simply looking through all the classes in your application for one that can handle the command message. This approach, which is called *command routing*, works only for **WM_COMMAND** messages—the messages generated by toolbars and menus. It doesn't work for other kinds of Windows messages.

Using command routing, **WM_COMMAND** messages are first sent to the currently active view, then to the document, then to the main frame window object, and finally to the application itself. If any object handles the message, it goes no further; if no object handles the message, then it's sent to Windows for default processing. For custom command messages, the default processing is (of course) to do nothing.

Using The Menu Editor

Using the Menu Editor, you can easily attach an action or command handler to a particular menu selection. Let's add the handler for the Clear Drawing menu selection. Here are the steps to follow:

1. Be sure that the MiniSketch project is open. Open the **IDR_MAINFRAME** menu in the Menu Editor and select the Edit|Clear Drawing menu item. Right-click, and then choose ClassWizard from the context menu.
2. In ClassWizard, select the Message Maps property page. The **ID_EDIT_CLEARDRAWING** resource ID should appear highlighted in the Object IDs list box. You must decide which class should handle the Clear Drawing command message. Because this command affects the contents of the document, let's put it in the document class. Select **CMSDoc** from the Class Name combo box.
3. You must now decide which kind of messages you want to handle. As you can see in the Messages list box, you can

choose either **COMMAND** or **UPDATE_COMMAND_UI**. Right now, you're interested only in the **WM_COMMAND** messages, so highlight **COMMAND**. Be sure your screen looks like Figure 13.7, then click on Add Function.

4. In the Add Member Function dialog box that opens, change the proffered name—**OnEditCleardrawing**—to **OnEditClearDrawing**, which is a bit easier to read. Click on OK when you're ready to continue, and you'll return to the ClassWizard dialog box. Click on Edit Code and you'll be taken to the text editor, which is ready to accept your commands.
5. In the text editor, enter the code highlighted in Listing 13.4.

Listing 13.4 The Clear Drawing command message handler.

```
void CMSDoc::OnEditClearDrawing()
{
    // TODO: Add your command handler code here
    m_data.SetSize(0, 128);
    SetModifiedFlag();
    UpdateAllViews(NULL);
}
```

Once you're finished, compile and run your program. Notice that:

- Unlike the File|New menu selection, choosing Edit|Clear Drawing doesn't cause the program to prompt you to save your old document.

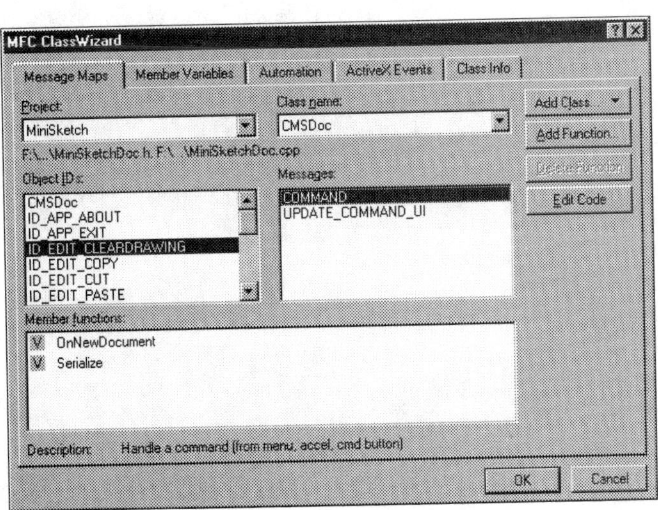

Figure 13.7
Adding the Clear Drawing command handler in ClassWizard.

- When you choose File | Save, you save the erased document under the existing name.
- The prompt string you specified appears in the status bar when you select the new menu item.
- You can select Clear Drawing using the keyboard shortcuts.

You can see the program running in Figure 13.8.

Behind The Scenes: What ClassWizard Did

Most of the time, you don't want to know what ClassWizard is doing behind your back. However, in the case of command messages, you do need to know, because sometimes you'll want to add your own command handlers. Fortunately, doing so is relatively straightforward.

To add a new menu command, ClassWizard performs three tasks. Let's take a look.

The Handler Prototype

ClassWizard begins by adding a prototype for the command-handler function to the class that handles the command. ClassWizard adds the prototype between special comment brackets that mark the prototype as property of ClassWizard (see the

Figure 13.8
Using the Clear Drawing command item.

highlighted lines in Listing 13.5). You can delete a ClassWizard prototype, but you shouldn't change it. Neither should you add a prototype within the special comment. To add a prototype, place it outside the special comment; to change a prototype, delete it and add your own outside the special comment.

NOTE

*MFC places the **afx_msg** prefix in front of generated message-map functions as a visual aid. When you see a function preceded by **afx_msg**, you know that function must also have a message-map entry. Apart from this, the **afx_msg** prefix does nothing, so you're free to omit it when you add your own message-map functions.*

Listing 13.5 Partial listing of the CMSDoc class definition.

```
class CMSDoc : public CDocument
{
// Class definition code omitted
// Generated message map functions
protected:
    //{{AFX_MSG(CMSDoc)
    afx_msg void OnEditClearDrawing();
    //}}AFX_MSG
    DECLARE_MESSAGE_MAP()
private:
    CArray<CPoint, CPoint> m_data;
};
```

The Handler Body

Second, ClassWizard adds the body for your handler function to the implementation (CPP) file for the class you've specified. Simple command handlers take no arguments and return no values, so ClassWizard simply needs to suggest a name and then use the name to write the function. If you add your own **WM_COMMAND** message handler, you can name it as you like—but its name must match the name you used in the class definition.

The ON_COMMAND Macro

Finally, ClassWizard associates your handler function with the resource ID for the related command. It does this by using the **ON_COMMAND()** macro, which it adds to the class message map.

As with the class prototype, ClassWizard inserts the **ON_COMMAND()** macro between special ClassWizard comment brackets. If you add a message map, you should add it outside these brackets. Listing 13.6 shows the message map entry for the Clear Drawing command.

Listing 13.6 The CMSDoc class message map.

```
BEGIN_MESSAGE_MAP(CMSDoc, CDocument)
    //{{AFX_MSG_MAP(CMSDoc)
    ON_COMMAND(ID_EDIT_CLEARDRAWING, OnEditClearDrawing)
    //}}AFX_MSG_MAP
END_MESSAGE_MAP()
```

Once you've written your function, you connect it to the particular command message you wish to process by placing an **ON_COMMAND** macro in the class message map. The **ON_COMMAND** macro takes two arguments: the resource ID for the command you want to handle and the name of your message-handler function. Notice that message map entries don't end in semicolons, even though they resemble function calls.

Now that you know how to make your menu items respond, let's go back and do some more work in the Menu Editor. Adding pen colors and pen widths to MiniSketch will allow us to explore most of the options.

The Return Of The Pens

In just a second, you're going to add a Pens menu to your program. Before you do, though, let's clean up the Edit menu.

When you left the Edit menu, it was happily coexisting with the Undo, Cut, Copy, and Paste menu items deposited there by AppWizard. Unlike most of the menu items provided by AppWizard, these don't do anything. If you want them to work, you have to hook them up yourself. In some programs (such as a text editor), these menu items are easy to activate. However, in a graphics program, doing so is a bigger job. For instance, to activate Copy, you must first provide a way for the user to select a portion of an image—not a trivial programming task.

In light of that, we're going to take the easy way out and delete all the menu items on the Edit menu except for Clear Drawing. Simply select the top item (Undo), then press the Delete key until all the menu items have been removed. Now that you've cleaned the cobwebs out of the Edit menu, you're ready to start working with Pens.

Adding A New Menu

The Pens menu is a new, top-level menu that will appear between the View menu and the Help menu. When the user clicks on Pens, menu items let the user select the color, thickness, and style of the pen.

Let's start by adding the Pens menu itself. Here are the steps to follow:

1. With the MiniSketch project loaded, open the **IDR_MAINFRAME** menu in the Menu Editor. You can add a new menu by selecting the dotted rectangle that appears to the right of the Help menu on the top line of the Menu Editor. Because you want the Pens menu to appear to the left of the Help menu, select the Help menu, then drag and drop it to the right of the insertion point. Figure 13.9 shows the Menu Editor while the Help menu is being dragged.
2. Select the insertion point with the mouse and begin typing the caption "&Pens". As soon as you start typing, the Menu Item Properties dialog box will open, as you can see in Figure 13.10. Notice that the Pop-up checkbox is selected, and the ID combo box is disabled—pop-up menus don't have (or need) unique IDs. When the Pens menu is selected, it doesn't fire a **WM_COMMAND** message; only menu items fire messages.

Pen Color: Adding Dialog Box Options

As soon as you added the Pens menu, a new menu item selection rectangle will appear below it. Here's where you enter the menu items for the Pens menu. You'll start by adding the menu item to select a new pen color.

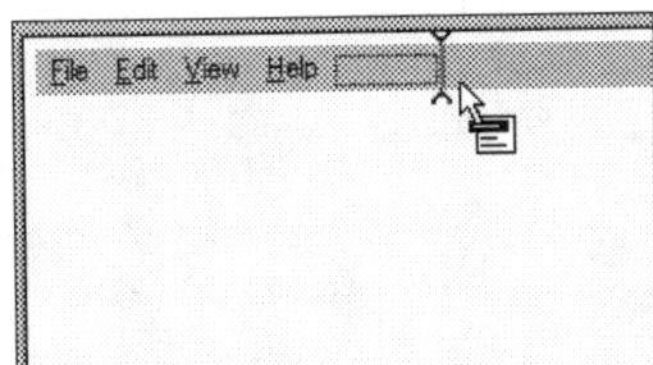

Figure 13.9
Dragging the Help menu past the new menu insertion point.

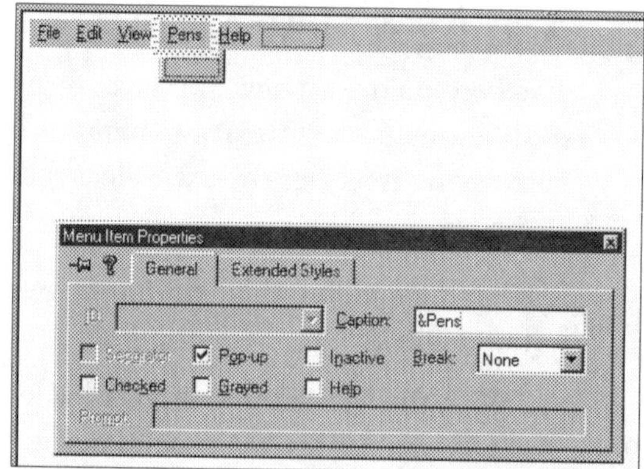

Figure 13.10
Adding the Pens menu caption.

Here are the steps to follow:

1. Select the new menu item and either double-click on it or simply start typing the caption "&Color...". You'll use the Windows common Color dialog to capture the pen color, just as you did in the PaintORama program.
2. Fill in the Prompt field with the text "Select the current pen for drawing\nPen Color". Drop down the ID combo box and be sure that **ID_PENS_COLOR** is selected. Once it is, you're ready for the next step: hooking everything up. Your screen should look like that shown in Figure 13.11.

Adding The Color Dialog Box Item

You've already seen how to add a command message handler by selecting the menu item and then choosing ClassWizard from the context menu (or by pressing Ctrl+W). Let's look at another way to add a message handler: using the WizardBar that you met in the very first chapter.

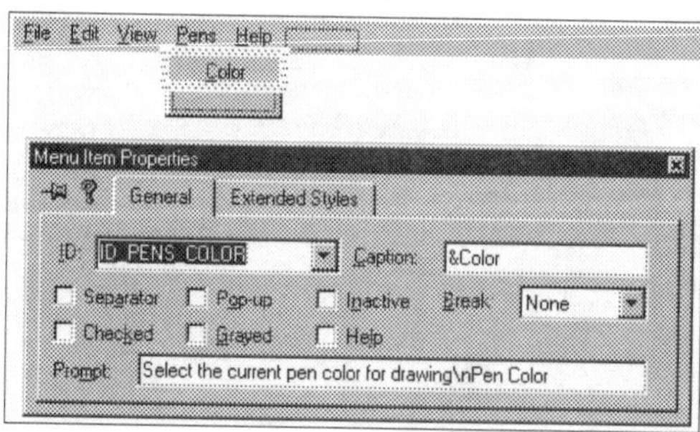

Figure 13.11
Adding the **ID_PENS_COLOR** menu item.

Visual C++ often gives you several ways to accomplish a goal. That way, you're able to choose the one that you find most convenient. Here are the steps to follow to add the new menu command handler using the WizardBar:

1. Be sure the MiniSketch project is loaded and that the **IDR_MAINFRAME** menu is open in the Menu Editor. Select the Pens | Color menu item.
2. In the WizardBar—which spans the window above the Workspace window and the editing window—select the **CMSView** class from the far-left combo box. When you do this, the far-right combo box will change to contain the **CMSView** class. Click on the WizardBar pull-down menu and choose Add Windows Message Handler. Your screen should look like that shown in Figure 13.12.
3. In the dialog box that appears (titled New Windows Message And Event Handlers For Class CMSView), select **ID_PENS_COLOR** from the Class Or Object To Handle list box and select **COMMAND** from the New Windows Messages/Events list box. When your screen looks like that shown in Figure 13.13, click on Add and Edit to continue.
4. When the Add Member Function dialog appears, accept the name **OnPensColor()** and click on OK. Add the lines shown in Listing 13.7.

Listing 13.7 The CMSView OnPensColor() function.

```
void CMSView::OnPensColor()
{
    // TODO: Add your command handler code here
    CColorDialog dlg(m_PenColor);
```

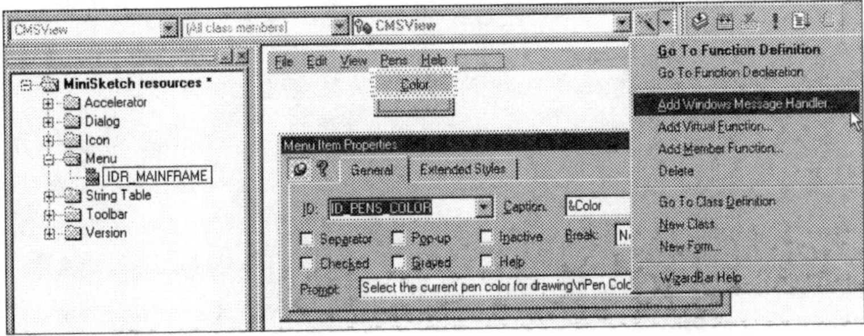

Figure 13.12
Adding a Windows message handler from the WizardBar.

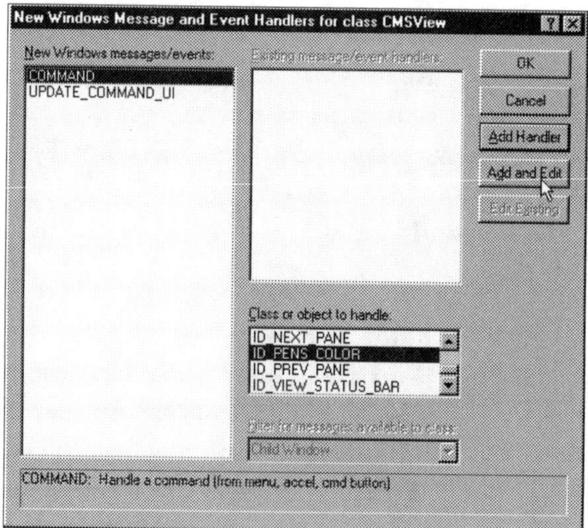

Figure 13.13
Selecting options for the pen color command handler.

```
    if (dlg.DoModal() == IDOK)
    {
        m_PenColor = dlg.GetColor();
        InitPen();
    }
}
```

The Supporting Cast

The code in **OnPensColor()** creates an instance of the Windows common Color dialog and displays it using **DoModal()**. If the user selects a color, the code retrieves the color and stores it in the **m_PenColor** variable, calling the **InitPen()** function to change the current drawing pen.

Unfortunately, this code has a few problems. Mainly, you don't yet have an **m_PenColor** variable or an **InitPen()** function. Before you can use the new menu, you need to erect some additional infrastructure.

Here's what you do:

1. Add the member variables shown in Table 13.1 to the **CMSView** class. You can use the Add Member Variable dialog box, or you can simply type them into CMiniSketchView.h by hand. All of the variables should be **private**. You may recall these variables—the PaintORama program used similar ones.

Table 13.1 Member variables for the CMSView class.

Type	Name	Description
CPen	**m_Pen**	The current drawing pen used by the **CMSView** class.
COLORREF	**m_PenColor**	The color of the current drawing pen.
int	**m_PenStyle**	The style of the current drawing pen.
int	**m_PenWidth**	The width of the current drawing pen.

2. Initialize each member variable by adding the code shown in Listing 13.8 to the **CMSView** constructor.

Listing 13.8 The CMSView constructor.

```
CMSView::CMSView()
{
    // TODO: add construction code here
    m_PenColor  = RGB(0,0,0);
    m_PenStyle  = PS_SOLID;
    m_PenWidth  = 1;
    m_Pen.CreatePen(m_PenStyle, m_PenWidth, m_PenColor);
}
```

3. Use the Add Member Function dialog box to add the **public InitPen()** function to the **CMSView** class. The **void** function takes no arguments and returns no value. Add the code highlighted in Listing 13.9 to complete the function.

Listing 13.9 The InitPen() member function.

```
void CMSView::InitPen()
{
    m_Pen.DeleteObject();
    m_Pen.CreatePen(m_PenStyle, m_PenWidth, m_PenColor);
}
```

4. Add the following line to the **CMSView OnMouseMove()** function, immediately after the line that constructs the **CClientDC**:

```
dc.SelectObject(&m_Pen);
```

Once you're finished, compile and run the program. As you can see in Figure 13.14, selecting Pen|Color from the menu opens the Windows common Color dialog. When you select a color, the program uses the new pen for drawing.

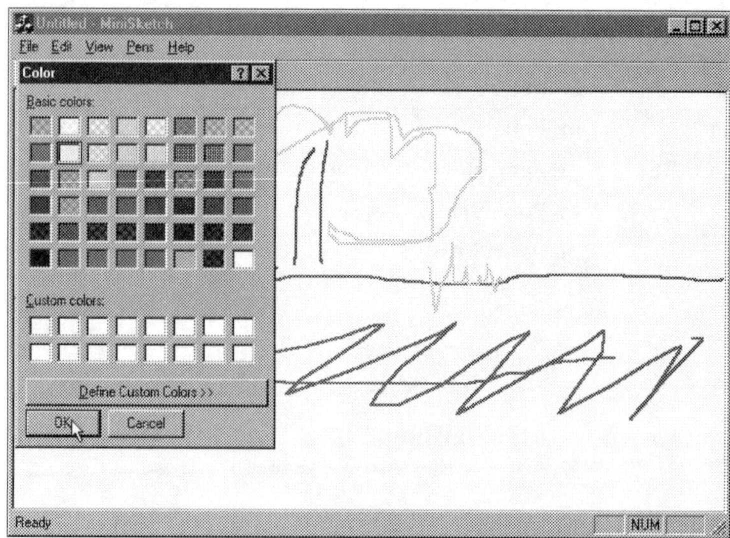

Figure 13.14
Using the Pens|Color menu selection to change the drawing color.

Of course, your document class doesn't yet keep track of the pen color used to create lines—so, when the image resizes or you save and restore a file, your colorful images revert to black and white. You'll handle that problem in the next few chapters, as you improve the view and document classes.

Pen Widths: Adding Cascading Menus

When you open the Windows Start menu, not all the options are immediately visible. For example, if you click on Programs, the Start menu displays another menu, and that menu may display another. These are called *cascading menus*. You can create cascading menus very easily in the Visual C++ Menu Editor.

In the PaintORama program, you used a spin control to specify pen widths. For MiniSketch, let's use a series of menu options instead: Thin, Medium, Thick, and Extra Thick. To avoid cluttering the Pens menu, you'll put these selections on their own, cascading menu. Then, you'll use a special form of the **ON_COMMAND** macro—**ON_COMMAND_RANGE**—to hook them up. Finally, you'll use Windows accelerators to give each pen thickness a hotkey.

Ready? Let's go.

Creating The Cascading Menu

First, you'll create the Pens|Width cascading menu. Follow these steps, and you'll be finished in no time:

1. Be sure the MiniSketch project is loaded, with the **IDR_MAINFRAME** menu open in the Menu Editor. Open the Pens menu, go to the bottom, and select the new menu item. Enter the caption "&Width" and check the Pop-up checkbox. When you do this, Visual C++ disables the resource ID combo box. You don't have to put ellipses after the caption: For cascading menus, Windows automatically inserts a right-arrow, instead. When your screen looks like that shown in Figure 13.15, you're ready for the next step.
2. On the pop-up menu attached to Pens|Width, use the values shown in Table 13.2 to add four menu items. Notice that each caption contains a hotkey designation following an inline tab (\t). Figure 13.16 shows the last menu item being added.

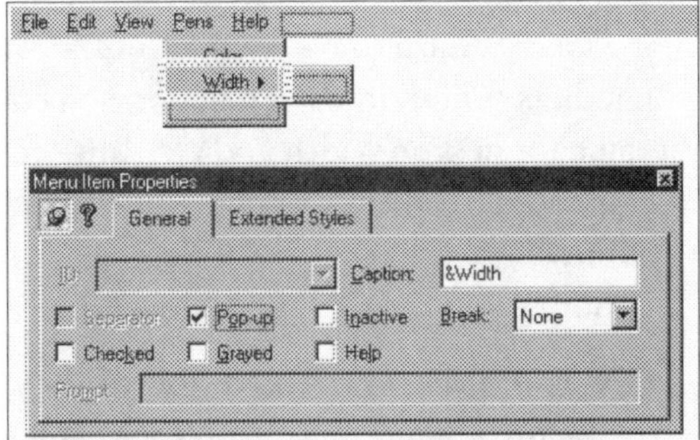

Figure 13.15
Adding the Pens|Width cascading menu.

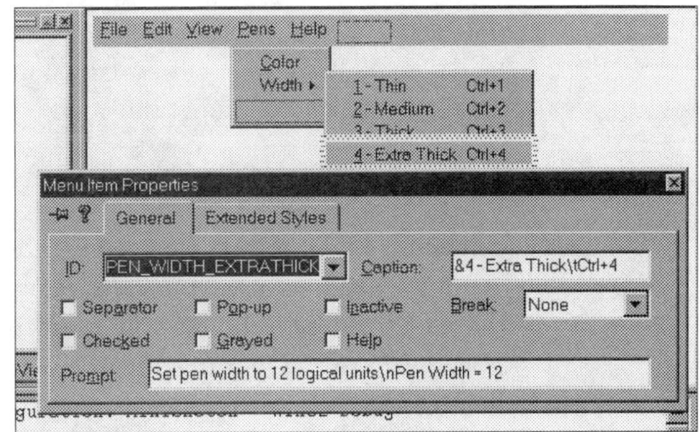

Figure 13.16
Adding the Pens|Width cascading menu items.

Table 13.2 Menu items for the Pens | Width menu.

Resource ID	Menu Caption	Prompt String
ID_PEN_WIDTH_THIN	&1 - Thin\tCtrl+1	Set pen thickness to 1 pixel wide\nPen Width = 1 pixel
ID_PEN_WIDTH_MEDIUM	&2 - Medium\tCtrl+2	Set pen width to 4 logical units\nPen Width = 4
ID_PEN_WIDTH_THICK	&3 - Thick\tCtrl+3	Set pen width to 8 logical units\nPen Width = 8
ID_PEN_WIDTH_EXTRATHICK	&4 - Extra Thick\tCtrl+4	Set pen width to 12 logical units\nPen Width = 12

Once you're done with this step, you can compile and run your application—but when you pull down the Pens | Width menu, all the items will be grayed out. That happens because you haven't yet attached any command handlers. Let's take care of that now.

Handling Pen Widths

You already know one way to handle menu selections: You could use ClassWizard to hook up four **ON_COMMAND** menu handlers. Then, in each handler, you could set the appropriate value for **m_PenWidth** and call **InitPen()**. Because the pen-width command handler doesn't do much, that's probably as good a way as any. But, as long as we're here, let's take a look at a second option: using the **ON_COMMAND_RANGE** method.

ON_COMMAND_RANGE() works when you have a series of consecutive menu IDs. With **ON_COMMAND_RANGE()**, MFC sends a whole range of commands to a single handler, rather than sending every command to a unique handler. To tell you which menu item the user selected, Windows sends the menu ID as an argument to the function.

When you define a set of menu items one right after another, like you did the Pens|Width menu items, Windows assigns them consecutive ID numbers. You can use the View|Resource Symbols menu to examine the ID numbers. As you can see in Figure 13.17, the resource IDs for the Pens|Width menu items are contiguous from 32773 to 32776. (You don't need to worry about the actual numbers.)

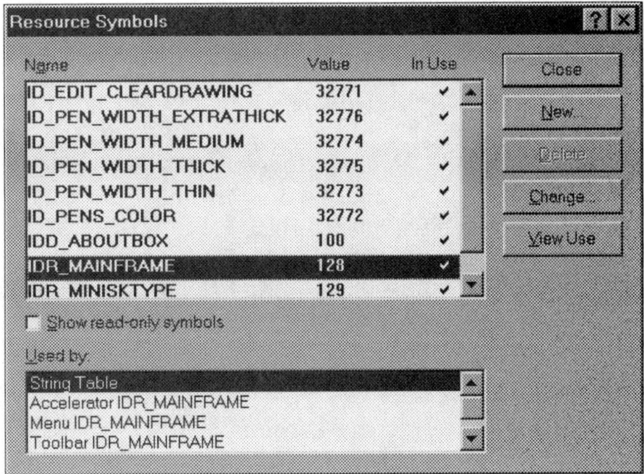

Figure 13.17
Viewing the Resource Symbols dialog box.

Now you know that the menu items' resource IDs are consecutive, so you can add a message handler for them. Here are the steps you need to follow:

1. Add the prototype shown in Listing 13.10 to the **CMSView** class definition. You need to add only the highlighted line—we show the other lines merely to provide context.

Listing 13.10 The OnPensWidth() prototype.

```
// Generated message map functions
protected:
    //{{AFX_MSG(CMSView)
    afx_msg void OnLButtonDown(UINT nFlags, CPoint
      point);
    afx_msg void OnLButtonUp(UINT nFlags, CPoint point);
    afx_msg void OnMouseMove(UINT nFlags, CPoint point);
    afx_msg void OnPensColor();
    //}}AFX_MSG
    afx_msg void OnPensWidth(UINT nCmd);
    DECLARE_MESSAGE_MAP()
```

2. Add the highlighted message-map entry shown in Listing 13.11 to the **CMSView** class message map.

Listing 13.11 The CMSView message map.

```
BEGIN_MESSAGE_MAP(CMSView, CView)
    //{{AFX_MSG_MAP(CMSView)
    ON_WM_LBUTTONDOWN()
    ON_WM_LBUTTONUP()
```

NOTE

You may notice the use of the continuation character (\) at the end of each line. These are macros, not functions—if you omit the continuation character, the program won't compile.

```
    ON_WM_MOUSEMOVE()
    ON_COMMAND(ID_PENS_COLOR, OnPensColor)
    //}}AFX_MSG_MAP
    ON_COMMAND_RANGE(ID_PEN_WIDTH_THIN, \
                     ID_PEN_WIDTH_EXTRATHICK, \
                     OnPensWidth)
    // Standard printing commands
    ON_COMMAND(ID_FILE_PRINT, CView::OnFilePrint)
    ON_COMMAND(ID_FILE_PRINT_DIRECT, CView::OnFilePrint)
    ON_COMMAND(ID_FILE_PRINT_PREVIEW,
CView::OnFilePrintPreview)
END_MESSAGE_MAP()
```

3. Add the **OnPensWidth()** function shown in Listing 13.12 to the MiniSketchView.cpp file. Add the function manually, rather than going through the Add Member Function dialog box, because you've already added the prototype to the class definition. In the listing, notice how the pen width is calculated by subtracting the actual ID chosen from the first possible value, and then multiplying the result by four. This calculation results in pen widths of 0, 4, 8, and 12. A pen width of zero results in a pen that is one pixel wide, no matter what the logical mapping mode—just what you want.

Listing 13.12 The CMSView OnPensWidth() command range message handler.

```
void CMSView::OnPensWidth(UINT nCmd)
{
    m_PenWidth = (nCmd - ID_PEN_WIDTH_THIN) * 4;
    InitPen();
}
```

Compile and run the program, and test each of the menu options. As you can see in Figure 13.18, you can change both the color and the width of the pen.

Where Do We Go From Here?

In this chapter, you've mastered almost all the basic menu-handling skills. You can add menu items and remove unused ones, insert menu shortcut keys, and use ClassWizard to hook up a function to a menu selection. You know how to create cascading

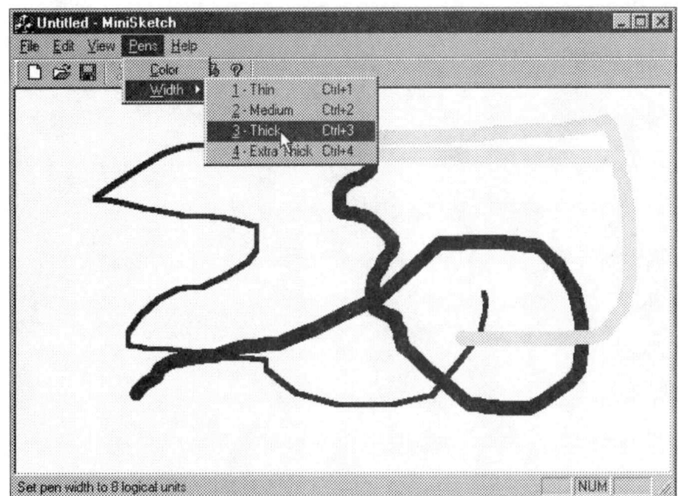

Figure 13.18
Running the MiniSketch program with the Pens|Width menu.

menus and menus that invoke a dialog box. You can add status bar menu help and tool tips, and even manually connect a range of menu commands to a single command handler. What else could be left?

Glad you asked. How about:

- *Checking the menu item that's currently selected*—How do you tell which pen width is in use, without drawing a line?
- *Disabling and enabling menu commands*—For instance, if you add styled pens, then the Pens | Width menu no longer makes sense, because styled pens are all one pixel wide.
- *Setting up the hotkeys you added to the Pens|Width menu*—To do this, you'll have to learn about the Windows Accelerator table.
- *Hooking up the toolbar for instant access to commonly used menu commands*.

Well, you get the picture. We've come a long way, but we haven't arrived yet. Take a breather and then let's go get them toolbars.

Chapter 14

Menus, Toolbars, And Status Bars

"You don't know what you've got till it's gone," sang Joni Mitchell in her hit song "Big Yellow Taxi." And it's true. That's why software developers never throw anything away. You can be certain that every last feature of GizmoMaster 1 will somehow survive in vestigial form down through GizmoMaster 13.

The downside to software's "survival of the fattest" is that a state-of-the-art word processor that fit on a 160K diskette in 1980 now consumes 60MB. Even though most of us use only a tiny fraction of the features offered by our current word processor, we know that when we buy the next upgrade, the box won't say "Now Does Less!"

Just as you fail to appreciate an existing feature until it's missing, sometimes you fail to appreciate what a new feature can do until you've used it a while. Take pull-down menus, for instance. When user-interface designers first introduced pull-down menus, they saw them as a comprehensive solution to all aspects of using a computer. They believed there was nothing that couldn't be done more easily and quickly by using pull-down menus. But, as pull-down menus became widely used, many shortcomings became evident, and designers added new features to address them.

In this chapter, we'll look at four enhancements to the basic menu system:

- *Command UI*—Lets programmers provide feedback to the user by manipulating the *menu user interface (UI)*.
- *Keyboard accelerators*—Let users bypass the menu system and select a command by pressing a combination of keyboard keys.
- *Toolbars*—Let users select commonly used menu commands by clicking on visible and easily accessible buttons. Together,

keyboard accelerators and toolbars bring menu-system interaction to the surface of the application, instead of burying it inside a multi-click menu sequence.

- *Status bars*—Bring important information to the attention of the user.

Command UI

If you've played with the MiniSketch program, you've noticed that you must draw an unwanted line to discover which pen is in use. The program would be easier to use if the Pens|Width menu displayed a check beside the currently selected pen width.

The Windows API has always included support for putting checks beside menu items. Just before a pop-up menu displays, Windows sends a **WM_INITPOPUP** message. When an application receives that message, it can iterate through the menu items, adding or removing check marks and enabling or disabling menu items as necessary.

Programming this operation in Windows isn't hard, but it is tedious. Fortunately, MFC makes this operation as easy as responding to a menu command. And, it uses a very similar method: the **UPDATE_COMMAND_UI** macro.

The **UPDATE_COMMAND_UI** macro instructs Windows to call a specified function when a menu item is about to be displayed. When it calls the function, Windows passes a pointer to a **CCmdUI** object, which you can use to enable or disable the menu item, or to set or clear a check mark.

You can update the menu system's command UI in three ways:

- Map each menu item to a particular command UI handler.
- Use the same command UI handler for several menu items.
- Map a range of menu items to the same command UI handler.

Let's take a brief look at each method as you add command UI handing to the Pens|Width menu. Your goal is to place a check mark beside the currently selected pen width and to remove check marks from all other widths.

Method 1: Individual UI Handlers

Let's start with the simplest method (it's simplest because ClassWizard most directly supports it). Note that simplest doesn't always mean best—this method may result in many lines of redundant code.

Here are the steps to follow:

1. Open the MiniSketch project, then open the **IDR_MAINFRAME** menu in the Menu Editor. Open the Pens|Width menu and select the Thin menu item. Your screen should look like that shown in Figure 14.1.
2. Use the right-click context menu to launch ClassWizard, then select **CMSView** from the Class Name drop-down list. Select **ID_PEN_WIDTH_THIN** from the Object IDs list and **UPDATE_COMMAND_UI** from the Messages list. Click on Add Function when your screen looks like the one shown in Figure 14.2.
3. When the Add Member Function dialog box opens, accept the proffered name—**OnUpdatePenWidthThin()**—as you can see in Figure 14.3. Click on OK and then click on Edit Code once you return to the ClassWizard window.
4. Add the code shown in Listing 14.1 to the **OnUpdatePenWidthThin()** function. The **SetCheck()**

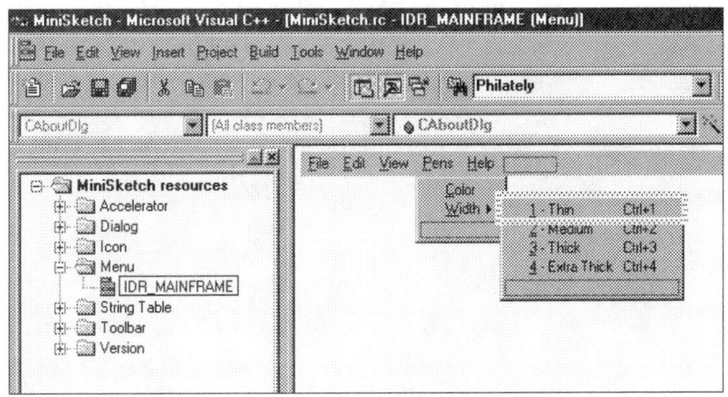

Figure 14.1
Opening the Pens|Width menu in the Menu Editor.

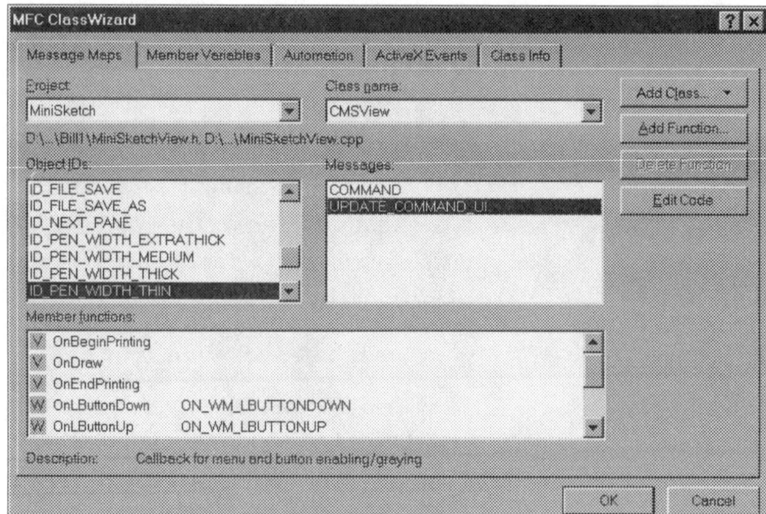

Figure 14.2
Adding an **UPDATE_COMMAND_UI** message handler in ClassWizard.

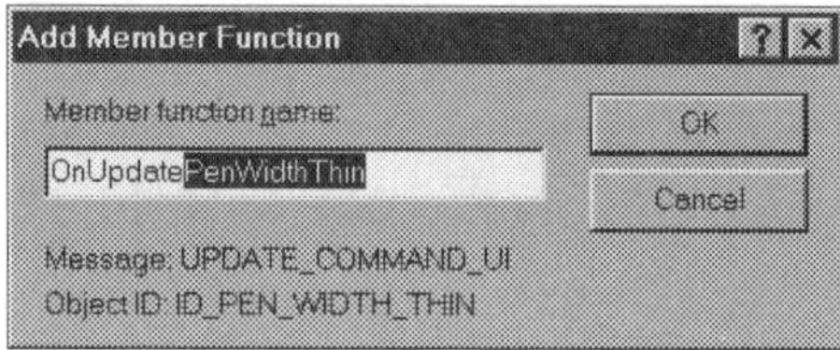

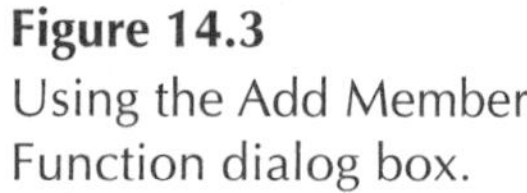

Figure 14.3
Using the Add Member Function dialog box.

method will put a check beside the menu item if its argument is true and remove the check if its argument is false. MFC calls the **OnUpdatePenWidthThin()** function when the Pens|Width|Thin menu item is about to be displayed. Your code will place a check on the menu item if the variable **m_PenWidth** is zero—the width of the thin pen.

Listing 14.1 The OnUpdatePenWidthThin() command UI handler for the thin pen.

```
void CMSView::OnUpdatePenWidthThin(CCmdUI* pCmdUI)
{
    // TODO: Add your command update UI handler code here
    pCmdUI->SetCheck(0 == m_PenWidth);
}
```

5. Repeat the same procedure for each of the other four menu selections on the Pens|Width menu. Use the same code for each selection, but check against the values 4, 8, and 12, rather than 0.

When you're finished, compile MiniSketch and take it out for a spin. As you select different menu items, you'll see the check mark follow the currently selected pen, as shown in Figure 14.4.

You might be surprised to discover that the MiniSketch Pens | Width menu starts out with no check mark displayed. Why is that? If you look at the constructor for the **CMSView** class, you'll discover that you initialize **m_PenWidth** to 1. Unfortunately, 1 isn't a value recognized by the command UI handlers—you can use only 0, 4, 8, or 12. Change the code in the **CMSView** constructor to initialize **m_PenWidth** to one of these values, and you'll see it work.

Method 2: Multiple Macros, One Handler

Because the four command UI handlers work similarly, you can map each of the **UPDATE_COMMAND_UI** macros to a single function. Your message map will have four entries, but each entry will call the same function.

To do this in ClassWizard, begin with a fresh copy of MiniSketch from Chapter 13. (Copy the program from this book's CD-ROM, if necessary.) Then, select each of the menu items exactly as you did previously. However, when the Add Member Function dialog box appears, don't accept the name offered to you—instead, use the same function name for all four entries.

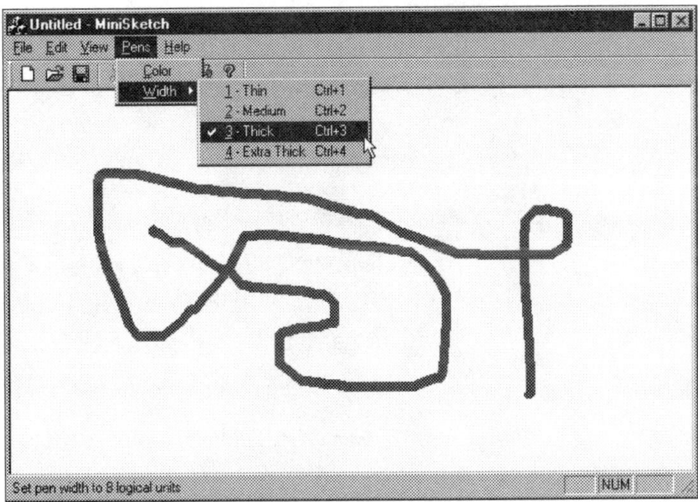

Figure 14.4
The Pens|Width command UI handlers in action.

A good name choice in this case is **OnUpdatePensWidth()**, because you can simply backspace over the additional characters presented by the Add Member Function dialog box. Use the calculation shown in Listing 14.2 to set **m_PenWidth**. Notice how the code uses **pCmdUI->m_nID** to discover the particular menu selection being interrogated.

Listing 14.2 The OnUpdatePensWidth() function.

```
void CMSView::OnUpdatePensWidth(CCmdUI * pCmdUI)
{
    int thisWidth = (pCmdUI->m_nID - ID_PEN_WIDTH_THIN) *
      4;
    pCmdUI->SetCheck(m_PenWidth == thisWidth);
}
```

Method 3: The ON_UPDATE_COMMAND_UI_RANGE Alternative

Even when you map multiple handlers to the same command UI handler, your code contains several message-map entries. However, you can eliminate the redundant map entries.

To facilitate this, MFC offers several extended UI handler macros. Unfortunately, if you choose to use them, ClassWizard won't help you at all—you have to code by hand. Still, the extra coding isn't difficult, and the result is much more elegant.

For this example, you'll use the extended command UI handler: **ON_UPDATE_COMMAND_UI_RANGE**. As with the **ON_COMMAND _RANGE** macro, you can use this macro only when your menu IDs are consecutive (you know that's the case here).

Here are the instructions:

1. As before, begin with the project you completed in Chapter 13. Add the member function declaration (prototype) for the message-handler function to the **CMSView** class header. Let's use the function from Listing 14.2:

   ```
   afx_msg void OnUpdatePensWidth(CCmdUI * pCmdUI);
   ```

2. Add the **ON_UPDATE_COMMAND_UI_RANGE** macro to the message map for the **CMSView** class. Place the new

macro in the MiniSketchView.cpp file, between the **BEGIN_MESSAGE_MAP** and **END_MESSAGE_MAP** macros. Your macro should look like this:

```
ON_UPDATE_COMMAND_UI_RANGE(ID_PEN_WIDTH_THIN, \
                           ID_PEN_WIDTH_EXTRATHICK, \
                           OnUpdatePensWidth)
```

Be sure you don't put a semicolon after the last parenthesis.

3. Add the **OnUpdatePensWidth()** function to the **CMSView** class implementation file, using Listing 14.2 as a guide.

When you compile and run the application, your program should work just as it did before.

Accelerators

Windows menus include a keyboard interface that you specify by placing an ampersand (&) in a menu item's caption. MiniSketch already has this capability. For instance, a user running MiniSketch can change to the extra-thick pen by pressing Alt+P (to open the Pens menu), W (to open the Width menu), and 4 (to select the extra-thick pen).

Keyboard shortcuts provide a way to access the menu system via the keyboard—but the user must still navigate the menu system. In contrast, accelerator keys offer an alternative way to issue a command to your program—one that doesn't require navigating the menu system.

When you defined the captions for the Pens|Width menu items, you included prompts for the keyboard accelerators following the tab escape character (\t). If you look at MiniSketch's menu, you'll see Ctrl+1, Ctrl+2, and so on. The user can select an extra-thick pen simply by pressing Ctrl+4. However, adding the accelerator-key prompts doesn't activate the accelerators themselves.

Here are the steps you need to follow to make the MiniSketch accelerator keys active:

1. Using your latest version of the MiniSketch project, select the ResourceView window and expand the Accelerator folder.

Double-click on **IDR_MAINFRAME** to display the Accelerator Editor window. Your screen should look like that shown in Figure 14.5.

2. Scroll to the end of the list of accelerator keys and double-click on the empty position at the end of the list. The Accel Properties dialog box will open, as shown in Figure 14.6.
3. Locate **ID_PEN_WIDTH_THIN** in the ID drop-down list.
4. Click on Next Key Typed, then press the 1 key when the Press Accelerator Key dialog box opens, as shown in Figure 14.7.
5. Check the Ctrl checkbox in the Accel Properties dialog box. The completed dialog box should look like Figure 14.8.

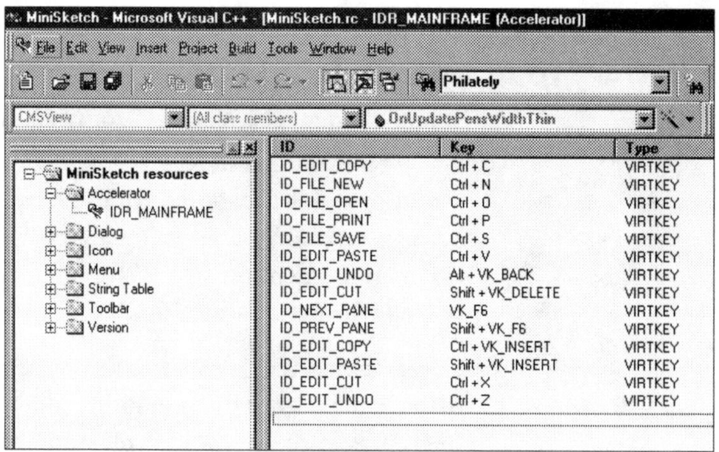

Figure 14.5
Opening the Visual C++ Accelerator Editor.

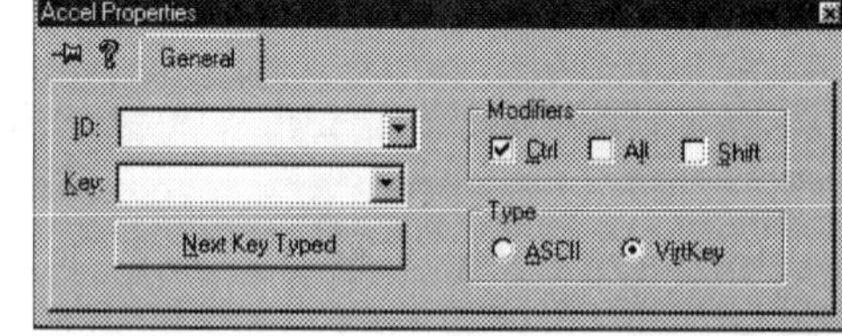

Figure 14.6
Opening the Accel Properties dialog box.

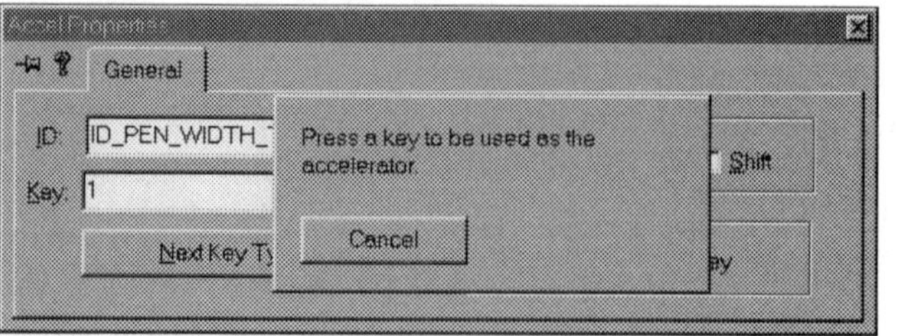

Figure 14.7
The Press Accelerator Key dialog box.

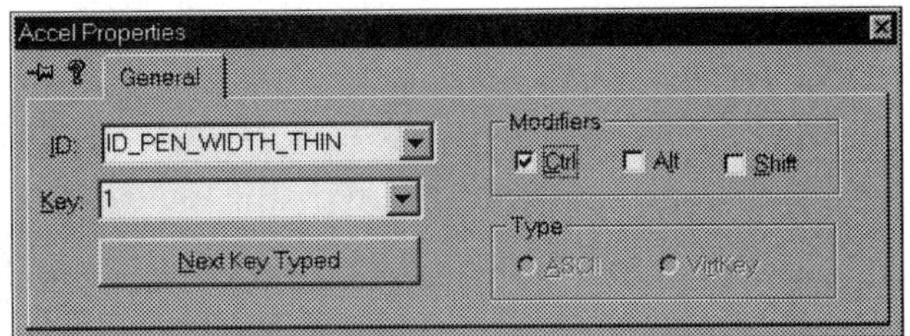

Figure 14.8
Completing the Accel Properties dialog box.

6. Follow the same pattern to add accelerator keys for the Medium, Thick, and Extra Thick selections, using Ctrl+2, Ctrl+3, and Ctrl+4, respectively. The finished accelerator dialog box should look like Figure 14.9.

When you finish, compile and run MiniSketch. You can now choose an extra-thick or thin pen without opening the Pens|Width menu.

As you look through the accelerator commands defined in the Accelerator Editor, notice that you can have multiple accelerators for the same command—**ID_EDIT_CUT**, for example. You can also define accelerators for non-menu commands. Accelerator commands that have no associated menu ID are accessible only via the keyboard.

Toolbars

A *toolbar* consists of small buttons displayed under the main menu at the top of the screen. The toolbar's buttons duplicate frequently

ID	Key	Type
ID_PEN_WIDTH_THIN	Ctrl + 1	VIRTKEY
ID_PEN_WIDTH_MEDIUM	Ctrl + 2	VIRTKEY
ID_PEN_WIDTH_THICK	Ctrl + 3	VIRTKEY
ID_PEN_WIDTH_EXTRATHIC	Ctrl + 4	VIRTKEY
ID_EDIT_COPY	Ctrl + C	VIRTKEY
ID_FILE_NEW	Ctrl + N	VIRTKEY
ID_FILE_OPEN	Ctrl + O	VIRTKEY
ID_FILE_PRINT	Ctrl + P	VIRTKEY
ID_FILE_SAVE	Ctrl + S	VIRTKEY
ID_EDIT_PASTE	Ctrl + V	VIRTKEY
ID_EDIT_UNDO	Alt + VK_BACK	VIRTKEY
ID_EDIT_CUT	Shift + VK_DELETE	VIRTKEY
ID_NEXT_PANE	VK_F6	VIRTKEY
ID_PREV_PANE	Shift + VK_F6	VIRTKEY
ID_EDIT_COPY	Ctrl + VK_INSERT	VIRTKEY
ID_EDIT_PASTE	Shift + VK_INSERT	VIRTKEY
ID_EDIT_CUT	Ctrl + X	VIRTKEY
ID_EDIT_UNDO	Ctrl + Z	VIRTKEY

Figure 14.9
Completed accelerator keys for the Pens|Width

used menu items. MFC toolbars are even more flexible—they're dockable, so users can move them around on screen. And, AppWizard thoughtfully generates a default program that includes a menu item to turn off the toolbar.

Think of toolbars as accelerator keys for those who prefer the mouse to the keyboard. Pull-down menus make a program easier to learn; users can explore the program's options with little risk. Keyboard accelerators and toolbars, on the other hand, don't make a program easier to learn—they make it easier to use.

The buttons on a toolbar can act in three ways: as push buttons, as checkbox buttons, or as radio buttons. When a toolbar button acts as a push button, it performs an action when you click on it. When a toolbar button acts as a checkbox button, it remains depressed when you click on it the first time, then springs back to the surface when you click on it again. To see a good example of a checkbox toolbar button, try the Bold, Italic, and Underline buttons that appear in your word processor.

When a toolbar button is part of a group of buttons, it may behave like a radio button. For instance, your word processor probably offers text-alignment buttons, such as Left-Align, Center-Align, and Right-Align. One of these buttons is always depressed. When you click on a button that's currently depressed, it doesn't spring back like a checkbox button—instead, you must click on one of the other buttons to make the previously selected button spring back.

Opening Color: A Push-Button Toolbar Button

Let's add a push-button-style toolbar button that displays the MiniSketch Pens|Color dialog box. Then, when you're comfortable creating a toolbar, you'll add a set of radio-button-style toolbar buttons for the drawing shape.

In Visual C++, you use the Toolbar Editor to create and manipulate toolbars. The Toolbar Editor is a three-pane graphics editor, similar to the Bitmap Editor or Icon Editor. In the top pane, you see a representation of the entire toolbar. Behind the scenes, the toolbar is represented as a single bitmap. When you work with the Toolbar Editor, you edit only one button at a time, and you can move and delete buttons as you like. To open the Toolbar Button Properties dialog box, simply double-click on the left pane. When you're finished, the Toolbar Editor reassembles your pieces into the single bitmap used by the program.

Let's get familiar with the Toolbar Editor now. Here are the steps to follow:

1. Open the MiniSketch project and select the ResourceView window. Open the Toolbar folder and double-click on **IDR_MAINFRAME** to open the Toolbar Editor. Figure 14.10 shows the Toolbar Editor as it appears with the default SDI toolbar that AppWizard generates.
2. Start by removing the Cut, Copy, and Paste buttons. To do so, select the Cut button (the button displaying a scissors icon). Pressing Delete or Cut doesn't remove the button—it merely erases the image. To delete the button, you must drag it off the toolbar and drop it elsewhere (it doesn't matter where), as you can see in Figure 14.11. Do the same thing to remove the other two buttons.
3. Select the far-right empty button, then drag and drop it to the left of the Help button. Select the Help button and drag it a little to the right so that the new button stands by itself. Figure 14.12 shows what your screen should look like.

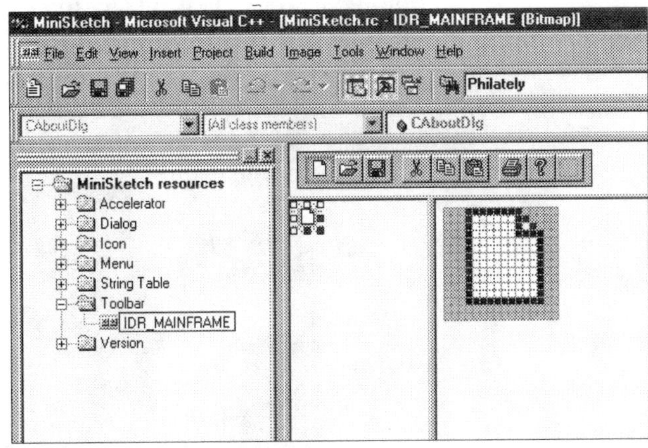

Figure 14.10
The Toolbar Editor with the default SDI toolbar.

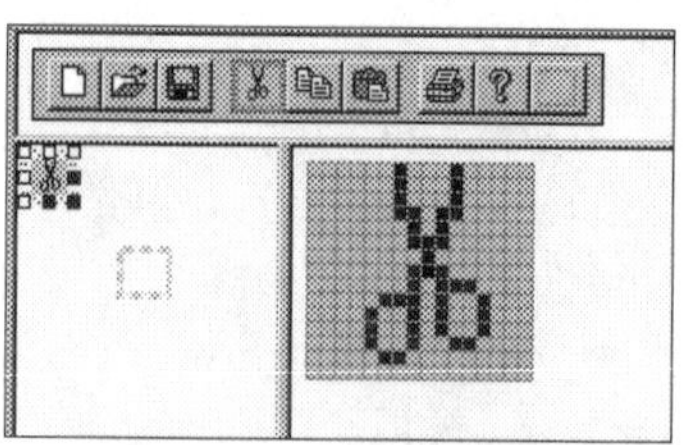

Figure 14.11
Deleting a toolbar button.

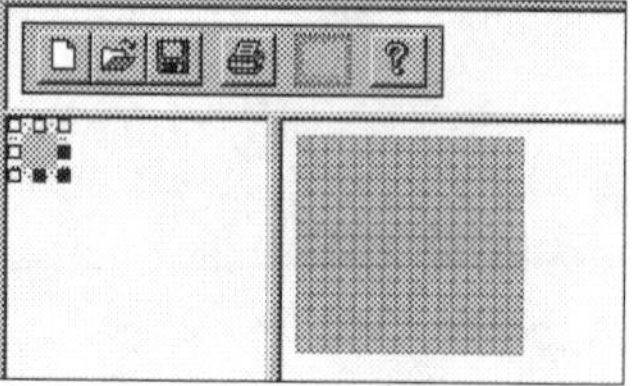

Figure 14.12
Positioning the new pen-color button.

4. Select the Pencil tool on the Graphics toolbar. Left-click on the yellow swatch on the Color palette. Draw a two-pixel-wide horizontal line, two pixels in from the left and right sides and two pixels down from the top.
5. One pixel below the yellow line, draw a similar green line. Below that, draw a blue and then a red line. The finished toolbar should look like that shown in Figure 14.13. (Note that the figure shows both the Graphics toolbar and the Color palette floating free, rather than as docked toolbars.)
6. Double-click in the left pane of the Toolbar Editor—anywhere but on the button bitmap—to open the Toolbar Button Properties dialog box. Note that the ID displayed in the ID drop-down list is an arbitrary integer. Open the list and select the identifier **ID_PENS_COLOR** (the same identifier used

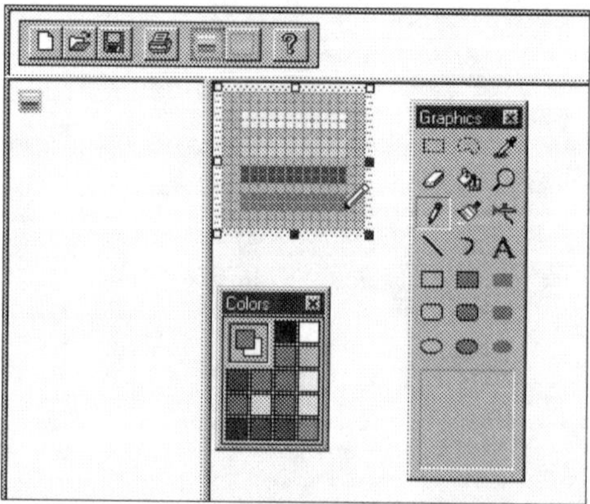

Figure 14.13
Drawing lines in the Toolbar Editor.

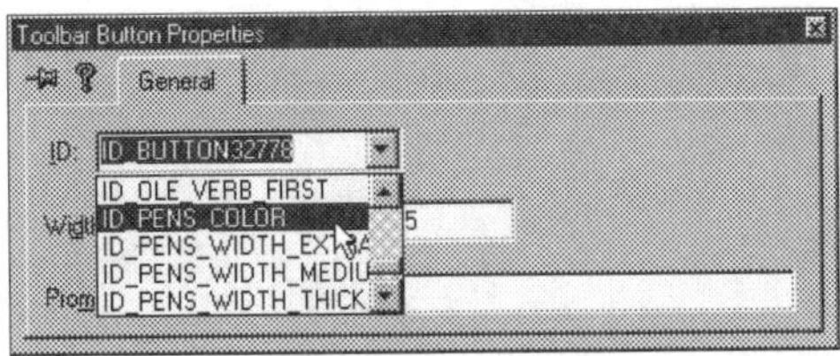

Figure 14.14
Changing the ID in the Toolbar Button Properties dialog box.

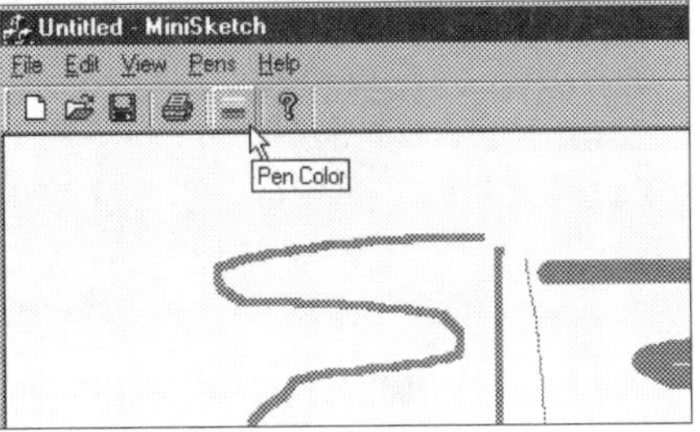

Figure 14.15
Running the MiniSketch program and using the pen-color toolbar button.

for the Pens|Color menu item), as shown in Figure 14.14. You don't need to make any other changes in this dialog box.

Compile and run the program. You can now change the pen color by using either Pens|Color menu command or the toolbar button. You can see the program running in Figure 14.15.

Adding Shape-Type Buttons: Radio Button Toolbar Buttons

When drawing shapes in the PaintORama program, you used a combo box—**m_ShapesCombo**—to hold the kinds of shapes your program could draw. When the program painted the drawing, it retrieved the value stored in the combo box, assigned it to a local variable called **drawMode**, and used **drawMode** in a **switch** statement to draw lines, rectangles, or ellipses as required.

You're going to do something similar in the MiniSketch program, but you'll use toolbar buttons to switch between drawing styles. When the user clicks on a toolbar button, you'll store the value in a variable called **m_ShapeType**.

Here are the steps to follow to add the shape-type buttons:

1. Add four more toolbar buttons in their own group. Draw a shape on each—straight line, freehand, oval, and rectangle—as shown in Figure 14.16.

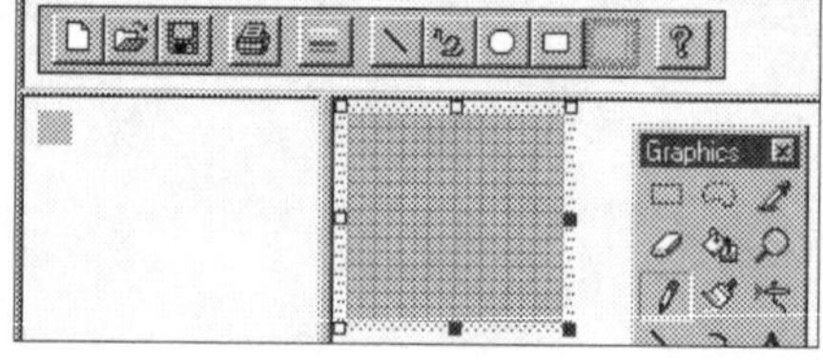

Figure 14.16
Adding the new shape-type toolbar buttons.

NOTE

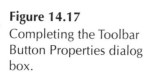

In this chapter, you'll hook up the user interface for the shape types. You'll have to wait until Chapters 15 and 16 to actually draw shapes.

2. For each of the four buttons, double-click in the left pane to open the Toolbar Button Properties dialog box. Create a new ID for each: **ID_SHAPE_TYPE_LINE**, **ID_SHAPE_TYPE_FREEHAND**, **ID_SHAPE_TYPE_OVAL**, and **ID_SHAPE_TYPE_RECTANGLE**, respectively. Include appropriate status-bar and tooltip help, as shown in Figure 14.17. (The status bar help appears first and is separated from the tooltip help by a newline (\n) character.)
3. Now that you've created the button IDs, it's time to handle the button messages. Start ClassWizard and select **CMSView** in the Class Name combo box. In the Object IDs list box, locate the four **ID_SHAPE_TYPE** IDs you just created. Add **Command** handler functions, as you can see in Figure 14.18.
4. Add the code shown in Listing 14.3 to the four command handlers. To save time, you can simply replace the skeleton code that ClassWizard generated.

Listing 14.3 Command handlers for the ID_SHAPE_TYPE toolbar buttons.

```
// Handle toolbar ID_SHAPE_TYPE_XX buttons
void CMSView::OnShapeTypeLine()
{
    m_ShapeType = ID_SHAPE_TYPE_LINE;
}
```

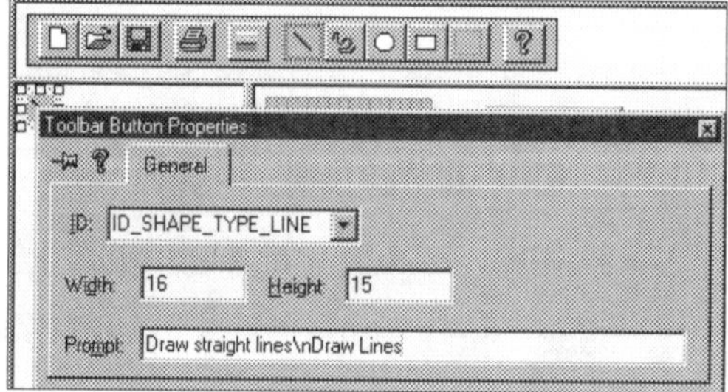

Figure 14.17
Completing the Toolbar Button Properties dialog box.

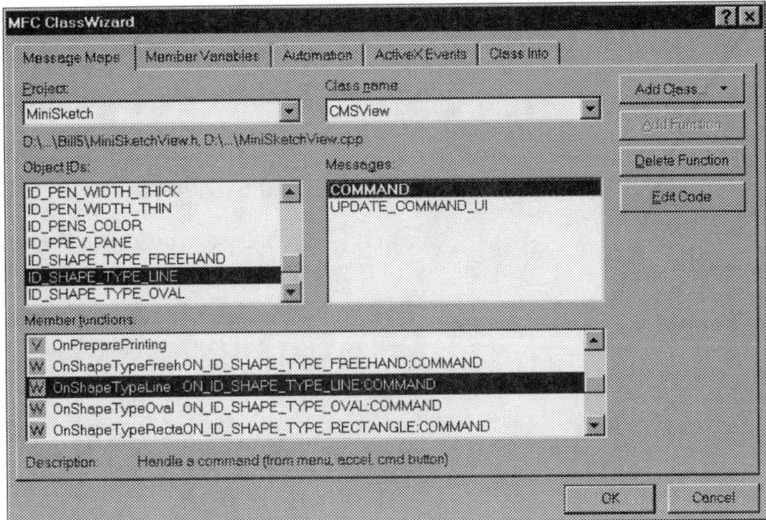

Figure 14.18 Adding command handlers for the **ID_SHAPE_TYPE** toolbar IDs.

```
void CMSView::OnShapeTypeOval()
{
    m_ShapeType = ID_SHAPE_TYPE_OVAL;
}

void CMSView::OnShapeTypeRectangle()
{
    m_ShapeType = ID_SHAPE_TYPE_RECTANGLE;
}

void CMSView::OnShapeTypeFreehand()
{
    m_ShapeType = ID_SHAPE_TYPE_FREEHAND;
}
```

5. Add the **m_ShapeType** member variable to the **CMSView** class. Make the variable type **UINT** and the access **private**.
6. Initialize the **m_ShapeType** member variable by adding the following lines to the **CMSView** class constructor:

```
// Initialize the shape type
m_ShapeType = ID_SHAPE_TYPE_FREEHAND;
```

The Shape-Type UI Handlers

The shape-type buttons act differently than the other toolbar buttons. When the user clicks on one, the program should take an action and leave the button depressed. Furthermore, if another shape-type toolbar button was previously depressed, it should now pop up. You can do all this by sending the selected toolbar button a **SetCheck()** message in an **UPDATE_COMMAND_UI** handler.

Here are the steps to follow:

1. Open ClassWizard and select the **CMSView** view class from the Class Name drop-down list. Click on **ID_SHAPE_TYPE_FREEHAND** in the Object IDs list, then choose **UPDATE_COMMAND_UI** from the Messages list and click on Add Function. In the Add Member Function dialog box that opens, change the name from **OnUpdateShapeTypeFreehand** to **OnUpdateShapeType**, as illustrated in Figure 14.19. Click on OK.
2. In ClassWizard, select each of the remaining **ID_SHAPE_TYPE** IDs and map them to the same function. To do so, click on Add Function and then enter "**OnUpdateShapeType**" as the function name in the Add Member Function dialog box. Your screen should look like that shown in Figure 14.20.
3. Add the code shown in Listing 14.4 to the **OnUpdateShapeType()** function.

Listing 14.4 The OnUpdateShapeType() command UI handler.

```
void CMSView::OnUpdateShapeType(CCmdUI* pCmdUI)
{
    pCmdUI->SetCheck(pCmdUI->m_nID == m_ShapeType);
}
```

That's all there is to it— compile and run the application. Now, when you click on one of the shape-type buttons, it stays depressed, giving you easily accessible control as well as feedback. You can see this feature in Figure 14.21.

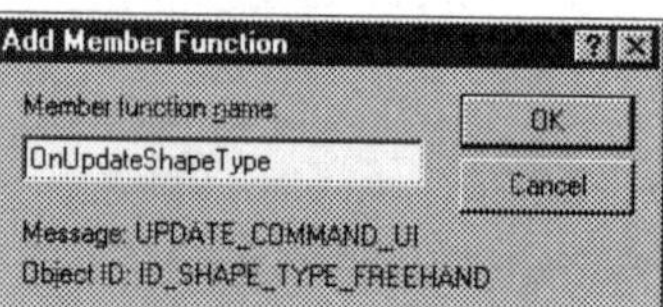

Figure 14.19
Adding the **OnUpdateShapeType()** command UI handler.

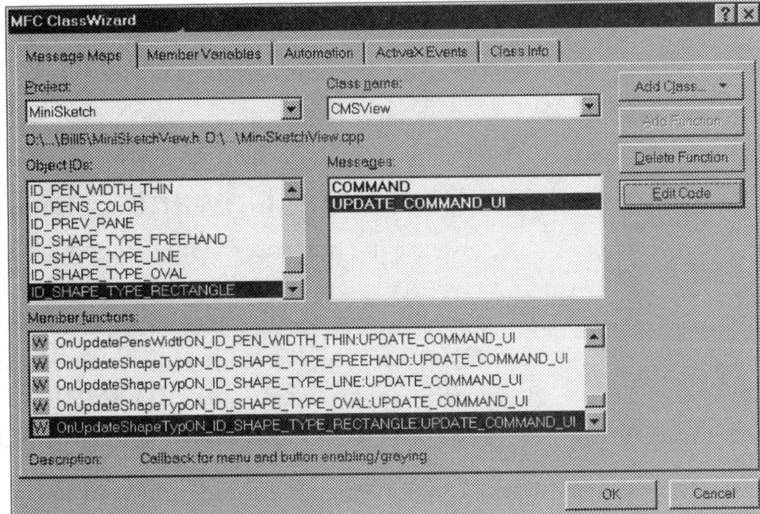

Figure 14.20
Mapped member functions for the **ID_SHAPE_TYPE** toolbar buttons.

Figure 14.21
Using the shape-type toolbar buttons.

Of course, the code that does the drawing doesn't yet take into account that **m_ShapeType** has changed. That recognition will come when you improve the document and view classes in the next few chapters. Despite this deficiency, however, it's nice to see that the toolbar UI works.

Status Bars

The last of the user-interface enhancements we'll study in this chapter is the status bar. A status bar doesn't issue commands as do toolbar buttons, menus, or accelerators. Instead, a status bar "talks back," keeping the user informed by providing ready access to important information.

As you've noticed, you don't have to do anything to create a status bar. MFC creates it for you—all you have to do is use it. In this section, you're going to modify the built-in status bar in three different ways:

- Remove the ScrollLock, NumLock, and CapsLock indicators.
- Add an indicator for pen width.
- Add an owner-drawn indicator to display the pen color.

Removing Unwanted Indicators

Removing unwanted status bar indicators is the simplest of our planned changes. MFC stores indicators as string resources in your application's string table. The indicators for the CapsLock, NumLock, and ScrollLock keys are already included in the string table under the IDs **ID_INDICATOR_CAPS**, **ID_INDICATOR_NUM**, and **ID_INDICATOR_SCR**.

You don't remove these indicators from the string table to disable them. Instead, you simply remove the references to them in the code that constructs the status bar.

The **CMainFrame** constructor creates the status bar by referencing a **static** array of string IDs created near the top of the MainFrm.cpp file:

```
static UINT indicators[] =
{
    ID_SEPARATOR,           // status line indicator
    ID_INDICATOR_CAPS,
    ID_INDICATOR_NUM,
    ID_INDICATOR_SCRL,
};
```

If you comment out (or remove) the highlighted lines, the status bar will omit the CapsLock, ScrollLock, and NumLock indicators.

Adding Your Own Indicators

Adding your indicators isn't quite as easy as removing the built-in indicators—but almost. In this section, you'll add a status bar indicator for pen width. The indicator should display the width of the pen in logical units: 0, 4, 8, or 12.

To add a new indicator, you follow a three-step process:

- Add a new resource ID for the indicator.

- Add a string-table resource tied to the resource ID. The length of this string will be used to size the indicator pane, so you may need to pad it with spaces.
- Add an **ON_UPDATE_COMMAND_UI** handler for the string ID. You have to do this manually—ClassWizard doesn't help with string table resource IDs.

Let's walk through these steps.

Add The Resource ID

First, you'll add a new resource ID. Windows will assign your resource a number, but you'll have to supply a name.

Here are the steps to follow:

1. Choose View|Resource Symbols. When the Resource Symbols dialog box opens, as you can see in Figure 14.22, click on New.
2. In the New Symbol dialog box, enter "**ID_STATUS_PEN_WIDTH**" and accept the default value for the Resource ID. Close both dialog boxes when you finish.

Add The String-Table Resource

Your second step in adding a status-bar indicator will be to create a new string-table resource. You can store string constants used

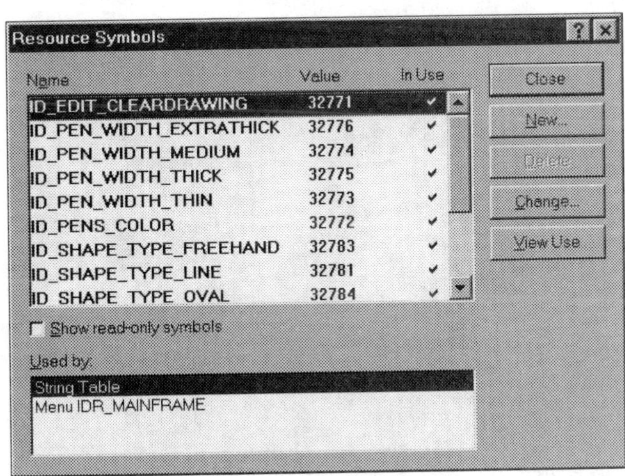

Figure 14.22
Adding a new resource symbol using the Resource Symbols dialog box.

throughout your program in the string table, rather than embedding them in your source code. If you consistently use the string table instead of embedded string literals, you can easily translate your interface to use a different language, simply by changing the string table's contents.

Follow these steps to add the new string-table resource:

1. Select the ResourceView pane in the Workspace window, then open the String Table folder. Note that no ID is associated with the string table. Double-click on the abc icon to open the String Table Editor, as illustrated in Figure 14.23.
2. Scroll to the bottom of the string table and double-click on the last (empty) entry. In the String Properties dialog box that opens, use the ID drop-down list to select **ID_STATUS_PEN_WIDTH**—the new resource ID you just created—and then provide the default text for the indicator. Type several spaces at the end of the text—doing so provides room for the string that will be displayed, because the indicator window won't expand at runtime. Your screen should look like Figure 14.24.

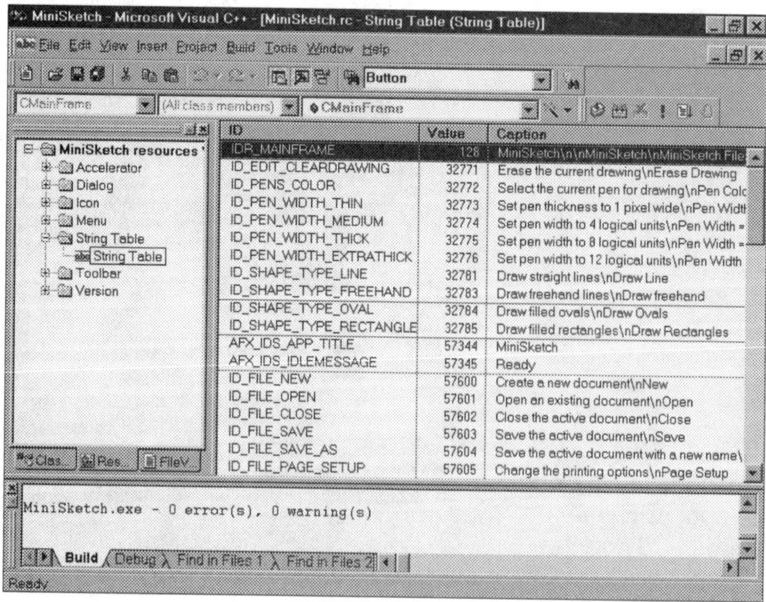

Figure 14.23
The String Table Editor.

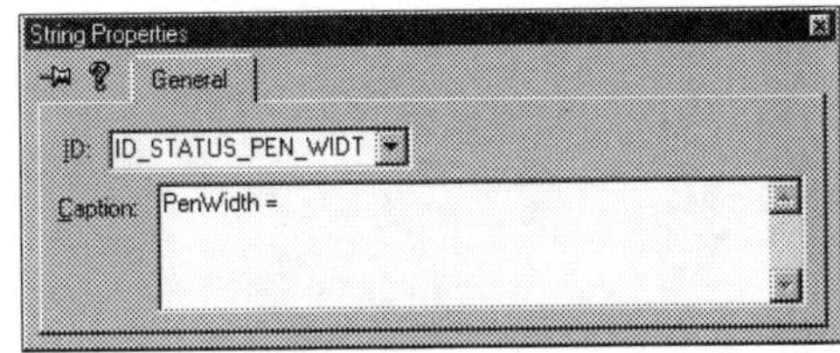

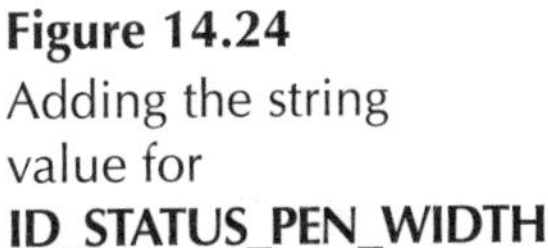
Figure 14.24
Adding the string value for **ID_STATUS_PEN_WIDTH**.

3. Edit the **indicators** array in the CMainFrame.cpp file. Add **ID_STATUS_PEN_WIDTH** after **ID_SEPARATOR**.

When you compile and run your program, you'll see the new indicator. It doesn't do anything yet, even if you change the pen width—activating the indicator is the third and final step to come.

Activating The Indicator

To activate the indicator, you simply write an **ON_UPDATE_COMMAND_UI** handler. You must do this by hand, because ClassWizard doesn't recognize resource IDs bound to string-table resources.

Fortunately, adding the handler is simple. Here's all you do:

1. In the **CMSView** class header, add the following prototype:

```
afx_msg void OnUpdateUIPenWidthIndicator(CCmdUI
  *pCmdUI);
```

2. In the **CMSView** class message map, add the following update handler macro (be sure you don't accidentally add a semicolon to the end of the handler):

```
ON_UPDATE_COMMAND_UI(ID_STATUS_PEN_WIDTH,
OnUpdateUIPenWidthIndicator)
```

3. Add the **CMSView** update UI handler as **OnUpdateUIPenWidthIndicator()**, as shown in Listing 14.5.

Listing 14.5 The OnUpdateUIPenWidthIndicator() update UI handler.

```
void CMSView::OnUpdateUIPenWidthIndicator(CCmdUI *
  pCmdUI)
{
```

```
    CString s;
    s.Format("Pen Width = %2d", m_PenWidth);
    pCmdUI->SetText(s);
}
```

Compile and run the application. Now, when you change the pen width—either through the menu system or by using the new accelerator keys—you'll see the indicator respond as shown in Figure 14.25. If the number is truncated, you need to add more spaces to the string defined in the string table.

You may be wondering how the status bar **ON_UPDATE_COMMAND_UI** macro can update the status bar when the status bar is displayed continuously. With menus, the macro calls the command UI handler each time the menu is displayed, using the **WM_INITPOPUP** message as a trigger. What does the command UI handler use when it's attached to a status bar?

Windows calls status-bar command UI handlers—as well as those attached to toolbars—during its idle processing. Idle processing occurs when your application doesn't have any more messages to process—when there's nothing left to do. You might think that this occurs infrequently, but, in fact, most interactive applications spend a lot of their time in idle processing.

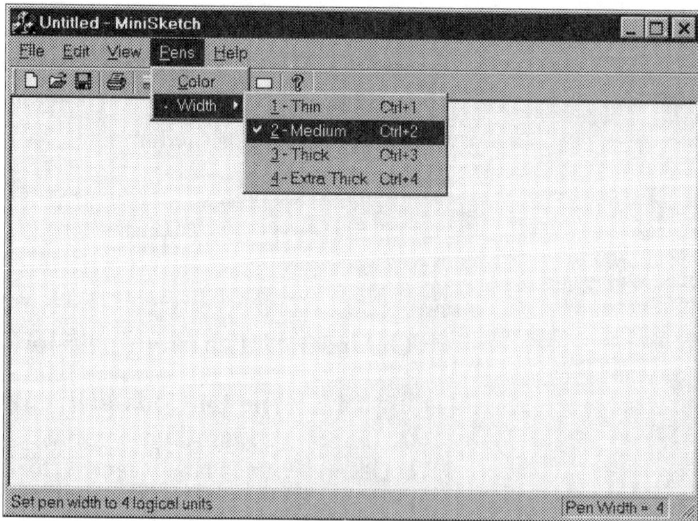

Figure 14.25
Running the MiniSketch application with the pen-width indicator.

However, because Windows calls toolbar and status-bar command UI handlers during idle processing, you may find situations in which a status bar indicator lags a little. This is never true for menu-command UI handlers.

Adding A Pen Color Indicator

Although the built-in **CStatusBar** class supports text-style indicators, it doesn't automatically provide support for graphic-style indicators like those you want to use to display the current pen color in MiniSketch. You can easily determine the shape-drawing mode, because you can see which of the shape-drawing indicators is depressed. And, with the pen-width indicator, you can tell how wide the current pen is. But, what about the pen color?

You could add another text-mode indicator that displays the RGB values of the current color, but that's not really very useful. You need a pen-color swatch like the one in the PaintORama—preferably, one that works a little better. Fortunately, that's quite easy to accomplish.

Up until now, you've relied on the four classes written by AppWizard. You've modified them, added member variables, and overridden virtual functions. What you haven't done so far is add an entirely new class to the MiniSketch project. You'll do that now.

When AppWizard adds a status bar to your project, it adds a protected member variable named **m_wndStatusBar** to the **CMainFrame** class. This variable is a member of the **CStatusBar** class and is constructed and attached to your main frame window in the **CMainFrame** constructor.

Because **m_wndStatusBar** is a **CStatusBar** object, and not a subclass created especially for your application—as are the **CMSView**, **CMSDoc**, **CMSApp**, and **CMainFrame** classes—you can't override any of **CStatusBar**'s virtual functions. You can send messages to **m_wndStatusBar**, but you can't change the way it works. However, if you create your own subclass of **CStatusBar** and use it in place of **CStatusBar** when creating the **m_wndStatusBar** variable, then you can make any changes you like. That's what you'll do to add a pen-color swatch to the status bar.

Creating The CMSStatusBar Class

You'll begin by creating the new class, then hook it to your application in place of the **CStatusBar** class. As you walk through these steps, you'll first create a **CMSStatusBar** class that works exactly like the built-in model. Then, you'll go back and make your changes.

Here's how you start:

1. Be sure the MiniSketch project is open. Open the ClassWizard (by pressing Ctrl+W or choosing View|ClassWizard from the menu). Click on Add Class when the ClassWizard dialog box opens, then choose New from the drop-down menu.
2. Type "**CMSStatusBar**" as the class name and select **CStatusBarCtrl** as the base class from the drop-down list. (You're actually going to use **CStatusBar** rather than **CStatusBarCtrl**, but you'll change the base class manually.) Click on OK when your screen looks like Figure 14.26. When the ClassWizard dialog box reappears, close it.
3. Select the ClassView pane in the Workspace window and double-click on the **CMSStatusBar** class. In the class header, change the reference to **CStatusBarCtrl** to **CStatusBar** :

```
class CMSStatusBar : public CStatusBar
```

4. Open the file MSStatusBar.cpp and find the class message map. Remove the reference to **CStatusBarCtrl**, replacing it with **CStatusBar**. The revamped message map should look like this:

```
BEGIN_MESSAGE_MAP(CMSStatusBar, CStatusBar)
    //{{AFX_MSG_MAP(CMSStatusBar)
    // NOTE - the ClassWizard will add and remove
    // mapping macros here.
    //}}AFX_MSG_MAP
END_MESSAGE_MAP()
```

5. In the ClassView pane, open and expand the **CMainFrame** class. Double-click on the **m_wndStatusBar** variable to go to the variable definition. In the Source Code Editor, change

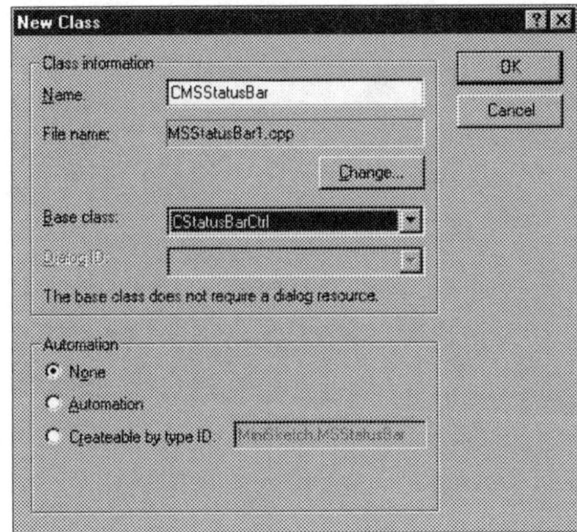

Figure 14.26
Adding the new **CMSStatusBar** class.

the declaration of **m_wndStatusBar** so that it's a **CMSStatusBar** rather than a **CStatusBar**. The new declaration should look like this:

```
CMSStatusBar  m_wndStatusBar;
```

6. Include the header file for the **CMSStatusBar** class in the header file that declares **m_wndStatusBar** (MainFrm.h). Simply add the following line before the **CMainFrame** class definition:

```
#include "MSStatusBar.h"
```

Compile and run your code. It should work exactly as it did previously.

Adding The Pen-Color Indicator

Next, you'll add a new indicator to the status bar when it's created. You'll add it after the pen-width indicator. The status-bar indicators are a zero-based array, so the new indicator will have an index of 2 (you'll use this index when you need to access the indicator).

Because you're going to simply paint a solid swatch of color, rather than write any text, it might seem strange to create a text indicator, as you did for the pen widths. But that's exactly what you have to do.

Here are the steps to follow (they basically reiterate the work you did for the pen-width indicator):

1. Using the View|Resource Symbols menu selection, add a new resource symbol named **ID_STATUS_PEN_COLOR**. Accept the default ID.
2. Add a new string resource to the string table, using the new ID. When you define the new string value, use a value of 5 or 10 spaces so that the swatch has a sufficient size.
3. Add the new string-resource ID to the **indicators** array defined near the top of MainFrm.cpp. Your new **indicators** array should contain these three lines (it may also contain the commented-out keylock indicators):

```
static UINT indicators[] =
{
    ID_SEPARATOR,            // status line indicator
    ID_STATUS_PEN_WIDTH,
    ID_STATUS_PEN_COLOR,
};
```

Compile and run your program. Be sure that your frame looks like Figure 14.27 before you continue.

Coloring The Indicator

To paint the pen-color indicator, you're going to override the virtual function **DrawItem()** in the **CMSStatusBar** class. In a status bar, Windows calls **DrawItem()** once for every pane that needs to be painted, passing it a **LPDRAWITEMSTRUCT** argument. For your purposes, you care about only three fields in the structure:

Figure 14.27
Running MiniSketch after adding the pen-color indicator.

- ***itemID***—Specifies the pane that's being painted. Because status-bar panes start at zero, you should color your swatch when this value is two.
- ***rcItem***—The rectangle that contains the "paintable" area. You'll use it to tell how big your swatch should be.
- ***hDC***—The device context for the status bar. To use it, you create a duplicate **CDC** object, and then call **Attach()** to use it and **Detach()** to free it.

In addition to overriding the **DrawItem()** virtual function, you need to give the pen-color indicator pane the **SBT_OWNERDRAW** style. You can do that by calling the member function **GetPaneInfo()** to get the basic information about the pane you're interested in, and then calling **SetPaneInfo()**, using a bitwise **OR** to add the **SBT_OWNERDRAW** style to your pane.

Here are the steps to hook up **DrawItem()**:

1. Add the following virtual function declaration to the **CMSStatusBar** class:

   ```
   virtual void DrawItem(LPDRAWITEMSTRUCT lpdis);
   ```

   You can't use ClassWizard's Add Virtual Function mechanism to add this declaration, but you can use the Add Member Function dialog box. Make the return type **void**, and check the Virtual check box. Ignore any warning generated by ClassWizard.

2. Add the code shown in Listing 14.6 to the body of the **DrawItem()** function. The comments explain what each line does.

Listing 14.6 The CMSStatusBar DrawItem() virtual function.

```
void CMSStatusBar::DrawItem(LPDRAWITEMSTRUCT lpdis)
{
// 1. Check to make sure we're dealing with the right
item
    if (lpdis->itemID == 2)
    {
        // 2. Create a DC to paint with
        CDC dc;
```

```
            // 3. Associate it with the lpdis DC
            dc.Attach(lpdis->hDC);

            // 4. Find the size of the rectangle we have to
            // paint
            CRect rect(lpdis->rcItem);

            // 5. Paint the rectangle
            CBrush brush(RGB(255,0,0));  // Create a red
            // brush
            dc.FillRect(rect, &brush);

            // 6. Disengage the DC
            dc.Detach();

            // 7. If we've painted, then return
            return;
        }
        // Not our pane? Let CStatusBar handle it
        CStatusBar::DrawItem(lpdis);
}
```

3. Add the style **SBT_OWNERDRAW** to the pen-color pane by using the **GetPaneInfo()** and **SetPaneInfo()** functions. Add the following lines to the **CMainFrame::OnCreate()** function, just before the final **return**:

```
// Initialize the custom status bar
UINT nID, nStyle;
int cx;
m_wndStatusBar.GetPaneInfo(2, nID, nStyle, cx);
m_wndStatusBar.SetPaneInfo(2, nID, nStyle |
  SBT_OWNERDRAW, cx);
```

Compile and run the finished application. The pen-color swatch should now be painted in red—the color that you hard-coded into the **DrawItem()** function. Now, you only need to hook up the swatch so that it uses the actual pen color instead of the hard-coded red brush.

Hooking Up m_PenColor

The last step reflects changes to the **m_PenColor** variable. This step is difficult because **m_PenColor** is a **private** member variable in the **CMSView** class, so you can't access it in the **CMSStatusBar** class. Even if you make **m_PenColor** a **public** variable—undoubtedly a bad idea—you'd still have difficulty connecting your status-bar object with your view object.

Probably the least complex solution is to create a copy of the **m_PenColor** variable in the **CMainFrame** class, because the **CMainFrame** object is the *parent window* for both your view object and the status-bar object. If you add **SetPenColor()** and **GetPenColor()** functions to the **CMainFrame** class, then both the status bar and the view can access the functions by calling the built-in **GetParent()** function to access the application's main window.

Here's how you do it:

1. Add a **private COLORREF** member variable named **m_PenColor** to the **CMainFrame** class.
2. Add **SetPenColor()** and **GetPenColor()** member functions to the **CMainFrame** class, using the code in Listing 14.7. The **GetPenColor()** function simply returns the value of **CMainFrame::m_PenColor**. The **SetPenColor()** function sets the value of **CMainFrame::m_PenColor** and then invalidates the status bar so that it will be repainted every time a new pen color is selected.

Listing 14.7 The CMainFrame GetPenColor() and SetPenColor() member functions.

```
COLORREF CMainFrame::GetPenColor()
{
    return m_PenColor;
}

void CMainFrame::SetPenColor(COLORREF color)
{
    m_PenColor = color;
    m_wndStatusBar.Invalidate();  // Repaint status bar
}
```

3. In the **CMSStatusBar::DrawItem()** function, change the line that creates the red brush so that it reads

```
// 5. Paint the rectangle
CBrush brush(((CMainFrame*)GetParent())-
  >GetPenColor());
dc.FillRect(rect, &brush);
```

4. Add the following line to the bottom of the **CMSView InitPen()** function:

```
((CMainFrame *)GetParent())->SetPenColor(m_PenColor);
```

5. Using ClassWizard, add a new member function to **CMSView**, overriding its inherited **OnInitialUpdate()** function with the code from Listing 14.8.

Listing 14.8 The CMSView::OnInitialUpdate() virtual function.

```
void CMSView::OnInitialUpdate()
{
    CView::OnInitialUpdate();
    InitPen();
}
```

6. Finally, include a reference to the MainFrm.h header file at the top of the MiniSketchView.cpp and MSStatusBar.cpp files by adding the following line to each file, right after the other **includes**:

```
#include 'MainFrm.h"
```

Compile and run the program. As you change pen colors, you'll see the new pen color reflected in the pen-color swatch on the status bar.

Coming Up Next

Well folks, we've had another big chapter. You can take a breather, but don't get too comfortable. The **OnDraw()** mechanism is still pretty flaky—it doesn't handle your pen widths and colors, for instance. The shape-type buttons work fine, but MiniSketch doesn't yet draw different shapes. And printing! Don't even ask about printing.

As you can see, there's a whole lot of work to be done, and the best way to start is to do a little idle processing yourself. Windows programs use idle processing to handle those important chores that get neglected while they're processing messages. So, get a hammock and take a nap—tomorrow will be here soon enough.

Chapter 15

Saving MiniSketch: Working With Documents And Files

In the DocView architecture, the document class has two responsibilities. On one hand, the document class defines the way that your program's data is stored in memory. On the other hand, it's responsible for determining the way that your program stores and retrieves data, using disk files and other secondary storage media.

Suppose you're writing a very simple DocView text-editor program. Your document class could store the text used by your program in several ways:

- *As a two-dimensional array of characters*—One dimension would be lines of text, and the other the individual characters.
- *As a single-dimensional array of* **CStrings**—Each line of text would be stored in a separate **CString**, and each element in the array would be a line of text.
- *As a single block of memory*—A newline character would mark the end of each line.
- *As a doubly linked list of arrays of bytes.*

The possibilities could go on for several pages. When you create a document class, you must decide how its data will be stored in memory. Each method has advantages and disadvantages—your job is to decide which structure is the most appropriate for the job at hand.

But, that's only half the problem. You must also decide how to store the data on disk, and how to translate between the permanent, disk-storage form of your document, and the in-memory, active form of your document. Again, you have several choices. You can store your data as a traditional text file, separating lines of text with newlines. You can write your data as a binary image that's simply read back into memory as a unit. Or, you can devise an alternative form, incorporating compression, encryption, or some other novel design feature.

When designing your document class, your choices regarding the document's in-memory representation frequently affect your choices regarding long-term, secondary storage. For instance, if you choose to store your textual data as a dynamically allocated linked list of **CStrings**, you can't use the binary block-write method to store your data on disk—when you read it back into memory, the pointers no longer point to valid memory.

As we work through the design of the MiniSketch document class—**CMSDoc**—we'll follow this pattern:

- You'll begin by creating the *elemental classes*—classes that store document data. For the MiniSketch program, you'll design a class hierarchy called **Shape**, which will store a single line, rectangle, or oval.
- Next, we'll look at MFC support for *collection classes*—classes designed to hold large quantities of elemental objects.
- Finally, we'll examine MFC support for *serialization*—storing and retrieving classes from disk. Along the way, we'll discuss MFC's support for POFH: Plain Old File Handling. When serialization appears too complex and confusing, you may find that a simple file-storage scheme simplifies your program. Fortunately, MFC makes file handling even easier than does C.

Let's get started by looking at the basic elements managed by the **CMSDoc** class.

Points And Shapes

When you think of a text editor, you can easily identify the basic document element: the character. Or is that it? Depending on your application, you may also need to track sentences, paragraphs, and sections. And—if you're writing a word processor instead of a simple text editor—you may have to manage font and formatting information, as well.

You're in a similar quandary with the MiniSketch program. At first glance, simply storing points in the document seemed adequate to let you repaint your pictures and read and write the information to disk. But, once you start adding pen widths and colors (not to mention the different shape types for which you added buttons in Chapter 14), storing points is no longer enough. You need to define a more complex document.

Classes And Attributes

Let's think about the information MiniSketch must store:

- *Freehand lines*—You've already seen that you can store freehand lines as an array of **CPoint** pairs. But, now you also want to store the color and width of the pen used to draw each line. You'll create the **Squiggle** class to store freehand lines.
- *Straight lines*—A straight-line object is much simpler than a **Squiggle** object. The **Line** object needs to store only the two end-points and the pen width and color.
- *Boxes and ovals*—The **Box** and **Oval** objects must store the dimensions of the bounding box used to draw the shape, as well as the pen used in the outline. Moreover, because boxes and ovals are filled shapes, the objects must store the brush used to fill the interior.

It's easy to create a class hierarchy that meets these requirements. Because each class needs access to pen color and pen width, you can create a base class—let's call it **Shape**—that contains only these data members.

Freehand lines and straight lines are both kinds of **Shape**s, so you'll use **public** inheritance to derive the **Line** and **Squiggle** classes from **Shape**. Each **Line** object contains data members specifying its endpoints, while each **Squiggle** object contains an array of **CPoint** objects—much like the current **CMSDoc** class.

Both the **Box** class and the **Oval** class are kinds of filled shapes, and they require the same member variables: They need to store the brush attributes used to paint the shape interior and the corner points of the bounding rectangle. If **Box**es and **Oval**s have the same data members, then how are they different? Well, as you'll see in a moment, when asked to display itself, a **Box** object produces a rectangle, and an **Oval** object produces an ellipse. Thus, because their behavior varies—even though their data doesn't—you'll create separate classes for **Box** and **Oval**, both descended from the **FilledShape** class.

The **FilledShape** class itself derives from **Shape**, and will contain the brush characteristics used to fill the shape. You don't store the bounding box dimensions in the **FilledShape** class, because you may later decide to derive a new **FilledShape**—such as an irregular region or polygon—that doesn't need a bounding box.

You can see the finished **Shape** class hierarchy in Figure 15.1.

The Behavior Of Shapes

In the last section, we decided that objects in the **Shape** class hierarchy should be able to draw themselves. You'll implement this requirement by supplying the **Shape** class with a **virtual Draw()** member function that each of the derived classes overrides. You'll write the **Draw()** function to take a pointer to a device context as an argument, so the function will be entirely self contained. Thus, **Box**, **Squiggle**, and **Oval** objects can render themselves appropriately.

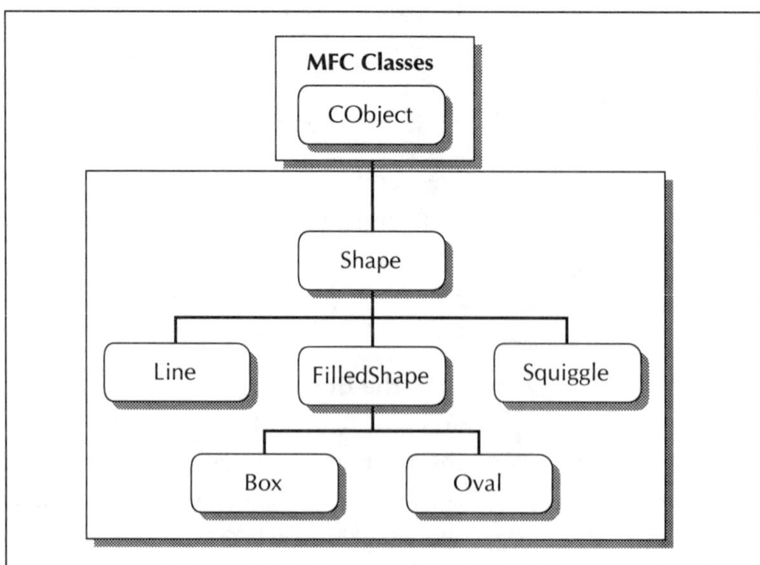

Figure 15.1
The **Shape** class hierarchy.

But that's not all! Because the **Draw()** function is virtual, you can use polymorphism to greatly simplify your program's painting logic. Here's how.

If you create an array (or list) of **Shape** pointers, as shown in Figure 15.2, C++ permits you to assign each of those pointers to a **Shape** object or *any object derived from the **Shape** class.*

Thus, the following code is legal:

```
Shape * list[3]; // Array of three Shape pointers
list[0] = new Squiggle(...);
list[1] = new Oval(...);
list[2] = new Box(...);
```

Not only is this code legal, it's amazingly useful—you can use it to implement late binding and polymorphism in C++. If you use the pointers stored in **list[0]**, **list[1]**, and **list[2]** to call a virtual function like **Draw()**, the **Draw()** function in the derived classes will be called, rather than the **Draw()** function in the **Shape** class.

Here's an example that takes up where the previous example left off:

```
list[0]->Draw(); // Calls Squiggle::Draw();
list[1]->Draw(); // Calls Oval::Draw();
list[2]->Draw(); // Calls Box::Draw();
```

Notice that, for this code to work, two conditions must be true. First, **list** must hold *pointers* to base-class objects, not base-class objects. Second, you must declare the **Draw()** function **virtual** in the base class—otherwise, the code will invoke the **Draw()** function in **Shape**, instead of the **Draw()** functions in **Line**, **Box**, **Squiggle**, and **Oval**.

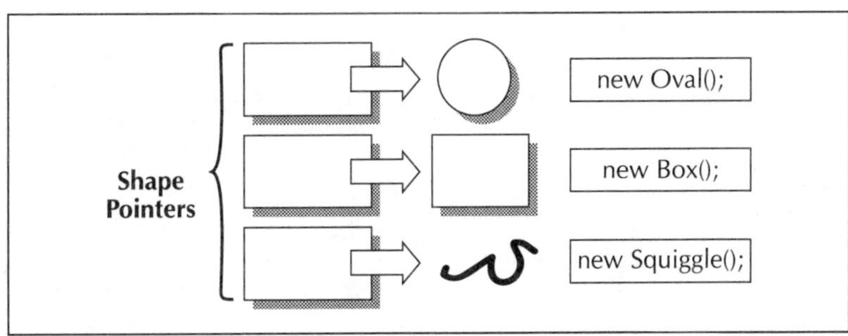

Figure 15.2
Polymorphic pointers, using the **Shape** class.

Defining The Shape Classes

If you look back at Figure 15.2, you'll see that we've derived the **Shape** class from the MFC **CObject** base class. There's no hard-and-fast requirement that you do this. In this case, we want to use the built-in support for serialization and dynamic object creation that the **CObject** class provides. On the other hand, using **CObject** imposes some constraints on the way you define classes, as you'll see shortly. Fortunately, the constraints aren't onerous, so there's no real reason *not* to derive from **CObject**.

Creating The Class Files

First, let's create a basic set of document class files. Once you've created the "skeleton" files, you can modify them to add the behavior and features you need.

Rather than creating header and implementation files for each class—Shape.h, Oval.h, Squiggle.h, and so on—you'll put all the class definitions in Shape.h and all the member function implementations in Shape.cpp. If you want to make things even simpler, you can add the definitions to the files used by the **CMSDoc** class. Of course, learning how to add a new, freestanding class is good for you, so that's what you'll do.

Here are the steps to follow:

1. Open the MiniSketch project. From the WizardBar drop-down menu shown in Figure 15.3, choose New Class or use the Insert|New Class menu item.

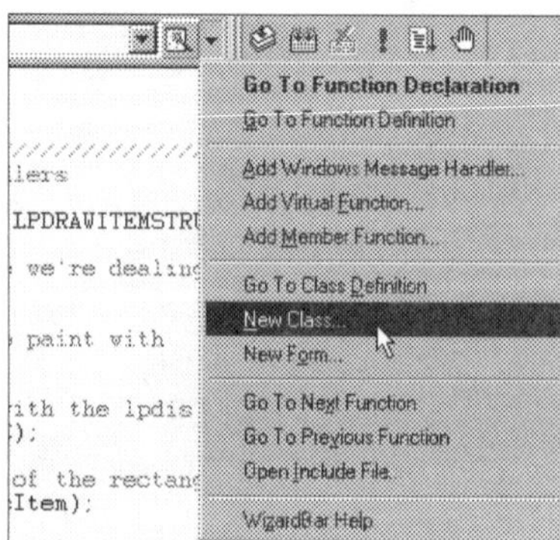

Figure 15.3
Adding a new class with the WizardBar drop-down menu.

2. In the New Class dialog box, select Generic Class as the class type. (This option isn't available if you launch the New Class dialog box from the ClassWizard instead of the WizardBar.) Name your class **Shape**, and derive from **CObject** using **public** derivation. Your finished dialog box should look like Figure 15.4. When it does, click on OK.
3. If a warning message appears, as shown in Figure 15.5, click on OK. Because this is a generic class, rather than an MFC class, ClassWizard doesn't know where to find the appropriate header files. You'll remedy that shortly.
4. Select the ClassView pane in the Workspace window and double-click on the new **Shape** class you find there. Add the following line immediately before the beginning of the **Shape** class definition as written by ClassWizard (that is, just before the line that begins **class Shape**):

```
#include "stdafx.h"
```

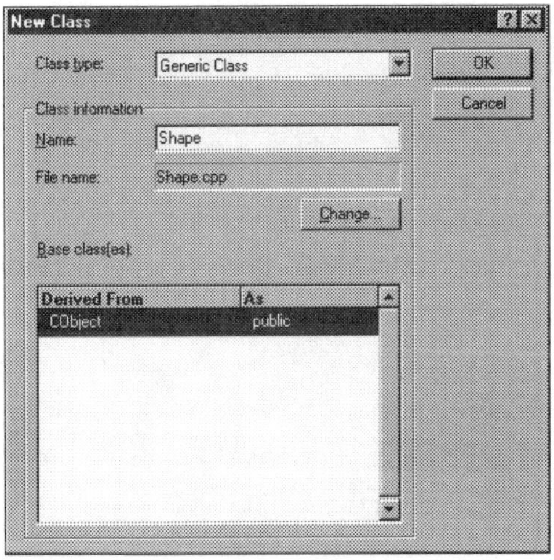

Figure 15.4
Adding the **Shape** class.

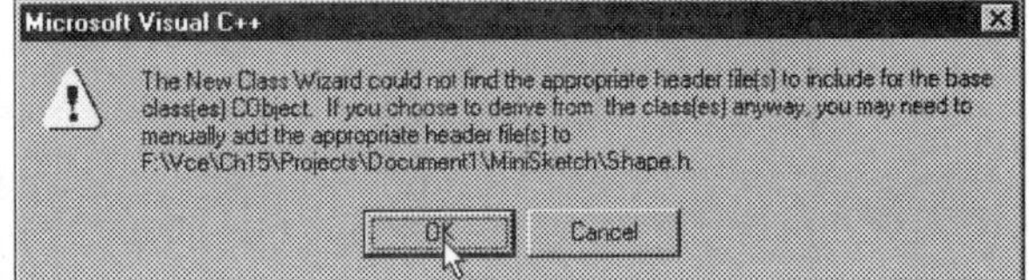

Figure 15.5
The header-not-found message box.

Why Won't This Link?

*If your program compiles fine, but you get linking errors after adding the **Shape** class, rebuild the entire project by choosing Build|Rebuild All from the menu.*

Visual C++ normally uses incremental linking when making your projects—it relinks only the code that has actually changed. Sometimes, especially after adding new classes, the incremental linker gets lost in the ozone. When you select Build|Rebuild All, Visual C++ re-creates your project from a clean slate.

This line remedies the error reported in Step 3. Compile your program, just to be sure everything works okay.

Now that you have the skeleton files, you need to implement each of the derived classes. You'll work on the **Shape** class first, because ClassWizard provides the skeleton functions you need. Then, you'll move on to the derived classes.

You'll create two listings for each class. Add the class definitions to the Shape.h file, after the **Shape** class definition, but before the closing **#endif**. Add the member function definitions to the Shape.cpp file.

The Shape Class Definition

To implement your classes, you must decide what member variables are required. When we designed the **Shape** class hierarchy, we determined that all the children of **Shape** require a pen—so, the **Shape** class has data members for pen width and pen color. Let's name the member variables **m_PenColor** and **m_PenWidth**, and make them **protected** so the children can access them without the need for accessor functions.

Only the **CObject** serialization mechanism will use the default **Shape** constructor, so it doesn't need to be **public**. Let's move it to the **protected** section. The class does need a constructor to set values for **m_PenColor** and **m_PenWidth**, so let's add a constructor in the **public** section.

The **Shape** class needs to override the **CObject::Serialize()** virtual function. To make **Serialize()** work, it also needs to invoke the **DECLARE_SERIAL()** macro within the class definition. (Be sure you don't inadvertently insert a semicolon after the invocation of the **DECLARE_SERIAL()** macro.) Finally, the **Shape** class needs two virtual functions of its own: **Draw()** and **Update()**. The **Draw()** function returns **void** and takes a **CDC *** as its only argument; the **Update()** function also returns **void** and takes a **CPoint** as its argument. You can see the completed **Shape** class definition in Listing 15.1. Modify Shape.h so that it conforms to the definition shown there.

Listing 15.1 The Shape class definition.

```
class Shape : public CObject
{
    DECLARE_SERIAL(Shape)
public:
    Shape(COLORREF color, int width);
    virtual ~Shape();
    virtual void Draw(CDC * pDC);
    virtual void Update(CPoint point);
    virtual void Serialize(CArchive &ar);
protected:
    Shape();

    COLORREF     m_PenColor;
    int          m_PenWidth;
};
```

The Line Class Definition

The definition for the **Line** class generally follows that of the **Shape** class. It contains the same functions, so you can get started easily by copying the **Shape** class definition and then changing every occurrence of **Shape** to **Line**.

After that, make the following changes:

1. Be sure that **Line** is derived from **Shape**, not **CObject**.
2. Remove the two member variables **m_PenColor** and **m_PenWidth**. **Line** will inherit these from **Shape**.
3. Add two **CPoint** member variables to mark the beginning and end of the line. Name the variables **m_LineStart** and **m_LineEnd**, and make them **protected**.
4. Add two additional **CPoint** arguments, named **start** and **end,** to the working constructor.

You can see the finished **Line** class definition in Listing 15.2. Add it to the **Shape** header file, following the definition of the **Shape** class.

Listing 15.2 The Line class definition.

```
// The Line Class
class Line : public Shape
{
```

```
    DECLARE_SERIAL(Line)
public:
    Line(COLORREF color, int width,
         CPoint start, CPoint end);
    virtual ~Line();
    virtual void Draw(CDC * pDC);
    virtual void Update(CPoint point);
    virtual void Serialize(CArchive &ar);

protected:
    Line();

    CPoint  m_LineStart;
    CPoint  m_LineEnd;
};
```

The Squiggle Class Definition

Squiggle and **Shape** differ only in the member variables they use. You can begin by making a copy of the **Shape** class definition and then changing all references from **Shape** to **Squiggle**. After you've done that, make these changes:

1. Change the parent class from **CObject** to **Shape**.
2. Remove the two data members and add a **CArray** of **CPoints** named **m_data** in their place. Each **Squiggle** object will store an array of points.
3. Add a third argument to the working constructor, representing the starting point of the **Squiggle**. Make its type **CPoint** and name it **start**.

You can see the finished definition for the **Squiggle** class in Listing 15.3. Add it to the **Shape** class header file.

Listing 15.3 The Squiggle class definition.

```
// The Squiggle Class
class Squiggle : public Shape
{
    DECLARE_SERIAL(Squiggle)
public:
    Squiggle(COLORREF color, int width,
             CPoint start);
    virtual ~Squiggle();
    virtual void Draw(CDC * pDC);
    virtual void Update(CPoint point);
    virtual void Serialize(CArchive &ar);
```

```
protected:
    Squiggle();

    CArray<CPoint, CPoint> m_data;
};
```

The FilledShape Class Definitions

The **Box** and **Oval** classes don't derive directly from the **Shape** class. Instead, they're derived from the **FilledShape** class.

Because all **FilledShape** objects use a brush, **FilledShape** defines the information needed to construct the brush. To make the MiniSketch project shorter, the **FilledShape** class stores only the **COLORREF** that defines solid brushes. However, you could easily include the information necessary to construct hatch brushes and other brushes.

To build the **FilledShape** class, follow the same procedures you used for **Line** and **Squiggle**:

1. Copy the **Shape** class definition, then replace all instances of **Shape** with **FilledShape**.
2. Change the base class from **CObject** to **Shape**.
3. Replace the **Shape** class member variables with a **COLORREF** variable named **m_BrushColor**.
4. Add a third argument called **brushColor** to the working constructor, to initialize the **m_BrushColor** variable.

The **FilledShape** class definition is shown in Listing 15.4. Add it to the **Shapes** header file, as well.

Listing 15.4 The FilledShape class definition.

```
// The FilledShape Class
class FilledShape : public Shape
{
    DECLARE_SERIAL(FilledShape)
public:
    FilledShape(COLORREF color, int width,
                COLORREF brushColor);
    virtual ~FilledShape();
    virtual void Draw(CDC * pDC);
    virtual void Update(CPoint point);
    virtual void Serialize(CArchive &ar);
```

```
protected:
    FilledShape();

    COLORREF    m_BrushColor;
};
```

The Box And Oval Class Definitions

The last two classes in the **Shape** class hierarchy have identical definitions, differing only in name. (However, as we mentioned earlier, each class *behaves* differently.) We'll walk through the definition of the **Box** class here.

Follow these steps to produce the **Box** class definition:

1. Copy the **Shape** class definition and replace all instances of **Shape** with **Box**, as you did previously.
2. Change the class so it derives from **FilledShape** instead of **CObject**. (Note that this step differs from the previous class definitions.)
3. Replace the **Shape** data members with two **CPoint** data members named **m_ULCorner** and **m_LRCorner**. (These will store the upper-right and lower-left corners of their respective shapes.)
4. Change the constructor to include three additional arguments: the **COLORREF brushColor**, which passes to **FilledShape** whenever a **Box** object is constructed; the **CPoint ulc**; and the **CPoint lrc**, which will initialize the **Box** member variables.

You can see the finished **Box** class definition in Listing 15.5. Follow the same instructions for the **Oval** class—but replace every instance of **Box** with **Oval**. (Or, you can copy the **Box** definition, select the copy, and use the Edit|Replace menu item to replace **Box** with **Oval** within the copy.) Add both definitions to the **Shape** header file.

Listing 15.5 The Box class definition.

```
// The Box Class
class Box : public FilledShape
{
    DECLARE_SERIAL(Box)
```

```
public:
    Box(COLORREF color, int width,
        COLORREF brushColor,
        CPoint ulc, CPoint lrc);
    virtual ~Box();
    virtual void Draw(CDC * pDC);
    virtual void Update(CPoint point);
    virtual void Serialize(CArchive &ar);

protected:
    Box();

    CPoint  m_ULCorner;
    CPoint  m_LRCorner;
};
```

Implementing The Shape Classes

Now that you've finished the header file, let's get started on the implementation file. ClassWizard has already created the necessary file—Shape.cpp—but you need to implement the member functions you defined in Shape.h.

Rather than present a huge code listing, we'll work on Shape.cpp incrementally. First, you'll create dummy functions (sometimes called *stubs*) so you can be sure that the basic structure is sound. Then, you'll go back and replace the stubs with actual working functions in the rest of this chapter and the next.

Stubbing Out Shape.cpp

Here are the steps to follow to create the dummy functions:

1. Be sure that the MiniSketch project is open. Select the ClassView pane in the Workspace window and double-click on the **Shape** class to open the Source Code Editor window for Shape.h.
2. Using your mouse, select the class definition in Shape.h. Copy it to the clipboard using Edit|Copy or by pressing Ctrl+C. You can see this in Figure 15.6.
3. Open the Shape.cpp file in the FileView pane. Use your mouse to mark the two functions already present in the file,

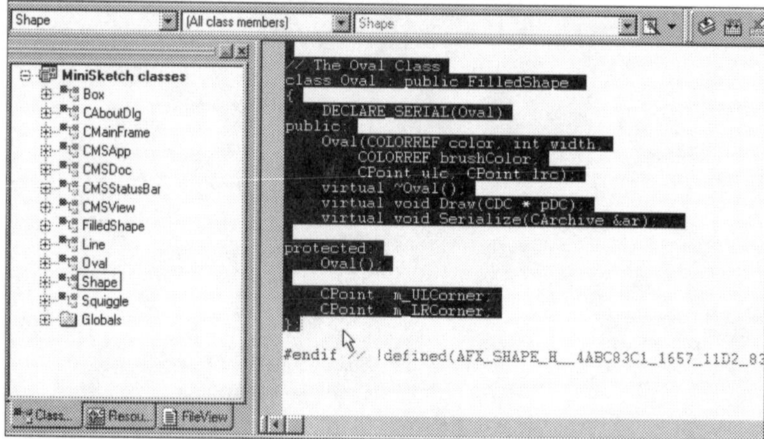

Figure 15.6
Copying the **Shape** class definitions.

and then use Edit|Paste or press Ctrl+V to copy the class definitions from Shape.h to Shape.cpp. (You may notice that the ClassView pane now contains duplicates for each of the **Shape** classes—you'll remedy that in the next step.)

4. Edit the Shape.cpp file, removing everything you added except the member function prototypes, the constructors, and the destructor. Add the scope resolution operator in front of each member function name, then remove the keyword **virtual** wherever it appears. (You declare a function **virtual** in the class definition, not within the member function.) Listing 15.6 shows how this code should look for the **Line** class; the other classes look similar. Add implementations for **Shape**, **Line**, **Squiggle**, **FilledShape**, **Box**, and **Oval**.

Listing 15.6 The Line class member functions after editing.

```
// The Line Class
Line::Line(COLORREF color, int width, CPoint start,
  CPoint
end);
Line::~Line();
void Line::Draw(CDC * pDC);
void Line::Update(CPoint point);
void Line::Serialize(CArchive &ar);
Line::Line();
```

5. After each member function prototype, remove the semicolon and add a pair of empty braces. Listing 15.7 shows how this looks for the **Line** class; the other classes are similar.

Listing 15.7 The Line class after adding empty function bodies.

```
// The Line Class
Line::Line(COLORREF color, int width, CPoint start,
  CPoint end){ }
Line::~Line(){ }
void Line::Draw(CDC * pDC){ }
void Line::Update(CPoint point) { }
void Line::Serialize(CArchive &ar){ }
Line::Line(){ }
```

6. Add the lines shown in Listing 15.8 to the bottom of the file. These macros add the support necessary to create each of the **Shape** objects using serialization.

Listing 15.8 The Shape class serialization macros.

```
// Serialization Macros
IMPLEMENT_SERIAL(Shape, CObject, 1)
IMPLEMENT_SERIAL(Line, Shape, 1)
IMPLEMENT_SERIAL(Squiggle, Shape, 1)
IMPLEMENT_SERIAL(FilledShape, Shape, 1)
IMPLEMENT_SERIAL(Box, FilledShape, 1)
IMPLEMENT_SERIAL(Oval, FilledShape, 1)
```

7. Write the working constructors for each of the classes. Except for the **Squiggle** class, none of the constructors needs a body. You can use initialization syntax to initialize each of the member variables within the class. The finished constructors are shown in Listing 15.9.

Listing 15.9 The Shape class hierarchy constructors.

```
// The Shape Class
Shape::Shape(COLORREF color, int width)
    : m_PenColor(color), m_PenWidth(width) { }

// The Line Class
Line::Line(COLORREF color, int width, CPoint start,
CPoint end)
    : Shape(color, width), m_LineStart(start),
m_LineEnd(end) { }

// The Squiggle Class
Squiggle::Squiggle(COLORREF color, int width, CPoint
start)
    : Shape(color, width)
{
```

```
    m_data.Add(start);
}

// The FilledShape Class
FilledShape::FilledShape(COLORREF color, int width,
  COLORREF brushColor)
    : Shape(color, width), m_BrushColor(brushColor) { }

// The Box Class
Box::Box(COLORREF color, int width, COLORREF brushColor,
         CPoint ulc, CPoint lrc)
    : FilledShape(color, width, brushColor),
      m_ULCorner(ulc), m_LRCorner(lrc) { }

// The Oval Class
Oval::Oval(COLORREF color, int width, COLORREF
brushColor,
           CPoint ulc, CPoint lrc)
    : FilledShape(color, width, brushColor),
      m_ULCorner(ulc), m_LRCorner(lrc){ }
```

After you've added the serialization macros and the constructors to Shape.cpp, you should be able to compile your project. Of course, you aren't using any of the new **Shape** objects in the program yet—that's coming up next.

Using The Shape Classes

Before you start slinging code, let's step back a bit and plan how to use the new **Shape** classes you've created. Having an idea where you're headed may help you avoid blind alleys.

Here's the overall plan for the **Shape** classes:

- When the user starts drawing by pressing the left mouse button, you'll create a new **Shape** object on the heap. You'll look at the **m_ShapeType** variable to decide what kind of **Shape** object to create.
- As the mouse is moved, you'll call the **Shape** object's virtual **Update()** method to keep it informed of the current mouse position. You'll also call its **Draw()** method to render the latest version of the **Shape** object.
- When the user stops drawing by releasing the mouse button, you'll store the **Shape** in your document class.

This design seems fairly straightforward, but there are a couple of things you need to pay extra attention to:

- Both the view class and the document class can create **Shape** objects. The view class creates **Shape** objects *explicitly* during the drawing operation, whereas the document class creates Shape objects *implicitly* during serialization.
- The document class is responsible for freeing the memory used by all **Shape** objects, whether they're created by the document class or by the view class.
- Your document class can't simply store objects, as it has done so far. Instead, you'll have to store *object pointers*. (If you used a **CArray** of **Shape** objects, all the polymorphic information specific to **Squiggle** objects or **Box** objects would be sliced off when you stored the **Shape** object in the document.)

That's the high-level view of where we're going. In the next chapter, we'll do more work to improve the MiniSketch view class. For now, let's turn our attention to the document class. What classes do you need in order to store your drawings? To find the answer to that question, we need to look at MFC's *collection classes*.

The MFC Collections

Collection classes are designed to hold objects—to collect them, if you will. Take an **Array** class, for instance. When you create an **Array**, it doesn't do anything more elaborate than provide a place for you to store objects, all of a single type. The **Array** itself doesn't care what kind of data you store in it, provided every element is the same kind.

A linked-list class is similar. The class isn't concerned about what kind of elements it holds—it merely provides functions to add an item, delete an item, or find an item. Classes like these—collection classes—are classes that manage data in a particular way.

If you look in the online help under *collections*, you're bound to get a shock. Rather than basic data-structure classes—linked lists, vectors, hash-tables, and binary trees—you'll see a bewildering assortment of almost two dozen classes, several of which seem to

Fortunately, the situation isn't as chaotic as it first appears. The 23 collection classes are easily categorized into groups that make choosing the correct container much less difficult. Let's take a look.

Non-Template (Inheritance-Based) Classes

The MFC library predates the addition of templates to the C++ language. Thus, the first MFC collection classes were based on inheritance and designed to hold entities of a single specific data type, such as **bytes** or **ints**. Seventeen of the MFC collection classes belong to this earlier non-template group.

The classes based on inheritance—**CObArray** and **CObList**—store *object pointers*; they can store only pointers to objects derived from **CObject**. These inheritance-based collections aren't *type-safe*. The compiler doesn't check the data types of object pointers you store in the array—if they derive from **CObject ***, that's good enough.

Let's look at an example. Suppose you want to store both **Line** objects and **Squiggle** objects in a **CObArray**. Here's how you'd go about it:

```
// Create the array object
CObArray ar;
// Create a new Line
Line * pLine = new Line(...);
// Create a new Squiggle
Squiggle * pSquiggle = new Squiggle(...);
// Add the Line to the array
ar.Add(pLine);
// Add the Squiggle to the array
ar.Add(pSquiggle);
```

So far, this looks great! When it comes to getting your information out, however, things are a bit more difficult. If you use the subscript operator on a **CObArray**, it doesn't return a pointer to a **Line** or **Squiggle**—instead, it returns a pointer to a **CObject**. You must cast the result before you can use it, like this:

```
// Get our Squiggle out of the array
pSquiggle = (Squiggle *) ar[0];
// Get our Line out of the array
pLine = (Line *) ar[1];
```

```
pSquiggle->Draw(pDC);                   // Draw the Squiggle
pLine->Draw(pDC);                       // Draw the Line
```

Sharp-eyed readers will note the problem with this code, above and beyond the awkward cast of the return value. When we stored the value in the array, we stored the **Line** object in element 0, and the **Squiggle** object in element 1. When we *retrieved* the objects, however, we accidentally reversed the indices, pointing to the **Squiggle** object with a **Line** pointer, and vice versa.

Because you're required to cast the pointer returned from a **CObArray**, the compiler can't help you by pointing out your error. After all, casts are *designed* to tell the compiler to mind its own business.

Template-Based Collections

The remaining six MFC collection classes are template-based, and thus provide type-safe access to your data. Generally, you should use a template-based class instead of a pre-template class.

However, the template classes aren't without their drawbacks. Every time you create an array or list from one of the template-based collection classes, the template invisibly creates an entirely new class, based on the argument types used to instantiate the template. Thus, if you create six **CArray** objects in your program, each storing a particular kind of object, the compiler will create six *different* classes. If you use **CObArray** to create your arrays, your program will contain only the code for the one class.

The six MFC template classes come in three *shapes*, with two varieties for each shape: one class that stores simple objects and another that stores object pointers. The three shapes are as follows:

- *Arrays*—Similar to the built-in arrays in most programming languages, the MFC template-based array classes automatically resize themselves when you add elements. You access the individual members of the collection using an integer index. The MFC **CArray** class stores objects, while the **CTypedPtrArray** stores object pointers.
- *Lists*—Implemented as a doubly linked list, the **CList** class (for simple objects) and the **CTypedPtrList** class (for object

pointers) provide a non-indexed data structure that must be serially traversed. You can move forward or backward, but you can't randomly access a particular element. Lists are the data structure of choice when the number of elements varies widely.

- *Maps*—Sometimes known as *dictionaries*, maps work much like their namesake. In a regular dictionary, you look up a word (called the *key*) and you retrieve a definition (called the *value*). Maps allow you to store any kind of value and retrieve it using any kind of key. However, when you create your collection, you must specify the type of key and value. If you create a map of **TelephoneRecord** types keyed on the **CString** name, the map won't let you retrieve or store values using the telephone number as a key. The two MFC map classes are **CMap** and **CTypedPtrMap**.

Saving The MiniSketch

So, which of these should you use to store your data in the **CMSDoc** class? Let's start by ruling out the non-template-based classes. You want to enlist the compiler's help to ensure you don't accidentally cast a **Line*** to a **Squiggle***. With the inheritance-based classes, the compiler can't help.

Your document must store polymorphic objects, so you can't use the classes that store simple objects—you'll have to use **CTypedPtrArray**, **CTypedPtrList**, or **CTypedPtrMap**. You can pretty well rule out the map version, so your choice boils down to an array or a list.

Each has advantages and disadvantages. The list version might be a little more efficient, but at the expense of slightly more programming complexity. In the interest of simplicity, let's use the **CTypedPtrArray** class to store the document.

Implementing The CMSDoc Class

Now that you've decided which data structure to use to store your data, let's implement the **CMSDoc** class. To get your document class working, you'll have to complete each of these tasks:

- Change the **CMSDoc** class member variable **m_data** to use the **CTypedPtrArray** class.
- Replace the **AddPoint()**, **NumPoints()**, and **GetPoint()** functions—which work only with **CPoint** objects—with a set of access functions that manage **Shape** objects. You'll call the functions **AddShape()**, **NumShapes()**, and **GetShape()**. The functionality will remain basically the same.
- Because your document now uses pointers and dynamic memory, you'll also need to write some code that cleans up the memory. To do this, you'll override the virtual **CDocument::DeleteContents()** function, which is called right before a document is destroyed and when you want to clear the current document.
- Finally, you'll have to deal with serialization. To do so, you don't have to make any changes to the **CMSDoc** class. But, when you ask the **CMSDoc** object **m_data** to serialize itself, it asks each object that it contains to serialize itself. The previous version of **CMSDoc** worked because you stored only **CPoints**, which know how to serialize themselves. To get the new version to work, you'll need to be sure all your **Shape** objects can store and retrieve their information from disk.

Adding A CTypedPtrArray Object

As is often the case, the first step is the easiest. All you have to do is change the **CMSDoc m_data** member variable from a **CArray** to a **CTypedPtrArray**. Like **CArray**, the **CTypedPtrArray** template takes two instantiation arguments.

In the case of **CTypedPtrArray**, the first argument is known as the *collection base type*. You may use either **CObArray** if you want to store pointers to objects (which you do), or **CPtrArray** of you want to store plain (**void**) pointers (which you don't).

The second template argument is the kind of pointer you actually intend to store. In this case, you're going to store **Shape** pointers. The finished declaration—which you should add to the end of the **CMSDoc** class definition, replacing the previous declaration of **m_data**—looks like this:

```
CTypedPtrArray<CObArray, Shape*> m_data;
```

Don't try to recompile your project after making this change. The member functions that worked with **m_data** no longer work, now that **m_data** holds pointers to **Shape** objects.

Replacing The Access Functions

The next step in the transformation of **CMSDoc** is to remove the **CPoint** accessor functions and replace them with functions that work with **Shape** pointers.

When you remove a member function, you have to delete both the declaration (contained in the class definition) and the function definition. The Visual C++ IDE can help you, by removing the function declaration and commenting out the function definition.

Here are the steps to follow:

1. With the MiniSketch project loaded, select the ClassView pane in the project Workspace window and expand the **CMSDoc** class. Locate the **AddPoint()** function and right-click on it. Choose Delete from the context menu that appears, as shown in Figure 15.7.
2. A message dialog box will open, explaining that the function body will be commented out and asking for confirmation. You can see this in Figure 15.8. Click on Yes.
3. Visual C++ will delete the function declaration from the class and place comment markers in front of each line of the function, as shown in Figure 15.9.

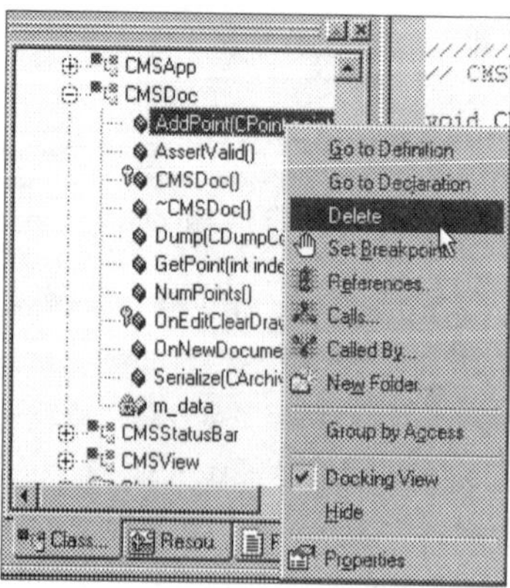

Figure 15.7
Deleting a member function.

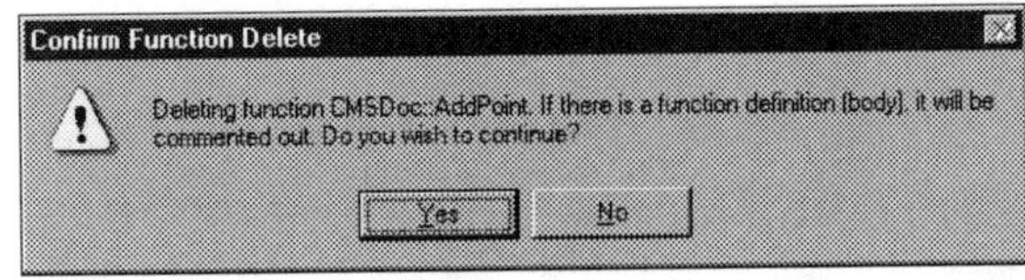

Figure 15.8
The Confirm Function Delete dialog box.

Figure 15.9
Comments placed in your source code.

4. Repeat the same operation for the **NumPoints()** and **GetPoint()** functions.
5. Right-click on the **CMSDoc** class in Class View and choose Add Member Function from the context menu. Add the three public functions shown in Listing 15.10.

Listing 15.10 The CMSDoc access functions for Shape objects.

```
Shape * CMSDoc::GetShape(int item)
{
    return m_data[item];
}

int CMSDoc::NumShapes()
{
    return m_data.GetSize();
}

void CMSDoc::AddShape(Shape *pNewShape)
{
    m_data.Add(pNewShape);
}
```

Cleaning Up The Pieces

Although both your view class and your document class can create **Shape** objects, the document object must clean up those objects. To do so, you simply walk through the **m_data** array, calling **delete** on each item it contains. To free the memory used by the pointers, you call the member function **RemoveAll()**.

Here are the two steps to follow:

1. Select the **CMSDoc** class in the ClassView window. Right-click to open the context menu, then select Add Virtual Function. In the New Virtual Function Override dialog box, shown in Figure 15.10, select **DeleteContents()** and click on Add And Edit.
2. Add the code shown in Listing 15.11.

Listing 15.11 Cleaning up the document class.

```
void CMSDoc::DeleteContents()
{
    int nItems = m_data.GetSize();
    for (int i = 0; i < nItems; i++)
    {
        delete m_data[i];
    }
    m_data.RemoveAll();
}
```

Now, when you clear a document, you can't simply use **SetSize(0, 128)**, as you did when you were working with the **CArray** class. When **m_data** was a **CArray**, it stored **CPoint** *objects*—not pointers—and so it was able to manage its memory automatically. Now that **m_data** is a **CTypedPtrArray**, it holds **Shape** *pointers* instead of objects; therefore, you need to iterate through the entire collection, calling **delete** on each item. As you **delete** each element, its destructor is called, and the object has an opportunity to free any resources that it has allocated.

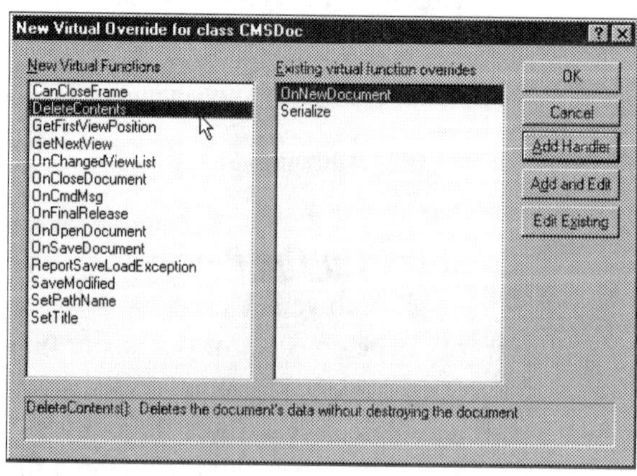

Figure 15.10 The New Virtual Function Override dialog box.

Serialization

Finally, you need to complete the serialization code for the **Shape** class hierarchy. Before you do that, let's take a higher-level view of why serialization is important and how it works.

Suppose that you have the following lines in your program, where **pDoc** is a pointer to your program's document object:

```
Shape *p = new Oval(RGB(255,0,0), 25,
                    RGB(0, 255, 0),
                    CPoint(0,0), CPoint(100, 100));
pDoc->AddShape(p);
```

When this code executes, space for a new **Oval** object is created on the freestore, and the **CObject**, **Shape**, **FilledShape**, and **Oval** constructors initialize all of the member variables. The code stores the address of the new **Oval** object in the pointer variable **p** and adds that pointer to your document class by calling the **AddShape()** function, which we wrote earlier in this chapter. You can then reuse **p** for some other purpose, because the document will take care of deleting the **Oval** object on the freestore. You can see this memory structure pictured in Figure 15.11.

Now, suppose you want to save your document as a disk file. What has to happen?

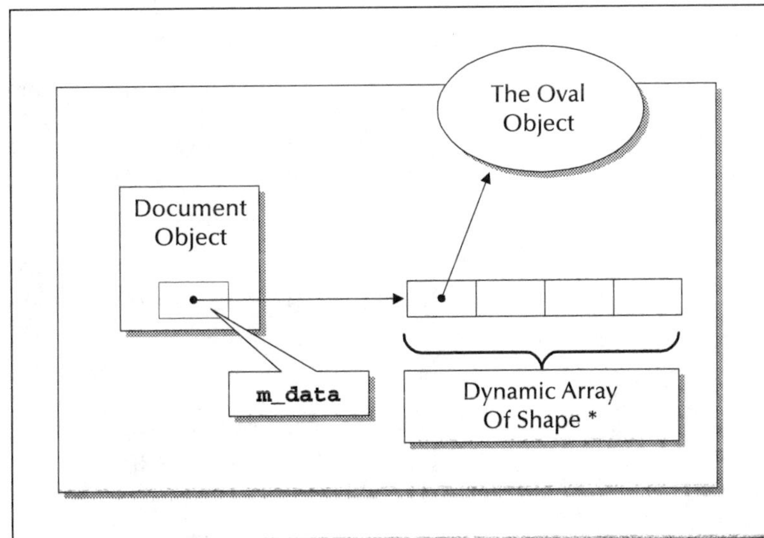

Figure 15.11
Shapes in memory.

Well, obviously, you can't simply write the value stored in **m_data** to disk. Behind the scenes, **m_data** points to an actual array of **Shape** pointers, located somewhere out on the freestore. Similarly, you can't simply write those **Shape** pointers to disk. The pointers simply store the locations of the current actual objects. Instead, you must retrieve the information stored in each object: the color of the pen, its width, the color of the brush, and the coordinates of the bounding rectangle. You then have *almost* everything you need to reconstruct the **Oval** object in a new setting when you read it in from disk.

Notice that we said *almost*. In addition to the data that goes into the member variables, you also need to store some *runtime-type-identification information* (RTTI). When you read back the data, you need to know that you must construct a new **Oval** object, not a new **Box** object. When the MFC serialization mechanism reads the RTTI information, it finds the specified class and constructs a new object using the default (no-argument) constructor. It then uses the rest of the information to populate the data fields, so that they contain exactly the same values they had when they were serialized.

MFC Serialization Details

The MFC **CObject** class contains built-in support for serialization. If you derive your classes from **CObject**, you can automatically save and retrieve your objects from disk by following a few simple rules:

- Your class must derive from **CObject**.
- Your class declaration must invoke the **DECLARE_SERIAL()** macro, to provide the forward declarations for the dynamic object-creation functions.
- Your implementation file must invoke the **IMPLEMENT_SERIAL()** macro for each serializable class. This macro adds the functions to match the forward declarations created by the **DECLARE_SERIAL()** macros.
- Your class must override the virtual **Serialize()** function, to save its data members to disk.

That's all there is to it. You've already taken care of the first three items. The only thing left to do is to write the **Serialize()** for your **Shape** classes.

Writing Serialize()

When MFC calls your **Serialize()** function, it passes a reference to a **CArchive** object. This **CArchive** object works much like the standard C++ input and output stream objects, **cout** and **cin**.

For any of the primitive types—like **int** or **float**—you can use the overloaded insertion operator (<<) to store values in the archive, or the extraction operator (>>) to retrieve values from the archive and store the values in variables. The insertion and extraction operators have also been overloaded for most simple, non-**CObject** based objects (such as **CPoint** and **CRect**). For some of the Windows-specific primitive types, you must cast the value to a generic primitive. For example, for **COLORREF**, you cast the value to a **DWORD**.

Rather than have separate input and output objects—like **cout** and **cin**—the **CArchive** object takes on both roles, but not at the same time. Before you use the insertion object, you must call its member function **IsStoring()**. If **IsStoring()** returns true, then the archive object is in output mode, and acts like **cout**. If **IsStoring()** returns false, then the archive object is in input mode and acts like **cin**.

Let's see how this works, by adding the code for **Shape::Serialize()**. Follow these steps:

1. Using ClassView, expand the **Shape** class folder and locate its **Serialize()** function. Double-click to open the Source Code Editor.
2. In any class, before you serialize your portion of the data, you must give the base class a chance to serialize its data. Thus, the first line in **Shape::Serialize()** should be a call to **CObject::Serialize()**. Pass the **CArchive** object as an argument.
3. The **Shape** class has two data members you need to store: the **int m_PenWidth** and the **COLORREF m_PenColor**. Neither

of these are **CObject**-derived, so you'll have to use the insertion and extraction operators, in combination with the **IsStoring()** function. In addition, you must cast **m_PenColor**, which is a **COLORREF** to a **DWORD**. The finished code for the **Shape::Serialize()** function is shown in Listing 15.12.

Listing 15.12 The Shape::Serialize() virtual function.

```
void Shape::Serialize(CArchive &ar)
{
    CObject::Serialize(ar);

    if (ar.IsStoring())
    {
        ar << (DWORD)m_PenColor << m_PenWidth;
    }
    else
    {
        ar >> (DWORD)m_PenColor >> m_PenWidth;
    }
}
```

If your object contains other **CObject**-derived objects as fields—such as the **m_data CArray** field in the **CSquiggle** class—you don't use the insertion and extraction operators to serialize them. Instead, you simply call the object's **Serialize()** function, passing the **CArchive** argument you received.

The **Serialize()** functions for the rest of the **Shape** classes are shown in Listing 15.13. Replace the stubs in Shape.cpp with them, and you're finished with the **CMSDoc** class.

Listing 15.13 The remaining Shape class hierarchy Serialize() virtual functions.

```
// The Line Class
void Line::Serialize(CArchive &ar)
{
    Shape::Serialize(ar);
    if (ar.IsStoring())
    {
        ar << m_LineStart << m_LineEnd;
    }
    else
    {
        ar >> m_LineStart >> m_LineEnd;
    }
}
```

```
// The Squiggle Class
void Squiggle::Serialize(CArchive &ar)
{
    Shape::Serialize(ar);
// This is the CArray in Squiggle
    m_data.Serialize(ar);
}

// The FilledShape Class
void FilledShape::Serialize(CArchive &ar)
{
    Shape::Serialize(ar);

    if (ar.IsStoring())
    {
        ar << (DWORD) m_BrushColor;
    }
    else
    {
        ar >> (DWORD) m_BrushColor;
    }
}

// The Box Class
void Box::Serialize(CArchive &ar)
{
    FilledShape::Serialize(ar);
    if (ar.IsStoring())
    {
        ar << m_ULCorner << m_LRCorner;
    }
    else
    {
        ar >> m_ULCorner >> m_LRCorner;
    }
}

// The Oval Class
void Oval::Serialize(CArchive &ar)
{
    FilledShape::Serialize(ar);
    if (ar.IsStoring())
    {
        ar << m_ULCorner << m_LRCorner;
    }
    else
    {
        ar >> m_ULCorner >> m_LRCorner;
    }
}
```

What's New To View?

You'll want to compile MiniSketch to make sure you haven't made any typing mistakes. Unfortunately, two functions in the **CMSView** class still make reference to the old document—the one that contained only **CPoint** objects. Comment out the code that uses the document class in **CMSView::OnDraw()** and **CMSView::OnMouseMove()**, and add the line

```
#include "Shape.h"
```

to MiniSketchDoc.h. Now you can compile your program.

Of course, it won't work—the **CMSView** class is responsible for creating **Shapes** for the document to save. That's where we'll turn our attention in the next chapter. By the time you've finished Chapter 16, the MiniSketch application will be complete.

Chapter 16

A Brand New View: Scrolling And Printing

Gutenberg failed to earn a substantial return on his remarkable invention. However, you'll profit greatly by learning how to use the MFC scrolling and printing facilities.

Johannes Gensfleisch Zur Laden Zum Gutenberg—known to history simply as Gutenberg—invented a method of printing with movable type. Gutenberg's fifteenth century method was so advanced that printers made no important improvements until the twentieth century.

Like modern entrepreneurs, Gutenberg used investors to finance the development of his method. One of those investors became concerned about his prospects for financial return and filed a lawsuit against Gutenberg. In 1455, the investor won a judgment forcing Gutenberg to repay the modest business loan of about 2,020 guilders. Later, the investor gained control of the type for Gutenberg's 42-line Bible—sales of this Bible yielded many times the sum owed. To spare Gutenberg from destitution, the archbishop of Mainz awarded him a pension in 1465.

Don't panic—we won't force you to such financial extremes before you can benefit from our printing lessons. In this chapter, you'll make the final improvements to the MiniSketch application. When you're done, users will be able to use your creation to print their masterpieces. They'll even be able to create wall-mural-sized artworks too large to view in a single window. Let's get to it!

What About Brush Colors?

Before you fix the view, you need to give the user a toolbar button that changes the brush color. Doing so will be short and sweet—you can think of it as a Chapter 15 review.

Here are the steps to follow:

1. Open the MiniSketch project and right-click on **CMSView** in the ClassView window. Choose Add Member Variable from the context menu. Create a private **COLORREF** named **m_BrushColor**. The Add Member Variable dialog box should look like that shown in Figure 16.1.
2. Using the same procedure, add a new private **CBrush** object named **m_Brush**. Using Class View, open the **CMSView** constructor in the Source Code Editor and add the following lines to the bottom:

   ```
   // Initialize the brush color
   m_BrushColor = RGB(0, 0, 0);
   m_Brush.CreateSolidBrush(m_BrushColor);
   ```

3. Switch to the ResourceView pane in the Workspace window, expand the Toolbar folder, and double-click on the **IDR_MAINFRAME** toolbar resource to open the Toolbar Editor. Drag the empty button at the right of the toolbar so that it lies next to the pen-color toolbar button. Figure 16.2 shows how your screen should look.
4. Using the pencil tool, draw four filled rectangles, each in a different color. This design will help the user to distinguish the icon used to change the brush color from the icon used to change the pen color. Your screen should look something like Figure 16.3.

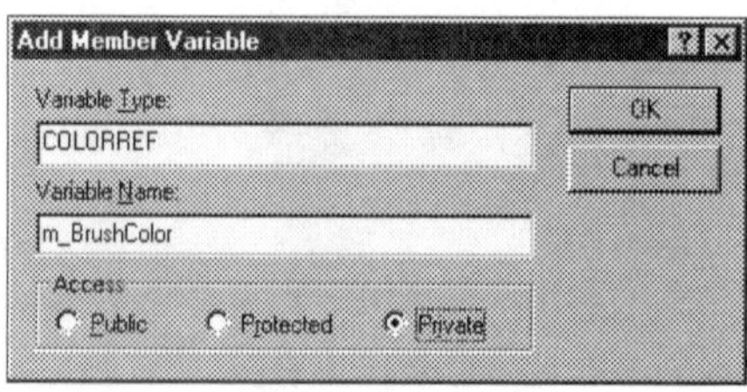

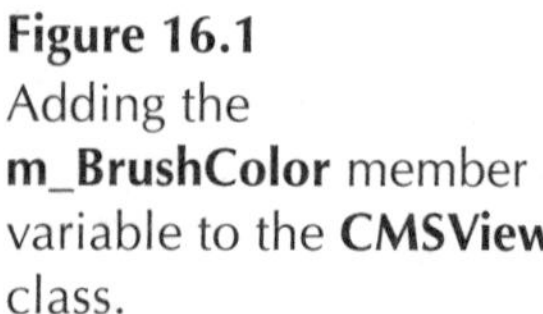

Figure 16.1
Adding the **m_BrushColor** member variable to the **CMSView** class.

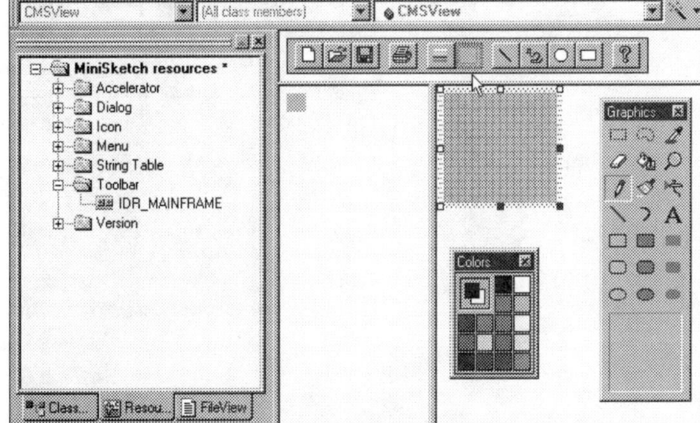

Figure 16.2
Adding a new toolbar button for brush color.

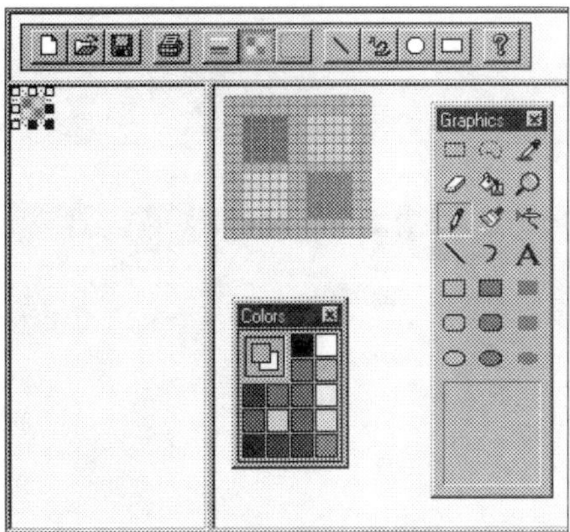

Figure 16.3
Drawing the brush-color toolbar button.

5. Double-click in the left-pane of the Toolbar Editor to display the Toolbar Button Properties dialog box. Enter the new resource ID "**ID_BRUSH_COLOR**". Set the prompt string to read "Set the brush color for filled shapes\nBrush Color". The dialog box should look like that shown in Figure 16.4.

6. From the WizardBar menu, choose Add Windows Message Handler. Be sure the dialog box that appears is titled New Windows Message And Event Handlers For Class CMSView. In the Class Or Object To Handle list box, locate and select **ID_BRUSH_COLOR**. In the New Windows Messages/Events list box, choose **COMMAND**. When your screen looks like that shown in Figure 16.5, click on Add And Edit.

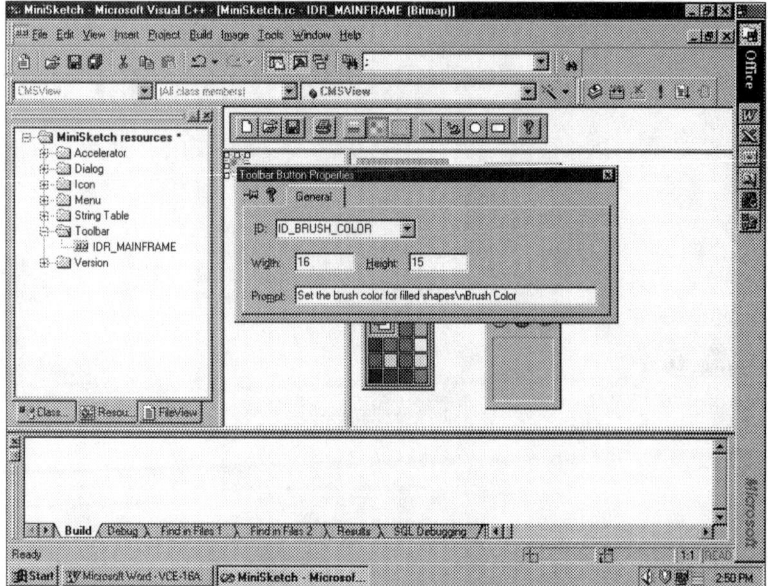

Figure 16.4
Completing the Toolbar Button Properties dialog box.

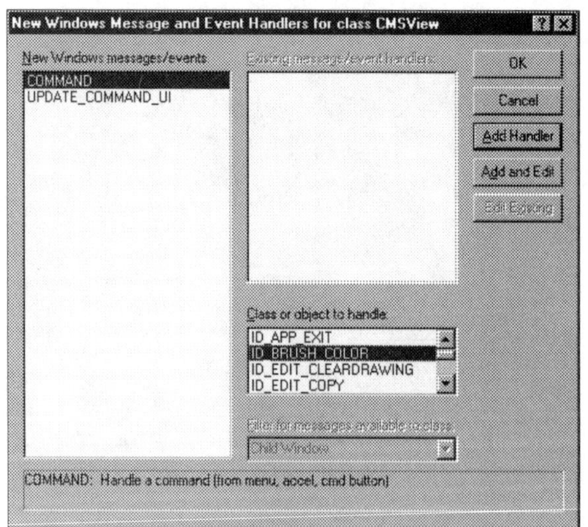

Figure 16.5
Creating the **ID_BRUSH_COLOR** handler.

7. Accept the file name offered by ClassWizard, **OnBrushColor()**. Click on OK when your screen looks like Figure 16.6.
8. Add the code shown in Listing 16.1 to the function written by ClassWizard.

Listing 16.1 The OnBrushColor() member function.

```
void CMSView::OnBrushColor()
{
```

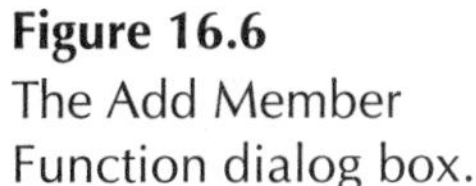

Figure 16.6
The Add Member Function dialog box.

```
    // TODO: Add your command handler code here
    CColorDialog dlg(m_BrushColor);
    if (dlg.DoModal() == IDOK)
    {
        m_BrushColor = dlg.GetColor();
    }
}
```

Now that you've provided users a way to change the brush color, you may want to add a brush-color swatch on the status bar, similar to that used to display the pen color. In the interest of forging ahead, we'll leave that as an exercise, and turn our attention to getting MiniSketch up and running.

Connecting The Doc With The View

If you remember the general plan from the last chapter, you know that you're going to modify your view class to create a **Shape** object—using the C++ **new** operator—when the user clicks the left mouse button in the client area. As the mouse is moved, you'll continually update the **Shape** object by calling its virtual function **Update()**. Finally, when the user releases the mouse button, you'll send the finished **Shape** to join its brethren in the **CMSDoc** class.

To do this, you must rewrite three of the **CMSView** functions: **OnLButtonDown()**, **OnLButtonUp()**, and **OnMouseMove()**. Let's start by looking at **OnLButtonDown()**.

Creating New Shapes

In **OnLButtonDown()**, you must create a new **Shape** object of the type indicated by the variable **m_ShapeType**. For instance, if **m_ShapeType** has the value **ID_SHAPE_TYPE_LINE**, you'll create a new **Line** object; if it has the value **ID_SHAPE_TYPE_RECTANGLE**, you'll create a new **Box** object. The default shape type will be a **Squiggle**.

Because you create the new shape in the freestore, using the **new** operator, you need to store the shape's address. You'll create a new member variable called **m_pCurShape** that points to the shape you're drawing.

Follow these steps to update **OnLButtonDown()**:

1. Open the ClassView window and locate the **CMSView** class. Right-click to bring up the context menu, then choose Add Member Variable. Add the **private Shape *** variable named **m_pCurShape,** and click on OK when your screen looks like Figure 16.7.
2. In the ClassView window, expand the **CMSView** class and locate the **OnLButtonDown()** member function. Double-click to open the Source Code Editor, then add the code from Listing 16.2. The highlighted code is new.

Listing 16.2 The CMSView::OnLButtonDown() member function.

```
void CMSView::OnLButtonDown(UINT nFlags, CPoint point)
{
    m_LineStart = point;
    SetCapture();
    switch (m_ShapeType)
    {
    case ID_SHAPE_TYPE_LINE:
        m_pCurShape = new Line(m_PenColor, m_PenWidth,
                               point, point);
        break;
    case ID_SHAPE_TYPE_OVAL:
        m_pCurShape = new Oval(m_PenColor, m_PenWidth,
                               m_BrushColor, point,
```

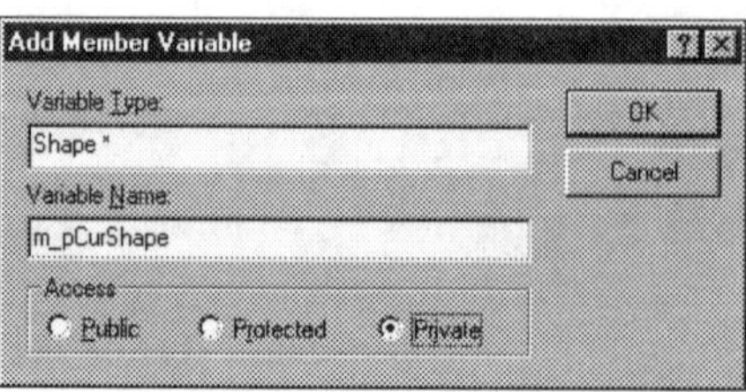

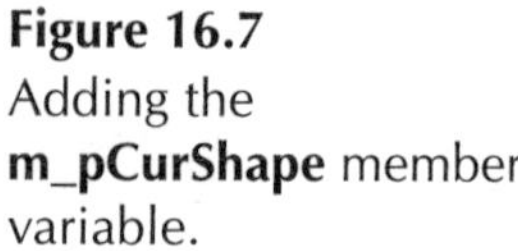

Figure 16.7
Adding the **m_pCurShape** member variable.

```
                                        point);
            break;
        case ID_SHAPE_TYPE_RECTANGLE:
            m_pCurShape = new Box(m_PenColor, m_PenWidth,
                                       m_BrushColor, point,
                                       point);
            break;
        case ID_SHAPE_TYPE_FREEHAND:
        default:
            m_pCurShape = new Squiggle(m_PenColor,
                                   m_PenWidth, point);
            break;
    }
}
```

Finishing The Shape

Previously, the **OnLButtonUp()** function simply released the mouse capture. In the new version, when the user releases the mouse button, you want to perform these three additional tasks:

- *Update the finished* ***Shape*** *by sending the last point to the* ***Shape*** *object.* You'll do that by calling the **Shape** class's virtual function **Update()**.
- *Send the finished* ***Shape*** *to the document object for safe keeping.* To do so, you'll call the **CMSDoc** function **AddShape()**.
- *Draw the finished* ***Shape*** *in the current view.* You could call the **Invalidate()** function, which would cause all **Shape** objects stored in the document to be redrawn. However, there's really no need to do so, and it's much quicker to draw directly. Now that you've stored your **Shape** in the document, it won't accidentally disappear the next time the screen is refreshed.

To add this new functionality, locate the **OnLButtonUp()** function, using the same method you used to find **OnLButtonDown()**. Add the highlighted code shown in Listing 16.3.

Listing 16.3 The CMSView::OnLButtonUp() member function.

```
void CMSView::OnLButtonUp(UINT nFlags, CPoint point)
{
    CClientDC dc(this);
    m_pCurShape->Update(point);
    m_pCurShape->Draw(&dc);
```

```
    ReleaseCapture();

    CMSDoc* pDoc = GetDocument();
    ASSERT_VALID(pDoc);
    pDoc->AddShape(m_pCurShape);
}
```

Rubber-Banding

The last member of your view-class drawing triumvirate is the **OnMouseMove()** function. As in the PaintORama application, you'll draw the current shape as the mouse moves, using shape stretching or rubber-banding. At every new mouse position, you draw a new **Box** or **Oval** and erase the previous **Box** or **Oval**. As before, you should do this only if you're *not* drawing freehand.

Here's how you go about doing that:

- If you're dragging, get a client-area device context (DC), using **CClientDC**.
- If you're *not* drawing freehand, change the drawing mode to **R2_NOT** and call the current **Shape**'s **Draw()** function. Recall that the **R2_NOT** mode simply reverses the current background, ignoring the pen color. Because you haven't yet updated the coordinates used by your **Shape**, the pen will redraw the **Shape** using **R2_NOT**, erasing the old image.
- Update the coordinates of the current **Shape** object by calling its **Update()** function, passing the current mouse coordinates as the argument.
- Call the current **Shape**'s **Draw()** function, passing the client DC you previously obtained. Remember, if you're not drawing freehand, then this DC will draw in **R2_NOT** mode.

To implement these changes, revise the **CMSView:: OnMouseMove()** function to agree with Listing 16.4. You'll need to delete a few lines and add the highlighted ones.

Listing 16.4 The CMSView::OnMouseMove() member function.

```
void CMSView::OnMouseMove(UINT nFlags, CPoint point)
{
    if (nFlags & MK_LBUTTON)
```

```
    {
        CClientDC dc(this);
        if (m_ShapeType != ID_SHAPE_TYPE_FREEHAND)
        {
            dc.SetROP2(R2_NOT);
            m_pCurShape->Draw(&dc);
        }
        m_pCurShape->Update(point);
        m_pCurShape->Draw(&dc);
    }
}
```

Figure Drawing

Although the user-interaction portion of MiniSketch is complete, you need to perform two more tasks before it will work:

- Teach your **Lines**, **Boxes**, and **Ovals** how to draw themselves, by writing code for each of their **Draw()** functions.
- Write the code that redraws the entire image when the **CMSView::OnDraw()** function is called.

Let's look at drawing each of the **Shape** classes first.

Self-Rendering Shapes

The code to draw each **Shape** class is fairly straightforward. Each class contains a virtual **Draw()** function, which is called from the view class through the **m_pCurShape** pointer. Because **m_pCurShape** is a pointer to a **Shape** (not a pointer to a **Line** or **Box**), it's important that the **Draw()** function be declared **virtual**—otherwise, the view class will call the **Draw()** function in the **Shape** class, even if **m_pCurShape** actually points to a **Line** or **Box** object.

When the view class calls **Draw()**, the view class passes a pointer to the DC for the **Shape** object to use in rendering itself. The first thing each **Shape** object must do is construct its own pen and select it into the DC. The **Shape** must also select the pen out of the DC when finished, like this:

```
CPen pen, *oldPen;
pen.Create(PS_SOLID, m_PenWidth, m_PenColor);
```

```
oldPen = pDC->SelectObject(&pen);
// Drawing code goes here
pDC->SelectObject(oldPen);
```

The variables **m_PenWidth** and **m_PenColor** are **protected** member variables inherited from the **Shape** class. If you add code to handle styled pens, you might employ an **m_PenStyle** variable rather than a hard-coded **PS_SOLID** value. The **SelectObject()** function returns a pointer to the old pen—the last line restores the old pen, removing the new pen from the DC in the process.

The classes derived from **FilledShape**—**Oval** and **Box**, in our example—must similarly construct a brush and select it into the DC. They should deselect the brush, just as they did the pen, before the **Draw()** function terminates.

To modify the **Draw()** functions, you can use the Workspace ClassView pane to locate the member function for each class. Then, enter the code shown in Listing 16.5. Note that there's no code for **Shape::Draw()** or **FilledShape::Draw()**—neither of those classes knows how to draw a *specific* shape. The body of each of these functions should contain a pair of empty braces.

Listing 16.5 The Draw() member functions for the Shape class hierarchy.

```
// The Line Class
void Line::Draw(CDC * pDC)
{
    CPen pen, *pOldPen;
    pen.CreatePen(PS_SOLID, m_PenWidth, m_PenColor);
    pOldPen = pDC->SelectObject(&pen);
    pDC->MoveTo(m_LineStart);
    pDC->LineTo(m_LineEnd);
    pDC->SelectObject(pOldPen);
}

// The Squiggle Class
void Squiggle::Draw(CDC * pDC)
{
    CPen pen, *pOldPen;
    pen.CreatePen(PS_SOLID, m_PenWidth, m_PenColor);
    pOldPen = pDC->SelectObject(&pen);
    int nPoints = m_data.GetSize();
    pDC->MoveTo(m_data[0]);
    for (int i = 1; i < nPoints; i++)
```

```
    {
        pDC->LineTo(m_data[i]);
    }
    pDC->SelectObject(pOldPen);
}

// The Box Class
void Box::Draw(CDC * pDC)
{
    CPen pen, *pOldPen;
    pen.CreatePen(PS_SOLID, m_PenWidth, m_PenColor);
    pOldPen = pDC->SelectObject(&pen);

    CBrush brush, *pOldBrush;
    brush.CreateSolidBrush(m_BrushColor);
    pOldBrush = pDC->SelectObject(&brush);

    pDC->Rectangle(CRect(m_ULCorner, m_LRCorner));

    pDC->SelectObject(pOldPen);
    pDC->SelectObject(pOldBrush);
}

// The Oval Class
void Oval::Draw(CDC * pDC)
{
    CPen pen, *pOldPen;
    pen.CreatePen(PS_SOLID, m_PenWidth, m_PenColor);
    pOldPen = pDC->SelectObject(&pen);

    CBrush brush, *pOldBrush;
    brush.CreateSolidBrush(m_BrushColor);
    pOldBrush = pDC->SelectObject(&brush);

    pDC->Ellipse(CRect(m_ULCorner, m_LRCorner));

    pDC->SelectObject(pOldPen);
    pDC->SelectObject(pOldBrush);
}
```

Handling Update()

In addition to knowing how to display itself, each **Shape** object has an **Update()** virtual function that the view class **OnMouseMove()** function calls. The actual behavior of the function varies by type. **Squiggle** objects, for instance, need to add the new point to their internal array of **CPoints**; **Line** objects need to update their **m_LineEnd** member variable; and **Oval** and **Box** objects both need to update their **m_LRCorner** member variable.

To add the necessary code, you can open Shapes.cpp using the Workspace FileView window, or locate each of the individual **Update()** functions using Class View. You'll have to write code for the **Line**, **Squiggle**, **Oval**, and **Box** classes, as shown in Listing 16.6. (No code is needed for the **Shape** or **FilledShape** classes.)

Listing 16.6 The Shape class hierarchy Update() member functions.

```
void Line::Update(CPoint newPoint)
  { m_LineEnd = newPoint;  }
void Squiggle::Update(CPoint newPoint){
m_data.Add(newPoint);  }
void Box::Update(CPoint newPoint)
  { m_LRCorner = newPoint; }
void Oval::Update(CPoint newPoint)
  { m_LRCorner = newPoint; }
```

Rewriting OnDraw()

If you compile and run your program at this point (commenting out the code within the **OnDraw()** function that references **NumPoints** and **getPoint()**), all the drawing modes will work. You'll even be able to save your work and retrieve it from disk. However, you won't be able to see it again, once it's saved. While some folks might consider this a feature (New! The only drawing program that shields your drawings from prying eyes) you should fix it before going on. That means rewriting the **CMSView OnDraw()** function.

The new **OnDraw()** function is simpler than the previous version, which dealt only with **CPoints**. It doesn't do any drawing—it merely retrieves each **Shape** from the document and tells the **Shape** to draw itself. What could be easier?

To add the new **OnDraw()** function to MiniSketch, locate and expand the **CMSView** class in the Workspace ClassView pane. Find and double-click on the **OnDraw()** function to open the Source Code Editor. Enter the code shown in Listing 16.7.

Listing 16.7 The CMSView::OnDraw() member function.

```
//////////////////////////////////////////////////////////////
////////////////////
// CMSView drawing

void CMSView::OnDraw(CDC* pDC)
{
    CMSDoc* pDoc = GetDocument();
    ASSERT_VALID(pDoc);

    int nShapes = pDoc->NumShapes();
    for (int index = 0; index < nShapes; index++)
    {
        m_pCurShape = pDoc->GetShape(index);
        m_pCurShape->Draw(pDC);
    }
}
```

Once you've finished with **OnDraw()**, you can compile and run the program. Try using different brushes and pens. Choose different colors. Save your drawings to disk, and reopen them. Use the print and print-preview options. As you can see, the MiniSketch application is complete and full-featured. Finally!

Well, more or less.

For instance, when you open a new document, or read a document from a file, the display doesn't immediately update itself. You can fix that by adding a call to **UpdateAllViews(NULL)** at the end of the **CMSDoc::OnNewDocument()** and **CMSDoc::Serialize()** functions. However, printing and print-preview have a more serious problem. Sure, they work, but Figure 16.8 shows a drawing image as it appears on screen and the same drawing as it appears in the print-preview window.

Obviously "What-You-See-Is-What-You-Get" (WYSIWYG) applies to MiniSketch only if you think that printed output should appear at a fraction of its on-screen size. Most of us prefer a closer match between the video display and the printed output.

Fortunately, Windows makes that easy, if not immediately obvious. Get ready to explore the fascinating world of Windows Mapping Modes.

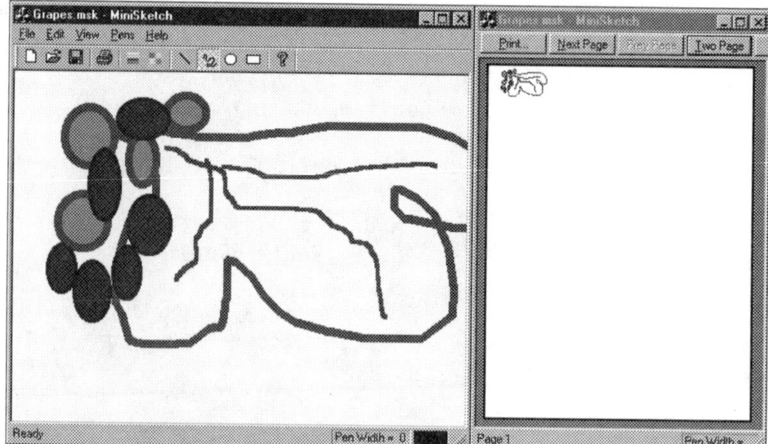

Figure 16.8
A drawing displayed in the MiniSketch using standard display and print-preview.

Alternative Views: Mapping Modes

One of the goals of Windows was device independence. Programmers shouldn't have to worry about whether the user's screen can display 640×480 or 1600×1280. Programmers shouldn't care whether output is going to a 300 dpi ink-jet printer or a 4,800 dpi film recorder. Programmers shouldn't need to worry about output devices *at all.*

Of course, as you've just seen, that device independence isn't automatic or built-in. Obviously, if you use the commands

```
dc.MoveTo(100, 100);
dc.LineTo(400, 400);
```

you'll get wildly different results on a film recorder (where the line will extend a little less than one-tenth of an inch) and an ink-jet (where it will extend just under an inch and a half.) How can GDI let your program work in both these environments, without requiring you to write specific code for each device? The answer lies in the difference between *device coordinates* and *logical coordinates*.

Device coordinates are the pixel or dot sizes used by a particular device. When you refer to a 640×480 dpi display, you're using device coordinates. Most Windows functions—the mouse-reporting functions, such as **WM_LBUTTONDOWN**, for example—work with device coordinates.

The output functions of the **CDC** class are exceptions to this rule. Device-context functions work with logical coordinates—so, when you write **dc.MoveTo(100, 100)**, you aren't necessarily moving 100 pixels down and 100 pixels over from the upper-left corner of your screen or printer. Instead, you're moving 100 positive logical units in the *x* direction and 100 positive logical units in the *y* direction. Exactly how large is a logical unit? It varies: The size of a logical unit is determined by the current mapping mode. So, to understand logical units, you must first understand mapping modes.

The MM_TEXT Mapping Mode

Windows has eight mapping modes, which are listed in Table 16.1. The simplest of these—**MM_TEXT**—is also the default. If you don't do anything, your DC mapping mode is **MM_TEXT**.

The **MM_TEXT** mapping mode has two defining characteristics. First, the unit of measure is the same as that used for device units—thus, when you move 100 logical units in **MM_TEXT** mode, you also move 100 device units, or pixels. That explains why the MiniSketch printed output is so much smaller than the on-screen output: The printer has many more pixels per inch than the screen.

Table 16.1 The GDI logical mapping modes.

Mapping Mode	Unit Of Measure	Sign Of The Y Axis
MM_TEXT	Pixel	Positive
MM_LOMETRIC	0.1 mm	Negative
MM_HIMETRIC	0.01 mm	Negative
MM_LOENGLISH	0.01 inch	Negative
MM_HIENGLISH	0.001 inch	Negative
MM_TWIPS	1/1440 inch	Negative
MM_ISOTROPIC	Variable	Variable
MM_ANISOTROPIC	Variable	Variable

Second, in **MM_TEXT** mode, the coordinates are interpreted similarly to the way English text is read on the printed page. If you think of a page as made up of rows and columns (as in a spreadsheet, perhaps) then the lower-numbered rows are at the top, and the lower-numbered columns are at the left. In **MM_TEXT**, as you increase the *x* value, the coordinate moves toward the right; as you increase the *y* value, the coordinate moves toward the bottom of the screen.

Beyond ease of use, the **MM_TEXT** mapping mode doesn't have much to recommend it.

The Device-Independent Mapping Modes

Two of the remaining mapping modes—**MM_ISOTROPIC** and **MM_ANISOTROPIC**—let you completely define the mapping between logical and physical coordinates, as well as the positive and negative orientation of each axis. The **MM_ISOTROPIC** mode requires you to use the same mapping characteristics for both the *x* and *y* axes. The **MM_ANISOTROPIC** mode lets you define each axis independently.

However, for most applications, you'll use one of the fixed-scale mapping modes. Each fixed-scale mapping mode has a predetermined scaling factor. If you draw a line 100 units long in **MM_LOENGLISH**, for instance, your line will appear about one inch long on screen as well as on your printer—whether your printer is 300 dpi or 3000. The other fixed-scale mapping modes work similarly. A 100-unit line in **MM_HIENGLISH** will be 0.1 of an inch long, in **MM_LOMETRIC** it will appear 10 millimeters long, in **MM_HIMETRIC** it will be 1 millimeter long, and in **MM_TWIPS** it will be just about .07 of an inch long.

By default, all mapping modes assign the coordinates (0,0) to the upper-left corner of the screen or printed page. You can change this, if you like, by using the DC functions **SetViewportOrg()** and **SetWindowOrg()**. **SetWindowOrg()** assigns a logical point to the upper-left corner of the display, while **SetViewportOrg()** maps the logical point (0,0) to the device coordinates passed as its arguments.

It's easy to get these confused, so here's a simple example. Suppose you want the upper-left corner of your display to be the logical point (100,100), rather than (0,0). Just call **SetWindowOrg(100,100)**. On the other hand, what if you want the logical point (0,0) to be 100 device units in from the left and down from the top? You'll call **SetViewportOrg(100,100)**.

All of the fixed-scale mapping modes use *Cartesian coordinates* to describe the *x* and *y* axes. Even if you aren't familiar with the term, you probably learned the Cartesian system when you studied graphs in algebra. In a Cartesian grid, the *x* and *y* axes cross at the point (0,0). The *x* axis increases as it moves right, and the *y* axis increases as it moves up.

Of course, that's different than **MM_TEXT** mode, where the *y* axis increases as it moves down. In **MM_TEXT** mode, the call **dc.Rectangle(0, 0, 100, 100)** draws a rectangle in the upper-left corner of the screen. Issuing the same call in any of the fixed-scale mapping modes results in no apparent output—the rectangle would appear above the (0,0) point, not below it. To draw the same rectangle in one of the fixed-scale mapping modes, you need to write **dc.Rectangle(0, 0, 100, -100)**. Note carefully the negative value of the last argument.

Mapping Comes To MiniSketch

Adding a mapping mode to the MiniSketch program doesn't involve a lot of code, but there are some details that can trip the unwary. The biggest of those details involves the need to translate between device and logical coordinates. You must translate because, except for the **CDC** output functions and a few isolated GDI functions, most Windows coordinates are expressed as device coordinates.

This isn't an insurmountable problem—Windows provides the **DPtoLP()** function to translate between device points and logical points, as well as the **LPtoDP()** function to translate in the reverse. The only question to answer is, where to perform the translation? Do you save device coordinates in your document class, and then translate them to logical coordinates on output?

Or, do you store logical coordinates in your document and translate the mouse-clicks and mouse-movements into logical coordinates? You can do it either way, but in this case, let's do the latter.

You'll convert MiniSketch to use the **MM_LOENGLISH** mapping mode, in which every unit represents 0.01 inch, both on screen and when printed. Follow these steps:

1. Open the MiniSketch project and locate the **CMSView** class in the ClassView window. Right-click to bring up the context menu, then choose Add Virtual Function. In the New Virtual Override dialog box, locate the **OnPrepareDC()** function. Click on Add And Edit when your screen looks like that shown in Figure 16.9.
2. Add the highlighted code shown in Listing 16.8 to the **OnPrepareDC()** function written by ClassWizard. The **SetMapMode()** function sets the mapping mode to **MM_LOENGLISH**. MFC automatically calls the **OnPrepareDC()** function before it calls **OnDraw()**.

Listing 16.8 The CMSView::OnPrepareDC() function.

```
void CMSView::OnPrepareDC(CDC* pDC, CPrintInfo* pInfo)
{
    // TODO: Add your specialized code here and/or call
    // the base class
    pDC->SetMapMode(MM_LOENGLISH);
    CView::OnPrepareDC(pDC, pInfo);
}
```

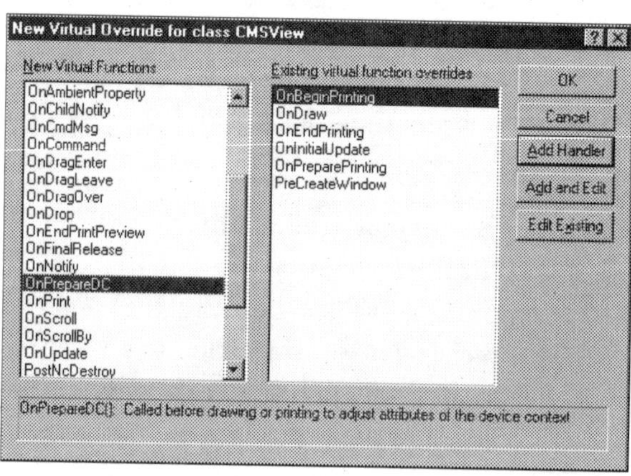

Figure 16.9 Adding the **OnPrepareDC()** function.

3. Even though MFC automatically calls **OnPrepareDC()** before **OnDraw()**, MFC doesn't automatically call it before other functions in which the program draws to the DC, such as **OnMouseMove()**. To take care of those cases, you need to modify the mouse-handling functions. Start by adding the three lines shown in Listing 16.9 to the beginning of the **OnLButtonDown()** function. Calling **OnPrepareDC()** after creating the DC ensures you're using the **MM_LOENGLISH** mapping mode, and calling **DPtoLP()** ensures that the mouse coordinate stored in **point** is correctly translated to logical units before being used.

Listing 16.9 Changes to the CMSView::OnLButtonDown() function.

```
CClientDC dc(this);
OnPrepareDC(&dc);
dc.DPtoLP(&point);
```

4. You need to add similar lines to **OnMouseMove()** and on **OnLButtonUp()**. In each function, add the two lines shown in Listing 16.10 immediately following the line that creates the DC. The changes from previous code are highlighted.

Listing 16.10 Changes to the OnMouseMove() and OnLButtonUp() functions.

```
CClientDC dc(this);
OnPrepareDC(&dc);
dc.DPtoLP(&point);
```

After you've made these changes, compile and run your program. What you see on screen is now, roughly, the same size as what appears on your printer. (Actually, what appears on screen is slightly larger than what appears on your printer. A 100-unit line in **MM_LOENGLISH** mapping mode will be exactly 1 inch long on your printer, but on screen it will be closer to 1.5 inches. This is the case because screen displays use a logical inch optimized to improve the legibility of the standard 10- to 12-point text.)

Scrolling Views

MiniSketch still has one small drawback. Unless you have a very high-resolution display, you can't create drawings that fill an entire 8.5×11-inch page when printed. The usual solution for this problem is to add scrolling, which allows you to create a very large document, yet view only a portion of it at any given time.

Adding scrolling to MiniSketch is even easier than changing the mapping mode from **MM_TEXT** to **MM_LOENGLISH**. If you'd planned ahead, you could even have told AppWizard to incorporate scrolling automatically by using the **CScrollView** class as the base class for **CMSView**, instead of **CView**.

Fortunately, adding scrolling is simple even after the fact. Just follow these directions:

1. Locate the **CMSView** class in the ClassView window and double-click on it to open the class definition. Change the class header so that **CView** is replaced by **CScrollView**, like this:

   ```
   class CMSView : public CScrollView
   ```

2. Open the **CMSView** implementation file—MiniSketchView.cpp—and locate the following two lines near the beginning of the file:

   ```
   IMPLEMENT_DYNCREATE(CMSView, CView)
   BEGIN_MESSAGE_MAP(CMSView, CView)
   ```

   Replace both instances of **CView** with **CScrollView**, as shown here:

   ```
   IMPLEMENT_DYNCREATE(CMSView, CScrollView)
   BEGIN_MESSAGE_MAP(CMSView, CScrollView)
   ```

3. Modify the **OnPrepareDC()** function by commenting out the call to **SetMapMode()** and changing **CView::OnPrepareDC()** to **CScrollView::OnPrepareDC()**. The finished function should look like that shown in Listing 16.11.

Listing 16.11 The revised OnPrepareDC() function.

```
void CMSView::OnPrepareDC(CDC* pDC, CPrintInfo* pInfo)
{
    // TODO: Add your specialized code here and/or call
```

```
    // the base class
    // pDC->SetMapMode(MM_LOENGLISH);
    CScrollView::OnPrepareDC(pDC, pInfo);
}
```

4. In a program that uses **CScrollView**, you don't set the mapping mode in the **OnPrepareDC()** function. Instead, you set it in the **OnInitialUpdate()** function, by calling **SetScrollSizes()**. **SetScrollSizes()** takes several arguments, but you need to provide only the first two. The first is the logical mapping mode—you'll use **MM_LOENGLISH**, as before. The second is the document size, using logical coordinates. You want to allow 8.5×11-inch pages, so you'll use the dimensions 800×1050. In **MM__LOENGLISH**, where 1 unit equals 0.01 inch, those dimensions will yield a width of 8 inches and a height of 10.5 inches, allowing a .25-inch margin on each side and a .5-inch margin on the top and bottom. The finished **OnInitialUpdate()** function is shown in Listing 16.12, with the new line highlighted.

Listing 16.12 The OnInitalUpdate() function to set the scrolling view.

```
void CMSView::OnInitialUpdate()
{
    InitPen();
    SetScrollSizes(MM_LOENGLISH, CSize(800, 1050));
}
```

After you compile and run the program, you'll be able to draw inside an 8.5×11-inch "virtual" canvas, accessing the different regions by using the scroll bars. As you can see in Figure 16.10, the printed output does, indeed, fill the whole screen.

If your application requires single-page output, like MiniSketch does, the combination of **CScrollView**, the device-independent mapping modes, and **OnDraw()** can meet all of your printing needs. However, for more complex printing requirements, you'll want to know a little more about how MFC handles printing. We'll explain that in the next section.

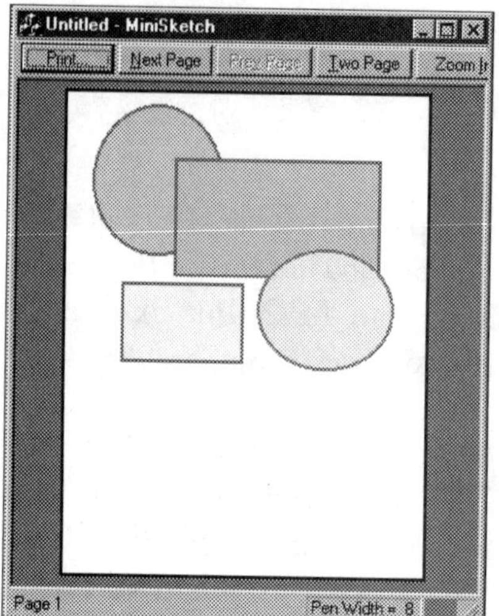

Figure 16.10
Print-preview using the scrolling view.

Printing And Print Preview

To be perfectly honest; printing under Windows is plain old nasty. It's not just a matter of getting a device context for your printer and then making some GDI calls. You have to worry about pagination, spooling, writing callback abort procedures, enabling and disabling the main window, and a whole lot of should-never-see-the-light-of-day details. MFC gives the process a facelift, but it still isn't what you'd call attractive.

The first thing you must understand about printing under Windows—whether you're using the API or MFC—is that printing is *page-oriented.* A page of output begins when you call the **StartPage()** function and ends when you call **EndPage()**. (The MFC application framework does this for you.) Between the calls, you use the same GDI functions used for screen output to compose your printed page. So, how does Windows know when to stop printing one page and move on to the next? Simple: It doesn't. Composing each page, telling the printer to move on, and arranging the text or graphics to print in the correct places on the correct page are all your jobs. As we said, it's not a pretty picture.

Under MFC, you don't have to worry about the low-level printing functions like **StartPage()** or **EndPage()**. Nor do you need to get a DC for your printer, spooling, or handling interruption. Basically, all you must do is override one or more of the virtual functions shown in Figure 16.11. Let's take a look at those now.

The MFC Printing Functions

When you use AppWizard to add print and print-preview support to your application, AppWizard overrides three of the five MFC printing functions. Here are the five functions, and their intended purposes:

- ***OnPreparePrinting()***—Displays the printer dialog box and gives you an opportunity to paginate your document.
- ***OnBeginPrinting()***—Called just before printing commences, this function gives you the opportunity to allocate the fonts, pens, and brushes that you want to use throughout your document, rather than re-creating them for each page.
- ***OnPrepareDC()***—Called just before drawing commences, this function moves the printing origin, so that you can print selected pages multiple times.
- ***OnPrint()***—Performs normal printing. If you don't override this function, the default version simply calls **OnDraw()**. If you override it, you can call **OnDraw()**, but add your own headers, footers, and page numbers.

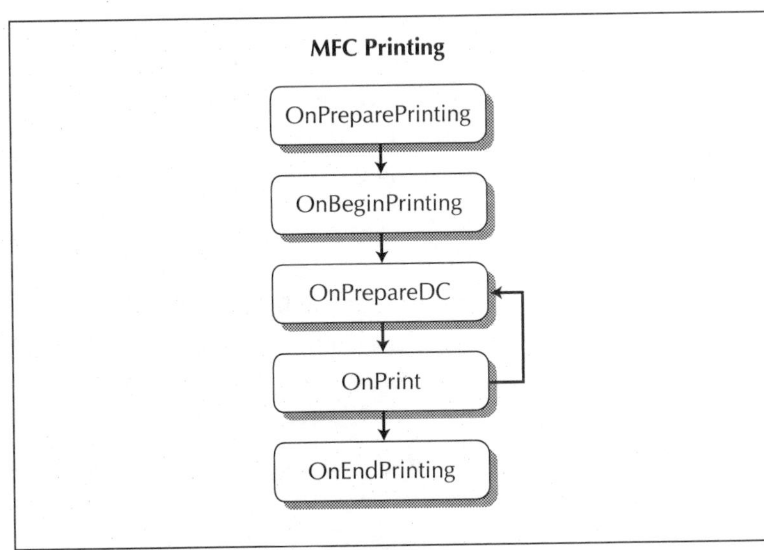

Figure 16.11
The MFC printing functions.

- ***OnEndPrinting()***—Called after the last page is printed, this function gives you a place to release any brushes, pens, or other resources you allocated in **OnBeginPrinting()**.

The OnPreparePrinting() Member Function

AppWizard automatically overrides the **OnPreparePrinting()** function, which calls the **DoPreparePrinting()** function. Here's the default implementation of **OnPreparePrinting()**:

```
BOOL CMSView::OnPreparePrinting(CPrintInfo *pInfo)
{
    return DoPreparePrinting(pInfo);
}
```

The **DoPreparePrinting()** function displays the Print dialog box and returns a printer DC that you can use. Canceling the Print dialog box or causing **OnPreparePrinting()** to return **FALSE** aborts printing.

When the framework calls **OnPreparePrinting()**—and when you call **DoPreparePrinting()**—a pointer to a **CPrintInfo** object is passed as an argument. This same **CPrintInfo** object follows the print job throughout its life-cycle. You can use it to determine the status of your print job—for instance, which page is currently printing.

OnPreparePrinting() primarily serves to provide you the means to tell the printing process how many pages should be printed. You do that by calling the **CPrintInfo** functions **SetMinPage()** and **SetMaxPage()**. After you set the minimum and maximum page, the print-preview mechanism uses the numbers in the Print dialog box to decide how many pages to display.

So how do you tell how many pages your document contains? That's the nasty part. There's no easy or automatic way. For instance, if you have a text file, you must calculate how many lines fit on a page (given your current font) and determine how many lines are in the file. Then, you can calculate how many pages you'll need. It's no easy task. If you don't know (as you often don't), you can use a flag in the **CPrintInfo** object to tell the printing framework whether to keep going to the next page.

The OnBeginPrinting() Member Function

If successful, the **DoPreparePrinting()** function creates a printer DC and a pointer to that DC, along with a pointer to the **CPrintInfo** object seen earlier, which is passed to the **OnBeginPrinting()** function.

OnBeginPrinting() and its companion function, **OnEndPrinting()**, allow you to allocate resources that will be used throughout the entire print job. They also give you a second chance to set the number of pages your document will require.

In the **OnPreparePrinting()** function, you don't have access to the DC used by the printer, so you don't know how large the printable area is. You can use the printer DC in **OnBeginPrinting()** to get that information, by calling the **GetDeviceCaps()** function with the arguments **VERTRES** or **HORZRES**. The **GetDeviceCaps()** function, as its name suggests, returns the printing area size in pixels. You'll have to convert those numbers to logical coordinates to calculate how many pages your printout will need.

The OnPrepareDC() Member Function

You've seen the **OnPrepareDC()** member function, which MFC automatically calls before each page of output, whether the output is going to the printer or to the screen. The **OnPrepareDC()** function is passed the same two arguments as **OnBeginPrinting()**: a pointer to the DC and a pointer to a **CPrintInfo** object. If **OnPrepareDC()** is called before screen output, then the **CPrintInfo** object is **NULL**. You could test for that condition, but it's easier to simply call the **CDC** member function **IsPrinting()**, which tells you whether output is going to the screen or printer.

By now, you're probably wondering why you should care if output is going to the screen or printer. After all, aren't you using the same printing code for each? Well, yes and no. If output is going to the printer, **OnPrepareDC()**—as well as the subsequent **OnPrint()** function—will be called once for each page of output. It's your responsibility in **OnPrepareDC()** to move the printing origin, and possibly set a clipping rectangle, so that the correct page is printed. To do this, you'll query the **CPrintInfo** object to retrieve its member variable **m_nCurPage**, and then adjust things accordingly.

The OnPrint() Member Function

The last of the printing framework functions we're going to discuss is **OnPrint()**. The default version of **OnPrint()** simply calls **OnDraw()**. If you don't need any headers, footers, or page numbers—and if you set your viewport and clipping region within **OnPrepareDC()**—you have no reason to override **OnPrint()**.

On the other hand, if you want to install a clipping region, or print headers and footers, then this is where you do it. AppWizard doesn't override this function for you—you'll have to use ClassWizard.

A MiniSketch Example

Well, there you have it. Simple and straightforward, huh? No, well, we guess not. But we do have time for a short example. That won't make things any prettier, but it may turn up the lights a bit.

In the last iteration of MiniSketch, you used **CScrollView** to create a document that was 8 inches wide by 10.5 inches tall. Let's take MiniSketch and make the document size *potentially* 24 inches wide and 21 inches tall. You could print the maximum size document: more than six pages, three wide and two high. However, you'll calculate the actual size of the document, then paginate accordingly.

Just follow these instructions, and you'll be on your way:

1. Creating the large, virtual document is the easy part. Open the MiniSketch project and locate the **CMSView::OnInitialUpdate()** function in the ClassView window. Double-click to open the Source Code editor, then change the arguments passed to the **SetScrollSizes()** function as shown in Listing 16.13.

Listing 16.13 The CMSView::OnInitialUpdate() function.

```
void CMSView::OnInitialUpdate()
{
    InitPen();
    SetScrollSizes(MM_LOENGLISH, CSize(2400, 2100));
}
```

2. To support pagination, you must determine how many of the six possible pages in your virtual canvas contain figures. If only the first page has drawing on it, you don't want to print all six pages. Add to the **CMSDoc** class a member function called **GetDocDimensions()**. This function, which is shown in Listing 16.14, steps through each **Shape** stored in the document and retrieves the *x*,*y* coordinates furthest from the document origin. It does so by calling each **Shape** object's **GetMaxSize()** function. As you retrieve the information from each **Shape**, you update the variables **x** and **y**. (When updating **y**, you use the **min()** function, because in the **MM_LOENGLISH** mapping mode, the *y* axis is negative.)

Listing 16.14 The CMSDoc::GetDocDimensions() function.

```
CSize CMSDoc::GetDocDimensions()
{
    int x = 0, y = 0;
    CSize temp;
    int nItems = m_data.GetSize();
    for (int i = 0; i < nItems; i++)
    {
        temp = m_data[i]->GetMaxSize();
        x = max(x, temp.cx);
        y = min(y, temp.cy);
    }
    return CSize(x,y);
}
```

3. For each of the classes in the **Shape** hierarchy, add a **virtual GetMaxSize()** function that returns a **CSize**. For the **Shape** and **FilledShape** classes, return a **CSize** initialized to (0,0). For the other classes, you need to find the furthest extent of the **Shape**. Listing 16.15 shows the code for the **Line** class's **GetMaxSize()** function. You can retrieve the others from the CD-ROM.

Listing 16.15 The Line::GetMaxSize() member function.

```
CSize Line::GetMaxSize()
{
    int x = max(m_LineEnd.x, m_LineStart.x);
    int y = min(m_LineEnd.y, m_LineStart.y);
    return CSize(x,y);
}
```

4. After you retrieved the document size, you'll need to use that to calculate how many pages to print. To store that information, add four new **private int** member variables to the **CMSView** class:

   - **m_PageWidth**—Stores the width of the printable page, retrieved from the printer DC.
   - **m_PageHeight**—Stores the height of the printable page, retrieved from the printer DC.
   - **m_nPagesWide**—Stores the number of pages in a single row.
   - **m_nPagesHigh**—Stores the number or rows to print.

5. Calculate how many pages to print. You can't do that in **OnPreparePrinting()**, because you don't yet have a printer DC. So, you'll have to calculate and set the page count in **OnBeginPrinting()**.

   Calculating the page count is fairly straightforward. First, find out how big each page is. (This will vary depending on what printer is in use and what paper and orientation are selected.) You retrieve page-size information by calling **CDC::GetDeviceCaps()** and store it in the **m_PageWidth** and **m_PageHeight** variables. Once you know each page size, you need to find out how big the document is. You calculate that by calling **GetDocDimensions()**, the **CMSDoc** class function you just wrote. Because **GetDeviceCaps()** returns device coordinates, and your document is stored in logical coordinates, you must convert the device coordinates to logical coordinates. Then, you can calculate the number of rows and columns you'll need, using **m_nPagesWide** and **m_nPagesHigh**. Finally, you call the **CPrintInfo** function **SetMaxpage()** to tell the printing mechanism how many pages to print.

Add the code for **OnBeginPrinting()**, which is shown in Listing 16.16.

Listing 16.16 The OnBeginPrinting() member function.

```
void CMSView::OnBeginPrinting(CDC* pDC, CPrintInfo*
  pInfo)
{
    m_PageWidth  = pDC->GetDeviceCaps(HORZRES);
    m_PageHeight = pDC->GetDeviceCaps(VERTRES);

    CSize docSize = GetDocument()->GetDocDimensions();
    CSize pageSize(m_PageWidth, m_PageHeight);
    pDC->SetMapMode(MM_LOENGLISH);
    pDC->DPtoLP(&pageSize);
    m_PageWidth  = pageSize.cx;
    m_PageHeight = -pageSize.cy;

    m_nPagesWide = 1 + docSize.cx / m_PageWidth;
    m_nPagesHigh = 1 + ((docSize.cy) / m_PageHeight);

    pInfo->SetMaxPage(m_nPagesWide * m_nPagesHigh);
}
```

6. Now that you've told the MFC printing mechanism how many pages to print, it will call the **OnPrepareDC()** and **OnPrint()** functions once for each page. Each time MFC calls one of these functions, the **CPrintInfo** member variable **m_nCurPage** will be incremented. You use this variable to determine which page to print, and call **SetWindowOrg()** to adjust the printing origin before calling **OnDraw()**. (Note that this isn't a particularly efficient way to print. Each time **OnDraw()** is called, it prints the entire document, but only the portion in the current printing DC clipping rectangle is visible.)

   To override the **OnPrint()** virtual function, locate the **CMSView** class in the ClassView window. Right-click to bring up the context menu, then choose Add Virtual Function. Add the changes shown in Listing 16.17, and you're done.

Listing 16.17 The OnPrint() member function.

```
void CMSView::OnPrint(CDC* pDC, CPrintInfo* pInfo)
{
    int row = ((pInfo->m_nCurPage - 1) / m_nPagesWide);
    int col = ((pInfo->m_nCurPage - 1) % m_nPagesWide);
```

```
    pDC->SetWindowOrg(col * m_PageWidth, row *
      m_PageHeight);

    OnDraw(pDC);
}
```

Well, that's it. Compile and run your program, and you can draw on a virtual canvas 24 inches wide and 21 inches tall. Your printing will be tiled across as many pages as needed to render your drawing. If you change the size of the paper or the orientation, the number of pages required will change—but the printout will still work. Figure 16.12 shows the famous neo-realistic drawing "The Eggs," as rendered in the MiniSketch print-preview window. Supposedly, this drawing was originally created for director Alfred Hitchcock for inclusion in the final scene of *The Birds*. Hitchcock reportedly found the idea too macabre, and the drawing languished on the back lot, occasionally providing inspiration for such films as *Aliens* and, more recently, *Godzilla*. Of course, this is all rumor—the original rendering of "The Eggs" is actually located on your CD-ROM. You can use it to try the printing capabilities of MiniSketch.

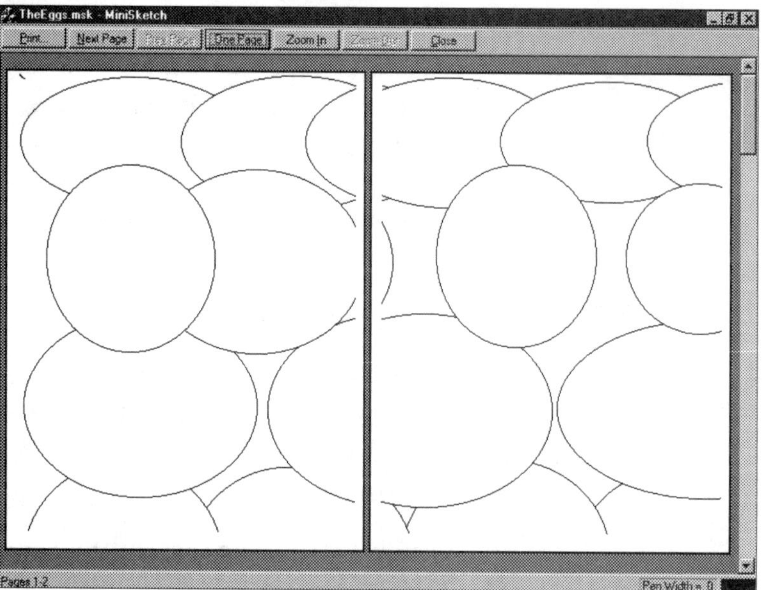

Figure 16.12
"The Eggs" rendered in the MiniSketch print-preview window.

Now For Something Completely Different

There are still plenty of improvements you could make to MiniSketch. You could use styled brushes and styled pens, add zooming to the scrolling by working with the mapping modes, or incorporate different dialog boxes. You could add a zillion features—and we hope you do.

For us, however, it's time to bid MiniSketch goodbye. In the next chapter, we'll return to dialog boxes and take a look at some of the rest of the Windows common controls. You'll learn how to work with text and use the rich edit control. From there, we'll move on to ActiveX controls, databases, and the Internet.

Are you coming?

Chapter 17

Software Reuse: Building An Application From Components

If a field as young as computer programming can lay claim to any "hoary old chestnuts," then the oldest and hoariest is undoubtedly, "Don't reinvent the wheel." For years, the homage paid to this tradition was mostly lip-service—every new generation of programmers seemed hand-crafted another variation on the same set of components. Visual Basic changed all that.

The year was 1990. Professional Windows programmers ridiculed the idea of writing Windows programs in Basic, "the toy language that comes free with your PC." As they saw it, if God had wanted Windows programs written in Basic, He wouldn't have written the Windows API in C. Moreover, Visual Basic programmers didn't program in the usual sense. Instead, they dragged little icons—called components—around the screen and used dialog boxes to set component properties. Only as a last resort did they write code, and then only small snippets. Professional Windows programmers were unimpressed.

However, two groups of people *were* impressed. First, the many business-applications programmers who used products like dBASE, Clipper, or Business Basic to create vertical-market applications—those that automated video stores and dental offices—saw Visual Basic as their ticket into the world of Windows. Second, a few professional Windows programmers saw Visual Basic not as a competitor, but as an opportunity to supply specialized software components to the growing number of Visual Basic programmers.

It's hard to say which came first, business programmers switching to Visual Basic or software developers offering new and improved components—but the combination proved explosive. If Visual Basic hadn't somehow tapped a deep reservoir of pent-up demand for easy-to-use Windows programming tools, the huge market in

Visual Basic components would never have developed. And, if Visual Basic hadn't been an open system that enabled companies to write components that worked within it, programmers wouldn't have adopted it.

Perhaps we can say, in the end, that it was neither the mass of programmers nor the wealth of third-party support that made Visual Basic a success: It was the component.

The first Visual Basic controls—called *VBX controls* because of their file extension—were 16-bit controls designed to work in Windows 3.1. VBX controls were tightly tied to Visual Basic. As the Microsoft operating systems moved from 16-bits to 32-bits with Windows NT, Windows 95, and Windows 98, Microsoft changed the underlying architecture of Visual Basic controls. Visual Basic's VBX controls were replaced by OCX controls, which are now known as ActiveX controls. VBX controls and ActiveX controls differ in many ways, but the primary difference is that ActiveX controls aren't tied to Visual Basic. Based on Microsoft's Component Object Model (COM), ActiveX controls now exist across the range of Windows software-development tools.

In Chapter 1, we told you that Visual C++ isn't a point-and-click visual programming environment like Visual Basic or Delphi. Perhaps we should have said that Visual C++ isn't *only* a visual programming environment, because it has been strongly influenced by the component revolution that Visual Basic spawned.

In this chapter and the next, we're going to look at how Visual C++ supports component software development. Visual C++ provides a much richer environment than Visual Basic, because it supports so many kinds of development. This is doubly true in the area of component software development, where Visual C++ supports two kinds of components:

- *Visual* C++ *components*—Let you easily add software features such as splash screens, progress bars, and property sheets to your MFC projects.
- *ActiveX controls*—Work in Visual C++ much as they do in Visual Basic.

We'll start our tour by looking at the Visual C++ Gallery.

Exploring The Gallery

The Visual C++ component and control Gallery provides a place for you to store components for future use. However, in the Gallery, the word *component* has a broader meaning than we've discussed so far. A Gallery component can be an ActiveX control, but it can also be a Wizard, a graphics file, a dialog template, or a class you've written for reuse. You can also purchase custom Visual C++ source-code components specifically designed to work with the Gallery.

When you first install Visual C++, the Gallery includes two folders: one containing links to all the ActiveX controls registered on your system and another containing links to Visual C++ components. When you add your own classes or resources, you create new folders to store them in. The links stored in the ActiveX and Visual C++ Components folders are dynamically re-created each time you open the component Gallery.

We'll start our tour of the Gallery by looking at some of the components in the Visual C++ Components folder. To help out, we're going to bring the venerable MiniSketch program back for an encore. After we retire MiniSketch for good, we'll start a new project called WordZilla, using the rich edit control.

Enhancing MiniSketch

The Visual C++ Gallery contains components designed to be added to existing components. In that sense, the Gallery resembles ClassWizard more than AppWizard. On the other hand, the Gallery is definitely a "one-way" tool. For example, after you use the Gallery to add a splash panel to your project, you can't go back and remove it by using the Gallery tools. Instead, you must search through the project and revise it manually. In this sense, the Gallery resembles AppWizard more than ClassWizard.

You'll see what we mean as you add a new capability to the MiniSketch program: dynamic splitter windows. Splitter bars allow the user to open a second, third, and fourth view onto a single document. Because they are all the same kind of view, you don't need to add new application code.

Are you ready? Let's split. (A big groan is not only permitted here, it's nearly mandatory.)

Adding Splitter Bars

As you know, the MiniSketch program is an SDI (Single Document Interface) program, so it can open only one document at a time. The MiniSketch program contains a single document and a single view. Splitter bars allow you to automatically add additional views to an SDI program.

You can easily add splitter-bar support to your program using the Visual C++ splitter component contained in the Gallery. Here's how:

1. Open the MiniSketch project. When you retrieve a component from the Gallery, it will automatically be added to the current project. If you don't have a project open, you can't open the component Gallery.
2. Finding the component Gallery is no easy task—it's hidden several levels deep in the main menu. Open the Gallery by choosing Project|Add To Project|Components And Controls from the main menu. Figure 17.1 shows the menu selection.
3. When you open the components and controls Gallery, the initial dialog box takes a little while to appear—Visual C++ is looking through your system and creating a list of registered ActiveX and Visual C++ components. When it finds a component, it stores a link to it in the Gallery's Registered ActiveX Controls folder or Visual C++ Controls folder. When it finishes, the Components And Controls Gallery dialog box opens, as shown in Figure 17.2.

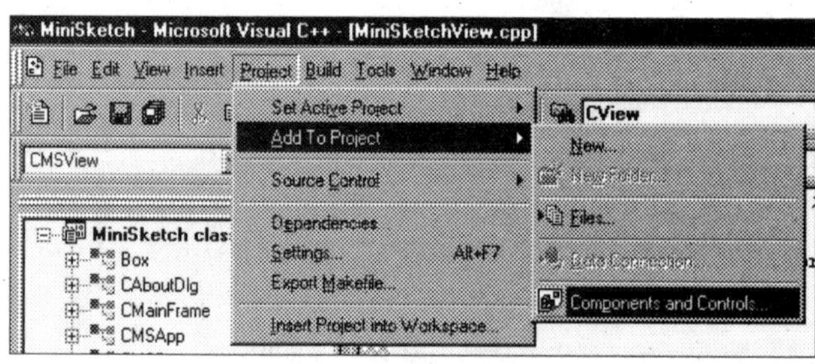

Figure 17.1
Opening the Visual C++ component Gallery.

4. Double-click on the Visual C++ Components folder to display the list of components you can automatically add to your project. Use the scroll bars to locate the splitter bar component, as you can see in Figure 17.3.

5. Once you've looked through online help, return to the Components And Controls Gallery dialog box and click on Insert. When you do so, Visual C++ runs the add-in program that writes the code to add splitter bars to your project. However, before the program can write the code, it needs some information from you. Figure 17.5 shows the Splitter Bar

▶Tip

Getting Information About Components

Notice that as you select a component, a prompt appears in the bottom panel of the Component And Control Gallery dialog box, describing the selected item. Online help is also available for most components. If the More Info button is active, you can click on it to display the online help. Figure 17.4 shows the online help for the splitter bar component.

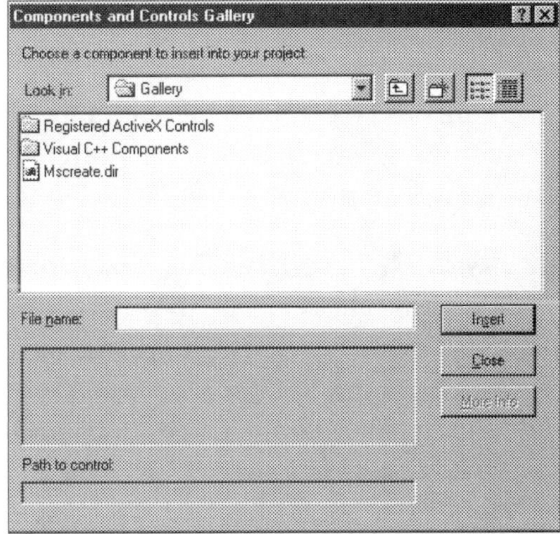

Figure 17.2
The Components And Controls Gallery dialog box.

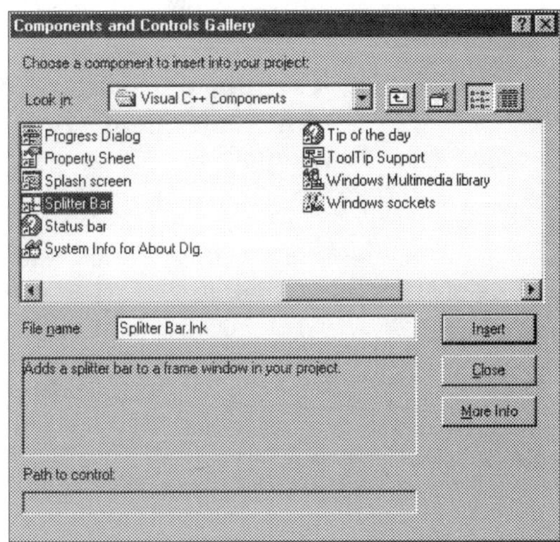

Figure 17.3
Selecting the splitter bar Visual C++ component from the component Gallery.

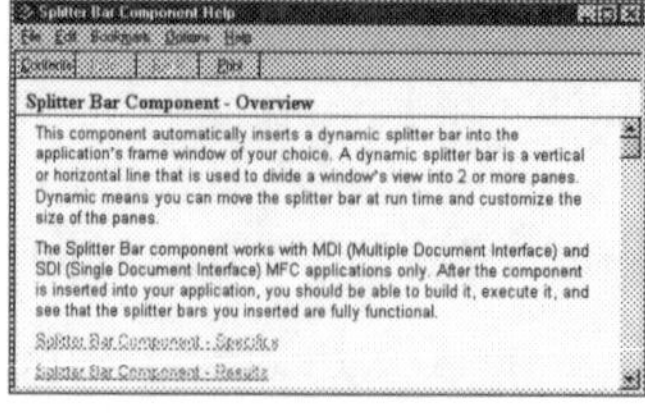

Figure 17.4
Accessing online help for the splitter bar component.

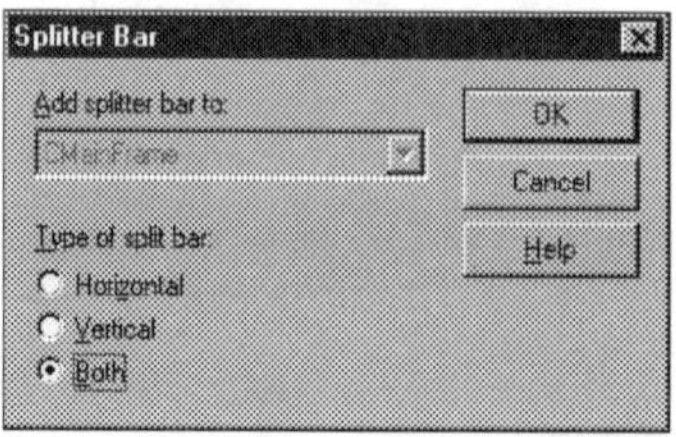

Figure 17.5
The Splitter Bar dialog box.

dialog box. As you can see, you can choose to add a vertical splitter, a horizontal splitter, or both. Select the Both radio button.

Inside The Splitter Bar Component

When you click on Insert, Visual C++ does two things. First, it adds a new protected member variable name **m_wndSplitter** to the **CMainFrame** class. This variable is a **CSplitterWnd** object. Next, it overrides the **CMainFrame::OnCreateClient()** function, which is called whenever the client area—that is, the view—of the main window is created. The **OnCreateClient()** code added by component Gallery creates the **CSplitterWnd** object, so that it overlays the **CMSView** window, as you can see in Listing 17.1.

Listing 17.1 Creating a CSplitterWnd in the OnCreateClient() function.

```
BOOL CMainFrame::OnCreateClient(LPCREATESTRUCT lpcs,
   CCreateContext* pContext)
{
    // CG: The following block was added by the Splitter
    // Bar component.
    {
        // TODO: adjust number of rows, cols
        if (!m_wndSplitter.Create(this,
                   2, 2,
          // TODO: adjust the minimum pane size
          CSize(10, 10),
                   pContext))
```

```
        {
            TRACE0("Failed to create splitter bar ");
            return FALSE;    // failed to create
        }
        return TRUE;
    }
}
```

Although the **TODO** code makes it appear that you can change the number of rows and columns allowed, you really have only three choices: one column and two rows, two columns and one row, or two rows and two columns. Every other combination is illegal for the kind of dynamic splitter windows the component Gallery creates. The Gallery bases the initial values on the radio button you check in the Splitter Bar dialog box.

Cleaning Up

Once the Gallery finishes adding code to your project, you can close the Gallery dialog box and recompile your program without problems. Unfortunately, if you try to run the program at this point, it will crash. This reveals a problem—not with the Gallery code, but with some assumptions you made when you added the pen-color swatch to the main window status bar.

If you look through the **CMSView** class and find the **InitPen()** function, you'll see that it contains the following line:

```
((CMainFrame *)(GetParent())->SetPenColor(m_PenColor);
```

This code worked fine before you added the splitter bars—but afterward, the parent of the **CMSView** object is no longer the **CMainFrame** window, but the **CSplitterWnd** object added in **OnCreateClient()**. To fix this problem, change the call from **GetParent()** to **AfxGetMainWnd()**—which will always work in an SDI application—like this:

```
((CMainFrame *)AfxGetMainWnd())->SetPenColor(m_PenColor);
```

Once you've cleaned that up, run the MiniSketch program. Notice the small bars that appear immediately above the vertical scrollbar and to the left of the horizontal scrollbar: Those are the splitter bars. Also notice the change in the mouse cursor when you move it over the splitter bar. If you drag the bar when the

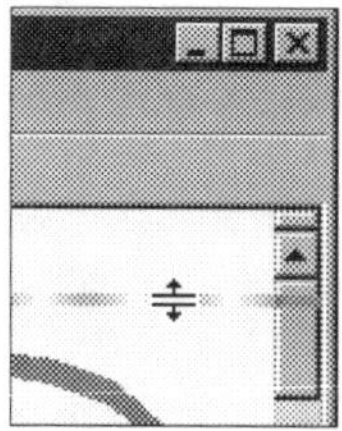

Figure 17.6
Using a splitter bar.

cursor changes shape, as you can see in Figure 17.6, you can divide your view into vertical and horizontal panes.

By dragging both the horizontal and the vertical splitter bars, you can create four semi-independent screen regions on one document. These regions are merely semi-independent because you don't have separate vertical and horizontal scrollbars for each of the four panes—the vertically aligned panes share the same horizontal scrollbar, and the horizontally aligned panes share the same vertical scrollbar. Figure 17.7 shows splitters at work in our drawing, "The Eggs." Each of the four panes in the figure shows one of the document's four corners.

Take your time exploring the Visual C++ components. On this book's CD-ROM, you'll find another version of MiniSketch that adds both a splash screen and system information with the help of the component Gallery. For now, though, let's look at something new.

Just When You Thought It Was Safe: WordZilla

We'll come back to the Visual C++ component Gallery in the next chapter. But now, let's look at another kind of component reuse: applications built using the Windows common controls.

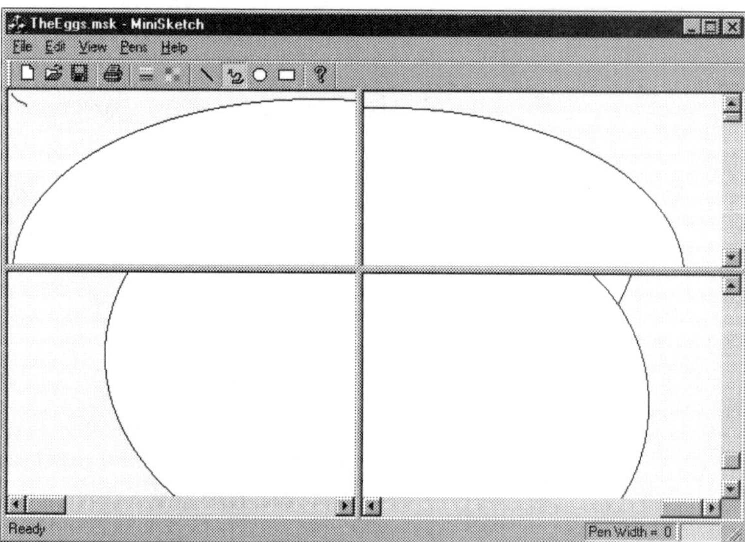

Figure 17.7
Splitting "The Eggs" four ways.

Actually, you've already seen an application that extends one of the built-in controls: The NotePod program was based on the **CEditView** class, which is based on the **CEdit** component, which is simply a wrapper around the Windows edit control.

Applications based on Windows controls differ from other DocView applications in one important way: Rather than storing their document as an external data structure, each control acts as a self-contained unit, storing its own data. The document class still exists in a component-based DocView application, but its role changes from storing data to transferring it.

Let's create a multifile text editor like NotePod, just as you did in Chapter 1. However, instead of using NotePod's **CEditView** class, you'll use the **CRichEditView** class, so your documents can use different text styles and fonts.

Because your program will be—more or less—a knock-off of WordPad, perhaps we should follow the precedent we set in Chapter 1, and call it WordPod. The NotePod program added a few new features to the basic Notepad program, so the name NotePod was appropriate. However, our new editor won't merely use the rich edit control—it will act as an experimental test-bed, while we explore the world of ActiveX controls. In all honesty, our program will very likely turn out to be a huge, hideous mutant. Only one name seems fitting under the circumstances: WordZilla.

Building WordZilla: A RichEditView Project

To build the new project, create a new MFC AppWizard project and name it WordZilla. Then, follow these instructions:

1. In the MFC AppWizard-Step1 window, accept the default MDI project with DocView support.
2. In the MFC AppWizard-Step 2 window, also accept the default: no database support.
3. In the Step 3 window, select the Container radio button, click on Yes for compound file support, and be sure the ActiveX

Controls checkbox is selected. When your screen looks like Figure 17.8, click on Next. (If you don't add compound-document container support to your application, you can't use the rich edit control.)

4. In the Step 4 window, accept the defaults, but click on Advanced to open the Advanced Options dialog box. Select the Document Template Strings tab and enter "wzi" for the File Extension. Change the Document Type Name to "WZilla" and expand all the other instances of "WordZi" to "WordZilla". When the dialog box looks like that shown in Figure 17.9, click on Close to return to the Step 4 window. Then, click on Next.
5. Accept the default values in the MFC AppWizard-Step 5 window.
6. In the Step 6 window, change the View Base Class to **CRichEditView**, using the drop-down list. Shorten each of the class names from "WordZilla" to "WZ". Your classes should be **CWZView**, **CWZDoc**, **CWZApp**, and **CWZCntrItem**. Leave the **CMainFrame** and **CChildFrame** classes as they are. Your screen should look like Figure 17.10. When it does, click on Finish, and then on OK.

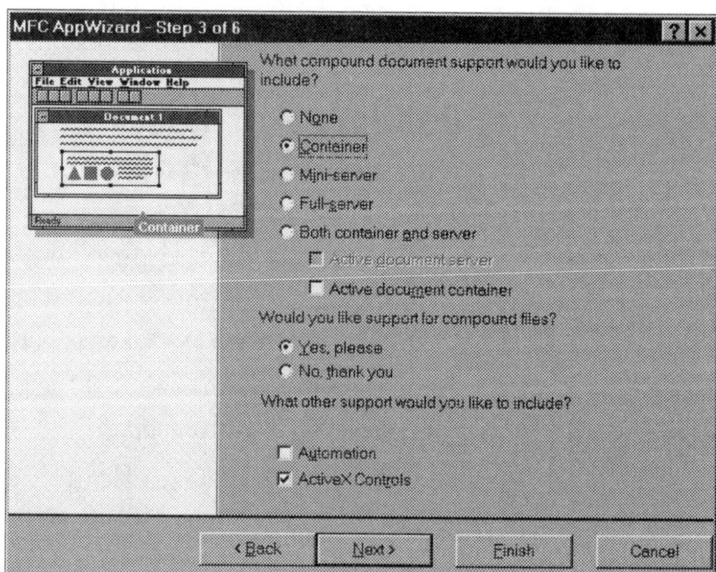

Figure 17.8
The MFC AppWizard-Step 3 window while building WordZilla.

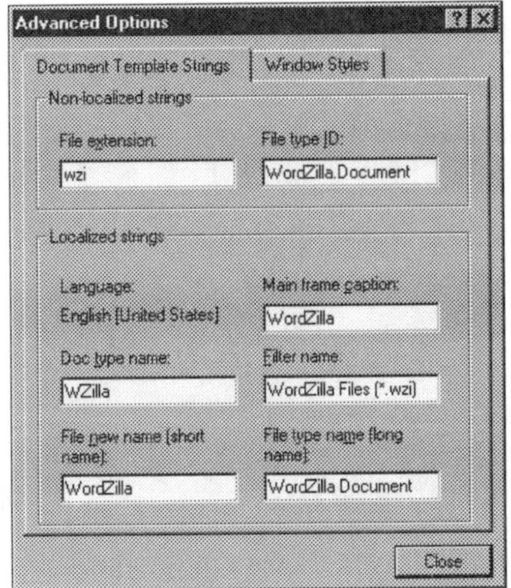

Figure 17.9
The WordZilla Advanced Options dialog box.

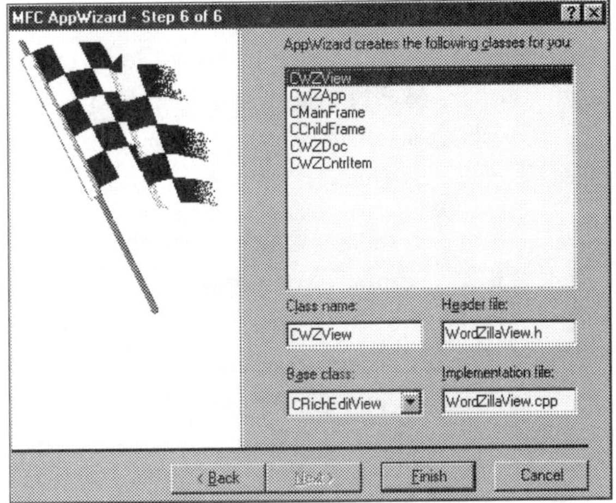

Figure 17.10
The MFC AppWizard-Step 6 window.

Exploring WordZilla

Once AppWizard has generated the code for WordZilla, go ahead and build it, then take it for a spin. As you can see in Figure 17.11, the program works almost exactly like NotePod.

You can open multiple files, each in its own child window. Print and print-preview both work, as do the Window menu and the Edit menu. And, you can save and retrieve documents. All the functionality contained in NotePod is already hooked up. However, despite the outward appearances, WordZilla is very different from NotePod.

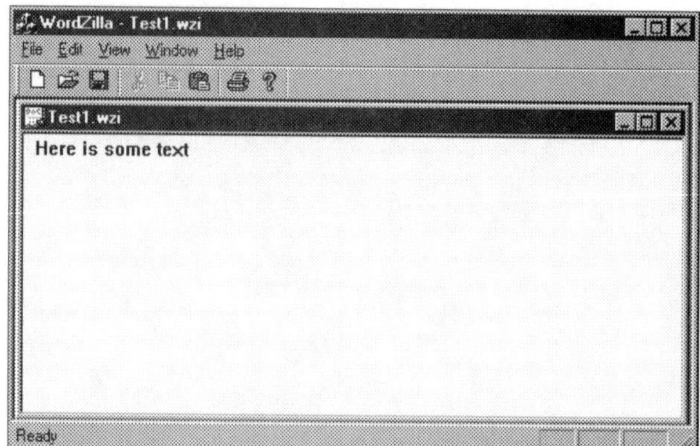

Figure 17.11
Running the WordZilla program.

One difference has to do with the document type. NotePod—and the **CEdit** control it's based on—manage plain ASCII text. The rich edit control that forms the basis for WordZilla works with a special kind of document called Rich Text Format (RTF). If you open an RTF file in a regular text editor, as shown in Figure 17.12, you'll see that the document structure is much more complex than that used by NotePod.

You can see a second difference between NotePod and WordZilla if you compare the contents of the Edit menu. While NotePod had only Cut, Copy, Paste, and Undo menu entries, the WordZilla menu includes several other sections—Select All and Paste Special commands, along with Find and Replace menu entries that you've already enabled. If you look below them, you'll see the real key to the power of WordZilla: the Insert New Object menu selection, shown in Figure 17.13.

In actuality, the rich edit control doesn't hold just formatted text: It can contain any kind of embedded COM or OLE object. You can embed Excel spreadsheets or Paint pictures, for instance. When you choose the Insert New Object command, WordZilla

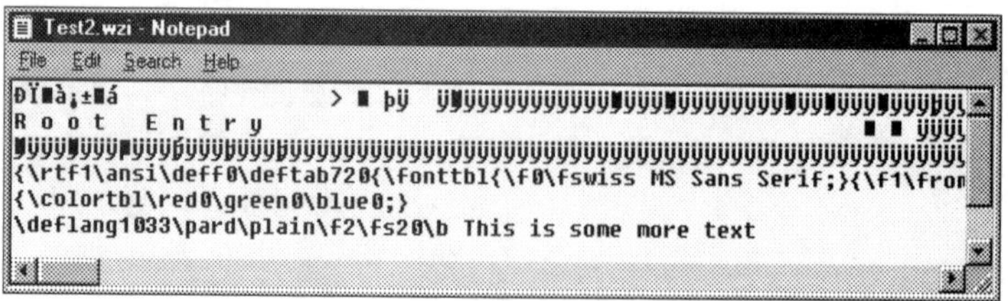

Figure 17.12
Looking at a WZI file using Notepad.

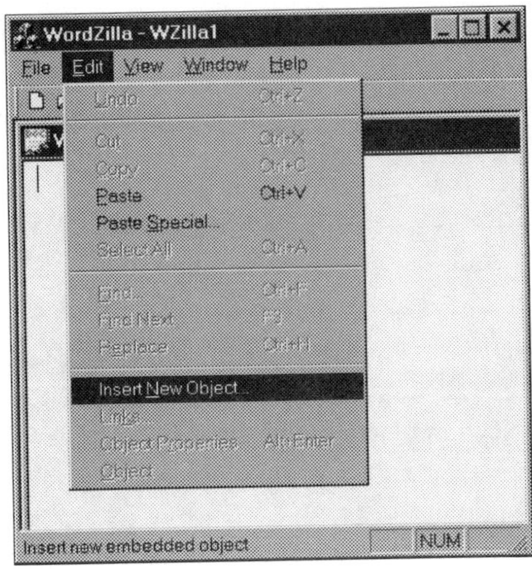

Figure 17.13
WordZilla's Insert New Object menu selection.

searches the Registry for applications that have registered their documents. The application lets you scroll through a list of available document types in the Insert Object dialog box—you can see this in Figure 17.14, where we've selected a Visio 5 document. The Insert Object dialog box allows you to create a new Visio object, right in your WordZilla document. You can also import an existing file by selecting the Create From File radio button.

When you click on OK, the Insert Object dialog box launches the selected application within the program you're using. For

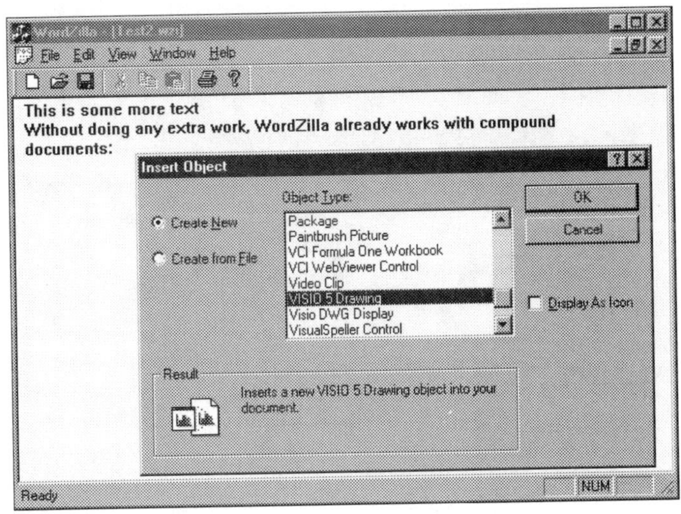

Figure 17.14
Inserting a new Visio 5 drawing into a WordZilla document.

instance, if you insert a new Visio document, Visio starts running in WordZilla. The Visio menus temporarily replace the normal WordZilla menus until you're finished editing the object, as you can see in Figure 17.15.

Once you're finished editing the COM object, it becomes part of your document. When you save your document, the object is saved as part of it. You can print the object and otherwise treat it as if it were native to your application. If you double-click on the embedded object, its application is launched—you can edit the object in place. As Figure 17.16 shows, you can format, size, move, and align the embedded object, without ever involving its application.

Improving WordZilla

Despite its impressive capabilities—especially its ability to host embedded objects—WordZilla still suffers from several shortcomings. It uses the same goofy system font that NotePod used. Although you can cut, copy, and paste, there's no way to change the attributes of the characters you select. Furthermore, you can't change the alignment of paragraphs.

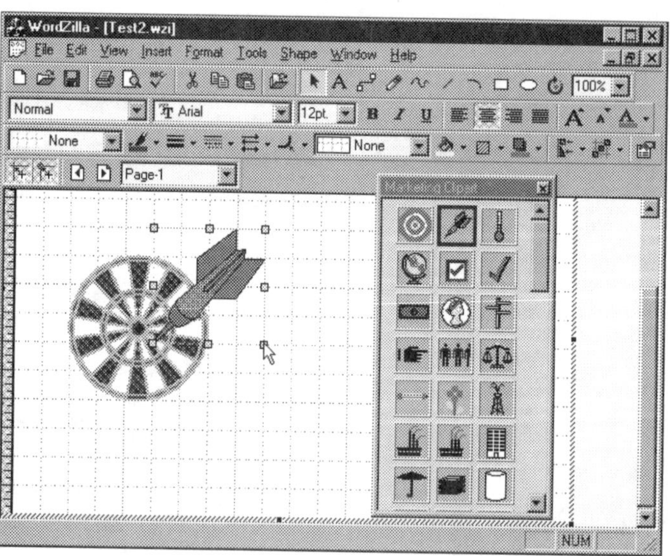

Figure 17.15
Editing a Visio object inside the WordZilla application.

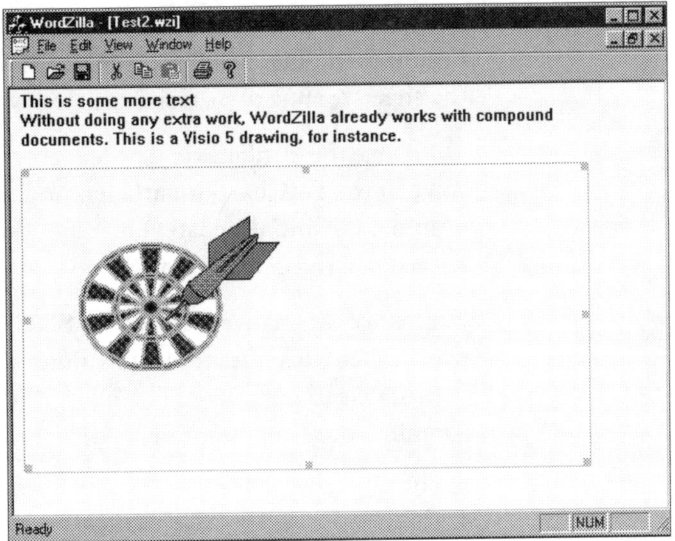

Figure 17.16
Formatting a Visio 5 document in a WordZilla application.

Before you add new components, let's make these improvements to WordZilla:

- Install a more attractive default font, such as Arial.
- Add the ability to choose a new font.
- Let the user change the character attributes—bold, italic, and underline—used by a text selection.
- Allow paragraph-alignment selections: left, center, or right.
- Add the ability to apply a bullet to a paragraph.

This seems like an awful lot of work—and, truthfully, it would be, if you had to build the changes from scratch. But, because you're using a pre-built component—the rich edit control—99 percent of the work has been done for you. All you have to do is hook up some identifiers and write a little code.

Let's address these items, one by one.

Installing A Default Font

Writing a program based on **CRichEditView** is straightforward, but you must address a lot of details. Unfortunately, the documentation doesn't make readily apparent which information is important and which is less important. All the information you need is there, but most of it is hiding in plain sight, obscured by the sheer volume of material.

To change the attributes of new text entered into a **CRichEditView**, you call the **SetCharFormat()** method. If you call this method from the **OnInitialUpdate()** method, the text characteristics you set become the defaults.

Because of the many text options, **SetCharFormat()**—along with many other **CRichTextView** functions—takes a **CHARFORMAT** structure as its argument. The **CHARFORMAT** structure contains three important fields that you should set:

- **cbSize**—Sets the size of the structure in bytes. You must set this.
- **dwMask**—Tells which of the remaining fields are valid. For instance, if **dwMask** has the value **CFM_FACE**, then the **szFaceName** field is valid. If **dwMask** doesn't have the value **CFM_FACE**, the **SetCharFormat()** function will ignore the value of **szFaceName**. You can specify several values in **dwMask** by **OR**ing them together.
- **dwEffects**—Sets text characteristics, such as bold, italic, and underlined. The value in **dwEffects** enables or disables each characteristic. For instance, if **dwMask** has the value **CFM_BOLD**—indicating that the bold value stored in **dwEffects** is valid—you can set **dwEffects** to **CFE_BOLD** to enable the bold characteristic, or set it to zero to turn off bold.

For WordZilla, you'll use a 10-point Arial font. You'll set **dwMask** to the value **CFM_FACE|CFM_SIZE|CFM_BOLD**, so it will pay attention to the name of the font, the size, and the bold characteristic you pass in. You can safely ignore everything else, except **cbSize**. Add the code shown in Listing 17.2 to the **CWZView::OnInitalUpdate()** method, to make each new document start out using 10-point Arial.

Listing 17.2 The CWZView::OnInitialUpdate() function.

```
void CWZView::OnInitialUpdate()
{
    CRichEditView::OnInitialUpdate();
```

```
    // Set the initial font
    CHARFORMAT cfm;
    cfm.cbSize = sizeof(cfm);
    cfm.dwMask = CFM_FACE | CFM_SIZE | CFM_BOLD;
    cfm.dwEffects = 0;  // Turn off Bold
    cfm.yHeight = 200;  // Size in TWIPs (1/20)
    strcpy(cfm.szFaceName,"Arial");
    SetCharFormat(cfm);

    // Set the printing margins (720 twips = 1/2 inch).
    SetMargins(720, 720, 720, 720);
}
```

Notice that **dwEffects** field is set to zero to disable the bold characteristic, which is turned on by default. This setting is necessary only because the default document you've inherited has bold turned on. The **yHeight** field is set to 200 TWIPs. Each TWIP is 1/20 of a point, so this value sets the font size to 10 points.

Selecting A New Font

Setting a default font wasn't so difficult, but allowing users to select any font they like is even easier. The necessary functionality already exists within **CRichEditView**—all you have to do is hook it up. Let's add a toolbar button to let the user change the font or font color. Here's how the button will work.

When the user clicks on the select-font button, the Windows common Font dialog box will appear, letting the user select any installed font. If the user selects a block of text and then selects a new font, only the selected block of text will be formatted in the new type style. The same goes for the select-font-color button. If, on the other hand, no text is selected, the newly selected font will be applied to new characters.

Here are the steps to follow:

1. Open the WordZilla project and select the ResourceView window. Open the Toolbar folder and double-click on **IDR_MAINFRAME** to open the Toolbar Editor.
2. In the Toolbar Editor, drag the new button so that it rests between the Print button and the Paste button. Move it

slightly away from either button, so the Toolbar Editor puts it in its own group.

3. Using the Text tool on the Graphics toolbar, select 12-point bold Times New Roman, then add a capital "A" to your button and center it on the face.
4. Double-click in the left Toolbar Editor pane to open the Toolbar Button Properties dialog box. Locate and select the **ID_FORMAT_FONT** resource ID in the drop-down list. If you like, you can also add a prompt. Your screen should look like Figure 17.17.

Once you've added the button, compile and run your program. The resource ID **ID_FORMAT_FONT** has already been pre-identified with the **OnFormatFont()** function defined in the **CRichEditView** class, so you don't need to use ClassWizard to hook it up. Add some text, and then select it. As you can see, you can use any font, in any style, without difficulty.

However, the Font dialog box offers a limited color selection. Let's add a button that opens the Windows common Color dialog box. Follow these steps:

1. Open the **IDR_MAINFRAME** toolbar in the Toolbar Editor and add another button to the right of the **ID_FORMAT_FONT** button.
2. Using the Graphics Text tool, add a red, 12-point Times New Roman "A" to this button.

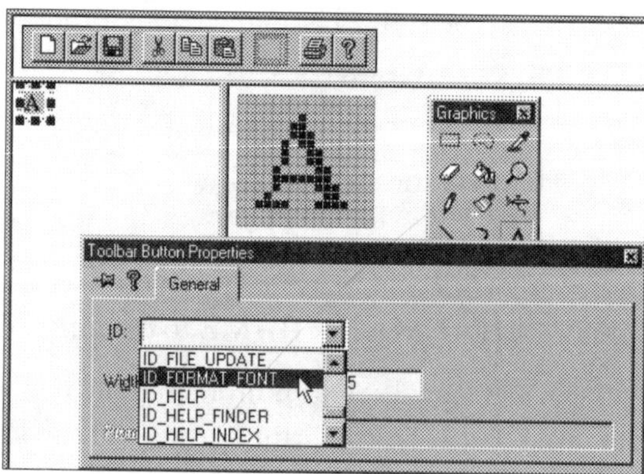

Figure 17.17
Adding the **ID_FORMAT_FONT** toolbar button.

3. Open the Toolbar Button Properties dialog box and enter the new resource ID "**ID_COLOR_PICK**". Set the prompt string to "Change the current font color\nFont Color". Your screen should look like that shown in Figure 17.18.
4. Open ClassWizard and choose the Message Maps property sheet tab. Select **CWZView** from the Class Name drop-down list. Locate **ID_COLOR_PICK** in the Object IDs list and select it. Select Command from the Messages list, and click on Add Function and then on Edit Code.
5. Add the code shown in Listing 17.3 to the **OnColorPick()** function written by ClassWizard.

Listing 17.3 The CWZView::OnColorPick() function.

```
void CWZView::OnColorPick()
{
  GetCharFormatSelection();
  CColorDialog dlg(m_charformat.crTextColor);
  if (dlg.DoModal() == IDOK)
  {
    m_charformat.dwMask = CFM_COLOR;
    m_charformat.dwEffects = NULL;
    m_charformat.crTextColor = dlg.GetColor();
    SetCharFormat(m_charformat);
  }
}
```

The **CRichEditView** class contains a **protected** member variable—**m_charformat**—that stores the current text attribute. This is a **CHARFORMAT** variable like the one you used to set the default

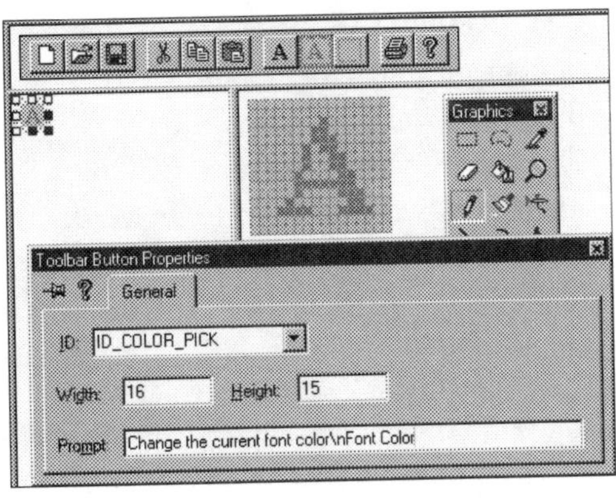

Figure 17.18 Adding the **ID_COLOR_PICK** toolbar button.

font in **OnInitialUpdate()**. To use the **m_charformat** variable, you first have to call **GetCharFormatSelection()**, which fills in each of its fields. The text color is stored in a field called **crTextColor**, which you can use to initialize a **CColorDialog** object, just as you did in previous chapters.

As before, you display the **CColorDialog** object by calling its **DoModal()** member function. If **DoModal()** returns **IDOK**, then the user selected a new color, and you update the current text-color attribute. To do that, you first set **m_charformat.dwMask** to **CFM_COLOR**, so the **SetCharFormat()** function knows that the **crTextColor** value is valid. You then set **dwEffects** to **NULL**, because you aren't applying bold or italic. Next, you retrieve the selected color from the **CColorDialog** object and store it in the **crTextColor** field. Finally, you pass the **m_charformat** structure back to **SetCharFormat()**.

Creating The Character-Attribute Buttons

Now that you can set any font, let's add character-attribute toolbar buttons, just like those on most word processors. You'll create three buttons: bold, italic, and underline. When the user clicks on a button, you'll add the corresponding characteristic to the current selection. Each toolbar button will act as a checkbox button—when you click on it, it will remain depressed until you click on it again.

In the last section, you learned how to use **GetChar FormatSelection()** and **SetCharFormat()**, along with the **CHARFORMAT** structure, to change individual attributes of a selection. However, for the attributes described in the **dwEffects** field, you can follow an even easier route by using the **OnCharEffects()** function. **OnCharEffects()** takes two arguments: the value to store in **dwMask** and the value to store in **dwEffects**. The **OnCharEffects()** function takes care of calling **GetCharFormatSelection()** and **SetCharFormat()** for you. The single call

```
OnCharEffects(CFM_BOLD | CFM_ITALIC, CFE_ITALIC);
```

makes the current selection italic and removes its bold attribute.

Here are the steps you need to follow to hook up the character-attribute buttons:

1. Open the **IDR_MAINFRAME** toolbar in the Toolbar Editor. Add three new buttons between the Print button and the Text Color button. Drag them slightly away from either side to form their own group.
2. Using the Type tool, select 10-point bold Times New Roman, then label the first button "B". Repeat this step and offset the second instance of the "B" to give the appearance of a single, fat letter. Open the Toolbar Button Properties dialog box and set the ID to **ID_CHAR_BOLD**. In the Prompt field, enter "Set the current selection to bold\nBold".
3. Change the Type tool to 10-point bold italic Times New Roman, then label the second button with an "I". Use the Pencil tool to enlarge the top and bottom serifs by one pixel in either direction. Give this button the ID **ID_CHAR_ITALIC** and set the Prompt field to read "Set the current selection to italic\nItalic".
4. Follow the same steps with the third button. Use 10-point bold Times New Roman to label the button with a 'U'. Using the Pencil tool, draw a single thin underline under the 'U'. Assign the button the ID **ID_CHAR_UNDERLINE** and change the Prompt to read "Set the current selection to underlined\nUnderlined". Figure 17.19 shows how the dialog box and your toolbar should look.

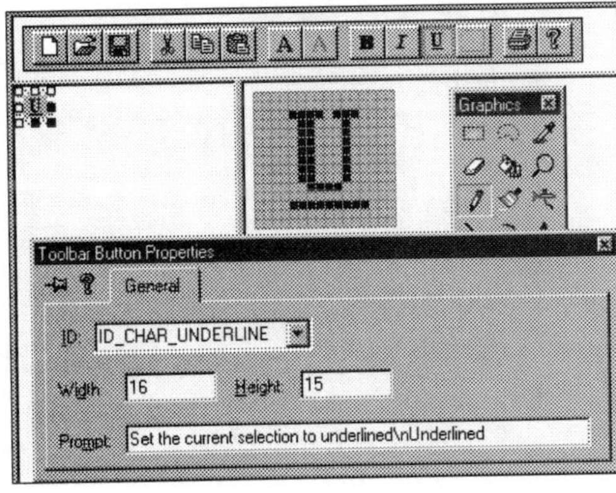

Figure 17.19
Adding the **ID_CHAR_UNDERLINE** button.

To hook up the character-attribute buttons, you need to write two functions for each button: a command handler and a command UI update handler. To do this quickly, open ClassWizard and be sure the **CWZView** class is selected in the Class Name drop-down list. Then, simply add **COMMAND** and **UPDATE_COMMAND_UI** handlers for each of the three buttons, without doing any editing.

Once you've done that, add the code from Table 17.1 to each of the functions. Recompile your program, and the character-attribute toolbar buttons will work.

Creating The Paragraph-Attribute Buttons

In the rich edit control, attributes such as text color and font apply to individual characters. If you wish, you can create a document in which every character is a different color. But, in addition to these character-level attributes, rich edit controls also support document-level and paragraph-level attributes. Margins, for instance, apply to an entire document—you can't set them separately for each paragraph or character.

For WordZilla, you'll add four paragraph-level toolbar buttons: three to control paragraph alignment—left, center, and right—and one to handle bullets. The alignment attributes are mutually exclusive, because a paragraph can't be both left- and right-aligned at the same time. However, you can combine the bullet attribute with any of the others.

Table 17.1 Character-attribute toolbar button handlers.

Function Name	Function Body
OnCharBold	OnCharEffect(CFM_BOLD, CFE_BOLD);
OnUpdateCharBold	OnUpdateCharEffect(pCmdUI, CFM_BOLD, CFE_BOLD);
OnCharItalic	OnCharEffect(CFM_ITALIC, CFE_ITALIC);
OnUpdateCharItalic	OnUpdateCharEffect(pCmdUI, CFM_ITALIC, CFE_ITALIC);
OnCharUnderline	OnCharEffect(CFM_UNDERLINE, CFE_UNDERLINE);
OnUpdateCharUnderline	OnUpdateCharEffect(pCmdUI, CFM_UNDERLINE, CFE_UNDERLINE);

Here are the instructions for adding the paragraph-attribute buttons:

1. Open the **IDR_MAINFRAME** toolbar resource in the Toolbar Editor. Add three new toolbar buttons in a group between the Underline button and the Print button.
2. Using the Pencil tool, draw a series of six horizontal lines spaced one pixel apart on the face of each button. Each button's lines should be of various lengths. On the first button, start each line in the third column, so the right margin appears ragged. On the second button, center each line, inset equidistant from both margins. On the last button, begin each line three pixels in from the right, so the left margin appears ragged. You can use a shortcut to make the last button—simply copy and paste the first button and then use Image|Flip Horizontal menu item. You can see the buttons illustrated in Figure 17.20.
3. From left to right, assign the buttons the resource IDs and prompt strings shown in Table 17.2.
4. Using ClassWizard (just as you did for the character attributes), add a **COMMAND** and an **UPDATE_COMMAND_UI** handler to each of the three buttons. Table 17.3 shows the handler names and their contents.

Adding The Bullet Paragraph Style

Adding the button and handler to apply the bullet paragraph style is even easier, because the **CRichEditView** class has already implemented the style. Here's all you have to do:

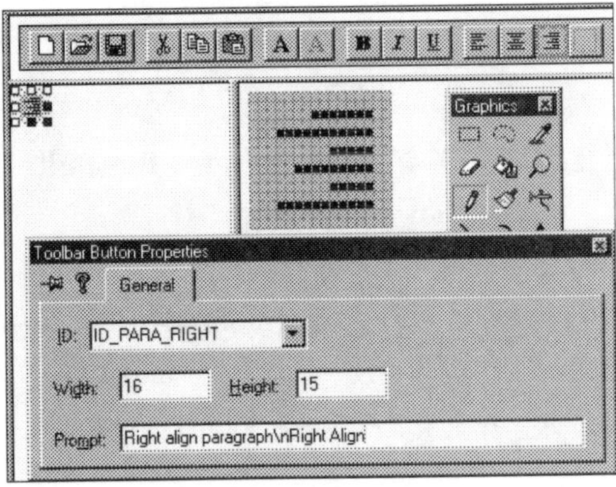

Figure 17.20
Adding the paragraph-attribute toolbar buttons.

Table 17.2 Paragraph-attribute toolbar button properties.

Resource ID	Prompt String
ID_PARA_LEFT	"Left align paragraph\nLeft Align"
ID_PARA_CENTER	"Center align paragraph\nCenter Align"
ID_PARA_RIGHT	"Right align paragraph\nRight Align"

Table 17.3 Paragraph-attribute toolbar button handlers.

Function Name	Function Body
OnParaLeft	OnParaAlign(PFA_LEFT);
OnUpdateParaLeft	OnUpdateParaAlign(pCmdUI, PFA_LEFT);
OnParaCenter	OnParaAlign(PFA_CENTER);
OnUpdateParaCenter	OnUpdateParaAlign(pCmdUI, PFA_CENTER);
OnParaRight	OnParaAlign(PFA_RIGHT);
OnUpdateParaRight	OnUpdateParaAlign(pCmdUI, PFA_RIGHT);

1. In the Toolbar Editor, add another button between the Print button and the Right Align button. Move it slightly so that it's in its own group, not attached to either the paragraph-alignment buttons or the Print button.
2. Draw a series of black crosses and dark-blue horizontal lines, as shown in Figure 17.21. These appear as bulleted lines of text when reduced to toolbar-button size.
3. Give the button the resource ID **ID_BULLET** and enter the Prompt "Set the current paragraph to bullet style\nBullets".
4. Using ClassWizard, add both a **COMMAND** and an **UPDATE_COMMAND_UI** handler, adding the code shown in Listing 17.4.

Listing 17.4 Handlers for the Bullet paragraph-attribute button.

```
void CWZView::OnBullet()
{
    CRichEditView::OnBullet();
}

void CWZView::OnUpdateBullet(CCmdUI* pCmdUI)
{
    CRichEditView::OnUpdateBullet(pCmdUI);
}
```

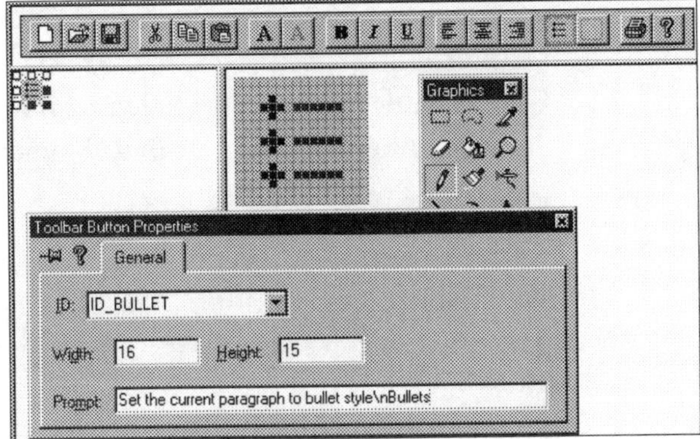

Figure 17.21
Drawing the Bullet paragraph-attribute toolbar button.

When you're finished, run WordZilla through the compiler and try it out. All the buttons should work, and you can apply different fonts and styles to characters, as well as to paragraphs. Figure 17.22 shows WordZilla using some of the available styles.

ActiveX At The Dialog Bar

In this chapter, you've seen three kinds of code reuse. First, the source-code components stored in the component Gallery's Visual C++ Components folder made short work of adding splitter bars to the MiniSketch program. Then, you extended one of the Windows common controls—in this case, the rich edit control—

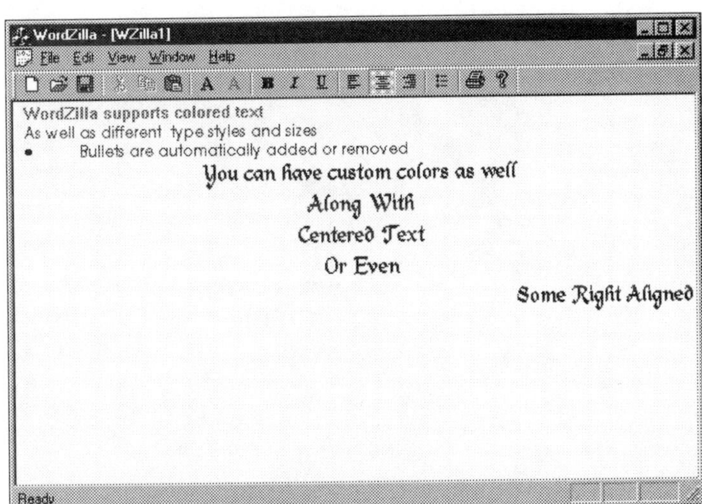

Figure 17.22
Running WordZilla with various character and paragraph styles.

to provide the basis for an entire program. Finally, you saw how pre-written components designed to do a specific job (such as **CFontDialog** and **CColorDialog**) can remove much of the drudgery inherent in performing common tasks.

But, the best is yet to come. Do you remember the thousands of ActiveX controls we mentioned at the beginning of the chapter? Well, ActiveX isn't just for Visual Basic anymore—Visual C++ programmers can now take advantage of the same component revolution.

In the next chapter, you'll pony up to WordZilla's dialog bar and try out some ActiveX.

Chapter 18

ActiveX And Component-Based Applications

Chances are, the last time you purchased a portable television or a coffee-maker, you didn't call an electrician to install it. Instead, you simply plugged it into one of the standard electrical outlets scattered around your house.

Standards make the mass-market appliance industry possible. If you want to manufacture a successful line of popcorn-poppers or hair-dryers, you had best be sure your product plugs into a standard outlet and runs on standard current. Most consumers won't install a special circuit, no matter how revolutionary your gadget.

Electrical appliances aren't the only standardized household item: Your bathroom fixtures have standard sizes and connections so you can easily replace a leaking faucet by using a standard part. Your telephone uses a standard connection, and so does your cable TV. In fact, you have such a powerful, yet inexpensive, computer on your desk due to standardization. Hardware component manufacturers can mass-produce high-performance subsystems like video or sound because the interfaces—the PCI bus, for instance—are standardized and well defined. And, computer manufacturers can easily assemble the finished product using these same standardized parts.

However, the software industry has developed in a different direction. A market (of sorts) has long existed for specialized function libraries in areas such as communications, numerical analysis, and graphics. However, until recently, most programmers have hand-crafted every line of every program. Without a standard way to connect software components, programmers had little use for them. When Visual Basic (VB) appeared, it convinced many people that such a "software bus" was a possibility.

However, VB components were too tightly tied to VB. In creating ActiveX—and the Component Object Model (COM) upon which it's based—Microsoft attempted to create a more universal and general way for components to connect and communicate with each other.

In this chapter, we'll look at components from the Visual C++ perspective. VB offers you one kind of form and one kind of component. In Visual C++, you can choose among several kinds of components:

- *Original Windows controls*—Such controls include buttons, checkboxes, and scroll bars.
- *Windows common controls*—These include controls first distributed with Windows 95, and those first distributed with Internet Explorer.
- *Source-code components*—Controls like these are available in the Visual C++ folder of the component Gallery.
- *ActiveX components*—Such controls operate in many environments.

In addition to a variety of components, Visual C++ also includes a wide range of containers that can host those components. You can use components in dialog-based applications, as you did in the first portion of this book. You can also use components in modal and modeless dialog boxes, as well as in property sheets and dialog bars. You can even use a special view class—**CFormView**—designed specifically to hold components.

To help you get a feel for how these options work, we're going to add a Paste Date menu command to WordZilla, solving one problem several ways. We'll introduce the new Windows common **CDateTimePicker** control and compare it to the ActiveX version of the same component. You'll also learn how to use these controls in modal and modeless dialog boxes. Seeing the same task done multiple ways should help you appreciate the pros and cons of each approach.

Ready? Let's go meet our date.

WordZilla Gets A Dialog Box

You're familiar with the Visual C++ Dialog Editor, because you used it extensively while building the dialog-based applications in Chapters 1 through 10. When you moved to a DocView application, you left the Dialog Editor behind, using it only to create toolbar buttons.

However, most DocView applications use dialog boxes for a wide range of tasks, from selecting document options in a property sheet to searching and replacing text. The simplest kind—and the one we'll begin with—is the *modal* dialog box.

A modal dialog box appears in response to a menu or toolbar command, allowing the user to perform an action or enter information. The user must close the dialog box before the program can continue. The Windows common Print and Color dialog boxes are good examples of modal dialog boxes—you *must* select a printer or pick a color before the show can go on.

The first version of WordZilla's new Paste Date command uses a modal dialog box that allows you to select a date using the **CDateTimePicker** component. If you close the dialog box by clicking on OK, the program pastes your selected date into the document. (Technically, the date *replaces* the current selection. If nothing is selected, then WordZilla simply inserts the date at the cursor location.) However, if you close the dialog by clicking on Cancel, your document doesn't change.

As usual, you'll put the program together first, and then come back and understand how it works.

Drawing The Select A Date Dialog Box

Three steps are necessary to add your new component to WordZilla:

- First, you'll use the Dialog Editor to design and place the components in your user interface.
- Next, you'll use ClassWizard to create a new C++ class, attached to the dialog resource created in the Dialog Editor. In

ClassWizard, you'll also create data-transfer variables to get the information into—and out of—the dialog box.

- Finally, you'll use the Menu Editor to add a new menu command, then have ClassWizard hook up the command to a **COMMAND** handler function. The handler function will display the dialog box; then, if you closed the dialog box by clicking on OK, the program will retrieve the new date from the dialog box and paste it into the current document.

Let's begin by drawing the new dialog box.

1. Open the WordZilla project and add a new dialog template by choosing Insert|Resource from the main menu. Select Dialog in the Resource Type list box, as you can see in Figure 18.1, and click on New.
2. Locate the Date Time Picker control on the Controls toolbar, as you can see in Figure 18.2. Drag and drop a date time picker near the top of the dialog box.
3. Open the Date Time Picker Properties dialog box by selecting the component and right-clicking, then choosing Properties

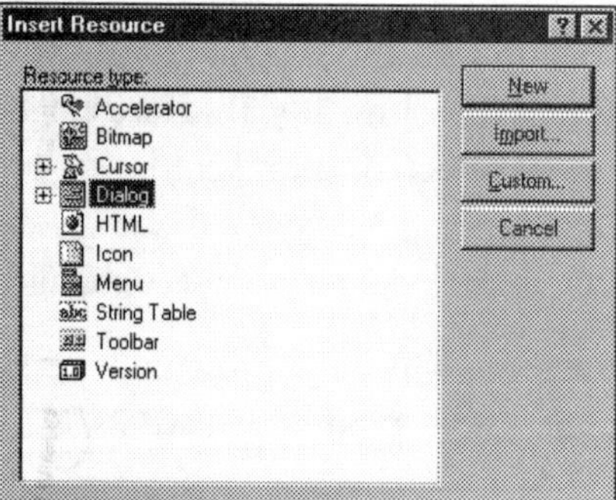

Figure 18.1
The New Resource dialog box.

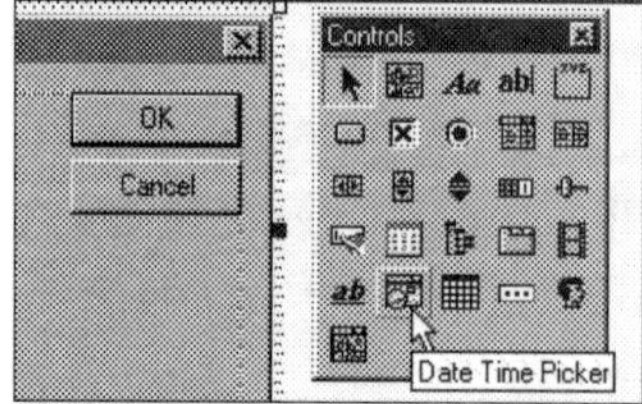

Figure 18.2
The Date Time Picker control.

from the context menu. (Alternatively, you can select the component and press Enter.) Select the Styles tab and choose Long Date from the Format drop-down combo box. Doing so causes the control to display the day of the week as well as the month, day, and year, as you can see in Figure 18.3.

4. Because the long-format date requires more space, make the dialog box wider and enlarge the control. Then, make it shorter to eliminate the wasted space at the bottom. Your finished layout should look like Figure 18.4.

5. In the Dialog Properties dialog box, enter the ID value "**IDD_PICK_DATE**" and the Caption "Select A Date", as shown in Figure 18.5.

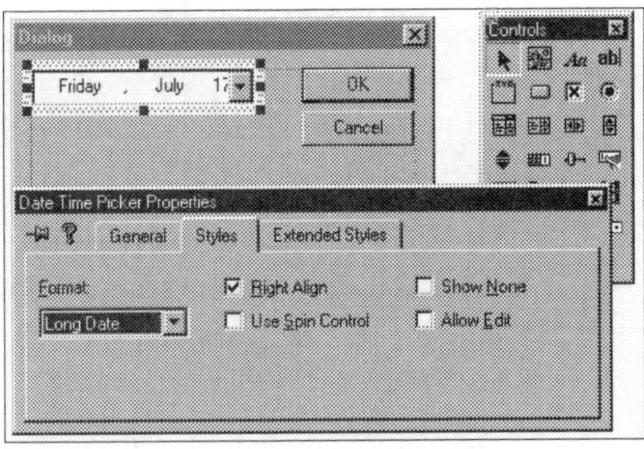

Figure 18.3
Changing the date time picker's **Format** property.

Figure 18.4
Changing the dialog-box dimensions.

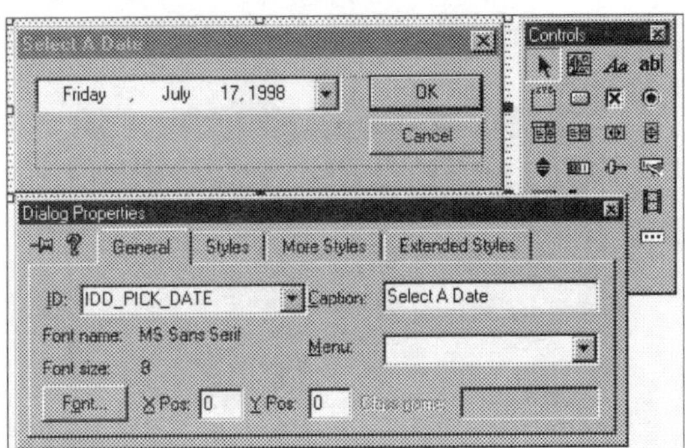

Figure 18.5
Changing the resource's ID and caption.

Creating The Dialog Box Class

To work with a dialog box, you generally create a new class, which contains public member variables you use to get information into and out of the dialog box. You derive the new class from **CDialog**.

If using **public** member variables makes you a little uneasy (as it should), you're free to make the variables **private** and write the necessary accessor and mutator functions. However, you must do this on your own, because the member variables created by ClassWizard are **public**.

Here are the steps to create the date-picker dialog box class:

1. Launch ClassWizard by pressing Ctrl+W or choosing View|ClassWizard from the main menu. ClassWizard will find that you've added a new dialog box, but that you haven't yet defined a class for it. As a result, ClassWizard will display the Adding A Class dialog box shown in Figure 18.6.
2. Select the Create A New Class radio button and click on OK. ClassWizard displays the New Class dialog box. Enter "**CPickDateDlg**" in the Name field and accept the default values for all the other fields. Click on OK to return to ClassWizard.

Figure 18.7 shows ClassWizard's Message Maps screen for the **CPickDateDlg** class. Notice that the class already has one virtual function: **DoDataExchange()**. This function automatically transfers information from components like the date time picker control to variables, so your program can access them.

Let's create some variables now, and you'll see how the dialog-box data transfer works. Here are the steps to follow:

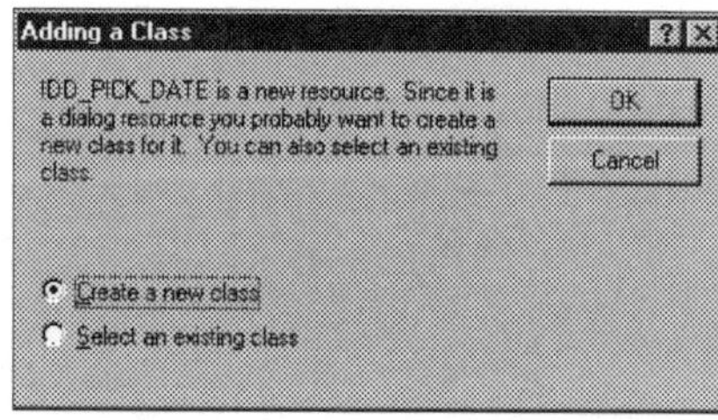

Figure 18.6
The Adding A Class dialog box for **IDD_PICK_DATE**.

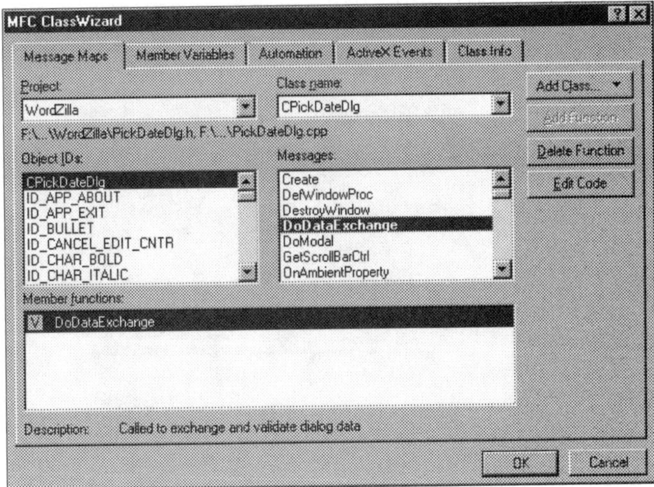

Figure 18.7
Looking at **CPickDateDlg** in ClassWizard.

1. While ClassWizard is still open, switch to the Member Variables tab. Locate the **IDC_DATETIMEPICKER1** resource ID, as shown in Figure 18.8. Click on Add Variable.
2. When the Add Member Variable dialog box opens, enter "**m_DateValue**" in the Member Variable Name field. Select Value from the Category drop-down list and choose **COleDateTime** from the Variable type drop-down list. When your screen looks like Figure 18.9, click on OK.

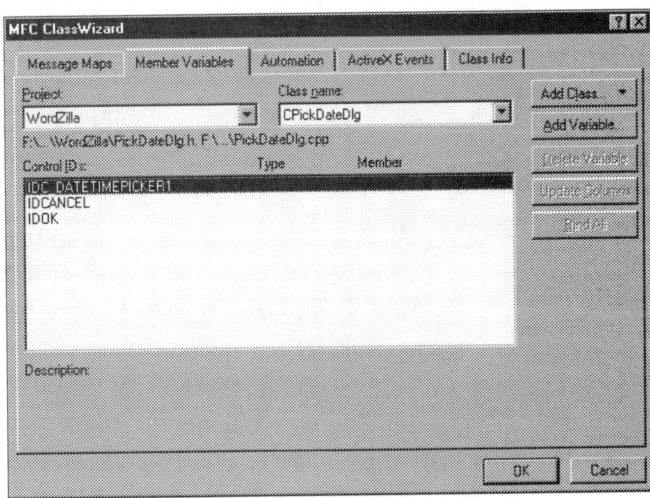

Figure 18.8
ClassWizard member variables for the **CPickDateDlg** class.

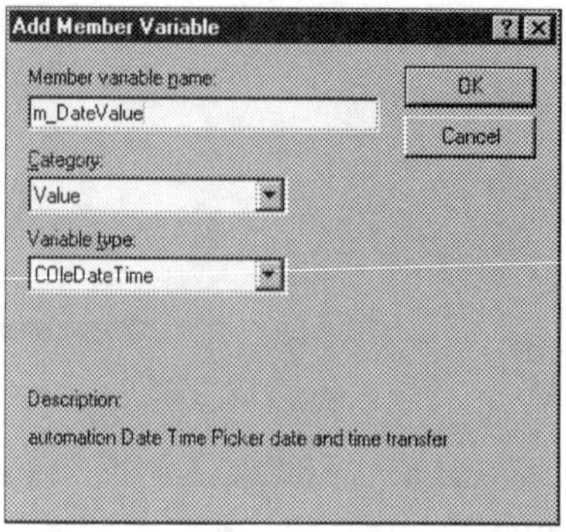

Figure 18.9
Adding the **m_DateValue CPickDateDlg** member variable.

Hooking Up The Dialog Box

You've completed all the steps necessary to use the new Select A Date dialog box. All that's left is to add a menu command and, in the menu command handler, display the dialog box. Here's how:

1. Select the ResourceView tab in the Workspace window and expand the Menu folder. Double-click on the **IDR_WZILLATYPE** menu. MFC displays this menu when a WordZilla document window is active. Because you want to paste a date only when a document is active, you won't add the command to the **IDR_MAINFRAME** menu.
2. Open the Edit menu and drag the new menu item at the bottom to a spot immediately beneath the Paste Special menu item. Enter "Paste &Date" as the menu caption and "**ID_EDIT_PASTE_DATE**" as the resource ID. The Prompt field should contain the text "Select and insert a date into your document\nPaste Date". When your screen looks like Figure 18.10, you're ready to go on.
3. With the Paste Date menu item still selected, open ClassWizard by pressing Ctrl+W. Click on the Message Maps tab. **ID_EDIT_PASTE_DATE** should already be selected in the Object IDs list box—if it isn't, select it now. Be sure the Class Name drop-down list displays **CWZView** (that's where you'll handle the menu command). Select **COMMAND** in the Messages list box and then click on Add Function. When the Add Member Function dialog box opens, accept the name offered by ClassWizard—**OnEditPasteDate**—as shown in Figure 18.11. Click on Edit Code.

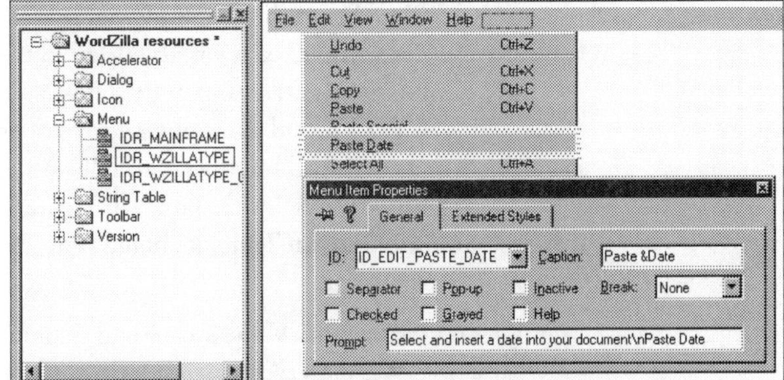

Figure 18.10
The Paste Date menu item properties.

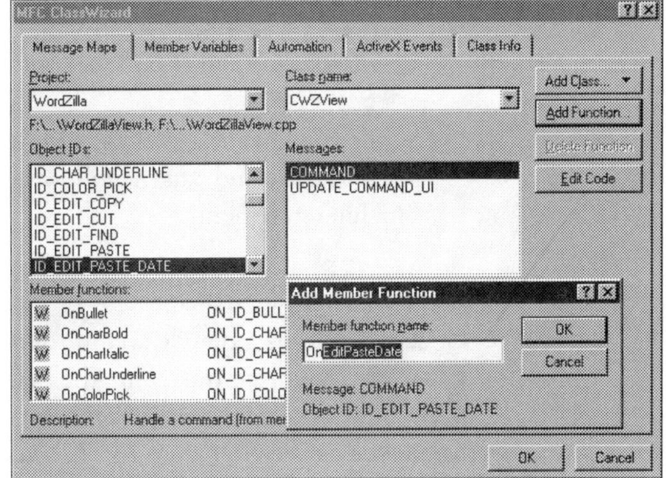

Figure 18.11
Adding the **OnEditPasteDate()** member function to the **CWZView** class.

4. Replace the **OnEditPasteDate()** function with the code shown in Listing 18.1. We'll discuss how the code works shortly.

Listing 18.1 The CWZView::OnEditPasteDate() menu command handler.

```
void CWZView::OnEditPasteDate()
{
    CPickDateDlg dlg;
    dlg.m_DateValue = m_PasteDate;
    if (dlg.DoModal() == IDOK)
    {
        m_PasteDate = dlg.m_DateValue;
        CString sDate = m_PasteDate.Format("%B %d, %Y");
        GetRichEditCtrl().ReplaceSel(sDate);
    }
}
```

5. In addition to the date variable stored in the **CPickDateDlg** class, you need a variable to hold the date when the dialog box isn't active. Open the ClassView pane and find the **CWZView** class. Right-click to open the context menu, then choose Add Member Variable. When the dialog box opens, fill in the fields as shown in Figure 18.12. The variable's type is **COleDateTime**, its name is **m_PasteDate**, and its access is **private**.
6. Using ClassView, locate and double-click on the **CWZView::OnInitialUpdate()** function. Add the following line to the end of the function:

```
// Initialize the current date
m_PasteDate = COleDateTime::GetCurrentTime();
```

7. While you have the WordZillaView.cpp file open, go to the top of the file and add the following line after all the other **#include** statements:

```
#include "PickDateDlg.h"
```

Once you're done, compile and run WordZilla. When you choose Edit|Paste Date from the menu, the Select A Date dialog box will open. Select the date time picker component to display a calendar, as you can see in Figure 18.13. You can use the arrow keys to scroll through the calendar, and the arrows on either side of the title bar let you change to a different month. When you click on a date in the calendar, the calendar closes, and the date changes in the date time picker.

You can open and close the date time picker as often as you like, but the dialog box remains open until you click on OK or Cancel. (You can also press Enter to select OK or Esc to select Cancel.) If

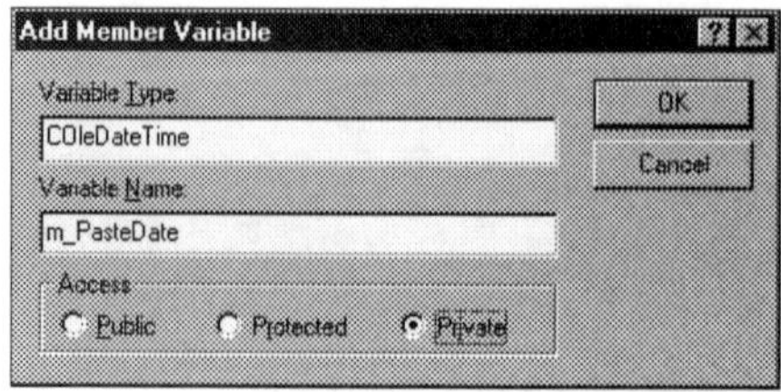

Figure 18.12
Adding the **m_PasteDate** member variable.

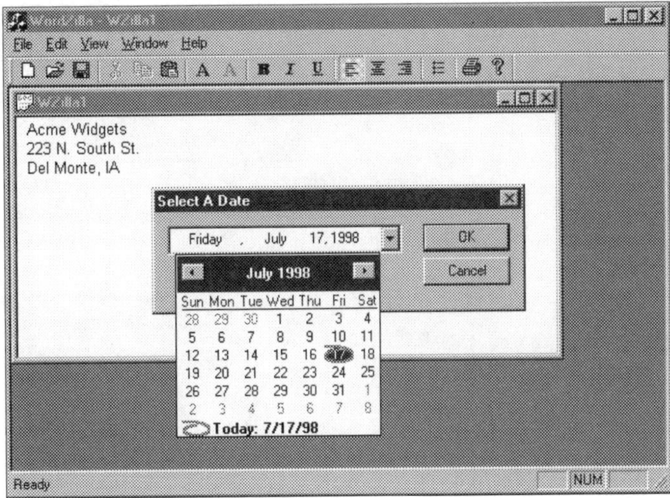

Figure 18.13
Using the Select A Date dialog box.

you click on OK, WordZilla pastes the new date into your document; the next time you choose Edit|Paste Date in the same document, the date time picker control will start with the date you previously selected.

How Modal Dialog Boxes Work

When you first look at the code for **CWZView::OnEditPasteDate()**, it seems simple and straightforward. Because it's so simple, it provides a good opportunity to understand dialog boxes in general, and modal dialog boxes in particular. Later, you'll see that the outward simplicity is deceptive: Much goes on behind the scenes.

Figure 18.14 schematically illustrates the life cycle of a modal dialog box, using the code in **OnEditPasteDate()** as an example. Notice that the illustration contains three columns, consisting of code in the **CWZView** class, code in the **CPickDateDlg** class, and code in the **CDialog** class. We've numbered each step so that you can use the illustration as a road map through the following discussion.

Constructing A Dialog Box

In MFC, when you construct a normal window, you make a variable from one of the **CWnd** classes and then call its **Create()**

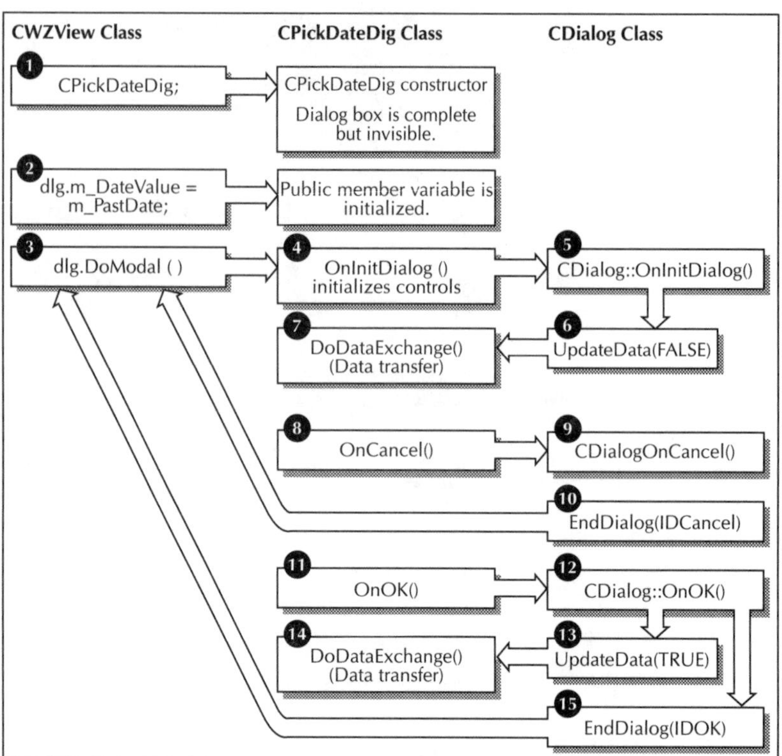

Figure 18.14
The modal dialog box life cycle.

member function. Dialog boxes don't work the same way. Dialog boxes are **CWnd**-derived windows—just like **CFrameWnd** windows—but they're created "on the fly" using the data contained in your program's compiled resource script. So, you simply create a dialog box variable, as shown in Step 1 of Figure 18.14.

When you construct an instance of your new dialog class, it calls the **CDialog::OnCreate()** function to read the specifications of your dialog box from the resource script, then creates and places each component. Consequently, you can't override the **OnCreate()** method as you did with the **CMainFrame** class: You must find another way to initialize the dialog box controls. At the time the **OnCreate()** method executes, the controls don't yet exist.

You can initialize dialog-box member variables after the constructor has finished running, as shown in Step 2 of Figure 18.14. At that time, the dialog-box object exists in memory, but isn't yet visible. In **OnEditPaste()**, for instance, you directly initialize the **CPickDateDlg** member variable **m_DateValue** by assigning the value stored in **m_PasteDate** (a data member stored in the **CWZView** class).

Displaying A Dialog Box

To display your dialog box, you call its **DoModal()** function, which sets off the chain of events shown as Step 3 in Figure 18.14. First, **DoModal()** calls the virtual **CDialog::OnInitDialog()** function. Because **CDialog::OnInitDialog()** is virtual, you don't have to create a message handler for it—you can simply override it.

Why might you override **OnInitDialog()**? You might need to manually initialize controls—populate a list box, for instance. However, **OnInitDialog()** isn't the place to initialize value variables associated with your controls. You'll soon see how to initialize them.

You also might override **OnInitDialog()** to make keyboard focus begin on a control other than the first control in the tab order, perhaps based upon some runtime value. In that case, you can use the **SetFocus()** function to set the keyboard focus to the control of your choice, and then return **FALSE** from **OnInitDialog()**. Otherwise, **OnInitDialog()** should return **TRUE**.

If you override **OnInitDialog()**, call **CDialog::OnInitDialog()** as the last line in your function. Otherwise, it will be called automatically, as shown in Step 5 of Figure 18.14. When **CDialog::OnInitDialog()** executes, it first calls the **CWnd::UpdateData()** function, passing **FALSE** as an argument (Step 6 in Figure 18.14). The **UpdateData()** function constructs a pointer to a **CDataExchange** object, then calls the **DoDataExchange()** function of the **CPickDateDlg**() class (Step 7 in Figure 18.14). Finally, **CDialog::OnInitDialog()** displays the dialog window, so that the user can work with it.

How Dialog Data Transfer Works

When you first look at the series of function calls initiated by calling **dlg.DoModal()**, you may find it confusing. However, if you understand the purpose of each call, the operation makes much more sense. In a nutshell, here's the purpose behind the **UpdateData()** and **DoDataExchange()** functions:

- **UpdateData()** transfers information between controls and member variables in a dialog-box class. If **UpdateData()** is called with **FALSE**, then the controls are initialized with the values stored in the member variables. If **UpdateData()** is called with **TRUE**, then the data transfer goes the other direction—moving from the Windows controls into the member variables.
- When **UpdateData()** transfers information between controls and member variables, it uses a *data map* to associate each control with each particular variable. This data map also describes what kind of conversion needs to occur when the information is transferred. This data map is contained in the function called **DoDataExchange()**.

Most of the time, you won't need to worry about the contents of **DoDataExchange()**—as you use ClassWizard to add member variables for your controls, ClassWizard writes the necessary entries in the **DoDataExchange()** function. But, understanding how the code works helps when you're troubleshooting. Listing 18.2 shows the **CPickDateDlg::DoDataExchange()** function.

Listing 18.2 The CPickDateDlg::DoDataExchange() function.

```
void CPickDateDlg::DoDataExchange(CDataExchange* pDX)
{
    CDialog::DoDataExchange(pDX);
    //{{AFX_DATA_MAP(CPickDateDlg)
    DDX_DateTimeCtrl(pDX, IDC_DATETIMEPICKER1,
      m_DateValue);
    //}}AFX_DATA_MAP
}
```

The **DoDataExchange()** function is bi-directional. When the function is called, it's passed a pointer to a **CDataExchange** object—constructed by the **UpdateData()** function—indicating the direction in which information should flow. **DoDataExchange()** passes this pointer (**pDX** in Listing 18.2) to the actual data-exchange function.

The data-exchange functions—called ***DDX** functions*—take three arguments:

- The pointer to the **CDataExchange** object, which indicates the direction information should flow.
- The resource ID of the control.
- The member variable that acts as the source or destination of the value to be transferred.

Specific **DDX** functions exist for each type of control and each control value data type.

You can specify a *validation code* for some controls. For instance, if your dialog box contains an edit control, ClassWizard gives you the option of associating several types of variables with that edit control. If you associate the control with a numeric value, ClassWizard allows you to specify a minimum and maximum value for the control. It writes a validation function—called a **DDV** function—and places it with the **DDX** function in **DoDataExchange()**. This **DDV** function prevents the user from closing the dialog box while the related control contains an invalid value.

Closing The Dialog Box

After **CDialog::OnInitDialog()** returns, you're free to navigate through the dialog box controls. If any control has an attached message handler, it's invoked when you use the control. Because this is a modal dialog box, control can't return to the calling program until you close the dialog box.

To close a modal dialog box, you invoke the **EndDialog()** function, passing one of two values: **IDOK** or **IDCANCEL**. **DoModal()** returns this value to its caller. The function that invoked the **DoModal()** function tests this value and takes action accordingly.

If you look back at Figure 18.14, you'll see that **OnCancel()** and **OnOK()** are virtual **CDialog** functions. You haven't overridden them in the **CPickDateDlg** class. If you had, you could use that opportunity to perform more extensive data validation than that provided by ClassWizard's **DDV** functions. If you choose to override either function, you should call **CDialog::OnOK()** or **CDialog::OnCancel()**, rather than call **EndDialog()** directly—this is especially important in the case of the **OnOK()** virtual function.

When you end a dialog box by clicking on OK, the **CDialog::OnOK()** function again calls **UpdateData()**, this time passing **TRUE** to indicate that data should be transferred out of your controls and into your variables. As before, **UpdateData()** calls your **DoDataExchange()** function. Finally, **CDialog::OnOK()** calls **EndDialog()**, passing **IDOK** so that **DoModal()** knows how things ended. Look back at Figure 18.14, Steps 11 through 14, to see this process illustrated.

Handling OK

When **DoModal()** returns, the **EndDialog()** function has already hidden the dialog box. It's no longer on screen, but the dialog-box object is still in memory. It won't be destroyed until the dialog box variable goes out of scope.

If **DoModal()** returns the value **IDOK**, you should immediately transfer information from the dialog variables to variables in the class that invoked the dialog box. Although the dialog-data exchange functions handle transfer between dialog-box controls and dialog-box member variables, they don't handle the transfer of information out of the dialog-box class and into the larger world. Once the dialog box object goes out of scope, that information is lost.

When the **CWZView::OnEditPasteDate()** function (see Listing 18.1) receives **IDOK** from the dialog object it constructs, it takes the opportunity to perform three tasks:

- Retrieve the **COleTimeDate** value stored in the dialog member variable **m_DateValue** and save it in the **CWZView** member variable **m_PasteDate**.

- Construct a temporary **CString** variable called **sDate**, using the **COleTimeDate** member function **Format()**. **Format()** works much like **printf()**, but it has a number of formatting options specifically designed to format dates. In **OnEditPasteDate()**, you use **%B** to print the full month name, **%d** to print the day as a decimal number, and **%Y** to print a four-digit decimal year. (To learn about the other formatting specifiers available, look up the **strftime()** function in the Visual C++ online help.)
- Insert the formatted date into the current view by calling the **CRichEditView::GetRichEditCtrl()** function to retrieve the underlying Rich Edit control, then call the **RichEditCtrl::ReplaceSel()** function to insert the newly formatted date.

Look Ma, No Mode

If you use WordZilla to write letters to your friends, you probably won't use the date-pasting feature often. For low-frequency operations such as this, the modal dialog box is a good solution.

But suppose that, rather than writing letters, you're using WordZilla to produce the weekly schedules for the Southwest Lawn Bowling Association, and that every schedule contains 20 or 30 dates. In that case, the modal dialog box seems less convenient. You need a dialog box that stays open until you're done with it: a *modeless* dialog box.

How Modeless Dialog Boxes Work

Modeless dialog boxes use the same dialog template as modal dialog boxes. MFC creates modal dialog boxes on the stack, whereas it creates modeless dialog boxes in the freestore. MFC automatically calls the destructor for a modal dialog box, but you must use **delete** on a modeless dialog box.

You display a modal dialog box by calling **DoModal()**, whereas you display a modeless dialog box by calling **Create()** and **ShowWindow()**. To close a modal dialog box, you call **EndDialog()**, either directly or indirectly. You can hide a modeless dialog box by calling **ShowWindow(SW_HIDE)** or destroy it by calling **DestroyWindow()**.

In a modeless dialog box, you must override the virtual **OnOK()** and **OnCancel()** functions to prevent MFC from calling the default **CDialog** versions. Because the **CDialog** version of **OnOK()** isn't called, you must manually call **UpdateData(TRUE)** to perform the **DDX** data transfer.

Let's see how this works by turning the Select A Date dialog box into a modeless version.

A Modeless Dialog Box For WordZilla

Before we get down to the specific steps, let's get a handle on where we're going. When your dialog box was modal, you created it in the view class's **OnEditPasteDate()** function. That worked fine, because you created and destroyed the modal dialog box within a single function.

This scheme won't work as well for a modeless dialog box, however, because nothing prevents the user from switching to another document or closing the current document while the dialog box is open. Instead, you'll create the dialog box in the **CMainWnd** constructor and delete it in the **CMainWnd** destructor. By doing so, you can be sure you have no memory leaks.

By default, dialog boxes are invisible when they're first created. So, you'll use **ShowWindow()** to display the dialog box when the user chooses Edit|Paste Date from the menu. In the overridden **OnCancel()** function, you don't really want to destroy the dialog box—you merely want to make it invisible, so you'll use **ShowWindow(SW_HIDE)**. Finally, you'll move the code that pastes the date from **CWZView::OnEditPasteDate()** to the **CPickDateDlg::OnOK()** function.

Changes To The CWZView Class

You must make only one change to the **CWZView** class: removing the **OnEditPasteDate()** function. This is a two-step process:

1. Open ClassWizard by choosing View|ClassWizard from the main menu or by pressing Ctrl+W and click on the Message Maps tab. Select **CWZView** in the Class Name drop-down list, then select the **COMMAND** handler for **ID_EDIT_PASTE_DATE**. When your screen looks like Figure 18.15, click on Delete Function.

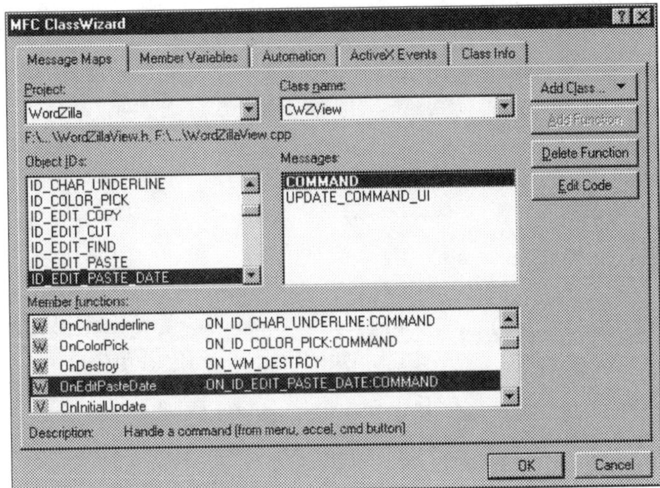

Figure 18.15
Removing the **CWZView::OnEdit PasteDate()** function.

2. ClassWizard will display the warning shown in Figure 18.16; click on OK. Open the ClassView pane and expand the **CWZView** class. Double-click on the **OnEditPasteDate()** function to open the Source Code Editor, then delete or comment out the **OnEditPasteDate()** function.

Changes To The CMainFrame Class

The **CMainFrame** class requires quite a few more changes. Here are the step-by-step instructions:

1. Open the WordZilla project and locate the **CMainFrame** class in the ClassView pane. Right-click on it to open the context menu, then choose Add Member Variable. Add a **private CPickDateDlg *** named **m_pPickDateDlg**. When your dialog box looks like Figure 18.17, click on OK.

2. Double-click on the **CMainFrame** class in ClassView to open the MainFrm.h header file. Add the following line before the **CMainFrame** class definition:

```
class CPickDateDlg;
```

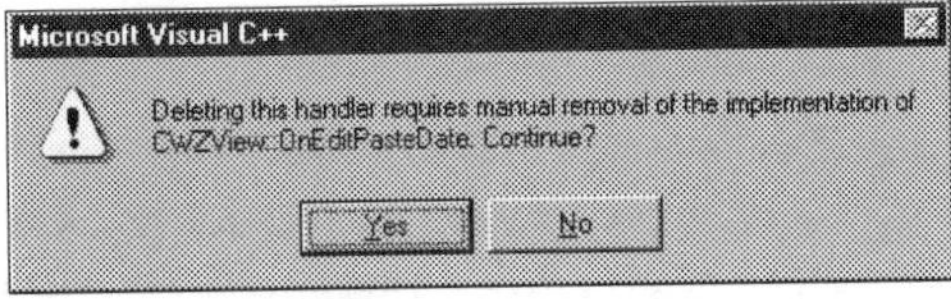

Figure 18.16
ClassWizard's manual class-deletion warning.

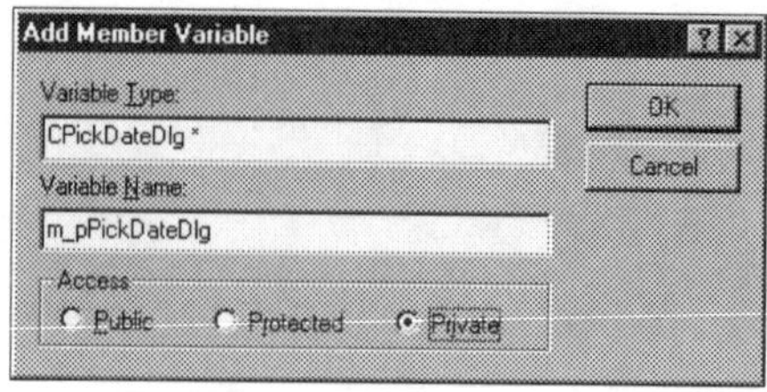

Figure 18.17 Adding the **m_pPickDateDlg** member variable to the **CMainFrame** class.

Such a line is called an *incomplete class declaration* or a *forward reference*. It gives the compiler sufficient information to parse the **CMainFrame** class definition.

3. Expand the **CMainFrame** class in ClassView and double-click on the **CMainFrame()** constructor. Add the highlighted code in Listing 18.3 to the constructor and destructor.

Listing 18.3 The CMainFrame constructor and destructor.

```
CMainFrame::CMainFrame()
{
    m_pPickDateDlg = new CPickDateDlg;
}

CMainFrame::~CMainFrame()
{
    m_pPickDateDlg->DestroyWindow();
    delete m_pPickDateDlg;
}
```

4. Locate the **OnCreate()** function and place the following line immediately before the return statement at the end of the file:

```
m_pPickDateDlg->Create(IDD_PICK_DATE, this);
```

(If you erroneously place this statement in the constructor, the dialog box won't stay on top of the main window when it loses focus.)

5. Go to the top of the file (CMainFrm.cpp) and add the following line after the other **#include** statements:

```
#include "PickDateDlg.h"
```

6. Open ClassWizard and select the **CMainFrame** class in the Class Name drop-down list. Select **ID_EDIT_PASTE_DATE**

in the Object IDs list box and **COMMAND** in the Messages list box. Click on Add Function, then click on OK when the Add Member Function dialog box opens, as you can see in Figure 18.18. Add the code shown in Listing 18.4 to the **CMainFrame::OnEditPasteDate()** function.

Listing 18.4 The CMainFrame::OnEditPasteDate() menu handler.

```
void CMainFrame::OnEditPasteDate()
{
    if (m_pPickDateDlg->IsWindowVisible())
    {
        m_pPickDateDlg->SetFocus();
    }
    else
    {
        m_pPickDateDlg->ShowWindow(SW_SHOW);
    }
}
```

Changes To The CPickDateDlg Class

You'll use the Dialog Editor to change the **CPickDateDlg** class, and you'll change some source code, as well. Here are the instructions:

1. Open the ResourceView pane in the Workspace window and expand the Dialogs folder. Double-click on the **IDD_PICK_DATE** dialog resource to open the Dialog Editor. Open the Properties dialog box for the Cancel button,

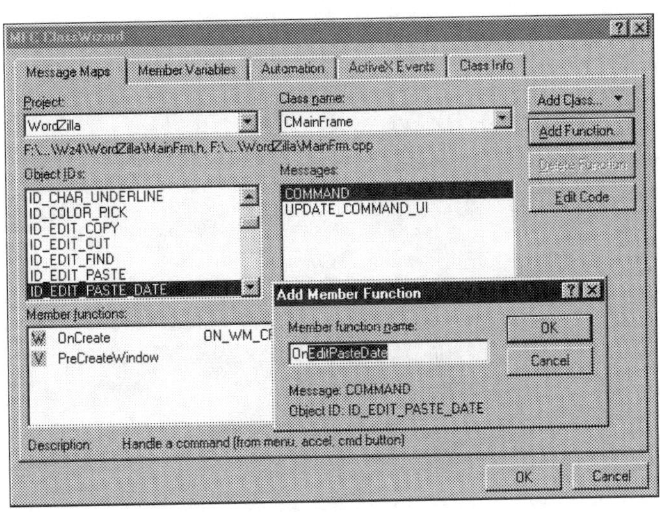

Figure 18.18
Adding the **OnEditPasteDate()** menu handler to the **CMainFrame** class.

then enter the Caption "&Close". Leave the ID set to **IDCANCEL**. Open the Properties dialog box for the OK button and change its caption to "&Paste". Leave its ID set to **IDOK**. Your screen should look like Figure 18.19.

2. Double-click on the Close button to create a new handler function. It's important to accept the offered name, **OnCancel()**—doing so lets you override the **OnCancel()** virtual function. Replace the generated code with that shown in Listing 18.5.

Listing 18.5 The CPickDateDlg::OnCancel() function.

```
void CPickDateDlg::OnCancel()
{
    ShowWindow(SW_HIDE);
}
```

3. Return to the Dialog Editor and double-click on the Paste button to create a new handler function. As with the Close button, accept the offered name, **OnOK()**—don't change it. Accepting the name lets you override the **CDialog::OnOK()** function, which you must do for a modeless dialog box. Replace the generated code with the highlighted code shown in Listing 18.6. As you can see, it's a little more complex than previous code, but you should be able to follow the steps if you read the comments.

Listing 18.6 The CPickDateDlg::OnOK() function.

```
void CPickDateDlg::OnOK()
{
    // 1. Get the data from the control to the variable
    UpdateData(TRUE);
```

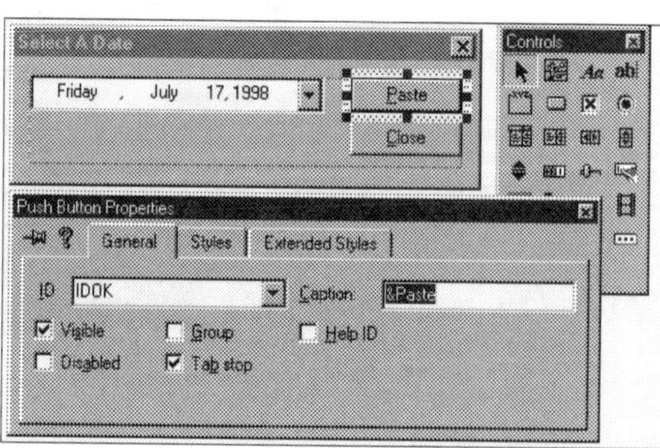

Figure 18.19
Changing the Select A Date dialog box button captions.

```
    // 2. Get the MainFrame window
    CMainFrame * pMain = (CMainFrame*)AfxGetMainWnd();

    // 3. See if there are any CChildFrames active
    CChildFrame * pChild = (CChildFrame*)pMain->
      GetActiveFrame();
    if (pChild == NULL)  // No active children
        return;

    // 4. Get the active view
    CWZView * pView = (CWZView*)pChild->GetActiveView();
    if (pView == NULL)  // No active view
        return;

    // 5. Format the date object
    CString sDate = m_DateValue.Format("%B %d, %Y");

    // 6. Get the Rich Edit Control and paste the date
    pView->GetRichEditCtrl().ReplaceSel(sDate);

    // 7. Set the focus to the Rich Edit Control
    pView->SetFocus();
}
```

4. Locate the constructor for the **CPickDateDlg** class and comment out the line that calls the **CDialog** constructor. The work previously done by the **CDialog** constructor is now done by **Create()**. The completed constructor should look like Listing 18.7, in which we've highlighted the changed line.

Listing 18.7 Changing the CPickDateDlg constructor.

```
CPickDateDlg::CPickDateDlg(CWnd* pParent /*=NULL*/)
//  : CDialog(CPickDateDlg::IDD, pParent)
{
    //{{AFX_DATA_INIT(CPickDateDlg)
    m_DateValue = COleDateTime::GetCurrentTime();
    //}}AFX_DATA_INIT
}
```

5. With the addition of the **OnOK()** function, the **PickDateDlg** class now refers to several classes that it previously didn't know about. You need to tell it what's up by adding the highlighted **#include** statements shown in Listing 18.8 to the top of the PickDateDlg.cpp file.

Listing 18.8 Adding header files to PickDateDlg.cpp.

```
#include "stdafx.h"
#include "WordZilla.h"
#include "PickDateDlg.h"
#include "MainFrm.h"
#include "ChildFrm.h"
#include "CntrItem.h"
#include "WordZillaDoc.h"
#include "WordZillaView.h"
```

Well, that's all there is to it. Compile and run WordZilla, and you'll see the Select A Date dialog box open, just as it did before. However, when you click on Paste, the dialog box doesn't close—it remains open, floating above your window. You can switch among several documents, and the Paste button will paste the date you select into the current document.

The ActiveX DatePicker

Now that you know how to make both modal and modeless dialog boxes, let's learn how to add a new type of control. ActiveX controls resemble regular Windows controls in several ways. The actual code for Windows controls isn't housed in your program, but rather in a separate dynamic-link library (DLL). For instance, the common controls introduced with Windows 95 are contained in the file Comctl32.dll, located in your Windows\System directory (if you're running Windows 95 or 98) or your Windows\System32 directory (if you're running Windows NT).

ActiveX controls are dynamically linked, like regular Windows controls. However, ActiveX DLLs normally use the extension .ocx. It's common for each OCX file to contain only a single control.

Internally, ActiveX controls are quite a bit different from regular Windows controls. However, when you use them in your MFC programs, you can treat them almost like the built-in controls—but only "almost." Let's replace the built-in date time picker control with the ActiveX version, so you can see how they differ.

Using ActiveX controls in an MFC program is a three-step process:

- First, you'll add the ActiveX control to the Dialog Editor's Controls toolbar. When you do this, Visual C++ will create

NOTE

ActiveX controls are added to the Control palette on a project-by-project basis, rather than being placed there permanently.

a proxy class for the new ActiveX control and add it to your project.

- Second, you'll use the Dialog Editor to add instances of your ActiveX control to your dialog box.
- Third, you'll use ClassWizard to write code in response to *events* generated by the control. You'll also use ClassWizard to associate the ActiveX control with an instance of the proxy class created when you first added the control to your project.

Let's walk through these steps as you add the ActiveX version of the Windows date time picker to WordZilla.

Adding ActiveX Controls

You begin by adding an ActiveX control to your project and generating a proxy class. The control then appears on the Dialog Editor Controls toolbar, just like a built-in control.

Here are the steps to follow to add the Microsoft date and time picker control to the WordZilla project:

1. Open the WordZilla project. Choose Project|Add To Project|Components And Controls to open the Components And Controls Gallery dialog box. Open the Registered ActiveX Controls folder, then select the Microsoft Date And Time Picker Control, Version 6.0 option. When your screen looks like that shown in Figure 18.20, click on Insert.

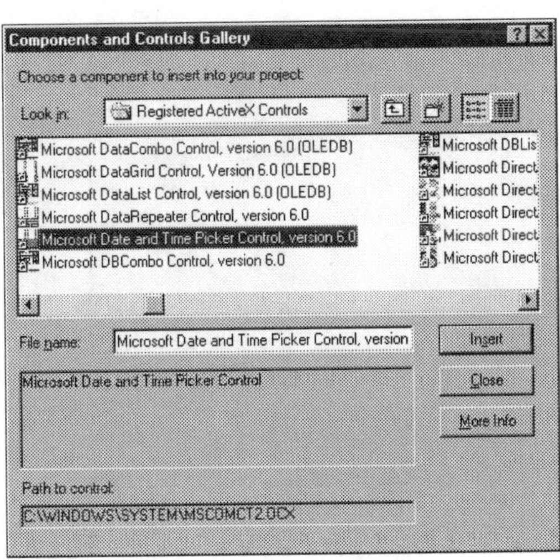

Figure 18.20
Adding an ActiveX control to your project.

Tip

Help Is Not Always Helpful

If an ActiveX control has an associated help file, MFC will activate the More Info button, as you can see in the figure. However, the documentation generally assumes you're using the component in VB (which is why it's important to understand the differences between using ActiveX controls in Visual C++ and using them in VB). Notice that this ActiveX control is contained in the MSCOMCT2.OCX file. If you write a program that uses this control, you must distribute this file with your program—otherwise, your program may not run.

2. You can deal directly with ActiveX controls in your Visual C++ program, but you *definitely* don't want to. (You'll see why shortly.) Instead, for every ActiveX control you add, Visual C++ generates *wrapper* or *proxy* classes that let you treat the ActiveX control as if it were a C++ object. Figure 18.21 shows the Confirm Classes dialog box that lets you select which classes to generate. Because you're adding only one control, just click on OK.

If you were adding several ActiveX controls to your project, they might all use the **COleFont** class, and you'd want to include the class only once. In such a case, you'd deselect the **COleFont** class in the list box. You can also change the name of the basic class that Visual C++ generates (although you can't change the names of helper classes like **CPicture** and **COleFont**, for obvious reasons.) For instance, if your project already had a **CDTPicker** class, you might want to change the class name.

That's it for the first step in using an ActiveX control in MFC. Close the Component And Control Gallery dialog box and get ready for the next step: using the ActiveX control in the Dialog Editor.

ActiveX Controls In The Dialog Editor

After you've finished with the Gallery, use the ResourceView pane in the Workspace window to open the **IDD_PICK_DATE**

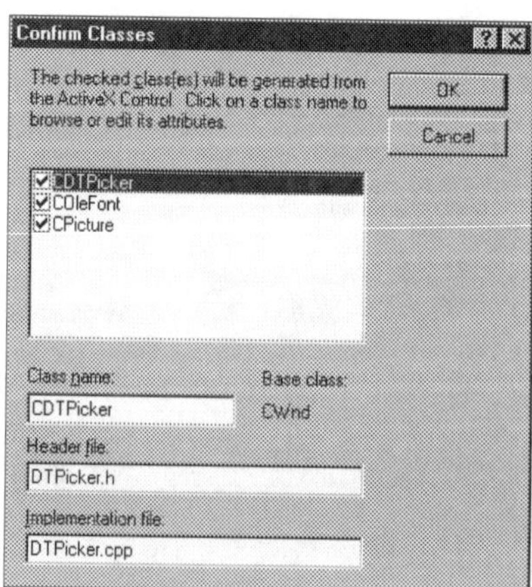

Figure 18.21
The Confirm Classes dialog box when adding an ActiveX control.

dialog box in the Dialog Editor. Select the Date Time Picker control—**IDC_DATETIMEPICKER1**—and press the Delete key to remove it.

Now, you're ready to replace the date time picker control with its ActiveX cousin. Here are the steps to follow:

1. Locate the new Date And Time Picker control on the Controls toolbar, as you can see in Figure 18.22.
2. Drag the control from the Controls toolbar to the Select A Date dialog box. Notice in Figure 18.23 that as you drag the component, the cursor changes to include an "X." This change indicates that you're adding an ActiveX control rather than a regular Windows control.
3. Position and size the component as you did the date time picker it replaces. Then, right-click to open the component's context menu. Notice that, in addition to the normal Properties menu item, a separate Properties DTPicker Object menu item appears. Select either one to open the ActiveX control's property sheet.

Date And Time Picker Properties

When the Date And Time Picker Properties dialog box opens, you'll immediately notice that you have many more options than you did with the built-in date time picker control. Because ActiveX controls are normally used in a "drag-and-drop" environment like VB, they usually have many options.

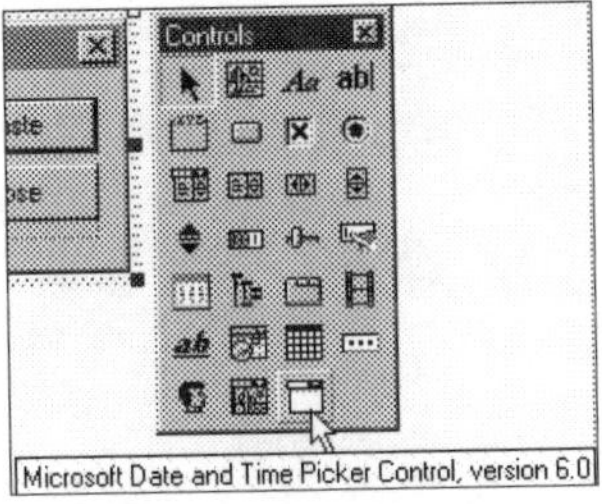

Figure 18.22
The Date And Time Picker control on the Controls toolbar.

Figure 18.23
Dragging an ActiveX control.

▶Tip

What About Year 2000?

*You might notice that the ActiveX component doesn't seem to be year-2000 compliant. If you try to change the **MaxDate** property, the control uses its own calendar to let you set the date. However, because its maximum date is set to December 31, 1999, you can't set a date past the millennium.*

*Don't worry: You can also access every property on every page through the property sheet's All tab, where you can simply type in a new value. Once you change **MaxDate** on the All properties page, you can enter any date up to December 31, 9999. Of course, if you need a year-10,000-compliant product, you'll have to look elsewhere.*

Let's explore some of the properties you can change.

1. Select the Control tab, then use the Format drop-down list to change the control's Format property to 3-dtpCustom. With the built-in date time picker, you could choose between long format and short format, but you couldn't precisely specify the desired format. With the ActiveX control, you can. After you change the Format property, enter "MMMM d, yyy" in the CustomFormat edit field. This custom format means that the control will use the same display format you insert into your rich edit control. (Use the control documentation to see what other formats are available.) Your screen should look like the one shown in Figure 18.24.
2. The Color tab, shown in Figure 18.25, allows you to change the colors used in various portions of the calendar that's displayed. However, you can't change the color of the combo-box portion of the control. You can choose between Windows system colors and the standard color sets, as well as define your own colors. Change the colors of several calendar elements: See if you can devise a color scheme that's easy to read but draws the user's attention to the calendar.
3. Finally, you can set the **Font** property used throughout the control. As with the color properties page, you might want to ask someone with some design sense before changing this property. On the other hand, a little 12-point Blippo never hurt anyone, as you can see in Figure 18.26.

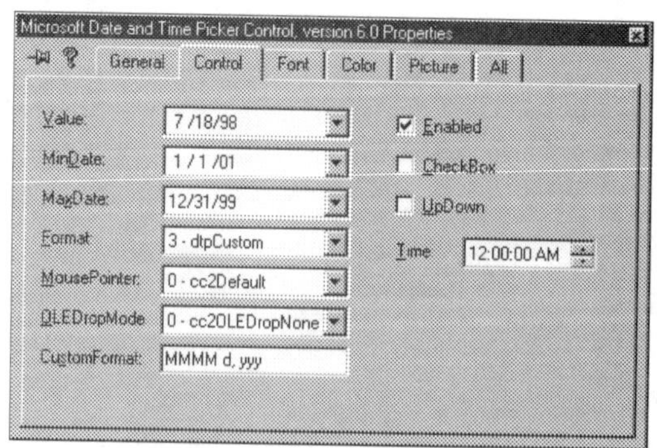

Figure 18.24
Changing the control properties of the date and time picker.

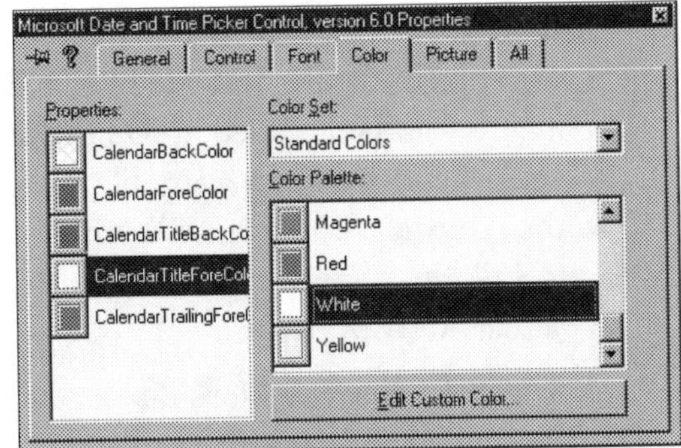

Figure 18.25
Setting the date and time picker color properties.

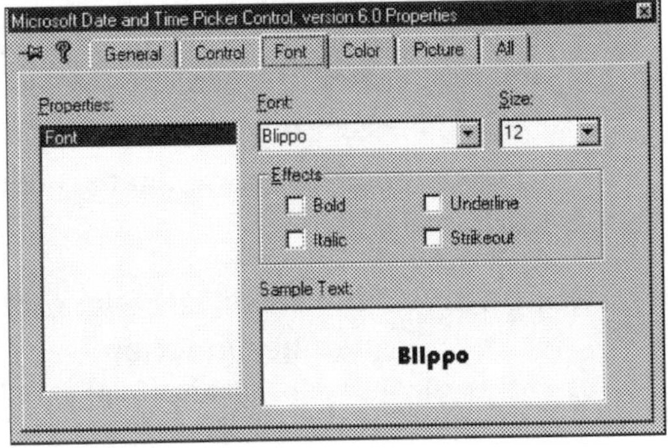

Figure 18.26
Changing the date and time picker **Font** property.

ActiveX Controls, Code, And ClassWizard

Before you can hook up your new date and time picker control, you must unhook the old one. You've deleted the control in the Dialog Editor, but the **CPickDateDlg** class still has an **m_DateValue** member variable that was attached to the old control.

The **CPickDateDlg** class will still need to store the date. So, after you remove the variable using ClassWizard, you'll bring it back for an encore as an unattached member variable.

Finally, rather than use the automatic **DDX** data exchange (which doesn't work with ActiveX controls), you'll intercept an ActiveX event, and then manually do the necessary data transfer.

Are you ready? Here are the steps to follow:

1. Open ClassWizard and select the **CPickDateDlg** class in the Class Name drop-down list. Change to the Member Variables tab and delete the **m_DateValue** variable associated with the

ID **IDC_DATETIMEPICKER1**. Then, select the ID for your new control—**IDC_DTPICKER1**—and add a new member variable called **m_DTPickerCtrl**, as shown in Figure 18.27. Notice that the variable you create is an instance of the proxy class you created earlier. You'll use the proxy object to call functions, and it will transparently forward them to the actual ActiveX object.

2. Select the Message Maps tab, locate **IDC_DTPICKER1**, and choose Change from the Messages list box. Each of the items appearing in this list box is an event, fired by the ActiveX control. The date and time picker control fires the **Change** event whenever the date changes in the control. Click on Add and accept the offered function name.Click on Edit Code and replace the generated code with that shown in Listing 18.9.

Listing 18.9 The CPickDateDlg::OnChangeDtpicker1() member function.

```
void CPickDateDlg::OnChangeDtpicker1()
{
    m_DateValue = m_DTPickerCtrl.GetValue();
}
```

Every time the date changes inside the ActiveX date and time picker control, the control will fire an event that calls

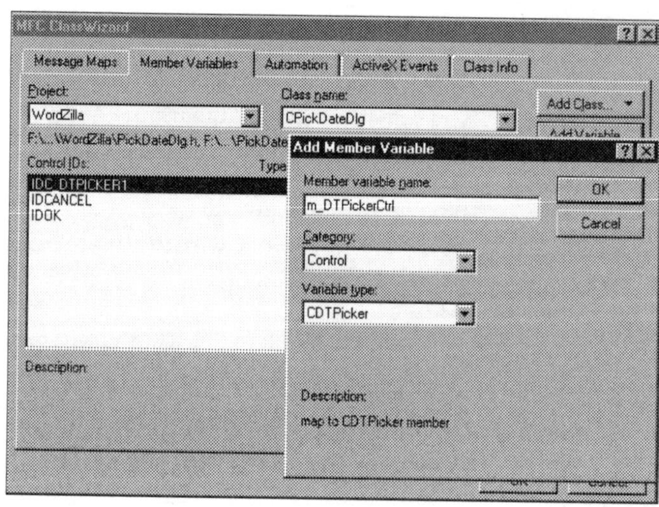

Figure 18.27 Adding the **m_DTPickerCtrl** variable to the **CPickDateDlg** class.

your function. Within the function, you call the **GetValue()** function—using your proxy object—and store the value back in the **m_DateValue** variable.

3. Locate the **CPickDateDlg** class in the Workspace ClassView window. Right-click on it to open the context menu, then add a new private **COleDateTime** variable named **m_DateValue**, as shown in Figure 18.28. This replaces the variable that was attached to the original date picker control.

Once you're finished, compile and run the program. As you can see from Figure 18.29, the new control works almost exactly like the earlier version—but it's much more colorful!

Properties, Events, And Methods

If you read the documentation for the date and time picker ActiveX control, you'll notice that—from a Visual Basic point of view—every control can have events, properties, and methods.

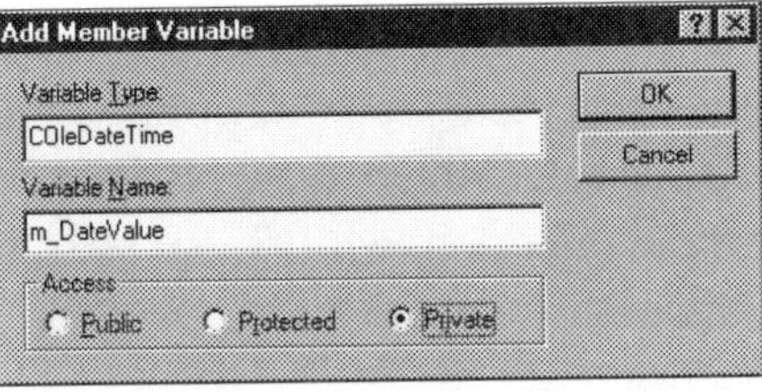

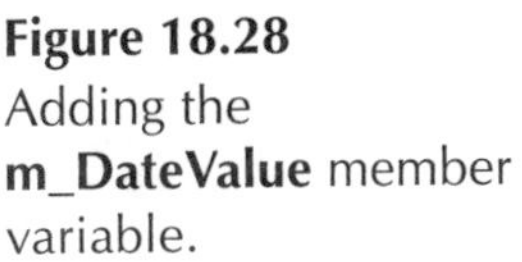

Figure 18.28
Adding the **m_DateValue** member variable.

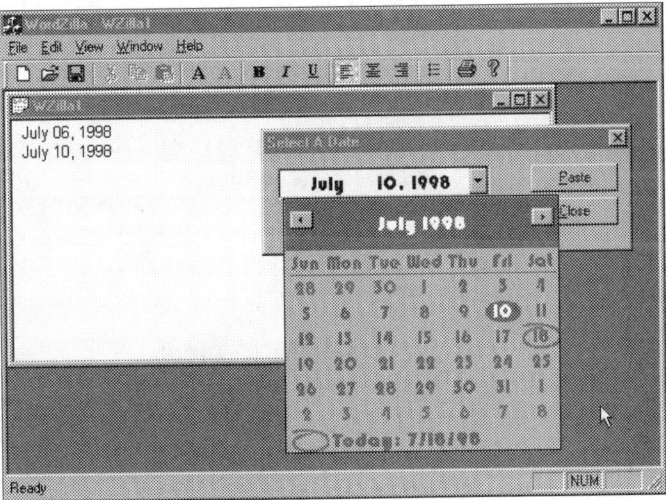

Figure 18.29
Running WordZilla with an ActiveX date and time picker.

In VB, properties are like member variables, so they're accessed directly. If you read the documentation for the **Value** property, for instance, it might lead you to write code like this:

```
m_DateValue = mDTPickerCtrl.Value;
```

If **Value** were a **public** member variable of the **CDTPicker** class, that would be correct. However, in Visual C++, properties aren't directly accessible **public** member variables. Instead, each property has a pair of functions—those for the **Value** property are called **GetValue()** and **SetValue()**—that let you retrieve or set the value of a property.

In an ActiveX control, a method is like a procedure—it's something you can tell the control to do. The date and time picker control doesn't have methods. If it did, you could call them using the proxy class, just as you'd access the object's properties. From the Visual C++ viewpoint, both properties and methods are functions you call to access the ActiveX control.

Events, on the other hand, let the ActiveX control communicate with your program. You can think of them as being similar to **WM_COMMAND** or **WM_NOTIFY** messages. Events are mapped to functions within your class, using a mechanism very much like the message maps you're familiar with. The ActiveX mechanism uses an **EVENTSINK_MAP** rather than a **MESSAGE_MAP**—but because you'll almost always let ClassWizard maintain the map for you, the difference is inconsequential. However, to satisfy your curiosity, here's the **EVENTSINK_MAP** that directs the **Change** event to your **OnChangeDtpicker1()** function:

```
BEGIN_EVENTSINK_MAP(CPickDateDlg, CDialog)
    //{{AFX_EVENTSINK_MAP(CPickDateDlg)
    ON_EVENT(CPickDateDlg, IDC_DTPICKER1, 2,
      OnChangeDtpicker1,
       VTS_NONE)
    //}}AFX_EVENTSINK_MAP
END_EVENTSINK_MAP()
```

ActiveX Again

In this chapter, we've shown you how to create dialog boxes that can hold normal Windows controls as well as ActiveX controls. In the next chapter, you'll learn how to use a view class based on the dialog template—the Form View—as the basis for building database applications. And, your ActiveX experience will prove invaluable, as you move on to work with the *data-aware* controls.

Before we move on, however, let's put all your newly won skills to work by using ActiveX controls to create one last version of WordZilla. As you've worked through these projects, we're sure that you've noticed WordZilla's one glaring deficiency. Well, the time has come to remedy that. Yes, you're going to create a *musical* About dialog box, using the ActiveX multimedia control.

We won't walk you through each step—we'll just go over the highlights. Here's what you need to do:

1. In the Components And Controls Gallery dialog box, select the Microsoft Multimedia Control (MCI) and add it to your project. (You already have the necessary **CPicture** class, so you don't need to re-create it.)
2. Open the About dialog box, then drag and drop onto it an MCI control and a regular button, as shown in Figure 18.30. Give the button the ID **IDC_NEW_FILE**, but accept the ID assigned to the multimedia control. Enter the button caption "New File".
3. Using ClassWizard, create a new member variable attached to your MCI control, as shown in Figure 18.31. Name your variable **m_MCICtrl**.

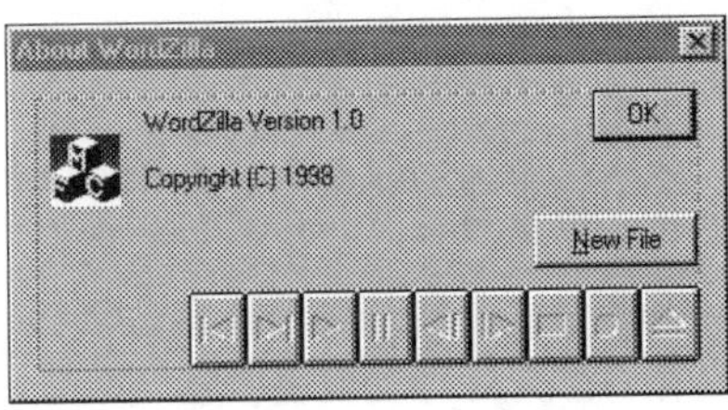

Figure 18.30
Arranging WordZilla's About dialog box.

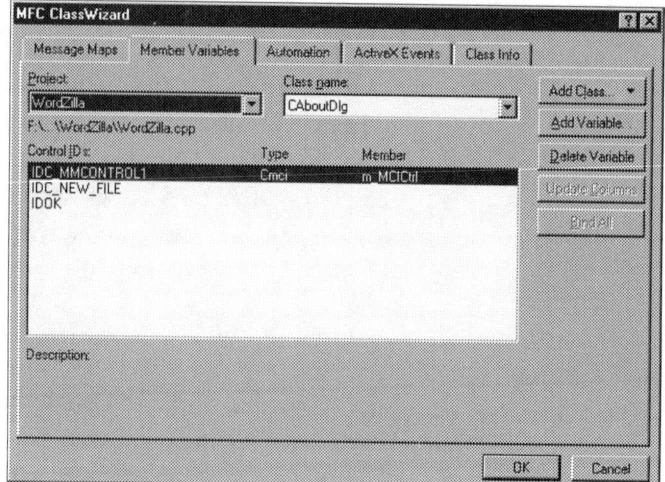

Figure 18.31
Adding the MCI control variable.

4. Manually add a **CString** member variable named **m_DefaultSong** to the **CAboutDlg** class. Initialize the variable in the **CAboutDlg** constructor to hold the value "Yeeehaaa.mid".

5. Double-click on the New File button and the OK button in the Dialog Editor to add new handler functions for those controls. Replace the generated code with that in Listing 18.10.

Listing 18.10 The OnOK() and OnNewFile() member functions.

```
void CAboutDlg::OnOK()
{
    // TODO: Add extra validation here
    m_MCICtrl.SetCommand("Close");
    CDialog::OnOK();
}

void CAboutDlg::OnNewFile()
{
    // TODO: Add your control notification handler code
    // here
    CFileDialog dlg(TRUE, "*.mid", m_DefaultSong);
    if (dlg.DoModal() == IDOK)
    {
        m_DefaultSong = dlg.GetPathName();
        m_MCICtrl.SetCommand("Close");
        m_MCICtrl.SetFileName(m_DefaultSong);
        m_MCICtrl.SetCommand("Open");
```

```
        m_MCICtrl.SetCommand("Play");
    }
}
```

6. Use ClassWizard to write a handler for the **WM_INITDIALOG** message. Add the code in Listing 18.11 to **OnInitDialog()**.

Listing 18.11 The CAboutDlg::OnInitDialog() member function.

```
BOOL CAboutDlg::OnInitDialog()
{
    CDialog::OnInitDialog();

    // TODO: Add extra initialization here
    m_MCICtrl.SetFileName(m_DefaultSong);
    m_MCICtrl.SetCommand("Open");
    m_MCICtrl.SetCommand("Play");
    return TRUE;  // return TRUE unless you set the focus
                  // to a control
                  // EXCEPTION: OCX Property Pages should
                  // return FALSE
}
```

That's it! Copy the MIDI files provided on this book's CD-ROM to the same directory in which the WordZilla executable is stored, and you'll be the envy of the civilized world. (If you're running the program through the IDE, the MIDI files must be located with the project source-code files, not with the executable.)

Coming Up: A Trip To The Reservoir

Data is the essential raw material of information systems: Most computer software is built to transport data and transform it into information. Because data is so important, most modern applications store their data in databases, which protect the data so that it can be safely shared. But, protection and convenience are sometimes at odds: Data protected in a database can be cumbersome to access. In the next chapter, you'll learn how to use several MFC facilities that let you tap into these data reservoirs and siphon off the data you need. We promise you'll have buckets of fun.

Chapter 19

Software At Work: Building Database Query And Update Applications

SQL, ODBC, DAO, ISAM, RDO, ADO, OLE DB.... If you are a fan of the X-Files *television series, database acronyms may remind you of the government agencies featured on the show—each hiding behind a cryptic set of initials, each concealing part of the truth. Reality is much more prosaic; the truth about database technology isn't to be found on television, but in the refrigerator.*

Mystery casserole: That's the fastest way to understand the latest database technology. You make a mystery casserole by combining the contents of the leftover containers in your refrigerator and baking at 350 degrees for half an hour. Sometimes it works fine, but sometimes you end up with sweet-and-sour pork cheese blintzes. Similarly, each new database technology corrects some deficiency in an earlier methodology, but you'll often find that the new technology retains the flavor of its predecessors.

Visual C++ is a remarkably versatile tool—if an application can be written, it can be written in Visual C++. You can't say the same for Visual Basic or Microsoft Access, for instance. But, you shouldn't write an application with a particular product merely because you can. For example, if you want to write business database applications, Visual C++ probably isn't the right product for the job—you should consider using Visual FoxPro, Powersoft PowerBuilder, or Borland Visual dBASE, instead. The database support in Visual C++ allows you to access databases in your C++ programs, but it doesn't turn Visual C++ into a database development environment.

Though you have the latest version of Visual C++, not all its constituent tools and technologies are up to date. Here's an example. When you use Open Database Connectivity (ODBC) to connect to a data source, you must specify the data source's location and the driver you want to use. When ODBC was originally introduced, you did that by using the ODBC Data Source Administrator tool to create a Data Source Name (DSN) on the user's machine.

As time went by and new versions of ODBC arrived, the shortcomings of this approach became apparent. In response, Microsoft developed File DSNs, which let people on the network share a DSN and thereby eliminate the need to install the DSN on each computer. If you use a Microsoft tool like Visual InterDev to connect to a database, it uses File DSNs by default. However, when you use MFC to connect to an ODBC database, you aren't given the option to use a File DSN. It's not that MFC ODBC support is obsolete—it just hasn't kept up.

Because there are so many options (and lots of places to get lost), let's take a few minutes to map out our trail. We've deliberately simplified most of the sample programs in this chapter, so you can see clearly where you're going. Rather than exploring one data-access option—such as ODBC with Microsoft Access databases—in depth, we want you to see the whole territory. To accomplish this, we'll look at ODBC, Data Access Objects (DAO), and OLE DB. In the next chapter, we'll show you how to use ActiveX controls to create much more sophisticated database applications, with much less work.

In this project-oriented chapter, we'll focus on *doing*. We'll show you how to write a database query-and-update application, but we won't talk much about Structured Query Language (SQL) or database design. For that, you'll have to wait until the next chapter.

First, Get Yourself Some Data

Visual C++ comes with many sample programs. Two of these programs, DAOView and DAOTable, let you create tables and examine the structure of Microsoft Access databases without using Access itself. Let's use these programs to explore a database. If you prefer to use Access, that's fine—but you'll have to find your own way down the trail.

For the programs in this chapter, we'll use the sample Access database Sampdata.mdb supplied with the DAOView application. Here's how to get the programs and the data:

1. While Visual C++ is running, press F1 to open MSDN online help, or select Microsoft Developer Network from the Windows Start menu.
2. Click on the Home button on the toolbar to go to the MSDN start page, and then click on the Visual C++ hyperlink. Doing so will transfer you to the Visual C++ start page.
3. Click on Explore The Samples in the right-hand column. You'll probably be instructed to insert the MSDN Disk 1 CD (the original CD you used to install MSDN, not the CD you used to install Visual C++ or Visual Studio). All the MSDN samples are on the first MSDN disk, while the documentation is on the second. When you've changed disks, click on OK.
4. When the Visual C++ Samples page appears, click on the MFC hyperlink, and then select Categorical List Of MFC Samples. Choose Databases from this list, then choose DAOVIEW.
5. When the DAOVIEW dialog box opens, click on Click To Open Or Copy The DAOVIEW Project Files. In the Visual C++ Samples dialog box, click on Copy All, choose an appropriate directory and make note of it, then click on OK.
6. Follow the same procedure to copy the DAOTable application to your hard disk.
7. When you've copied all the files, start Visual C++ and open the DAOView project.
8. Choose Build|Set Active Configuration from the main menu. In the Set Active Configuration dialog box, change from Daoview - Win32 Unicode Debug to Daoview - Win32 Release. (If you're using Windows NT, you can use the Win32 Unicode Release option—but don't do that on Windows 95 or 98.)
9. Build the DAOView application. Create a data directory and drag into it a copy of the Sampdata.mdb database, from the

DAOView project directory. (Be sure to copy the file rather than move it. That way, you don't have to reinstall the sample files if you damage your working copy.) Drag a shortcut to DAOView to your desktop so you can access it easily. Open it, then use the program to navigate to your copy of Sampdata. Figure 19.1 shows how you can use the program to examine the structure of Sampdata's tables and queries.

No-Code Records With ODBC

For our next trick...er...lesson, you'll learn how to connect to a database using ODBC, and how to create a form that allows you to navigate through a database table, editing the data as you go. Actually, it isn't much of a trick, because AppWizard does most of the work. You'll do some pointing and clicking, but you won't have to write any code.

First, you need to hook up Sampdata as an ODBC data source. To do this, you must have the 32-bit ODBC Data Source Administrator installed on your machine. You can confirm that it's installed by looking in the Control Panel, where you'll see an icon that looks like the one shown in Figure 19.2. If you don't have the ODBC Data Source Administrator application installed, install it from your original Windows 95, Windows NT, or Windows 98 CD-ROM.

Step 1: Creating A Data Source Name

ODBC allows you to write programs that work similarly, regardless of whether the actual data is stored in an Oracle database, a Microsoft Access database, or Indexed Sequential Access Method (ISAM) files (such as those supported by dBASE and Paradox).

To use ODBC, you first instruct the ODBC Data Source Administrator to create a DSN. The DSN specifies the type of database you'll be working with, the location of the data files, and the driver used to access the files. In your MFC programs, you'll pretend that the DSN is your database—but, in reality, you'll be communicating with a database driver that forwards your database requests to the database system.

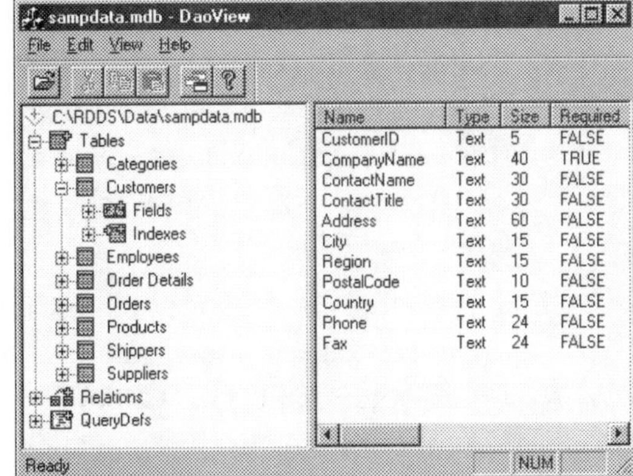

Figure 19.1
Using the DAOView application to examine the Sampdata database.

Figure 19.2
Locating the ODBC Data Source Administrator in the Windows 95 Control Panel.

In this chapter, you'll create a DSN called BucketOStuff. It's important to remember that BucketOStuff isn't a database—it merely *refers* to a database. This indirection provides an advantage: You can isolate your entire application from the specific characteristics of the database that stores the data. Initially, you'll connect BucketOStuff with the Sampdata.mdb database, using the Microsoft Access 7.0 driver. Later, you could redefine BucketOStuff to refer to a SQL Server or Oracle database—as long as all the field names and types were identical—and your application would continue working.

Follow these steps to create the BucketOStuff DSN:

1. Start the 32-bit ODBC Data Source Administrator by double-clicking on its icon in the Control Panel. When the program window opens, select the User DSN tab. You can see this tab in Figure 19.3. (It would be better to use a File DSN or System DSN, but AppWizard supports only User DSNs.) Click on Add.
2. The ODBC Data Source Administrator needs to know which driver you want to use. Figure 19.4 shows the Create New Data Source dialog box. Choose Microsoft Access Driver (*.mdb) from the list box and click on Finish.
3. Each available driver has a slightly different set of options, but they all let you name your data source and add a short description. When the ODBC Microsoft Access 97 Setup

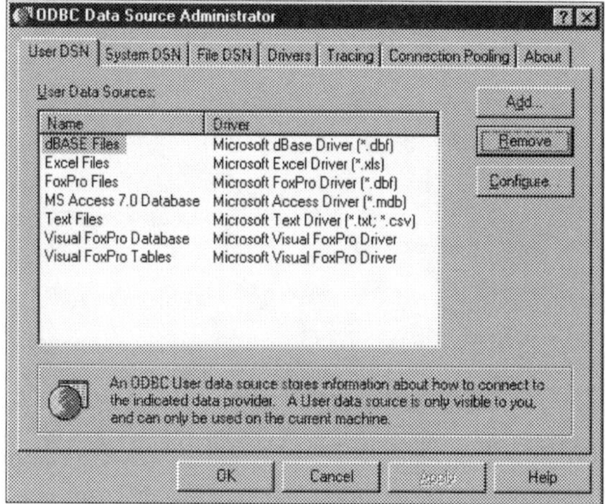

Figure 19.3
Adding a new ODBC data source.

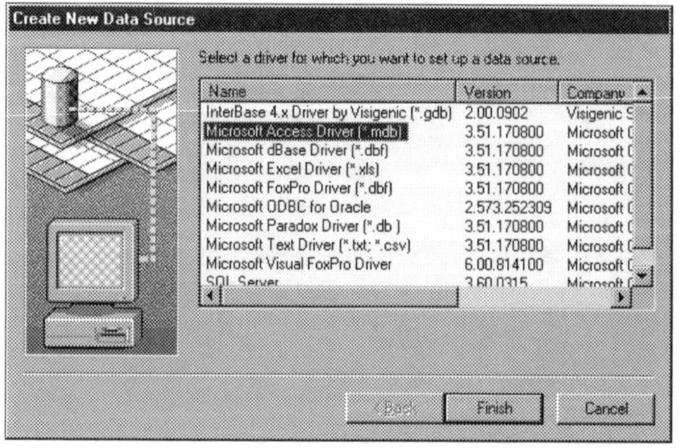

Figure 19.4
Selecting an ODBC driver.

dialog box appears, as shown in Figure 19.5, enter the data-source name "BucketOStuff". You can add any description you like. If you want to protect your database with a password, you can add a user name and a password by clicking on Advanced.

4. After you've named your data source, you need to connect it to a database. Click on Select; the Select Database dialog box shown in Figure 19.6 allows you to navigate your hard disk, looking for the necessary file. Locate the copy of Sampdata.mdb you stored in your data directory, select it, and then click on OK.
5. The new BucketOStuff User DSN now appears in the ODBC Data Source Administrator. Click on OK to close the application.

Now, let's go to AppWizard and build a database application.

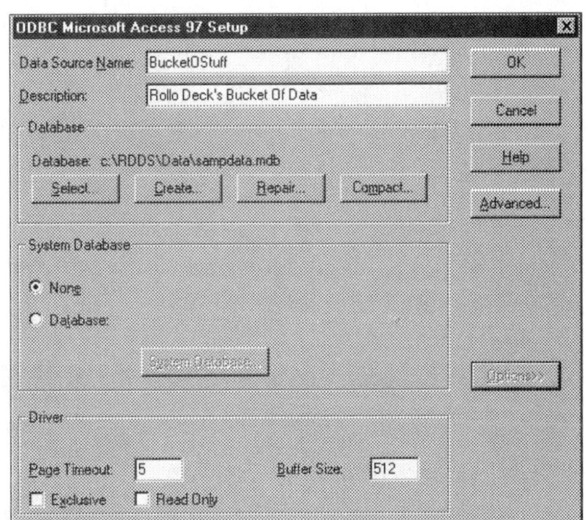

Figure 19.5
Naming and describing your data source.

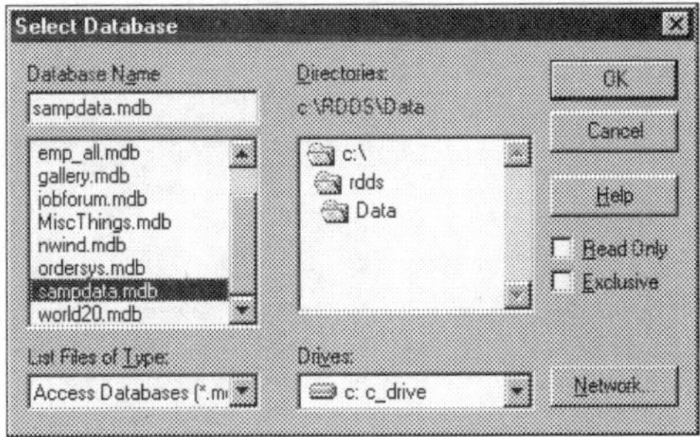

Figure 19.6
Telling ODBC where the files are.

Step 2: Creating An ODBC Application With AppWizard

Your first application is named OBos. (This intriguing acronym stands for **O**DBC **B**ucket**OS**tuff, of course.) Later, you'll follow up with DBos (**D**AO **B**ucket**OS**tuff) and EBos (OL**E** DB **B**ucket**OS**tuff). You'll eventually add ABos (**A**DO **B**ucket**OS**tuff) and **R**Bos (**R**DO **B**ucket**OS**tuff), as well. By the time you're done, believe us, you'll be tired of *Stuff*.

Begin by running AppWizard to create a new MFC App Wizard (exe) project. Name the project OBos, and then follow these instructions:

1. In the MFC AppWizard - Step 1 dialog box, choose an SDI application with DocView support.
2. In the MFC AppWizard - Step 2 dialog box, choose Database View Without File Support. (You choose With File Support when your application reads and writes regular files and works with data stored in a database.) When your screen looks like Figure 19.7, click on Data Source.
3. In the Recordset Type group box, click on Dynaset. Whereas a snapshot merely provides access to a copy of data from the database, a dynaset lets you directly update the database. In the Datasource group box, click on the ODBC radio button,

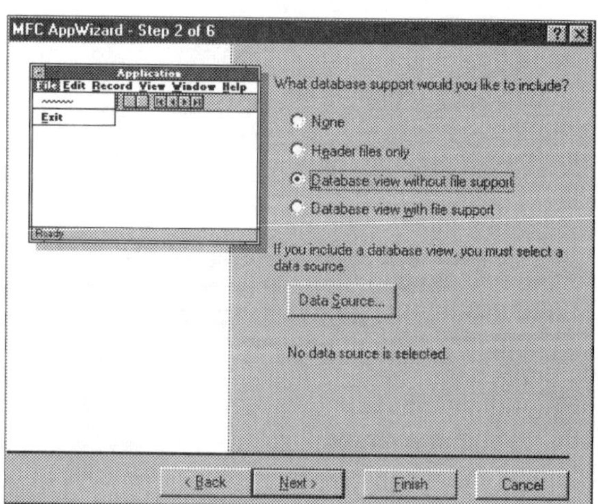

Figure 19.7
Selecting the database options.

and then choose BucketOStuff from the drop-down list, as you can see in Figure 19.8. Click on OK.

4. AppWizard will open the database to determine its structure. It takes the information it retrieves and stores it in a list box in the Select Database Tables dialog box. Despite its title, the list box includes entries other than tables, such as database queries and views. Locate Customers in the list, as shown in Figure 19.9, and click on OK. (If you look back at Figure 19.1, where you used the DAOView application to look at Sampdata, you'll see the structure of the Customers table—the table you'll work with.) When the MFC AppWizard - Step 2 screen opens, click on Next.
5. Accept the defaults in the MFC AppWizard - Step 3, Step 4, and Step 5 dialog boxes. When the Step 6 screen appears (see Figure 19.10), notice two things. First, the base class used for the view is **CRecordView**. **CRecordView** is a subclass of **CFormView**, which allows you to create your interface using the Dialog Editor, much like the dialog-based applications we began with in this book. Second, a fifth class—**COBosSet**—

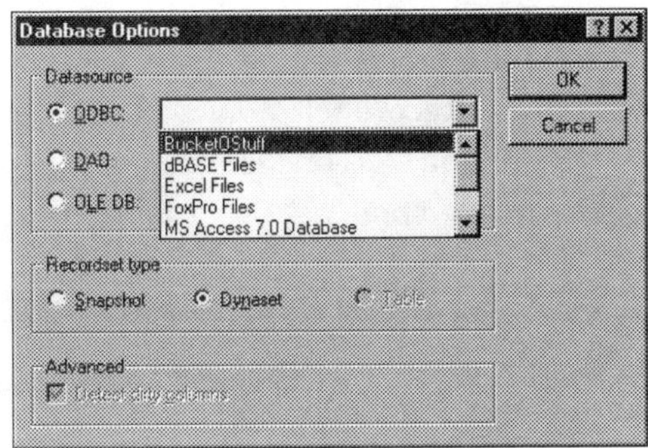

Figure 19.8
Selecting an ODBC data source.

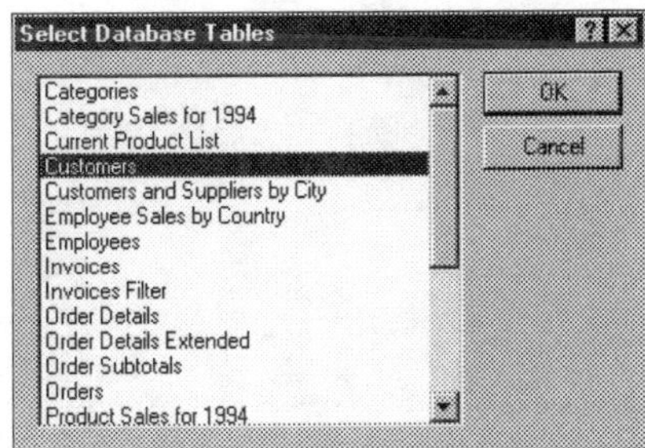

Figure 19.9
Choosing a database table.

supplements the four classes that normally comprise an SDI application. **COBosSet** is a subclass of **CRecordSet**; you'll use **COBosSet** as a proxy to read and write database information.

What Do You Mean, Tables?

If you're very attentive, you may have noticed the "s" on the end of the name of the Select Database Tables dialog box. If you're adventurous, you may even have tried selecting several tables, and found out that it works just fine. But, here's a word of advice: Don't select multiple tables.

When you select multiple tables in the Select Database Tables dialog box, the AppWizard generates an application that uses an SQL query to retrieve the Cartesian product of all of the tables you've selected. The result can easily contain an enormous number of records.

*If you want to work with multiple tables, identify the primary table using the Select Database Tables dialog box. Then, add additional classes derived from **CRecordSet** after AppWizard creates the application.*

Step 3: Creating Your Form

Click on Finish and then on OK to let AppWizard generate the application. Once AppWizard finishes writing the files, it will launch the Dialog Editor so that you can design your new form. **CRecordView** applications are built around a dialog box that acts as the main window of the application. You use the main dialog box like a form, to display the values stored in the fields of a single database record.

To help you, the AppWizard **CRecordView** application also includes toolbar buttons and menu selections that allow you to traverse the database by moving to the next, previous, first, or last record. As you move from record to record, the fields on your form are refreshed with the values stored in the database table. If you enter a new value in one of the controls on your form, the value you entered is written to the table when you move to a new record.

To help this process along, every **CRecordView** application has at least one **CRecordSet**-derived class. This class (which is created by AppWizard) has one member variable for each field (or column, if you prefer) in your table. You can see these proxy

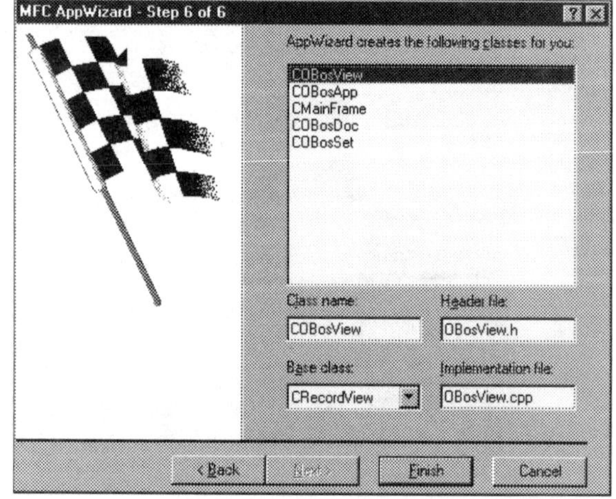

Figure 19.10
The OBos classes.

variables by pressing Ctrl+W to start ClassWizard, changing to the Member Variables tab, and then selecting the **COBosSet** class from the Class Name drop-down list.

Figure 19.11 shows the member variables of the **COBosSet** class. In this case, all the variables are **CString** objects, but that isn't always—or even normally—true. Each variable created by AppWizard usually has a type similar to that of the corresponding database field. In addition to creating the member variables, AppWizard writes a set of data-exchange functions—similar to the **DDX** functions used in dialog boxes—to transfer information between the controls used to display the information and the database fields defined in the **CRecordSet** class.

Here are the steps to create the OBos main form:

1. Be sure the OBos project is open. Open the ResourceView pane in the Workspace window and expand the Dialogs folder. Locate the **IDD_OBOS_FORM** resource and double-click to open the Dialog Editor. Delete the To Do static-text control.
2. You won't use all the fields in the record set. Instead, you'll create a dialog box that displays the information found on a mailing label. Drag and drop a groupbox control onto your form, expand it around the perimeter, and add the caption "Mailing Labels".

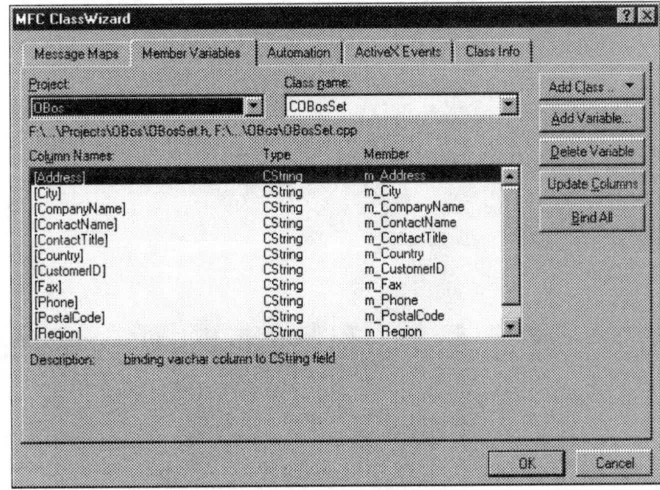

Figure 19.11
Examining the **COBosSet** variables in ClassWizard.

3. Drag four static-text controls to the form and arrange them in a column down the left side. Use the Alignment tools to line them up and space them evenly. Leave the ID of each control set to **ID_STATIC**, but change their alignment to Right, and give them the captions "Name", "Address", "City, State, Zip", and "Country".
4. Drag and drop six edit controls onto your form and arrange them as shown in Figure 19.12. Change the IDs of the controls to match the database fields you're using. Your IDs should be **IDC_COMPANYNAME**, **IDC_ADDRESS**, **IDC_CITY**, **IDC_REGION**, **IDC_POSTALCODE**, and **IDC_COUNTRY**. Once your form looks like Figure 19.12, you're ready to go onto the next step—hooking up the code.

Step 4: Hooking Up The Pieces

To make the data transfer work, you need to associate each edit control with the **COBosSet** variable representing the database field. You make this association by means of a *foreign connection*: an indirect mapping between a Windows control and a member variable in the **COBosSet** class.

You already know how to use ClassWizard to associate a control like **IDC_ADDRESS** with a **CString** member variable like **m_Address**. If you do this in a dialog box, any changes made to **m_Address** are copied into (or out of) the **IDC_ADDRESS** control during the **DoDataExchange()** function.

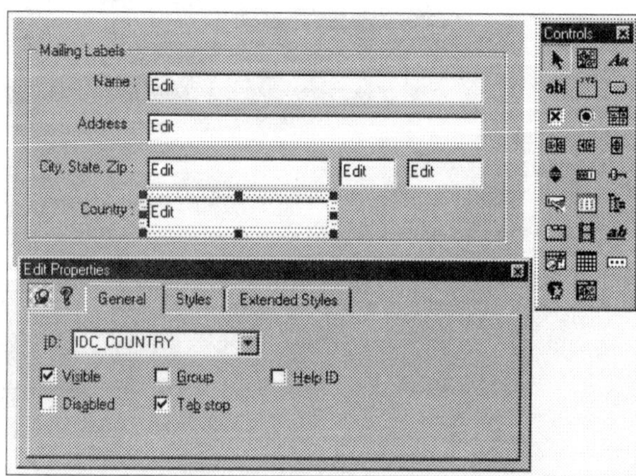

Figure 19.12
Adding edit fields.

However, when you use a **CRecordView**, ClassWizard lets you associate a control with one of the member variables in the **COBosSet** class. You do so via the **COBosView** class member variable **m_pSet**, which points to your program's **COBosSet** object.

Here are the steps to follow:

1. Open ClassWizard by pressing Ctrl+W or choosing View|ClassWizard from the main menu. Select the **COBosView** class in the Class Name drop-down list. Select the Member Variables tab so you can see the resource IDs of the edit controls you just added.
2. Select each of the resource IDs in turn and click on Add Variable just as if you were working in a regular dialog box. Notice that when the Add Member Variable dialog box appears, the Member Variable Name field is no longer a simple Edit field—it's now a drop-down list, containing indirect variable references like **m_pSet->m_Address**. You can see this illustrated in Figure 19.13. Hook up each control to its correct **CRecordSet** field by using a **CString** member variable that holds its value.
3. Each foreign variable added by ClassWizard lets you include a length validation. This is important when you create a **CRecordView** application. When fields are written back to the database, you must be careful to send no more characters

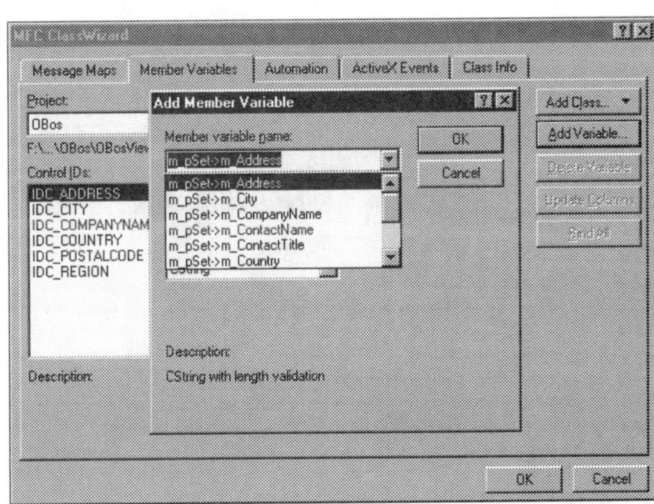

Figure 19.13
Making foreign connections with ClassWizard.

than will fit. If you look back at Figure 19.1 (or run the DAOView application on Sampdata.mdb once again), you'll see that each field in the Customers table has a maximum length. Enter those lengths in the Maximum Characters field to add validation to each of the foreign variables defined in the **COBosView** class, as shown in Figure 19.14. Your application will validate the data before shipping it to the database.

Now, compile and run the program. Look at Figure 19.15, and notice that you can navigate through the database using the VCR-style toolbar buttons. You can also navigate by using the commands on the Record menu. If you change the data, the application writes your changes to the database when you move off the current record. All this—and you didn't write a single line of code.

However, to make OBos a fully functional table-maintenance utility, you'll have to add some code. In the next section, you'll first see how to filter your data, thereby displaying only those records you're interested in. Then, we'll show you how to add code that adds and deletes new records.

Adding Code To OBos

In a **CRecordView** application, the document class has little to do, because the database stores and retrieves information. Thus,

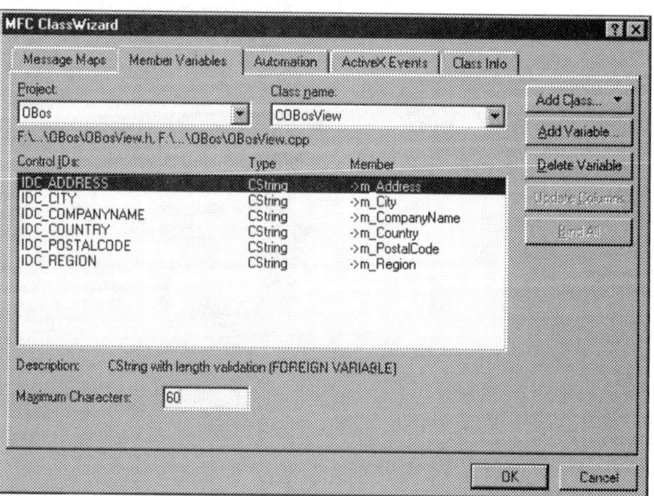

Figure 19.14
Validating input fields with ClassWizard.

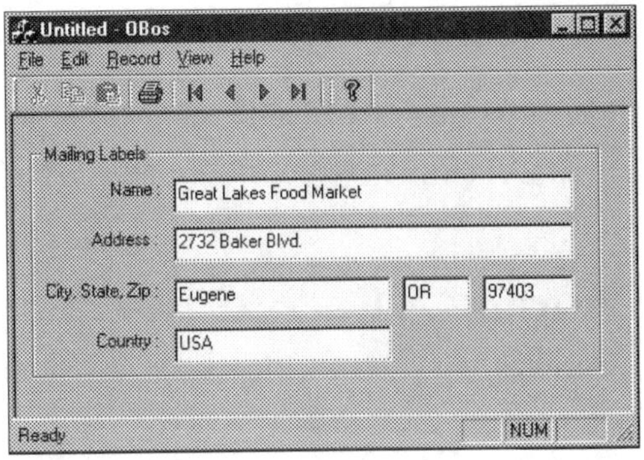

Figure 19.15
Running the OBos application.

for instance, the **COBosDoc** class has no serialize function. The document class merely holds a **CRecordSet** object as a public member.

When your application begins, the view class's **OnInitialUpdate()** function stores the address of your document's **CRecordSet** object in its **m_pSet** data member, like this:

```
m_pSet = &GetDocument()->m_oBosSet;
```

Then, it calls the base class **OnInitialUpdate()** function, which fills the record set with data from the database, constructs each control on your form, and transfers the data from the first record in the record set into the controls. Only then does the function make your application's window visible.

After your view class retrieves the **CRecordSet** object—but before it calls **CRecordView::OnInitialUpdate()**—you have an opportunity to specify how records are retrieved, by setting the value of the **m_strFilter** and **m_strSort** fields in the **CRecordSet** object. The **m_strFilter** value specifies which records are retrieved, and the **m_strSort** value specifies the order in which they're retrieved.

Here's how it works. Suppose you want to display only records for customers located in the USA. Add this line right before the call to **CRecordView::OnInitialUpdate()**:

```
m_pSet->m_strFilter = "Country = 'USA'";
```

Similarly, suppose you want to sort the records by PostalCode value. Simply add the line

```
m_pSet->m_strSort = "PostalCode";
```

If **m_strFilter** and **m_strSort** are empty (the default), your record set contains all the records in the table in no particular order: It's just a BucketOStuff.

Adding A Record Filter

Rather than hard-wiring the values for **m_strFilter** or **m_strSort**, let's add an edit control that lets you specify at runtime what records you'd like to see. Here are the steps to follow:

1. Open the OBos project and bring up **IDD_OBOS_FORM** in the Dialog Editor. Enlarge the dialog box and move the existing controls down, to allow room for the new controls at the top.
2. Drag and drop a static-text field, an edit control, and a push-button control onto the form. Place them as shown in Figure 19.16.
3. Change the caption of the static-text control to "Country". Set the resource ID of the edit control to **IDC_COUNTRY_FILTER**. Enter the caption "&Filter" for the push button and change its resource ID to **IDC_FILTER**.
4. Using ClassWizard, add a member variable to the edit control. Name the variable **m_CountryFilter**, set its Category to Control, and make its Variable type **CEdit**. When your screen looks like Figure 19.17, click on OK. Then close the Class Wizard.
5. Double-click on the **IDC_FILTER** push-button control and create a new **COBosView** class handler called **OnFilter()**. Enter the code shown in Listing 19.1.

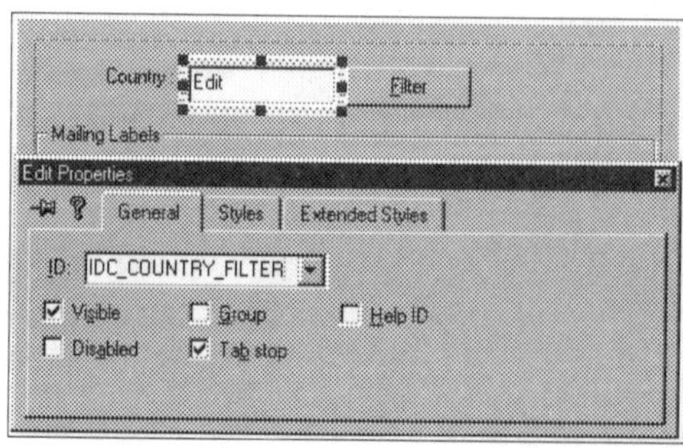

Figure 19.16
Adding the record filter fields.

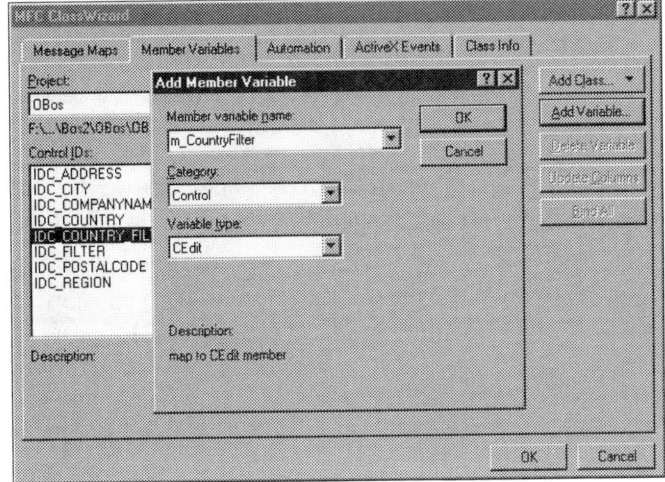

Figure 19.17
Connecting the filter edit control.

Listing 19.1 The COBosView::OnFilter() member function.

```
void COBosView::OnFilter()
{
    CString filter = "";
    m_CountryFilter.GetWindowText(filter);
    if (filter == "")
    {
        m_pSet->m_strFilter = "";
    }
    else
    {
        m_pSet->m_strFilter = "Country = '"+filter+"'";
    }
    m_pSet->Requery();
    UpdateData(FALSE);
}
```

How OnFilter() Works

The **OnFilter()** handler first extracts the text from the **IDC_COUNTRY_FILTER** edit control by using the **GetWindowText()** function. When the control is empty, the code selects all the records by setting **m_pSet->m_strFilter** to "". If the edit control contains a value, the code concatenates the value with the "Country=" string that restricts the values retrieved from the database.

After you construct a record set, changing the value of its **m_strFilter** or **m_strSort** member won't change the values or order of values in the record set. MFC reads the **m_strFilter** and **m_strSort** values when it retrieves data. To tell your **COBosSet** object to build a new record set, you simply call its **Requery()** method.

After all this, one nagging little problem remains. The record set has changed, but the program still displays a record from the old record set. To refresh the display, you must exchange the data in the record-set variables with the controls in your dialog box by calling **UpdateData(FALSE)**.

Go ahead and run the new version of OBos. When you first start the application, it retrieves all the records from the Customers table. If you type "USA" in the Country edit box and then click on Filter, the application displays only customers with USA as their Country value.

Adding And Deleting Records

You can't yet use the OBos form to add data to the Customers table, because the form lacks some of the necessary fields, such as CustomerID. Let's create a special form, just for data entry. In the process, you'll learn how to use a regular dialog box, along with a **CRecordView** form.

Here are the steps to follow to create the Add A Record dialog box:

1. Be sure the OBos project is open and then select Insert|Resource from the main menu. When the Insert Resource dialog box appears, select Dialog in the Resource Type list box, then click on New.
2. Change the caption of the dialog box to "Add New Record" and change its resource ID to **IDD_ADD_NEW**.
3. Drag and drop 11 static-text controls and 11 edit controls onto your dialog box. Arrange the controls as shown in Figure 19.18. Leave the static-text controls' resource IDs set to **IDC_STATIC**. Change the caption of each static-text control and the Resource ID of each edit field to reflect the name of the corresponding field in the Customers table. For

example, give the first edit field the Resource ID **IDC_CUSTOMER_ID**.

4. Hold down the Ctrl key and double-click on the first edit control, **IDC_CUSTOMER_ID**. ClassWizard will notice that you don't have a class defined for the **IDD_ADD_NEW** dialog resource. Select New Class and click on OK. When the New Class dialog box opens, use **CAddNew** for the class name and base your class on **CDialog**, as shown in Figure 19.19.
5. Add member variables for each control in the Add New Record dialog box. Give each variable the same name as the corresponding variable in the view class, if one exists. Make the variables **CStrings**—add validation in ClassWizard to ensure that the length of each field matches the length of the corresponding record in the Customers table. (To determine the proper field lengths, look at Figure 19.1 or use the DAOView utility program.)
6. Open the **IDR_MAINFRAME** menu in the Menu Editor and add a separator after the Last Record menu item. Add two new menu items. Make the first item's caption "&Add New" and its resource ID **ID_RECORD_ADD_NEW**, as shown in Figure 19.20. Caption the second menu item "&Delete" and give it the resource ID **ID_RECORD_DELETE**.
7. Use ClassWizard to hook up **COMMAND** handlers in the **COBosView** class for **ID_RECORD_ADD_NEW** and

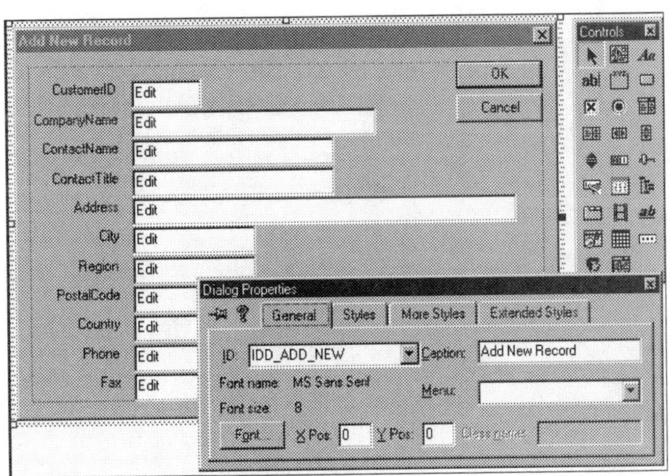

Figure 19.18
Creating the Add New Record dialog box.

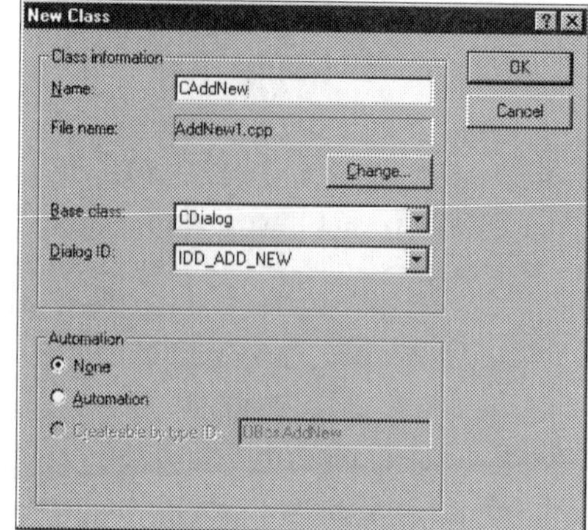

Figure 19.19
Creating the **CAddNew** dialog class.

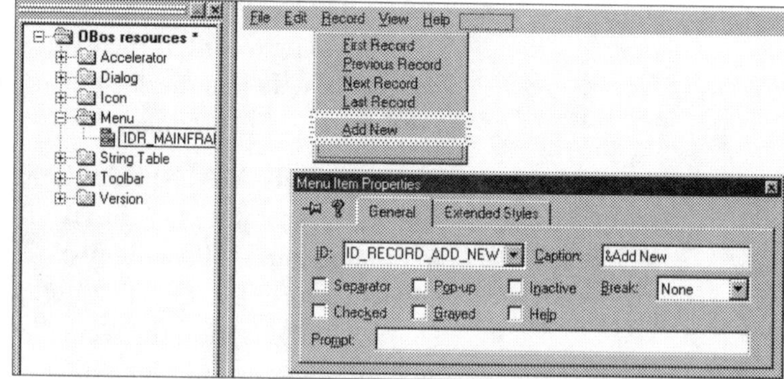

Figure 19.20
Creating menu items for Add New and Delete.

ID_RECORD_DELETE—name them **OnRecordAddNew()** and **OnRecordDelete()**. Add the highlighted code shown in Listing 19.2.

Listing 19.2 The OnRecordAddNew() and OnRecordDelete() functions.

```
void COBosView::OnRecordAddNew()
{
    // 1. Create a new Add Dialog
    CAddNew dlg;
    if (dlg.DoModal() == IDOK)
    {
        // 2. Check to make sure the required field is
        // not empty
        if (dlg.m_CompanyName.IsEmpty())
        {
```

```
            MessageBox(
                "Cannot add without company name");
            return;
        }
        // 3. Add a new record to the record set
        m_pSet->AddNew();

        // 4. Transfer the field values from the dialog
        // to the record set
        m_pSet->m_Address       = dlg.m_Address;
        m_pSet->m_City          = dlg.m_City;
        m_pSet->m_CompanyName   = dlg.m_CompanyName;
        m_pSet->m_ContactName   = dlg.m_ContactName;
        m_pSet->m_ContactTitle  = dlg.m_ContactTitle;
        m_pSet->m_Country       = dlg.m_Country;
        m_pSet->m_CustomerID    = dlg.m_CustomerID;
        m_pSet->m_Fax           = dlg.m_Fax;
        m_pSet->m_Phone         = dlg.m_Phone;
        m_pSet->m_PostalCode    = dlg.m_PostalCode;
        m_pSet->m_Region        = dlg.m_Region;

        // 5. Write the changes out to the database
        m_pSet->Update();

        // 6. Position on our new record
        m_pSet->MoveLast();

        // 7. Update the display
        UpdateData(FALSE);
    }
}

void COBosView::OnRecordDelete()
{
    // Try to delete a record
    try
    {
        m_pSet->Delete();
    }
    catch (CDBException* error)
    {
        AfxMessageBox(error->m_strError);
        error->Delete();
        m_pSet->MoveFirst();
        UpdateData(FALSE);
        return;
    }
    // Move to a new record
```

```
    m_pSet->MoveNext();
    if (m_pSet->IsEOF())
        m_pSet->MoveLast();

    UpdateData(FALSE);
}
```

8. Add the following line near the top of OBosView.cpp, immediately after the other **includes**:

```
#include "AddNew.h"
```

9. Compile and run the application.

How Adding Records Works

To add a new record to the database, the code constructs a new **CAddNew** dialog object, then calls its **DoModal()** function. If **DoModal()** returns **IDOK**, the code attempts to add the new record, but first it makes sure the user has supplied a company name. If not, it prints a polite message and returns. If you want to add more validation, you can do so.

To add a new record to a **CRecordSet**, the code calls the **AddNew()** member function, which creates a new, blank record. After creating the new record, the **OnRecordAddNew()** function transfers each field from the **CAddNew** dialog box to the new, blank record in the record set.

Once a new record is added to the record set, it isn't actually written to the database until the **Update()** function is called. Before you try to update the database, you should call **IsUpdatable()** to check whether updates are allowed. The update may also fail for other reasons. For instance, if you use the same CustomerID value for two records, you'll see the error message shown in Figure 19.21.

Once **Update()** writes the data to the database, you can go to the new record by calling **MoveLast()**. Even if the record set is sorted or filtered, new records are added to the end of the record set. If you want to put a particular record "in its place," you must call **Requery()** after calling **Update()**. However, if you do so, there's

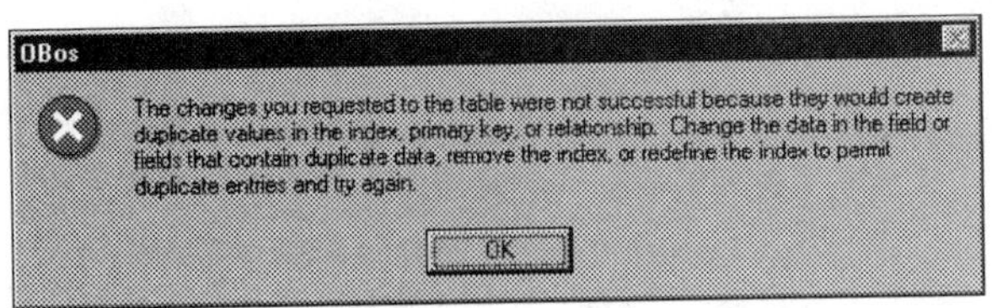

Figure 19.21
Attempting to add a duplicate record to the Customers table.

no way to position your form on the newly added record, short of searching the entire table to find it.

How Deleting Records Works

Deleting a record is a little easier than adding a new one. You simply call the **Delete()** member function—which deletes the current record in the record set—and then move to a new record. In the **OnRecordDelete()** function, the code moves to a new record by calling **MoveNext()** and then testing the end-of-file value using the **IsEOF()** member function. If **IsEOF()** returns true, then you've just deleted the last record; you need to use **MoveLast()**, rather than **MoveNext()**. You may be tempted, but don't try to rewrite the code like this:

```
if (m_pSet->IsEof())
    m_pSet->MoveLast();
else
    m_pSet->MoveNext();
```

As reasonable as this code seems, it won't work: The end-of-file flag isn't triggered until you attempt to move forward *past* the last record.

It might seem that less could go wrong when deleting a record, but that isn't really true. If you delete a customer record while the customer still owes you money, your business is going to be in big trouble—you'll have invoice records showing that *someone* bought those new computers, but you won't have any idea who it was.

To avoid these kinds of problems, database-management systems enforce *referential integrity rules*, which prevent programs from deleting a record that other records depend on. When you try to do so, a **CDBException** exception is thrown. The code in **OnRecordDelete()** places the **Delete()** function call in a C++

try-catch block—if an error occurs, the program prints a message and moves to the first record. Figure 19.22 shows the message produced after we failed to delete a record.

Using DAO

When you create a database application using ODBC, your program talks to an ODBC driver, and the driver talks to a database or other source of data, such as a text file. This indirection promises quite a bit of flexibility—just reconfigure your ODBC data source, and your program can work with anything from a PC database to a client-server mainframe database.

On the other hand, this flexibility comes at a price. If the database you're using includes special features, you may not be able to access them through the ODBC driver. Even if you can, you thereby lose the portability you gained by using ODBC in the first place. In addition, when you're working with PC databases like Visual FoxPro and Access, access via ODBC usually isn't as fast as directly connecting to the PC database engine. That's what Microsoft's Data Access Objects (DAO) lets you do.

With DAO, you can use the Access (Jet) database engine directly to read and write Access databases. In addition, the Jet engine can directly read and write a variety of PC desktop files, such as FoxPro and dBASE. (However, this capability isn't directly supported by the AppWizard.) You can even use Access to attach to remote ODBC data sources, although doing so is somewhat inefficient.

Apart from efficiency, DAO offers several other advantages over ODBC. The DAO classes are generally more capable. You can easily search a record set for a particular value or save your place with a bookmark. In addition, you can use Data Definition Language (DDL) commands to add tables and change the structure of your database. Finally, DAO provides an object-oriented interface that's an especially good match for C++.

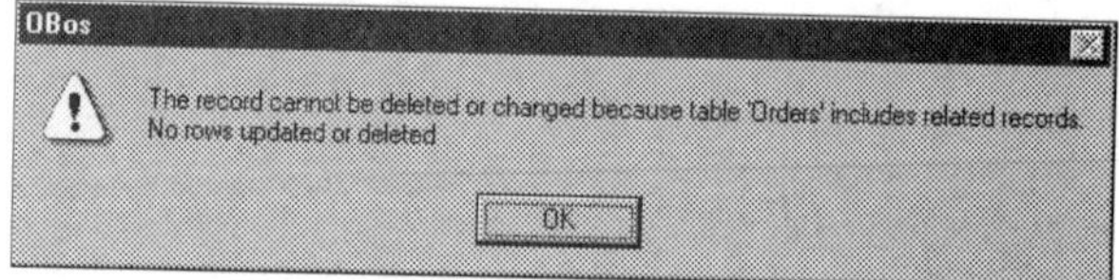

Figure 19.22
Attempting to delete a record that has related records.

Creating A CDaoRecordView Application

The structure of an MFC DocView application that uses the DAO classes is similar to one that uses the ODBC classes. A few class names change. For instance, your application uses a **CDaoRecordView** rather than a **CRecordView**. You work with a pointer to a **CDaoRecordSet** object, rather than a pointer to a **CRecordSet** object. Other than the differently named classes, little else changes—the names of class data members and the way that ClassWizard interacts with data fields stay the same. If you pay little attention to class names, you might not even notice the difference—at least, until time to use the **CDaoRecordSet**. Then, you'd notice the presence of additional functions like **FindFirst()** and **Seek()**.

To give you a feel for working with the **CDaoRecordView** class, let's build another simple browsing application. This one will use the Shippers table from the same Sampdata.mdb database you used in the previous example. The Shippers table has only three fields, as you can see in Figure 19.23.

Here are the steps to follow:

1. Create a new AppWizard MFC project and name it DBos. Make it an SDI application with DocView support. In the MFC AppWizard - Step 2 dialog box, choose Database Without File Support. Click on Data Source to display the Database Options dialog box, shown in Figure 19.24. Click on the DAO radio button, and select the Table radio button in

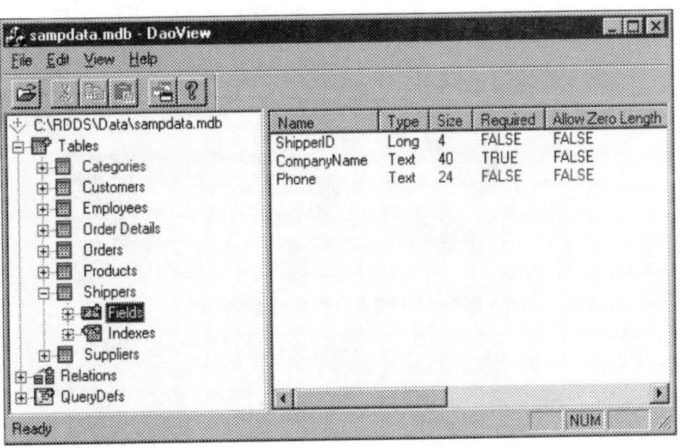

Figure 19.23
Examining the Shippers table in the DAOView application.

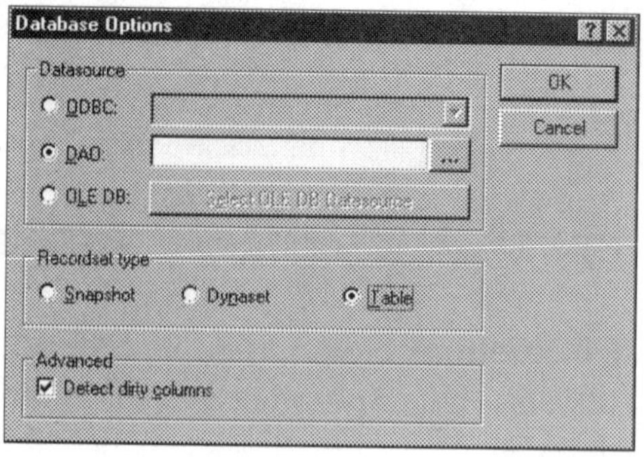

Figure 19.24
Filling in the Database Options dialog box for the DBos application.

the Recordset Type section. DAO lets you work directly with the underlying tables—something you can't do using ODBC. Click on the button with the ellipsis, select your database, and click on OK.

2. A list of database tables will open. (If you'd chosen Dynaset or Snapshot as your record source, you'd also see a list of database queries in this list box.) Choose the Shippers table, as you can see in Figure 19.25, and click on OK.
3. Accept the default values in the rest of the AppWizard steps. Notice that rather than **CRecordView**, your application is based on **CDaoRecordView**. Once AppWizard finishes generating the files for your application, open ClassWizard and look at the fields generated for the **CDBosSet** class. As you can see in Figure 19.26, AppWizard creates a field for each column in the database. Note that this time, not all the member variables are **CStrings—m_ShipperID** is a **long**.
4. Open the main form dialog box in the Dialog Editor, delete the To Do static-text control, and place three static-text labels and three edit controls on the dialog box. Name the

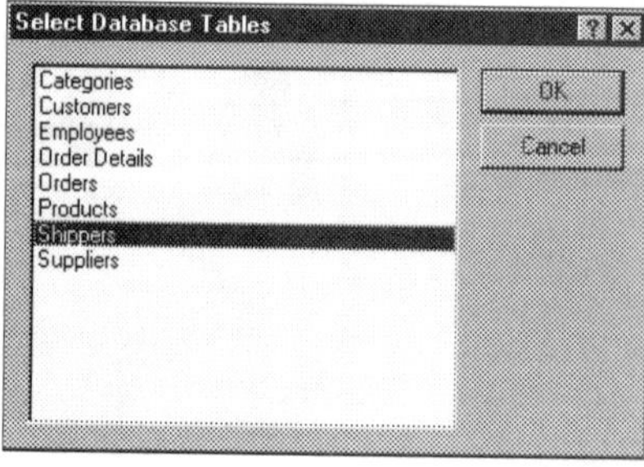

Figure 19.25
Selecting a database table in the DBos application.

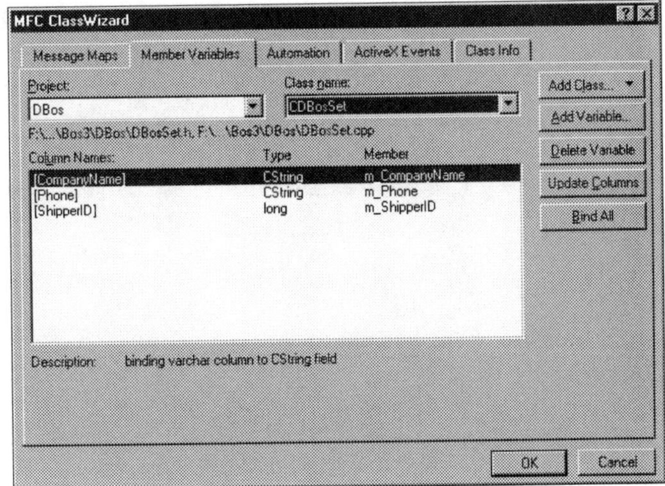

Figure 19.26
The **CDBosSet** member variables.

edit controls **IDC_SHIPPER_ID**, **IDC_COMPANY_NAME**, and **IDC_PHONE**. Set their label captions to "ShipperID", "CompanyName", and "Phone", respectively. Arrange the components and use the Layout|Tab Order menu command to set the tab order as shown in Figure 19.27.

5. Using ClassWizard, associate each edit control with one of the foreign variables in the **CDBosSet** class, as you can see in Figure 19.28. In the Add Member Variable dialog box, use the drop-down list box to select the name of each foreign variable. Set the length of the Company Name field to 40 and the length of the Phone field to 24. Don't specify a minimum or maximum value for the ShipperID field.

Compile and run the program. As before, you should be able to traverse the database and change the data items—all without writing any code. As before, though, you might want to make some improvements. This time, we'll skip the filter and sorting logic, and just work on Add and Delete.

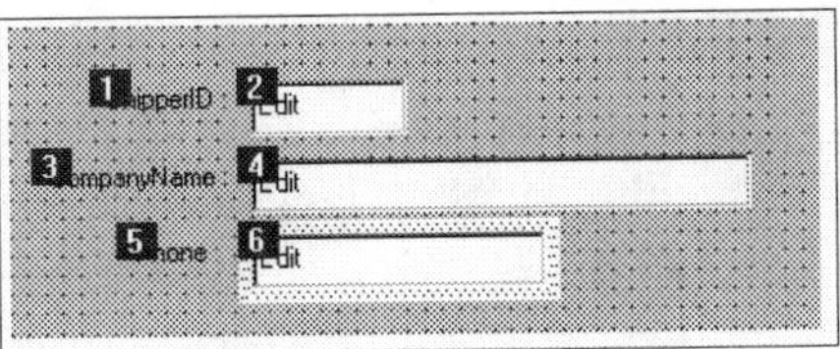

Figure 19.27
Laying out the controls for the DBos application.

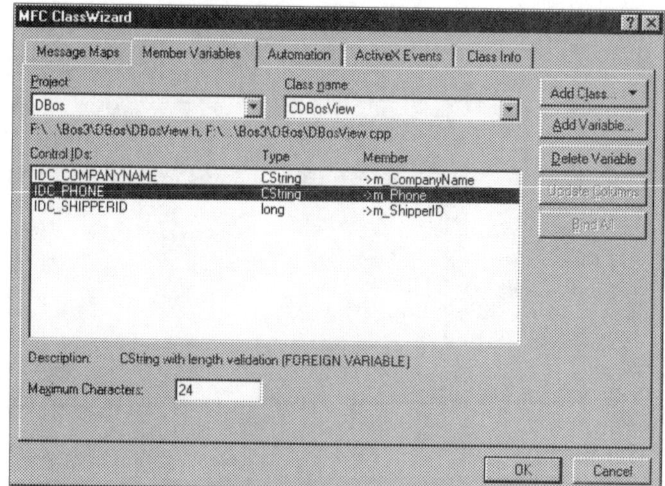

Figure 19.28
Adding member variables for your database fields.

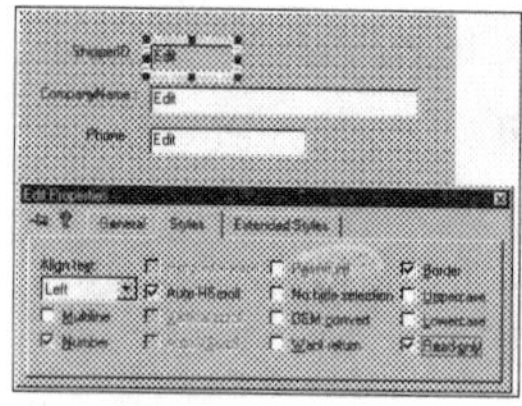

Figure 19.29
Protecting the ShipperID field from accidental injury.

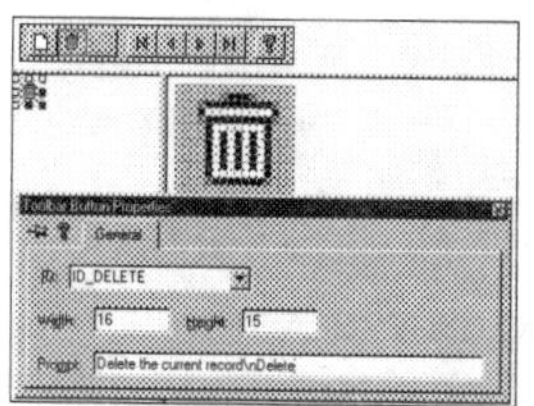

Figure 19.30
Creating the Add and Delete toolbar buttons.

Improving On DBos

You'll begin the improvements by changing the supplier ID from read-write to read-only. You don't have to add any code to do this—simply open the form in the Dialog Editor and select the Read-Only property checkbox for the **IDC_SHIPPER_ID** field, as shown in Figure 19.29. Since the field is read-only, you don't really need to select the Number style as well, but doing so doesn't hurt.

Rather than use the menu this time, let's attach the Add and Delete commands to toolbar buttons. Here are the steps to follow:

1. Open the **IDR_MAINFRAME** toolbar resource in the Toolbar Editor.
2. Remove the Cut, Copy, Paste, and Print buttons from the toolbar. Recall that you can remove a toolbar button by simply dragging it off the toolbar and dropping it in a pane other than the Toolbar Editor.
3. Add two new toolbar buttons to the left of the navigation arrows. On the first toolbar button, draw an outline of a sheet of paper. On the second, draw a small trash can. You can see how this is done in Figure 19.30. Assign them the resource IDs **ID_ADD_NEW** and **ID_DELETE**, respectively. Add an appropriate prompt for each button.

4. Add a new public **bool** member variable called **m_IsAdding** to the **CDBosView** class. Initialize the variable to **false** in the **CDBosView** constructor. Use ClassWizard to create a **COMMAND** handler for both **ID_ADD_NEW** and **ID_DELETE**, as you can see in Figure 19.31. Add the highlighted code shown in Listing 19.3 to the functions written by AppWizard.

Listing 19.3 The OnAddNew() and OnDelete() member functions.

```
void CDBosView::OnAddNew()
{
    m_pSet->MoveLast();
    long newID = m_pSet->m_ShipperID + 1;

    m_pSet->AddNew();
    m_pSet->SetFieldNull(&(m_pSet->m_ShipperID), FALSE);
    m_pSet->m_ShipperID = newID;
    UpdateData(FALSE);
    m_IsAdding = true;
}

void CDBosView::OnDelete()
{
    m_pSet->Delete();
    m_pSet->MoveNext();
    if (m_pSet->IsEOF())
        m_pSet->MoveLast();
    UpdateData(FALSE);
}
```

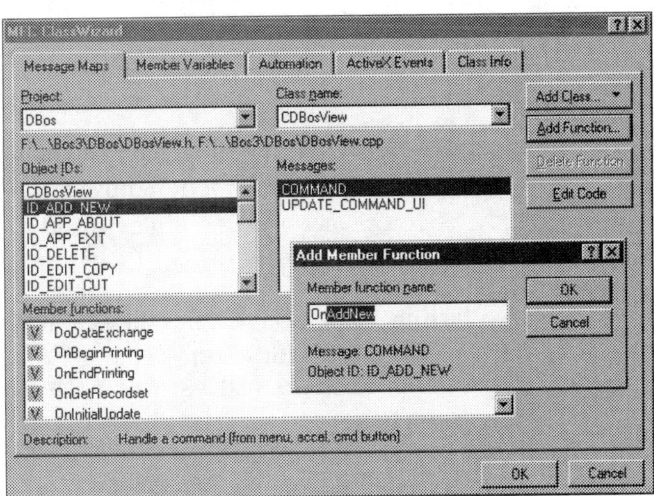

Figure 19.31
Adding command handlers.

Add And Delete In DBos

Back in the OBos application, you used a modal dialog box to add new records to the database. When the user clicks on Add New in DBos, the program goes to the last record in the file, extracts the ShipperID value as a key for the next record, and then calls **AddNew()**. Rather than have the user enter a new ShipperID, you calculate a new value and store it in the **m_ShipperID** field. Notice how the **SetFieldNull()** function prevents the system from blanking the ShipperID field.

Once you've set the key field, **OnAddNew()** sets the **m_IsAdding** field to **true** and returns. The **OnMove()** function—which calls the **CDaoRecordSet::Update()** function—writes the records to the database.

Unlike the OBos version of Delete, the **DBosView::OnDelete()** function lets the system deal with exceptions; it simply deletes the current record and then calls **MoveNext()**.

One Last Move

With a modal dialog box, such as the one you used in the OBos add-record routine, you can update the database when the dialog box is closed. However, when you use a regular, non-modal form like the DBos view class, you must look for another opportunity to write the data. As is often the case, you can write the data when the user moves off a record. To write the data, you must override the **OnMove()** function. Here's how:

1. Open ClassWizard and select the **CDBosView** class. Select the virtual **OnMove()** function in the Messages list box. Click on Add Function, as you can see in Figure 19.32.
2. The **CDaoView** class generally updates records satisfactorily. You want to take action only when you've added a new record, and the user is moving off it. Add the highlighted code shown in Listing 19.4 to implement this behavior.

Listing 19.4 The CDBosView::OnMove() overridden virtual function.

```
BOOL CDBosView::OnMove(UINT nIDMoveCommand)
{
    if (m_IsAdding)
    {
```

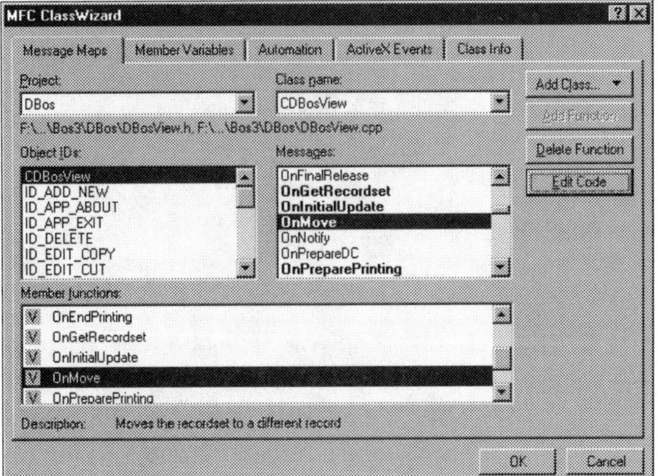

Figure 19.32
Overriding the virtual **OnMove()** function.

```
        UpdateData();
        try
        {
            m_pSet->Update();
        }
        catch (CDaoException* err)
        {
            AfxMessageBox(err->m_pErrorInfo
              ->m_strDescription);
            m_pSet->MoveLast();
            err->Delete();
        }
        UpdateData(FALSE);
        m_IsAdding = false;
        return TRUE;
    }
    return CDaoRecordView::OnMove(nIDMoveCommand);
}
```

Go ahead and take the program out for a spin, as you can see in Figure 19.33. Add and delete some records, and see how it works.

Using OLE DB

As you built the OBos and DBos applications, you probably noticed another available choice when you selected a data source: OLE DB. OLE DB is the latest Microsoft technology: It provides a single interface to all your data, whether it's on the Web, in a legacy system, or coming from a relational database.

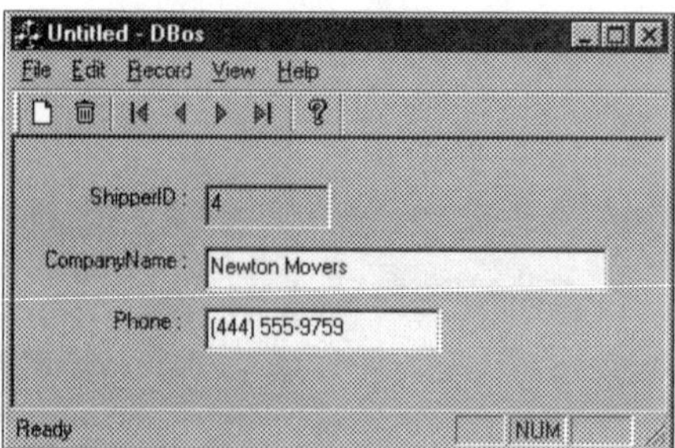

Figure 19.33
Running the DBos application.

Setting up your application to use an OLE DB data source is just as easy as setting up ODBC or DAO. After you select OLE DB in AppWizard, you choose an OLE DB provider and provide the necessary information to make a connection. Then, just as before, you select the table you want to work with, and AppWizard generates a skeleton application.

When you use the OLE DB classes, AppWizard generates a class based on the **COleDBRecordView** class. This is a **CFormView**-derived class that works very much like **CRecordView** or **CDaoRecordView** classes. You add controls to a dialog-based form, and the **COleDBRecordView** class retrieves data and navigates the database for you.

COleDBRecordView differs from the others primarily in that ClassWizard provides no support for mapping foreign fields to your controls—you must enter the code manually. Doing so isn't especially difficult, but it's tedious.

Our CD-ROM contains an EBos project that's similar to those you've created before. It uses the OLE DB classes to navigate through the Sampdata.mdb Products table. If you're interested in writing applications that use the OLE DB templates, then look at the code, paying special attention to the **DoDataExchange()** function. Also, run the program so you can see how it works.

Coming Up: ActiveX And Easy Street

As we come to the end of this chapter, you may feel that database handling in Visual C++ isn't all it could be. Writing database programs is certainly more difficult than it would be using Visual FoxPro, Visual Basic, or Access.

And, even though your Visual C++ programs are more efficient than programs written in those other languages, they're also much more simplistic. You haven't tackled multi-table joins, scrolling tables, or master-child forms. Actually, looking at the applications generated by AppWizard, it's not even clear where you'd *begin* to write such applications.

In the next chapter, rather than modifying more AppWizard generated code, you'll see why database development is so much easier in Visual FoxPro and Access. You'll leave behind the hard-coded AppWizard generated record sets and say hello to ActiveX database development.

You'll be pleasantly surprised.

Chapter 20
Relational Databasics

"When I use a word," Humpty Dumpty said, in a rather scornful tone, "it means just what I choose it to mean— neither more nor less."
"The question is," said Alice, "whether you can make words mean so many different things."
"The question is," said Humpty Dumpty, "which is to be master— that's all."

If you've lately come from another part of the programming universe to the world of relational databases, you can be forgiven if you feel a little like Alice in Lewis Carroll's *Through the Looking Glass*. Here, you'll find a plethora of terms— some of which, such as *database*, have several meanings.

A database is simply an organized collection of information. However, over time, the term has come to also refer to the software that manages that information. Technically, the software isn't a database, but a *database management system* (DBMS).

Database information can be organized in several ways. Early DBMS products arranged data in either a hierarchical or a networked pattern. Then, in the 1960s, Dr. E.F. Codd (working for IBM) invented the *relational database*, which organizes its information by using tables, rows, and columns.

In this chapter, we'll take you on a quick tour of relational database concepts and technology, including the use of Structured Query Language (SQL) to retrieve information from a database. And, on the way back from database-land, we'll stop on the ActiveX asteroid to learn about some strange creatures: data-bound controls.

What *Is* A Relational Database?

In a relational database, all information is stored in *tables* (technically called *relations*). As you can see in Figure 20.1, these tables look a great deal like spreadsheets—they consist of cells organized into rows and columns. Each table holds information about a single kind of information. You may have one table for your customers, another for your employees, and yet another for invoices.

Each *row* within the table (technically called a *tuple* and sometimes called a *row*) describes a single instance of the kind of object contained in the table. (Sometimes, rows are called *records*.) Each row in the Employees table would hold information about a single employee, for instance. Moreover, you'll generally design your tables such that every row contains some distinct value. Your Employees table would hold only one record for each employee.

Each row in a table can contain multiple *columns*, with each column storing the value for some attribute of the record. For example, columns in the Employees table would probably include the employee's name, address, job classification, and salary. (Columns are often called *fields* or *attributes*.)

Those Scheming Schemas

You'll benefit from using a DBMS, rather than a collection of random tables, because the DBMS software keeps track of the important details about the databases it manages. For instance, it

Employee ID	Name	Address	Job Class	Salary
1235	Dot Matrex	1234 South Street	Programmer	50,000
1305	Kay Sera	733 East 5th Street	Planner	150,000
1427	Barb Dwyer	12809 Mar Vista	Security	15,000
1811	Neil Doughn	623 Breckenridge Dr	Chaplain	15,000
1912	Paul Murkey	126 Oxford	Pollster	100,000
1011	Les Moody	119 Foothill Blvd	Psychologist	150,000
1112	Marge Novera	118 East Slauson Ave	Statistician	75,000

Figure 20.1
A database table.

knows the names of the tables it contains and the names of the columns contained in each table.

This kind of information is called *meta-data* (data about data). Like everything else in a relational database, it's stored in tables—in this case, tables used by the DBMS. The tables that describe the structure of the database are called the database *schema*. They allow your programs to discover what tables and fields are contained inside the database. Very large databases may have multiple schemas, grouped as a *catalog*.

In a database, all the values in every row of a particular column must have the same type. In the Employees database, for instance, the **Salary** column can hold only numeric values, never text. In this way, database tables are unlike spreadsheets—values stored in a spreadsheet column can be any type.

With many DBMS programs, however, you can go further than simply restricting a column to a specific type of value, such as numeric or text. You can also specify a *domain*: the set of acceptable values for the column. To describe the domain of a column, you define a special set of rules called *constraints*, which the DBMS subsequently enforces. For example, you could constrain the Salary column by specifying that every value must be greater than $10,000 and less than $1,000,000. Domain constraints help you avoid storing bad data in your database.

The Key Concept

Most tables are designed to include one particular column that's guaranteed to have a unique value. Your company may have many Employees named Jane Smith, for instance—but by including a unique **EmployeeID** column, you can keep from getting them confused.

Such a unique column is known as the table's *primary key*. No two rows within the Employees table can have the same **EmployeeID** value. Sometimes, no single column in a table holds unique values, ruling out the use of a single column as a primary key. In such a case you may designate a *composite primary key*, composed of values from multiple columns.

Primary keys ensure that every row in your table contains a unique value. Because of this, you can use the primary key of one table as a column in another table. If you have a Products table, for instance, your Invoice table doesn't need columns for **ProductName** and **ProductPrice**. Instead, you can simply insert the primary key from the Products table into a field in your Invoice table, and thus store the Products information in only one place.

When you use the primary key of one table as a linking field in another table, the field is called a *foreign key*. Figure 20.2 shows how primary and foreign keys are related. Unlike primary keys, values of foreign keys need not be unique. For example, several invoices may contain entries for Widgets.

We've introduced quite a few new terms in this section; Table 20.1 summarizes the most important ones. Check to be sure you understand each of the terms before proceeding to the next section. If a term is unclear, re-read its earlier description.

Part Table

Part No	Description	U/M	Unit Cost
414	Thingy	Case	150.00
550	Bobbin	Dozen	15.00
723	Widget	Gross	1.50

Primary Key

Invoiceline Table

Invoice No	Customer No	Part No	Qty
1211	312	723	15
1212	315	414	5
1215	214	723	150

Primary Key

Foreign Key

Figure 20.2
Primary and foreign keys.

Table 20.1 Relational database terms.

Term	Meaning
Table	A single kind of entity, consisting of rows and columns.
Row	A part of a table that represents some object, physical or conceptual.
Column	A part of a table that holds a single attribute of the table; attributes describe properties of objects.
Meta-data	Data about data. Allows a database to contain information describing itself.
Schema	Meta-data that describes the contents of a database, including its tables and their structures.
Catalog	A collection of schemas.
Domain	The acceptable range of values of a column.
Constraint	A rule intended to restrict data values; enforced by the DBMS.
Primary key	A column (or combination of columns) that yields a value unique to every row within a table.
Foreign key	A column (or combination of columns) that references the value of the primary key of a table.

Looking At A Database With DAO

Although the method for retrieving information from relational databases is somewhat standardized, there's no standard way to learn about the contents of a database. However, you can use the MFC DAO classes to take a look inside Microsoft Access databases. Let's see how this works by examining an example database.

Each year, the U.S. Department of Energy's Energy Information Administration (EIA) collects statistics about energy production and consumption throughout the world. The EIA then publishes this information in the International Energy Annual. The raw data used to create this annual report is available as a Microsoft Access database; you can download it from the EIA Web site at http://www.eia.doe.gov/emeu/world/main1.html. To save you the effort of downloading the relatively large files involved, we've included the current edition of the World Energy Database on the CD-ROM. You'll find two versions of the file: World20.mdb (in the older Microsoft Access 2.0 format) and World97.mdb (in the newer Access 97 format). We'll use World Energy Database for all the examples in this chapter.

The DBExplore Example

Using the MFC DAO database classes is easy. You first create a **CDaoDatabase** object and call its **Open()** member function, passing it the name of the Access database you want to work with. The **CDaoDatabase** object contains a collection of tables, queries, and relationships. By using the **CDaoDatabase** member functions, you can retrieve those objects or get information about them. Once you're done, you call the **Close()** method to free the connection to the database.

So far, all the database programs you've written have used hard-coded database names. However, with the help of **CDaoDatabase**, you can use the **CFileDialog** class to allow the user to open any Access database and explore its contents. Let's name the program DBExplore—here are the instructions for building it:

1. Use AppWizard to create an SDI DocView application named DBExplore. In the Step 2 dialog box, choose Header Files Only, as shown in Figure 20.3. Click on Next.
2. Accept the defaults in the Step 3 dialog box and deselect the Printing check box in Step 4. Accept the defaults in Step 5.

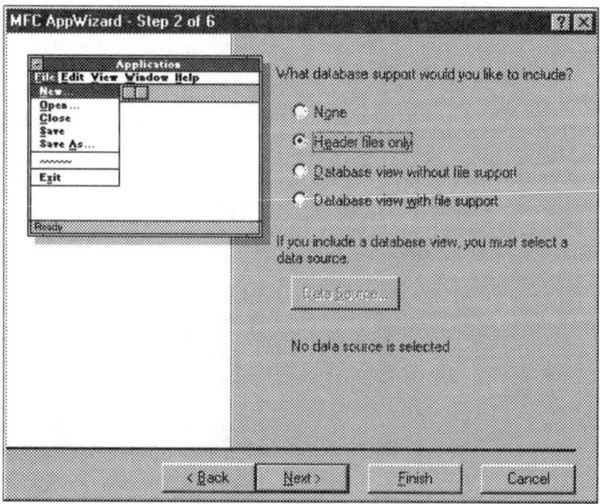

Figure 20.3
Database options for the DBExplore project.

In the Step 6 dialog box, change the view base class to **CFormView** and change each of the class names to **CDBEXXX** (with the exception of the **CMainFrame** class), as you can see in Figure 20.4.

3. Open the main form in the Dialog Editor and add two static-text labels, an edit field, and a list box. Size and arrange the items as shown in Figure 20.5. Caption the static-text labels "Database" and "Tables". Name the edit box **IDC_DBNAME** and the list box **IDC_TABLE_LIST**.
4. Use ClassWizard to add member variables for each control to the **CDBEView** class, as shown in Figure 20.6. Name the edit box **m_DBName**; make its Category value Control and its Type **CEdit**. Name the list box **m_TableList**; make its Category value Control and its Type **CListBox**.
5. Open the Menu Editor and remove the Edit Menu, as well as the File|New, File|Save, and File|Save As menu items. Your finished menu should look like Figure 20.7.

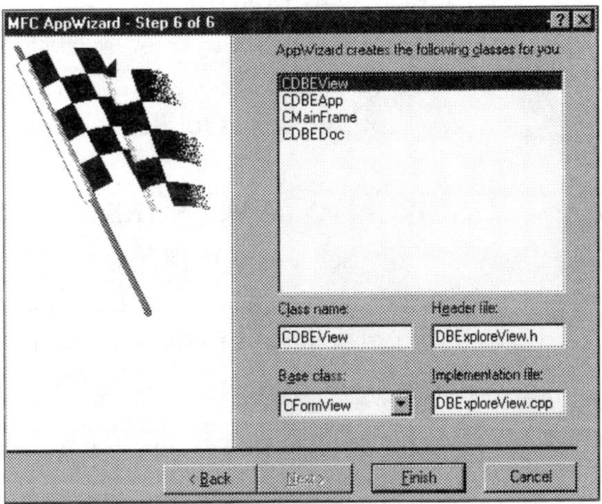

Figure 20.4
The DBExplore classes.

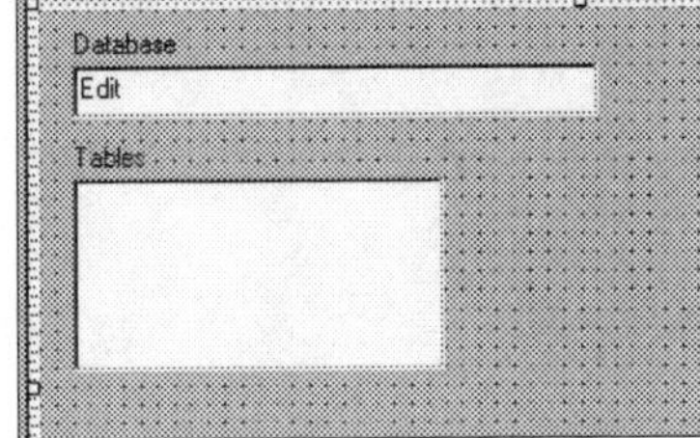

Figure 20.5
The DBExplore dialog box.

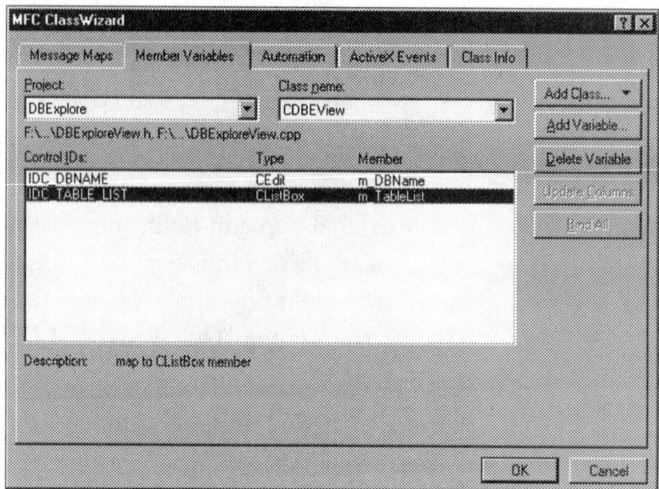

Figure 20.6
Control variables for DBExplore.

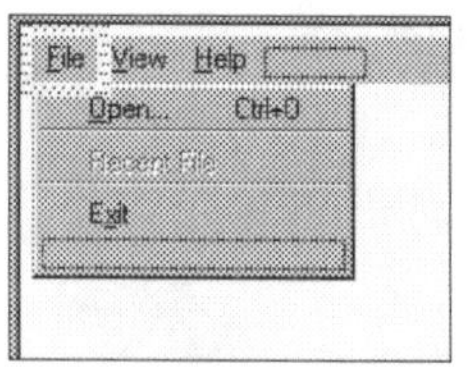

Figure 20.7
The DBExplore menu.

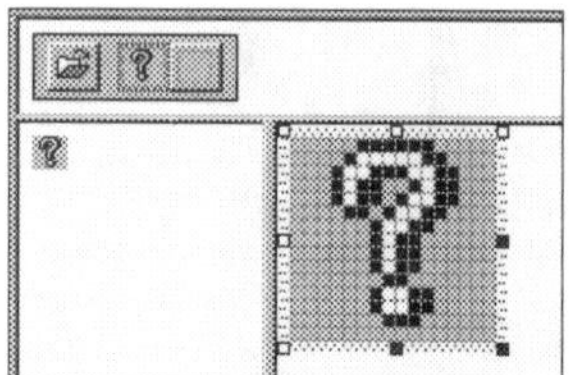

Figure 20.8
The DBExplore toolbar.

6. Remove the same items from the toolbar, leaving only the File Open and Help buttons. Your toolbar should look like Figure 20.8.
7. In ClassWizard, select the Message Maps tab, then select **CDBEView** from the Class Name drop-down list. Select **ID_FILE_OPEN** in the Object ID list box, choose **COMMAND** in the Messages list box, and click on Add Function. Accept the name **OnFileOpen**, as shown in Figure 20.9.

Using The DAO Classes In OnFileOpen()

When the user selects File|Open or clicks on the File|Open toolbar button, you first create a **CFileDialog** object, passing ".mdb" as the third argument to the constructor so that the dialog box will display only Access database files. The code looks like this:

```
CFileDialog dlg(TRUE, "Open a Database File", "*.mdb");
```

Next, you call the **DoModal()** function and check that the return value is **IDOK** and that the opened file has the .mdb extension. (For the latter, you can use the **GetFileExt()** function.) If either of these conditions isn't met, you skip the rest of the steps. Here's the code:

```
if (dlg.DoModal() == IDOK && dlg.GetFileExt() == "mdb")
{
```

```
    // Rest of the code goes here
}
```

Once you have the name of the database, you can retrieve the name from the dialog box by using **GetPathName()** and store it in the **m_DBNames CEdit** field by using **SetWindowText()**. You need to delete any table names left in the **m_TableList CListBox**. The code to perform these tasks is as follows:

```
m_TableList.ResetContent();
m_DBName.SetWindowText(dlg.GetPathName());
```

To access the database, you need to create a **CDaoDatabase** object, then call its **Open()** method. When you're done with it, you call **Close()**. The code should look like this:

```
CDaoDatabase db;
db.Open(dlg.GetPathName());
// Actions on database occur here
db.Close();
```

You need to fill the **m_TableNames** list box with the names of all the tables in the database. All the table definitions are contained in the **TableDef** collection. To retrieve each table definition, call **GetTableDef()**. You don't need to retrieve the complete table definition, which includes all the information about the table's columns in the table—all you want are the names. To do so, you

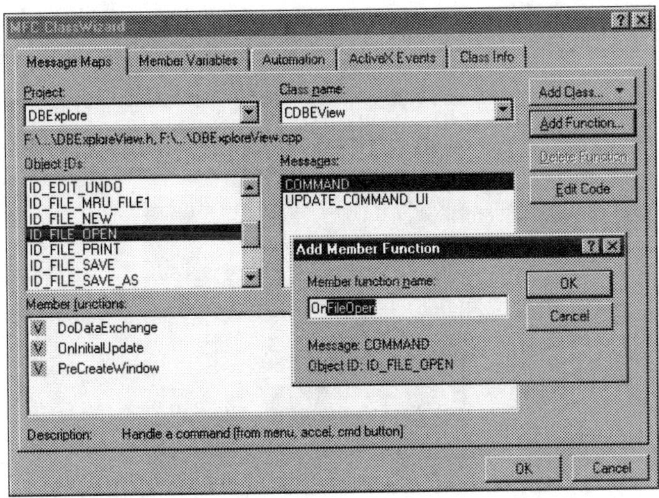

Figure 20.9
Adding the **OnFileOpen()** menu handler.

can create a **CDaoTableDefInfo** object and call the function **GetTableDefInfo()**. Then, step through each table definition by using the **GetTableDefCount()** function to initialize a counter. Once you've done that, you can use the **m_strName** member to populate the list box. Here's the code that meets these requirements:

```
CDaoTableDefInfo info;
int nTables = db.GetTableDefCount();
for (int i = 0; i < nTables; i++)
{
    db.GetTableDefInfo(i, info);
    m_TableList.AddString(info.m_strName);
}
m_TableList.SetCurSel(0);
```

Add this code to **OnFileOpen()**, being sure to put the actions before the call to **close()**. Then, compile the program and use it to open the World Energy Database. You should be able to scroll through the list of tables, as you can see in Figure 20.10.

When you call **GetTableDefInfo()**, it returns the definition of the requested database table by using a structure called **CDaoTableDefInfo**. (Despite the "C" prefix on the name, **CDaoTableDefInfo** is a simple structure, not a class.) You use the **m_strName** field in this structure to populate the list box.

You might also be interested in another field—**m_lAttributes**—which describes several characteristics of the table the structure refers to. By using the bitwise **AND** operator (&) with the following constants, you can test for specific table characteristics:

- ***dbAttachExclusive***—An external attached table, opened exclusively.

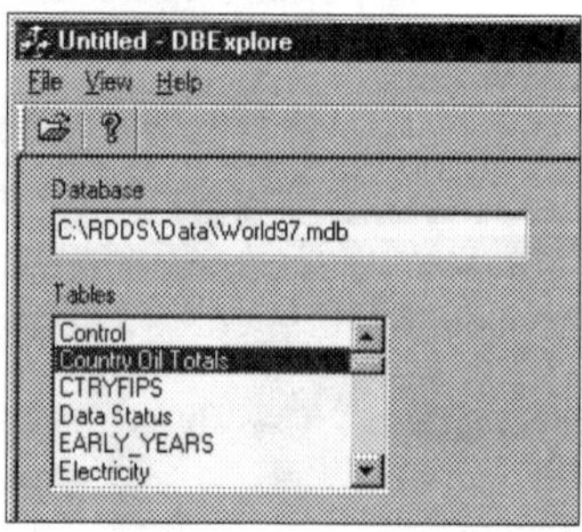

Figure 20.10
Running the DBExplore program.

- ***dbAttachSavePWD***—User ID and password are saved with the connection information.
- ***dbSystemObject***—An Access system table (read-only).
- ***dbHiddenObject***—An Access hidden table for temporary use (read-only).
- ***dbAttachedTable***—A table in an attached, non-ODBC database.
- ***dbAttachedODBC***—A table in an attached ODBC database.

By putting the code that adds table names to the **m_TableList** within an **if** statement

```
if ((info.m_lAttributes & dbSystemObject) == 0)
{
    m_TableList.AddString(info.m_strName);
}
```

you can ensure that the table list displays only non-system tables.

Exploring Other Objects

In addition to tables, the **CDaoDatabase** object stores a collection of queries and relations. You can modify them, add new ones, and delete existing ones. You won't do any more work with **CDaoDatabase** at this time; let's move on and explore the **CDaoTableDef** class.

You can use a **CDaoTableDef** object to retrieve the field, index, and validation information about each table in your database. A **CDaoTableDef** object can also change the structure of an existing table or retrieve the information from the table.

Let's use this class to retrieve information about a table when the user selects it in the **m_TableNames** list box. Here's what you need to do when the list selection changes:

- Create a new **CDaoDatabase** object, using the name saved when all the tables were enumerated.
- Retrieve the name of the table to open and pass it to the **CDaoDatabase** object, to construct a **CDaoTableDef** object.

- Call the **GetFieldCount()** function to find out how many fields are in the table. Iterate through the field list, extracting the name of each field and its type. Then, store that information in the **m_FieldList CListBox** object (which you'll construct shortly.)

That doesn't look so hard. Here's how you go about it:

1. Open your main form in the Dialog Editor. Add to your dialog box a static-text label captioned "Fields" and a list box named **IDC_FIELD_LIST**. Make the Fields list box a bit wider than the Tables list box. Your screen should look like Figure 20.11. Check the Use Tabstops checkbox on the Styles tab of the List Box Properties dialog box.
2. Use ClassWizard to create a control **CListBox CDBEView** member variable named **m_FieldList**.
3. Use ClassWizard to add a handler function for the **LBN_SELCHANGE** message and attach it to the **IDC_TABLE_LIST** list box. The handler function should be in the **CDBEView** class, as shown in Figure 20.12.
4. Add the code shown in Listing 20.1 to the **OnSelchangeTableList()** message handler. Although the code is long, it's straightforward—you should be able to follow the numbered comments and tie them back to the discussion in this chapter.

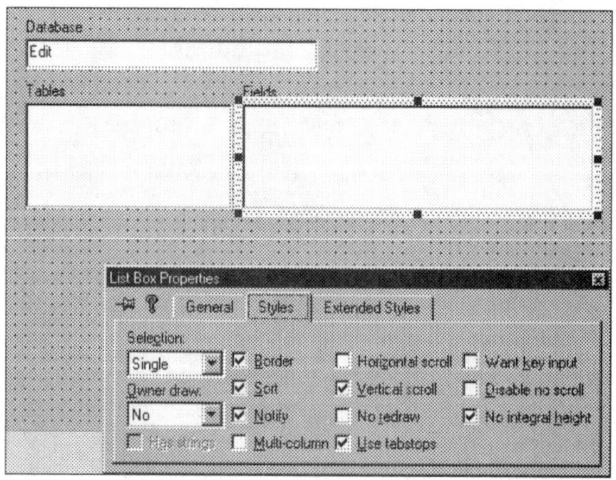

Figure 20.11
Adding the Fields list box to your dialog box.

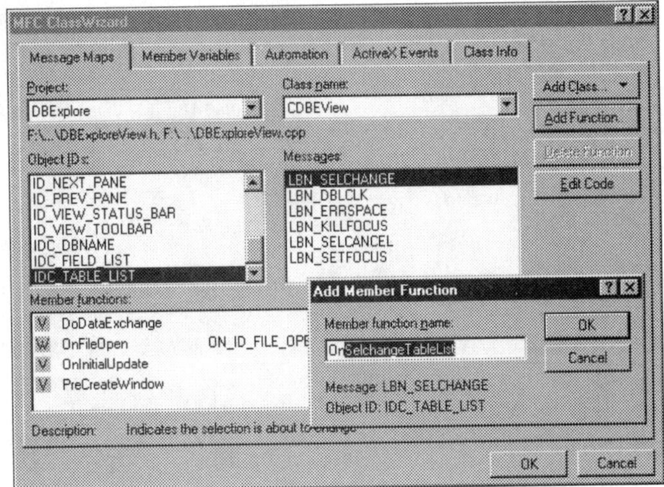

Figure 20.12
Adding the **OnSelchangeTableList()** message handler.

Listing 20.1 The CDBEView::OnSelChangeTableList() message handler.

```
void CDBEView::OnSelchangeTableList()
{
    // 1. Construct a CDaoDatabase object & open it
    CDaoDatabase db;
    CString name;
    m_DBName.GetWindowText(name);
    db.Open(name);

    // 2. Construct a CDaoTableDef object and open it
    CDaoTableDef table(&db);
    m_TableList.GetText(m_TableList.GetCurSel(), name);
    table.Open(name);

    // 3. Clear the Field list box and set the tab stops
    m_FieldList.ResetContent();
    m_FieldList.SetTabStops(110);

    // 4. Ask the table how many fields it contains
    int nFields = table.GetFieldCount();
    CDaoFieldInfo info;   // Store field info in this
    CString sType;        // Store type info desc in this

    // 5. Loop through the databse
    for (int i = 0; i < nFields; i++)
    {
        // 6. Retrieve field from the field
        table.GetFieldInfo(i, info);
```

```
        // 7. Set the type info description for the field
        switch (info.m_nType)
        {
        case dbBoolean: sType = "Boolean";
          break;
        case dbByte:    sType = "Byte";
          break;
        case dbInteger: sType = "Integer (2 bytes)";
          break;
        case dbLong:    sType = "Long (4 bytes)";
          break;
        case dbCurrency:sType = "Currency";
          break;
        case dbSingle:  sType = "Single (4 bytes)";
          break;
        case dbDouble:  sType = "Double (8 bytes)";
          break;
        case dbDate:    sType = "Date/Time";
          break;
        case dbText:
            sType.Format("Text %ld", info.m_lSize);
              break;
        case dbLongBinary:  sType = "Long Binary";
          break;
        case dbMemo:    sType = "Memo";
          break;
        case dbGUID:    sType = "GUID";
          break;
        }

        // 8. Add the name and type to the list
        m_FieldList.AddString(info.m_strName + "\t" +
          sType);
    }
    // 9. Close everything up
    m_FieldList.SetCurSel(0);
    table.Close();
    db.Close();
}
```

Relational Databases: The Sequel

Some PC DBMS systems (such as dBASE or Paradox) include both a data-storage model and a programming language. Programmers soon realized that this is a bad idea—if your company decides to change programming languages, it probably doesn't want to leave its data behind.

Most DBMS programs support SQL, which lets you access your data using COBOL, C++, or even Snobol, if you're so inclined. (You can pronounce the abbreviation "S-Q-L" or "sequel".) SQL provides two levels of commands: those that let you manipulate data (Data Manipulation Language, or DML) and those that let you manipulate the database schema (Data Definition Language, or DDL).

We lack the space to cover SQL comprehensively, but as a C++ and MFC programmer, you'll often be called upon to understand the SQL commands that retrieve data from a database. To understand them, you must understand the SQL **SELECT** command.

Some SELECT SQL

The most basic SQL command is **SELECT**. To retrieve all the rows and columns from a table called Oil—which you'll do shortly—you simply write this code:

```
SELECT * FROM Oil
```

You can write SQL keywords—**SELECT** and **FROM**, in this case—in either uppercase or lowercase, but uppercase is often used to distinguish the keywords from other parts of the SQL syntax. Enter non-keywords in an SQL query (such as **Oil**) the same way you entered them when you created the table. Some DBMSs are more forgiving than others in such matters, but it's best to get in the habit of writing portable queries that a variety of DBMSs will accept.

The **SELECT** command tells the SQL interpreter:

- What table to access
- What columns to retrieve
- What rows to include in the result

If you look closely, you'll notice that nothing in the **SELECT** statement tells the SQL interpreter what *database* contains the Oil table. You identify the database in the code that establishes the database connection and invokes the SQL command.

The last part of this simple **SELECT** command is the asterisk (*). When used in a **SELECT** statement, the asterisk simply says, "get everything." As a result, this query returns all columns and all rows. Often—in fact, almost always—that's not what you want. Instead, you'll specify *exactly* which rows and columns you want to retrieve. Here's how.

Choosing Fields

To select which columns are returned, you include the name of a table column—or a list of column names, separated by commas. For example, if you want to retrieve the crude-oil production for all the countries in the Oil table, you could write this statement:

```
SELECT Country, Year, [Crude Production] FROM Oil
```

If a field name contains spaces (as **Crude Production** does), simply enclose the field name in brackets. The SQL interpreter returns the columns in the order you specify in your **SELECT** statement. If you want to place the year in the left-most column, you simply write:

```
SELECT Year, Country, [Crude Production] FROM Oil
```

This form of **SELECT** can be much more efficient than the all-columns form, especially if the table contains long text strings or other large values. But, it offers an even more important advantage: When you explicitly list the fields you want retrieved, you always get the same fields in the same order, even if the structure of the table changes. If you simply say **SELECT ***, then every change to the table structure changes the result of the **SELECT**. In the best case, your MFC program ignores any new fields; in the worst case, a new field can crash your program.

Choosing Rows: Using The Where Clause

Even when you explicitly use **SELECT** to return specific columns, every query returns all the rows in the table. If the table contains a few hundred records, this isn't a problem. On the other hand, if you're connected to a remote server database, you may find yourself with thousands or even millions of records. Needless to say, performance can suffer in such a case. Sending a million records across the Internet when you need to access only a single record may not be a criminal act, but it won't win you many friends.

To select specific rows from a table, you simply include a **WHERE** condition in your **SELECT** statement, like this:

```
SELECT Year, [Crude Production] FROM Oil WHERE Country
  = 'Zimbabwe'
```

This query returns only those records for which the value of the **Country** field is Zimbabwe. Notice that you specify the value of the field (a text string) using single quotes—omitting the single quotes, or using double quotes, will cause the query to malfunction. Furthermore, notice that the comparison operator is the single equal sign (=). This SQL syntax can cause real fits for MFC programmers, because C++ uses double quotes for strings and double-equal (==) to compare for equality.

Predicate This

The art of writing useful **WHERE** clauses consists mainly of deciding what records you need, then accurately writing a condition that identifies them. This condition is referred to as a *predicate*, because it's either true or false for any record. If the condition tests true for a given record, the record is included; otherwise, the record is excluded. Predicates are often called *relational expressions*, because they usually involve relational or comparison operators.

Fortunately, the rules that govern the writing of predicates in SQL are quite similar to those for writing conditions in C++. The next section fills you in on the most common differences.

Comparison Operators

The most common form of SQL predicate compares values. Table 20.2 shows the comparison operators you'll use to write SQL

Table 20.2 SQL comparison operators.

Operator	Meaning
=	Equal
<>	Non-equal
<	Less than
>	Greater than
<=	Less than or equal (that is, not greater than)
>=	Greater than or equal (that is, not less than)

queries. They're the same as those used in C++, except that non-equality is represented using <> rather than !=, and equality is represented using = rather than ==.

Most values used in comparisons are either numbers or strings. It's important that both operands of a comparison operator have the same type: You should compare numbers with numbers and strings with strings. Mixing types leads to errors or wrong results.

String Comparisons

Although you can easily write comparison predicates that use strings, such comparisons involve two subtleties. First, SQL string comparisons are case sensitive, just as they are in C++.

Second, computers encode character information differently, using *collating sequences*. If you're attached to a table on a mainframe database, for instance, you might find that the character "9" follows the letter "Z", while on a PC database, "9" precedes "Z". Ideally, your SQL queries shouldn't depend on the collating sequence, because any query that does so may work on one database host but fail on another. However, when your application demands that such comparisons be performed, be sure to check with the database administrator and ask about collating sequences.

Compound Comparisons

Sometimes, a single comparison isn't enough. For instance, you may want to retrieve all the oil statistics for Zimbabwe and Angola. In such a case, you can use Boolean operators to combine relational expressions to form compound relational expressions.

Table 20.3 shows SQL's Boolean operators. For example, you could write

```
SELECT [Crude Production]
FROM Oil
WHERE Country = 'Zimbabwe' OR Country = 'Angola'
```

to generate the desired result. Notice that, as the query gets longer, you'll find it helpful to put each clause on its own line. You can use parentheses, just as you would in C++, to control the order in which comparisons are evaluated.

Additional Predicates

Most SQL implementations include other predicates that make it easier to write SQL queries that return exactly the results you want. Table 20.4 summarizes these additional SQL predicates; we'll explain them in the following sections.

Table 20.3 SQL Boolean operators.

Operator	Result Is True If:
AND	Both predicates are true
OR	Either predicate is true, or both are true
NOT	The predicate is false

Table 20.4 Additional SQL predicates.

Predicate	Meaning
BETWEEN ... AND	Include records with a field value within the specified range.
NOT BETWEEN ... AND	Exclude records with a field value within the specified range.
LIKE	Include records with a string field that matches the specified pattern.
NOT LIKE	Exclude records with a string field that matches the specified pattern.
IN	Include records with a field value contained in the specified list.
NOT IN	Exclude records with a field value contained in the specified list.
IS NULL	Include records with an omitted (null) value for the optional field.
IS NOT NULL	Exclude records with an omitted (null) value for the optional field.

The **LIKE** predicate lets you specify "wild card" patterns like those used for DOS file names. In a pattern, you use an underscore (_) to stand for any single character and a percent sign (%) to stand for any string of characters.

For example, the following query would return the crude-oil production from all countries with names ending in "ia":

```
SELECT [Crude Production]
FROM Oil
WHERE Country LIKE '%ia'
```

The **IN** predicate lets you specify a list of values in place of a long sequence of **OR** and **AND** conditions, like this:

```
SELECT 'Crude Production'
FROM Oil
WHERE Year IN (1990, 1992, 1994, 1996)
```

The **NOT IN** predicate provides the complementary result, including only records with a field value *not* in the specified list.

NULL

When you design a table, you designate whether each field is required or optional. When you update a record, the DBMS won't let you skip a value if it's required. On the other hand, if you omit an optional field value, you won't get an error—instead, the DBMS will store a special value called a *null* in the field. (A null field isn't the same as a numeric field with zero value or a string field containing an empty string or a blank string.)

You can use the **NULL** predicate to identify records without optional field values—that is, with null fields. The form of the query is:

```
SELECT [Crude Production]
FROM Oil
WHERE Units IS NULL
```

The corresponding **IS NOT NULL** predicate specifies records with non-null optional-field values.

ActiveX Database Controls

As you've seen, the SQL **SELECT** statement lets you retrieve values from your tables. In MFC, you can store the result of a query in a record-set object. Each MFC database class includes its own version of the record set: the ODBC-oriented **CDatabase** class has the **CRecordset**, and the DAO-oriented **CDaoDatabase** class uses **CDaoRecordset**.

All the record sets you saw in the last chapter were, essentially, static. The AppWizard generated a specific variable for each column in the result set, and the automatic field exchange transferred data from the record set into variables. That process is fine, as far as it goes, but it isn't very flexible.

You can make your programs more flexible by using the DAO classes to identify the fields in the table you want to display, and to create your database form "on-the-fly." Doing so is quite a lot of work, however, and there's a much easier way: Use the ActiveX *data-bound controls*.

Visual C++ 6.0 comes with two sets of data-bound controls: Remote Data Objects (RDO) and ActiveX Data Objects (ADO). You use the RDO controls to connect to SQL-based relational database systems through ODBC. ADO controls are the latest thing; they use OLE DB. Microsoft has indicated that RDO controls will no longer be improved, and that future development should use ADO. However, the ADO controls that ship with Visual C++ show signs of being "Release 1.0" products. You may want to hedge your bets when you commit to a particular set of components.

DataBound Basics

ActiveX data binding requires two kinds of controls. First, you need a *data-source control* that connects to the database and manages scrolling through the database records. You'll have one data-source control for each data connection in your program.

Second, you need a *data-bound control* to automatically display the results retrieved by a data-source control. Data-bound controls come in two varieties: simple controls, which display the values from a single record, and complex controls, which display the values from several records at once.

You'll have a data-bound control for each data-source control, as well as several controls that you can use with any data-source control. Table 20.5 lists the data-bound controls. The RDO and ADO columns indicate whether the control works with the ADO data control and the RDO data control.

Table 20.5 The data-bound ActiveX controls shipping with Visual C++ 6.0.

Name	RDO	ADO	Description
DataCombo	No	Yes	Links a field in an ADO record set to a drop-down combo box.
DataGrid	No	Yes	Provides a text-oriented, scrolling, spreadsheet-like view on an ADO record set.
DataList	No	Yes	Links a field in an ADO record set to a list box.
DataRepeater	No	Yes	Provides a method of using controls in a scrolling grid.
Hierarchical FlexGrid	No	Yes	Displays tabular data, including strings and pictures.
Chart	No	Yes	Displays an array of data from a record set as a chart.
DBCombo	Yes	No	Links a field in an RDO record set to a drop-down combo box.
DBGrid	Yes	No	Provides a text-oriented, scrolling, spreadsheet-like view on an RDO record set.
DBList	Yes	No	Links a field in an RDO record set to a list box.
FlexGrid	Yes	No	Displays tabular data, including strings and pictures, in a read-only display.
Calendar	Yes	Yes	Connects to a date field in an ADO or RDO record set.
Date and Time Picker	Yes	Yes	Connects to a date or time field in an ADO or RDO record set.
Masked Edit	Yes	Yes	Allows display of formatted text (this control is accessible only using Visual Basic).
RichText	Yes	Yes	Allows display of RTF and most OLE objects.

Adding ActiveX To DBExplore

The fastest way to learn how ActiveX data-bound controls work is to use them. Let's take the DBExplore program and make it into a full-fledged query-and-edit tool. To do that, you'll use the ADO data control and Microsoft's datagrid.

You'll complete the project in several steps:

- First, you'll add both the ADO Data control and Microsoft's DataGrid to the project. You'll do that through the component Gallery, just as you did for the other ActiveX controls you've used.
- Then, you'll add several controls to the DBExplore main form: a multi-line edit box in which you can type queries, an Execute Query button, and an ADO data control.
- Next, you'll create a dialog box that displays the results of your query. You'll add the ADO DataGrid component to the dialog box.
- Finally, you'll write the code that executes the query by activating the ActiveX data control and displaying the new dialog box containing the grid.

Step 1: Adding The ActiveX Data Controls

To add the ActiveX data controls to your project, just follow these instructions:

1. Be sure the DBExplore project is open in Visual C++. Select Project|Add To Project|Components And Controls to open the Components And Controls Gallery dialog box. Open the Registered ActiveX Controls folder and select the Microsoft ADO Data Control, version 6.0, as shown in Figure 20.14. Click on Insert to add the control to your project.
2. Click on OK when the Confirm Classes dialog box appears, as shown in Figure 20.15. These are the ActiveX wrapper classes that Visual C++ will add to your project.
3. Locate and select the Microsoft DataGrid Control, Version 6.0, as shown in Figure 20.16, then click on Insert. Be sure you don't select the DBGrid control by mistake: DBGrid

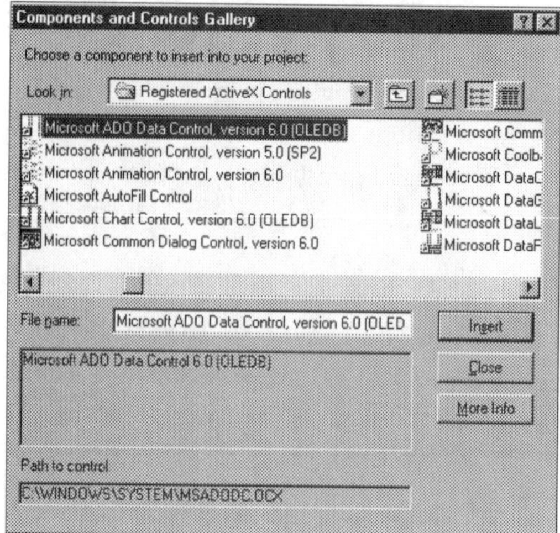

Figure 20.14
The Microsoft ADO data control.

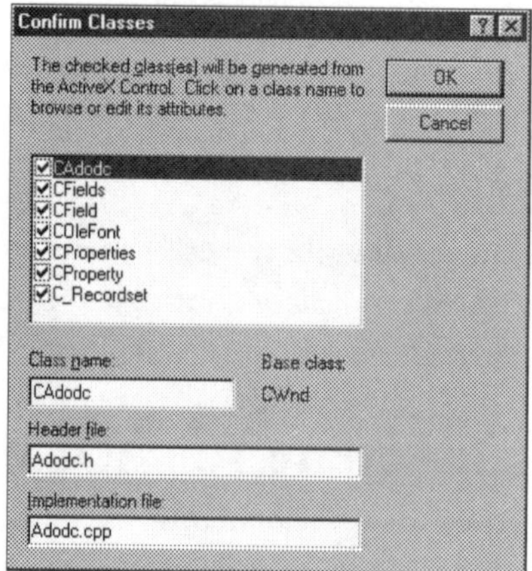

Figure 20.15
ActiveX wrapper classes for the ADO data control.

works only with the RDO data control, not with the ADO data control.

4. Click on OK in the Confirm Classes dialog box, just as you did for the ADO control. Figure 20.17 shows the classes that Visual C++ will add to your project to support the DataGrid control. Dismiss the Components And Controls Gallery dialog box by clicking on Close.

Step 2: Adding Components To The Main Form

Once you've added the DataGrid and the ADO data control to your project, each of them appears on the Controls palette. You

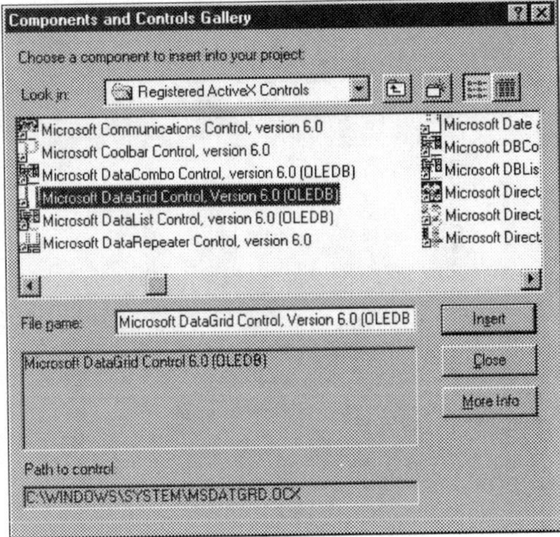

Figure 20.16
The Microsoft DataGrid control.

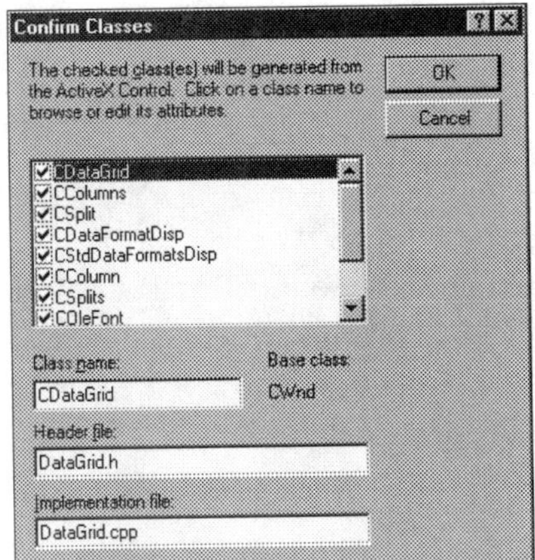

Figure 20.17
ActiveX wrapper classes for the Microsoft DataGrid control.

can simply drag and drop them onto your form. However, these controls present a few pitfalls that await the unwary—follow closely, and you'll be able to avoid them.

Here are the steps to add and configure the new components:

1. Drag and drop the following controls on your main form: an ADO data control, an edit control, a static-text label, and a push button. Arrange the controls as shown in Figure 20.18. Add the caption "SQL Query" to the static-text control "Execute Query" to the push button, and "The ADO Grid" to the ADO data control. Change the resource ID of the Execute Query button to **IDC_SELECT**.

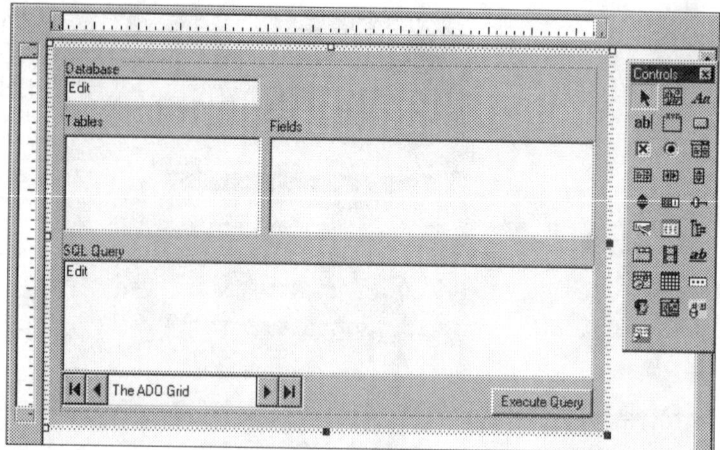

Figure 20.18
Arranging components on the main form.

2. Open the property sheet for the new edit control. Change the resource ID to **IDC_QUERY**. On the Styles tab, select the Multiline checkbox, deselect the Auto HScroll checkbox, and check the Want Return checkbox. The dialog should look like Figure 20.19.

3. Open the property sheet for the new ADO data control. Change the resource ID to **IDC_DB** and deselect the Visible checkbox on the General tab. On the Control tab, check the Use Connection String radio button, as you can see in Figure 20.20, and click on Build.

4. When the Data Link Properties dialog box appears, select the Microsoft Jet 3.51 OLE DB Provider, as shown in Figure 20.21. Don't click on Next—instead, click on OK. Open the property sheet for the ADO data control and select the text in the Connection String edit field and use Edit|Cut or Ctrl+X to clear the edit box. Use ClassView to locate the CPP file for the **CDBEView** class, then paste the connection string at the bottom of the file using Edit|Paste or Ctrl+V.

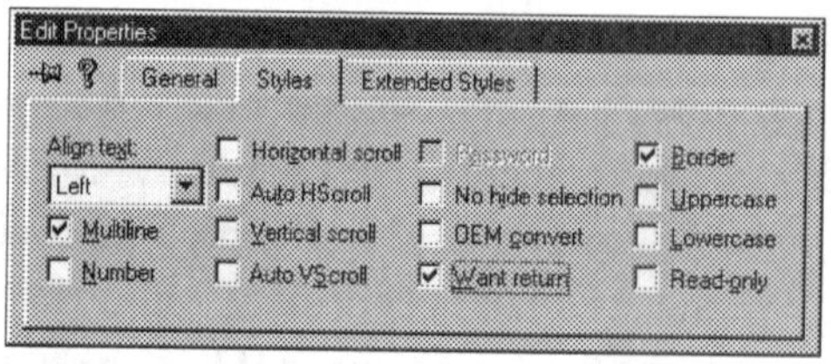

Figure 20.19
Changing the Edit properties for the **IDC_QUERY** edit control.

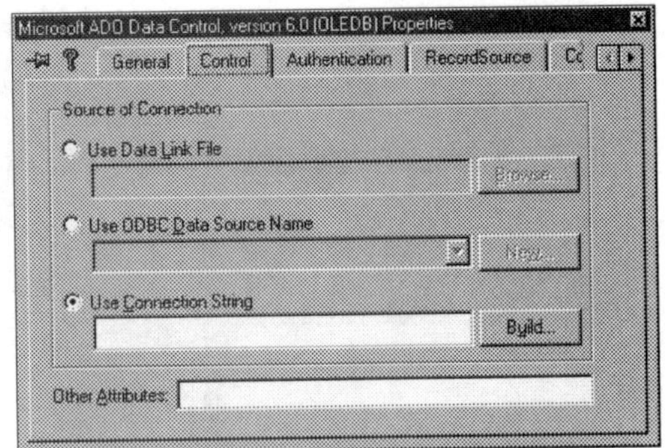

Figure 20.20
Setting the data control Control properties.

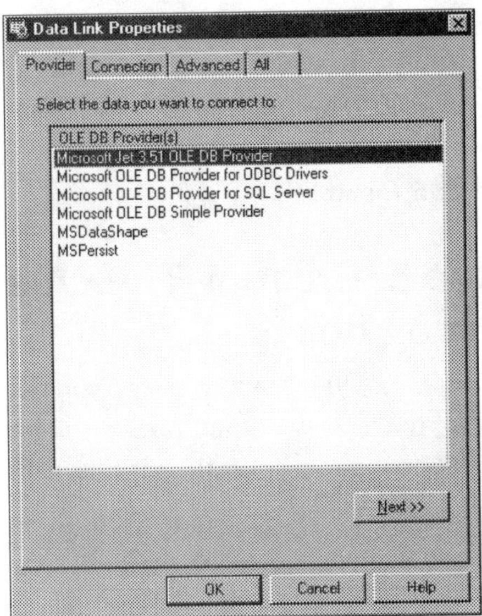

Figure 20.21
Selecting an OLE DB provider.

Place comment markers around the text: You'll come back later and get it.

5. Scroll the ADO Data Control Properties dialog box until you locate the RecordSource tab. In the Command Type drop-down list, select 1 - adCmdText, as shown in Figure 20.22. This setting tells the control to expect a SQL query. You won't provide one just yet, because you need to let the user type in a query at runtime. (If you want to use DBExplore only for editing tables, change the Command Type appropriately—the component will automatically open a table when it's selected in the DBExplore table list box, just as you do now with fields.)

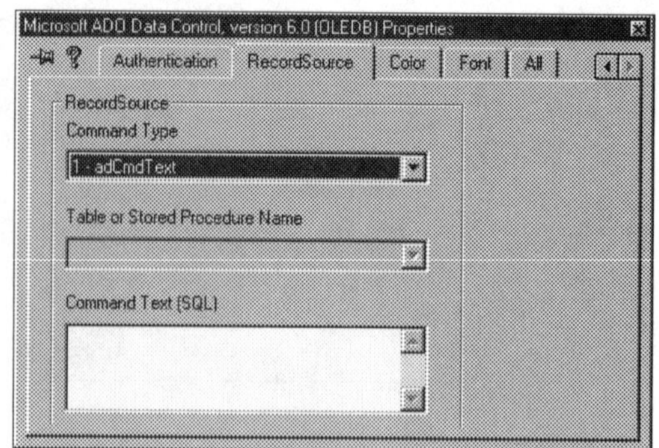

Figure 20.22
Setting the ADO control Command Type property.

6. Once you've set the control properties for both the **IDC_QUERY** control and the **IDC_DB** control, use ClassWizard to add control variables for each component. Name the edit control **m_Query**, and name the ADO data control **m_DB**.

Step 3: Creating The Query Results Dialog Box

Whenever you run a new query, you need to display the results in a new, resizable window. To keep the program simple, you'll use a modal dialog to display the result set. Here's how you go about it:

1. Choose Insert|Resource from the main menu and then choose Dialog from the Insert Resource list box. Remove the buttons from the dialog box, clear the Caption box, then drag and drop a DataGrid control. Size the dialog box and the control as shown in Figure 20.23.

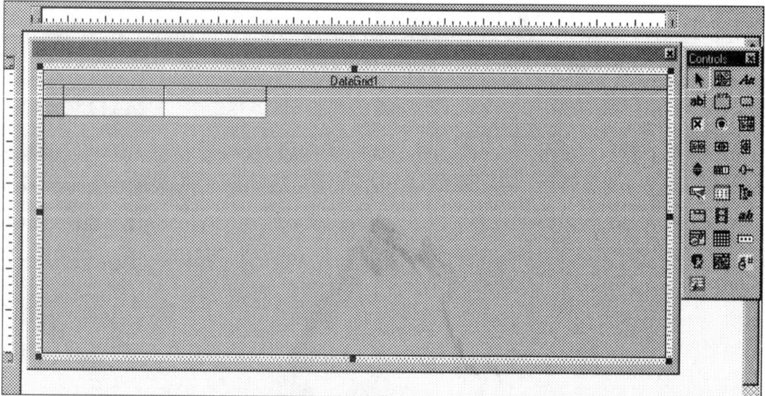

Figure 20.23
Creating the grid dialog box.

2. Open the Dialog Properties dialog box and set the resource ID to **IDD_GRID_DLG** on the General tab. On the Styles tab, select Resizing from the Border drop-down list. On the Extended Styles tab, check the Tool Window checkbox. Your property sheets should look like those shown in Figure 20.24.
3. Open the DataGrid Properties dialog box and change the resource ID to **ID_GRID**. On the Control tab, shown in Figure 20.25, check the AllowAddNew and AllowDelete checkboxes, so you can use DBExplore to add and delete records to your tables.
4. Start ClassWizard by choosing View|ClassWizard or pressing Ctrl+W. Because this is a new dialog box, ClassWizard will ask if you want to create a new class. Click on OK; name your class **CGridDlg**, derived from **CDialog**, when the Add New Class dialog box opens. Click on OK. When ClassWizard appears, select the Member Variables tab and add a new **CDataGrid** variable called **m_Grid**, as you can see in Figure 20.26.
5. Before you close ClassWizard and start writing code, add Windows message handlers for the **WM_INITDIALOG** and

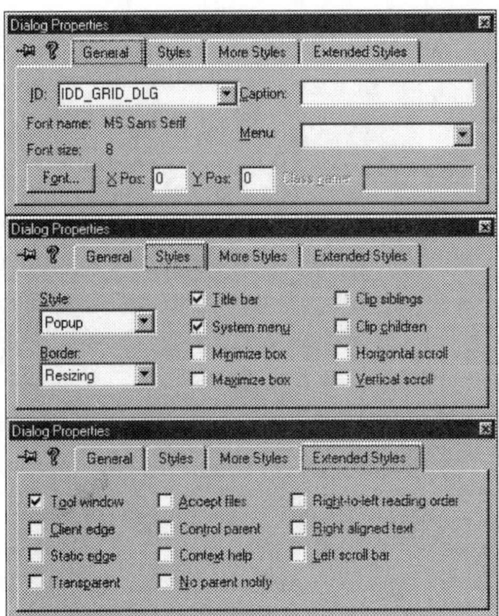

Figure 20.24
Properties for the **IDD_GRID_DLG** dialog box.

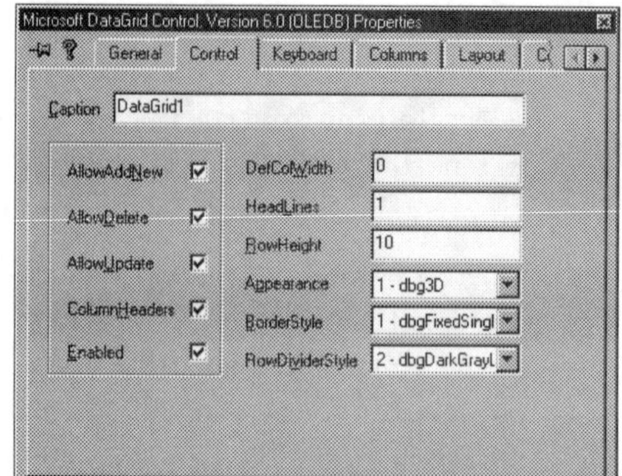

Figure 20.25
The DataGrid Control properties.

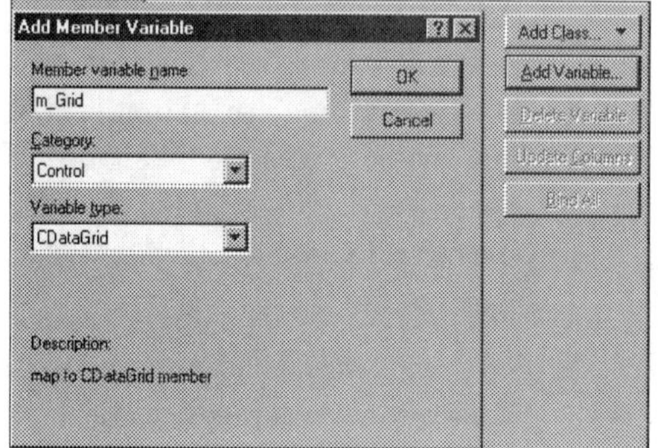

Figure 20.26
Adding the **m_Grid** member variable.

WM_SIZE messages to the **CGridDlg** class. You'll add the code in the next step.

Step 4: Activating The Query Button

Finally, you need to hook the parts together so the DBExplore program works. You'll simply add a couple of variables and then write the code for the Execute Query button. Here's how to do that:

1. Open the main form in the Dialog Editor and double-click on the Execute Query button. Click on OK in the Add Member Function dialog box. Add the code shown in Listing 20.2 to the **OnSelect()** function. Notice that we've commented the code with the steps you need to perform and highlighted each step. Use the text you saved at the bottom of the file to initialize the first two lines of Step 3: These may be different if you chose a different OLE DB provider.

2. Before you leave the **CDBEView** class, go to the top of the file and add

```
#include "GridDlg.h"
```

so that the code in Step 6 will compile.

Listing 20.2 The CDBEView::OnSelect() member function.

```
void CDBEView::OnSelect()
{
    // 1. Get the query text from the m_Query control
    CString query;
    m_Query.GetWindowText(query);

    // 2. Get the database name from the m_DBName control
    CString db;
    m_DBName.GetWindowText(db);

    // 3. Get the rest of the provider info
    CString connect =
      "Provider=Microsoft.Jet.OLEDB.3.51;";
    connect += "Persist Security Info=False;";
    connect += "Data Source=" + db;

    // 4. Set the ConnectionString and RecordSource
    // properties
    m_DB.SetCommandType(1); // SQL
    m_DB.SetConnectionString(connect);
    m_DB.SetRecordSource(query);

    // 5. Read the data
    m_DB.Refresh();

    // 6. Display the Grid
    CGridDlg dlg;
    dlg.m_pCursor = m_DB.GetDSCCursor();
    query.Replace("\r\n", " ");
    dlg.m_Caption = query;
    dlg.m_Title = db;
    dlg.DoModal();
}
```

3. After you've added the necessary code to the view class, you also must add the companion code in the **CDialog** class, **CGridDlg**. Locate the **OnInitDialog()** and **OnSize()** functions you added when you created the **CDialog** class, then add the code shown in Listing 20.3.

Listing 20.3 The CGridDlg OnInitDialog() and OnSize() member functions.

```
void CGridDlg::OnSize(UINT nType, int cx, int cy)
{
    CDialog::OnSize(nType, cx, cy);

    // TODO: Add your message handler code here
    CRect rect;
    GetClientRect(rect);
    if (m_Grid.GetSafeHwnd() != 0)
        m_Grid.MoveWindow(rect);
}

BOOL CGridDlg::OnInitDialog()
{
    CDialog::OnInitDialog();

    // TODO: Add extra initialization here
    m_Grid.SetRefDataSource(m_pCursor);
    m_Grid.SetCaption(m_Caption);
    SetWindowText(m_Title);
    return TRUE;  // return TRUE unless you set the focus
                  // to a control
                  // EXCEPTION: OCX Property Pages should
                  // return FALSE
}
```

4. Add three public member variables to the **CDialog** class: **m_pCursor** is of type **LPUNKNOWN**, and **m_Title** and **m_Caption** are **CStrings**.
5. Compile the finished code and use it to try some of the SQL you learned earlier in this chapter. In Figure 20.27, you can see a sample query as it runs.

How It Works—The Abbreviated Version

Three properties determine how the ActiveX ADO data control works. The first property is the connection string, which determines the characteristics of the DB OLE provider that sends data to the control. You used the data control to build most of the string. You retrieved the last portion of the string—the data-source argument—from the **m_DBName** text box. You set the property by calling the control's **SetConnectionString()** function.

The **connect** property tells the data control *where* to look for its data, but the **RecordSource** property tells it *what* data to retrieve.

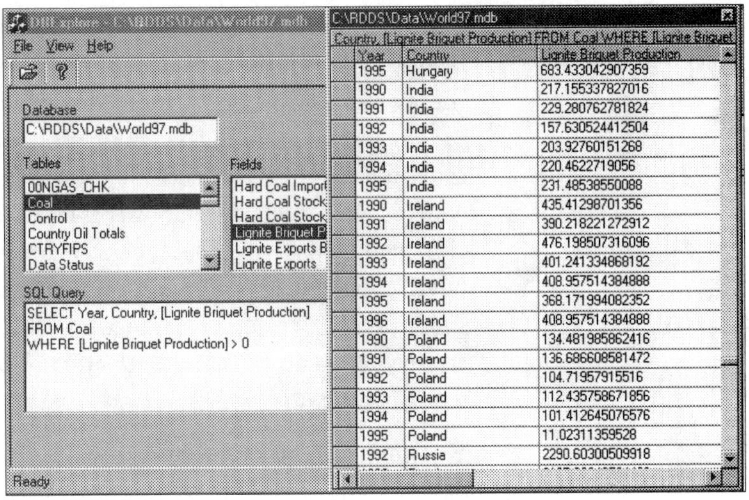

Figure 20.27
Running a sample query with DBExplore.

In the program, you retrieve the SQL statement from the **m_Query** edit control. Once you have the query text, you send it to the data control by calling its **SetRecordSource()** function.

You can use the **RecordSource** property to retrieve data in three ways: by using a **SELECT** statement, as you've done here; by retrieving all the records from a particular table; or by running a stored procedure located on the database server. You switch between these three different meanings by setting the **Command** property using the **SetCommandType()** function. If you pass 1, the **RecordSource** field is interpreted as an SQL query.

Once you've set those three properties for your data control, you only have to call the control's **Refresh()** method—it will retrieve the records you've requested. Of course, unless you have some way to display them, this doesn't help a lot. Here's where the DataGrid comes in.

How The DataGrid Works

The DataGrid has many properties, but we're interested only in its **DataSource** property. The **DataSource** property binds the DataGrid to a data provider, such as the ADO data control. If you connect the properties in your data control at design time—that is, if you know exactly what data you want to retrieve ahead of time—then you can simply connect your DataGrid to your data control using the property sheet.

On the other hand, if you don't know what the **DataSource** will be until you run the program—as is the case with DBExplore—then you must set the property at runtime, which poses a bit of a problem. If you search the wrapper classes produced when you imported the ActiveX controls, you'll find that the DataGrid control has a **SetRefDataSource()** method. Unfortunately, you can't simply pass it a reference to your data control. Instead, you have to call the **CWnd** function **GetDSCCursor()**—using your data control—to get a reference to the data set produced by the control. You can then use **SetRefDataSource()** to make the grid use those records.

You might wonder how you'd ever discover this fact, because the documentation for the data control and the DataGrid neglects to mention it. The answer is simple: Look through the sample programs included on the Visual C++ CD. When it comes to using ActiveX controls with Visual C++, the documentation is rather sparse—but you can be almost certain that someone has created a sample program that shows you how to do exactly what you want.

Next Stop, The Web

As you can see, using ActiveX data controls makes database programming in Visual C++ much easier and more flexible than simply writing the code by hand. There are a few caveats, of course.

Because most ActiveX controls were written for Visual Basic, documentation on how to make them work in Visual C++ is often terse. Some controls (the Microsoft masked edit control, for instance) don't work correctly when you use them in a Visual C++ container. Others (notably the new DataGrid and the date-and-time picker) don't work correctly in the Dialog Editor, but will work fine in your programs.

ActiveX controls not only make you a more productive database programmer, they can ease your way into the world of the Internet. In the next chapter, you'll see how the new **HTMLView** class makes displaying HTML content simple, and how the ActiveX controls that come with Internet Explorer make building your own Web browser a matter of a few mouse clicks.

Chapter 21

Programming For The 'Net: Browsers And Other Clients

If you used one of the first available Web browsers, which were merely somewhat reliable, you may know what dog browser *means. However, in this chapter, the phrase takes on new meaning.*

Not long ago, the word *browser* referred to a casual shopper. Today, almost everyone understands that *browser* refers to a type of software. But, browsers haven't yet invaded the everyday world of programmers, most of whom see browsers as mysterious black boxes. Microsoft's HTMLView control changes all that.

An HTMLView Of The World

Visual C++ makes it easy for you to build Web browsers and other network clients. Just as the **CEditView** class helped you build a Notepad clone and the **CRichEditView** class let you mimic the WordPad application, the **CHtmlView** class (new in Visual C++ 6.0) lets you create your own version of Internet Explorer—without writing a single line of code.

When you use AppWizard to create an application based on the **CHtmlView** class, your program automatically connects to the Internet when you run it. Your program will render Hypertext Markup Language (HTML), follow hyperlinks, and even run Java programs. You don't *have* to write any code to get this functionality. However, you'll probably want to add features like forward and back buttons, and perhaps a history list.

Before you jump in, you need to consider one caveat. The **CHtmlView** class works much like the **CRichEditView** class, which uses the rich-edit control as the basis for its view. The **CHtmlView** class uses the Internet Explorer 4.0 (IE4) Web browser control, contained in the file SHDOCVW.DLL. Unlike many ActiveX controls you might use in your application, you can't distribute the IE4 Web browser control with your program. Instead, you must distribute the entire IE4 installation program, or your customers must already have IE4 installed on their systems—if your customers don't install IE4, they won't be able to run your program. To distribute IE4 with your applications, you'll need to sign a license agreement; contact Microsoft for more information.

Building A Web Browser

You might want to build an application based on the **CHtmlView** class for any of several reasons. Perhaps you'd like to add Web support to an existing application, or you might need to create a customized browser dedicated to a particular purpose. Let's take a look at how you'd go about doing that.

Suppose you belong to a dog-owner's club. Using **CHtmlView**, you can build a browser that links your fellow members to the American Kennel Club (AKC) Web site and provides special facilities for recording information about dogs they own. For example, you can use the Visual C++ database features we discussed in the last few chapters to let members store their pets' pedigree information and health records. You might also add an accounting module to track pet-ownership costs, and so forth.

If you're really zealous, you could even include special blocking technology—filtering out all sites containing the word *cat*, for instance. We won't show you how to do that, but we will show you how to build a basic Web browser.

Our project will be called Bowser—the all-canine Web browser. Here are the steps to follow:

1. Start a new MFC AppWizard (exe) project and name it Bowser. In the Step 1 dialog box, choose Single Document with DocView support. Accept the defaults in Step 2, Step 3, Step 4, and Step 5. In Step 6, change the base view class to

CHtmlView, and change the names of your classes to **CBView**, **CBDoc**, and **CBApp**. When your Step 6 screen looks like Figure 21.1, click on Finish.

2. Using ClassView, expand the **CBView** class and double-click on the **OnInitialUpdate()** method to open the Source Code Editor. Find the line that reads

```
Navigate2(_T(
  "http://www.microsoft.com/visualc/"),NULL,NULL);
```

and change it to point to the home page for the American Kennel Club:

```
Navigate2(_T("http://www.akc.org"), NULL, NULL);
```

Compile your changes, and then run the program. If you're permanently connected to the Internet, your program will locate the AKC Web site and display the home page. Otherwise, your system may attempt to connect you by dialing into your Internet Service Provider (ISP), as shown in Figure 21.2. Of course, if you haven't configured your system for automatic dial, you'll need to manually connect to your ISP.

If you don't have an ISP, or if you cancel the connection, your program automatically displays an error message and then displays the built-in navigation error Web page. Notice that the program

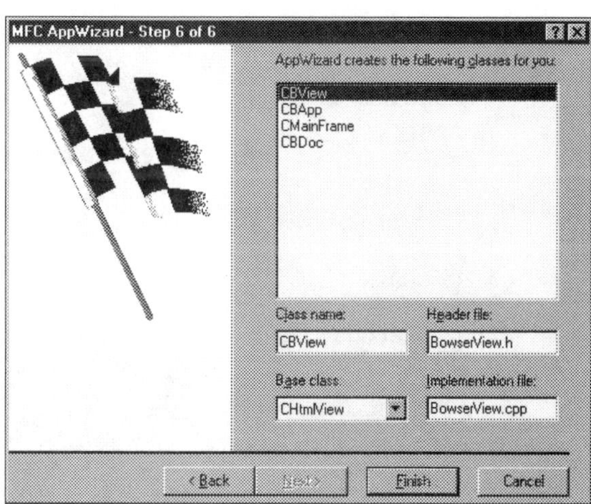

Figure 21.1
Setting up the classes for the Bowser browser.

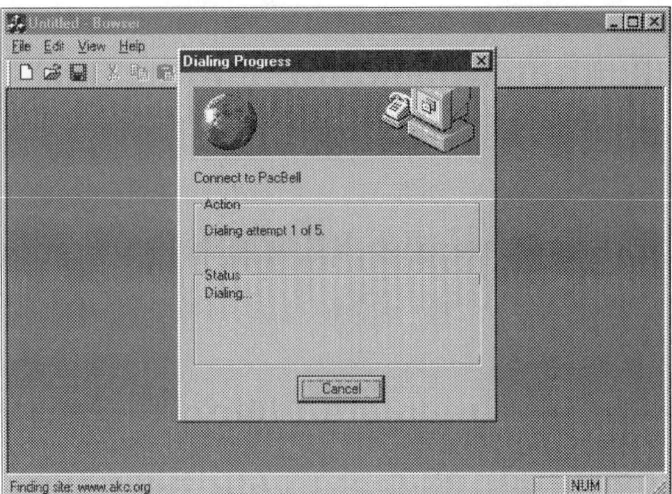

Figure 21.2
Dialing into an ISP.

includes a status line, which displays a message as each file is retrieved. You can see Bowser's initial screen in Figure 21.3.

Giving Bowser A Home Page

Bowser obviously has a few deficiencies: It provides no forward or back button, for instance. We'll correct its problems shortly, but let's start our improvements in another area: a default home page.

In a way, it's nice that Bowser connects to the Internet automatically—that's one less thing you have to worry about. On the other

Figure 21.3
Browsing the Web with the Bowser browser.

hand, it isn't polite of Bowser to pick up the phone without asking, even if the user has configured automatic dial. (Perhaps you've noticed that some topics in the Visual C++ help system display the same behavior.)

You could put your users in control by making the program start with a modal dialog box. Or, even better, you can simply display a local "home" page that's specifically designed for Bowser. Your system dials your ISP when Bowser calls the **Navigate2()** function using a non-local URL. When you create a local home page for Bowser to display at start-up, your system won't dial your ISP until the user clicks on one of the (clearly marked) Internet links.

Let's begin this home-page project by adding a new HTML file to the project and writing some HTML code using the Source Code Editor. You can, of course, use a WYSIWYG (What You See Is What You Get) editor such as Microsoft FrontPage or Netscape Composer to create your home page. But, even though it's not WYSIWYG, the Visual C++ Source Code Editor understands HTML, and its syntax-highlighting feature points out HTML syntax errors in much the way it points out C++ syntax errors. Furthermore, when you open a new HTML file, Visual C++ writes a starter file for you.

The Home Page Source Code

Here are the steps to follow to create Bowser's new home page:

1. Be sure the Bowser project is open in the Visual C++ IDE, and select File|New from the main menu. When the New dialog box opens, the Files tab will be selected. (If you choose File|New with no project open, the Projects tab will be selected, instead.) In the Files list box, select HTML Page, as you can see in Figure 21.4. Be sure the Add To Project check-box is selected and that the Bowser project appears in the drop-down list. Name your file Bowser.html. Use the browser to select the Debug directory of your project, then click on OK.
2. As you can see in Figure 21.5, Visual C++ creates the new HTML file, provides a basic skeleton, and then turns you loose with the admonishment, "Insert HTML here". Take the

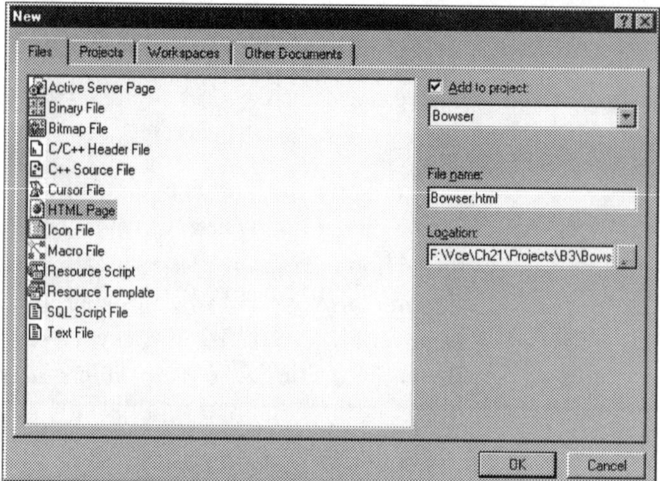

Figure 21.4
Adding a new HTML page to your project.

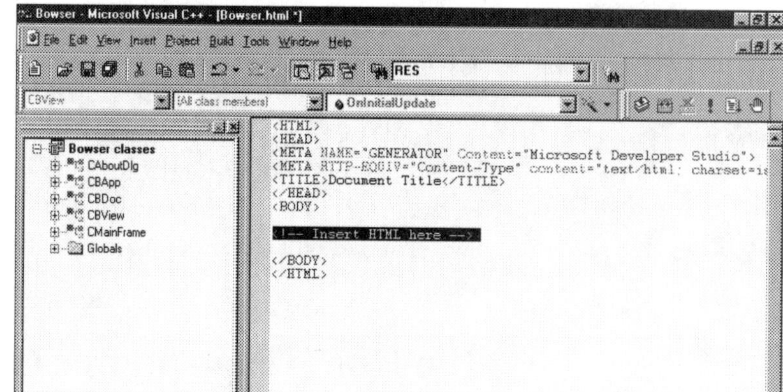

Figure 21.5
Visual C++ created this skeleton HTML file.

hint, and add the code shown in Listing 21.1 to Bowser.html. The changed lines are highlighted.

Listing 21.1 Bowser.html.

```
<HTML>
<HEAD>
<META NAME="GENERATOR" Content="Microsoft Developer
Studio">
<META HTTP-EQUIV="Content-Type"
  content="text/html; charset=iso-8859-1">
<TITLE>The Bowser Home Page</TITLE>
</HEAD>
<BODY>

<!-- Insert HTML here -->
```

```
<CENTER>
<IMG SRC=Dalmatian.gif ALIGN=LEFT>
<H1>The Bowser Home Page</H1>
<H2>All Dogs - All the Time</H2>
<P>
<HR ALIGN=LEFT>
<H2>Internet Links</H2>
</CENTER>
<H3>
<DL>
<DD><A HREF="http://www.akc.org">
<IMG SRC=./Collie.gif ALIGN=CENTER>
 The American Kennel Club</A>
<DD><A HREF="http://www.tiercom.com/">
<IMG SRC=./Chihuahua.gif ALIGN=CENTER>
 Tiercom Veterinary Information Service</A>
<DD><A HREF="http://www.avma.org/">
<IMG SRC=./Hound.gif ALIGN=CENTER>
 The American Veterinary Medicine Association</A>
<DD><A HREF="http://www.napcc.aspca.org">
<IMG SRC=./Poodle.gif ALIGN=CENTER>
ASPCA - The National Animal Poison Control Center</A>
</DL>
</H3>
</BODY>
</HTML>
```

3. An HTML file can contain references to external files, including images that must be in either the JPEG or GIF format. The Bowser home page displays five GIF files: Dalmation.gif, Collie.gif, Chihuahua.gif, Hound.gif, and Poodle.gif. Locate these files on the CD-ROM and copy them into the directory that contains Bowser.html.
4. As you work, you'll probably want to see how your page will appear when your program runs. To do so, right-click on the HTML file and select Preview from the context menu. You can see this in Figure 21.6.
5. When you select Preview, Visual C++ launches IE4 and displays your Web page, as you can see in Figure 21.7. If you do this several times, you may notice that Visual C++ doesn't save your HTML file before launching IE4—if you want to see your latest changes, you need to save the file manually. Visual C++ does save all the files in your project when you build the project.

Figure 21.6
How to preview an HTML file.

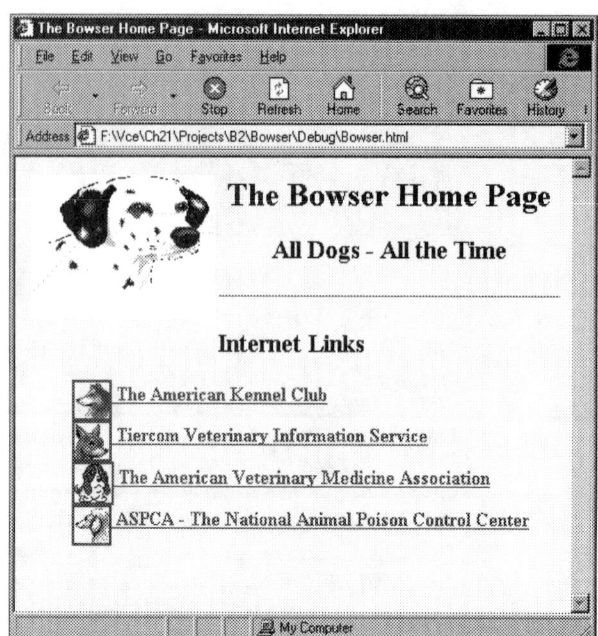

Figure 21.7
Viewing the Bowser home page in IE4.

Understanding HTML

If you're already an HTML guru, you can skip to the next section, in which we hook Bowser to its home page. For the benefit of those who've never done any HTML programming, we'll briefly go over the basics.

HTML is the language used to create Web pages. Web pages normally reside on a *Web server*, although—as you've seen—you can store them on your local hard drive, instead. The program that displays a Web page is called a *client*; the most familiar client is the ubiquitous Web browser.

A Web server sends a Web page like Bowser.html to a client (such as IE or Bowser) as plain text. It's up to the client—that is, the browser—to format the page according to the HTML instructions contained in the plain-text Web page.

Tags

HTML uses keywords, just like C++. In HTML, the keywords are called *tags*—you always place them between angle brackets. For example, Bowser.html contains the tags **<HTML>**, **<HEAD>**,

<TITLE>, and **<BODY>**. Most HTML tags aren't case sensitive, and white space within and around them isn't significant.

Most tags come in pairs. An opening tag (such as **<HEAD>**) marks the beginning of a section, and its opposite number (**</HEAD>**) marks the end. The three *structural tags*—**<HTML>**, **<HEAD>**, and **<BODY>**—delimit the basic parts of an HTML file. **<HTML>** tags indicate the start and end of the file. The **<HEAD>** section contains the title and various meta-information, whereas the **<BODY>** section holds most of the visible text (with the exception of the title).

HTML Text

As we mentioned, the client formats the body text of your HTML document. If you create long lines of text in your HTML file, the browser will wrap the text to fit in the display window. On the other hand, if your source-code lines are very short, the browser will combine those lines to form longer lines that fill the window—a kind of reverse word wrapping. Whatever the length of your lines, your Web browser will display them just right.

Of course, if all the text in your documents ran together, your Web page would look like a jumbled mess. To force a line break, you can use the **
** tag (which stands for Break) or the **<P>** tag (for Paragraph). Neither requires a matching closing tag.

HTML Heads And Text Styles

In addition to plain body text, you can specify six levels of headlines: **<H1>** is the most prominent, and **<H6>** is the least prominent. All the headline styles require that you supply both an opening and closing tag.

When you use a headline tag, an implicit line break is inserted before the **<Hn>** tag, and another after the **</Hn>** tag. For instance, the HTML line

```
<H2>This<H1>IS</H1>Just Fine</H2>
```

produces three lines of output. The word "This" appears on one line in the **H2** headline style, the word "IS" appears on the next line in **H1** style, and the phrase "Just Fine" appears on the third line, again in **H2** style. If text followed the closing **</H2>** tag, it would appear on the next line in plain-text style.

In addition to body text—which requires no tag—and headline styles, you can specify the **<PRE>** style (for Preformatted) to produce code listings or other fixed-position output. You must end a block of preformatted text with the **</PRE>** tag. Finally, you can use character styles to make specific text bold (**<B></B>**), italic (**<I></I>**), or underlined (**<U></U>**).

HTML Images

You can display images on your HTML pages by using the **<IMG>** tag. HTML requires no closing **</IMG>** tag; instead, **<IMG>** uses a *parameter*, which is a keyword that specifies additional information used by the tag. The **<IMG>** tag requires only one parameter: **SRC**. **SRC** specifies the Uniform Resource Locator (URL) that contains the image, which must be either a JPEG or GIF file. The URL can refer to a file in the same directory as the HTML file, like this:

```
<IMG SRC="SomePicture.GIF">
```

The URL can also refer to a directory relative to the location of the HTML file. When you specify directories, you use the Unix forward-slash path separator (/), rather than the DOS back-slash separator (\ ). Here's an example that uses a relative URL to specify the source of an image:

```
<IMG SRC="../images/AnotherPicture.jpg">
```

Finally, you can specify the source name using an absolute URL. If the URL starts with /, it's an absolute path on the same host machine that served the HTML file. If the URL starts with *http://*, it must specify the host name, as well. Here's an example of an image link that uses an absolute URL:

```
<IMG SRC="http://www.nasa.gov/images/jglenn.gif">
```

Of course, if you include a reference to an absolute URL (especially one on a server that you don't control), don't be surprised if the image isn't at that location tomorrow—or even sooner. If you include an image in your HTML page, the actual image remains where it is. When the Web browser downloads your page, it retrieves the image, using the **SRC** argument you provided.

The **<IMG>** tag uses several parameters besides **SRC**. You can change the scale of the image on the fly, for instance—or align the image against one edge, while text flows around it, as we've done in Bowser.html.

Hyperlinks

Besides making it easy to use images with your Web page, HTML also lets you include *hypertext links*. Like an **<IMG>**, a hypertext link (or *hyperlink*) is a reference to another document—a document that may be on the same server as the HTML that references it, or on another server half-way around the world.

A hyperlink doesn't cause the browser to retrieve the referenced document. Instead, the browser (usually) displays the reference in a distinctive color, indicating that the text or image is "hot," or "live." If the user clicks on the hyperlink, the Web browser attempts to retrieve and display the document that the link refers to.

You create a hyperlink by using the **<A></A>** tag pair (**A** stands for Anchor). Any text or images appearing between the tags become part of the hyperlink hotspot. Like the **<IMG>** tag, the **<A>** tag requires an additional parameter: **HREF**. **HREF** specifies a relative or absolute **URL**, just like **SRC**. But, **HREF** usually points to an HTML file, rather than a JPEG or GIF file. If an **HREF** points to a JPEG or GIF file, your browser will display the image when you click on the hyperlink.

This hyperlink opens an HTML page located in the same directory as the page that contains the hyperlink:

```
<A HREF="Page2.html">Go to page two</A>
```

When the browser renders this hyperlink, it displays only the words "Go to page two", usually in a distinctive color—the user won't see the tags or the target URL. The linked files don't need to be on the same server as the file that contains the hyperlink. Moreover, the hyperlink URL needn't completely specify a file: The **HREF** parameter can be a file, a directory, or a Web server.

If the URL names a directory or Web server, the server returns a default file specified by the server administrator (frequently index.html, default.htm, or Default.asp). The following are valid **HREF** arguments:

```
<A HREF="http://www.microsoft.com">Microsoft</A>
<A HREF="http://www.microsoft.com/visualc/">Visual C++
  page</A>
<A HREF="http://www.microsoft.com/misc/
  cpyright.htm">Rules</A>
```

Helping Bowser Find Home

Now that you know enough HTML to be able to decipher Bowser.html, let's hook the file to the Bowser program. Even though your home page works in IE, you must tell the Bowser program to use the new page instead of the Internet page you specified earlier. You've probably guessed that you need to change the starting location used in the **OnInitialUpdate()** function—the question is, what do you put there?

If you enter just the name of the file, Bowser will think it's the name of a server somewhere on the Web and will try to connect to it. If you enter the complete path to the Bowser.html file, IE will be smart enough to recognize it as a local resource. But, you don't want to hard-code the location, because when the dog-club members install Bowser on their machines, each one may put the program in a different directory.

You can solve this problem by storing the HTML file in the same directory as the executable. Use the **__argv[0]** global variable to retrieve the full path name of the program executable, and use the **_splitpath()** function from the C Runtime Library (RTL) to extract the executable's drive and path names. Finally, you can paste the name of the file you want to use—Bowser.html, in this case—on the end, and call **Navigate2()** just as you did previously.

Listing 21.2 shows you the code you need to add.

Listing 21.2 The CBView::OnInitialUpdate() function.

```
void CBView::OnInitialUpdate()
{
    CHtmlView::OnInitialUpdate();
```

```
    char drive[_MAX_PATH];
    char dir[_MAX_DIR];
    char fname[_MAX_FNAME];
    char ext[_MAX_EXT];

    _splitpath(__argv[0], drive, dir, fname, ext);

    CString path(drive);
    path += dir;
    path += "Bowser.html";

    Navigate2(path,NULL,NULL);
}
```

New: HTML Resources

When you ship the Bowser application, you must send all the extra image files, as well as the main HTML home page. Wouldn't it be nice if you could bind your HTML page and all the images it uses into the executable, just as you do toolbars and icons? Now you can, thanks to HTML *resources*—another new feature in Visual C++ 6.0.

HTML resources allow you to bind HTML pages—as well as the images they refer to—as part of your executable. You can include any number of pages, and the pages can be linked. In addition, you can include in the executable the image resources used by your HTML.

Where Did You Say That Was?

If you look in the online help for information about the global variable **__argv**, you'll probably come away a little frustrated. It's not exactly an undocumented feature, but it's well hidden. One Knowledge Base article—"HOWTO: Obtain the Program Name in a Windows-Based Application" (Article ID: Q126571)—deals with **__argv**. The index and other documentation provide no additional information, even though at least 10 of the sample programs use **__argv**. To find the solitary article, type "__argv" in the Search window, being sure to include the two leading underscores.

If you think the documentation may be skimpy because you can determine the program path another way, you're at least partially right. You can call the Windows API function **GetCommandLine()** to retrieve the command line. **GetCommandLine()** returns the program argument in quoted form—a quote character is the first character of the program path. You must increment your pointer to skip over the quote before you call **_splitpath()**.

But, before you rush off and abandon plain-old HTML pages, consider the tradeoffs. If you bind your HTML resources into your executable, you'll have to recompile and redistribute a new EXE every time the links change. When you maintain separate HTML files, you can simply ship an HTML page update. On the other hand, if your material is relatively static, HTML resources make the job of distributing your application much easier.

Importing Bowser.html

Follow these steps to make Bowser use an internal HTML file (the same file you've already created):

1. Open the Bowser project and choose Insert|Resource from the main menu (or press Ctrl+R). When the Insert Resource dialog box opens, select HTML, as shown in Figure 21.8, and then click on Import.
2. The *Import* Resource dialog box opens—not to be confused with the *Insert* Resource dialog box you just left. Locate the Bowser.html file by first choosing HTML Files from the Files Of Type drop-down list. Be sure the value in the Open As drop-down list is Auto. When the dialog box looks like Figure 21.9, click on Import.

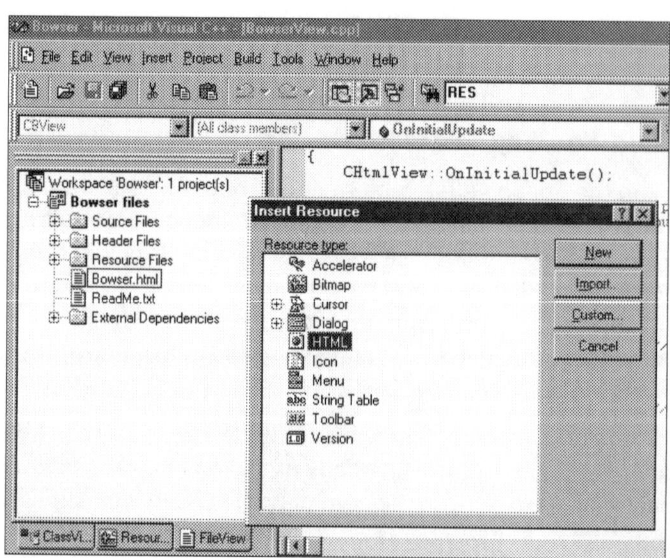

Figure 21.8
Inserting Bowser.html as an HTML resource.

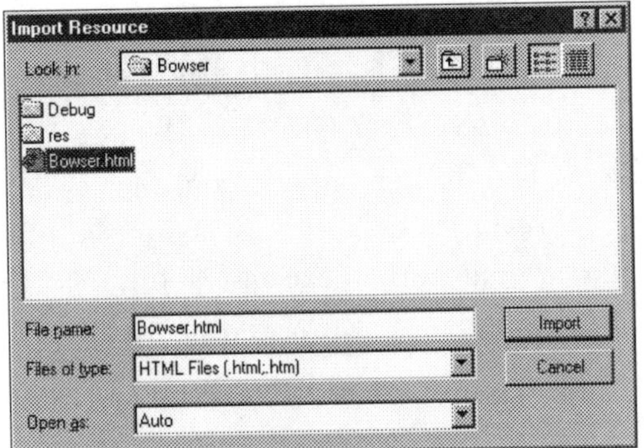

Figure 21.9
Importing Bowser.html as an HTML resource.

3. Switch to the ResourceView pane in the Workspace window, and you'll notice a new HTML folder. Open the folder to display **IDR_HTML1**. Right-click on **IDR_HTML1** to display the Custom Resource Properties sheet, then change the Resource ID to **IDR_HOME_PAGE**. When the property sheet looks like Figure 21.10, close it.

That's all it takes to add an HTML resource. However, you need to bundle all the graphics files, as well as the HTML file. That step requires a little more work.

Importing Graphics Files

In the section on HTML, you learned that Web pages can display graphics files only if the files contain JPEG or GIF images. Unfortunately, Windows bitmap resources aren't JPEG or GIF images. You'd be out of luck, except for two facts:

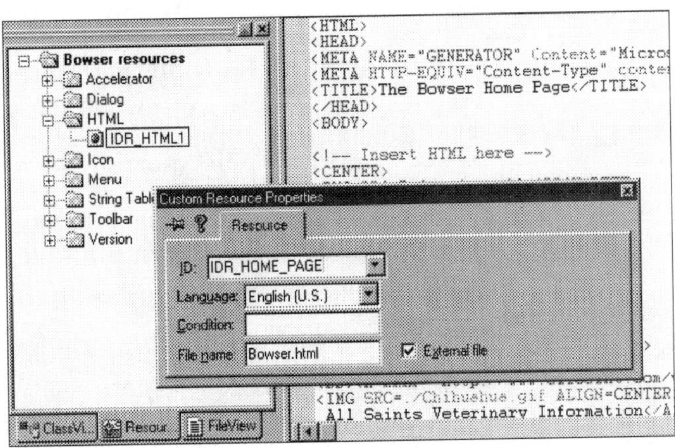

Figure 21.10
Setting the HTML properties for **IDR_HOME_PAGE**.

- Visual C++ allows you to open GIF and JPEG files and save the contents as BMP files. This means you can easily convert all the images to BMP format.
- The IE Web browser control supports a special protocol—the **res:** protocol—for displaying Web content stored as a bitmap resource in an executable file.

To bind your images with the Bowser.html file, you must perform two tasks: Convert all your images to BMP files, and then change Bowser.html to refer to the new resources, rather than the original GIF files.

Here's how you do it:

1. Copy all the GIF images into your project's res directory. This directory already contains your application's toolbar bitmap and document icon. Use File|Open to open each GIF file in the Bitmap Editor, then save the file with a .bmp extension, as you can see in Figure 21.11.
2. Once you've converted all the images, choose Insert | Resource (or press Ctrl+R) to open the Insert Resource dialog box. Select Bitmap as the Resource Type, and then click on Import. Navigate to the res directory and load your bitmaps. As you load each bitmap, change its resource ID to match the name of its file. In Figure 21.12, you can see the last image being loaded.

Using The res: Protocol

When you load the images as bitmaps, the **SRC** parameters you used in Bowser.html become invalid. Now, you must change each parameter to point to its new image using the **res:** protocol.

When you refer to a file using the **res:** protocol, you must answer three questions:

- *Where is the resource located?* In your case, it's located in Bowser.exe. If you like, you can refer to bitmaps outside the executable.
- *What kind of resource are you loading?* The Winuser.h file gives the default values. If you want to see them, just search for ***RT_***.

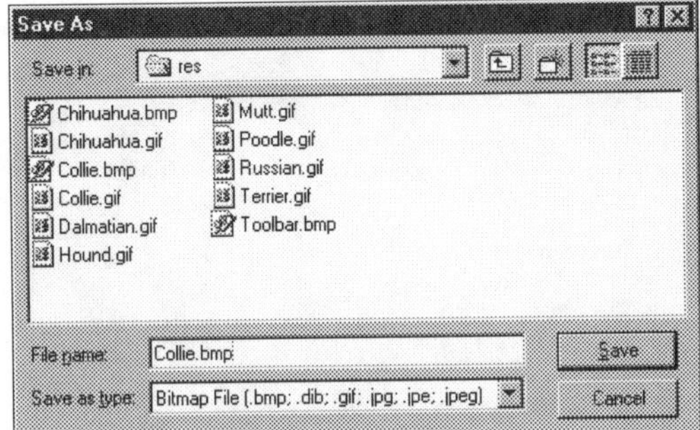

Figure 21.11
Converting GIF images into BMP images.

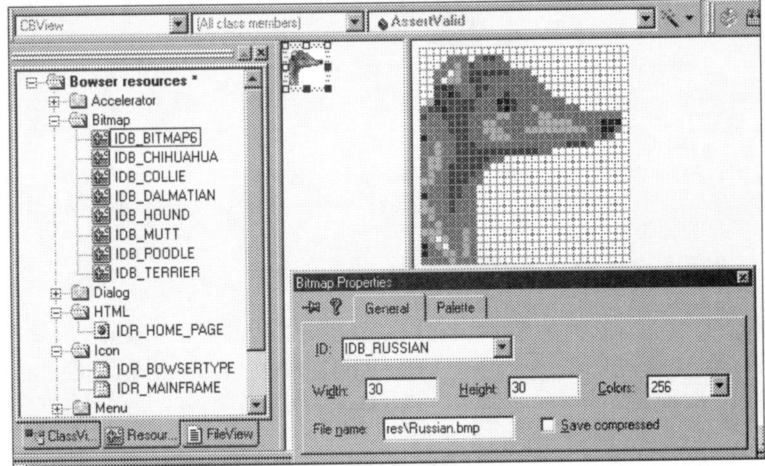

Figure 21.12
Loading the image bitmaps.

You need the two resource types **RT_BITMAP** and **RT_HTML**, which have the values 2 and 23, respectively. To use one of these values in a **res:** protocol tag, enter the actual number preceded by the # symbol—you can't use the symbolic name.

- *Which resource do you want to load?* As with the resource-type protocols, you enter the actual number, preceded by a # symbol—you can't use a symbolic name, such as **IDR_POODLE**.

Here are the steps to modify Bowser.html and hook it up:

1. Select View|Resource Symbols from the main menu and write down the actual ID Value for each bitmap resource. Figure 21.13 shows the numbers assigned in our project; your numbers may be different.
2. Use the resource editor to access Bowser.html, and replace each occurrence of

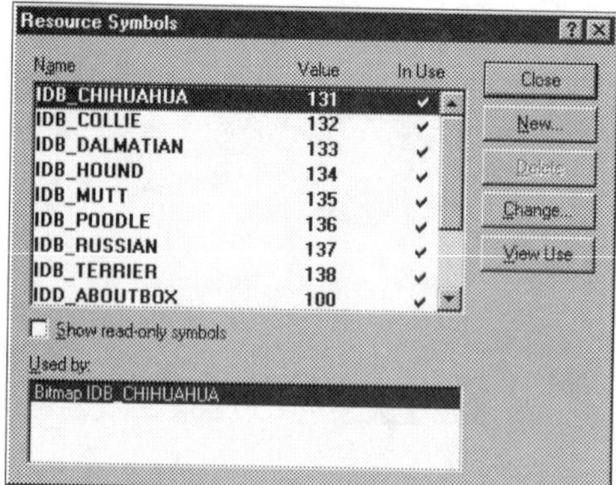

Figure 21.13
Examining the resource IDs.

```
SRC="somefile.gif"
```

with

```
SRC="res://Bowser.exe/#2/#nnn"
```

where ***nnn*** is the resource ID of the image.

3. Locate the **CBView::OnInitialUpdate()** function. Replace the whole complicated function with the simple two-liner shown in Listing 21.3.

Listing 21.3 The OnInitialUpdate() function.

```
void CBView::OnInitialUpdate()
{
    CHtmlView::OnInitialUpdate();
    LoadFromResource(IDR_HOME_PAGE);
}
```

4. Compile and run your program. Now it will work anywhere, without bringing the HTML and image files along. Moreover, just like the previous version, it's well behaved—it doesn't dial your ISP until you click on an Internet link.

Exploring Navigation

Now that Bowser's a little better trained, it's time to turn your attention to the program's menus and toolbars. As Bowser is currently written, you can return to a previous page only via a hyperlink on a following page. Because Bowser's home page is an internal resource, no page in the known universe is likely to link back to it. In other words, once you leave the home page, you can't get back. So, your next improvement will be a Back button that returns Bowser to the last URL you visited.

Of course, after you use the Back button, you might change your mind and want to return to the original page—so, you'll also add a Forward button. While you're at it, you'll add three other buttons:

- *Stop button*—Lets you cancel a download that's taking too long.
- *Web button*—Displays a dialog box in which you can type a URL.
- *Search button*—Automatically opens a search engine.

You'll also make the File Open dialog box work.

This might seem like a lot of effort—but, as it turns out, creating the toolbar buttons is the hardest part. When it comes time to write the actual code, you'll see that the **CHtmlView** class includes functions that implement most of what you need.

Creating The Toolbar

First, you'll create the toolbar buttons and menu items needed to implement each command. Rather than draw the toolbar images by hand, you'll use the graphics files included with Visual C++. The files you need reside in your Visual Studio directory, in the Common\Graphics\Icons subdirectory. (If you didn't install the graphics files when you installed Visual C++, you can read the files directly from the installation CD-ROM; again, look in the Common\Graphics\Icons subdirectory.)

Follow these steps to create Bowser's new toolbar and menu items:

1. Be sure you have the Bowser project open. Select the ResourceView pane in the Workspace window, expand the Toolbars folder, and double-click on the **IDR_MAINFRAME** resource. Remove the New, Cut, Copy, and Paste buttons; leave the Open, Save, Print, and Help buttons.
2. Choose File|Open from the main menu and navigate to the Visual Studio Common\Graphics\Icons subdirectory. In the Open dialog box, select Image Files from the Files Of Type

drop-down list. In the Arrows subdirectory, select the files Arw04lt.ico and Arw04rt.ico, as shown in Figure 21.14; click on Open. Similarly, retrieve the file W95mbx01.ico (a white X in a red circle) from the Computer subdirectory. Retrieve Earth.ico from the Elements subdirectory, and Binoculr.ico from the Misc subdirectory.

3. You won't add these icons to your project. Instead, you'll use the images on the faces of your toolbar buttons. Each icon file contains two versions of the same icon—a 32×32 standard-size icon (measurements are in pixels) and a 16×16 small icon. Although toolbar buttons are usually 16×15, you'll enlarge yours slightly to accommodate the images at hand. Use the Window menu to display each of the five icons and select its Small icon, as shown in Figure 21.15.

Creating Toolbar Buttons

Next, you'll create a new toolbar button for each icon image. Repeat these steps for each of the five new images:

1. Using the Window menu, select a page that contains one of the new icons. Click in the left pane to select the actual-size

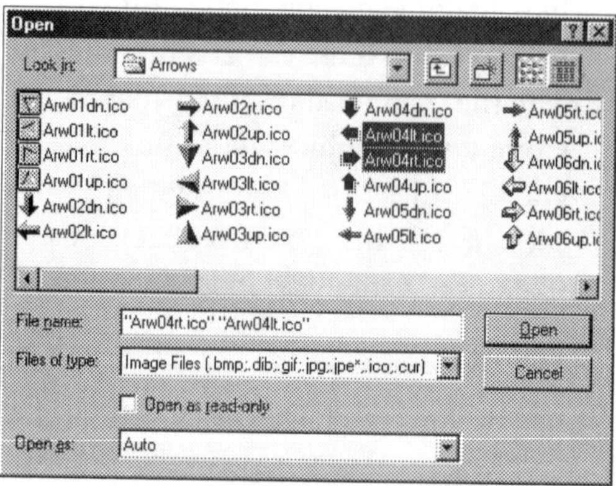

Figure 21.14
Retrieving graphics files from the Visual C++ distribution disk.

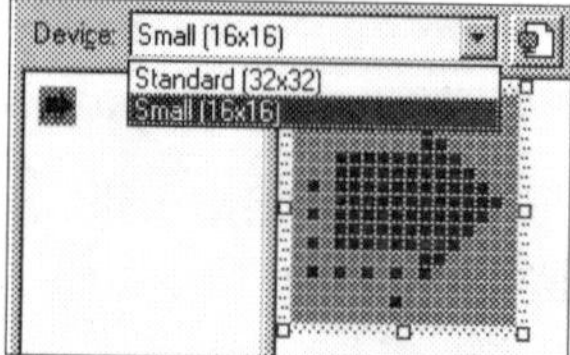

Figure 21.15
Selecting small icon images.

icon. Press Ctrl+C (or choose Edit|Copy from the menu) to copy the icon image to the clipboard.

2. Display the toolbar in the Graphics Editor. To do this, double-click on the **IDR_MAINFRAME** toolbar resource ID in the ResourceView window, or select the toolbar window from the Window menu. Create a new toolbar button and make it the active button. The actual-size button and the enlarged button should appear as a plain, solid-gray rectangle. Choose Edit|Paste from the menu (or press Ctrl+V) to paste the icon image onto the new toolbar button. The first time you do this, Visual C++ will warn you that the bitmap is too large and ask if you want to enlarge it. Click on OK to enlarge all the toolbar buttons to 16×16.
3. Repeat Steps 1 and 2 until you have five new toolbar buttons, as you can see in Figure 21.16. Fill in each button's Resource ID and Prompt according to the information shown in Table 12.1.

Creating Menu Items

You also need to hook up a menu command for each toolbar button, to accommodate club members who don't want to use a mouse. (The mouse reminds many club members of distasteful cats.) Follow these steps:

1. Add an Open Web Site menu item to the File menu, just after the Open menu item; use **ID_WEB_OPEN** as the Resource

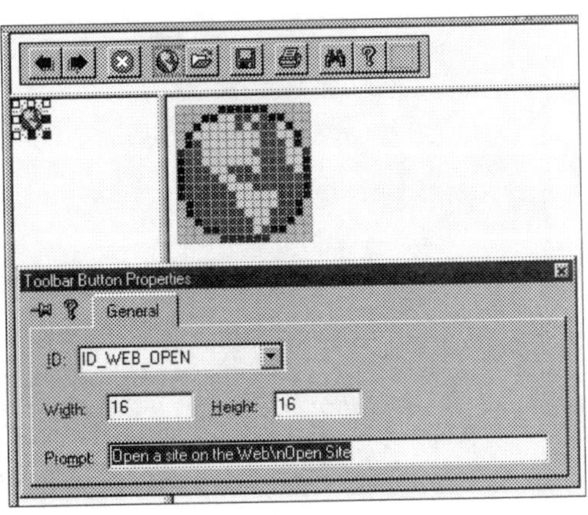

Figure 21.16
The Bowser toolbar buttons.

Table 12.1 Bowser toolbar buttons.

Image	Resource ID	Prompt String
Arw04lt.ico	ID_WEB_BACK	Return to the previous Web page\nBack
Arw04rt.ico	ID_WEB_FORWARD	Move to the next Web page\nForward
W95mbx01.ico	ID_WEB_STOP	Stop loading the current Web page\nStop
Earth.ico	ID_WEB_OPEN	Open a site on the Web\nOpen Site
Binoculr.ico	ID_WEB_SEARCH	Search for a location on the Web\nSearch

ID. While you're at it, remove the Save menu item from the File menu. Your menu should look like that shown in Figure 21.17.

2. Remove the Edit menu by selecting Edit and then pressing Delete. Click on OK when Visual C++ asks if you really want to delete the pop-up menu, as well.
3. Add a new Navigate menu with Back, Forward, and Stop items, as shown in Figure 21.18. Be sure you use the same resource IDs you used for the toolbar buttons.
4. Add the last command—**ID_WEB_SEARCH**—to the Help menu, just below the About menu item. Use the caption "&Search the Web".
5. Open the **IDR_MAINFRAME** Accelerator table, then use the Use Next Key Typed feature to add accelerator keys for the three menu items on the Navigate menu. Press

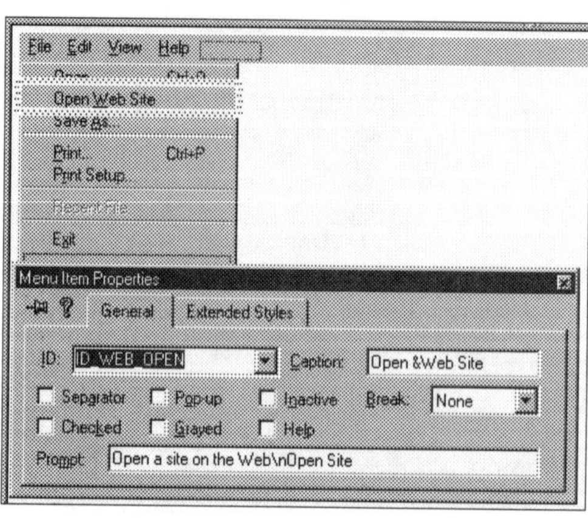

Figure 21.17
Adding the Open Web Site menu command.

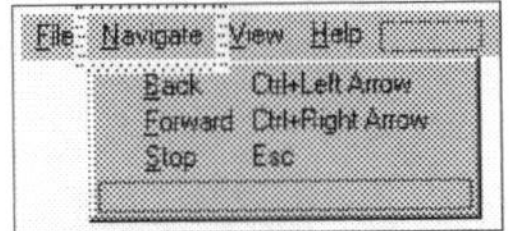

Figure 21.18
Adding the Navigate menu.

Ctrl+Right Arrow for Forward, Ctrl+Left Arrow for Back, and Esc for Stop.

Adding The Code

Rather than simple, small buttons, let's create large buttons that display text with the icon. You can do that by calling the **CToolBar::SetButtonText()** function. **SetButtonText()** takes two arguments: the button offset (starting at 0, numbered from the left) and the string to display.

The first time you use **SetButtonText()**, you may be confused because the text and buttons don't match up. This happens because every separator on the toolbar—like the space between the Forward button and the Stop button—counts as an ordinal position.

Here's the code to add to the **CMainFrame** class's **OnCreate()** function, just before the toolbar is docked:

```
m_wndToolBar.SetButtonText( 0, "Back");
m_wndToolBar.SetButtonText( 1, "Forward");
m_wndToolBar.SetButtonText( 3, "Stop");
m_wndToolBar.SetButtonText( 5, "Web");
m_wndToolBar.SetButtonText( 6, "File");
m_wndToolBar.SetButtonText( 8, "Save");
m_wndToolBar.SetButtonText(10, "Print");
m_wndToolBar.SetButtonText(12, "Search");
m_wndToolBar.SetButtonText(13, "About");
```

Once the buttons display text, you need to attend to one last detail: You must resize them by calling the **SetSizes()** function. **SetSizes()** takes two **CSize** objects as arguments: The first specifies the overall size of the button, and the second specifies the size of the images. Enter this code immediately after the previous block:

```
m_wndToolBar.SetSizes(CSize(56, 40), CSize(16,16));
```

Handling CBView

Now that you've finished the toolbar interface, let's hook up the code for the buttons. Here's what you do:

1. Using ClassWizard, add **COMMAND** message handlers for the new **ID_WEB** resource identifiers. Be sure you add the handlers to the **CBView** class, not the **CMainFrame** class.

The ClassWizard screen should look like Figure 21.19 when you're done.

2. While ClassWizard is open, select **CBView** in the Object IDs list box and **OnDocumentComplete** in the Messages list box. Click on Add Function to override this **CHtmlView** virtual function. ClassWizard should look like Figure 21.20 when you finish this step.

3. Add the code shown in Listing 21.4 to the functions generated in the **CBView** class by ClassWizard. Notice that the code doesn't include the **OnWebOpen()** function—we'll address it later. (We've formatted the code to save space—you're free to use conventional formatting, of course.)

Listing 21.4 Handling the Bowser commands in CBView.

```
void CBView::OnWebBack()    {    GoBack();      }
void CBView::OnWebForward() {    GoForward();   }
void CBView::OnWebSearch()  {    GoSearch();    }
void CBView::OnWebStop()    {    Stop();        }
void CBView::OnDocumentComplete(LPCTSTR lpszURL)
{
    CHtmlView::OnDocumentComplete(lpszURL);
    AfxGetMainWnd()->SetWindowText(GetLocationName());
}
```

Each **CBView** member function simply calls the appropriate **CHtmlView** member function. MFC calls the

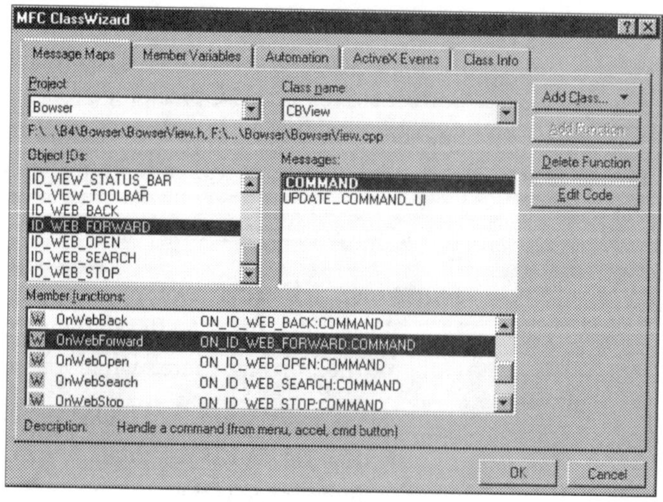

Figure 21.19
Adding **COMMAND** message handlers for Bowser.

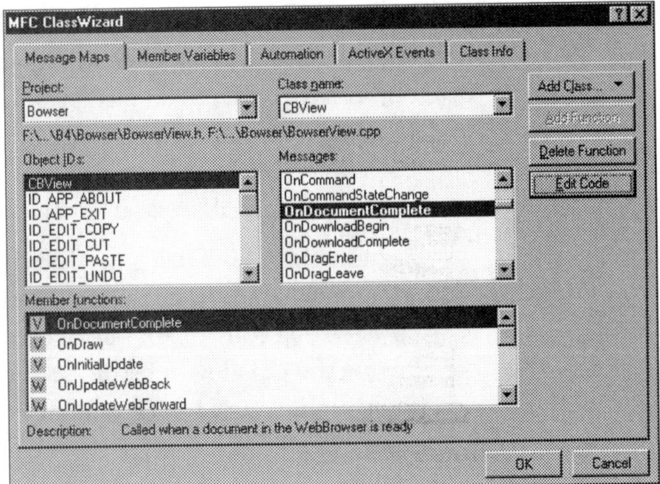

Figure 21.20
Adding the **OnDocumentComplete()** virtual function to the **CBView** class.

OnDocumentComplete() function whenever it finishes loading a document. When the program calls **OnDocumentComplete()**, it passes the **CHtmlView** object the URL of the loaded page. If you want to create a history list, you can use the **lpszURL** argument.

In this case, once a page has loaded, you simply need to set the main Bowser window title to the title of the current HTML page. The second line in **OnDocumentComplete()** does that by calling the **CHtmlView** function **GetLocationName()**.

Handling The Open Dialog Boxes

You need to complete two items before moving on. First, although the File Open button works, it doesn't load an HTML file. Second, you need to create a dialog box to open URLs.

The fact that File Open doesn't work is actually good news, because it gives you a chance to fix an undesirable IE "feature." Every time you open a local HTML file in IE, you have to navigate from the root to your file's location. If you want to open several files in the same directory, the inefficient navigation can be annoying. Your improved File Open dialog box will always open where you opened the last file.

Let's tackle the File Open problem first. Here's how.

1. Rather than create a new **CFileDialog** object each time you open a file, your view class will have a single **CFileDialog** object as one of its data members. Using ClassView, locate the **CBView** class and right-click to open the context menu. Select Add Member Variable from the menu, then create a **private CFileDialog** variable named **m_FileDialog**.

2. Because the **CFileDialog** needs to be initialized in its constructor, you must use the initialization syntax to call the **CFileDialog** constructor before the **CBView** constructor runs. Locate the **CBView** constructor and add the highlighted lines shown in Listing 21.5. (Be sure to include the colon in front of **m_FileDialog**.)

Listing 21.5 Initializing m_FileDialog in the CBView constructor.

```
CBView::CBView()
: m_FileDialog(TRUE, "*.html", "*.html",
               OFN_HIDEREADONLY | OFN_OVERWRITEPROMPT,
               "HTML Files (*.html)|*.htm;*.html||")
{
    // TODO: add construction code here
}
```

3. Using ClassWizard, add a handler function to the **CBView** class for the **ID_FILE_OPEN** identifier (called **OnFileOpen()**). Add the code shown in Listing 21.6 to display your File Open dialog box and navigate to the new site if the user clicks on OK.

Listing 21.6 The CBView::OnFileOpen member function.

```
void CBView::OnFileOpen()
{
    if (m_FileDialog.DoModal() == IDOK)
        Navigate2(m_FileDialog.GetPathName(), NULL,
        NULL);
}
```

The Open A Web Site Dialog Box

Visual C++ doesn't come with a built-in Open A Web Site dialog box (rather surprising, given all the emphasis on the Internet). Fortunately, building your own isn't difficult.

Here's all you need to do:

1. From the main menu, choose Insert|Resource or press Ctrl+R. Choose Dialog in the Insert Resource list box and click on New.
2. Title the new dialog box "Open A Web Site" and give it the resource ID **IDD_OPEN_WEB**. Add a static-text label and an edit control to the dialog box. Give the edit control the resource ID **IDC_URL**, and caption the static text "URL". Arrange the controls as shown in Figure 21.21.
3. Start ClassWizard and click on OK when Visual C++ asks if you want to create a new class. Name your class **CURLDlg**. (Actually, because this is a dog-oriented browser, we should probably call it **CURDlg**.) The base class should be **CDialog**, as shown in Figure 21.22. Click on OK.

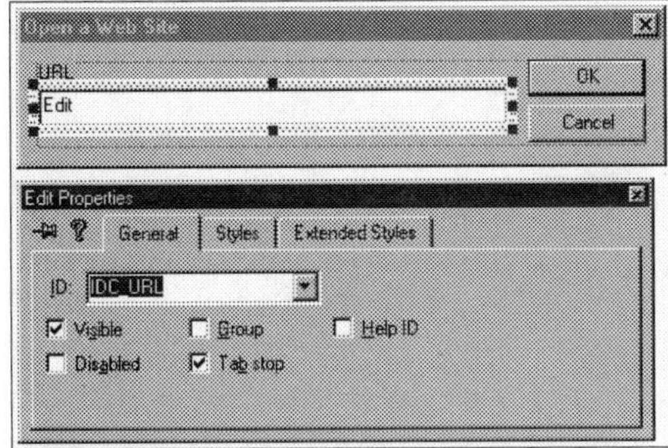

Figure 21.21
Creating the new Open A Web Site dialog box.

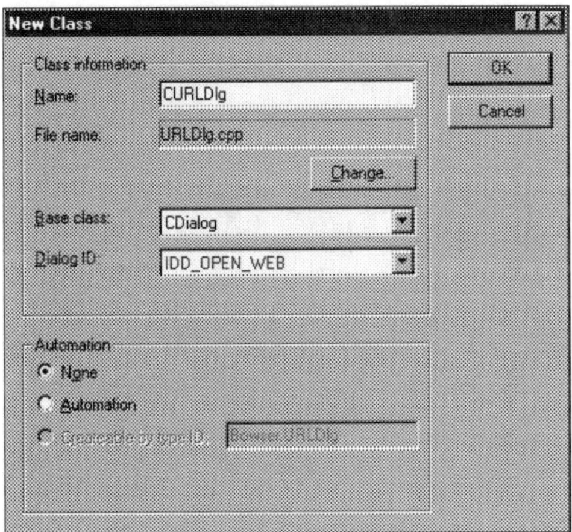

Figure 21.22
Adding the **CURLDlg** class.

4. Once in ClassWizard, be sure your new **CURLDlg** class is selected, then switch to the Member Variables tab. Select **IDC_URL** and click on Add Variable. In the Add Member Variable dialog box, shown in Figure 21.23, name the variable **m_URL**, select Value from the Category drop-down list, and select **CString** from the Variable Type drop-down list.
5. Switch to ClassWizard's Message Maps tab. In the Class Name drop-down list, select **CBView** once again; locate the **OnWebOpen()** member function, then click on Edit Code. Add the code shown in Listing 21.7 to that generated by ClassWizard.

Listing 21.7 The CBView::OnWebOpen() member function.

```
void CBView::OnWebOpen()
{
    CURLDlg dlg;
    if (dlg.DoModal() == IDOK)
        Navigate2(dlg.m_URL, NULL, NULL);
}
```

6. While BowserView.cpp is open, go to the top of the file and add the following line to let the **CBView** class know exactly what a **CURLDlg** object is:

```
#include "URLDlg.h"
```

Once you're done, compile the program and take Bowser out for a walk. As you can see in Figure 21.24, your browser looks almost like the store-bought variety. Even better, if you don't like the way something works, you can change it!

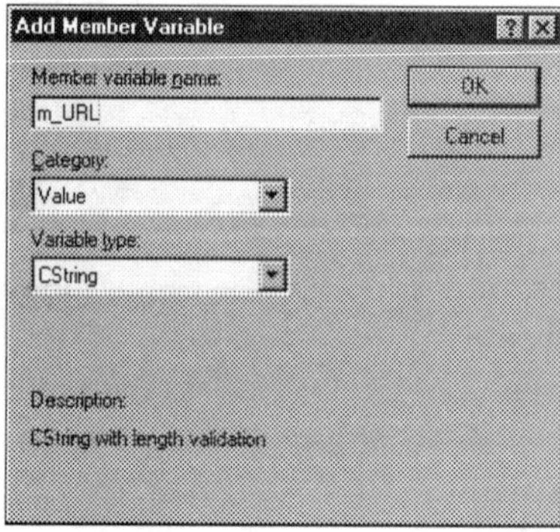

Figure 21.23
Adding the **m_URL** member variable to the **CURLDlg** class.

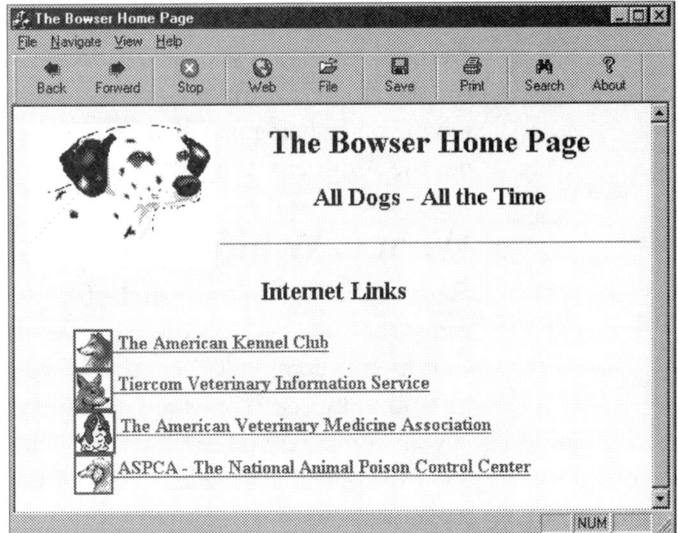

Figure 21.24
Running the Bowser browser.

Using The WinInet Classes

If you read the documentation for the **CHtmlView** class and look at the samples, you'll undoubtedly notice that when you use Bowser (or the MFCIE example on the Visual C++ CD-ROM) to save an HTML file, the result leaves a little to be desired. If you click on Save As, Bowser creates a file—but *it's empty*. You don't have to go far to find out why. Take a look at the **CBDoc::Serialize()** method: There's nothing there! Obviously, the **CHtmlView** class—that is to say, the IE Web browser control—loads the HTML code for the page. After all, your Web pages *do* appear. Perhaps there's some way for you to tap into the IE control, get hold of the HTML code that it's displaying, and then write the HTML to disk.

Unfortunately, although that seems easy (especially when you notice that the **CHtmlView** class has a **GetHtmlDocument()** method), you'll quickly find yourself in a quagmire. The function **GetHtmlDocument()** doesn't return the *text* representation of a Web page—instead, it returns an ActiveX **IDispatch** pointer to the document. You must call the OLE function **QueryInterface()** to get a pointer to an **IHtmlDocument2** interface to work with the document. And, after you've done that, things just *begin* to get complicated....

You really don't want the HTML document in the DocView, ActiveX sense—all you need is the plain text document saved on the server. As it turns out, you can get this text easily, without relying on IE being installed on the client machine. You'll simply use the WinInet (Windows Internet Extension) classes.

What Is WinInet?

Suppose that you want to send a file over the Internet to a friend across the country. How does the file get from your computer to your friend's computer? Very simply, your computer breaks the file into "chunks," each of which contains both the Internet address of your computer and the Internet address of your friend's computer (as well as some additional information).

Your computer transmits these chunks to your ISP, which retransmits them to your friend's ISP (most likely with several relays in between). Finally, your friend's ISP sends the data chunks to your friend's computer, which reassembles the pieces. The magic that choreographs all of this chunking, unchunking, sending, and receiving is called a *protocol*. The Internet uses a particular protocol called *transmission control protocol/internet protocol (TCP/IP)*.

Although you can program with raw TCP/IP, doing so involves myriad details. So, most programmers work at a higher level, with *sockets*—logical connections between two computers over a network. One of the computers acts as a data *source*, and the other acts as a data *sink*. If you've used file redirection, you know that a console-mode program can get its input either from a file or the keyboard, but you can treat the data sources the same. Network sockets work in a similar way: You open a socket, write to it or read from it, and then close it. To use sockets in your Windows programs, you use the Winsock (or Winsock2) interface.

Programming with sockets is much easier than raw TCP/IP programming, but it still involves many details. The MFC WinInet classes encapsulate most of the repetitive work required to establish a socket connection between two computers and monitor the various errors that can occur while data is exchanged. With WinInet, socket programming is as easy as reading and writing to local files.

Simple WinInet

Believe it or not, you can create a simple Internet client application in four easy steps:

- Create a **CInternetSession** object, which connects you to your ISP if you aren't permanently connected to the Internet.
- Create a pointer to a **CStdioFile** and initialize it by passing a string representation of a URL to the **CInternetSession OpenURL()** function. The pointer you get back is a specialized form of **CStdioFile** or **CInternetFile**, but you normally won't care; you'll treat it like a regular file.
- Read from the file using either **Read()** or **ReadString()**.
- Close the file and the Internet session.

You may not believe that Internet programming can be this simple, but it is. To convince you, let's build a simple Web browser that downloads and displays the text of any HTML page, anywhere in the world. You can do it in 10 minutes, and you won't even use any ActiveX controls.

Here are the steps to follow:

1. Using AppWizard, create an SDI application named SimpleNet that contains no ActiveX support, based on the **CEditView** class.
2. Use Insert|Resource to add a new dialog box. Add an edit control and a static-text label. Give the edit control the resource ID **IDC_URL**; arrange and caption your controls as shown in Figure 21.25.
3. Use ClassWizard to create a new **CURLDlg** class for your dialog box, just as you did in Bowser. While still in ClassWizard, create a **CString** value variable named **m_URL** for your edit control.
4. Open the file SimpleNet.cpp and locate the message-map entries for File Open and File New. Place comments in front of each line. They should look like this:

```
//    ON_COMMAND(ID_FILE_NEW, CWinApp::OnFileNew)
//    ON_COMMAND(ID_FILE_OPEN, CWinApp::OnFileOpen)
```

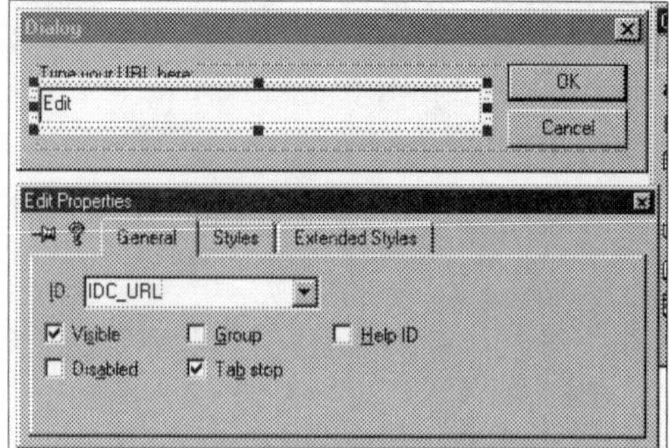

Figure 21.25
Adding an Open URL dialog box.

5. Use ClassWizard to create a Windows **COMMAND** handler in the **CSimpleNetView** class for **ID_FILE_NEW**. Call your handler **OnFileNew()**, and map **ID_FILE_OPEN** to the same handler. Add the code shown in Listing 21.8 to **OnFileNew()**.

Listing 21.8 The CSimpleNetView::OnFileNew() message handler.

```
void CSimpleNetView::OnFileNew()
{
    // TODO: Add your command handler code here
    CURLDlg dlg;
    if (dlg.DoModal() == IDOK)
    {
        CWaitCursor wait;
        CInternetSession session("Simple Net");
        CStdioFile * pFile = NULL;
        pFile = session.OpenURL(dlg.m_URL);
        if (pFile != NULL)
        {
            SetWindowText("");
            CString str, allText, crlf = "\r\n";
            while (pFile->ReadString(str))
            {
                allText += crlf + str;
            }
            SetWindowText(allText);
            pFile->Close();
        }
        session.Close();
    }
}
```

6. While SimpleNet.cpp is open, add the following two lines at the top of the file, so that the WinInet classes and your **CURLDlg** class will be recognized:

```
#include "URLDlg.h"
#include <afxinet.h>
```

7. Locate the **OnPreCreateWindow()** function and comment out the line shown below (doing so turns off word-wrapping, so your HTML file source looks normal):

```
BOOL CSimpleNetView::PreCreateWindow(CREATESTRUCT& cs)
{
    BOOL bPreCreated = CEditView::PreCreateWindow(cs);
//  cs.style &= ~(ES_AUTOHSCROLL|WS_HSCROLL);
    return bPreCreated;
}
```

Compile and run the program. Choose Open from the menu, and then type a URL in the edit box. Click on OK, and the program will connect with your ISP (assuming you've configured your system for automatic dial—otherwise, you'll need to establish the connection). It will then download the HTML source code into the main window. You can use the printing functions or the Save As button to save each page as a file. Figure 21.26 shows SimpleNet connected to the Coriolis Group Web site.

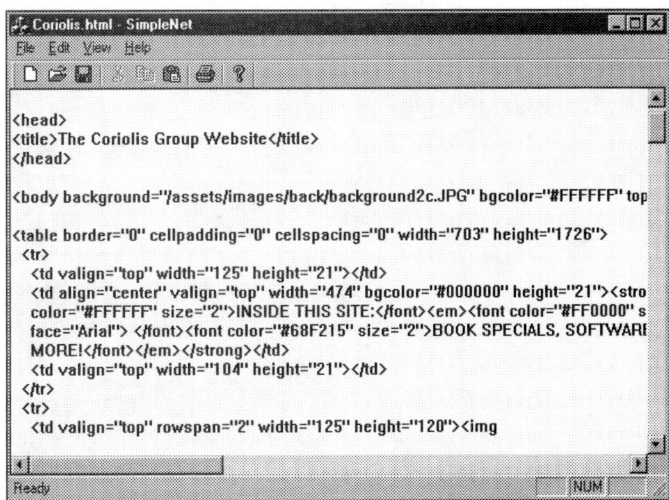

Figure 21.26
Running the SimpleNet program.

Other WinInet

WinInet can do much more than this simple example illustrates. You can, for instance, derive your own class from **CInternetSession** and automatically receive status reports about the state of your connection by overriding the **OnStatusCallback()** function.

WinInet automatically handles FTP (File Transfer Protocol) sessions just as easily as it does HTML files, allowing you to write to and read from an FTP server. Rather than using **GetURL()**, you use **GetFtpConnection()**, which lets you download a file from a remote computer with a single call to **GetFile()**—you do even less work than you did in SimpleNet.

Saving Private Bowser

Before we take our final leave, let's finish up the Bowser application. Here's all you have to do:

1. Add a public **CString** member variable to the **CBDoc** class. Name the variable **m_URL** and initialize it to the empty string ("") in the **OnNewDocument()** function.
2. Add the code shown in Listing 21.9 to the **CBDoc::Serialize()** function.

Listing 21.9 The CBDoc::Serialize() function.

```
const MAX_BUF = 1024;
void CBDoc::Serialize(CArchive& ar)
{
    if (ar.IsStoring())
    {
        if (m_URL.Left(4) == "res:")
        {
            AfxMessageBox(
              "Cannot save internal HTML files");
            return;
        }
        if (! m_URL.IsEmpty())
        {
            char buf[MAX_BUF];
            CInternetSession session;
            CStdioFile * pFile = NULL;
            pFile = session.OpenURL(m_URL);
            int nBytesRead;
```

```
            while ((nBytesRead = pFile->Read(buf,
                    MAX_BUF))  > 0)
            {
                ar.Write(buf, nBytesRead);
            }
            delete pFile;
            session.Close();
        }
    }
    else
    {
        // TODO: add loading code here
    }
}
```

3. Add an **#include <afxinet.h>** line to the top of the BowserDoc.cpp file.
4. Add the highlighted line in Listing 21.10 to the **CBView::OnDocumentComplete()** function.

Listing 21.10 The CBView::OnDocumentComplete() function.

```
void CBView::OnDocumentComplete(LPCTSTR lpszURL)
{
    CHtmlView::OnDocumentComplete(lpszURL);
    AfxGetMainWnd()->SetWindowText(GetLocationName());
    (GetDocument())->m_URL = lpszURL;
}
```

Compile your new Bowser browser, load some interesting pages, and save them. You'll find that Bowser now saves the HTML perfectly. Of course, if the page refers to resources such as image files by using relative URLs, the saved page won't function properly if you load it, because the resources won't be present on your local hard drive. Certainly, you could add code to Bowser that scans the HTML code for such resources and saves them with the HTML code. But, that's another story—and, perhaps, another book.

A Final Goodbye

Congratulations on making it to the end of the trail. We trust you've enjoyed the journey, whitewater and all. And, we hope the information and examples we've presented prove to be worth the time you've invested—we're confident they will. You now have a solid foundation for continuing to learn about MFC. You'll find many further delights as you go off-trail and explore on your own. Keep reading, keep learning, and keep programming. So long, pard!

Index

Numbers

Symbols

A

B

C

D

E

F

G

H

I

J

K

L

M

N

O

P

Q

R

S

T

U

V

W

Learn More Faster

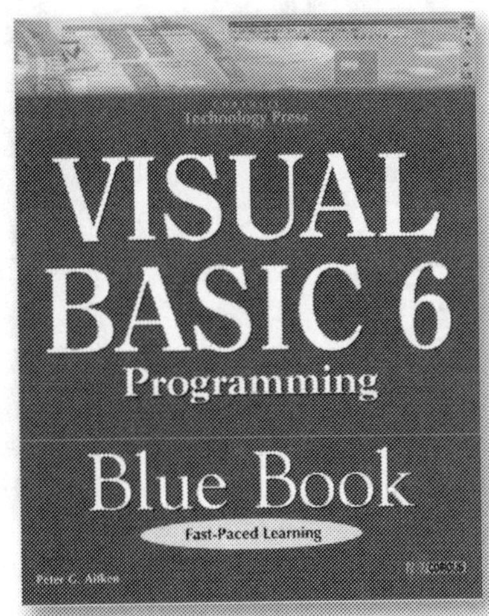

ISBN: 1-57610-281-5
$49.99 U.S. • $69.99 Canada
Available Now

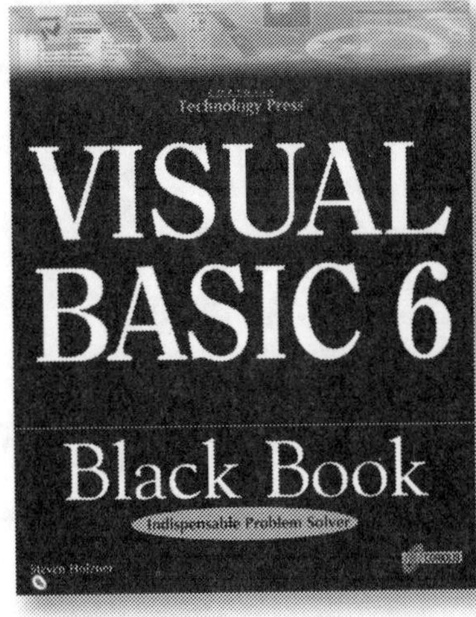

ISBN: 1-57610-283-1
$49.99 U.S. • $69.99 Canada
Available Now

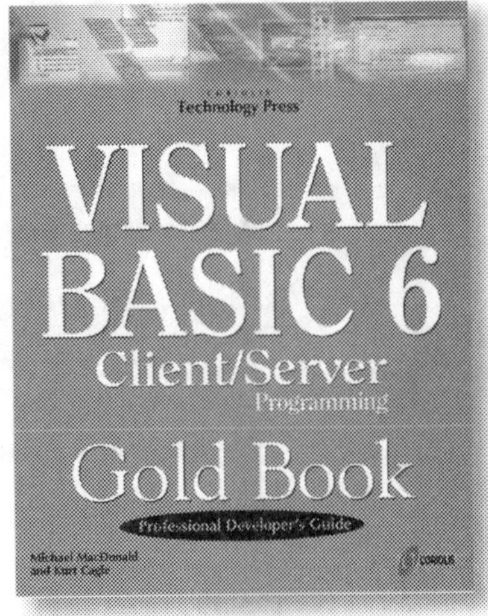

ISBN: 1-57610-282-3
$49.99 U.S. • $69.99 Canada
Available Now

In addition, you are sure to find relevant tips, techniques, and topics faster as well.

CORIOLIS
Technology Press™

Blue, Black, and Gold books. Novice, intermediate, advanced. Easy-to-identify classifications for an innovative new concept in technology publishing.

A completely new series. Each title written to address the specific needs of the system developer, user, or engineer—at the level of his or her concern.

ACQUIRE MORE KNOWLEDGE

When you are learning a new technology, Blue Books are the complete, hands-on tutorials you'll want to reach for first. Their highly interactive, project-based, "learn-by-doing" approach helps ensure that you will learn more at a much faster rate than you can with other tutorials.

USE YOUR KNOWLEDGE

Black Books are indispensable problem-solving guides. Their unique format, which provides very thorough, in-depth, highly technical overviews followed by highly practical "immediate solutions," will help you quickly complete any task: large or small, simple or complex.

EXPAND YOUR KNOWLEDGE

Gold Books are the professional-level guides you'll turn to when you want to expand your horizons. Their highly conceptual but practical approach will teach you how to think in new ways and push your skills to a new level.

Blue, Black, and Gold. They're comprehensive, illustrated, and easy to understand. Experience the difference. Look for these and other soon-to-be-released titles from Coriolis. Of course!

Available at Bookstores and Computer Stores Nationwide

Telephone 800.410.0192 • International callers 602.483.0192
www.coriolis.com

Prices are subject to change without notice. ©1998 The Coriolis Group, Inc. All rights reserved. 8/98

THE *ONLY* MONTHLY POWERBUILDER RESOURCE SINCE 1994!

Don't Miss a Single Issue!

In Each Issue, PBDJ Offers its Readers the Most

- **Insighful and Timely Information**
- **Coverage of Management Issues Affecting Business Application Developers and IS Professionals**
- **Reviews of New and Innovative Client/Server and Database Techniques and Solutions**

www.PowerBuilderJournal.com

SYS-CON Publications, Inc.
39 East Central Ave Pearl River, NY 10965
Tel: 914-735-1900 Fax: 914-735-3922

SUBSCRIBE NOW!

❑ **1 Year PBDJ $119** (12 Issues)
❑ **2 Years $188** (24 Issues)
❑ ***FREE* Trial Subscription (Three Months)** With No Obligation

SAVE $25 off the Single Issue Price!
SINGLE ISSUE PRICE: $144 YOUR PRICE: $119

Name:
Title:
Company:
Address:
City: St: Zip:
Tel: Fax:

❑ M/C ❑ Visa ❑ Amex
Card#:
Expiration Date:
Signature:

*PowerBuilder Developer's Journal one year is a total of 12 issues. PBDJ basic annual subscription rate is **$119.00** in American funds, and must be drawn on a U.S. Bank. NY, NJ, CT residents, please add sales tax. Canada/Mexico **$139**; all other countries **$179**. Subscription begins upon receipt of payment. Please allow 6-8 weeks for delivery of first issue. International subscriptions must be payable in U.S. dollars.*